Reasoning and Writing Well

Reasoning & Writing Well

A Rhetoric, Reader, and Handbook

Betty M. Dietsch
Marion Technical College

Mayfield Publishing Company
Mountain View, California
London • Toronto

Copyright © 1998 by Betty M. Dietsch

Library of Congress Cataloging-in-Publication Data

Dietsch, Betty M.
  Reasoning and writing well : a rhetoric, reader, and handbook / Betty M. Dietsch.
    p. cm.
  Includes indexes.
  ISBN 1-55934-953-0
    1. English language—Rhetoric.   2. English language—Grammar.   3. Report writing.
4. College readers.   5. Reasoning.   I. Title.
PE1408.D5437   1997
808'.0427—dc21   97-40705
                                                                      CIP

Manufactured in the United States of America

10   9   8   7   6   5   4   3   2

Mayfield Publishing Company
1280 Villa Street
Mountain View, California 94041

Sponsoring editor, Renée Deljon; developmental editor, Mark Gallaher; production editor, Melissa Kreischer; manuscript editor, Joan Pendleton; art director, Jeanne M. Schreiber; text and cover designer, Linda M. Robertson; art manager, Robin Mouat; permissions editor, Pam Trainer; manufacturing manager, Randy Hurst. The text was set in 10/12 Berling Book by G&S Typesetters, Inc. and printed on acid-free 45# Chromatone Matte, PMS color 542, by Banta Book Group.

Acknowledgments and copyrights continue following the handbook on pages C1–C4, which constitute an extension of the copyright page.

A Note to Instructors

Students, especially those at colleges and universities with an open-door policy, tend to have a practical mindset. More and more ask, "How is this course related to my career?" Yet too few seem to realize that the ability to write well can affect not only their grades but also their careers. Six years of research on communication in the workplace, including nearly a hundred interviews with employers and employees from dozens of different businesses, have influenced *Reasoning and Writing Well*. This rhetoric is overtly relevant to the workplace as well as to the academic environment. The primary educational goals are to enable students to:

- Write with a purpose that considers the rhetorical situation
- Write clearly, concisely, and accurately
- Use language appropriately
- Research a topic using electronic and other sources
- Apply principles of documentation
- Analyze and evaluate logically and objectively
- Write with confidence
- Appreciate the value of effective writing

Reasoning and Writing Well is a comprehensive process-centered rhetoric that demystifies the art of writing and offers an abundance of engaging readings. The self-help features and group activities work well for individual study, collaborative work, or computerized settings. The text takes the student all the way from sentence structure to researched argument, literary analysis, and job-related writing. Logical and critical thinking, causal analysis, problem solving, and persuasion receive extensive coverage. Strategies of organization are shown as options to combine creatively. Other important features include:

- *Readability.* The light, friendly tone, sprinkled with humor, sets the scene for enjoyable and thoughtful reading. The clear explanations make the text suitable for students with a wide range of abilities. Whether valedictorian or average student, each reader should be able to understand and complete the assignments. Equally important, each student should be challenged.

- *Flexible*. This text has been designed for and tested with a multicultural audience. Every reader should be able to identify with some of the examples.

- *Numerous student, as well as professional, models*. Exemplary student writing is featured throughout. Examples of introductions, conclusions, and entire papers illustrate various rhetorical strategies.

- *In-depth coverage of expository writing*. Students gain an overview of the writing process before each step is explained and illustrated. They are taught how to shape material according to purpose, audience, and occasion. Each major rhetorical strategy is allotted a full chapter, going from less to more complex.

- *Creativity*. Heuristics to generate ideas and details will enable students to start writing quickly. They are encouraged to use figures of speech and other literary devices.

- *Revision*. Revision is treated as an integral part of the writing process. Checklists for revision appear periodically. By the time students finish the course, they should be convinced that revision is a vital part of writing.

- *Diction*. The book provides extensive treatment of levels of formality, colloquialisms, jargon, sexism, positive/negative words, and concrete/abstract words. Students are encouraged to develop proficiency in professional English to succeed in college and the workplace.

- *Writing in response to literature*. Students learn how to write papers of reaction and analysis in response to essays, fiction, and poetry. The chapters explain not only how to take and defend a position but also how to discuss the elements of fiction and common literary devices.

- *Résumé and employment letter writing*. Up-to-date options for résumés emphasize skills and abilities. Students learn to analyze the needs of employers and tailor the statement of their qualifications accordingly. They also learn how to write impressive application, thank you, and refusal letters as well as compile an effective list of references.

- *Study aids*. Chapter summaries, tables, guidelines, and checklists assist students in preparation. "Test Yourself" exercises provide opportunities for quick feedback.

- *Activities*. Creative activities encourage and enhance analysis and discussion. Suggestions for peer review, role plays, and case problems provide opportunities to learn collaboratively. Suggestions for practice writing and papers stimulate thinking and originality.

- *Extensive help for computer users*. Tips and precautions alert users to possible pitfalls. Students learn how to create documentation for material from CD-ROMs, online services, and the Internet.

- *Reader*. This rhetorically arranged reader (that parallels the rhetoric's organization) contains 39 engaging readings. The selections for each rhetorical mode progress from the readily accessible to the more challenging. Charles Kuralt, Eudora Welty, C. S. Lewis, and Elisabeth Kübler-Ross are among the authors represented.

- *Handbook: A Guide to Usage*. The concise handbook provides quick answers to common questions about grammar, punctuation, mechanics, spelling, and usage. Common correction symbols are listed inside the back cover.

- *The Idea Book*. This unusual instructor's manual provides objectives, teaching strategies, activities, keys to exercises, and other features to interest students and to lighten the load of the instructor. For example, twenty-seven transparency masters and fourteen grammar work sheets are ready for duplication.

The philosophy of *Reasoning and Writing Well* has been shaped by education at Ohio State University, research, professional writing, experience in the workplace, and twenty years of teaching at Marion Technical College. Recently, a joint effort in workplace education by MTC and Whirlpool Corporation gained international recognition, winning a gold medal. A similar effort by MTC and Med-Center Hospital received the Governor's Workforce Excellence Award. *Reasoning and Writing Well*, tested locally for three years, has played a part in these and other achievements. This unusual rhetoric, reader, and handbook can also help your students to develop their potential.

A Note of Appreciation

This book could not have been written without the generosity of the many students who have contributed their work. Heartfelt gratitude is also extended to professors Nancy Gilson and Leslie Weichenthal, my coworkers, and to librarians David Evans and Nannette White. Also lending expertise as well as encouragement were family members—George, Neil, Jeanne, Julie, and Christine. Appreciated too, is the assistance of Linda K. Wendling, University of Missouri-St. Louis, for helping to compile the Reader. Finally, my thanks go to the reviewers: Patricia Blaine, Paducah Community College; Julie Ann Doty, Southeastern Illinois College; Linda Jarvis, Kilgore College; Sharon Poat, Paducah Community College; Jonah Rice, Southeastern Illinois College; and Marilyn Terrault, Macomb Community College, for their suggestions.

Contents in Brief

Contents

READER

HANDBOOK: A GUIDE TO USAGE

Rhetoric

PART 1

The Writing Process

CHAPTER 1

The Writing Process

An Overview

Genius, that power which dazzles mortal eyes,
Is oft but perseverance in disguise.

—Henry Willard Austin

The ability to write well is not a mystical talent, conferred upon a lucky few, but a skill that is learned and developed through perseverance. Although effort is required, the results are richly rewarding. Skill in writing is crucial for succeeding in college and for advancing a career. Various surveys have found that white-collar workers spend from 10 to 70 percent of their time writing. For example, a study conducted at California State University at Chico found that technical graduates, "regardless of their job duties, all spend half or more of their career time writing." Technological advances have increased, not decreased, the demand for employees who can write effectively.

Whether you relish or dread writing, you will be relieved to find that *Reasoning and Writing Well* will aid you not only in preparing for college assignments but also for writing in the workplace. You'll learn shortcuts to ease the task of transferring thoughts from your mind to paper and to help you develop your ideas. You'll sharpen both your writing and thinking skills, refining your ability to reason logically, solve problems, write persuasively, and conduct research. As you expand your repertoire, you will be better prepared to write college papers, as well as enhance your résumé and compose effective letters and reports. Mastery of the writing process will allow you to shine when written communication is required.

Effective writing is focused, fresh, and appropriate. The purpose and organization are clear; words and sentences reflect a sense of style; words mean what they are intended to, spelling observes standard usage, grammatical structures fit the ideas they house, and punctuation makes relationships clear. As you progress through this book, you will learn more about each of these elements.

Anything worth achieving is seldom a snap. And writing is no exception; you may need intensive practice. But keep in mind that you will be building on what you already know. If you are already proficient in grammar, college writing may be easier than expected. Whether words flow from your fingers or each syllable is a struggle, the key is not to compare yourself to others, but to evaluate your own achievement step by step. There is a tiny lesson in each mistake. Master these mini-lessons, and you will make steady progress.

THE RHETORICAL SITUATION

Writing a paper is a little like rafting down an unfamiliar river. Although both the writer and the rafter have a purpose, they are unsure of the route and risks that lie ahead. They must plan the trip and take necessary equipment. Usually, each has a companion (the writer has the reader) whose interests must also be considered. Even when the course is smooth, there are decisions to be made and work to be done. A writer must select the best channel for ideas; taking a wrong fork leads to confusion. Shoals, eddies, and rapids must be navigated. Listening to sounds is essential for a successful passage.

And just as a rafter must consider his or her surroundings if the trip is to be successful, so too a writer must consider the *rhetorical situation* or context. Some types of writing stress certain elements of the rhetorical situation more than others. Nevertheless, five factors influence any piece of writing:

1. The occasion for writing
2. The purpose for writing
3. The topic
4. The audience or reader
5. The writer

Occasion

The occasion is the circumstance or condition that causes you to write, whether an assignment by an instructor or the result of a need or problem that arises in the course of your job or day-to-day life. Different occasions require different writing strategies. The occasion of writing a letter to thank a relative for a birthday gift, for example, is very different from the occasion of writing a performance review of a subordinate at work or the occasion of writing a research paper for a marketing course. Much college writing is *expository writing*, which explains, conveys information, or establishes the truth of a statement. It includes many of the techniques described in this book: process analysis, comparison, definition, determination of cause and effect, illustration, and division and classification. Your responses to these occasions would vary considerably, as would your rhetorical decisions.

Purpose

Purpose refers to a writer's reason for composing. The purpose directs the writer in selecting and shaping ideas so that they unite and flow toward an appropriate conclusion. The *general* purpose may be to entertain, to express feelings, to inform, to evaluate, to persuade, or some combination of these. Writing also has a *specific* purpose that in academic and other kinds of formal writing may be reflected in a thesis statement (chapter 3). As you revise and edit your writing, knowing your general and specific purpose will help you to focus your drafts.

Topic

In the workplace and in day-to-day life, topics for writing spring from an occasion that often takes the form of a need or problem. In the classroom an instructor may assign a general purpose for a paper, but often students are free to select their own topics. The first guideline is to select a topic you care about. The second is to narrow the topic so that you can focus the paper and develop it satisfactorily (chapter 2).

Audience

The writer's *audience* is the reader. Knowing the general characteristics of the person or group who will be reading the writing assists the writer in meeting the reader's needs. A writer can also visualize a typical reader and write directly to him or her. If a writer ignores readers and neglects their needs, however, they will respond by ignoring the writing. A keen awareness of how readers think and feel will assist you in shaping your writing purpose and in finding an appropriate *voice*.

The Writer and the Writer's Voice

The *voice* of the writer refers to how the writing sounds. Each of the rhetorical decisions you make influences your written voice. Your written voice is affected not only by what you believe but also by how you feel about the act of writing, about the reader, and about the topic. It is important that you be aware of how your written voice affects your reader's responses. Few readers want to be bored, baffled, ignored, or insulted. Readers seem to prefer a clear, knowledgeable voice that respects, understands, and accommodates (chapter 6).

Three Criteria for Effective Writing

Over the years you have been taught dozens of rules governing the use of the English language. The rules are designed to produce clear, concise, appropriate writing. To maintain a sense of direction (and sanity!), however, keep in mind these three chief standards:

1. Is the purpose apparent?
2. Is the treatment of the topic clear?

3. Are the writing and the writer's voice appropriate for the occasion, purpose, topic, and audience?

All three criteria are important not only during revision but also during drafting. The sooner you can focus and organize a draft, the faster the writing will proceed. As you revise and proofread, remember the adage "Learn to use the language before you abuse it." True, you may sometimes choose to overlook a rule if it interferes with your effectiveness, but such exceptions are few.

THE WRITING PROCESS

An excellent way to gain confidence in writing is to dispel any myths you may have heard and to understand the writing process. Then, you will be less likely to become entangled in the "perfect draft" approach, expecting to perfect each sentence the first time you put it on paper. This approach is tedious and exasperating. Those who use it proceed at a snail's pace and miss the elation of finishing a first draft rapidly. Nor will you be lulled by the false belief that inspiration alone can transform a first draft into a final draft without revision. High-quality papers require more than an hour or two of work. The reality is that writing is a process of growth. A first draft requires nurture and development, strengthening through revision and editing, before the paper can mature and withstand the rigor of evaluation.

Although there is no one way to write, there are ways to make writing easier and more effective. The stages of the writing process are flexible, accommodating a variety of techniques and writing styles. Seasoned writers select a mode of writing that works best for a particular purpose or occasion. They combine a variety of techniques, according to what is most effective. And they randomly shuttle back and forth between stages of writing. Rarely is writing a neat linear procedure, even though it may seem so if you have thought long about a subject. Although writing is not a process in the technical sense of a set procedure, the writing process has been divided into distinct stages. For clarity and convenience, four are identified here as prewriting, drafting, revising, and editing/proofreading.

Prewriting

Prewriting can be an antidote for writer's block. During this first stage of writing, you discover ideas that can lead to a topic and details to develop it. Prewriting can be done whenever and however you like—on paper, at a keyboard, or with a tape recorder. Mystery novelist Agatha Christie did much of her prewriting while washing dishes, pausing at intervals to jot down notes. One writer keeps a tape recorder in his car to save ideas while driving. When ideas are elusive, some writers like to walk along a quiet street or path to let their thoughts settle before they attempt any writing. Yet it is essential to prewrite and pin ideas down before they flit away.

Drafting

In this second stage of writing, some writers scribble a "discovery draft," exploring ideas uncovered in prewriting. For them, drafting is an irregular, zigzag process in which they zip from one idea to another, finding out what they think and how it may apply to the piece they will write. Other writers, who have a clear purpose and audience in mind, are more focused. Their objective in a first draft is to expand the main idea as quickly as possible. They follow a loosely organized outline, delineating major ideas and minor details. Still other writers— particularly those who know their topic well—set up a tentative order, leaving the fleshing out of details for a later draft. There is no one method of drafting that works for every writer, and methods vary with different rhetorical situations.

Revising

Revision is the reworking of the larger aspects of a piece of writing. Revision requires a shifting of mental gears. In this stage you become your own editor, working however you wish. You may want to revise the body of the paper first— adding an anecdote, example, reason, or concrete details and leaving your introduction and conclusion for later. Or perhaps you feel revising the introduction first will help you find a better structure for the rest of the paper. You may rearrange whole sections. You may toss out an entire section and write a replacement. When you revise, you examine the overall structure and style of the work. You work through successive drafts until the writing includes all necessary information and sounds the way you want (and most college instructors expect).

Editing and Proofreading

After revision comes the final task: fine-tuning the smaller aspects of the manuscript and hunting for errors. Editing and proofreading require an eagle eye. You watch for any irregularities in word choice, spelling, punctuation, agreement, reference, sentence structure, and transition. This final stage is rarely accomplished in one sitting.

Once you recognize the stages of the writing process, you will be better prepared to encourage and pace yourself.

A WORD OF ENCOURAGEMENT

If you consider how much you already know about the process of writing and the English language, you should be encouraged. You are not attempting to learn something completely new. And as you write, you'll recover much that now lies hidden in your memory files.

The task of writing is exacting, yet exciting. No matter how much experience a writer has and how similar the assignments, each writing task differs somewhat.

Writers have to think and plan what to say, then find how to say it best. What a challenge! There is, of course, no quick formula for success. *This book is not about formulas or rules, but about options.* It is about trolling for ideas, selecting the best, and dressing them to suit the reader's taste. As you embark on the craft of writing, this book will show you the ropes so that you can succeed.

Summary

Writing effectively is a skill you can learn. Good writing is focused, fresh, organized, and appropriate. To write effectively, a writer must consider the rhetorical situation, which has five elements: the occasion, the purpose, the audience, the writer, and the topic.

The three main standards for effective writing are clarity, appropriateness of style, and fulfillment of the writer's purpose.

Awareness of the stages of writing—prewriting, drafting, revision, and editing/proofreading—can forestall frustration and increase efficiency. Prewriting before (and possibly during) drafting can save time in the long run. The chief purpose of drafting is to get ideas on paper. Revision refines the larger aspects of a draft; editing/proofreading, the smaller aspects.

Take heart! In learning to write better, you are honing a skill that will multiply your chances for success whenever and wherever you communicate.

Key Terms

rhetorical situation	audience	prewriting
occasion	writer's voice	drafting
expository writing	three criteria	revision
writer's purpose	writing process	editing/proofreading

Practice

Prewriting Activities

Directions: Select a suggested activity or one of your own. Then note as many sights, sounds, smells, and tastes as possible. Finally, write a paragraph, using your concrete details.

1. Look out a window. What do you see?
2. Hang out at a mall and note what you see and hear.
3. Take a walk around your neighborhood or campus.
4. Eat a pizza or other favorite food slowly. Savor the fragrance, appearance, texture, and taste.

5. Take a bus or train ride.

6. Observe a person who is very different from you.

7. Early in the morning or late in the evening, go outside your home and listen.

8. Visit a garden, forest, or park.

9. Visit a farm and observe an activity or animal there.

10. Visit a tourist attraction or historical site for the first time.

11. Visit an antique shop, quilt show, flea market, country store, cheese factory, art show, or museum.

12. In a restaurant, listen to people's voices and the emotions their voices convey.

13. Visit the produce section of a supermarket and check out unusual vegetables.

14. Listen to the rain.

15. Pretend you are a bug as you watch a freeway. What might you think?

Writing Ideas

Directions: Describe an interesting event or thought. Perhaps the suggestions below will foster an idea.

1. Wisdom learned from a cat

2. The art of snow sculpture

3. Ads in personal columns

4. An interesting one-day trip

5. Thoughts of an oak tree

6. A great moment in . . .

7. Music in my life

8. My favorite object

9. An unusual party

10. The dog who loved to fish

CHAPTER 2

Discovering and Devising

A writer needs three things, experience, observation, and imagination,
any two of which, at times any one . . . , can supply the lack of the others.

—William Faulkner
Writers at Work: First Series

Your experience, observation, and imagination can fuel your writing. You can take amusing, unusual, or perhaps eerie incidents that have happened to you or someone you know and transform them into essays. Often, however, student writers are reluctant to write because they don't know how or where to start. The invention techniques explained in this chapter will help you start writing. They can help to divert the flood of anxiety that often overwhelms inexperienced writers.

OVERCOMING ANXIETY

When an instructor assigns a paper, does your stomach contract into a tight knot? If it does, remember that you are not alone. Inexperienced writers often carry a heavy bundle of anxiety that impedes the effectiveness of their writing. If you lack training in writing or if you have been away from the classroom for several years, you may feel as student Tom Ledwick did:

> Writing is an underused form of communication for me. I avoid it whenever possible. . . . I leave myself open to misinterpretation when writing. Many of the ideas are not expressed in the same manner as in speaking. The written word is much more permanent and unchangeable. It requires more specification and clarification than talking. I fear that what the writer writes will not be the same as what the reader reads. Perhaps I may never have a chance to make my position clear in direct discourse and will go forever misunderstood.

Another student confided, "I don't know what's the matter, but when I walk into this classroom, I become so frightened." When asked if she was afraid of the instructor, she smiled and said, "No, but if I don't get over this feeling, I'll have to drop the course." Yet she came to every session and did excellent work. Late in the quarter during a practice assignment, she wrote about the sources of her anxiety:

> Finally, I've realized why I was so scared of this class. I was haunted by the memory of a high school literature class where we had to memorize poetry. I had learned my poem well, but when my turn came to stand and recite, I drew a blank. I could not remember a word. The teacher became angry and bawled me out in front of the class. It's taken me fifteen years to exorcise this old ghost.

Perhaps the ogre that menaces you is the dread of evaluation. You may long to write a perfect paper that will receive no criticism; and each time you write, you feel inadequate and bewildered. Lu Ann Montz felt this fear:

> Writing, for me, can be very frightening—in particular, that writing which is going to be evaluated. . . . When the pressure is on, the deadline is nearing, and I don't know what my next sentence is going to be, I become frightened. Being extremely concerned about grades, I strive to do my best. Since there are few clear-cut right or wrong answers in writing, with the exception of grammar, I often have an insecure feeling upon turning in an assignment.

Insecurity never vanished for John Steinbeck, the prolific American novelist and Nobel Prize winner. In a letter, Steinbeck wrote, "I suffer as always from the fear of putting down the first line [of a book]. It is amazing the terrors, the magics, the prayers, the straitening shyness that assails one. . . . A strange and mystic business, writing." Later, as Steinbeck was about to finish a book, he again became apprehensive over whether or not he had achieved his purpose. He described his fear as being "as natural as breathing." Eleanor Roosevelt was sometimes criticized for her lack of beauty and her strong personality in an era when women were expected to be ornamental and retiring. Yet she did not succumb to fear of criticism. The first lady wrote, "You gain strength, courage, and confidence by your experience in which you really stop to look fear in the face."

By acknowledging fear and finding the cause, you, too, can control it. Once you begin to prewrite and pace yourself throughout the writing process, chances are your fear will shrink. Dana White described how she manages fear and assumes responsibility for her writing:

> When I do not achieve as high a grade as expected, fear begins to creep in. For a while I feel inadequate. Then I become more positive as I begin to analyze why I did not reach my goal. Maybe it was poor timing, or I did not put my whole self into my writing. For whatever reason, I do not place the burden on anyone else; it always falls on my shoulders. By realizing my mistakes, I start to alleviate them. I work hard to overcome these problems so that my fear does not keep me from doing what I want to accomplish.

Criticism is a fact of life for all of us. Professional writers, too, encounter criticism. Not every manuscript is published, nor are published pieces always received kindly by critics. The best way to dull the pain of criticism is to view errors and comments as a doorway to revision. Then they become opportunities to learn. The more you think and write, the more your awareness and insights will deepen, and the easier writing will become. As your writing improves, bubbles of confidence will buoy your spirits. You may even discover you enjoy writing.

FINDING A TOPIC AND IDEAS BY PREWRITING

An excellent way to ease the frustration of finding a topic is to prewrite. To discover ideas in the nether regions of the brain, there is no substitute for prewriting. Prewriting can condense the swirling mists of your thoughts into written words, helping you retrieve information you already know. This first step of the writing process uncovers raw material to shape and polish later. Prewriting is a stage of planning, of assessing the rhetorical situation and proposing possibilities.

The beauty of prewriting is that it enables you to find possible topics and ideas quickly. While you are prewriting, there is no need to think about order or correctness—*the objective is to produce as many ideas as possible.* In prewriting, general ideas lead to specific topics and details. As you become more specific, you will find that formulating a thesis becomes easier.

Invention techniques are ways to jump-start ideas. By trying all six techniques described in this chapter, you will find out which ones work best for you. All can be done on a word processor or with pen and paper, whichever is most comfortable for you.

Brainstorming

An efficient way to start your mind moving is to brainstorm, either alone or in groups. The secret of success in brainstorming is to think fast and forgo criticism. Remarks such as "That won't work" or "We've tried that before" dampen enthusiasm and dam the stream of ideas. In brainstorming, all ideas are respected and recorded, no matter how wild. You can brainstorm by beginning with one general topic or more.

For one topic, write it at the top of your paper. Or if you have two or more topics, just fold a sheet of paper in sections, one for each topic. Then begin brainstorming wherever you wish. The objective is to fill *one* section to the brim. Whichever section yields the most details indicates the topic you know best (see table 2.1).

Freewriting

Like brainstorming, freewriting is uncensored writing. Unlike brainstorming, freewriting is more developed; it may be in sentence form. Freewriting often

TABLE 2.1 Brainstorming Four General Interests

telling ghost stories
sitting around the fire
sleeping in the wild
tent camping
        CAMPING
looking at the stars
skunks parade past our tent
	feel fit
	more confident
	for women
	    WEIGHT LIFTING
	look masculine?
	takes discipline

can start small—with a tub
  add fantail goldfish
  large multicolored snails
  water plants:
    Japanese iris
    miniature water lilies
    water lettuce—floats!
stones, gravel
water gets scummy; must clean
  must empty tub in winter
raccoons eat fish/snails
    WATER GARDENS
I would like a pool with a
  waterfall or a fountain.
  pump, pool liner, rocks
  shrubs at back
  frogs, turtles, fish—safer
  more places to hide
  can leave them out all winter
  don't have to change water
Expensive. Work to install.
	show cats
	  clean, intelligent
	  affectionate pets
	      CATS
	beautiful

works well for writers whose thoughts flee at the sight of a fresh sheet of paper. Freewriting enables anyone to start writing immediately. To freewrite, just empty your mind and write about anything. Record bits and pieces of ideas as they drift by. Here is an example:

> What to write? There's so much debris in my mind. Clutter. The files are over-flowing—it's no wonder I can't find anything to write about. What is significant? Let's see. Life is significant—very, very, very much so. Yet some individuals toss it away so lightly. Just last week in our town, two guys in their twenties carried out a suicide pact. They had been drinking and doing drugs. A bartender overheard them planning the night before. But he didn't do anything or tell anyone. Probably thought they were just talking—old saying, you know, that those who talk about it won't. But the truth is they often do. How sad—only one chance and they throw it away. They jump into eternity without a parachute, not knowing where they will land—or if they will ever land.

This freewriting sample has unearthed three general topics: the value of life, suicide, and the possibility of another life after death. The writer might go on to take one of these three topics as the subject for a second round of freewriting. Freewriting in this way is called *focused freewriting* because rather than starting with whatever is in his or her head, the writer has already established a focus to freewrite about.

Note that freewriting may not be the best technique for writers who are under time constraints: it may take much longer than other techniques. To avoid a time trap while freewriting, set a timer for ten minutes. Shut off your conscious editor and write quickly. When the timer rings, stop, examine your catch, and develop whatever seems promising.

Clustering

Clustering is the favorite prewriting device of many students. Devised by Gabriele Rico, clustering is uncensored brainstorming combined with doodling. This combination produces a web of connections. Clustering enables you not only to generate ideas but also to establish visible links between them. A page of clustering produces an overview of a general subject, suggests specific topics, and yields related details.

To begin clustering, take a fresh sheet of paper and write one subject in the center. Then circle the word. As each new thought bursts forth, jot it near the word that prompted it. Circle the new word. Next draw a line and attach it to its predecessor. Continue as quickly as possible, filling the page with ideas, details, and examples. As you review the cluster, one segment should yield a suitable topic. The sample cluster (fig. 2.1) began with the subject of birds. That central idea branched out, leading to the specific topic of birdwatching.

Questioning

To use questioning at its best, try projecting yourself into the role of a reporter. What questions could you ask to elicit information from other people?

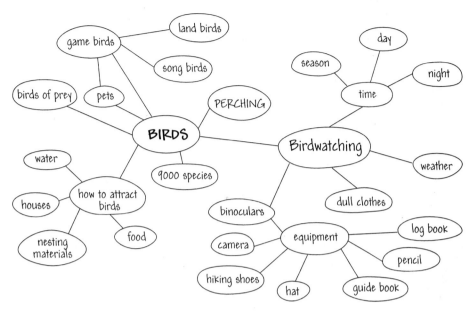

Figure 2.1 Clustering

Then try the questions on yourself. Whenever your writing stalls, ask questions to restart the flow of details. The traditional "five W's and an H" (who? what? when? where? why? how?) can be expanded to full-fledged questions:

- Who was involved?
- What happened?
- When did it happen?
- Where did it happen?
- Why did it happen?
- How did it happen?
- Who is interested?
- When did it end?
- What will be its effect?
- How will it affect the participants?
- What does it mean?
- What can be learned?
- What is the subject?
- What are some examples of it?
- What is the subject like or unlike?
- What caused it?

- What can it cause?
- When did you (or other people) become aware of it?
- Where did it originate?
- Where is it going?
- Why does it exist?
- Why are you (or other people) interested in it?
- How has it changed over time?
- How does it affect you (or other people)?

List-Making and Scratch Outlining

List-making and scratch outlining are speedy devices to capture and organize ideas. List-making can be a godsend when you know so much about a topic that you feel overwhelmed. With a list you can narrow a broad range of possibilities. To start listing, place your topic at the top of a page or computer screen. Then list details that might be relevant. If you sort details as you write, place each group in a short column. If you spy an item that does not belong, simply cross it out or delete it from the screen.

Below is one student's list of ideas about the ducks she raised on her family's farm as a child:

received two Pecan drakes as a gift

ducks were noisy

ducks were also affectionate and intelligent when they matured

quacking to call me when they were hungry

digging worms to feed them

ducks will not obey

locked them in the yard while my friends went to the woods, but they escaped and found us

grew fast

went through ugly, awkward stage

changes in colors and feathers

sleek appearance in maturity

Dad didn't like it when they polluted the horse trough

Lesson learned: no eggs, no income

Lists often have no apparent order. When you start placing ideas in order, you are beginning a *scratch outline*. This primitive outline is simply a revised list that herds ideas into a tentative order. To develop a scratch outline, first scan your details, looking for some logical order. This may be a chronological sequence or a grouping of details according to topical categories. As you find labels or headings for groups, place the headings at the top of columns. These headings will become your main points. Now recopy your points into one column, leaving several spaces between points to insert related details. Your scratch outline will enable you to predict the shape of your paper. The scratch outline that follows groups details from the previous list under topical headings.

Scratch Outline: A Child's Lesson in Economics

1. Intro: Gift of two noisy newborn Pecan drakes

2. Duck adolescence:
   feeding, digging worms, fast growth, ugly awkward stage, changes in color and feathers.

3. Duck habits:
   what Dad didn't like: polluting the horse trough and ducks will not obey.

4. Duck maturity:
   sleek, affectionate, intelligent. Quacking at the back gate to call me when they were hungry. Locking them in yard while my friends and I went to the woods. How the ducks escaped and found us.
   No eggs, no income.

5. Conclusion:
   the fate of my beloved pets

A Tip for Computer Users: Check your word-processing package to see if it has an integrated outline function. This function allows you to develop and reorganize an outline easily. This way you can start a scratch outline and quickly move to a working outline.

Combining Invention Techniques

As you prewrite, play around with ideas. Many writers find that combining invention techniques is even more productive than using one technique alone. For instance, while clustering, you might try asking yourself brief questions to increase the flow of ideas: What? Where? What next? What else should be said? Who? How? What else? What is interesting? Funny? When? Why? So what? What does the reader need to know?

GATHERING INFORMATION

All of the discovery techniques mentioned here are useful, but for most college work, you will also need other methods of gathering information. One very practical method is to keep a journal to store writing material. Interviewing can yield considerable information, too. Reading, of course, can put a variety of information at your fingertips.

Keeping a Journal

A journal is a private account of conversations, events, perceptions, reactions, or anything else a writer cares to record. In some ways a journal is similar to a diary, but journals tend to be more developed and thoughtful. Some writers also save quotations, funny stories, or poems. Any of these items may prove valuable for later writing.

Keeping a journal has additional advantages. A journal can be a safe place to pour out your feelings. Regular journal entries enable you to track problems and trace how you communicate, maintain relationships, and handle concerns. In the process of writing journal entries, you will develop self-awareness and gain insights. Actually, a journal can serve as a personal progress report. Note that some instructors require journals for class assignments. If instructors or other people will be reading your journal, you may want to monitor it, perhaps keeping separate pages for material you consider private.

To start a journal, you need a notebook small enough to be convenient, but big enough to give you space to write easily. To begin an entry, jot down the date, then describe any significant events or interesting thoughts that occurred during your day. The crucial factor in journal keeping is to record facts and perceptions while they are fresh. That way you preserve your initial impressions and observations. If they should change, note the change and the cause. Also record other people's reactions and comments. As you do, you will be developing your analytical abilities.

Interviewing

When a writer lacks information, an interview with a knowledgeable person can be a valuable resource. Interviews may be informal or formal. For example, an informal interview with friends or family might elicit unknown bits of family history. A formal interview with a local historian might uncover further information. Prepared questions are helpful for guiding the interview and uncovering specific information. Telephone interviews are seldom as rewarding as face-to-face interviews. Most people seem less inclined to reveal personal details and beliefs or give out much information over the telephone. Then, too, a conversation from a distance lacks intimacy; being face to face provides the visual cues that yield bits of information about how the informant feels.

When you wish to interview someone, ask for an appointment so that the interviewee will be relaxed, comfortable, and prepared to talk. While making the appointment, briefly state the purpose of the interview and ask a question or two to start the person thinking about the topic. You might also request permission to tape-record the interview and so avoid the distraction of note-taking. If you do, assure the interviewee that the tape will be erased as soon as your writing is completed. Finally, remember that interviews, like quotations from written material, require documentation (see chapter 22).

Reading

When factual information is required for an assignment, a library may be the best place to go. If you have access to the Internet or other online services, those may also be useful. In fact, many libraries provide access to online services. In the library you can browse through computerized listings, the card catalog (if there is one), and various indexes. If you decide to do library research, turn to chapters 21, 22, and 23 *before* you begin. These chapters will guide you through the search process, giving tips and showing how to incorporate information into your papers effectively.

CONSIDERING THE RHETORICAL SITUATION

After you finish reading, but before you start the first draft, consider the rhetorical situation. In particular, you need to ask yourself three questions: What is the purpose of the writing? Who is your audience? How do you want your writing voice to sound?

Thinking about Your Purpose

As mentioned in chapter 1, the *purpose* of the writer refers to the *reason* for writing. To find your purpose, think about what you wish to accomplish in the paper. Completing a class assignment is not purpose enough. The real purpose for writing arises from a situation that requires clarification, definition, problem solving, or some other approach to meeting your readers' needs. To find a writing purpose, you might ask: What result do I wish to achieve for the reader and for me? The answer will help you approach the topic in a way that will interest and serve the reader.

The most common general purposes of writing are to inform, to persuade, to evaluate, to entertain, or to express an opinion, feeling, or belief. Note that these purposes can be combined. Many student writers find it helpful to write their purpose statement down before they begin a first draft. That way they can also refer to the statement from time to time to help them focus. The format for a purpose statement has only two basic parts: general purpose + specific purpose, as shown here:

>   [general]   [specific]
> - Purpose: To *inform* readers *about ways to decrease cholesterol.*
>   [general]   [specific]
> - Purpose: To *persuade* readers *to vote for a bill requiring deposits on and recycling of all glass beverage bottles.*

Considering Your Audience

To accomplish your purpose, you must recognize and respect your readers' needs. The more you can learn about your readers, the more appropriate and interesting you can make your writing. Writing that is addressed to no one in particular will lack a sense of purpose.

On the job, your readers are probably people you have met or talked to on the telephone. If not, you might inquire of a coworker or an administrator. In the classroom, your instructor may assign a type of audience. If no audience is assigned, you should select one and keep that reader in mind as you write. To assess your reading audience, you might ask the following questions.

Questions to Assess Readers

1. *To whom am I writing?* What do I know about the age, gender, education, social class, economic status, interests, and attitudes of the readers? How should these characteristics affect the voice and content of my writing?

2. *Why will they read this piece of writing?* How can they benefit? Will they gain information? Be entertained? Learn more about conflicting views of an issue? Any other benefit? How can I shape the writing to their needs?

3. *How much do they need or want to know?* How much can I assume they already know about the subject? What terms should be defined? How much should I say?

4. *How will they feel about the subject?* How should their current feelings affect my word choice and strategy?

5. *How will they react to my point of view?* How should their probable reaction to my position affect my writing?

A helpful tactic in assessing your audience is to deliberately shift your perspective from writer to reader. Try to put yourself into the reader's role—to feel and think as the reader might. In "Don't Blame the Editors," Sloan Wilson explains this dual role of writer/reader:

> Each of us is both writer and reader, and no reader has mercy for dullness. My editor, who as politely as possible had told me that my work was boring, had learned to speak for millions of readers, and I was grateful to him for making me clean up my act before putting it before the world's sleepy eyes. . . . Those listeners would start getting restless if I confused them; they demanded clarity above all else.

A seasoned writer selects words with care, listening to both their meaning and their music. Precise words specify exactly what you mean. Little surprises in word sounds dispel dullness and delight the reader. The sound of the voice behind the words is also important.

Listening to Your Own Written Voice

To be respected by your readers, you must find a voice that not only serves your purpose but also reflects sincerity, integrity, acuity, and (at times) empathy. Readers expect understanding and trust, and they are usually quick to recognize insincerity, incompetence, and arrogance. To better understand voice in writing, think about what you do when chatting with a friend face to face. You automatically adapt your voice to the occasion. Your tone is pleasant and friendly. You welcome your friend by your words and manner. When writing informally, you might think of the reader as a friend.

Of course, not all writing carries the mark of a writer's personality. Some writing is distant and impersonal, devoid of the writer's presence. You are familiar with the matter-of-fact tone found in encyclopedias, other reference works, and some textbooks. For most of your college writing, however, you will be expected to have a clear, appropriate voice, not completely distant but not overly informal either.

Naturally, the quality and tone of a writer's voice may vary from one writing situation to another; the expectations of the audience play a considerable role in determining the voice a writer presents. But as Dona J. Hickey points out in *Developing a Written Voice*, "We must live with one tension between what pleases the writer and what pleases the audience." In other words, although we conform to certain conventions and write to reach the reader, we also include what pleases us. Sometimes there is a conflict that must be resolved. Hickey explains, "Pleasing audiences is part of a writer's skill. Creating voices is how it is done."

Summary

Prewriting is a practical way to manage fear of writing. When a writer faces fear and starts prewriting, progress has begun. Prewriting is the first stage of the writing process, your opportunity to discover ideas and write them down. Six common invention techniques useful in prewriting are brainstorming, freewriting, clustering, questioning, list-making, and scratch outlining.

You may also gather information for writing from journal writing, interviews, or reading. After you gather material, you shape it according to your purpose and audience. Knowing your readers' backgrounds, interests, and viewpoints will help you to find an appropriate writing strategy and voice. Your written voice affects whether or not the audience accepts your thesis. Your written voice should be appropriate for the writing situation.

Key Terms

brainstorming	questioning	purpose statement
freewriting	list-making	
clustering	scratch outline	

Practice

Ideas for Ten-Minute Writings

Directions: Free-write for ten minutes about anything you wish. The following suggestions may be helpful.

1. Softly falling snow is like . . .
2. Sometimes I feel . . .
3. When I see . . . I remember . . .
4. When I hear . . . I think of . . .
5. I wonder . . .
6. Tomorrow . . .
7. I can't . . . but I can . . .
8. Once I . . . but now . . .
9. When I see . . . I think of the time . . .
10. Raindrops remind me of . . .
11. My territorial behavior
12. Death of a cardinal
13. Neighborhood brats
14. Letter from a . . .
15. A little . . . is . . .

Ideas for Journal Writing

1. Describe an amusing event that happened at work.
2. Write a reaction to your day. Then set objectives for tomorrow.
3. Describe a problem in communication. What was said? What might have been meant? What, if anything, should be done?
4. Describe a person you have met recently. What qualities or characteristics impressed you?
5. Write a short poem.
6. Recount a dream. What might it mean? (You may want to borrow a book on dreams to aid in interpretation.)
7. Describe an unusual occurrence.
8. Copy a quotation you would like to keep.
9. React to an article or a book you have read. You might begin by summarizing the main points, then add your reactions.
10. Sketch a career plan. What additional experience, training, or education will you need? How can you gain them?
11. Describe a happy event and your thoughts about it.
12. Describe a problem and map out a strategy to solve it.
13. Summarize your worst mistake. What have you learned from it?
14. Describe your greatest success. Why was it so meaningful?
15. What would you most like to do? How might you do it?

CHAPTER 3

Drafting

*Writing and rewriting are a constant
search for what it is one is saying.*

—John Updike

WRITING A FIRST DRAFT: AN OVERVIEW

Drafting is the time to rummage through the ideas you have accumulated during prewriting and unfold them into sentences and paragraphs. Developing an exploratory draft can be exciting—hours may seem like minutes. You may glance at an old idea and suddenly see it in a new light. You may conceive a delightful comparison or find a bit of irony or an unusual twist. As you combine and create, you may grope for words and settle for temporary substitutes. You may thumb through prewriting notes, hunting for details. Although there may be moments when you are unable to see the way clearly, it is important to keep writing. The purpose of a first draft is to expand ideas on paper as quickly as possible without interruption by a personal censor or other noise.

Fleshing Out Your Prewriting Notes

Before you begin to write, find a secluded spot. Make up your mind not to be disturbed by the telephone or other distractions. Do whatever you can to ensure privacy. To start a first draft, you need a block of uninterrupted time, at least an hour, when your mind is keen. Start wherever you wish—beginning, middle, or end. That way, there is no worry about wording a thesis statement, supplying transitions, or other concerns. There is no need to correct or do anything that will disrupt your concentration. Just glance at your prewriting notes whenever you need more ideas.

Perhaps the best advice is to let ideas go where they will. Don't be overly concerned if your first draft wanders into byways. Unnecessary details and mistakes may litter the path of your main idea. That's all right. This draft is for your eyes only. It lets you explore. You can rearrange and clean up later. If your inner censor will not allow you free rein, then circle suspicious spellings or mark questionable words, but move on quickly. If a word or idea eludes you, just draw a short line and spurt on. Carefree, you will be more apt to experience the fun of discovering what you know as you write.

When Ideas Disappear

As you roam the hills and valleys of your memory, collecting bits of experience (incidents, anecdotes, examples, and other specific details) for your exploratory draft, sometimes there is little to find. That may be the time to stop and take an exercise break. Whether you do isometrics or pushups, jog in place, or ride an exercise bike, the deep breathing and increased blood flow will decrease muscle tension and fatigue. Refreshed, you can return and restart. To focus and find more material, try asking yourself questions:

- What people, places, objects, or ideas might I write about?
- Why am I interested in this topic, event, or experience?
- How do I feel about these?
- What has influenced my feelings?
- What do I want my readers to know or feel? What should I include to achieve this purpose?

Or if you find that you are completely blocked, a break may be the only solution. Before you stop, schedule a specific time to resume writing.

FOCUSING AN EXPLORATORY DRAFT

If writers have a distinct sense of purpose, they are often able to focus their exploratory drafts surprisingly well. A clear central idea unifies the material, so that it progresses in a logical way. Other writers circle aimlessly around a general topic, unsure of how or where to proceed. If they can pause to limit the topic and write a thesis statement, however, they are able to establish a direction for their writing.

Narrowing a Topic

When you narrow a topic, you focus on a segment that you can develop well. You write more about less. If you find yourself rambling or lost while exploring your topic, stop and consider the range you are covering. Is the topic too broad? Can it be covered adequately in the required number of words? To be manageable, a topic should be whittled down to fit the assignment and the rhetorical situation. The pyramid below shows how a very broad topic (top of pyramid) can be narrowed.

Ohio

touring Ohio

touring the Ohio River

steamboats on the Ohio River

my steamboat ride on the Ohio River

CASE STUDY

JUANITA NARROWS HER TOPIC

Juanita wishes to research solar energy. Over the years she has read a few articles on the subject, but she wonders what has been discovered recently. She suspects that her general readers are also hazy about the topic. And they may not care one way or the other. She asks several of her classmates and verifies both inferences. How can she interest them in the topic? How might they benefit from reading about it? She writes down the latter question and starts a list to come up with ideas and narrow the topic.

Question: How might readers benefit by learning more about solar energy?

Narrowing: General-to-Specific

solar energy

practical applications for solar energy

solar heating for homes

solar heating during construction of new homes

solar heating for existing homes

As Juanita reviews her list, she realizes that every reader is a potential home owner. At first she considers discussing applications for new home construction, but then she thinks about budget constraints. Few of her readers will be building their first home. Most will buy older homes and repair or remodel them. At this point, she briefly describes her audience and writes a purpose statement.

- *Audience:* College students who are potential buyers of existing homes and who are interested in comfort at a reasonable cost.

- *Purpose:* To inform the reader of solar heating applications for existing homes and to evaluate practicality.

Writing a Thesis Statement

The thesis statement presents the main idea of a paper. It also acts as a contract with the reader, making a promise that sets forth the specific purpose and the intent of the writer. Because there is no simple formula for thesis statements, only a few examples are shown here. (You will find dozens more throughout the book.) Whatever form they take, however, thesis statements perform four specific tasks:

Four Tasks of a Thesis Statement

1. Identify the subject.
2. State a claim, an approach, or an attitude.
3. Suggest the direction of the writing.
4. Set the tone.

An analysis of a thesis sentence from a paper by student Michele Flahive demonstrates the four tasks:

Thesis: For the dedicated player, the challenge, the enjoyment, and the camaraderie make softball a game worth playing.

Subject: Playing softball

Claim: For the dedicated player, softball is worth playing.

Direction: Focus on three main points—challenge, then enjoyment, then camaraderie

Tone: Middle level of formality

Notice that Michele's thesis sets up her three main points. An easy way to draft this type of thesis sentence is to make a list like the one that follows and fill in the blanks.

Subject: _____

Main points: _____

    _____

    _____

Claim/approach/attitude: _____

Write in the best possibilities to fill the blanks, and then combine the results to make a complete sentence. Experiment, and soon you will have a tentative thesis statement. Even if it doesn't seem quite right, be patient. It can still act as your controlling idea and assist in organizing an exploratory draft. If you are not dividing your topic into points, skip line 2 of the pattern above. *The sooner you write a tentative thesis statement, the fewer drafts you are likely to need.*

Where Should the Thesis Statement Go?   Usually, the thesis statement is placed in the introduction, often in the opening paragraph of short papers. Sometimes it appears at the beginning but more often at the end of the opening paragraph. There it can forge a tight link to later paragraphs. In research or other long papers, the introduction may contain two or more paragraphs. In that case, the thesis sentence generally appears at the end of the introduction.

Omitting a Thesis Statement   Some kinds of writing have a thesis that is never specified but is clearly implied. The omission is not a lapse; careful planning and considerable skill are required to keep the controlling idea apparent without stating it openly. Omission of a thesis sentence is hazardous for a budding writer, especially for the kinds of writing often done in college. Most instructors expect an explicit thesis.

SEVEN COMMON ORDERS

Whether you are explaining a process or arguing for one side of an issue, you have to develop your thesis idea. Every completed manuscript should have a logical order. Well-organized details improve clarity and readability. There is no one order to fit all writing; you must decide what is appropriate for a particular purpose, audience, and occasion. As you sort through your prewriting notes and reread your first draft, watch for a pattern to emerge. Does your thesis statement contain a clue to the order needed? Look closely at any transitions you have included. Do they refer to time? To location? To cause and effect? Are some points more important than others? Any of these signs may give clues to the order that is needed for your paper.

Once you understand the seven common orders listed below, you will be better equipped to focus your drafts.

Seven Common Orders

1. Chronological order
2. Order of importance
3. General to specific (or reverse)
4. Whole to parts (or reverse)
5. Spatial order
6. Concrete to abstract (or reverse)
7. Familiar to unfamiliar

Chronological Order

Telling the reader *when* something happens over the course of time promotes clarity and provides continuity. In a narrative, *time* controls the order of events; the story usually moves forward (chronological order) or backward (reverse chronological order). Once in a while, a lateral shift in time may be made with words such as *meanwhile* or *at the same time*. In process analysis (for example, in writing instructions), the sequence in which steps occur governs their order of presentation (first to last). Résumés usually reverse the sequence, moving from most recent to earliest position held. All of these arrangements are variations of chronological order.

Spatial Order

Description uses an order of space to locate details for the reader. Details are presented in a sequence according to physical layout or design. For instance, any of the following spatial orders (or their reverse) might be used for a description:

head to toe	outside to inside	clockwise
bottom to top	north to south	circular
left to right	up and down	horizontal

Order of Importance

Newspaper articles typically use *most-to-least-important* order, beginning with the most important information and leaving the least important details until last. Editors know that readers often read only the first few paragraphs of an article or only what is on the front page. For other writing, *least-to-most-important* order is sometimes used. This order places the emphasis on the final point. For example, you might use least-to-most-important order in essays of classification, illustration, or argument.

General-to-Specific Order

Explanatory paragraphs and essays sometimes begin with a generalization that is placed in the opening topic sentence or thesis statement. The specific supporting details are presented to explain the opening generalization. This order can be reversed to *specific-to-general* order, with the generalization concluding the paragraph or essay. Moving from specific details to a general conclusion can pave the way for an idea that readers might otherwise be reluctant to accept.

Whole-to-Parts Order

An overview of a subject before an explanation of the parts is often helpful. For example, a narrative might begin with a description of a small town and its residents to give readers an overall sense of where the story takes place. An analysis often starts by presenting an object or concept as a whole before examining its individual parts. An argument may begin with a summary of an issue or problem, then move on to look at particular elements. Sometimes this order is reversed, moving from parts to the whole, especially in description.

Concrete-to-Abstract Order

Concrete words refer to actual (physical) data about a condition, event, experience, object, animal, or person. We perceive material evidence of these elements through our five senses. Most of us are able to see, hear, touch, taste, and smell to obtain firsthand proof that concrete items exist. For example, tears are concrete: we can see them, feel them, even taste them. Tears may sometimes *indicate* sadness, but sadness is an abstraction.

Abstract refers to ideas we conceive that have no physical referent, nothing material to prove they exist. We can think and talk about abstractions, but we *cannot* see, hear, taste, touch, or smell them. For example, patriotism, love, and integrity are all abstractions. The only way that we can infer they exist is to look for *concrete* evidence that *implies* their existence.

Writers of description often move from the concrete to the abstract, presenting physical details about a subject that lead to an understanding of it as appealing or unappealing, peaceful or warlike, beneficial or harmful (abstractions). Sermons, political speeches, and other such persuasive writing may use concrete images and stories drawn from life to lead into discussions of abstract concepts such as generosity, fairness, and the like. Or they may use concrete objects that have come to be closely associated with or symbolic of abstract ideas, as our flag is a symbol of patriotism and a rose is a symbol of love.

This order can be reversed to *abstract to concrete*. For example, an essay of illustration or definition might begin by introducing an abstract concept—such as friendship or bravery—and then move on to provide concrete instances and examples.

Familiar-to-Unfamiliar Order

Movement from the known to the unknown is an effective way to explain an unusual topic. By starting with the familiar, what readers already know and accept, you can orient them before explaining the unfamiliar and strange. Likewise, you might move from the old to the new, from easy to difficult, or from simple to complex.

FROM OUTLINE TO DRAFT

When you are ready to organize your exploratory draft, a scratch outline is a practical tool that can save you considerable time. Rearranging parts of an outline is much simpler than rearranging whole chunks of text. To make a scratch outline, go back to your prewriting and underline the most important points. Next, list these points on another sheet in a temporary order, leaving a few lines between them. Then, sort out the details belonging to each point and write them in under the appropriate heading. When you have finished, take a short break or work on something else to let your thoughts settle. When you come back, reconsider the order. Can you find a better way to arrange the main points? Is the order of details in each group consistent? Are your headings appropriate? At this point, rearrange and flesh out your points to create a working outline for your draft.

The following examples show the progression from a scratch outline to a working outline and from an exploratory draft to a revised draft.

Scratch Outline (Order of main points: unpleasant to pleasant)

Title: Kinds of People Who Attend Swap Meets

Type A
Usually dealers who resell. Gather around as we unload at 4 a.m. Give us a hard time. Looking for bargains.

Type B
Arrive late, often at closing time. Complain. Years ago we'd unload. They still didn't buy.

Type C
Looking for hard-to-find parts. Ask price. Buy or move on. Come about 8 a.m. Nice folks.

In the working outline that follows, the types noted in the preceding scratch outline have been renamed, and the order has been changed. The writer decided that chronological order would work better than his previous choice because the time when customers arrive correlates with their behavior. Details within paragraphs have also been reorganized for consistency and balance.

Working Outline (Chronological order)

Title: Swap Meets—It Takes All Kinds

1. Early Birds
   Arrival: 4 a.m.
   Purpose: Buy cheap for resale.
   Behavior: Buy little. Give us a hard time.

2. Buyers
   Arrival: 8:00 a.m.
   Purpose: Find parts they need themselves.
   Behavior: Pleasant, polite.

3. Sightseers
   Arrival: Late afternoon till closing time.
   Purpose: Look around.
   Behavior: Complaining.

EXPLORATORY DRAFT

People Who Flock to Swap Meets

Jack, my son, and I have decided there are three types of people who attend swap meets—the early birds, the buyers, and the sightseers. Swap meets are like flea markets, except these swap meets are for car parts only. Set-up times usually start at 4 a.m. This is the time when the early birds try to buy our car parts. They start gathering around our truck while we are trying to unload—crowding around and getting in the way. They hope to run across a good deal. They are usually dealers who have an eye out for a fast buck. They stand around and drink coffee and give us a hard time in general—making sarcastic remarks in a joking manner. A few may offer to help unload. They don't buy much.

The buyers don't arrive until 8 o'clock or thereafter. They usually look for hard-to-find parts to fix up an old vehicle they are working on. Often they are restoring a classic car in their garage in their spare time, and they like to tell us about it. Sometimes they are with their families. They take their time and hunt carefully through the boxes and piles of parts. They are serious buyers and do not give us a hard time. They ask how much a part costs, and if they don't want it, go on. Otherwise, they buy. They are pleasant. Some are almost like old friends—we see them regularly.

Sightseers generally come late in the afternoon, often at closing time. They are always complaining about something. Either they can't find what they want—there's not too much left by then—or they gripe because we are busy loading the truck to go home. Years ago we used to unload parts so they could see them, but then we noticed they would not buy anything anyway. They just wanted to sightsee.

Swap meets are enjoyable because Jack and I get together, make a little money, and meet some fine people.

—Roger Moore

Roger's exploratory draft was well developed. Like all early drafts, it needed revision, particularly in the introduction and conclusion, as his subsequent draft shows.

REVISED DRAFT

People Who Flock to Swap Meets

In the summertime my son and I load my panel truck with auto parts every Saturday and head for a swap meet. Swap meets are like flea markets, except these swap meets are for car parts only. At swap meets Jack and I not only make a little money and enjoy the time together, but we also meet some interesting people. We have found that three types of folks usually attend: the early birds, the buyers, and the sightseers.

The early birds start flocking around the truck as we begin unloading and setting up at 4 a.m., before daybreak. They are usually dealers who are out for a fast buck. They crowd around, getting in the way, hoping to strike a good deal. A few may offer to help unload, but most stand around, drinking coffee and giving us a hard time. Often they make sarcastic remarks in a joking way. They don't buy much.

The buyers don't arrive until 8 o'clock or so. They generally look for difficult-to-find parts to repair an old vehicle they are working on in their spare time. Often they are restoring a classic car in their garage, and they like to tell us about it. We've heard some surprising stories about how much money they made from restoring a junked car. Some of them return regularly; they are almost like old friends. Sometimes they bring their families. They take their time, hunting carefully through boxes and piles of parts. They are serious buyers who ask how much a part costs. If they don't want it, they go on to the next display. Otherwise, they buy.

Sightseers usually come late in the afternoon, often near closing time. It seems they can always find something to complain about. Seldom do they find what they want, and they often become irritated when we are too busy loading the truck to help them. Some even ask us to unload so that they can look over the rest of the parts! Years ago we tried unloading the parts for them to see, but we noticed they would not buy anything anyway. They just wanted to sightsee.

Despite the little irritations, swap meets are still a good place to spend a leisurely Saturday, visiting with my son and meeting interesting people.

—**Roger Moore**

DRAFTING AN INTRODUCTION

Whether you draft your introduction first or last, be prepared to give it careful thought. An effective introduction affords a graceful entry into a topic. The opening sentence arouses interest and induces the reader to continue. The writer's voice sets a suitable tone for the writing, inviting the reader to consider the topic.

Because of the many options for openings, inexperienced writers may be unsure of how to proceed. You will find a wide array of introductions throughout this book, showing many ways to start a story or a paper. Seven common types of introductions are described in the following sections.

Begin with an Anecdote That Sets the Scene

An anecdote, or a brief story, can be particularly effective in capturing a reader's attention. When inexperienced writers use such openings, however, they often skip the important first step of setting the scene. To orient readers and forestall puzzlement, state *when* and *where* the experience happened. Sometimes just a few carefully chosen details will give a sense of time and place, as in this introduction:

My Worst Job

When I was sixteen, my cousin suggested I take a job at a dress factory where she worked. Because she liked the people and the wages, I hired on. For a country girl who had never been inside a factory, the first day was overwhelming. Rows and rows of sewing machines whirred while hundreds of women worked at a furious pace. Finding me an empty chair, the trainer demonstrated how to operate the machine and sew a facing on the bodice of a cotton dress. Since I had made my own clothes for years, the task was simple. Outwardly, the power sewing machines somewhat resembled the old Singer at home. But the piece of technology in front of me was as much like my old machine as a Mercedes is like a Model T. Careening around the curves, I hung onto the cloth and somehow guided it under the presser foot. By lunch time, however, I had mastered the machine and the five-minute task that was my only responsibility. Day after day for an interminable week, I repeated that mind-numbing procedure.

A narrative opening not only provides interest, but also aids in avoiding "I" as the first word in a paper, which is irritating to many readers. The following rule will assist you in using first person with discretion:

> *Dietsch's Rule:* Never use *I* to open a letter, paper, or paragraph: find a better way.

Instead, look at the rest of the sentence for a word or phrase that can be moved up and placed before *I*. Even one word, such as *yesterday, although,* or *when,* will provide a smoother opening than a reference to yourself. Just tell when and where the action takes place. To help you start, here are some ideas.

Opening Words to Set the Scene

References to Time	References to Place
Ten years ago	From my window
When I was a small child	While working as assistant manager at
After I graduated	In the green hills of
In 1932 my grandfather	Near the Bay of Biscayne
Last month my life	On Kelly's Island
During my teen years	

Begin with a Description

A few words of artful description at the beginning of a paper can explain, illustrate, or provide a bit of background. For example, in the following introduction, Joe Norton involves the reader and sets the scene as he briefly describes the San Diego area, which he divides into three landscapes:

Adventures around San Diego

Anyone with a sense of adventure will find living in sunny southern California anything but boring. With all of the natural beauty in the San Diego area, there hardly seems time enough for exploring. Even the most jaded person can find something new, whether in the desert, in the mountains, or on the beaches.

In the next opening, Kenny Patrick sets the scene and involves the reader with vivid words that explain the fascination of his favorite sport:

Hooked on a Tradition

Icy water swirls around the wading fly fisherman. With experience gained from thousands of casts, he deposits the tiny brown deer hair fly directly beneath an overhanging branch at the water's edge. His pulse quickens as he gently twitches the tip of the rod. Like a living being, the tiny fly dances across the surface. Suddenly, a bronze torpedo erupts from the depths and snatches the small offering. The fisherman feels the solid pull of a feisty small-mouth bass and sets the hook. With a powerful thrust of its tail, the large fish launches itself into the air. Shaking its head, the bass dislodges the hook. Hands trembling, the fisherman is left with just a memory. Moments like this make fly fishing a frustrating, yet fascinating and educational sport.

Begin by Stating a Problem

Stating a problem can be a practical way to open. For example, Janet Edington begins by briefly summarizing a problem pet owners have. She begins by referring to pet owners generally and then smoothly switches her focus to her own experiences:

Safety First!

Pet owners are frequently faced with the challenge of transporting their pets to the veterinarian. This task can be not only nerve-wracking, but also hazardous, particularly if they are transporting a nervous cat or a large animal. The following suggestions are offered to spare anyone the "battle scars" I carry today.

Begin with an Interesting Experience

The key to beginning with an experience is to make sure that it will pique your reader's interest. Be a bit creative. Lisa Malone, for example, creates interest by relating the experience that led to her cats' names:

A Tale of Two Kittens

In our household two annoying but appealing feline members reside. Christopher was named after Christopher Columbus because he was the first kitten of the litter to explore outside their box. His brother Duke received his title because he ruled the kittens' domain. Although both of these scalawags have stripes, mitten paws, and the same gender, they differ in color, energy, and temperament.

The next writer confides how she learned a very painful piece of personal information:

A Shattering Secret

For the first twenty years of my life, I believed "Jay" was my biological father. Two years ago, however, I learned the truth, quite by accident. During a conversation with a family friend, she referred to Jay as my stepfather. She assumed that my mother had long ago told me the secret of my parentage. In those few shattering seconds, the cause of my years of emotional turmoil was finally revealed to me.

Begin with a Surprising Statistic
or Striking Bit of History

Beginning with a surprising statistic can spur a reader's curiosity, as the following example suggests:

Mitral Valve Prolapse

Although approximately 40 percent of the women in the United States suffer from a condition known as mitral valve prolapse, many of them remain unaware of its name or the nature of their illness. They do not connect their fatigue, occasional dizziness, or other symptoms to this valve, located deep within the heart.

A little-known but significant fragment of history can also provide an intriguing introduction, as in this opening by Kathy Cordle:

Kicking the Habit

In 1604 King James I of England officially condemned the use of tobacco. An 1859 report about dangers of tobacco stated that of the sixty-eight persons suffering from cancer of the mouth and throat in a hospital in Montpellier, France, all were tobacco users. Obviously, concern about the hazards of tobacco is not new.

Begin by Disputing a Common Belief or Defying a Stereotype

The writer who surprises readers with a statement that disputes a common belief or an example that defies stereotypes will grab their attention. Jenny Somerlot uses this technique when she starts by noting what people expect and then goes on to what they do not expect:

A Pair of Parakeets

Parakeets seem to be calm, loving, and predictable. But our family has found that not every parakeet is docile or the perfect pet. Our parakeet, Flash, is unfriendly not only to people but also to his cage mate, Rosco. With a flip of his beak, Flash can escape from the cage, leaving Rosco alone. While Flash soars around the room like a wild-eyed eagle, receiving all the attention, Rosco sits quietly on his perch, ignored.

In a variation of this technique, Paul Giacalone expresses a view that runs counter to a commonly held belief when he suggests that not everyone in a family need love the family pet:

The Trials of Tia

Recently my father brought home a very small and very ignorant animal. My parents named it Tia, and they have tried to convince me that it is a dog—I swear it is a rat. Actually, Tia is half rat terrier and half poodle.

Paul's offbeat perspective and critically amused tone surprise readers and hook their curiosity.

Begin with a Question

A provocative question can be used to pique readers' interest. Jack Buroker opens his paper with such a question:

Twin Troubles

Why do many people seem to think that just because twins are identical, they think and act alike? Even people who've known my twin brother and me for twenty-six years still confuse us, calling Mack, "Jack," and me, "Mack." They seem not to notice that we differ slightly in appearance and greatly in personality and goals.

In an introduction for a process paper, Dixie O'Rourke opens with a question that establishes common ground with her readers:

Cleaning House for an Unexpected Guest

Have you ever decided to take a day off from housework and just relax? It seems that on those days you get a call from a friend, who just happens to be in town, six blocks away, and would love to stop by. Now if you do, there is no need to panic. There is a simple procedure which will help you to get ready for the friend's visit.

Revising Sluggish Openings

If you are dissatisfied with your draft's introduction, first consider a bit of rearranging. You might put the thesis at the beginning and then amplify it a bit. Or try moving the thesis to the end and building up to it. Reword sentences; use active verbs. Or just leave a blank space and go on; the right words may come easily the next time you write.

Unless sluggish openings are revised, readers may have to stumble through unnecessary words, vague generalities, or other nuisances. One common cause of sluggishness is the overuse of empty expressions such as *there is*, *there are*, or *it is*. These words can spread like toadstools. Uproot them and rephrase the sentence. For example, "There is a strange house at the end of our street" can be rewritten as "A strange house stands at the end of our street."

Trite phrases are another fungus to avoid. Examples such as the following should *not* be inflicted on any reader:

There are not many people who go through life without a best friend. It is important for everyone to have a friend. True friends are hard to find, and they stick by you. To have a true friend, you must be a friend. Good friends have special qualities.

Prewriting can prevent sluggish openings. If you still don't find what you want, try stepping back and considering another perspective or angle on the subject. For example, the opening above might have been recast as an unusual comparison:

Friendships are a little like puppies. To thrive, both require time, nourishment, and affection.

WRITING AN EFFECTIVE CONCLUSION

An effective conclusion indicates that you have finished what you have to say; it does not rehash opinions or recite the obvious. No new material intrudes. An effective ending flows logically and smoothly from the body, giving a sense of completeness or *closure*. Seven basic ways to conclude are described here.

End with an Unexpected Twist

A conclusion that creeps up on readers, catching them off guard, can surprise and delight. When well done, such an ending seems spontaneous and appropriate. A brief comment or fact can pose an absurdity or profundity that causes the reader to smile or think. Paul Giacalone ended with a twist in his paper about his parents' dog Tia:

> I feel the only solution to this problem is either I go or the dog does. After I discussed this with my parents, they went out and bought me a set of luggage for Christmas.

Although a twist may be appropriate for personal writing, it is rarely appropriate for business writing. Customers, employees, and managers need to know what to expect and to understand the writer's purpose.

End with a Humorous Comment

A humorous ending catches the reader off guard and neatly completes the piece of writing. Such endings are often very short, much like the punchline of a joke. After presenting her final steps, Dixie O'Rourke finished her essay about cleaning for an unexpected guest with one sentence:

> By now your guest has probably arrived. Spray the air freshener, and open the door. Greet her with a confident smile.
> A final word of caution: Make sure you aren't still wearing your old robe and fuzzy slippers!

As with unexpected-twist endings, humor should be used with discretion.

End with a Reference to a Benefit

A paper may conclude by referring to a value, advantage, or benefit. Diane Zachman points out the benefits of a good manicure:

> The process of manicuring, when done correctly, gives your nails a vibrant, healthy appearance and keeps them from becoming weak and brittle.

End by Referring Back to the Thesis

To provide a satisfying ending, writers often refer briefly to the thesis. Notice that this device is an allusion, *not* a repetition of the entire thesis. By reworking an old cliché and repeating key points, Nora Lee Corbett is able to establish *closure:*

> **Thesis:** We raise Leghorn laying hens for their hardiness, longevity, and egg production.
> **Conclusion:** On our farm the chicken comes before the egg. And we have learned over the years that the best chicken according to hardiness, longevity, and egg production is the Leghorn.

End with a Personal Response

Writers sometimes confide their feelings to the reader. Especially at the end of a paper, they may express a sense of sadness, embarrassment, satisfaction, elation, or some other response to a situation. For example, the student who described her "worst job" concluded with the following:

> On Friday I was still doing the same mind-numbing procedure. By then my hands guided the cloth under the pressure foot with ease, but I knew I could not continue unless I underwent a lobotomy. So at quitting time I picked up my paycheck, inhaled the fresh air of freedom, and left with a light heart, knowing I would never go back.

End on a Note of Optimism

A note of optimism can create a satisfying conclusion. It might be a note of encouragement to yourself or to the reader, or it might be a look toward the future. Sue Taylor concluded "Breaking the Habit" with a congratulatory note to herself:

> Since November 7, I have not had one cigarette. Yes, there are times when I still want one, and I am struggling to drop those extra pounds, accumulated from eating all that candy, but I feel really good about myself. I am a winner!

End with a Suggestion

A suggestion or recommendation may be the best place to end a persuasive paper or a piece of business writing. Jack Buroker ends his call for more awareness of identical twins with this bit of advice:

> To someone who has a problem distinguishing twins, I suggest getting to know them. Chances are that if time is spent with each one, differences in their futures, tastes, behavior, and personalities will become much more apparent, especially to observant family members and friends. Twins are not carbon copies; they are simply individuals who happen to resemble each other.

DRAFTING ON A COMPUTER

Almost every quarter an agitated student knocks on my office door with a request for more time and a tale of the perils of using a computer. Most stories have a common theme: the failure to provide a backup file. Yet simple precautions can prevent the shock of lost text and erased or defective floppy disks or other disasters. Even if you are an experienced user, read on. Overconfidence and fatigue can contribute to this predicament.

Tips for Security of Computer Files

1. *Save files frequently.* Keep in mind that a power failure can cause the loss of all material in a file that has not been saved. Even if power failures seldom occur in your area, don't take the risk. An accident (by a car or a squirrel) or a sudden storm could cause a disruption of power.

2. *Make a backup copy right away.* Periodically save files to a second storage medium, such as a diskette. Even if you are working at home, saving on your hard drive is not enough. Loss can result from hardware, software, or user errors.

3. *Print out a copy of your draft early.* To safeguard your exploratory draft, print it out at the end of the first session. Do not wait for a completed draft. That way, if you should lose or damage your disk, you still have a copy.

4. *Take special precautions in a computer lab.* To preserve your privacy and maintain security, take *two* diskettes so that you can make a backup copy immediately. Save *only* on your floppy disks. Number them 1 and 2. Then always save on disk 1 first and load with disk 1 first. That way, if you forget to save the latest version on disk 2, you will still have it on disk 1.

Do not save on a hard drive in a lab and expect your writing to be safe. Lab personnel regularly erase student work from hard drives to keep them from filling up. Then, too, another student might gain access to your writing, which might prove embarrassing or lead to theft. (If you do not know how to save on a floppy disk, consult with a lab assistant.)

A NOTE OF REASSURANCE AND A BRIEF REVIEW

Drafting should bring a sense of adventure and exploration. To relieve any feelings of anxiety, remind yourself that drafting is the second stage in the writing process, not the last. You don't have to get everything right the first time; you will have chances to go back and revise. So focus on your central idea, follow the suggestions below, and your work should proceed fairly fast.

Summary of Tips for Writing a Draft

1. *Schedule a block of time for writing an exploratory draft.* Start early so that you will have plenty of time to revise, edit, and proofread.

2. *Study your prewriting notes to determine whether or not the topic is adequate for the assignment.*
   a. Is the topic significant?
   b. Has it been narrowed adequately?
   c. Will it interest the audience?
   d. Are there enough facts, examples, and details for support?
   e. How can the topic be presented in an interesting way?

3. *Think about how you want your written voice to sound.* Do you want to sound playful? Serious? Amused? Outraged? Or how? Your attitude toward a topic (and perhaps the assignment) will be reflected in your written voice.

4. *Begin composing anywhere in the exploratory draft.* Write in a way that is comfortable for you.

5. *Double-space and leave wide margins.* Allow room to mark changes and comments on the draft.

6. *After finishing the first draft, leave it for a day, if possible.* If not, leave it for at least an hour while you have lunch or work on another assignment. You need time to distance yourself intellectually and emotionally before revising.

7. *Save all drafts until you receive the graded paper back.* A paper may go astray. Saving drafts helps avoid losing all your work.

Summary

Drafting, the second stage of the writing process, is the time to explore ideas uncovered during prewriting. To start ideas flowing, glance back over your prewriting notes. Then write as quickly as you can without interruption and without thought to rules or restrictions. Revision and editing can come later.

A thesis statement identifies the subject; states a claim, an approach, or an attitude; suggests the direction; and sets the tone.

As you find related ideas, you can begin to group them in some sort of logical order such as chronological order, spatial order, and order of importance. You can also order ideas from general to specific, whole to parts, concrete to abstract, and familiar to unfamiliar.

An outline helps a writer to visualize the shape of a draft and to reorganize details easily. A scratch outline can be revised into a working outline, which is a plan for a draft.

An effective beginning is a necessity. You might begin with a narrative, a description, a statement of a problem, an interesting fact, a striking statistic, or a question. You might end with a twist, a bit of humor, a benefit, or another device to establish closure.

Ensure against lost text when writing on a computer by saving files regularly, making a backup copy on a floppy disk, and printing out copies of drafts soon.

Key Terms

exploratory draft	spatial order	concrete to abstract
narrowing a topic	order of importance	familiar to unfamiliar
thesis statement	general to specific	working outline
chronological order	whole to parts	closure

Practice

Ideas for Writing Activities

1. Prewrite, using one of the techniques explained in chapter 2.
2. Sketch a scratch outline from an example of prewriting.
3. Develop a scratch outline into a working outline.
4. Write an exploratory draft from a working outline.
5. Critique the exploratory draft.

Ideas for Ten-Minute Writings

1. I wish . . .
2. The magic of a music box
3. My favorite fragrance is the smell of . . .
4. If I had my way, . . .
5. My job
6. My earliest memory
7. If I could buy a ticket to anywhere, I would . . .
8. My grandfather's . . . was a tool to him, but for me it is a symbol of his . . .
9. Snails (or what else?) are wonderful creatures because . . .
10. If I had more free time, I would . . .

CHAPTER 4

Revising and Editing

A piece of writing is never finished. It is delivered to a deadline, torn out of the typewriter on demand, sent off with a sense of accomplishment and shame and pride and frustration. If only there were a couple more days, time for just another run at it, perhaps then. . . .

—Donald Murray
"The Maker's Eye:
Revising Your Own Manuscripts"

Professional writers rewrite constantly, perhaps reworking one draft dozens of times. How much a writer revises and edits depends on the situation, the importance of the writing, and the deadline. During revision a writer expands, expunges, shapes, and polishes ideas until they are clear and interesting. Although most instructors do not expect Donald Murray's level of dedication, they do expect several revisions of papers. Yet, too many student writers skip or skimp on revision and editing, turning in unfinished drafts. No matter how pleased you are with an early draft, keep looking for ways to improve it. After your euphoria wears off, you will find many imperfections.

Revision is circular, recurring until you are satisfied with your work or until the deadline looms. During revision you not only refine existing material but also discover more. You may prewrite again or review early notes if details seem sparse. Revision may take various forms—the only requirement is that it bring your writing closer to completion.

The final stage of the writing process, editing and proofreading, is the time to concentrate on precision and correctness. You check for accuracy of content, and you tackle distractions and errors in sentence structure, word choice, grammar, and punctuation. The goal of revision and editing is to refine writing so that it accomplishes your purpose and effectively reaches your audience.

REVISING AND FOCUSING ORGANIZATION

Revision literally means "re-seeing" a draft. To revise effectively, you must be open, detached, and disciplined. In this stage of the writing process, you shift your role from writer to reader. You might imagine yourself as an editor, evaluating an article for publication, or as a manager, evaluating a subordinate's work. What would you suggest to improve the draft? Does every detail support the central idea? What else does the reader need to know? How does the voice of the writer sound?

As your own editor, strive for a balance between culling and coddling. Weigh ideas and toss out the lightweights. Insist that pet ideas which have settled in odd places move to their proper place. A questioning mind, a sharp eye, and a keen ear are needed to uncover flaws and strengthen a manuscript.

Scanning the Draft

Probably the best way to start revision is to scan your entire draft and consider its larger aspects first. Hold off on any drastic action. Just pencil brief notes and alternatives in the margins or list possible changes on another sheet of paper. If your exploratory draft is one long paragraph, mark off logical units of thought as paragraphs. Next, check the progression of the paragraphs. Are they arranged in the most logical sequence? If you find some out of place, number them in the desired order.

If the present arrangement seems fine, scan the paper again as a reader might. Is it clear? How could it be improved? Sometimes a new perspective, a different angle on the topic, may clarify the thesis and make a piece more interesting. Also watch for gaps in thought and skimpy paragraphs. Early drafts tend to be underdeveloped, needing more information, examples, or transitions in strategic spots. Asking questions will help you to assess a draft.

➤ Checklist for Assessing a Draft

1. Is there one clear central idea?
2. Does the written voice sound considerate, knowledgeable, and appropriate?
3. Is each paragraph clearly related to the thesis and to other paragraphs?
4. Are paragraphs arranged in a logical order? What principle of order do they follow?
5. Do sufficient details support each topic sentence?
6. Does the conclusion flow logically from the body? Does it seem consistent with the beginning?

Outlining

After examining your exploratory draft, you may decide to rearrange entire sections. Paragraphs or sentences may need to be recast, cut, spliced, or inverted to highlight or to de-emphasize ideas. Rather than committing mayhem on your draft, you can save time and energy by testing organizational changes on an outline first.

If you are working on a computer, print out a scratch outline early. Mark small changes on the hard copy by hand. As large (and numerous) changes occur, save them under a different file name (for example, Outline 2). Then print out a revised copy so that you always have a clear road map to track the direction of your main idea. This precaution is particularly important for writers who see only a small portion of the text on screen. If you are working by hand, write out or type your revised outline so that you have a clear copy to follow.

If your revised outline requires major changes in the order of your manuscript, you can make an extra copy (printout or photocopy) to experiment on. The old cut-and-tape method is speedy and practical. Just cut up the sections of the paper, rearrange, and tape together in the new order.

If the new order seems logical, then revise the manuscript on screen or retype. *A precaution for computer users:* duplicate a file of the manuscript and save under a *different* name and number before attempting to move any material. This precaution will prevent loss in case of interruption and allow you to determine whether or not the organizational changes are effective.

Focusing the Title

A focused title attracts the attention of readers and suggests the approach the writer will take. A good title specifies and limits the topic, whereas an unfocused, general title gives only a vague idea. Let's consider some examples of titles for research papers:

Unfocused	*Focused*
The Internet	Using the Internet in the Classroom
Nutrition	Nutrition for the Elderly Who Live Alone

The unfocused titles are so broad that the topics could not be covered adequately in a paper. But the focused titles offer a feasible scope.

You can compose a title at any time during drafting or revision. Whenever inspiration strikes, jot down an idea. Then focus the best title when you are ready. As the next case study shows, the choice of an appropriate, focused title can be an integral part of the revision process.

FORMAL OUTLINES

Some instructors may require that you draft formal outlines, which are not only more detailed but also better balanced than scratch or working outlines. Formal outlines may be written in fragments or sentences. How detailed an outline is depends on the writer and the assignment, but here's a word of warning: Shy away from elaborate outlines. You can invest so much time and energy on outlining that you may be reluctant to revise. (For examples of outlines, turn to chapters 12, 15, 17, 19, 20, and 23.) Both topic outlines and sentence outlines use the following format with numerals and letters to distinguish parts and subparts:

I.
  A.
    1.
      a.
      b.
    2.
      a.
      b.
      c.
  B.
    1.
      a.
      b.
    2.
      a.
      b.
II. (Repeat as needed)
III. (Repeat as needed)

POINTERS FOR MAKING OUTLINES

- Begin with a large roman numeral. Follow with a capital letter, then an arabic number.
- For subtopics, use small letters.
- Use periods after each of the above.
- If you have an A, then you need a B. If you have a 1, then you need a 2.

A Series of Student Drafts

While drafting a paper about the various types of single men she encountered at parties and clubs, Stephanie Herrold had difficulty finding a central idea to tie her observations into a coherent whole. After typing her second draft, she attached a working title, "The Men," and added a tentative conclusion. In her third draft, Stephanie discarded her most annoying category, deciding to focus on the controlling idea of amusement.

By her fourth draft, Stephanie was vaguely dissatisfied with the direction the essay was taking. Going back to her exploratory draft, she noticed that the character type she had discarded might have come from the television program *Saturday Night Live*. This discovery afforded a new focus, as well as a new title. Stephanie reinserted the fourth category, rearranged the order of categories, added more details, and wrote a new ending. After the fifth draft, she was finally satisfied with her work. Here are her first, third, and final drafts.

Draft 1

The Men

Recently my brothers introduced me to college night life. I have come across four types of men and the lines they will use. The first type is every girl's dream boat, the gentleman type. They kind of bashfully stroll up, head slightly bowed, and smile nonchalantly. He seems wonderful till he opens his mouth. One guy, however, said, "Are your feet tired? "No," I replied, "Why? "Because you've been running through my mind all evening."

The second one is completely annoying. He comes waltzing up with a can of Budweiser in one hand with remnants left on his wrinkled shirt, and a camel nonfiltered cigarette, carefully balancing a one-inch ash. When this type approaches it's just known that the CroMagnon man is probably an idol or a close relative. "Hey Babe," is usually the best they can come up with. They don't give up, they just sit down and come up with more stuff. Believe me, it doesn't take long for me to leave.

The third type are the conceited ones. They are well groomed puppies, who are spoiled rotten and expect women to fall at their feet. This guy seemed nice at first. He extended his hand but quickly retracted it and said, "oh, I will let you catch your breath." I said sarcastically, "Yes, you do blow me away," but he may have taken it as a compliment because then he came up with most tacky lines that ever came out of the sixties: "What's your sign?" "I'm paper, you're glue." "My place or yours?"

The fourth type is the senior citizen. They are trying to recapture their youth with a younger woman. They come shuffling up with bifocals sliding down their nose and their hearing aid turned up to ten. They usually say, "If I were thirty years younger—" If this guy was 30 years younger, I wouldn't be born!

— Stephanie Herrold

DRAFT 3

Four Types of Men

During a recent trip to Ohio University to see my brothers, they introduced me to the night life there. Upon doing so, I have come across four types of men and the lines they will use. The first type is every girl's dream—the gentlemen. These are the ones that are bashful, slowly strolling up with head slightly bowed. They casually offer to get me a drink. One guy came up and introduced himself, which was a refreshing change. He used a clever line which was unique he asked, "Are your feet tired? I replied, "No, why? and he said, "Oh because you've been running through my mind all day"

The second type is completely annoying. The Kool Kat comes strutting up, in one hand a can of Budweiser with remnants left on his wrinkled shirt, and a camel nonfiltered cigarette carefully balancing a one-inch ash between his lips, and his hair—well the Exxon oil spill has nothing on this guy. When he approaches it is just a known that the CroMagnon Man is probably an idol or a close relative. "Hey Babe," is usually the best they can come up with. They do not stop there they just continue to use more lines to reel me in.

The third type is the senior citizen. These guys are actually trying to recapture their youth with a younger woman. They come shuffling up to me with their bifocals sliding down their nose, and their hearing aid turned up to ten. Apparently the line for these guy is, "If I was thirty years younger." Now if this guy were thirty years younger, I would not be born. Suddenly, the fishing game ceased to be amusing.

— Stephanie Herrold

FINAL DRAFT 5

Saturday Night Live

During a recent trip I made to Ohio University, my brothers introduced me to weekend night life around the campus. At parties and other places, I encountered four types of men and the lines they use.

The first were the Gentlemen. Rather bashful, they slowly strolled up, head slightly bowed. With a little smile, they politely offered to get me a drink. They were attractive, but seldom could they make small talk. One,

(continued)

however, excelled. He introduced himself, which was a refreshing change, and asked, "Are your feet tired?"

"No," I replied, "Why?"

"Because you've been running through my mind all evening." He was fun to talk to.

The second type was completely annoying, almost a cardboard stereotype. Joe College came strutting up, carrying a can of Budweiser and smoking a Camel nonfiltered cigarette. He carefully balanced the one-inch ash. His wrinkled shirt was splashed with beer. His hair looked as if it had washed up from the Exxon oil spill. "Hey Babe," was the best line he could find to greet me. Getting no response from me, he didn't give up, just sat down and spouted more drivel. It didn't take long for me to leave.

The third type was Over-the-Hill Harry. Trying to recapture his youth with a younger woman, he shuffled toward me, bifocals sliding down his nose and hearing aid turned up. He stopped and smiled. I did not smile back. "If I were thirty years younger . . . ," he began, but trailed off, peering at me expectantly. (If he were thirty years younger, I would not have been born.) I hastily excused myself and moved on.

The fourth and most annoying were the Conceited Pups. Handsome, well groomed, and overly confident, they seemed to expect women to collapse at their feet at the mere sight of them. One of the C.P.'s seemed nice at first. He introduced himself politely. But then he extended his hand and retracted it before I could respond. Grinning from ear to ear, he said, "Oh, I'll let you catch your breath."

His arrogance far exceeded his attractiveness. Here was a guy who not only lacked respect for women but was downright rude to boot. My reply was tinged with sarcasm: "I was born during a tornado, but you blow me away." Perhaps he took it as a compliment, for that didn't stop him.

He began tossing the tackiest lines from the sixties at me: "What's your sign?" "I'm paper, you're glue." "My place or yours?" Giving him a frigid glance, I turned on my heel and sought out my brothers. Saturday night live had ceased to be amusing.

—Stephanie Herrold

Finding a Fresh Perspective

In one episode of P. M. Brady's comic strip "Rose Is Rose," Pasquale, a preschool child, was tired of his toys and pleaded for a new one. His father listened, then showed him to the door, hinting that there was a big toy outside. Wading through newly fallen snow, Pasquale looked around and asked where the toy was. His father replied that Pasquale was standing in it.

We are all standing knee-deep in ideas for invigorating our writing. And like Pasquale, we often overlook them. Creativity involves taking everyday experience and transforming it. As writers we can benefit by stepping back to get an offbeat view of our lives; we can pause to gain a fresh perspective.

Sometimes an ordinary topic can be invigorated by looking at it from an angle the reader does not expect. For example, John Yeoman decided to give an imaginative spin to a story about his grandfather by writing from the perspective of his two-year-old self:

Babysitting for Grandfather

Everyone except me was getting ready to go somewhere. Being the youngest of the family and a member in good standing of the club known as "the terrible twos," I was used to receiving a lot of attention. But that night my four-year-old sister, dressed in a lacy white dress and black patent leather slippers, was the center of attention. In her hands, she carried a beautiful bouquet of fresh flowers for her role in a wedding.

Of course, so unusual a perspective as John's will not be appropriate for every writing situation. But when a draft you are working on seems dull or lifeless, trying out different perspectives can lead you to interesting breakthroughs you might not find otherwise.

IMPROVING PARAGRAPH STRUCTURE AND DEVELOPMENT

When you are pleased with the focus and organization of your draft, it is time to check the structure and development of individual paragraphs. Each paragraph should be a logical unit with one main idea. Usually, one sentence—called the topic sentence—announces the central idea and makes a claim about it. Supporting sentences provide evidence for the claim. They undergird the topic sentence with explanations, examples, anecdotes, reasons, and facts.

If you should find more than one central idea in a paragraph, you can either split it into two paragraphs or discard the less important idea. You may find paragraphs so long they are tiring to read. Divide overly long paragraphs at a logical place. (See chapter 7 for a discussion of writing effective paragraphs.)

~ *Checklist: Revising Paragraphs*

1. Is each paragraph organized around *one* central idea?
2. Does each supporting sentence closely relate to the topic sentence?
3. Is each sentence placed in the most logical spot?
4. Is any transition needed to connect sentences?
5. Does any paragraph need more explanation, examples, or details?
6. Is the same topic discussed in different places? Should any paragraphs be combined?

EDITING SENTENCES AND PROOFREADING FOR ERRORS

Revision is concerned with the larger aspects of the manuscript; editing and proofreading are concerned with smaller elements at the sentence level. *Editing* is a broad term that means "to prepare for publication or presentation by amending errors or revising." *Proofreading* means "discovering small errors and making corrections." Thus the terms overlap somewhat.

Editing and proofreading focus on accuracy and error detection as well as on meaning and readability. As you edit and proofread, you strengthen and clarify weak sentences, refine word choice, improve transitions, and correct errors in grammar, spelling, and punctuation.

Making Sentences Interesting and Clear

An essential part of editing is looking closely at the structure and overall clarity of individual sentences. You may find that you can strengthen a sentence by adding, deleting, or rearranging words or phrases. Editing sentences may also involve dividing very long complicated sentences into two sentences and combining short, choppy sentences.

The writing of effective sentences is covered in detail in chapter 8. The following checklist summarizes some of the information presented there.

～ Checklist: Editing Sentences

1. *Is the sentence clear?* Does a word need to be defined for the reader?

2. *Does the sentence make sense?* Dangling and misplaced modifiers can sabotage the logic of sentences. (These are discussed in the Handbook.)

3. *Does a sentence seem to ramble?* If so, cut extra words. Rewrite passive verbs into active verbs if possible. Suspect wordiness when you see *type of, number of, in view of,* or similar phrases.

4. *Does the sentence read smoothly?* Extra words and unbalanced structure cause awkward sentences. Coordinates (such as *either . . . or, not only . . . but also*) require parallel structure.

5. *Is the sentence too long?* If so, look for a logical spot to divide it into two complete sentences and insert a period.

6. *Are important words placed in positions of emphasis?* The beginning and end of a sentence are the most emphatic spots. The reader may miss an idea placed in the middle.

7. *Are there too many short, choppy sentences? Too many simple sentences?* If so, try combining related ideas into compound sentences. Parallel sentences provide balance and give equal status to similar ideas. Or you might enliven your writing by using other sentence types—but always for a pur-

pose. Complex sentences are excellent for stating two ideas when one idea is more important than the other. A periodic sentence combines related ideas in a climactic sequence, with the most important idea near the period (see chapter 8).

Finding Fresh, Concise Language

Improving word choice and using language innovatively can go a long way toward enlivening humdrum sentences, yet less experienced writers tend to be reluctant to experiment with new ways of expressing their thoughts. Chapter 9 discusses word choice in detail. Here, the focus is on using language thoughtfully and imaginatively to help invigorate your writing.

Create a Simile or Metaphor You might dress a plain idea in a simile, a metaphor, or other figure of speech. Similes and metaphors are unusual, non-literal comparisons that use familiar images to lead readers to see or understand less familiar ones. Similes and metaphors are found not only in literature but also in business and technical writing. A novel comparison not only clarifies an idea but also intrigues readers, allowing them to share, perhaps playfully, the writer's inventiveness, as the following student examples suggest:

- "My tires, *smooth as the soles of worn-out tennis shoes*, have cracks in the sidewalls." (simile by Kim Coffey)
- "Spade, whose pedigree was a mystery, had a tail eighteen inches long that *he could use like a whip*." (simile by John Spillman)
- "Seldom did I have anyone to talk to about my concern. I was *imprisoned in a bubble*, all alone with no way out." (metaphor)

A simile is an explicit (or stated) comparison of two unlike items or ideas, using *like* or *as*. For example, Lowell Ponte, writing about sunburn, uses a simile in this passage: "Like suicidal lemmings rushing to the sea, we bare our bodies to the first warm flushes of solar radiance—and then we bear the consequences."

A metaphor is a figure of speech that contains an implicit (or suggested) contrast. Our language is filled with metaphors we often take for granted. In conversation, we use many metaphors, such as "His last car was a lemon." The names of some automobile models and other consumer products are metaphors: Falcon, Cougar, Dove, Caress, Tide, and so forth. A person's name can be a metaphor: Rocky, Angela, Daisy, Heather, Opal, Ruby, and Forest—all imply comparison. Verbs, too, can contain metaphors: the motor *purred;* employees *support* their manager's decisions. Metaphors can also serve a complex function in a sentence: She needed *hip boots to wade through* his flattery. Metaphors are less easy to spot than similes because there are no signal words to announce them.

Experiment with Alliteration and Rhyme Distinctive phrasing can transform an ordinary sentence into an amusing one. In a speech titled "Run-of-the-Mill

Miracle," Gary Fenton used *alliteration* to comment on the birth of his daughter: "No doubt about it. Having a baby is not easy. If it were, we would refer to it as leisure, not labor." *Alliteration*, the repetition of initial consonant sounds occurs both in Fenton's title (*mill* and *miracle*) and in the emphatic final phrase (*leisure* and *labor*). In addition, *leisure* and *labor* rhyme in their final syllables. Another interesting combination is "No doubt about it." In this snappy phrase two words rhyme: *doubt* and *about*. Alliteration and rhyme are pleasing as long as they are not overdone.

Experiment with Old Sayings   Although clichés are usually avoided in effective writing, they can provide interest when revitalized. Changing or adding a few words can energize an old saying. For example, in one essay Robin Allen reworked "I never laid a hand on him" to "Sidney was a quiet cat and basically gentle. Even when I gave him a bath, which he hated, *he never laid a paw on me.*"

In a paper about "babysitting" for his grandfather, John Yeoman surprises the reader with a revitalized cliché:

> What about me? Why couldn't I go? This is when the plot thickened. Someone had to stay home and watch grandfather, or "Popo" as I called him. It was the classic, though crude, method of reverse psychology. Having a limited amount of reasoning ability at age two, I fell hook, line, and baby bottle.

Understate or Overstate for Effect   Understatement and overstatement, when effective, bring a smile to the lips of the reader who appreciates a good jest. Understatement is commenting on a subject in a way that deliberately downplays or minimizes the truth for an ironic effect. For example, when a tourist staying at a bed-and-breakfast inn in Scotland was served one small slice of toast with a trace of honey, he teased the hostess with understatement, "I see you keep a bee."

Overstatement, on the other hand, is gross exaggeration, embellishing the truth for a comic effect, as in "Her eyes were as big as saucers." In her book, *Seasons in the Sun*, Christina Ferchalk uses overstatement in an anecdote about a neighbor and a mouse:

> He was sitting in the middle of her kitchen floor, equally unprepared for his encounter with Edna, but instead of making a dash for freedom he remained seated, willing to negotiate.
>
> Edna took the defensive. In typical cartoon fashion, she jumped on the nearest chair and started screaming bloody murder. The mouse kept his cool under pressure. It wasn't until Edna had screamed herself hoarse and the kitchen was once again quiet that the mouse made his move. He sat up on his little hind legs, gave a small squeak and fell over stone-cold dead. No autopsy was performed, but it is assumed he succumbed to a massive mousey coronary. Edna was just too much for that little mouse.

To be successful, understatement and overstatement should be used with familiar subjects about which readers will know the truth. Then, when the truth is greatly minimized or exaggerated, readers recognize the joke.

In the workplace, understatement and overstatement ordinarily occur during casual conversation or informal meetings. Unsuitable for most business writing, these devices are best used verbally, face to face, to establish rapport and develop relationships.

Be Concise and Exact   You can keep sentences vigorous by deleting any unneeded words, especially favorites that seem comfortable but are redundant:

Redundant	*Edited*
absolutely essential	essential
actual truth of the matter	truth
advance warning	warning
blended together	blended
cancel out	cancel
connected together	connected
extreme hazard	hazard
foreign imports	imports
free gifts	gifts
kneel down	kneel
mutual cooperation	cooperation
past history	history

Also, always try to find specific nouns and power verbs to make your writing colorful. For instance, instead of *walked*, you might substitute *ambled*, *sauntered*, or *strode*. And don't try to sneak a pet colloquialism, such as "mess up" or "stuff," past the reader by wrapping it in a set of quotation marks. Redundancies and vague words are signs that a draft needs more work.

Proofreading for Grammar, Punctuation, and Spelling

No piece of formal writing—whether a college paper, a report to your boss, or a business letter—can be considered complete until it has been carefully proofread for errors, including typographical errors. Lapses in grammatical usage, punctuation, and spelling undercut your credibility as a writer and call into question your commitment to your work. In college these errors may result in lowering your grade; at work they may damage your career prospects.

The first step to developing proofreading skills is to learn the rules of correct grammar, punctuation, and spelling and to pay attention to examples of correct usage as you read. An excellent second step is to write examples of your own, based on models from a writer you admire. Lab practice in your college writing center can also help to refine your skills.

While it is always possible to have friends or family members proofread your writing, you cannot be certain they will catch every error. You need to take responsibility for your own work. Try to recognize the kinds of errors you are likely to make so that you can proofread for them specifically.

In addition, get in the habit of reviewing your marked papers soon after they are returned. Look up any rules you are unsure of. (Your instructor may use marks and symbols keyed to the chart in the inside back cover of this book, which will guide you to the appropriate discussion in the Handbook.) Then, correct every marked error soon after it is returned. Look up misspelled words, and write them ten (or twenty) times to rivet the correct spelling in your memory.

You can create an excellent tool to assist in proofreading by keeping a list of errors that are pointed out to you in your marked papers. Include hand-corrected versions of grammar and punctuation errors, as well as a list of words you have had trouble spelling. Review the list regularly, particularly before you begin to proofread written work. Armed with an awareness of the specific errors that often mar your writing, you will be better prepared to write well.

Estimating Total Words

An instructor may assign a minimum number of words for a paper so that students develop adequate support for their theses. Here's a tip: To allow for revision and editing, write an extra hundred words. If the total number of words should slip below the minimum, however, look at your prewriting notes to elicit more details.

To determine word count using a computer, look for your word-processing program's word-count command; most programs have one. To determine an approximate total, estimate each page by counting the lines and multiplying by the average words per line. To find the average words per line, count the words in three typical lines and divide by three. (For example: 10 + 11 + 12 words = 33, or an average of 11 words per line.) Next, multiply the average words per line by the lines per page. (Example: 11 words per line $\times$ 27 lines = 297 words per page.) Finally, add the page estimates together to find the approximate total: $3 \times 297 = 891$.

REVISING AND EDITING WITH A COMPUTER

The following advice about revising and editing with computers is based on some hard-won personal wisdom. Perhaps these suggestions will smooth your writing path and cushion you from similar jolts. The secret is to know the pitfalls and to avoid risky shortcuts that can devour time and elevate blood pressure.

Saving Early Drafts

Sometimes writers discard early material and regret its loss. Intent on saving space on the hard drive, they keep only their latest draft. To save time, they neglect to make a backup copy. To save paper, they neglect to print out periodically. These short-sighted measures can result in a minor catastrophe. Therefore, it is important to observe commonsense precautions.

To prevent loss of text, save different versions under different file names (for example, Research 1, Research 2) in the *same* file folder. Note that if you save in more than one file folder, you risk having different versions under the same title. Be sure to number or date the drafts so that you are sure to print the latest one. A student once submitted a long formal report with his graphics misplaced, along with other problems. When he received a C−, he realized he had not printed out his final version!

Saving sequential drafts is useful because you can retrieve discarded material if needed. It is a good idea to save everything until your paper is graded and returned. That way, if the instructor has any questions, you have everything you need.

Moving Text without Losing It

Most writing software packages have a feature that allows you to copy text, store it temporarily, or take it to another spot. This feature is a wonderful advantage, but it can pose problems for the neophyte and overtired users. If you copy and cut (delete) a portion of text and forget to paste (dump it onto the screen in another spot), the text is erased from the storage area when the computer is turned off. This means that if you forget about storing text and shut down the computer, you cannot retrieve the stored text. To be safe, do not cut the copied portion from the original spot until you have pasted (inserted) it in the new spot. (If you have made a backup copy, you can go back to that.)

Although some older software allowed users to copy material from several spots and to place it together for temporary storage, many new programs do not. For example, Clipboard will take only one bunch of copy at a time, which must be "pasted" into the document before moving more text. Otherwise, if you copy more material, the first bunch is lost.

Take special precautions when moving documentation such as works cited entries in a research paper. *When moving any text, double-check to be sure you have inserted every line back into the manuscript.* Keeping old printed drafts will ensure against loss and confusion.

Editing and Proofreading on Screen

Printing and submitting a paper without looking it over carefully is extremely risky. One risk, already described, is that you may submit an old version. Another risk is that you may overlook errors on a computer screen that you would notice on a printed page. Or you may not add all the corrections from your revised draft. As you make corrections on screen from printed copy, check off each correction. Several marked-up printed drafts may be required to achieve the quality of work you and your instructor desire.

Keep in mind that a word-processing spelling checker will flag typing errors and misspellings but you cannot rely on a spelling checker to alert you to informal spellings, such as *thru* for *through*. Nor will it alert you to a usage error such as *there* for *their* or *effect* for *affect*.

Also be sure to run a spelling check each time you revise. During revision you make numerous changes, and with every change there is a chance of introducing a new error.

GUIDELINES FOR PEER REVIEW

Writing is a painstaking task, but you are not alone. This book and your instructor will provide guidance and encouragement. In addition, your class may have informal peer reviews. Published writers often receive input from writing groups, agents, editors, or reviewers. This assistance predicts how an intended audience may receive a manuscript. Peer review in a classroom provides similar assistance. The job of a peer reviewer is to pinpoint problems, not to solve them. Peer review enables class members not only to help each other but also to sharpen their skill at identifying rough spots in their own writing.

Reviewing someone else's work is much easier than critiquing your own. As you word your comments in peer review, however, keep in mind how you would feel if you received them. Feedback that is vague, unnecessarily blunt, or overly critical can be worse than none at all. But feedback that is diplomatic and perceptive is invaluable. Learn to be tactful and resolve to benefit from any peer response you receive.

The difference between callousness and tact lies in the way comments are phrased. Vague reactions such as "I don't like the opening" or "Confusing" or "Needs something more" or "Dull" are not very helpful. Do *not* give your *general* impression of the writing. If you do, chances are that the listener will not understand well enough to correct the concern. Your task as a reviewer is to point out trouble spots and possibly their cause, not make corrections. Revision, editing, and proofreading are the responsibility of the writer. Responses should be specific so that the writer understands where and what the problem is, but they should not be so blunt as to be offensive. Responses can be softened in two ways:

1. *Be tentative*. Rather than issue a final decree, offer your comments as an opinion.
2. *Ask polite questions:*
   - Where is the thesis statement? (Not "You don't have a thesis sentence.")
   - I wonder if this paragraph fits here? (Not "Your draft rambles.")
   - Does this technical term need to be redefined?
   - Might an example here help the reader understand?
   - Might this sentence be shortened or condensed?
   - Should these verbs be parallel?
   - Can you find a more specific word?

- Is punctuation needed here?
- Have you checked the spelling of this word?

Writers who are mentally prepared to accept constructive criticism can learn much from peer review. Regard it as a free service to help you improve your draft. It is not a reflection on you personally, only an opinion regarding your draft at the stage of review. The usefulness of feedback is that you can use it thoughtfully to help polish your draft. That is indeed a benefit, and the reviewer should be thanked for the service. Still, peer responses to a piece of writing should not be taken as gospel. As you revise, evaluate the quality of each response and extract what is useful.

To assist you in preparing for peer review, both as reviewer and reviewee, here are six guidelines:

Suggestions for Peer Review

For Reviewers

1. *Identify concerns rather than provide whitewash.*
2. *Be tactful.*
3. *Consider one aspect of the writing at a time.* Focusing on a single aspect should increase your comfort and efficiency.

For Reviewees

4. *Listen to or read responses to your work carefully.* Be open to the need for possible changes. Ask questions about any comment that seems unclear.
5. *Evaluate responses thoughtfully.* When several readers agree about a concern, you are probably safe in following their suggestion—if you feel it is sound. If in doubt, ask for more information. *Why* do the reviewers respond as they do?
6. *Be willing to seek further help if you think it might be useful.* Make an appointment with your instructor or at the campus writing center.

A FINAL WORD

Revision doesn't sound as if it's as exciting as writing an exploratory draft, but revision is often the stage where you discover the perfect phrase, the ideal title, the best organization for getting your message across. It is a time for refining ideas—and even a time for discovering that they are more profound than you originally thought. Spend enough time revising, and you will be rewarded.

Checklist for Revising Drafts

Purpose

- Has the topic been limited to one controlling idea?
- Are the claim and direction of the thesis clear?

- Does the thesis set an appropriate tone for the writing?
- Is the purpose clear?

Audience

- For whom is the writing intended? Will it be clear?
- Is the word choice suitable?
- Will the voice of the writer seem appropriate to the audience?

Organization and Paragraph Development

- Is the opening relevant and interesting?
- Can the opening be improved?
- Does the order seem right for the topic and purpose?
- Does each body paragraph have a clear topic sentence?
- Does each body paragraph have strong supporting details?
- Is the order of paragraphs logical?
- Does the ending provide a sense of completeness?

Content

- Do any terms need to be defined?
- Is the information accurate?
- Are all points and examples relevant?
- Are there enough specific details and examples for support?
- Does the writing flow well?
- Is the writing interesting? Or are there slow spots?
- Is documentation (if needed) adequate and correct?
- Are any words unnecessary?
- Does anything else need to be said?

Summary

Students often slight revision and editing. Yet these stages of writing greatly influence the quality of their papers and the grades they earn.

During revision you add, expand, trim, and delete ideas and examine the internal order and development of each paragraph. Reworking an outline is an efficient way to check the order of a draft.

During editing and proofreading, you scrutinize, correct, and improve. You focus on sentence structure and on using vivid, concise language, as well as on grammar, punctuation, and spelling.

When revising and editing on a computer, you should take precautions when moving text and making backup files. Keep printed copies of all drafts to prevent valuable material from being discarded.

Peer review can assist in revising and editing. When giving feedback, a reviewer should be tentative, tactful, and helpful. To take advantage of feedback, a writer should be open and appreciative of the service.

Key Terms

revision	simile	understatement
editing	metaphor	overstatement
proofreading	alliteration	peer review
formal outline		

Practice

Peer Review Suggestions

1. Select one of your practice writings to revise and edit.
2. After you finish, find a partner and exchange papers.
3. Reread "Guidelines for Peer Review."
4. Using the "Checklist for Revising Drafts," write your responses and suggestions on a separate sheet.
5. Return the paper along with the peer review.
6. Question your reviewer about anything you are unsure of.
7. Later: Revise your paper again, applying any of the suggestions you think will be beneficial.

Ideas for Writing

Directions: Write a description of an incident, experience, or tradition that is significant to you. Use one of the following suggestions if you wish:

1. The earliest childhood scene or event that you can recall
2. Your first day of school
3. A hair-raising teen-age experience
4. Results of hanging out at the mall
5. The Roadkill Cafe
6. How you felt when you . . .
7. A frightening experience
8. A family tradition
9. The kindest person you know
10. The job that you would like to have in five years

CHAPTER 5

Checking Accuracy

Distinguishing Fact from Opinion

Truth is a hard deer to hunt.

　　—Stephen Vincent Benet

Witnesses testifying in courts of law traditionally swear "to tell the truth, the whole truth, and nothing but the truth." Yet determining what is "true" is tricky. We must first recognize the distinction between proven facts and unproven inferences that may be facts. We must also understand that value judgments and other opinions can never hold "true" for everyone. Finally, we must be alert to other pitfalls along the path of logical thinking.

Two of those pitfalls are the grapevine and the gossip mill, which exist in most groups and organizations. During breaks and lunches, after classes or meetings, the grapevine and the gossip mills operate. Yet the two are not the same. By listening carefully, you can soon spot the differences. The grapevine is an informal communication network whereby information about administrative actions, current events, and politics circulates. Although such news must be taken with a large grain of salt, experts estimate the grapevine is about 80 percent accurate. This is not true for gossip, which may have little basis. Since gossips trade rumors about private lives, this careless talk has the potential to harm both the victim and the purveyor. To be safe, you should never tell anyone anything you would not want seen in print. Never put such items in writing lest they come back to haunt you.

Your credibility as a writer, as well as an employee, rests upon your ability to distinguish fact from opinion and misinformation. Expository writing is inherently factual and accurate. The writer is obligated to tell the reader the truth. To find truth, you may have to sift through a mixture of fact, inference, value judgment, and inaccuracy.

HOW CAN FACT BE DETERMINED?

Statements or assertions that have been rigorously tested and finally accepted are said to be *established facts*. They have passed criteria for determining truth. When you think something is probably true, ask whether or not it is an established fact. If not, then it is still in the realm of opinion. Mathematical facts can be checked for accuracy by reversing computation. Scientific experiments are accepted as fact if they can be replicated under the same conditions by other professionals in the field. Other types of data are not so easily verified.

Technology that records measurable facts is widely used in the pursuit of truth. Yet even electronic devices are not foolproof. Sports announcers know that the angle of a camera lens can affect their perception of an umpire's call. Temperature and other factors can hinder the performance of equipment. Or someone may tamper with photographs, tapes, or other evidence.

In court, sworn evidence and the ever-present threat of punishment for perjury should keep witnesses truthful. Yet there can still be problems in accuracy. An eyewitness may recount an observation from memory, and another eyewitness may dispute the testimony, yet both people may think they are telling the truth. How can this happen? Perhaps one witness did not see all parts of the event. Or perhaps both saw the same event, but interpreted it differently. Then too, recollections fade with time, and the memory sometimes has strange quirks that make it unreliable. Legally, fact is based on three types of evidence; our courts decide cases by the admission of

1. Eyewitness reports sworn under oath
2. Expert opinion by an authority in the field
3. Material evidence (physical items that can be tested)

Without a doubt, material evidence is the most reliable of all. Hair samples, body fluids, fingerprints, voiceprints, tire casts, and other materials can all be carefully analyzed. Usually, the results are accurate, but once in a while human error does intrude. Although expert opinion seems to be reliable most of the time, even experts in the same field occasionally disagree. And, of course, eyewitnesses can be mistaken; often they confuse inference with fact.

INFERENCES ARE UNPROVEN

A temporary employee, fresh out of school, was standing by a paper shredder. A passing secretary noticed his puzzled expression and asked, "Would you like to know how the thing works?"

The "temp" thanked her and handed over a thick report. The secretary turned on the shredder and shoved in sections of the report. After a moment the temp asked, "When will the copies be ready?"

As far-fetched as this story sounds, it illustrates a common occurrence. We tend to make assumptions without questioning their accuracy. We take an untested inference and treat it as fact. How can such misperceptions be avoided? Perhaps if we keep in mind that an *inference is theory (opinion) until proven*, then we can distinguish it from established fact. Sometimes perceptions can be tested. For example, on a subzero morning a neighbor's car fails to start. This is the only time in two years the engine has refused to budge. He checks the gas gauge. Since it registers half full, he *infers* that the battery is weak. Then he calls the local service station for a quick charge. After the battery charge, the motor starts. A check of the battery reveals a faulty cell. Thus, the inference has been verified and found to be fact.

Sometimes faulty inferences creep into student essays:

> When his owner's red pickup truck approaches his pen, Buck realizes raccoon season must be here. During hunting season, his mind is strictly on tracking coon, but other times his chief pleasure is chasing cats.

What are the problems here? For one, dogs cannot understand the concept of "raccoon season" (although they could associate the truck with hunting). A second problem is that the word *strictly* means 100 percent, which is doubtful. Dogs, like humans, have a limited attention span; they are distracted by noises, other animals, and hunger pangs. The final statement "his chief pleasure is chasing cats" is not an established fact. (Eating might be the dog's favorite activity.) The statement could be made accurate by revising it to "*seems* to be chasing cats."

UNDERSTANDING VALUE JUDGMENTS

Lew Wallace's familiar words, "beauty is altogether in the eye of the beholder," point out the elusive nature of value judgments. Too often we regard these opinions as fact. Actually, they are perceptions, which can be illogical and unpredictable. Often we assume other people have (or should have) the same values we cherish. The problem is that value judgments often masquerade as fact.

A value judgment is an opinion about the worth of something, an estimate of value. Frequently, we rate items as bad or good, cheap or expensive, ugly or beautiful. Or we consider actions wrong or right, immoral or moral, according to our own perspective and experience. Yet value judgments are imprecise and variable. They vary from person to person and change with the times. For instance, baseball cards were originally just prizes collected by elementary school children from packs of bubble gum. Now the cards are valuable and sought by adult collectors. They are regarded from a different point of view.

Point of view refers to the angle from which something is perceived—the perspective. We form different value judgments based on our differing points of view. Sinclair Lewis, in his early novel *Main Street*, describes two young women who see the town of Gopher Prairie through very different eyes. The impressions of Carol Kennicott, a city girl from Minneapolis, reveal her point of view:

She glanced through the fly-specked windows of the most pretentious building in sight, the one place which welcomed strangers and determined their opinion of the charm and luxury of Gopher Prairie—the Minniemashie House. It was a tall lean shabby structure, three stories of yellow-streaked wood, the corners covered with sanded pine slabs purporting to symbolize stone. In the hotel office she could see a stretch of bare unclean floor, a line of rickety chairs with brass cuspidors between, a writing desk and advertisements in mother-of-pearl letters upon the glass-covered back. The dining room beyond was a jungle of stained tablecloths and catsup bottles. (34)

At the same time Bea Sorenson, "bored by farm work," walked along the other side of Main Street, thinking about the "excitements of city life" and the Minnie-mashie House. Her impression reveals very different judgments and a very different point of view:

A hotel, awful high, higher than Oscar Tollefson's new red barn; three storied, one right on top of another; you had to stick your head back to look clear up to the top. There was a swell traveling man in there—probably been to Chicago lots of times. (39)

Although Carol and Bea gaze at the same building, they form contrasting impressions. Coming from varying backgrounds, they view the town differently. Later they make value judgments about Gopher Prairie, based on their points of view. Carol thinks: "I must be wrong. People do live here. It can't be as ugly as—as I know it is! I must be wrong." But Bea reasoned that even if she didn't receive a salary of six dollars every week, she would work for much less "to be allowed to stay here" (40).

LISTENING TO THE TONE OF WRITING

A writer's point of view may range from essentially *objective* to highly *subjective* depending upon the purpose and the topic. Certain kinds of writing require an impersonal tone that presents the facts squarely. The front pages of most American newspapers, for example, carry factual reports in which the writers attempt to relay news stories objectively. The purpose is to report what happened—the facts—not push a particular view. The tone of objective writing is impartial, unslanted, and unbiased; readers seldom get a sense of the writer's opinion or personality.

The purpose of a newspaper's editorial pages, on the other hand, is to allow writers to express their individual points of view about the stories presented factually elsewhere. In editorials, columns, and letters to the editor, writers interpret facts subjectively, based on their own political, ethical, and economic values. They offer opinions and judgments; they praise and criticize; they urge specific courses of action. For example, the tone may convey passion, conviction, anger, or joy.

TABLE 5.1 **Characteristics of Fact, Inference, and Value Judgment**

Fact	*Inference*	*Value Judgment*
Act, deed, event, state or condition of reality	Assumption, generalization, or decision derived from evidence	Opinion or estimate of worth, an evaluation or rating
Objectively proved by observation, experiment, eyewitness, or expert opinion	Has not been proved; has possibility of being proved or discredited	Cannot be proved; will always be an opinion

A degree of subjectivity is inevitable in almost any writing, but it should be controlled and appropriate for the writing situation. As a critical reader, writer, and thinker, you need to recognize the difference between objectivity and subjectivity. It is important to know the difference between facts and the inferences, judgments, and opinions that may be formed from those facts. Then you will be well prepared to present information fairly, clearly, and accurately (see table 5.1).

FOUR WAYS MISINFORMATION ARISES

Misinformation is not necessarily conveyed deliberately. Here are four ways misinformation commonly comes to be accepted as fact.

Expert Opinion Occasionally Changes

We all know that one should not swim for an hour after eating—or do we? This bit of advice was published by the American Red Cross over fifty years ago. A lifesaving manual claimed that a swimmer who ate immediately before a dip risked stomach cramps or even death. Now the Customer Service Manager of the American Red Cross's Health and Safety Division, Earl Harbert, says his department "has no problem whatsoever with people swimming directly after eating a meal." Similarly, the *Journal of Health, Physical Education, and Recreation* disputes the idea of "stomach cramps." A prominent physical educator was quoted as saying, "I have never seen a case of so-called stomach cramps, although I have observed hundreds of thousands of persons swimming immediately after eating."

Medical opinions, as well as other expert opinions, sometimes change over the years. As we grow up, we hear folk wisdom, propaganda, myths, superstitions, and other inaccuracies presented as fact. Steeped in these beliefs, we tend not to question them, and so we accumulate much misinformation without realizing it.

Facts Are Overstated

Unintentional overstatement sometimes occurs. We may not recall exactly what we read or heard and may overstate the facts. Or we may paraphrase, using synonyms that give an impression different from the one we intended. And some people exaggerate for emphasis, possibly without being aware of it. For example, the student who wrote the following paragraph was convinced it was absolutely true:

> Lack of participation by the American people in their government is the number one cause for their loss of control over their own affairs. They say: "I don't care." "My vote doesn't matter." "I didn't have time to vote." These are some of the excuses given for not carrying out one of the most important rights given to the people, the right to vote.

The examples are authentic; such reasons are often voiced. But a partial truth has been stretched by overstatement ("number one cause"). This "statistic" is not an established fact.

Stereotyping Shuts Out Fact

A writer must also be on guard against various stereotypes: gender, ethnic, generational, religious, racial, or other. Stereotyping is pigeonholing, classifying someone or something into a tight little box. A stereotypic belief supposedly typifies a group, place, issue, or event. Although the characteristic attributed to the group may be true for some individuals, it is not true for all. Consider the following statements carefully. Then mark each one true or false.

_____   1. Redheads have quick tempers.
_____   2. Men are stronger than women.
_____   3. Politicians can't be trusted.

If you marked all of the statements true, you have probably grown up hearing these stereotypes presented as fact, taking them for granted. If you marked some answers false, you are to be congratulated on your growing skepticism. If all the statements are marked false, you are very alert and rate an A. Why are all three statements false? They are untrue because none allows for an exception. These statements are *absolute* or all-inclusive: they claim to apply 100 percent of the time. Think about it. Do *all* redheads in the world have quick tempers? Are *all* men stronger than *all* women? Isn't there even one politician who can be trusted? To further complicate matters, item 2 contains an *undefined term*. What kind of strength are we talking about—physical, emotional, intellectual, or spiritual?

Experienced speakers and writers avoid stereotypic thinking, for it is not only unfair and undiplomatic; it is also inaccurate. Stereotypes shut out new information that conflicts with old, embedded beliefs. Stereotypic thinking is a quagmire that can lead to charges of sexism and discrimination as well as hurt feelings.

A Small Survey Is Inadequate Proof

Sometimes we hear someone generalize after surveying a few friends or considering a few unusual incidents. It's the old story of "everyone else is getting a new prom dress but me." But a small sample is hardly a reliable survey. Let's take a weather example. If Williamsburg, Virginia, were to have three consecutive frigid winters within a twenty-year period, then the second and third times you might hear generalizations such as "Williamsburg's weather is as bad as Chicago's."

But three very cold years would not be a *representative sample*. To be representative, a sample must be typical of a reasonable number of cases. For a representative sample of people, the group should represent (be typical of) the general population in age, gender, background, location, economic level, employment status, and other pertinent factors. Otherwise, the sample would be unrepresentative and unreliable.

Overstatement, stereotypic thinking, and generalizing from an unrepresentative sample can lead to the fallacy of hasty generalization. *A hasty generalization is a broad statement, an inference, that lacks sufficient proof.* A hasty generalization can occur when a *trend* or a *tendency* is overstated as if it were true for an entire group or population. Although assumed to be true, a hasty generalization is not an established fact. (This fallacy and others are explained in chapter 18.)

WRITING RESPONSIBLY

Responsible writing presents the truth. Readers should not have to grope through a fog of misinformation to determine the facts. Once you become aware of the slipperiness of fact, you can take precautions to avoid misstatement. First, remind yourself that adequate support must be available for any claim or generalization stated in writing. If proof is not available, the statement is unacceptable and needs to be scaled down. Second, check to see that you use absolute terms accurately. Third, identify inferences and other forms of opinion.

Limiting Generalizations

To be accurate and useful in writing, generalizations must be factual. If they are too broad (overstated), you need to limit or "qualify." *Qualifiers are words or phrases that allow for exceptions and modify meanings.* Qualified generalizations often serve as topic sentences and thesis statements. The generalizations below were used successfully as thesis sentences in student essays. (Qualifiers are italicized.)

Some outstanding women have graced history with their heroic feats during battle.

In today's hurried pace, the giving and receiving of love is *often* overlooked.

Crash dieting *seems* to be the surefire approach to coping with obesity.

To limit an overly broad generalization, you may need a verb such as *may*, *might*, *tend*, *seem*, or *appear* to make your claim acceptable. Other qualifiers refer to number. To indicate a *majority* (over 50 percent), you can use terms such as the following:

most	largely	overall
usually	primarily	typically
chiefly	generally	as a rule

To indicate a *minority*, use less specific words. Note, however, that the size of a minority can vary and influence your word choice. If in doubt about the appropriateness of a qualifier, consult two or more good desk dictionaries for fine distinctions in meaning. Terms such as those below can be used to indicate less than 50 percent:

many	rarely	often
few	frequently	irregularly
some	sporadically	sometimes
several	seldom	occasionally
relatively few		

Using Absolute Terms Accurately

Absolute terms are inflexible words that state or imply *all* or *none*. These words mean zero or 100 percent. When you revise, examine every statement that contains an absolute term. Be sure that you consider what the word means, not just what you intend. If you overstate your case by misusing an absolute, the reader will be apt to take the literal meaning unless you plant a clue that the statement is ironic or joking. The lists below will help you recognize absolute terms:

all	always	everyone
none	never	only
every	completely	exact
no one	same	anything

PEANUTS reprinted by permission of United Feature Syndicate, Inc.

Other kinds of words can also be all-inclusive. Verbs and adjectives like the following can also lead to overstatement and misstatement:

is	perfect*	greatest
are	unique*	smallest
was	worst	opposite
were	best	exact

Identifying Inferences and Other Opinions

In workplace writing and college assignments, you may be asked to "draw a conclusion" (inference) from a set of facts, to "write a reaction" (see chapter 26), or to "interpret facts" (explain what you think they mean). To complete such assignments successfully, you need to know how to identify inferences and other types of opinion. Qualifiers like those below indicate inferences:

theory	probably	apparently
conjecture	possibly	it appears that
assumption	evidently	the evidence suggests
premise	seemingly	surmise
presume	seems	suggest
indicate	imply	infer

Opinion can be expressed in several ways, not just as inference. As you revise, check to see that no opinions are presented as facts. For example, a widely held belief that is unproven should be identified as opinion. Phrases such as "a common belief" or "the conventional wisdom" indicate the nature of such statements. Other terms that identify opinion include the following:

current thinking	viewpoint	reaction
appraisal	impression	feeling
point of view	estimate	prediction
perception	folk wisdom	view

REVISING FOR ACCURACY

Whether you write a report, an essay, a research paper, or some other document, double-check every item to be sure it is logical and accurate. In the flurry of pinning down ideas during prewriting and drafting, it is easy to leave out a word,

---

*Something is either perfect or imperfect; unique or not unique.

transpose a number, overstate a generalization, or commit some other blunder. Develop the habit of being thorough, of questioning information that doesn't quite ring true or seems suspicious. The checklist below should be helpful:

➤ Checklist for Revising for Accuracy

1. Are all data established facts?
2. Have inferences, value judgments, and other opinions been identified?
3. Do any generalizations need to be limited?
4. Are all words accurate?
5. Does the tone sound appropriate?
6. Have any significant facts been omitted? Are any more needed?

Only when we learn to think logically and critically, to analyze carefully our own ideas as well as the ideas of other speakers and writers, can we begin to approach "the whole truth." That is what the writing process is all about.

Summary

Truth is not always easy to recognize. Our courts accept three kinds of evidence as fact: eyewitness accounts, expert opinion, and material evidence. Still, there can be problems with all three kinds.

Inference and value judgment (special types of opinion) can be mistaken for fact. Inferences are unproven assumptions. Value judgments are evaluations that reflect a writer's point of view. Responsible writers distinguish opinion from fact; they identify inferences and other forms of opinion. They present facts objectively and accurately, limiting unfounded generalizations. Opinion adds subjectivity to writing. The tone of writing should be appropriate to the situation.

Misinformation can arise in various ways; among them are changes in expert opinion, overstatement, stereotypes, and generalization from a small sample. Sometimes inaccuracy can be avoided by careful word choice. Checking for accuracy is an important element of revision. Responsible writers present the truth.

Key Terms

established fact	objective	hasty generalization
inference	overstatement	qualified generalization
value judgment	stereotype	qualifier
point of view	representative sample	absolute
subjective		

Test Yourself

Fact, Inference, or Value Judgment?

Directions: To check your understanding, visualize a Red Delicious apple or examine one. Then mark "F" (fact), "I" (inference), or "VJ" (value judgment) below. Check your answers with the key at the end of the chapter.

_____ 1. This apple has four bumps (protrusions) on the bottom.

_____ 2. This apple is attractive to the eye.

_____ 3. This apple has a shiny red skin.

_____ 4. This apple will taste good.

_____ 5. This apple contains dark brown seeds. (The apple is uncut.)

Opinion or Observable Fact?

Directions: Write "O" for opinion or "F" for observable fact in the blanks. Then check your answers with the key at the end of the chapter.

_____ 1. The fender was *dented*.

_____ 2. Peggy is *pretty*.

_____ 3. The lighting was *adequate*.

_____ 4. Larry's eyes are *blue*.

_____ 5. The rock is *moss-covered*.

_____ 6. The painting is *ugly*.

_____ 7. The table is *oval*.

_____ 8. Joe *looks like a bum*.

_____ 9. The speech was *boring*.

_____ 10. Chartreuse is a *horrible* color.

Practice

Collaborative Learning I: What Are the Facts?

Directions: Mark the following items as Fact (F), Inference (I), Value Judgment (VJ), or overstatement/misstatement (O):

The 6 p.m. newscast on New Year's Eve alerted listeners to falling snow with a possible change to freezing rain. According to the State Patrol, all side roads were snow-covered and slippery, but most major highways had been cleared and salted. At 10 p.m. the highway patrol reported a two-vehicle accident had occurred on Route 22 on an overpass five miles south of Blinksville. Both cars were headed north. The second car hit the rear of the first car, causing heavy damage to both cars. One driver was cited for having an open container in the car.

_____ 1. The accident occurred at 10 p.m.

_____ 2. The highway patrol had reported freezing rain and icy conditions on side roads and major highways.

_____ 3. Two cars were involved in the accident.

_____ 4. The driver of the second car was careless.

_____ 5. No one was injured.

_____ 6. The icy overpass contributed to the accident.

_____ 7. All major highways had been cleared and salted.

_____ 8. The second driver was following too closely.

_____ 9. Both cars suffered heavy damage as one hit the other.

_____ 10. One driver was cited for DUI.

Collaborative Learning II: Fact, Inference, or Value Judgment?

Directions: Mark each item as fact (F), or inference (I), or value judgment (VJ). If both fact and inference, mark I; if both fact and value judgment, mark VJ. Discuss any disagreement.

_____ 1. Great Britain is an island, not a continent.

_____ 2. Many exquisite bays line Britain's coast.

_____ 3. The beautiful white cliffs of Dover, overlooking the English Channel, are composed of chalk.

_____ 4. The Isle of Man lies in the Irish Sea between Northern Ireland and England.

_____ 5. If you mention hunting to a Brit, he or she will immediately think of fox hunting.

_____ 6. Most Americans are surprised to learn that a subway in London is an underground passageway for pedestrians.

_____ 7. If you want a delicious meal in London, order fish, not steak.

_____ 8. The Tower of London is the most fabulous sight in the city.

_____ 9. In the spring after a rain, Paris has a delicate shimmering beauty.

_____ 10. The Louvre, the largest art museum and palace in the world, is located on the north bank of the River Seine in Paris.

Test Yourself Answers

Fact, Inference, or Value Judgment?

1. _F_
2. _VJ_
3. _F_
4. _VJ_
5. _I_

Opinion or Observable Fact?

Items 1, 4, 5, and 7 are observable facts. The others are opinions.

CHAPTER 6

Finding an Appropriate Voice

Great formality seems to be the hallmark of the still-insecure, the not-quite-arrived, the semi-accepted.

—Rudolf Flesch, *The Art of Readable Writing*

At the turn of the twentieth century, written English was more formal and involved than is common today. Often a reader did not sense a writer as an individual presence or personal voice. As the pace of our culture has quickened over the years, however, writers' voices have become more apparent. Now much written work is fairly informal, and the style of most writing is closer to speech, with shorter sentences and simpler word choice than in the past.

Simplicity and clarity are the heart of an effective writing style. Winston Churchill, possibly the greatest orator of the twentieth century, kept his speeches relatively simple and free of jargon, shunning unnecessary formality. Churchill chose words with care and labored long, spending as many as eight hours preparing a forty-minute speech. Where another speaker might have written "a bilateral agreement has been reached," Churchill said the two sides "joined hands together." Churchill knew that plain standard English has dignity and clarity.

A command of language is necessary not only for heads of state but also for most white-collar workers and college students. In the workplace and in college classes, you will be expected to write appropriately according to the occasion, purpose, reader, and topic. To fulfill this expectation, you observe conventional rules of usage and grammar and find an appropriate voice.

WHAT IS VOICE?

Voice is the distinctive sound of the writing—the presence of the writer as perceived by the reader. The voice of the writer reveals an attitude toward both the reader and the topic, radiating from word choice, phrasing, and sentence style.

As writers develop proficiency, they listen to the nuances of words—the subtle shades of meaning, feeling, or tone. These slight gradations affect the writer's voice. Voice is the net result of all the stylistic decisions a writer makes. In this chapter, we look at standard usage, levels of formality, and prescriptive tone.

USAGE: STANDARD AND NONSTANDARD

With each new invention and technological advance, new words flow out over the airwaves and into cyberspace, changing our language. Makers of dictionaries scramble to keep up with the flood of new words by bringing out revised editions every few years. To maintain a semblance of order, they classify words in various ways according to usage. All dictionaries have two broad categories of usage: standard and nonstandard.

Standard Usage

Most of the words in our language are standard usage, meaning they are widely accepted by educated speakers and writers. These words follow conventional spellings and rules of grammar. Standard usage varies widely, ranging from informal to formal words. Often language is a mixture of the informal and formal, the technical and nontechnical. Sometimes the status of words changes; a word can gain or lose acceptance or acquire new meaning. For example, the word *punk* has several colloquial or slang meanings but in recent years *punk* as applied to a style of dress and music has become standard English.

A word may also have no usage label for one meaning, indicating that it is standard usage, while another meaning may be labeled as nonstandard. A standard usage meaning for *learn*, for example, is "to gain knowledge." Many dictionaries, however, also include "to teach" as a definition of *learn* (as in, "That will learn him") but label this usage as nonstandard.

Sometimes dictionary makers cannot agree on the status of a word. For example, *complected* is listed as "regional dialect" or "substandard" in several dictionaries whereas Merriam-Webster's Collegiate Dictionary, tenth edition (1996), states, "Not an error, nor a dialectal term, nor nonstandard—all of which it has been labeled—*complected* still manages to raise hackles."* If you are trying to decide whether to use such a word, it is safer to be conservative. Avoid it lest the reader, unaware of the diversity in opinion, regard the word as an error.

Nonstandard Usage

As a rule, nonstandard words are not used in writing, although they may be heard in casual conversation. This level of usage includes taboo words that are inappropriate for college or workplace writing, such as obscenities, crudities, and

---

*By permission. From *Merriam-Webster's Collegiate® Dictionary*, Tenth Edition ©1996 by Merriam-Webster, Inc.

racial, ethnic, or gender slurs. Speakers sometimes use such language to make a social statement or to fit into a group. This variety of nonstandard usage is flamboyant, somewhat like ragged jeans with gaping holes and a T-shirt bearing an offensive phrase, designed to shock. Although nonstandard words are sometimes used to lend a sense of realism to novels, plays, or short stories, they are generally out of place in workplace and college writing.

Nonstandard usage also includes dialect and regional variations. Dialect is the natural way some folks talk, using colloquialisms such as "hit the road," regionalisms such as "down the road a piece," and fractured grammar such as "didn't never" or "them books." Although this language may be comfortable and inoffensive, rather like the careless attire worn around home to paint or work in the yard, its usefulness is limited. While dialect can be appropriate in writing to suggest regional or informal speech, it should generally be avoided in academic and professional work. Nonstandard usage can be ungrammatical, distracting, and difficult to understand.

Most dictionaries label words, or particular uses of words, that are considered nonstandard. The labels and their explanations are generally found in the introduction of the dictionary. There, too, you can find other notes explaining how to read the various abbreviations that appear in entries throughout the dictionary. For example, words used chiefly in conversation are often labeled *colloquial*, while those limited to a geographic area are identified as *dialect* or *regional*. Here are nonstandard usage labels and their common abbreviations that you may find in dictionaries:

N.S. or nonstd.	=	nonstandard
substand.	=	substandard
dial.	=	dialect
vul.	=	vulgar (common)

If no such label appears with an entry, then the word is widely accepted as standard usage.

LEVELS OF FORMALITY

With language, as with clothing, no one level of formality is suitable for all occasions. In fact, within the realm of standard usage, there are three broad levels of formality: informal, formal, and a level in between that includes most words. Dictionary entries usually label informal words, but not always with the same designations; you may find either of two labels to denote *informal* usage:

inf.	=	informal
colloq.	=	colloquial (conversational)

The level between informal and formal, which contains the most words in English, goes *unlabeled* in all dictionaries. Thus if you look up a word and find no status label, you know the word is standard in both grammatical usage and formality. For many years this middle level has been referred to as "Standard English." But that is gradually changing because all three levels of accepted usage have standard grammar. To prevent confusion, some writers call this level "Edited American English." Others prefer "Professional English," the designation used in this book.

Formal English is usually *not* labeled in dictionaries. It includes archaic words, Latin or other foreign phrases, and specialized terminology common to particular academic and professional disciplines and technical professions. If you find the following labels, you will know that the words are formal:

arch.   =   archaic (antiquated or rarely used)

obs.   =   obsolete (used chiefly before 1775)

poetic (found in poetry)

Technical terms, in particular, may begin life at the formal level; they are known only to the professionals who use them. Later, however, as they are widely quoted by the media and adopted by the general public, they enter the middle level, designated here as Professional English, or even the informal level. For example, such terms as *CD-ROM* and *Internet*, known only to specialists a few years ago, are now understood by many schoolchildren. In the following sections the three levels of formality in standard English are discussed in some detail.

Informal Standard English

Educated speakers and writers use not only Professional English but also Informal Standard English, the language of conversation. A large majority of words are acceptable at both levels. Along with standard words, Informal Standard English includes slang, contractions, and colloquialisms. Chiefly spoken, Informal Standard English has a casual, often friendly tone. This level is comfortable, rather like slacks and a sports shirt with rolled-up sleeves, open at the neck. Writers use Informal Standard English in many popular magazines, novels, short stories, poems, comics, ads, and newspaper articles because of its broad appeal and ease in reading.

Informal Standard English may also be found in personal essays, journals, memos, letters, instruction booklets, travel brochures, and other materials. Let's take a look at an example from *Frommer's Ireland on $35 a Day:*

> From picnics in St. Stephen's green to pub grub to Tourist Menu meals to elegant Big Splurges, Dublin offers wide variety in cuisine as well as price. . . . The Stag's Head, 1 Dame Court, is a real beauty. Built in 1770, its last "modernization" was in 1895. Lots of gleaming wood, wrought-iron chandeliers, stained-glass skylights, huge mirrors, and (need I say it?) mounted stags' heads.

Did you note the conversational tone? And did you spot the fragment in the line beginning "Lots of"? Although Informal Standard English may include a well-placed fragment, the verb forms, pronoun agreement, and other grammatical structures are standard. Pronouns in first person (*I*) and second person (*you*) are present when the reader is addressed directly.

There are different varieties of Informal Standard English. Business letters and many printed materials require complete sentences. The tone is often a bit more formal than Frommer's—more like Stuart M. Berger's *What Your Doctor Didn't Learn in Medical School:*

> The word *hypoglycemia* is the kind of six-syllable medicalese word that my patients hear and tell me: "That's Greek to me, doctor." Well, in the case of this word, it really is Greek! But just in case your ancient Greek is a tad rusty, let's review: *hypo* means "too little"; *gly* is the Greek root for "sugar"; and the suffix *-emia* means "of the blood." String them together, and you have "too little sugar in the blood." (The disease is the polar opposite of diabetes, which creates too much sugar in the blood.)

Although both selections are Informal Standard English, they differ in word choice and tone. "Pub grub" is less formal than "a tad rusty." And the voice of Frommer ("need I say it?") is much more personal than Berger's ("the polar opposite"). Berger's writing is closer to Professional English.

Professional English

Professional English marks a writer as well-educated and knowledgeable. Just as a well-tailored suit is often a requirement in workplace situations, so too is this level of formality. The written language of the professional world requires conventional grammar and standard words. Professional English is found in business reports, annual reports to stockholders, many newspaper articles, textbooks, and much academic writing. *The hallmarks of Professional English are complete sentences, correct grammar, and standard word choice.* Although first-person pronouns may be used, third person predominates, as in the following example from the *Wall Street Journal:*

> The white founder of an artificial Christmas tree company fills his work force with minority-group members. The black owner of a computer-management company hires a retired white corporate executive who says the job is the best he ever had. The female owner of a bakery-catering business takes pride in calling herself the firm's token Jew and her husband and partner its token Protestant.
>
> Owning a small business can give the boss the ability to hire and promote people whom other employers often shun. Some entrepreneurs take that challenge—determined to show that a diversified work force is valuable not only socially, but financially as well.
>
> —Dorothy J. Gaiter, "Equal Opportunities"

Did you notice that there are no contractions or informal words? Although this example and the next one are both written in third person and both appeared in the *Wall Street Journal,* the voice of the next writer is quite different:

The recent public offering by BET Holdings may mark a turning point for African-American business. The holding company for the Black Entertainment Television cable network is only the third black-owned enterprise ever to go public, and the first on the New York Stock Exchange. Most big black-owned companies have been family-built enterprises wary of Wall Street and its disclosure requirements.

—**Leon E. Wynter, "Business and Race"**

The voice of the second selection is more impersonal than that of the first. For readers unfamiliar with the stock market, the information may be meaningless. ("Go public" is technical jargon, meaning to issue stock in a corporation for sale to the public.) Technical words, which may be found at any level of formality, mute the voice of the writer.

Formal English

Rather like the tuxedo and long evening dress, Formal English is used for special purposes and occasions. Stately in tone, Formal English rarely includes first-person pronouns except possibly to describe primary research. Formal English has the major hallmarks of Professional English: correct grammar, standard word choice, and complete sentences. But some words in Formal English are scholarly and less known. Some may be archaic. Formal English may include foreign phrases, literary allusions, and specialized or technical terms unknown to the average reader. The sentence structure tends to be long and complex. All of these characteristics tend to make the voice of the writer less personal.

Formal English is primarily written. It is the language of technical and graduate-level textbooks, professional journals, symposiums, formal reports, many insurance policies, and legal and government documents. The following passage from a legal decision written in Formal English by former U.S. Supreme Court Chief Justice Earl Warren is easier to understand than many other legal documents:

The plaintiffs contend that segregated public schools are not "equal" and cannot be made "equal," and that hence they are deprived of the equal protection of the laws. Because of the obvious importance of the question presented, the Court took jurisdiction. Argument was heard in the 1952 Term, and reargument was heard this Term on certain questions propounded by the Court.

—**The School Segregation Decision of 1954**
Brown versus Board of Education of Topeka, Kansas
347 U. S. 487–496 (May 17, 1954)

You may be familiar with some varieties of Formal English. If enrolled in pre-law, paralegal, education, premed, nursing, data processing, engineering, or other such programs, you may read Formal Technical English in your textbooks. Or you may work in a profession where it is spoken and written daily. Let's take a look at technical language from the early 1980s, found in the Apple IIe Manual *Extended 80-Column Text Card Supplement:*

The memory mapping for double high-resolution graphics is similar to the normal high-resolution mapping described in Chapter 2 of the *Apple IIe Reference Manual*, with the addition of the column doubling produced by the 80-column display. Like the 80-column text mode, the double-resolution graphics mode displays two bytes in the time normally required for one, but it uses high resolution-graphics Page 1 and Page 1X instead of text Page 1 and Page 1X. (19)

Although this computer jargon is relatively simple, it would be unintelligible to anyone lacking computer savvy. Other factors also make the paragraph difficult to read. Did you notice the length of the sentences? The first contains 39 words; the second, 40 words. In fact, there are only two sentences in the entire paragraph. All varieties of Formal English tend to have long sentences, which contribute to the level of reading difficulty. In Formal English the author's voice is distant or nonexistent. Difference in voice is just one way focused writing differs from conversation.

FOCUSED WRITING DIFFERS FROM CASUAL CONVERSATION

Casual conversation ambles along at a leisurely pace, wordy and repetitive at times. Sometimes it becomes sidetracked, never getting to the point. Often fragmented and abbreviated, conversation may omit transitions and significant information. When this happens, the listener may frown, raise an eyebrow, or ask a question. Then the speaker has the opportunity to backtrack and explain.

Since few writers have the chance to observe nonverbal feedback or to ask questions of the reader, they must exert more effort than conversationalists to be clear and complete. Focused writing is much more specific, concise, and complete than casual conversation. Even when the style is informal, focused writing has a logical order.

A factor that complicates word choice for beginning writers is that each of us has three distinct vocabularies—speaking, writing, and reading. Our speaking vocabulary is the smallest and most general. Our reading vocabulary is the largest and most specific. Awareness of the levels of formality and your own three distinct vocabularies can help you select an appropriate voice for each writing task. The following list can help you gain a sense of the level of formality generally expected in different writing tasks for most workplaces. Note that there are some overlaps between the columns. For example, memos and letters may be written in either Informal or Professional English, depending on the audience and purpose. A memo inviting staff members to a surprise birthday party for a fellow worker would likely be informal, while most memos relating to company business would be more formal. Likewise, professional reports may be written in Professional English or Formal English, depending on the purpose and audience.

Levels of Formality in the Workplace

Informal	Professional	Formal
memos	memos	technical documentation
customer letters	letters	specialized papers and reports
newsletters	newsletters	laws, statutes
sales talks	bids, proposals	legal notices
letter reports	professional reports	proposals
informal speeches	contracts	contracts, legal documents
newspaper articles	forms	technical manuals
conversation	presentations	motivational speeches
	policy statements	policy statements
	manuals	court opinions
	bulletins	

TWO COMMON CONCERNS WITH VOICE

Just as the level of formality should be appropriate for the occasion, so too should the writer's voice. Although colloquialisms may give an air of friendliness, they are inappropriate for much college writing. Colloquial language has a very limited place in most nonfiction writing. Inappropriate prescriptive language may be perceived as having an abrasive tone.

Colloquialisms

Although Professional English is usually expected in college writing, colloquialisms (conversational usage) sometimes slip into student papers. This sudden downshift to a lower level of formality is jarring for the unsuspecting reader. Such shifts need to be made carefully and only for a sound reason. To help you avoid some common colloquialisms, consider the following list. The left column includes examples of colloquialisms, and the right column gives their standard counterparts.

Colloquial	*Standard*
The client *really wants* to sell.	The client *is eager* to sell.
She got a *good deal* on her car.	Her Ford Escort was a *bargain*.
His *phone* has been *tied up*.	His *telephone* has been *busy*.
Our flight left *around* 7:30 a.m.	Our flight left *at approximately* 7:30 a.m.
I'd hate to see her do that.	*I would prefer* she not do that.

Erin is an *awfully* good doctor.	Erin is a *very* good physician.
Jason added his *two cents' worth.*	Jason added his *opinion.*
Alright, I'll go.	*All right,* I *will* go.
When did Sue *get* married?*	When did Sue *marry?*
He takes his *kids* to the office.	He takes his *children* to the office.

Other colloquial expressions to avoid in expository writing are listed below, along with standard alternatives.

Colloquial	*Standard*
a lot of	many, much
sort of	rather, somewhat
headache (also has standard usage)	problem, concern
a couple of	two
fight (verbal)	argument, quarrel
really good	very good, excellent
mad	angry, upset
ballpark figure	estimate
stuff	items, articles, materials

Another pitfall in writing is the colloquial use of standard words. Sometimes standard words acquire slang meanings. Take for example, the word *turkey*, that delectable bird which has long been a mainstay of American menus. Informally, the word is used in two ways. "Talk turkey" means to speak frankly, to get down to basic facts. "You turkey!" refers to a person who blunders or who is considered inept or undesirable. Most beginning writers are probably aware of these distinctions and would realize when they were using the word colloquially.

However, many unsuspecting writers misuse the term *great*. "She's a great dancer," "I feel great!" and similar examples sometimes creep into college writing. The standard meanings of *great* include "very large in size," "large in quantity or number," and "extensive distance or time." Only informally does *great* mean "wonderful" or "excellent." If you are tempted to use slang or other colloquialisms but are not sure whether they are appropriate for the expected level of formality, ease your doubts by consulting a dictionary.

Prescriptive Tone

A prescriptive tone lends authority to a statement. Prescriptive language is used in giving directions, establishing rules and laws, or issuing commands. Just

---

*Get is not a helping verb.

as a doctor prescribes medicine, a prescriptive writer offers advice, makes suggestions, or requires the reader to do something. In a class or at work, you may be required to explain a procedure, to supply advice for a client, or to provide other kinds of directions. If you manage or supervise, you will be responsible for seeing that employees fulfill their duties. You may train new workers, relay orders, or make recommendations.

Whenever prescription is a part of your job, your voice should be calm and confident, not overly authoritative. In other situations, however, prescription is inappropriate. Then it merely intrudes and irritates. To avoid using prescriptive words inadvertently, you need to be keenly aware of them. Prescriptive language can often be identified by the words *must, should, ought,* or *need,* although these words can be implied. In other instances an order or command is issued. The examples below illustrate prescriptive language in different voices:

Business etiquette manual: The boss *should* issue the first invitation to a lunch, dinner, or party.

Doctor: Forceps, please. (Implied command)

Parent: *Clean up* your room before the health department issues a quarantine.

Boss: Those letters *need* to be typed by 2:30 p.m.

Neighbor: You *ought* to give your garage a coat of paint when you get time.

Pet owner: Rover, *sit!*

Did you notice the abrasive tone of some of these examples? Inappropriate prescription is annoying. Adults tend to resent being told what to do and being treated like children. Unnecessary orders, advice, or suggestions can be barriers to communication. Sometimes inappropriate prescription emerges in student essays, as in the first example below. The second example shows how prescription can be reworded as description (giving the facts):

Prescriptive: Setting goals should be a person's most important objective in life. (The student writer projects her priority onto everyone.)

Descriptive: Setting goals is an important part of my life. (Here the writer identifies the priority without projecting it onto everyone.)

CONCLUSION

With practice, you will be able to select an appropriate level of formality and voice for each piece of writing. To find an appropriate voice, you determine the purpose of writing, size up the situation and the audience, then adjust your written voice accordingly. To refine word choice, you need to know the precise meaning of words and listen to their nuances or undertones. Since the English language may range all the way from street talk to archaic phrases, you need a good desk dictionary. The more you learn about language and the more you write, the more flexible your writing voice will be.

≫ *Checklist for Revision: Listening to Your Written Voice*
_____

To check the tone of your writing, read it aloud, ask yourself these questions, and consider your answers carefully.

1. Is there prescription? If so, is it necessary?
2. Is the voice appropriate for the purpose, topic, and situation?
3. How might the reader perceive the voice?
4. Can I substitute other words that might improve the voice?

Summary

Clarity and simplicity are the heart of effective writing style. Writers are expected to find an appropriate voice for the rhetorical situation. Voice is the result of all the stylistic decisions a writer makes, including level of formality. To find a suitable level of formality and an appropriate voice, consider the occasion, purpose, audience, and topic.

Words are classified as either nonstandard or standard in usage. Standard usage comprises three levels of formality: Informal Standard English, Professional English, and Formal English. In the workplace, standard usage is expected and all three levels are used at various times. Sometimes language is a mixture of informal and formal words. For college papers, you will be expected to use Informal Standard English or Professional English, according to the assignment. A good desk dictionary can provide you with important information about usage and level of formality.

Focused writing is more orderly, concise, and complete than casual conversation. For workplace and college writing, avoid slang, colloquialisms, and unnecessary prescription. Descriptive words are safer to use than prescriptive words because they do not give unsolicited advice or unnecessary orders.

Key Terms

voice	slang	Informal Standard English
standard usage	level of formality	Professional English
nonstandard usage	archaic	Formal English
colloquial	obsolete	prescriptive tone
dialect		

Test Yourself

Recognizing Nonstandard Usage

Directions: Underline the nonstandard or colloquial terms. Then substitute a standard term. (To check your answers, turn to the end of the chapter.)

1. The crick in the pasture is almost dry.
2. Come on. Mom said it was alright to go.
3. The party was great, but I could of done without the singing telegram.
4. He is shy, but he enjoys playing with other kids after he opens up.
5. When she gets mad, she becomes very quiet.

Identifying the Level of Formality

Directions: Identify the level of formality of each example, then check your answers.

1. "Some editors may use the phrase "We can't use it right now" merely to soften the letdown, and many writers take the words as literal truth. However, some editors may mean the phrase literally, so if an editor writes, "We can't use it right now" write back and ask, "When can you use it?" If you receive encouragement from an editor, ask "If I changed the ending (or whatever change the editor suggests), would you be interested in seeing it again?"

    —Kenneth Atchity, "Dealing with Rejection"

2. Linda Ronstadt: "When we were little, we spoke Spanish at home. . . . My Spanish is very rudimentary—child's Spanish, really. But I sing in Spanish, and my new album is all Spanish *canciones* [songs], and I sing two songs in the movie *The Mambo Kings*."

    —James Brady, "In Step with: Linda Ronstadt"

3. "Fighting a stubbornly high inflation rate stoked by climbing wages, Hong Kong said it would nearly double the number of trained foreign workers who will be permitted to work. . . . The quota, now allowing for 13,000 foreign employees, will be expanded to 25,000."

    —"World Wire," *Wall Street Journal*

4. "Between eye-wiping and nose-blowing, I told him, 'I don't ever want another dog. It hurts too much. . . .' 'You're right about the hurt, son,' he answered, 'but that's the price of love.'"

    —Fred Bauer, "The Price of Love"

5. "Local historians say tea and cookies have been served ever since the five-acre Japanese preserve of dwarf trees, cherry blossoms and lily pads was

constructed 97 years ago in Golden Gate Park by gardener Makoto Higi-wara as a blissful refuge from the frenetic city pace."

—Jim Carlton, "For True San Franciscans,
It Was More Than a Tempest in a Teapot"

6. In Leeds, Maine, "Amy Dacyczyn has six kids, a $125,000 farmhouse, no debt and this advice: Don't throw away the lids to frozen-juice cans. . . . While the rest of the country seems to have spent the 1980's spending money, Mrs. Dacyczyn was stretching her husband's $30,000 salary as a petty officer in the Navy by reusing disposable vacuum-cleaner bags and buying oatmeal in feedstore lots."

—Clare Ansberry, "A Thrifty Couple Teaches Tightwads to Be Skinflints"

Practice

Rewriting Colloquialisms and Contractions

Directions: When you find colloquialisms or contractions below, rephrase the sentence into Professional English. If the sentence is already Professional English, mark with a C.

1. Around 11:30 I'll stop by your office so that we can go to lunch.
2. Since his head injury, Rick has been behaving sort of funny.
3. Tara and Jeanne had a fun time at the flea market.
4. Ray'll pick up the kids from the day care center on his way home from work.
5. Yesterday Lance had a client who was a big headache.
6. In the employees' lounge are some awfully good cinnamon rolls.
7. That's a ballpark figure.
8. He made a lot of punctuation errors in that letter.
9. I heard Scott and Julie got married last week.
10. Brent bought a really good sound system.

Collaborative Activity:
Choosing Levels of Formality for Different Audiences

Directions: Read the case problems below. Then decide which level of formality would be best for each case.

1. You are a newspaper reporter interviewing Bill Cosby for a feature in the Sunday paper about how he became a comedian. What level of formality will you use when you write the article?
2. You are a systems analyst, and your boss, who has a similar background, has assigned you to a systems project that will take approximately six

months. He has asked for a weekly memo report and a long report with graphics when the project has been completed. What level of formality would be appropriate for each of the reports?

3. You are writing a cover letter to mail with your résumé. What level of formality will you use?

4. You are writing a television commercial for antifreeze. You want to appeal to everyone who drives a car, so you have decided to feature a mechanic at a neighborhood garage. At which level of formality will you have him speak?

5. Imagine you are a physician writing an article that describes a new treatment for cancer. The article will appear in a medical journal that is read primarily by other doctors. What level of formality will you use?

Test Yourself Answers

Recognizing Nonstandard Usage

1. *The creek in the pasture is almost dry.*
2. *Come on. Mother (My mother) said it was all right to go.*
3. *The party was fun, but I could have done without the singing telegram. or The party was enjoyable, but I would have preferred no singing telegram.*
4. *. . . with other children once he becomes acquainted.*
5. *When Laura becomes angry, she becomes very quiet.*

Identifying the Level of Formality

1. *Informal*
2. *Professional*
3. *Professional*
4. *Informal*
5. *Professional*
6. *Informal*

CHAPTER 7

Writing Effective Paragraphs

Discipline and focused awareness . . . contribute to the act of creation.

—John Poppy

Paragraphs may not be as diverse in pattern as snowflakes are, but they offer a multitude of opportunities for creativity and variety. Paragraphs come in assorted designs and sizes to reflect their varying functions. Opening and concluding paragraphs act as a frame for an essay or report. Body paragraphs focus on making specific points and presenting information in a complete and coherent way. Transitional paragraphs provide connections between different ideas. A single well-developed paragraph by itself may even form a complete brief essay, exam answer, or business communication.

Effective opening and concluding paragraphs of essays are discussed in chapter 3. Chapter 7 discusses the elements and qualities of effective body paragraphs within essays, as well as single paragraphs, paying special attention to some specific patterns of development.

ELEMENTS OF AN EFFECTIVE PARAGRAPH

Good writing is not as exact as a chemical formula. The patterns for a good paragraph do not have to be followed every time you write. Still, to be effective, a paragraph must be centered on one main idea. And regardless of whether the paragraph comes in the body of an essay (or other piece of writing) or whether the paragraph stands alone, it contains certain elements. For clarity, most paragraphs have a topic sentence.

The Topic Sentence

The topic sentence contains the main idea of a paragraph. This sentence tells the reader *what* will be covered and *why*. Some topic sentences also tell *where* or *when*. A basic topic sentence has two essential functions:

1. *To limit the subject to one main idea* that can be developed in the paragraph.
2. *To make a claim, assertion, or statement of opinion.* This part of the topic sentence may be a belief, impression, generalization, or recommendation.

Let's consider a topic sentence that performs both these functions:

Uncle Jake, who came uninvited, was a difficult house guest.

The subject of this topic sentence is "Uncle Jake," and the claim is that he was "a difficult house guest." This topic sentence sets up the expectation that the writer will describe Uncle Jake's behavior. In the body of the paragraph, readers will expect support—examples of what he said and anecdotes of what he did so that they can see for themselves how difficult Uncle Jake was.

Support Sentences

Support sentences explain the main idea of the topic sentence. They supply evidence to convince the reader of the soundness of the claim, assertion, or opinion. The evidence may be in the form of facts, reasons, examples, illustrations, definitions, or other logical support. The minimum for support sentences is generally three or four; often there are more. As you search for support, keep in mind that *quality* is more important than *quantity*. A few excellent examples are worth more than a dozen mediocre ones. Established facts and valid reasons provide credible evidence. Appropriate illustrations and anecdotes increase readers' interest, understanding, and conviction.

A Concluding Sentence

Besides the two basic parts just discussed—the topic sentence and support sentences—some paragraphs have a third part. This final part is a concluding sentence that serves a different function than the sentences of support do. This final sentence may be a summary or an overview of the points made in the support sentences. It can also serve as a *clincher*, providing the paragraph with a sense of completeness by commenting on the subject in an interesting, surprising, or humorous way. In the following student paragraph, the clincher alludes to the opening topic sentence:

Climb Aboard!

The magic of a carousel has a way of turning men and women into children again. As they approach the carousel house, their steps and their hearts suddenly become lighter. Tots tug at adult hands, eager to climb aboard this remnant from a fairy tale. The magnificent carousel stands with hundreds of lights reflected in mirrors on the brightly painted rounding boards. Adventurous riders select mounts from rows of prancing horses or from the menagerie of bears, big cats, goats, ostriches, rabbits, a zebra, a giraffe, or a hippocampus. The timid and the elderly seem to prefer the sedate pace of the two chariots. When all riders are seated, the calliope signals the ride is about to begin. As the carousel gains speed, whirling faster and faster, the riders' faces are transformed by smiles. Their cares seem to disappear as they are charmed by the magic of the carousel.

—Bonita M. Goings

THE QUALITIES OF AN EFFECTIVE PARAGRAPH

Effective paragraphs have five distinctive features: interest, unity, coherence, completeness, and clarity. To remember these five characteristics, just think: I-U-C-C-C.

Interest

Above all, an effective paragraph is worth reading. The topic is significant and the development interesting. A secret of good essay writing is to remember that readers like to be entertained. That does not mean you have to be amusing. It means you try to capture readers' attention and make them eager to continue. Before beginning a draft, think about how you might stimulate interest. Can you approach your topic in an unusual way? What might readers like to know? What detail might hook their interest? Scan your prewriting; you may find an over-looked gem that will be just the hook you want. Then use action verbs and con-crete nouns to help the reader share your impression (see chapter 11).

Unity

To write effective paragraphs, resist the temptation to create thickets of words, lest your main idea become lost. Focus on the major thought so that each paragraph is clearly unified. Place your major idea in the topic sentence, where it can control and limit the paragraph. Each of the other sentences in the paragraph should support the major idea of the topic sentence through examples, facts, sta-tistics, opinion, or reasons. During the drafting stage, don't worry unduly about unity. At that stage your goal is to expand ideas on paper. But when you start to revise, unity becomes a prime consideration. To check a paragraph for unity, ask yourself three questions:

- What is the purpose of the paragraph?
- Does each support sentence help to achieve the purpose?
- If not, what needs to be deleted?

Coherence

You might think of a paragraph as a jigsaw puzzle—each piece must fit. If not, the paragraph lacks coherence; it does not flow smoothly. If words, phrases, or sentences are in the wrong places, they must be rearranged. If there are gaps between ideas, you need to add transitions and other words to provide connections. Other ways of achieving coherence are by repeating key words and by using parallelism.

Signpost Transitions   Like signs on a highway, signpost transitions direct the reader. Often these signal words and phrases appear at the beginning of sentences. Some common signpost transitions are listed here as a quick reference:

To show time: once, years ago, later, soon, now, today, then, before, when, while, after, meanwhile, as, next, first, second, and so forth

To add: too, also, and, another, besides, in addition, furthermore

To show difference: but, yet, however, still, otherwise, even so, although

To show similarity: like, likewise, similarly, both, resemble, identical

To show effects or results: because, for, therefore, as a result, since, thus

To emphasize: in fact, indeed, above all, again, regardless, nonetheless

To point out examples: for example, for instance

Note the use of transitions indicating *time* in the following student paragraph by Sonny Dyer:

Playing Possum

While defending an ambush position in Vietnam, I was run over by a tank. Hurt and bleeding, I was left lying in a rice paddy. My buddy, *after* routing the ambush against "Charlie," took off in pursuit, believing I was dead. *After an hour*, which seemed like an eternity, night fell. *A few hours later* the sky was pitch black. There was no moon nor stars, just blackness. Suddenly I heard someone sloshing through the paddy. It was Charlie. *As* I lay there motionless, I heard the Viet soldier rummaging through my Jeep. *After* he finished with the Jeep, he started to strip the dead. *Before* I knew it, he was standing over me. *While* lying there playing dead, trying not to breathe, I was sure he could hear the blood rushing from my wounds. Luckily for me, he was in a hurry and just stripped off my watch, flak jacket, lighter, and cigarettes. *After* he left, I took a big breath and let out a sigh of relief. *Hours later, as* dawn broke, a patrol finally happened across my Jeep and discovered the bodies lying around. Tears came to my eyes *as* I heard a U.S. soldier say, "Medic, this one is still alive!"

Key Words, Natural Relationships, Synonyms, and Pronouns   Repeating key words, substituting synonyms, and using pronouns that refer to key words help to focus a paragraph on the main idea and thus achieve coherence (see "Using Embedded Transition" in chapter 14). By consistently referring to the main idea of the paragraph, you ensure that readers can follow your line of thought. Note how repetition of key words, synonyms, and pronouns helps make the following paragraph coherent:

> *My mother* was the eldest of *her* generation—of nine children—and came from a slightly more elevated social station in Jamaica. *She* had a high school education, which *my father* lacked. . . . Before emigrating, *Mom* had worked as a stenographer in a lawyer's office. *Her* mother, Gram McKoy, was a small, lovely woman whose English wedded *African cadence* to *British inflection*, the sound of which is still music to my soul. The McKoys and the Powells both had *bloodlines* common among *Jamaicans*, including *African, English, Irish, Scotch*, and probably *Arawak Indian*. *My father's side* even added a *Jewish strain* from a Broomfield *ancestor*.

> —**Colin Powell**, *My American Journey*

Parallelism   Parallel structures provide balance in writing and contribute to coherence. Possibly without thinking, you already use parallelism in several ways: for items in a series, coordinate phrases and clauses, compound sentences, and pairs of related sentences (see chapter 8). You may sense that parallelism smooths sentence structure and gives equal emphasis to coordinate ideas. To check the coherence and parallelism of your paragraphs, read them aloud. The ear is often a better detector of imbalance than is the eye. Note the use of parallelism in the following descriptive paragraph by student Nancy Smathers:

Through a Child's Eyes

A tall, husky man has long been a very special person in my life. *His hair is the color of bricks in a schoolhouse*, while *his eyes are the color of hickory nut shells*. *Above his eyes* he wears a permanent frown, but *in his smile* I can see his inner warmth peeking through. *When he speaks*, his voice sounds like a semi-truck going through a tunnel at a high rate of speed. The low, gravelly tones echo like a bouncing tennis ball in an empty room. *When he enters a room*, he resembles a bear just waking from its winter slumber. But *when he sits*, a lap appears that would never turn away a child who wished to crawl upon it. When sitting there, I can detect the faint scent of Old Spice. *His big, muscular arms* make me feel safe from any possible harm. *His huge, powerful hands* are *like vise grips*, but when wiping tears away, they are *like soft cotton*. As rough as this man appears *on the outside*, *on the inside* he is soft and gentle, just like a newborn kitten. . . . This very dear person is my dad.

Completeness

An effective paragraph does not weary readers nor waste their time. Details appear for a valid reason. To be complete, a paragraph must supply adequate and appropriate information. But how much is adequate? What is appropriate? You, the writer, must decide the answers to these questions according to each writing situation. Whether your professor assigns a single paragraph or a lengthy paper, you will have to assess the audience and the occasion. To decide how much you need to say to be complete, you might consider the following points:

- How much are readers likely to know?
- How much more do they need to know?
- Why? How will the information be used?
- Are there enough examples, reasons, or anecdotes to be interesting?
- Is there enough specific support to make my point?

A word of caution: Include details only for a legitimate reason. A surplus of minor details will bore readers.

Clarity

Some writing is like bright sunlight. The main idea shines through the words clearly. Good writing requires that readers be able to determine the meaning upon a first reading. True, they may need to reread to recall specific details, but the main idea should be apparent the first time. Clarity is the most important aspect of expository writing. Clarity is the end result of correctly assessing the reader, unifying ideas, achieving coherence, and being complete. Other important influences on clarity are the level of language, voice of verbs, sentence structure, sentence length, and positions of emphasis (see chapter 8). Keep in mind that lack of clarity can result from lack of thoughtful analysis; check each of your paragraphs carefully for unity, coherence, and completeness.

PREWRITING AND DRAFTING PARAGRAPHS

If you are writing a body paragraph in an essay, the topic sentence introduces one segment of your thesis statement (central idea of the essay). Although this chapter shows some body paragraphs, they are explained in part 2. Mainly, this chapter focuses on single student paragraphs.

Narrowing a Topic Sentence

How to whittle down a general topic is a frequent problem for beginning writers. Narrowing a topic requires selecting one significant aspect. The problem may be that you know so much, you can't decide where to start. For example, a first attempt might read: "I like horses." But you realize the sentence is boring and too broad. Your mind spinning with ideas, you begin to prewrite. Soon you have a list that yields a suitable topic. Your efforts might look like this:

horses
riding horses
riding horses I have owned
my first riding horse

Draft topic sentence: I'll never forget my first horse.

First revision: Pinto was my first riding horse; actually, he was a pony.

Second revision: My first riding horse was actually a pony, but to my five-year-old eyes, Pinto was the finest of horses.

For most topic sentences, a limit of twenty words or so usually works well. A topic sentence that is too long may overwhelm the reader.

Positioning the Topic Sentence

Once you have drafted a topic sentence, your next concern is where to place it in the paragraph. Before positioning the topic sentence, consider its function and the effect you want to obtain. Will you place it at the beginning, the middle, or the end?

The Topic Sentence at the Beginning   Most expository paragraphs follow the direct approach: the topic sentence is placed at the beginning. There the topic receives more emphasis than in the middle, and the reader knows immediately what the writer will explain. Yet topic sentences sometimes wander into odd places. While revising this book, I have been surprised now and then to find a topic sentence huddled in the middle of a paragraph for no apparent reason. Unless I found a reason to leave it there, I yanked it back to the beginning. Check your drafts to see that your topic sentences are in the most effective position for the purpose and audience.

The Topic Sentence in the Middle   Sometimes a writer may wish to take a leisurely path to the main idea. Then the topic sentence may appear in the middle of a paragraph. Placed there, the major idea receives less emphasis than at the beginning or end. In a paragraph of comparison, for instance, a topic sentence might be located midway between the two subjects. There it can identify the purpose and connect the items being compared. Or the topic sentence may be in the middle for other reasons, as in the following paragraph, which describes nonverbal communication:

> Mrs. Clark, who teaches math, is explaining an essential aspect of the subject. She notices that Fred is staring at her with unblinking eyes, his body taut and erect, his feet flat on the floor. She discerns no motion whatever from Fred. Do you think that Fred is listening to the lecture, evaluating what Mrs. Clark is saying? *If you think he is interested, you are wrong.* A young teacher unaccustomed to this posture might fall for it, but a more experienced educator would not. Fred has turned his teacher off and is using a cover-up technique to convince her that he is "all ears."
>
> —Gerard I. Nierenberg and Henry H. Calero
> *How to Read a Person Like A Book*

Placing a topic sentence in the middle of a paragraph does carry a *risk*, however. The danger is that if readers are impatient or in a hurry, they may skim over the middle and miss the key thought. If the idea is very important, place it at the beginning or end.

The Topic Sentence at the End   At the end of an expository paragraph, the topic sentence acts as a summary, spelling out the controlling idea that is implicit in the sentences that precede it. The following paragraph, for example, builds up to a concluding topic sentence that offers a startling and bleak statistic:

> Many illiterates cannot read the admonition on a pack of cigarettes. Neither the Surgeon General's warning nor its reproduction on the package can alert them to the risks. Although most people learn by word of mouth that smoking is related to a number of grave physical disorders, they do not get the chance to read the detailed stories which can document this danger with the vividness that turns concern into determination to resist. They can see the handsome cowboy or the slim Virginia lady lighting up a filter cigarette; they cannot heed the words that tell them that this product is (not "may be") dangerous to their health. *Sixty million men and women are condemned to be the unalerted, high-risk candidates for cancer.*

> —Jonathan Kozol, "The Human Cost of an Illiterate Society"

A topic sentence at the end of a paragraph requires the reader to look at the support before considering the main idea. The writer takes time to explain the reasons before making the claim, so readers are less likely to reject the assertion. You might also place a topic sentence at the end to let readers know how and why you arrived at a decision.

Unifying a Paragraph without a Topic Sentence

Not all paragraphs have a topic sentence. Nonetheless, the main idea must be clear. In narrative writing topic sentences are often lacking, but a general point will still be strongly implied, as in the following paragraph:

> In the spring of 1948, in the first softball game during the afternoon hour of physical education in the dusty schoolyard, the two captains chose teams and, as always, they chose other boys until only two of us remained. I batted last, and first came to the plate with two or three runners on base, and while my teammates urged me to try for a walk, and the players on the field called Easy out, Easy out, I watched the softball coming in waist-high and stepped and swung, and hit it over the right fielder's head for a double. My next time at bat I tripled to center. From then on I brought my glove to school, hanging from a handlebar.

> —Andre Dubus, "Under the Lights"

The paragraph has no topic sentence, but its point is clearly implied and might be stated as "Without warning, I had become a good baseball player."

Diplomacy may be an excellent reason for omitting a topic sentence. Some business letters, such as a credit refusal, may not state the main idea directly. Instead, the refusal is *implied* in a subordinate clause. Unless there is a good reason to omit a topic sentence, however, include one.

Adjusting Paragraph Length

Reportedly, when Abraham Lincoln was once asked "How long should a man's legs be?" he answered, "Long enough to reach the ground." A similar answer comes to mind when students ask, "How long should a paragraph be?" A paragraph should be long enough to adequately cover the central idea according to the needs of readers and their purpose in reading.

For example, paragraphs in newspapers and magazines tend to be short, whereas those in some novels may be very long. Introductory paragraphs of short papers (500 words or less) usually range from three to five sentences, while paragraphs of definition or transition may contain fewer sentences. Body paragraphs are generally more substantial, ranging from five to eight sentences. Conclusions tend to be rather brief, perhaps three to five sentences. Paragraphs in research papers tend to be longer than those of short papers. Complexity of the subject also influences length; difficult subjects may require more explanation. As a general rule, avoid one- and two-sentence paragraphs as well as a series of short paragraphs. These will give your writing a choppy, careless appearance.

If a paragraph becomes quite long, consider the needs of the reader, the purpose of the writing, and the level of detail required for the subject. If division is needed, look for a shift from one aspect of an idea to another, according to the following suggestions.

Suggestions for Dividing Long Paragraphs

1. *Divide when a paragraph has more than one main idea.* Divide where the second idea or a shift to another facet of the major idea begins.

2. *Divide where there is a lapse in time.* Time provides a natural break. Tip: Look for transitions of time or a shift in verb tense.

3. *Divide if there is a shift in person of pronouns.* First, check to see that the shift is necessary. If it is, that may be an excellent spot to divide.

4. *In dialogue, start a new paragraph for each speaker.*

ORGANIZING AND DEVELOPING PARAGRAPHS

You can organize the details in a paragraph in any pattern that is clear and reasonable. Narrative and process paragraphs are generally in *chronological* (time) order with events and steps presented in sequence as they naturally occur. Descriptive paragraphs are generally arranged in *spatial* order according to location or design. For example, in describing objects, animals, or people, you might go from head to toe, left to right, outside to inside, or in another direction. (See "Through a Child's Eyes," earlier in this chapter, for an example of spatial order.) Paragraphs may also be organized in other logical or sequential orders, as explained in chapter 3. Some of these orders are listed following:

order of importance (from least-to-most important or vice versa)

level of complexity (least-to-most complex)

level of generality (general to specific or vice versa)

level of familiarity (most-to-least familiar)

emphatic order (bad to worst or good to best)

In organizing and developing paragraphs, you can use the same strategies that are used to develop essays. The student paragraphs that follow are organized according to strategies of narration, description, process analysis, illustration, and comparison/contrast.

Narrative Paragraphs

Narrative paragraphs tell a story or relate an event or anecdote. The details are generally arranged in chronological order. At the beginning the writer often sets the scene, telling who or what, when and where. Description, dialogue, or illustrations may be included to kindle interest and to clarify. Action verbs keep a story moving. Narratives often build suspense and reserve a surprise until the end. They may reveal rather than explain, letting the reader interpret the meaning, or they may direct attention to a social or political concern that has universal relevance (see chapter 10). The following narrative paragraph by Suzanne Omaits suggests a fear we all might experience:

Home Alone

Quiet holds many sounds. I never knew how many until I found myself alone one Friday night. Was that the wind rubbing a bare branch against the house, I wondered; or was that the front step groaning under someone's weight? I tried not to think about the sound and turned on the television set. But something compelled me to turn in my chair and look over my shoulder at the window. Slowly I turned, dreading what I might see yet afraid not to look. For a moment I froze! Through the fogged glass, I saw a man's face pressed against the window pane, staring at me. Leaping to my feet, I flipped off the lights and the television. Then he began to pound on the window. Realizing he could still see me dimly, I ran to the back room and hid. After a moment I knew I had to get help. Fearfully, I crawled back to the living room to use the telephone. My hands trembled so I could hardly dial. Clutching the receiver to my ear, I anxiously waited for the familiar voice of my neighbor. Suddenly the pounding stopped. Minutes dragged by until my neighbor arrived. After he checked the area around the house, he reassured me the intruder was gone. At that moment a car drove into the driveway. Never was I so glad to hear my parents call, "We're home!"

Descriptive Paragraphs

Descriptive paragraphs capture the essence of a person, place, or object through *significant* physical details. Concrete words reveal perceptions obtained through the five senses: seeing, hearing, touching, tasting, and smelling (see chapter 11). An effective description has a specific purpose; details are not just a pleasant filler. Often the point of a description appears in the final sentence.

In addition, descriptive paragraphs should focus on a single dominant impression to unify the various details, as the following paragraph does:

The Old Rocking Chair

In the corner of our living room sits an old wooden rocking chair. The chair is made of solid maple, varnished and trimmed in gold. The arms are worn smooth, as if someone had used the finest of sandpaper on the wood. On the edges of its arms, I can see indentations in the wood where little tykes did their teething. As I rock back and forth, the old chair squeaks and creaks; but the sounds are soothing. This rocking chair has served several purposes. It has helped to console our three children, countless nieces, nephews, and children of friends. It has rocked babies to sleep for naps and at bedtime. With its soothing rhythm, it has comforted and quieted them when they were restless or sick. Now that the children have grown older, the old chair is seldom used. Yet it sits patiently, awaiting the years when it will hold our grandchildren.

—Michael Schnitzler

Process Analysis Paragraphs

Process analysis explains how to do something or how something happens, such as how to use a software package or how mitosis occurs. Chronological order is the clearest way to organize process analysis. Just list steps or actions in sequence as they normally occur, including enough details for the reader to understand (see chapter 12). *If there is a risk during any part of the procedure, give a precaution early.* For conciseness and clarity, use second person (mainly the understood "you"), as in the following example, which is directed to someone who has never used a coin-operated car wash. Notice how the writer takes an ordinary topic and transforms it into an interesting paragraph:

How to Get the Best Shine from a Coin-Operated Car Wash

Whether your car is a prized possession or a necessary nuisance, it deserves an occasional wash. By following five simple steps, you can make your vehicle sparkling clean in just five minutes. First, vacuum the interior with the hose located outside the entrance of the car wash. Be sure the hose inhales every crumb, pebble, and gum wrapper. Second, drive into the wash cage to clean the exterior. Third, before you add coins, read the directions for operating the wand. Then turn the dial to "Prewash." Now add the coins and be ready to work fast. Fourth, spray all the exterior once. This light mist will break up grime. Fifth, switch to "High Pressure Soap" and grip the wand tightly. As you move around the car, spray the top, hood, sides, wheels, and trunk. Sixth, change the mode to "High Pressure Rinse." To prevent streaking, rinse all suds off. Next, switch to "Spot-free Final Rinse." This final step will prevent water spots and ensure a brilliant shine. If you are very dedicated to your four-wheeled friend, then take the time to wipe off excess water with the old bath towel you brought along. After that you will probably head down the highway only to be greeted with a gift from a passing bird!

—Kristi Gruber

Illustration Paragraphs

Illustration paragraphs—also called paragraphs of exemplification—present a *series* of examples to support the topic sentence. To maintain unity, every example is closely linked to the controlling idea. As you read the next paragraph, notice the order of the examples:

The Fearsome Rabbit

Bathsheba was not the typical Easter bunny. Sheba, her nickname, was a Newfoundland flop-eared rabbit. Having a large appetite, she soon grew into a fat fur ball. At maturity, she weighed close to thirty-five pounds—more than my two-year-old nephew! Our guests loved to watch her hop down the hall, then stand on her hind legs while she washed her face. With her long floppy ears hanging down, she always had a sad, gentle look, which was deceiving, for she seemed bent on destroying our property. One day we came home to find her sitting in the kitchen, chewing on a camera bag, which belonged to my husband. He yelled, "If I didn't love that rabbit so much, she would be dinner tonight!" The camera bag was not the only thing she found to destroy. Electrical cords, woodwork, wooden chairs, books, and other objects soon bore the marks of her sharp teeth. As a result, we learned to keep a close eye on her at all times. As Sheba grew older, she developed a mean streak when children were around. One day our son, who was six, went into her territory near her litter box. Soon he came running out—Sheba hopping close behind. As she nipped his bare heel, he screamed, "HELP!" After this incident she would hop toward him, and he would leap onto the couch. He had become afraid of her. Soon Sheba became too much of a problem; and we took her to a farm that raised rabbits, where she seems fat and happy.

—Sharon K. Cleveland

Comparison/Contrast Paragraphs

Comparison includes both similarities and differences, while *contrast* refers to differences only. The key to writing a good comparison or contrast paragraph is first to select two subjects that might make an interesting pair. Then list specific, significant features of each, matching every detail you list for one subject with a corresponding detail for the other.

Comparison/contrast paragraphs are arranged in either *alternating* or *block* format. The alternating method places parallel details side by side; it alternates the details. The block method, however, covers all details about the first subject in one block followed by a transition, such as "in contrast," to indicate a shift to a comparable block of details about the second subject. (For outlines of the two methods, see chapter 15.) The example below uses the alternating arrangement:

The Eye of the Beholder

This year when the first warm days of April began, I overflowed with energy. I wanted to make our family room as fresh as the spring buds outside. In a frenzy, I started to throw out one piece of junk after another, but each time Jerry would intervene to save a "treasure." First, I discarded a faded, cracked plate; but he rescued his family heirloom. Then I seized the tattered quilt; he returned his comforter for cold nights to its rightful place on the couch. Next I tossed out the stack of old *Time* and *Newsweek* magazines from the coffee table; he retrieved them because he might need a reference for a "current" event. And so it went. Finally, I said, "That sagging old couch we bought at a garage sale simply has to go!" But he objected sharply, "That's my favorite spot to watch football!" Refusing to argue, I stopped. But the first day he goes golfing, I'm calling Goodwill for an immediate pickup. . . . I may keep the plate.

—**Peggy Walker**

Transitional Paragraphs

Sometimes a special paragraph of transition is needed to connect two major ideas. In the middle of an essay or paper, you may need a paragraph of transition to bridge a gap or to direct the reader to a shift in thought. For example, Patty Seigneur wrote a brief transitional paragraph for a paper contrasting two good friends:

Sue is a wonderful person and friend, but I found myself wanting a friend more like myself. Then I met June. Quickly, she and I became good friends. We both realized how alike we are and how much we enjoy each other's company.

Notice that only one signpost transition, *then*, is used in this transitional paragraph. But the writer repeats key terms and uses pronouns to establish clear *embedded* transition.

Essay Exam Paragraphs

The principles you have learned in this chapter can be applied when you write essay exam answers. To answer an exam question completely, follow these four steps: (1) Read the question *twice*. (2) *Underline* key words such as *define, explain,* and *compare or contrast.* (3) If the question has more than one part, *number the parts.* (4) *Check off the number* of each part after you answer it. The example below shows how you can use an expository paragraph to answer an essay question on an exam.

Exam question: Define *information interview*. How does it differ from an employment interview? State three specific advantages of this interview.

Exam answer: An information interview is a meeting with an employer for the direct purpose of gaining information about a career field, not for the purpose of getting a job. The information interview has three distinct advantages. It provides firsthand information about a position you hope to be working in some day. It allows you an inside look at a company to see whether or not you would enjoy working there. It allows access to employers whom you might not be able to contact otherwise. You may even be asked to bring in your résumé or to come in for an employment interview. In fact, that is what happened to me last week; I start my new job as a medical transcriptionist tomorrow. The information interview is truly an excellent technique for uncovering the "hidden jobs" that are never advertised.

Summary

Paragraphs come in various designs and sizes. The two basic elements of a standard paragraph are the topic sentence and support sentences. Some paragraphs have a third part, a concluding sentence. The topic sentence identifies the subject and makes a claim about it. The support sentences supply proof. The concluding sentence gives a sense of completeness.

Effective paragraphs have five distinct features: interest, unity, coherence, completeness, and clarity. A topic sentence should be narrowed sufficiently to interest the reader and unify the paragraph. Although most topic sentences are placed at the beginning, they may appear in the middle or at the end of the paragraph. In special circumstances, a paragraph may not have a topic sentence.

Paragraph length is determined by audience, subject, and purpose.

Paragraphs may be arranged according to chronology, importance, complexity, generality, familiarity, emphasis, or some other logical order. Paragraphs can be developed using the same organizational strategies used for essays. A special type is the transitional paragraph, which may serve as a bridge between ideas in an essay.

The principles in this chapter can be applied to essay exam answers.

Key Terms

topic sentence	spatial order	process analysis
support sentences	order of importance	illustration
concluding sentence	level of complexity	comparison
clincher	level of generality	contrast
unity	level of familiarity	alternating method
coherence	emphatic order	block method
signpost transition	narrative	transitional paragraphs
parallelism	dominant impression	embedded transition
chronological order		

Practice

Small Groups: Narrowing Broad Topics

Directions: Narrow the following topics so that they could be covered in a paragraph. Write your topic sentences here and share with your group.

1. Children are unpredictable.
2. Things changed after I moved to a new school.
3. Grandpa's life was never easy.
4. Over the years I have owned several cats.
5. Comic strips are often commentaries on life.
6. Blind dates
7. Cars I have owned
8. Antiques
9. Baseball cards
10. Garage sales

Identifying Effective Topic Sentences

Directions: Mark the sentences that would make *good* topic sentences. If in doubt, consider the basic parts of a topic sentence.

_____   1. Cutting the Brazilian rain forest is causing weather problems.

_____   2. Living with a roommate who is an employed musician is exasperating.

_____   3. Every Thursday night I watch my favorite television program at 8 p.m.

_____   4. The older I become, the more I appreciate the wisdom of my old neighbor.

_____   5. Overnight the red amaryllis, which my son had given me, opened one large trumpet.

_____   6. Mr. Inskeep is my favorite teacher.

_____   7. My motto "play before work" received a severe blow this week.

_____   8. I found footprints in the snow outside my living room window.

_____   9. Finding footprints outside my window was a shock.

_____   10. From the size of the footprints, I knew the stalker was a large . . .

Forty Ideas for Paragraphs

1. How to milk a dairy cow
2. How to saddle a horse
3. How to change a flat tire safely
4. Compare and contrast two views of the same object
5. Describe the joy of creating a . . .

6. Homemade yeast bread
7. The clock in the tower
8. My happiest moment
9. My first date
10. My first day on a new job
11. My funniest experience
12. My first encounter with a garter snake
13. An unusual pet
14. The best baseball game I ever attended
15. A prank at summer camp
16. How to buy a good used car
17. How to put together an attractive outfit at garage sales
18. How to be assertive with an over-friendly neighbor
19. Why I chose . . . as a career
20. Why I like to go . . .
21. The first time I rode the tallest roller coaster at Cedar Point
22. Carlsbad Caverns
23. How to bottle-feed a baby lamb
24. Cutting virgin redwood forests
25. Raising grazing fees for ranchers
26. An encouraging word
27. Puppy love in third grade
28. A one-room school
29. The boss who . . . .
30. The girl who loved flowers
31. The second mile
32. A family of bald eagles at . . .
33. How to plant a wildflower garden
34. How and where to find arrowheads
35. The neighbor who hated cats
36. The dog who loved to fish
37. The raccoons and the water garden
38. The day I almost drowned
39. White water rafting at . . .
40. What my generation has to be optimistic about

CHAPTER 8

Revising Sentences

Style is the dress of thoughts; and let them be ever so just.

—Lord Chesterfield, *Letter to His Son*

Styling sentences is a challenging task, but it is the mark of a proficient writer. Effective sentences can be plain or ornate, simple or complex, short or long. The design and strength of sentences depend on the topic, the needs of the audience, the occasion for writing, and the voice of the writer. The clarity of sentences depends not only on the sentence pattern and word choice but also on correct punctuation, which is discussed briefly along with sentence structure.

As you revise at the sentence level, you will be trying to clarify ideas, to emphasize major ideas, and to add interest, variety, and style to your writing. To do so, substitute concrete action verbs for passive verbs and forms of *be*; vary sentence structures; create parallel forms; eliminate unnecessary wordiness; and consider sentence form, sentence length, and position of ideas within sentences.

EFFECTIVE USE OF VERBS

Although sentences can do without some parts of speech, a verb is always required. Even nouns can be omitted—leaving a verb to stand alone as a one-word sentence. For example, "Go!" "Heel!" and "March!" are each a complete sentence. The verbs you select will influence the strength and clarity of your writing.

Favoring the Active Voice

Strong action verbs can invigorate writing. Action verbs show movement and help readers to imagine an activity, whether physical or mental. For example, *ski*, *swim*, and *skate* show physical activity whereas *think*, *know*, and *dream* show mental activity.

102

Action verbs can be written in either the active or passive voice. Usually, the active voice is preferred, for it is direct and concise. Active voice simply means that the subject of the sentence is *performing the action*, as in the example below:

Active voice: Johnny *shot* the bear.

However, a verb is in the *passive* voice when the subject *receives the action*. Something or someone else is performing the act or deed. The passive voice consists of a *be* verb and a past participle so that a verb in the passive voice always consists of two (or three) words.

Passive voice: The bear *was shot* by Johnny.

Which sentence do you prefer, the one in active voice or the one in passive voice? Why? You probably noticed that the sentence in active voice gives the sharpest image of the event. And perhaps you noted that the sentence in active voice has only four words, whereas the one in passive voice contains six words. Although passive voice is useful at times, it lessens the impact of a sentence. To make writing clear and direct, experienced writers prefer the active voice in most situations.

Why Use the Passive Voice?

1. *The person responsible wishes to remain unknown.*
   Example: The new rule was enacted to tighten security.
2. *The one who does the action is unknown.*
   Example: The oriental rug was made in China.
3. *To place emphasis on an important word.* Passive voice allows the important word to become the subject of a sentence.
   Example: The *needs* of the student should be considered.

Replacing Forms of *Be*

The forms of *be* indicate a state of being or existing here on this planet. They do not show action. Although *be* verbs are sometimes necessary, too many of them tend to make a piece of writing seem wordy and lifeless. The main forms of the verb *be* are *is, am, are, was, were, be, been,* and *being*. To remember them easily, practice saying them in this order:

Say	Remember	Say	Remember
is	(one *i*)	be	(three *b*'s)
am	(two *a*'s)	been	
are		being	
was	(two *w*'s)		
were			

With a little thought, you can often replace a *be* verb with an action verb. Such revision not only shortens the sentence but also strengthens it. The following examples illustrate why action verbs are generally preferred:

Be verb: Sammy Davis, Jr., *was* a famous entertainer who entertained millions with his singing and comedy. (14 words)

Action verb: Sammy Davis, Jr., *entertained* millions with his singing and comedy. (9 words)

SENTENCE VARIETY

Verbs are an essential part of all sentence patterns. There are three basic sentence patterns: the simple sentence, the compound sentence, and the complex sentence.

Simple: Interviewers often inquire about weaknesses. (one independent clause)

Compound: Interviewers often inquire about weaknesses, but savvy applicants prepare for this question. (two independent clauses)

Complex: Since interviewers often inquire about weaknesses, savvy applicants prepare for this question. (dependent clause + independent clause)

Using all three structures adds interest to your writing, clarifies relationships among ideas, and emphasizes major points.

The Simple Sentence

A simple sentence contains a single subject (which may consist of more than one noun) and one or more verbs. The simple sentence is an *independent* clause— one complete thought that can stand alone. At its "simplest," such a sentence may consist of only a subject and verb:

Eagles soar.

More often though, simple sentences will contain other sentence parts, including objects, prepositional phrases and other modifiers, and perhaps additional verbs:

Eagles build *large nests*. (subject + verb + direct object)

Eagles build large nests *in isolated places*. (+ prepositional phrase)

Most commonly, eagles build large nests in isolated places. (+ adverbs)

Most commonly, eagles build large nests in isolated places and *lay two or three eggs*. (+ second verb and object)

The simple sentence is the primary sentence structure. In a piece of expository writing, as many as two-thirds of the sentences may have this pattern. When only simple sentences are used, however, writing can become boring, and ideas can seem disconnected. As you revise your drafts, look for ways to expand simple sentences into complex sentences or to combine two simple sentences into a compound sentence. With effective revision, you can clarify related ideas.

The Compound Sentence

Two related simple sentences can be joined to form a *compound* sentence. The compound sentence gives the clauses *equal* rank because both clauses contain important ideas. This means that a compound sentence has two main subjects and two main verbs. Often the two clauses are connected by a coordinating conjunction, as italicized in the following examples:

Geraniums are easy to grow, *for* they are quite hardy.

Mammoth Cave is the largest cave in the United States, *but* Carlsbad Caverns are the most colorful.

Minarsi entered the New York state turnpike at Buffalo, *and* she followed it until Rochester.

Coordinating Conjunctions   Coordinating conjunctions link similar elements such as clauses, phrases, or nouns. There are only seven coordinating conjunctions to learn. An easy way to remember them is to memorize the acronym *fanboys: for, and, nor, but, or, yet, so.*

The conjunction you use between clauses in a compound sentence depends on the relationship between the ideas in the two clauses. If the second clause provides additional information, use *and.* If the second clause is in contrast to the first, use *but, or, yet,* or *nor.* If the second clause has a cause-and-effect relationship with the first, use *for* or *so.*

Punctuating Compound Sentences   If you look at the length of the clauses in a compound sentence, punctuating a compound sentence can be less complicated. If *both* clauses are four words or less, you may join the clauses without a comma before the coordinating conjunction. If one or both have *five* words or more, you have three options:

1. Connect the two independent clauses with a *coordinating conjunction* preceded by a *comma:*

   The hidden job market consists of an estimated 80 percent of available jobs, *but* most jobs seekers seem unaware that it exists.

2. You can use a *semicolon* between two independent clauses when the connection between the ideas is so close that no conjunction to explain the relationship is needed:

   The hidden job market consists of an estimated 80 percent of available jobs; only 20 percent or so of the available jobs are ever advertised.

3. Use a *colon* to indicate that the second clause of the compound sentence will explain the first clause:

> The astute job seeker compiles a packet of employment search documents: the packet can contain an up-to-date résumé, cover letter, follow-up letter, and sheet of references.

It is incorrect to link independent clauses with only a comma and no coordinating conjunction. The resulting error is called a *comma splice*. If all punctuation is omitted between two independent clauses in a compound sentence, the error is called a *fused sentence*.

> **Comma splice:** Terrariums are costly at a flower shop, they are inexpensive to make at home.
>
> **Correct:** Terrariums are costly at a flower shop, *but* they are inexpensive to make at home. (comma and conjunction)
>
> **Comma splice:** Weather bulletins warned of ice-glazed roads, however, some drivers ignored the warning.
>
> **Correct:** Weather bulletins warned of ice-glazed road; however, some drivers ignored the warning. (semicolon)
>
> **Fused Sentence:** The ordinance won wide support it was passed by a two-thirds vote.
>
> **Correct:** The ordinance won wide support; it was passed by a two-thirds vote. (semicolon)

While compound sentences are often effective, they should not be overused. Also remember that a compound sentence gives both clauses equal weight. When the idea in one clause is more important, then two clauses should be combined into a complex sentence.

The Complex Sentence

A *complex* sentence consists of an independent clause and one or more dependent clauses. The complex sentence ranks a major idea and a minor idea. The major idea appears in the independent clause; the minor idea appears in the dependent clause. To the untrained eye, a dependent clause may look like a complete sentence because both have a subject and a verb. But the dependent clause has a word at the beginning that makes the (minor) idea incomplete. Thus *a dependent clause is always a fragment.*

Fragments

That has white forepaws

When the doorbell rings

Because McDaniel Motors gives dependable service

Sentences

The black cat that has white forepaws is Jeff's.

When the doorbell rings, my dog barks.

Because McDaniel Motors gives dependable service, Jason goes there.

Adjective Clauses   Adjective clauses are dependent clauses that refer to nouns or pronouns. These clauses are easy to identify because they always start with one of five relative pronouns: *who, whom, whose, which,* or *that.* (Think: four *w*'s and a *t.*) Adjective clauses can add either essential or nonessential information about the word they modify:

Essential: The car *that he prefers* has bucket seats.
The young woman *who is wearing blue jeans* is Mary's sister.

Nonessential: The yellow truck, *which is a Dodge,* represents her life savings.
Terry, *who is my brother,* is an avid photographer.

Did you notice that the sentences with *essential* clauses need no commas? But *the sentences with nonessential clauses require a pair of commas.* These commas act like tiny parentheses to set off extra material, which could be removed. To test whether or not a clause is essential, try covering it with your hand and reading the rest of the sentence. Does the basic meaning of the sentence change? If so, no commas are needed; the clause is essential. If the meaning does not change, set off the extra material (the nonessential clause) with commas.

Tips:
1. *That* is always used to indicate essential information. Sometimes *that* is omitted for the sake of conciseness if the meaning is clear. *That* can refer to people, animals, or things.
2. *Who* and *whom* refer only to people. *Which* is used to refer to animals or things. *Which, who,* and *whom* can introduce essential or nonessential clauses.

Adverb Clauses   Adverb clauses, like adverbs, tell *when, where, why, how,* or *under what conditions.* Adverb clauses begin with *subordinating conjunctions.* Some introduce reasons or explanations (*because, since, whereas, although*). After you learn to recognize the common subordinating conjunctions, you will be able to identify adverb clauses easily.

Common Subordinating Conjunctions

---

when	although	if	as	whether
while	even though	until	as long as	before
where	so that	unless	as though	than
since	because	as if	after	whenever

The adverb clause may come before or after the independent clause in a complex sentence. Look at two versions of a sentence with the dependent clause italicized:

When the big Doberman snarled, I slammed the door.

I slammed the door *when the big Doberman snarled*.

Which sentence do you prefer? Actually, the first sentence has two advantages: (1) the ideas appear in chronological order; (2) *I* appears in the middle of the sentence, where emphasis is minimized.

Note the following rules for punctuating sentences with adverb clauses:

1. When a long adverb clause (five words or more) appears at the beginning of a sentence, *place a comma after the clause*. If a misreading is possible, use a comma with fewer words as well.

2. When an adverb clause appears at the end, usually no comma is needed.

PARALLELISM: A BALANCING ACT

Grammar rules decree that when two or more parts of a sentence are coordinated, they must be parallel. In other words, you place sentence parts of equal rank in the same grammatical form: Nouns are matched with nouns, active verbs with active verbs, passive verbs with passive verbs, and *be* verbs with *be* verbs. Phrases are matched with phrases, and clauses are matched with clauses. This balance is called *parallelism*.

Undoubtedly, you have used parallelism in your writing without realizing it. You may have chosen parallel forms because they sounded clear or right. Experienced writers use parallelism not only for clarity but also for balance and emphasis. Winston Churchill, John F. Kennedy, and other great speakers used parallelism frequently in their speeches. Kennedy's most famous words, "Ask not what your country can do for you; ask what you can do for your country," serve as a prime example.

As you revise, be alert for instances of faulty parallelism. The next few sections discuss situations where parallelism is required.

Parallelism with Items in a Series

Items in a series require parallelism. Regardless of whether the items are single words, phrases, or clauses, all must be parallel: Every item must be matched according to grammatical form. The following example from *Coping with Difficult People*, by Robert M. Bramson, illustrates parallel adjectives in a series:

> Three factors in the Complainers' view of the world combine to convert useful problem solving into complaining: They find themselves *powerless, prescriptive*, and *perfect*.

Abraham Lincoln's famous phrase from the Gettysburg Address illustrates parallel prepositional phrases:

> . . . and that government *of the people, by the people, for the people,* shall not perish from the earth.

Note that in Lincoln's phrase all three prepositional phrases begin with a different preposition. When the same preposition applies to all three phrases, it may be stated before every item or stated only at the beginning of the first phrase:

I spend most of my time *at* work, *at* school, or *at* home.

I spend most of my time at work, school, or home.

Finally, a famous sentence from the Declaration of Independence illustrates parallel subordinate clauses in a series:

> We hold these truths to be self-evident, *that all men are created equal, that they are endowed by their Creator with certain unalienable Rights, that among these are Life, Liberty, and the pursuit of Happiness.*

As you revise, make sure that all items in a series are parallel. Reading your writing aloud can help you to detect unbalanced phrasing. The final item in the following series is not parallel; note how it can be corrected:

Not parallel: I enjoy listening to music, taking long walks, and *also like to work crossword puzzles.*

Parallel: I enjoy listening to music, taking long walks, and *working crossword puzzles.*

Parallelism with Items in Pairs

When a coordinating conjunction is used, the structures on each side should be parallel. The following examples from *Coping with Difficult People* show parallel nouns and parallel verbs:

> It pays to follow up any *complaint* or *suggestion* with an inquiry about what's happened.

> Your coping reply should be to ask, "Is that a *decision* or just your *opinion* at this stage?"

> Those Difficult People . . . [would-be experts] just can't *stand* such uncertainty and *strive* even harder to impose their own order on everything they can.

Notice that parallelism with verbs is more complex than with nouns. *To be parallel, verbs must be the same tense, the same form, and the same voice.* Different tenses should not be mixed. One-word verbs should not be mixed with verb phrases. Passive voice should not be mixed with active voice. The underlined verbs below are parallel:

> The students *are protesting* parking fees and *are requesting* free parking. (Both verbs are present tense, active voice.)

The students *protested* campus parking fees and *requested* free parking. (Both verbs are past tense, active voice.)

Note that *paired phrases and clauses* should also be parallel:

For richer or for poorer, in sickness and in health (prepositional phrases)

To run a company profitably and *to treat the environment responsibly* need not be conflicting goals. (infinitive phrases)

Changes in the workplace could mean *that workers will have more varied duties* and *that they will learn more varied skills.* (adjective clauses)

Parallelism with Correlative Conjunctions

Correlative conjunctions work in pairs to link words, phrases, or clauses. These conjunctions add grace and emphasis to a sentence by requiring parallel structure. Common correlative conjunctions include these pairs:

not only . . . but also

not . . . but

either . . . or

neither . . . nor

both . . . and

In a *compound* sentence, the final correlative conjunction is preceded by a comma. If the sentence is not compound, a comma is unnecessary before the final conjunction:

Not everyone received a bonus, but everyone received a raise. (compound sentence)

David has been outstanding not only in football but also in academic work. (simple sentence)

The examples below illustrate how parallelism is used with correlative conjunctions:

You must pay either *the parking fee* or *a penalty.*

The defendant was charged not only *with breaking and entering* but also *with resisting arrest.*

Our flight *did not arrive* on time but we *did arrive* safely despite minor problems in the air.

Neither the *teacher* nor the *students* saw the dog enter.

The talk was both *interesting* and *inspirational.*

Not parallel: It was both an interesting talk and inspirational.

Parallelism with Comparisons

Comparisons formed using *as* or *than* should be in parallel structure: the two subjects being compared should share the same grammatical form.

Running a spelling check is not as accurate as *proofreading carefully.*

Real wages are lower today than *they were twenty years ago.*

Look for faulty parallelism in comparisons as you revise. Note how the faulty parallelism in the first sentence below can be revised in two ways:

Not parallel: It is better *to do school work throughout a semester* than *cramming the night before an exam.*

Revised: It is better *to do school work throughout the semester* than *to cram the night before an exam.*

Revised: *Doing school work throughout the semester* is better than *cramming the night before an exam.*

CHOPPING OUT DEADWOOD

Even professional writers have to revise because their rough drafts ramble and repeat. Although Ernest Hemingway's finished writing is sparse and clean, he worked long and hard to bring it to that state. Hemingway was once questioned about how often he had revised the ending of his novel *A Farewell to Arms.* He said it had taken thirty-nine revisions for him to be satisfied. Revision is also a necessity for student writers, who often find deadwood in their papers. Some common sources of wordiness are discussed in the following sections.

References to Self

Self-confident persons may refer to themselves frequently in conversation. In writing, however, this tendency should be monitored. If an *I* appears at the beginning of a sentence, then the writer can invert the sentence or revise it some other way. Placing *I* in the middle of a sentence makes the reference to self less noticeable. Oftentimes unnecessary words can be deleted with no change in meaning, as in the example below:

Original: I will graduate on June 12 and will be available for employment after that. (14 words)

Revised: After graduation, June 12, I will be available for employment. (10 words)

When a rough draft has two sequential sentences that begin with *I*, try to combine the sentences and delete one of the *I*'s as well as any unnecessary words. This strategy will make your writing more concise and smooth.

Original: I use Microsoft Word daily to write letters. I also use Quicken for other tasks. (15 words)

Revised: Daily I use Microsoft Word and Quicken. (7 words)

Still another way to bypass *I* is to substitute *me* or *my* when a reference to self seems necessary.

Original: I can type accurately, perform basic accounting functions, and answer the telephone courteously, as you requested in your ad for a receptionist. (22 words)

Revised: My keyboarding skills, training in telephone etiquette, and experience with accounts payable/receivable should be assets for your position of receptionist. (21 words)

Instead of overusing first person singular, some people go to another extreme; they completely avoid *I*, *me*, *my*, or *mine*. They may resort to stilted phrases such as "the writer" or "the author of this paper." Experienced writers use *I* sensibly and sparingly.

Prepositional Phrases

Another source of wordiness may be unnecessary prepositional phrases in a sentence. If you find more than two prepositional phrases in a sentence, check for wordiness. Although using several prepositional phrases may not affect clarity, there may be a clearer, more concise way to make your point. Consider the following sentences before and after revision:

Original: A new type of compact, the Stallion II by CMG, was rated the safest in recent collision tests for compacts. (19 words)

Revised: CMG's new Stallion II was rated the safest in recent collision tests for compacts. (13 words)

Common phrases such as "this *type of* car" or "this *kind of* oven" or "*in the amount of $10*" may be shortened to "this car" or "this oven" or "$10."

Adjective Clauses

Sometimes there is little justification for an adjective clause, and the sentence can be made more effective by trimming the clause down to an appositive. Or you might substitute an adjective for an adjective clause. Consider the following examples:

Original: Dr. Goldberg, *who has been our physician since I was a child*, is going to retire. (adjective clause)

Revised: Dr. Goldberg, *our long-time family physician*, is going to retire. (appositive)

Original: My Appaloosa mare, *which is only two years old*, placed first in the "Best Trained Horse" trials. (adjective clause)

Revised: My *two-year-old* Appaloosa mare placed first in the "Best Trained Horse" trials. (adjective)

SENTENCE STYLE

The style of a sentence is influenced by the sentence pattern, the length of the sentence, and the position of the most important idea(s). In addition to the three major sentence patterns discussed earlier, you can use an occasional periodic sentence to provide interest and emphasis.

Periodic Sentences

A periodic sentence affords an opportunity to combine several related ideas into one grand sentence. This sentence pattern builds anticipation and suspense by presenting less important details before the major idea. This means that the major idea always appears just before the period. Although the subject may be placed early in the sentence, *the verb is always delayed*. Periodic sentences provide not only a refreshing change of pace, but also emphasis. Sometimes they are the ideal structure for a concluding sentence. James Herriot uses a periodic sentence at the end of his story "The Strychnine Episode at Darrowby":

> To me, the outbreak is a sad memory of failure and frustration. Fergus was my only cure. But over the years, when I saw the big dog striding majestically in his harness, leading his master unerringly around the streets of Darrowby, I always had one good feeling.

In the final sentence, Herriot builds to a climax, saying in one sentence what someone else might have said in three. Yet the periodic sentence is not an everyday sentence—it should be used for a significant idea. The next two examples of periodic sentences are taken from James Kelly's article "Rocky Mountain High":

> In Sandpoint, Idaho, a favorite refuge of disillusioned Californians, boutiques and craft shops flourish and stores sell wooden tubs for outdoor bathing.

> Of the eight states, Montana, Idaho, Wyoming, Nevada, Utah, Colorado, New Mexico and Arizona, which occupy 863,524 sq. mi., an area considerably bigger than all of Western Europe, Washington [the U.S. government] owns about 80% of the resources and nearly one-half of the land.

Sentence Length

Since Elizabethan times, sentences have been shrinking. In the 1600s the average sentence had about 45 words. One early English writer named Hakluyt actually wrote sentences that averaged 90.5 words. By Victorian times, the average sentence was down to 29 words. Now the average sentence length, according to Rudolph Flesch, is 17 words. ("Average" does not mean you should make every sentence the same length. Vary your sentences to produce variety and a change of pace.)

The length of a sentence is influenced by the kind of idea it houses. Brief sentences emphasize key ideas. Long sentences are like baskets, collecting several less important details. Each type has its place, but neither should be overused. Too many short sentences cause choppiness whereas too many long sentences interfere with clarity.

Position of Words within Sentences

Important words should be placed in *positions of emphasis*, either at the beginning or end of a sentence. Likewise, important sentences are usually placed at the beginning or end of a paragraph. The reader may skim over the middle. Ordinarily, the end position of a sentence or a paragraph carries more emphasis than the beginning; the middle carries the least of all. Of the three examples below, which one do you prefer? Why?

Snatching a field mouse, the spotted owl swooped down, wings outstretched.

Swooping with outstretched wings, the spotted owl snatched a field mouse.

Wings outstretched, the spotted owl swooped and snatched a field mouse.

The first sentence is anticlimactic and the least interesting. The second sentence is an improvement because the events are in chronological order, and the major action is emphasized. In the third sentence, *swooped* and *snatched* are parallel verbs in chronological order, which gives a vivid picture of the action.

Summary

The ability to style sentences that fit the rhetorical situation is the mark of a proficient writer.

Action verbs show movement. They can be written in either the active or passive voice. Usually, active voice is preferred because it is powerful and concise. *Be* verbs refer to a state of being or existing. Both the passive voice and *be* verbs lessen the impact of a sentence and frequently contribute to wordiness.

There are three basic sentence types: simple, compound, and complex. A simple sentence has one independent clause. A compound sentence has two independent clauses, which are equal in rank and parallel. A complex sentence has an independent clause and at least one dependent clause.

In a complex sentence, the dependent clause is either adjectival or adverbial. Adjective clauses begin with a relative pronoun. An essential adjective clause does not need commas. Nonessential clauses are set off by commas. Adverb clauses begin with subordinating conjunctions. A long introductory adverb clause is set off with a comma.

Coordinating conjunctions and correlative conjunctions link sentence elements of equal rank. These conjunctions require parallel structure. To be parallel, similar sentence elements must be in the same grammatical form. If not, the sentence will be unbalanced.

The time to trim wordiness is during revision. Too many references to self, unnecessary prepositional phrases, or other unneeded words slow down the pace of a sentence. Sometimes an adjective clause can be condensed to an appositive, or several ideas can be combined into a periodic sentence.

Sentence style is influenced by the sentence pattern, the length of the sentence, and the position of important ideas. The beginning and end of a sentence are the most prominent positions. For clarity, important ideas should appear in these emphatic positions. Short sentences highlight important ideas. Less important ideas can be combined into long sentences.

Key Terms

action verbs	independent clause	relative pronouns
active voice	dependent clause	adverb clause
passive voice	coordinating conjunction	subordinating conjunction
be verbs	comma splice	parallelism
simple sentence	fused sentence	correlative conjunction
compound sentence	fragment	prepositional phrase
complex sentence	adjective clause	periodic sentence

Test Yourself

Parallelism

Directions: Make the italicized segments parallel. You may have to delete. To check your answers, turn to the end of the chapter.

1. Peach orchards dot the south-central shore of Lake Erie in Ohio, but *grapes are grown* along the eastern shore in New York.
2. Ohio's principal crops are corn, soybeans, and *sometimes wheat is also grown.*
3. Raising soybeans is much more profitable than *to raise corn.*
4. To produce a pound of meat on chickens costs much less than *producing a pound of meat on beef cattle.*
5. Canola, which yields an edible oil, is grown more often than ordinary rape, *yielding a similar oil.*

Punctuation and Capitalization

Directions: The paragraph below has no punctuation and incorrect capitalization. Insert both as needed. Then turn to the end of the chapter and see how Annie Dillard wrote this excerpt from *Pilgrim at Tinker Creek.*

> It is the first of February and everyone is talking about starlings starlings came to this country on a passenger liner from europe one hundred of them were deliberately released in Central Park and from those hundred descended all of our countless millions of starlings today according to Edwin Way Teale "their coming was the result of one man's fancy that man was Eugene Schieffelin a Wealthy New York Drug Manufacturer his curious hobby was the introduction into America of all the birds mentioned in William Shakespeare" the birds adapted to their new country splendidly

Practice

Comma Splices

Directions: In the sentences below, punctuate the comma splices correctly. Mark the correct sentence(s) with a "C."

1. In some early primitive cultures, the people realized that while on the march they could not afford to be held back by a sickly pregnant woman or an unhealthy child.

2. As a matter of survival, it was necessary to prevent either occurrence so that the resources of the tribe would not be depleted by caring for a member who was ill, therefore the custom was for the entire tribe to share the responsibility of providing a pregnant woman with an adequate supply of the best foods available.

3. For the first few years of the child's life, he was also provided for in the same manner, these customs have transcended time in the Greek culture.

4. In a Greek restaurant where my mother once worked, she witnessed a fulfilling of the first custom.

5. There was a woman that Nick, the restaurant owner, disliked so strongly that he would not serve her in his place of business, he spat on the sidewalk once as she walked by.

6. Because of this attitude, Mother was very surprised one day when the same woman came into the restaurant, she just sat at a table looking at the fresh fruit behind the counter.

7. Nick took a generous serving of the fruit to the kitchen, prepared it himself, and took it to her.

8. When my mother expressed her bewilderment, Nick explained that he knew the woman to be pregnant, in Greece when a pregnant woman has

a need for any food, the community provides for her when she cannot provide for herself.

9. She came again whenever she needed nourishing food, Nick always gave it to her without charge.

10. He also left instructions with the employees that she was to be given any food she might ask for, in the event that he was out of the restaurant.

(*Note:* These sentences were taken from a research paper by Diane Patch and edited.)

Parallelism

Directions: Rewrite the sentences so that the parts are concise and parallel.

1. Alaska *was purchased* by Secretary of State Seward for about two cents an acre, but many Americans *complained*.

   Problem: One verb is in passive voice; the other in active voice.

   Correct: Secretary of State Seward *purchased* Alaska. . . .

2. The gold rush was started in 1898, but many prospectors found little gold.

3. Many of the new prospectors succumbed to epidemics of pneumonia, typhoid, and thousands of cases of smallpox.

4. Living conditions were unsanitary, and the state lacked police protection.

5. Alaska has large amounts of important minerals, forests, and an abundance of petroleum.

6. Alaska has become famous for its oil, for its fish, and the scenery which is beautiful.

7. To explore Alaska by car is impossible, but flying across Alaska is possible.

8. Alaska is popular not only with tourists, but also big game hunters like it.

9. At Fort Yukon in northeastern Alaska, extreme temperatures have been recorded: −75°F in winter and one summer reached a high of 100°F. (*Tip:* Examine the structures on each side of *and*.)

10. Alaska has the highest cost of living in any U.S. state, and Hawaii's cost of living ranks second highest.

Test Yourself Answers

Parallelism

1. *Peach orchards dot the south-central shore of Lake Erie in Ohio, but* grape fields line *the eastern shore in New York. (or another verb)*

2. *Ohio's principal grain crops are soybeans, corn and wheat.*

3. *Raising soybeans is much more profitable than* raising corn.
4. *To produce a pound of meat on chickens costs much less than* to produce *a pound of meat on beef cattle.*
5. *Canola, which yields an edible oil, is grown more often than ordinary rape,* which yields a similar oil.

Punctuation and Capitalization

It is the first of February, and everyone is talking about starlings. Starlings came to this country on a passenger liner from Europe. One hundred of them were deliberately released in Central Park, and from those hundred descended all of our countless millions of starlings today. According to Edwin Way Teale, "Their coming was the result of one man's fancy. That man was Eugene Schieffelin, a wealthy New York drug manufacturer. His curious hobby was the introduction into America of all the birds mentioned in William Shakespeare." The birds adapted to their new country splendidly.

—Annie Dillard, *Pilgrim at Tinker Creek*

CHAPTER 9

Revising Word Choice

Words play an enormous part in our lives. . . . Words have power to [mold] . . . thinking. . . . Conduct and character are largely determined by the nature of the words we currently use to discuss ourselves and the world around us.

—Aldous Huxley

Selecting words is rather like shopping in an enormous supermarket. But instead of roaming the aisles for groceries, a writer thumbs through the pages of a dictionary or thesaurus, searching for the right words. Both the shelves and the pages are well stocked; the English language has more words than any other language. Whether a writer wants plain bread-and-butter words, sweet words, tart words, tasteless words, kosher words, gourmet words, or playful words—they are all there for the taking, free of charge. Because there are so many words to choose from, a writer has countless opportunities to be creative, whether writing papers, letters, reports, poetry, or short stories. True, some writing offers more opportunities for creativity than expository writing does, but all rhetorical situations afford leeway in phrasing and sentence structure.

Reading widely and often will help you to become more aware of the nuances and subtle meanings of words. Frequent use of a good thesaurus and dictionary during revision will help you maintain an appropriate tone. Your awareness of the delicate distinctions in words will increase as you study this chapter. Your skill in detecting inappropriate words and in selecting appropriate words will be honed. With regular practice, your writing will become more precise and positive.

WORD MEANINGS: DENOTATION AND CONNOTATION

For years you have been looking up *denotations* in dictionaries. Denotations are the specific, literal meanings of words. If you were to look up the denotation of *coelacanth* in *The American Heritage Dictionary*, you would find it is a category of fish "known only in fossil form until a living species, *Latimeria chalumnae*, of African marine waters, was identified in 1938." Denotations seldom cause confusion when writers know a language well and take the time to edit carefully. Denotations seldom change; and when a few do, the changes often take place over a century or more.

Connotative meanings, however, are more difficult to pinpoint than are denotative meanings. *Connotations* are the hidden meanings beyond the denotation. These subjective meanings are imprecise. Connotations are associations, the emotional overtones attached to words. Our friends may agree with us on some connotations but may disagree on others. A further complication is that connotations can change rather suddenly or gradually.

Culture, education, gender, and generation influence one's perception of connotative meanings. Most men use some words differently than most women do. People of dissimilar backgrounds may have varying associations for the same words. Individual differences also influence thought and style of expression. Thus connotations contribute not only to meaning but also to the tone of writing. Connotations may be positive or negative, depending on the perception of the audience.

NEGATIVE AND POSITIVE WORDS

Sometimes the tone of writing is more important than the content. A negative word or an inappropriate word can contaminate an entire message, causing readers to misunderstand. Or readers may become so irritated that they stop reading and distort the message. As a safeguard, never send a note, memo, or letter without thinking carefully about word choice. When a situation is sensitive, take a day to mull over the best way to phrase the message. Experienced writers check to see if what they write is what they mean.

Focusing on the Positive

During revision, the old adage "Tell them what you can do, not what you can't" is helpful. Often an idea can be restated indirectly in positive words to soften unpleasant news, as in the examples below:

Negative: We are *out* of the Fullmark multistrike ribbons you requested. They will *not* be available for three days.

Positive: Your Fullmark multistrike ribbons *will* be here in three days.

Negative: I *don't* have my paper finished. I had to work seven days last week.

Positive: Professor James, although I worked seven days last week, I *do* have a typed draft. *May* I have another day to *polish*? Or would you *prefer* the rough draft now?

Courtesy words enhance the tone and effectiveness of messages, oral and written. For example, sprinkling courtesy words at the beginning and end of memos and letters helps to create goodwill. Yet we sometimes overlook several positive words that could improve our messages:

advantage	cooperate	gratitude	prompt
appreciate	cooperation	help	save
appreciation	courtesy	invite	succeed
assistance	encourage	may	success
benefit	enjoy	please	thank you
care	glad	pleasure	thanks

Positive words tend to elicit pleasant responses, whereas negative words risk offending. Some common offenders are found in the list below. The words in the "More Favorable" column will improve the tone of your writing.

Improving Word Choice

Unfavorable	More Favorable
wrong	incorrect, inaccurate
omitted, forgot	overlooked
failed	missed
failed (paper)	needs revision
mistake	error
advice	suggestion, recommendation
complained	reported
claimed	stated
problem	concern, challenge
deal	bargain, offer, opportunity

If you're struggling to find a positive word, try looking up the negative word in a thesaurus and checking antonyms. Or if you have reason to state a negative idea directly, then you can soften the impact somewhat by using a negative prefix. There are nine common negative prefixes: *non-, un-, im-, in-, dis-, il-, ir-, a-, ab-*. All enable a writer to delete *not*. For example, instead of *not perfect*, you might say *imperfect* or *irregular*.

Do Euphemisms Have a Place?

In the cartoon on the following page, Sally, with childhood innocence, was very direct in her thank you note. For the sake of politeness, however, she would have done well to use euphemisms. Euphemisms are words with usually favorable connotations. Euphemisms are terms that are often substituted for unpleasant words, words that might offend or cause pain. Harsh words sometimes injure self-esteem and rupture relations. For example, the instructor or manager who bluntly evaluates work as "poor" or "sloppy" will undermine morale and

PEANUTS reprinted by permission of United Feature Syndicate, Inc.

productivity. But the evaluator who allows the person to save face with a euphemism such as "needs to improve" or "can do better" and who encourages with constructive suggestions will have a better chance of motivating.

If a euphemism is needed in a touchy situation, that is fine—as long as there is no deception. There is a big difference between tact and deceit. Honesty is an important element of professionalism in almost any career as well as in college writing. Regardless of where you are or what you do, there will be times when euphemisms will be appropriate.

Over the years, as words lose their favorable connotations, new euphemisms are coined. For example, dealers once sold "used" cars. Later the cars were referred to as "secondhand," but now they are referred to as "pre-owned" or "previously owned." In the 1940s the person who cleaned, maintained the plumbing, and tended the heating system was a "janitor." In the 1960s he or she became a "custodian." In this decade the same job may carry the title of "maintenance engineer."

In conversation you may refer to someone, saying she is "expecting." In college writing, however, many instructors prefer direct words to euphemisms—in this case, *pregnant*, not *expecting*. But informal language that is intended to shock, such as sexual slang or obscenities, has no place in expository writing. It would sound inappropriate to the reader and would disrupt the tone.

Connotations of a word can change, becoming either negative or positive. For example, "Dear Madam" was once a polite salutation for a business letter. Now hopelessly outdated, the term is marred by negative connotations. In contrast, the term "Ms." was unpopular in the 1970s, but is now widely accepted in the United States as a polite form of direct address for both single and married women. With the acceptance of "Ms." has come a new awareness of sexist language.

SEXIST LANGUAGE AND TABOO TERMS

Just as society and culture change, so too does language. One of the biggest changes in the United States in the last forty years has been the recognition that women have the same legal rights that men do. With this legislation has come the idea that language should reflect equality by being gender-free or gender-neutral.

Replacing Sexist Terms with Gender-Free Terms

The Civil Rights Act of 1964 forced the U.S. Department of Labor to revise its *Dictionary of Occupational Titles* to eliminate sexist and ageist terms. Likewise, the Bureau of the Census modified 52 of the 442 categories of work. Newspapers have even changed column titles of advertisements from "Help Wanted—Male" and "Help Wanted—Female" to one column titled "Help Wanted."

New words—*sexism* and *sexist*—were coined to refer to language that discriminates on the basis of gender. Sexist language refers to gender (male or female) in a stereotypical or offensive way. Although not everyone is convinced on this point, still current usage, consideration, and professionalism rule out the use of sexist terms. For example, phrases such as "the fair sex," "my girl" (for secretary), and "career girl" are now archaic and taboo.

Some words carry sexist overtones because they contain the root *man:* fireman, policeman, mailman. But these forms are gradually being dropped in favor of gender-free counterparts such as firefighter, police officer, and mail carrier. The following list gives other outmoded words and their updated counterparts.

Sexist and Nonsexist Terms

Outdated	Updated
mankind	humanity
manpower	workforce
man hour	work hour
man, men (if applied to both sexes)	person, people
average man	average person
chairman	chair, chairperson
male nurse	nurse
girl, gal, chick	woman (adult)
man and wife	husband and wife
repairman	repairer
waitress/waiter	server

Although masculine nouns and pronouns (*he, his, him*) were used for centuries to include women, this usage is also outmoded. One way to avoid this faux pas is by writing in the plural—for example, "players . . . they." But the plural is not always possible. Then one "he or she," or one "his or her" is relatively unobtrusive. Often the best and simplest way is to use gender-neutral words, omitting any reference to gender.

Plural: The *deans* are to bring *their* projected department budgets.

Gender-specific: Every dean should bring *his* projected department budget. (Correct only if all deans are male.)

Gender-free: Every dean should bring *a* projected department budget.

Dodging Taboo Terms

Some words indicate discrimination on the basis of ethnicity, religion, race, skin color, or other factors. Other words may not actually be discriminatory, but may be unwise in terms of both politeness and the law. Employers are required to prohibit a "hostile environment," which includes verbal harassment. The definition of what constitutes verbal harassment varies. Nonetheless, in the workplace, as well as elsewhere, we need to be careful when mentioning personal attributes, especially physical characteristics, such as body parts, body size, attractiveness, race, and skin color.

The purpose here is not to provide a list of offensive racial terms, for most readers are well aware of them, but to alert you to rapidly changing usage. According to dictionaries and the media, the preferred usage given here is current. Only the most common terms that seem to be losing or have lost acceptance over the years are given. Although *white* is still widely used, it is less frequent than in the past, probably to de-emphasize color. *Black* is still current usage, but some prefer *African American* or *person of color*. Probably the best advice is to notice the accepted usage in your geographical area. If you are unsure, the following list can serve as a guide.

Usage: Past and Present

Past	Present
minorities	people of color
Indian	Native American
Chicano	Hispanic American, Spanish American, Mexican American
yellow races, oriental	Asian
colored	person of color
Negro	African American or Black
Anglo-Saxon	European descent, Anglo-American, or white

GOBBLEDYGOOK AND TECHNICAL JARGON

The word *gobbledygook* was used by early Pennsylvania Dutch settlers to signify a concoction of leftovers. Maury Maverick, director of a World War II agency, borrowed the term to refer to a mixture of euphemistic and jargon-laden language. He described gobbledygook in this way, "When concrete nouns are replaced by abstraction, simple terms by pseudo-technical jargon, the result is gobbledygook."

Since Maverick's early definition, gobbledygook has been branded as the language of bureaucracy and has been defined in various ways. Two dictionary definitions are "pompous, wordy, involved, and full of Latinized words" and "unclear, often verbose, usually bureaucratic jargon." Pretentious language obscures a writer's actual meaning. For example, "operationalize" has been used instead of *start* and "predawn vertical insertion" for *invasion*. But gobbledygook is not limited to government writing. It also appears in insurance policies, academic publications, and legal documents.

Often discussed along with gobbledygook is technical jargon. *Technical jargon* is the professional or formal language of a trade or profession. Technical jargon among peers causes no problems. But when a message is intended for someone else, unfamiliar jargon may make the message unclear. For example, nurses and physicians often use medicalese that is unintelligible to many patients. Translating technical jargon is not always easy. In fact, many large companies hire writers to rewrite rough drafts by technical personnel.

Where does one draw the line between gobbledygook and technical jargon? The answer seems to hinge upon two questions:

1. Can the language be understood by the intended audience?

2. Does the language serve a technical purpose?

If the answer to both questions is affirmative, then the language is technical jargon, and it does have a valid purpose.

TRITE LANGUAGE AND CLICHÉS

In everyday casual greetings and small talk, we often hear the same familiar words. Trite, overworked phrases such as the following echo in our ears daily:

richly rewarding	last but not least	enclosed please find
each and every	tip of the iceberg	tell you in a heartbeat
to the tune of	is always on the go	never meets a stranger

Three visiting exchange students from Germany and Denmark remarked that many Americans use *nice* to excess: "Nice to meet you," "You have a nice smile," "You speak nice English," "Isn't this nice weather?"

Other overused and misused words are *a lot* and *get*. Although *a lot* is frequently heard, it is informal. "Alot" is a common misspelling. Instead, you can use a synonym such as *many, much, several, various, some,* or *considerable.* The word *get* has numerous informal and slang meanings that are unsuitable for college writing. Although phrases such as "gets to me" or "got over" are usually detected, phrases such as "got married" are less apparent. (*Tip:* Remember that *get* is *not* a helping verb.)

Why risk boring or antagonizing the reader with repetitive or outworn words and phrases when fresh ones can be located easily? As you search for suitable words, also beware of clichés. Like favorite recordings, clichés become worn from overuse. Although they were once original, clichés have become familiar—now they are ingrained in our daily language. Many of William Shakespeare's brilliantly descriptive lines, written four hundred years ago, are now clichés. How many of the following have you used?

Famous Lines	Source
The naked truth	*Love's Labour's Lost*, 5.2.715
Out of the jaws of death	*All's Well That Ends Well*, 3.1.396
Parting is such sweet sorrow	*Romeo and Juliet*, 2.2.184
A dish fit for the gods	*Julius Caesar*, 1.1.173

Perhaps you are familiar with other clichés such as "fresh as a daisy," "happy as a lark," "solid as a rock," or "his bark is worse than his bite." For most conversations and some informal writing, a cliché now and then may be acceptable. In academic and professional situations, however, clichés do not belong except when used creatively for a reason.

MAKING THE MESSAGE CLEAR AND APPROPRIATE

Heads of state are expected, even when speaking informally, to have an excellent command of language. Abraham Lincoln's ready wit, John F. Kennedy's apt rejoinders, and William Clinton's ability to make small talk served them well during casual conversation and interviews. But George Bush was not so gifted. For instance, during the Gulf War, this president habitually used the phrase "the Saddam thing." This habit not only trivialized the subject, but also undercut his effectiveness and professional image.

Making Abstractions Concrete

Thing is a shapeless blob of a word, for it is purely abstract. *Thing* can refer to a monster or a gnat, a flask of poison or a glass of buttermilk, a viper or a star. Because *thing* can mean a condition, quality, vegetable, animal, mineral—or any bit of matter on or off this planet—people tend to overuse this elastic word. Using *thing* serves as a substitute for thinking. Shrewd speakers and writers shun *thing* and limit their use of abstractions generally. *Abstractions* are general words that identify categories, qualities, or ideas. Some abstractions refer to the intangible— concepts undetectable through the senses, such as *honesty, patriotism, fear,* and *courage.* Certainly, these broad terms have their place, but using unexplained abstractions or too many without concrete examples makes language vague and unclear.

Words that represent tangible qualities, objects, or activities are said to be *concrete*. Concrete words describe details that can be perceived through one or more of the five senses. You can see the delicate perfection of a purple crocus, the luminous rings of a lunar eclipse, and the muted hues of a rainbow. You can hear the whir of a hummingbird's wings or the thump of a human heart. You can smell the fragrance of honeysuckle or the pungent odor of an annoyed skunk. You can touch the fur of a baby rabbit or feel the grit of sandpaper. You can taste the sweetness of raspberry jam or the piquancy of horseradish. Concrete words stimulate the imagination and evoke vivid imagery.

As you revise, look particularly for abstract adjectives (*beautiful, terrible, impressive, delicious, unpleasant,* and the like) that can be replaced by concrete sensory words. Because some topics such as sunsets and love have been so popular, it is difficult to find a fresh way to describe them. In that case, you might choose another topic or devise an unusual comparison that uses concrete imagery:

Abstract: We watched a beautiful sunset.

Concrete: As we watched, the sun, like a huge gold coin, slipped into the slot of night.

Questions to Find Concrete Words

1. How did *X* look? Size? Shape? Color? Length of hair/coat?
2. Does *X* make a sound? Volume? Rate? Pitch?
3. How does *X* feel? Texture?
4. Does *X* have a fragrance or odor? Pungent? Faint? Pleasant?
5. If *X* is edible, how does it taste? Sweet? Sour? Tangy? Acid? How does it feel on the tongue?

Moving from General to Specific

If your friend tells you she purchased a new car, you have no mental image of the car. To obtain further information, you might ask, "What kind?" Perhaps she responds with "a Buick." And so the conversation continues until you eventually learn that she has purchased a dark red, two-door Buick Regal Brougham. Although the word *car* is concrete, it is general, lacking descriptive information.

Likewise, other general terms such as *cat, dog,* or *horse* tell very little about a specific animal. For example, do you mean a lion or a domesticated cat? And if you mean the latter, is the cat a mixed breed or registered breed? A barn cat or a house pet? Is it male or female? What age, size, and color is it? Writers need to be specific so that the reader comprehends quickly. Normally, a specific word or phrase is more appropriate than a general word as long as you don't drench the reader with nonessential details.

In the sentences below, note the differences in the effects of general words and specific words:

General: A *dog* went into a *building* and lay down in a *room*.

Specific: A *Dalmation* entered the side door of the *brick firehouse* and stretched out in a corner of the *kitchen*.

General: *Walking* is a good way to enjoy the *wonder of nature*.

Specific: *Hiking* in Sandy Cove Park is a good way to enjoy the *brilliance of an Indiana autumn*.

SCHOLARLY OR SIMPLE WORDS?

A woman went up to Adlai Stevenson after a speech. Enthusiastically, she said, "Oh, Mr. Stevenson, I think your speech was absolutely superfluous!"

He replied, "Thank you. I think I shall have it published—posthumously."

"Fine!" she said. "The sooner, the better."

Leafing through a thesaurus, some students select scholarly or other unfamiliar words without consulting a dictionary. The results may be disastrous or unintentionally amusing. Even if used correctly, words may be inappropriate for a piece of writing. Novelist Kurt Vonnegut says: "Simplicity of language is not only reputable but perhaps even sacred. The Bible opens with a sentence well within the writing skills of a lively fourteen-year-old: 'In the beginning God created the heavens and the earth.'" Vonnegut recommends simplicity for most writing.

Dr. Lewis Thomas, an editor and contributor to the *New England Journal of Medicine*, used simple language to explain a complicated process in his book *The Lives of a Cell*:

> Everything in the world dies, but we know about it [only] as a kind of abstraction. If you stand in a meadow, at the edge of a hillside, and look around carefully, almost everything you can catch sight of is in the process of dying, and most things will be dead long before you are. If it were not for the constant renewal and replacement going on before your eyes, the whole place would turn to stone and sand under your feet.
>
> There are some creatures that do not seem to die at all; they simply vanish totally into their own progeny. Single cells do this. The cell becomes two, then four, and so on, and after a while the last trace is gone. It cannot be seen as death; barring mutation, the descendants are simply the first cell, living all over again. . . .

Since Dr. Thomas is writing for a lay audience, he is careful to select words they will understand. He begins with a statement about death and relates it to his readers. Then he compares the familiar process of death to that of cell division, which is unfamiliar. Because he supports the abstractions with concrete examples, the result is beautifully clear. For most college writing, don't use a long, obscure word when a short, familiar one will do.

As you reconsider your word choice for college writing, consider how your readers might perceive the message, then revise accordingly. After any revision, reread each sentence to be sure that it says what you mean. Don't use a long word when a short word will do, but do not sacrifice meaning for conciseness. Clarity should remain top priority.

Summary

A good command of language makes a positive, lasting impression. Being keenly aware that words have both denotative and connotative meanings can help you improve your word choice. Denotations are the literal, precise meanings that are always defined in the dictionary. Denotations seldom cause confusion.

Connotations are the emotional overtones, the hidden meanings that people attach to words. Negative connotations sometimes interfere with a message because people tend to add meanings. Negative connotations may cause misunderstanding and rupture relationships. Therefore it is particularly important to choose specific words free from undesirable connotations. Positive words improve the tone of writing. Selecting positive words and de-emphasizing negative words is an important part of diplomatic communication. Euphemisms have a place in communication as long as they do not mislead or deceive.

Sexist language contains gender preferences with negative connotations. Sexism can be avoided by writing in the plural, by using one unobtrusive *he or she*, and by using gender-neutral language. Other taboo terms referring to ethnicity, religion, race, or other personal characteristics should be avoided. Outdated terms can be offensive; instead, use current terms.

Gobbledygook can confuse and mislead. Technical jargon, however, has a valid use. Clichés were once fresh and original, but they have become stale from overuse. Trite, outworn language is unsuitable for most writing in the workplace and in the classroom.

Abstract words may cause misunderstanding when unexplained. *Thing* is the most abstract word of all; it and other vague abstractions should be avoided in writing. Concrete words and examples clarify abstract concepts and provide interest.

Simple words are usually preferable to scholarly words. Accurate, precise word choice is necessary to communicate. Don't sacrifice clarity for conciseness.

Key Terms

denotation	gender-neutral	trite
connotation	gender-free	cliché
euphemism	gobbledygook	abstract words
sexist, sexism	technical jargon	concrete words

Test Yourself

Can You Find the Concrete Terms?

Directions: Underline the concrete words in the following excerpt from "Living Like Weasels" by Annie Dillard. Then check your answer against the key at the end of the chapter.

> Weasel! I'd never seen one wild before. He was ten inches long, thin as a curve, a muscled ribbon, brown as fruitwood, soft-furred, alert. His face was fierce, small and pointed as a lizard's; he would have made a good arrowhead. There was just a dot of chin, maybe two brown hair's worth, and the pure white fur began that spread down his underside. He had two black eyes I didn't see, any more than you see a window.

Practice

Collaborative Activity: Favorable and Unfavorable Words

Directions: Strong active verbs are needed on a résumé to identify work skills. Select the word in each group that sounds most favorable to you. If disagreement occurs, group members can explain their opinions.

ran	made	refined	prepared
managed	developed	redid	made ready
supervised	set up	revised	furnished
trained	operated	took appts.	planned
showed	ran	scheduled	arranged
instructed	used	telephoned	laid out

Using a Dictionary

Directions: Using a dictionary, find the entry word and the requested information.

1. *Find more than one spelling:*

judgment	theater	catalog
gray	color	epilogue
lovable	hallo	labor

2. *Pronounce these words, sounding all syllables correctly. Notice where the main stress lies:*

introduce	convenience	government
lexicographer	primitivism	onomatopoeia

3. *Look up parts of speech:*

hame	postulate	permissible
nix	prime time	nitrobacteria

4. *Discover the etymology:*

Gypsy   galaxy   video

sauté   salsa   votive

5. *Check idiom:*

catch   set   bring

cut   drop   pound

Write a Description Using Concrete Words

Directions: In one paragraph, write a description. Give concrete details and examples. If you wish, describe one of the following topics:

1. The footwear you are wearing

2. A "white elephant" in your home

3. A vehicle you use or have used

4. An animal you have owned

5. A favorite hideaway

6. A vacation spot

7. An unusual teacher

8. A family heirloom

9. A frightening moment

10. Your favorite time of day

Test Yourself Answer

Weasel! I'd never seen one wild before. He was ten inches long, thin as a curve, a muscled ribbon, brown as fruitwood, soft-furred, alert. His face was fierce, small and pointed as a lizard's; he would have made a good arrowhead. There was just a dot of chin, maybe two brown hairs' worth, and the pure white fur began that spread down his underside. He had two black eyes I didn't see, any more than you see a window.

—Annie Dillard, "Living Like Weasels"

PART 2

Options for Organization

CHAPTER 10

Narration

Recounting Events

The narrative impulse is always with us; we couldn't imagine ourselves through a day without it.

—Robert Coover, *Time Out*

Since prehistoric times, people have told stories not only to entertain but also to educate and to convince. Everyone from toddlers to grandparents, from doormen to diplomats, loves a good story. Wherever people gather—whether around a dinner table, over a back fence, or at the water cooler—they tell stories. The narratives may be jokes or yarns or true tales; they may recount a single action or a series of actions. Narration is used to relay news of a neighborhood and news of a nation. Stories are a powerful tool to attract, charm, and captivate an audience. Narratives stir emotions, evoke memories, and lend support to opinion. An effective narrative recounts action for a purpose. If the purpose is to entertain and establish camaraderie, then it may not matter whether the account is fiction or fact. But when the purpose is serious—primarily to inform or persuade—then accuracy is important.

Narration may be used as a major or minor writing strategy. If major, then narration dominates; the action is most important. For example, narration is the major strategy in reports of patients' progress. Managers keep brief narrative histories of employees' performance. Law enforcement officers write narratives of events prior to an arrest. Although these reports may include description as support, the major strategy is narration. If narration is minor, it supplements another strategy. For example, an anecdote (brief episode) might be inserted into a paper of description or comparison.

You may already use narration in college writing or in writing on the job. Workplace narratives, like narrative fiction, describe an action, a problem, or a conflict. Your main concern as a writer is not to worry whether a strategy is major or minor but to select and combine strategies to fit your purpose and audience.

POINT OF VIEW IN NARRATION

How a writer views a subject, from what angle and mind-set, influences the telling of the narrative. The writer must also decide how close or how far the narrator should be from the story. Using first person places the narrator up close to the scene of the action.

First-Person Narration

A writer may tell a story from either a first-person or third-person point of view, depending on the purpose and the situation. Whether you choose first person (*I*, *me*, *my*, *mine*, *we*, or *ours*) will depend upon your role in the story. Is it about you? Or were you involved in someone else's story? Either way, first-person narration will lend a sense of immediacy, giving the reader a front-row seat on the action. In first-person narration, an observer or a participant relates the tale. This eyewitness account is often written in a conversational tone. First-person point of view works well for autobiographies and personal essays. Mae Mattix uses first person when she recalls a playful incident that had unexpected consequences:

The Lesson of the Cornstalks and the Well

The biblical axiom of "He that spareth his rod hateth his [daughter]" was heeded in our home to some extent. Although Mother spanked us children once in awhile, the spankings were so mild, they had little effect. Discipline from Dad, however, was not mild. His large hand could cover our bottoms with stinging hand prints that would keep us obedient for months. Still, the most effective disciplinary lesson occurred when he implemented the principle of cause and effect: If we made a mess, we had to clean it up.

The most dramatic lesson occurred one day when my sister and I were six and seven. Earlier we had played with our cousins on grandfather's farm near a well from which he watered cattle. The ground near the well was littered with cornstalks. An iron pump with a handle stood on the ill-fitting wood cover of the well. We children would lie on our stomachs, peer through a crack at the dark water below, shout, and listen to our echoes. That day someone decided it would be fun to see if a cornstalk could reach the water. Soon we were taking turns poking cornstalks into the well. Although we did not tell our parents, Dad somehow discovered the mischief. But he did not scold us. Until he took us to the well the following Saturday, we thought our secret was safe.

There our father told us we had to take out the cornstalks while he held us by the ankles! Numb with fear, we said nothing, not even to protest the unfairness of two kids having to undo the mischief of six. I had to go first. Can you imagine being held by the heels, suspended over the dark depths of a well? Although I knew my father was very strong, I was terrified. Frantically, I grabbed as many cornstalks as my arms would hold, and he hauled me to the top. Then I had to repeat the fearsome feat. After that it was my sister's turn. Without crying or screaming, we removed all the cornstalks from the well. On the way home, no one said a word. Ashamed, I was thankful that Grandpa had not come out to witness our indignity and humiliation. That lesson was imprinted for life.

Third-Person Narration

Writers or narrators who are not involved in a story adopt a third-person point of view. They restrict pronouns to words such as *he, she, it, they,* and *them.* Third-person narration puts distance between the reader and the topic, producing a more detached tone than first person provides. A professional response, such as those found in many business and technical reports or research papers, usually requires third-person point of view. There the goal is to focus on facts and results, not on feelings or opinion. Reporters, biographers, and historians use third person for the same reason.

The following third-person narrative recounts a disastrous 1981 accident at the Hyatt Regency Hotel in Kansas City. Think how differently a narrative of the accident by a first-person survivor would have sounded.

> At 7:05 P.M. on Friday, July 17, 1981, the atrium was filled with more than sixteen hundred people, most of them dancing to the music of a well-known band for a tea dance competition, when suddenly a frightening, sharp sound like a thunderbolt was heard, stopping the dancers in mid-step. Looking up toward the source of the sound, they saw two groups of people on the second- and fourth-floor walkways, observing the festivities and stomping in rhythm with the music. As the two walkways began to fall, the observers were seen holding on to the railing with terrified expressions on their faces. The fourth-floor walkway dropped from the hangers holding it to the roof structure, leaving the hangers dangling like impotent stalactites. Since the second-floor walkway hung from the fourth-floor walkway, the two began to fall together. There was a large roar as the concrete decks of the steel-framed walkways cracked and crashed down, in a billowing cloud of dust, on the crowd gathered around the bar below the second-floor walkway. People were screaming; the west glass wall adjacent to the walkways shattered, sending shards flying over 100 ft. (30 m); pipes broken by the falling walkways sent jets of water spraying the atrium floor. It was a nightmare the survivors would never forget.

> —**Matthys Levy and Mario Salvador**
> *Why Buildings Fall Down*

There may be a time when you decide to write in the third person about an experience you participated in. Perhaps the topic is still painful, even heart-rending. To gain distance and objectivity, you might write about yourself in the third person, perhaps using a pseudonym. Or you might write a narrative essay in third person and switch to first person in the last paragraph—if there is a good reason as there was in the student paper "Just a Walk," printed later in this chapter.

WRITING A NARRATIVE PAPER

Sometimes beginning writers have no idea that a narrative requires just as much preparation (or more) as an expository paper. Prewriting, drafting, and revising are all part of writing a narrative.

Selecting a Topic and Prewriting

You have a treasure trove of stories just waiting to be told, some sad, some happy. Prewriting will help you find them. If you decide to describe an unpleasant or painful experience, however, you may find you are too close to see the implications and to shape the narrative accordingly. Before you start, consider the nature of the experience; it may not be a suitable topic for you. If a recent event has been traumatic, beware. You can become so entangled in emotion that you hit a writing block and lose the point. A year or more may be needed before you can describe such an event effectively. Time allows you to distance yourself from disturbing events and gain perspective. Implications, perhaps as a lesson or moral, often become apparent. Might one be hidden in your writing topic? Mull over the effect of the experience and consider:

- How did the experience influence me?
- What did I gain or learn?
- Am I happier? Wiser? What?
- Can I find a lesson or moral?
- How might the narrative affect someone else?
- Does the experience remind me of an event in the public eye?
- If so, what is the connection?

Once you have chosen a topic, there are other preliminary decisions to make. How to begin a narrative and how much to tell are not always easy decisions to make. Probably the simplest way to start prewriting is to list key events in the order they occurred. Leave two inches or so of space between items so that you can go back and insert related details. Organizing your notes will limit sorting later. After listing the key events, jot down significant details about each one. Ask questions to guide you in selecting details to start your draft:

- What is the source of tension or conflict?
- What is the purpose of the narrative?
- Who are the readers?
- Where is the best spot to start?
- How much do readers need to know?
- What details should be omitted to preserve the unity and advance the point?
- Can I think of a symbol that would help to unify the actions?
- Should the story be told in first person or third?
- What tone is appropriate?

Drafting an Introduction

Many writers compose the beginning and ending of a narrative first. This tactic allows them to gain an overview of the story quickly and save time. They select a definite segment of action and cut it off at a precise point. Then they plot the movement between the two points. This tactic cuts down on false starts and rambling.

Budding writers often tell too much too early. They give events away in either the title or first paragraph of the narrative. Stating a thesis too soon may siphon the reader's interest and make the story dull. Instead, the thesis may come at the end. Or you may imply, rather than state, your thesis. In beginning a narrative, you have considerable latitude, although the opening usually sets the stage for action. In other words, you identify the central person or character, place, and time. As the action starts rolling, description is usually sparse. Only essential details are shown. Gradually, necessary bits of background are woven in and conditions revealed.

Opening with Action   To create interest, successful writers often open with an action, weaving in brief glimpses of background as the story proceeds. An *action opening* plunges the reader into a story with no unnecessary details or explanations. Right away the main person or character is faced with a decision or immersed in a predicament that must somehow be resolved. (For an example, see "Just a Walk" at the end of the chapter.) Other types of openings reveal the action, problem, or conflict gradually.

Opening with a Quotation   If you find an appropriate quotation that *specifically* relates to your main idea, then you can easily tie it to the beginning of a narrative. Be sure that any explanation does not delay the action unduly. Do not belabor the point of the quotation lest the reader perceive it as talking down. If you want to use a quotation that relates in a *general* way to your main idea, then you may have to look long and hard to connect it adequately. The excerpt from Proverbs is about "sparing the rod," which is *not* the main idea of Mae's narrative, although related. Yet she manages to connect the quotation to her topic by using the *"is not"* technique. By mentioning examples that were *not* as effective as the principle of cause and effect, she prepares the reader for the dramatic lesson.

Opening with a Comparison   An unusual comparison in the title or first paragraph can hook the reader and serve as a unifying thread throughout the narrative. An effective comparison is introduced early and alluded to periodically. Sometimes a comparison may involve a symbol rich in connotations. For instance, one student wrote a moving tribute to her mother entitled "Clipper Ship Mom." Along with this striking symbol, the writer used water imagery: matrimonial seas, rough seas, tears, and similar images in developing her paper (see chapter 13).

Organizing and Developing a Narrative Paper

Narratives need a clear focus. Each event and detail you include should function to advance the narrative point. Avoid extraneous details, no matter how interesting. Make sure that everything contributes to the unity of the narrative and helps to establish a coherent design. If you limit your focus early by deciding the point you want your narrative to make, then you will find it easier to decide what to include—and what not to include.

In most narratives the action is presented chronologically. *Chronological order* sets forth a sequence of actions in a logical progression, starting at one point in time and moving forward to the conclusion of the experience or event. Sometimes, however, a writer may disrupt the chronology by a sudden shift to the past, or *flashback*. For example, you might begin a narrative at a dramatic moment near its conclusion, then flash back to relate how events led up to this point. Keep in mind, though, that flashbacks are tricky to manage effectively because of the special transition and plotting required. As a novice writer of narrative, you may want to stick to chronological order.

Another common feature of narrative is *dialogue*. Selected dialogue can brighten a narrative and give clues to the personality of the speaker. Dialogue enables the reader to view the action more closely. It should have the ring of real conversation but move more quickly. Actual conversation often ambles along, backtracks, circles, and stops for a while. To create realism, copy the way a person talks, perhaps using slang or fragments or pausing briefly. Or clip excerpts from actual conversation and shape them into dialogue for your narrative purpose. Of course, all dialogue should advance the point.

When writing dialogue, minimize the use of "he said" and "she said." As long as the identity of the person who is talking is clear, no other identification is needed. Just indent for a new paragraph with each new speaker, no matter how short the exchange is. Set off the dialogue with quotation marks. For examples of dialogue, see "How to Convince a New Neighbor You Are Insane" later in the chapter.

The trick to writing an effective narrative is to keep it interesting for readers. You can maintain interest by including *concrete details* of the setting and action, thus giving life to the story and allowing readers to participate in what happens. Then they can feel as if they know the people involved. Use strong action verbs, along with specific nouns and modifiers that will appeal to your readers' sense not only of sight but also of hearing, touch, taste, and smell. As with dialogue, however, beware of including unnecessary description that may distract or bore the reader. Another way to keep readers interested is to build *suspense:* you can hint at something to come but withhold crucial details in order to reveal them at a strategic moment. (Reba Herr Spana does this in "How to Convince a New Neighbor You Are Insane.") You can also build tension by pacing your narrative in such a way that readers are kept wondering what will happen next. By the end, however, all loose threads should be clearly connected and the conflict or problem resolved.

Writing a Conclusion

Although endings of narratives vary widely, every ending should have a sense of completion. It should flow logically from the previous events so that readers are not baffled, confused, or doubtful of the writer's skill. The ending should leave readers satisfied, convinced, empathetic, hopeful, amused, thoughtful, or wiser. Usually, the problem or conflict is resolved at the end. (See "Off with His Head!" later in this chapter.) To resolve matters successfully, the writer must tell enough but not too much. If an ending is too long and wordy, it may become tiresome or confusing. Underdeveloped endings may leave readers feeling frustrated or cheated. Readers should not be left hanging without a clue to what happened.

Ending with a Hint or a Hope   Even if the full story remains untold or the conflict is not resolved, there should be a clue so that readers can draw their own inferences. For example, sometimes the problem is not solved, and the story ends at a low point. In *Gone with the Wind*, Rhett is leaving Scarlett, and she is agonizing over his departure. Yet the reader is offered a hint and a hope that life will get better. The novel closes with these words:

> She could get Rhett back. She knew she could. There had never been a man she couldn't get, once she set her mind upon him.
> "I'll think of it all tomorrow, at Tara. I can stand it then. Tomorrow I'll think of some way to get him back. After all, tomorrow is another day."

Ending with a Surprise   An unusual incident or twist may bring a story to a satisfying close. The surprise ending contains something the reader does not expect. The surprise may be amusing, embarrassing, enlightening, romantic, or dramatic as long as it is appropriate. To be effective, the unexpected event should grow out of the action, problem, or conflict. For example, Shasta Scharf used a surprise ending that sprang from a key event in "Just a Walk" (at the end of the chapter).

Ending with a Reaction   Sometimes a narrative ends with a *reaction*, a focused response or thoughtful commentary, an opinion of the writer. The opinion may express emotion, inference, speculation, suggestion, generalization, or a combination of these. A reaction ending may spell out influences or implications of the action. There may be an attempt to explain extenuating circumstances or underlying motives. Columnists, biographers, historians, novelists, and other writers often explore the motives precipitating an event. (For help in using opinion, see chapter 5. To write a paper of reaction see chapter 26.)

In her essay "The Lesson of the Cornstalks and the Well," Mae Mattix ended with a reaction. She linked her experience to a news event that reverberated worldwide:

> A few years ago an American lad in Singapore was imprinted in more ways than one. He received a caning, which caused scars he will bear for life. He was caught spray painting parked cars. Although the young man knew the law of the land, he still committed the crime, showing disrespect for authority as well as for property. How much better and easier life would be for such youngsters if they had been introduced to the principle of cause and effect. By having to mend minor mischief at an early age, they might think twice about committing major infractions later.

Until we are enmeshed in the consequences of our misdeeds, the principle of cause and effect seems to have little meaning.

Flip back to reread Mae's paper. What is she advocating? How does she establish transition from her experience to that of the young man? (*Hint:* What word is repeated?) Also think about the switch from third person to first-person plural in the last sentence of the reaction. Why is *we* more effective than *they* would have been?

Writing the ending of a narrative may require painstaking effort. In fact, you may attempt more than one conclusion before finally being satisfied. If in doubt about your ending, try asking these questions:

- What is my narrative point?
- What did I learn from the experience?
- Do I need to state the point at the end?
- Or can I allude to or imply it?
- Are there any loose ends to resolve?
- Would a reference to the future be appropriate?
- Was there an unexpected result?
- Does the ending seem complete?
- How do I want my voice to sound?

Spend time in thought and on revision. The spot where you stop should seem just right, even if it means omitting pet details. (For more about endings see chapters 3 and 4.)

Revising a Narrative

When you revise your narrative, look at the larger items first. Check the shape of the story. Does it flow well? Is the direction clear, or are transitions of time needed? Watch for complicated sentences that slow the pace unnecessarily. When the action is fast-paced, use short sentences. When movement slows, you can often combine ideas so that longer sentences reflect that pace. The checklist below will help you revise:

∼ *Checklist for Revising a Narrative*

1. Have I clearly identified the conflict?
2. Is the action arranged in the most effective order? Or should some events be rearranged?
3. Might I use more dialogue to reveal some of the action?
4. Have I developed only details that advance the point?
5. Have I summarized minor details sufficiently?
6. Are there enough transitions to clarify the time sequence? (For example, *five years ago, an hour later, the next day.*)

7. Does the pace of the sentence reflect what is happening?

8. Does the ending give a sense of completion?

THREE SAMPLE NARRATIVE PAPERS

In the first paper, Janet Phillips's opening explanation sets the scene and gives the reason for the action. Sensory imagery burnishes the scene.

Off with His Head!

After living all of my seventeen years in the city, I suddenly found myself trying to become a good country wife. One gruesome task would help me prove I was becoming more countrified; I decided to kill my first chicken. I had witnessed my mother-in-law perform this chore many times. It seemed simple. Before daybreak she took a flashlight to the chicken house, caught an unresisting rooster, carried him to the chopping block, and with an ax hacked off his head.

At 4:30 a.m. one spring morning, flashlight in hand, I stepped out of our log cabin in Kentucky. Confidently, I entered the old wood shed. There I found, hanging on a bent rusty spike, a blood-stained ax. Carefully, I lifted it down and shivered. The ax seemed quite large and much heavier than I remembered. Placing it beside the jagged chopping block, I gripped the flashlight with a little less confidence and crept toward the hen house.

But the door squeaked as I opened it, and the chickens started clucking nervously. Flashing the light in each startled face, I soon found my victim—a large multi-colored rooster with a bright red comb. Like a king upon his throne, he sat erect, perched high above the other chickens. Blinding him with my light, I grabbed him by the throat and jerked him from the roost.

Next came chaos. The chickens squawked and flapped their wings, causing a storm of feathers and dust. Frantically, I held the struggling rooster by his churning feet. Then I dropped the flashlight and grabbed his throat again. Flapping his huge wings, he squawked loudly. For several minutes we fought. Three times he scraped my arm with his long spurs, and the gashes oozed blood. But I finally crushed him to my body and gained control.

As I carried the panting warrior, both of our hearts were beating rapidly. Cautiously, I laid him down with his neck stretched over the chopping block. Trembling, I held the ax handle in my sweaty palm. The beautiful rooster lay quiet. One bright black eye watched as I raised the ax over his head. Then with all my remaining strength, I brought the ax swiftly down toward his outstretched neck. Just before the weapon reached its mark, I jerked it back. I looked at the ax, then at the silent rooster. Sobbing, I sank to the ground.

After awhile, I wiped my eyes with my soiled apron. Picking up the king, I returned him to his throne. After replacing the ax on the rusty nail, I walked back to the cabin. As I shut the back door, a loud crow greeted the new day.

—**Janet Phillips**

Questions for Discussion

1. Is Janet's title effective? In what ways is it ironic?

2. How well does Janet set the scene? Note any particularly striking examples of vivid storytelling.

3. Were you surprised by the ending? How does the final sentence serve as a fitting conclusion?

The second paper creates suspense by opening with a reference to "catastrophes" the writer will go on to relate.

How to Convince a New Neighbor You Are Insane

Several years ago there began a string of small catastrophes that led my new neighbor to wonder if I was deranged. Through financial necessity, my teenage sister and I had moved into an apartment desperately in need of repair. At the close of a long first day of cleaning and unpacking, we were extremely disheveled and dirty. My sister decided she would avail herself of the shower first.

She went into the bathroom, undressed, and turned on the hot-water faucet, whereupon the faucet broke off the wall, allowing a mighty stream of hot water to flood the bathroom. Never being of sound mind while under stress, I bolted down the hallway and knocked on the first door.

A handsome young man, immaculately dressed, opened the door. Giving no thought to dignity or decorum, I gasped, "My hot . . . is running. Can you stop it?" I was so upset, I omitted the word *water*.

Raising one eyebrow, he smiled and said, "Lady, I'm not certain, but I'm willing to give it a try."

Without enough wit to retreat gracefully, I grabbed him by one arm, saying, "Come with me—quickly!" I practically dragged him down the hall and into my apartment. Then came the next phase of the fiasco. Not realizing my sister was trapped in the bathroom—the inner doorknob was broken—I yanked open the bathroom door. This released a flood and revealed an enraged, half-hysterical stark naked girl standing in a cloud of steam. Regaining my presence of mind, I jerked her from the bathroom and shoved her into the bedroom.

Then I looked at our neighbor. He was standing, immobilized, in water up to his ankles, staring at me with incredulous disbelief. Only then did I realize that during this whole crazy episode he may well have thought he was being dragged into a strange apartment by a full-fledged nymphomaniac!

—**Reba Herr Spana**

Questions for Discussion

1. Did the title of Reba's narrative grab your attention? Would you suggest a different title?

2. How effective is her use of dialogue? Does it sound realistic? Is there enough dialogue to tell the story completely?

3. What about Reba's narrative technique made you want to keep reading? How does her introduction create suspense?

4. What was your response to the conclusion? Was it satisfying for you, or would you suggest any changes?

The final paper is written in the third person, with a satisfying shift to first person in the conclusion.

Just a Walk

Jimmy was seventeen the day he joined the armed forces. Fresh from the coal mines of West Virginia, with only a sixth grade education and six weeks' survival training in Massachusetts, he was flown over 3,000 miles to Corregidor. Suddenly, his life became a battleground for survival. The day that General MacArthur left the Philippines, Jimmy shot his first enemy warrior. "This," he said, "was the first time I walked through Hell." As the Japanese took possession of the Philippines, the Bataan Death March began. Jimmy was near the head of the line. For over ninety days, he and the other U.S. soldiers suffered severe malnutrition, dysentery, malaria, and abuse as they walked to a prison camp. This was another walk through Hell. For three years, Jimmy was the camp interpreter. Being the interpreter gave him the chance to send messages to and receive them from the United States Army covertly. The Japanese never knew that "Jimpie," as they called him, was using their equipment for spying.

In 1945 Jimmy and the others left the Philippines via three "Hell Ships." Over 1700 men were crowded into quarters intended for 600. Each ship was designed to hold 200 passengers. Only 482 men walked off the ships in Osaka, Japan. Poor ventilation, no food, no water, and no place to lie down had taken a heavy toll.

When Jimmy reached the United States, he was decorated for bravery and given a six-day pass to see California. He and three friends drove up to Mt. Shasta to ski. There he beheld "a sight that restored [his] sanity." With seven years of hell behind him, Lake Shasta and the snow-capped mountain in front of him, Jimmy came face to face with a young deer. Only five feet away, the fawn stared straight into Jimmy's eyes. Tears flowed down his cheeks as he gazed at the most beautiful scene he had encountered in his twenty-four years of life.

After his experience at Mt. Shasta, Jimmy's life became less chaotic. He went back to the dark, damp coal mines with his father and brothers. Since mining coal is a "filthy, unsafe job and most people do not live to regret their old age in the mines," Jimmy soon headed north to Ohio and the steel mills. . . .

Jimmy's dream included having a home, a wife, and a daughter, but after marrying "Kat," two sons were born within three years. He loved his sons, yet his heart yearned for a daughter, one who would never engage in combat or shoot another human being. One evening two years later, a girl was born to him and his wife.

The birth certificate was not signed until Jimmy got home from work after midnight, eight hours after the birth. As he stared at his newborn daughter in amazement, he whispered, "She is the most beautiful sight I have ever seen." Recalling that earlier moment of overwhelming joy and peace, my father named me Shasta.

—Shasta Scharf

Questions for Discussion

1. Discuss the function of Shasta's title. Give a reason for your opinion.

2. Why does she place quotation marks around certain statements? What is the effect of these passages?

3. Discuss the switch from third person to first person in the last line. Do you think first person throughout would have been more or less effective? Why?

4. Shasta could have ended with her father's death from black lung disease as his final walk through Hell. Would this ending have been more or less effective? Why do you think so?

Summary

The purpose of a narrative may be to entertain, inform, explain, or persuade. You may use a narrative format in college writing or on the job, depending on the purpose and the audience. A narrative does not have to have a thesis statement; often the thesis is implicit. The action opening is often used to hook readers' attention. This opening shows a part of the action immediately. Beginning with a quotation delays the action.

A narrative may be told in first person by a participant in the story or in third person by someone outside the tale. Switches in person should be done skillfully and for a reason. Chronological order is common in narratives. The action begins and proceeds in a natural sequence. Sometimes the chronology is disrupted by a flashback, a sudden shift to the past. If a flashback occurs, it should be for a crucial incident.

To write a narrative paper, select a topic you know well and can shape purposefully. Decide when the story should begin, perhaps starting with an action, a quotation, or a comparison. Dialogue, carefully edited, can advance the action and heighten interest.

Narrative endings vary. Usually, the conflict or problem is resolved in some way. If not, there should be a clue so that the reader can surmise what will happen. A surprise ending should grow out of the action. The reaction ending is a thoughtful commentary, an opinion, that may spell out implications, explore motives, or speculate about causes. The reaction ending may connect a personal experience to one with universal implications.

When you revise, check the larger elements first, particularly the sequence and development. Prune any surplus words or excessively long sentences that slow the pace of the narrative. Check the ending to be sure it is satisfying and complete.

Key Terms

narrative	action opening	dialogue
first-person narration	chronological order	surprise ending
third-person narration	flashback	reaction ending
unity		

Practice

Write a News Story

Assume you are a reporter for your campus or hometown newspaper. Write a news story. You may want to conduct interviews to gain specific details. The following suggestions may stimulate an idea you can use:

1. New construction, new business, or restaurant
2. Plans for an activity such as May Day, a concert, or pig roast
3. A rash of robberies
4. Assaults after dark
5. Profile of the president of the university or college
6. Student interviews about campus concerns
7. Spring Cleanup: How We Can Spruce Up Our Town!
8. Historical highlight: A story from the city's history
9. Periodic flooding
10. Profiles of two opposing political candidates

Write a First-Person Narrative

Select an incident from your experience that may have caused you to laugh, to cry, to run, to show courage, or to learn. Then do some prewriting about the key events, including your reactions. After that, write a unified paragraph or short narrative. Perhaps one of the suggestions below will help you to find a suitable topic:

1. A family joke
2. A learning experience—gulp!
3. A spooky experience
4. A wonderful day
5. A prank at work
6. An unusual occurrence
7. Finding a . . .
8. First day at . . .
9. Meeting my future spouse
10. An embarrassing moment

Forty Ideas for Narrative Papers

1. My most frightening experience
2. My worst date
3. My favorite one-day trip
4. A prank that backfired
5. How I met my best friend
6. How my mother met my father
7. A strange experience
8. My most embarrassing experience

9. My first taste of defeat
10. My first experience as a . . .
11. My first day on a new job
12. The first time I rode a . . .
13. The day I lost my . . .
14. My worst punishment
15. My experience with . . .
16. My first encounter with a . . .
17. Why I left my job
18. I was my brother's keeper
19. The secret in . . .
20. My worst day
21. The day I won . . .
22. How I outfoxed a telemarketer
23. Revenge is sweet!
24. Sadder, but wiser
25. Out of the mouth of a toddler
26. How I learned to live with a jokester
27. . . . weren't meant for . . .
28. A narrative report you might write on the job
29. How not to succeed in/at . . .
30. Confession of a penny collector (or anyone else)
31. How I handled harassment
32. The lesson of the . . . experience
33. Fatherhood is not for sissies
34. Motherhood is not for . . .
35. The tale of a hound dog
36. My first apartment
37. A new bride's first home-cooked dinner
38. . . . is not what I expected
39. There was a young woman who lived in a . . .
40. The black sheep came home

CHAPTER 11

Description

Conveying Impressions

The background must never swamp the action,
nor must the aura of a place interfere with
the progress of the story.

—Rosalind Laker
"Imagination and the Past," *The Writer*

Effective description at the right spot can be potent. Sensory details evoke images in the reader's mind and trigger emotional responses. We all respond to strong sensory stimuli whether on the printed page or in reality. The fragrance of lilacs might take us back in time to the huge bush of purple blooms in grandmother's yard, where we frolicked with small cousins, spied a nest of newborn bunnies, and received that first kiss. Or the distant moan of a locomotive might remind us of picking wild strawberries along a railroad track long ago. The screech of chalk may conjure memories of flying spitballs, passed notes, and whispered chatter while the teacher wrote on the chalkboard. As sensitive human beings, we react to emotional stimulation. As writers we can guide the emotional responses of readers by describing sensory impressions.

Successful description has a purpose: hand-picked details reinforce the central idea. To develop your descriptions, choose essential details that will appeal to the audience. Think about what they will need to know to understand and appreciate the experience. Resist the temptation to toss in too many details lest the reader's attention stray from your writing purpose. The background should never obscure your point. Whether you write a college paper, lab report, technical manual, grant application, news story, advertising copy, or something else, descriptive details should strengthen the core idea.

This chapter explains the use of description as the major strategy in a piece of writing. In much writing, however, description plays a minor role, supporting a major strategy such as narration, process analysis, or comparison. Then descriptive details are used to make abstract ideas more concrete or to develop the point made in the thesis.

CREATING A DOMINANT IMPRESSION

When description is the chief writing strategy, it conveys a dominant impression, a mood that prevails throughout the piece. Then sensory details unite to produce an overall feeling, such as delight, fear, repugnance, rage, curiosity, or challenge. A dominant impression is often implied rather than expressed directly. In *Gift from the Sea*, description plays a major role. Anne Morrow Lindbergh creates an implicit dominant impression as she describes a shell she has found on the beach and compares the shell to her life:

> The shell in my hand is deserted. It once housed a whelk, a snail-like creature, and then temporarily, after the death of the first occupant, a little hermit crab, who has run away, leaving his tracks behind him like a delicate vine on the sand. He ran away, and left me his shell. It was once a protection to him. I turn the shell in my hand, gazing into the wide open door from which he made his exit. Did he hope to find a better home, a better mode of living? I too have run away, I realize; I have shed the shell of my life, for these few weeks of vacation.
>
> But his shell—it is simple; it is bare, it is beautiful. Small, only the size of my thumb, its architecture is perfect, down to the finest detail. Its shape, swelling like a pear in the center, winds in a gentle spiral to the pointed apex. Its color, dull gold, is whitened by a wash of salt from the sea. Each whorl, each faint knob, each crisscross vein in its egg-shell texture, is as clearly defined as on the day of creation. . . .
>
> My shell is not like this, I think. How untidy it has become! Blurred with moss, knobby with barnacles, its shape is hardly recognizable any more. Surely, it had a shape once. It has a shape still in my mind. What is the shape of my life?

As Lindbergh describes her life and the lives of others throughout the book, she continues to refer to the shell and to other sea imagery. These images establish a thread of continuity, creating unity as well as interest. The dominant impression is complex, far-reaching, and harmonious. In the author's search, there is a tranquillity and an acceptance of change as she collects insights along with shells.

Subjective and Objective Description

Description may be subjective or objective. A *subjective* description, such as Lindbergh's, reveals how the writer feels about the subject. Subjectivity refers to a personal view, which includes attitude and opinion as well as fact. The purpose of a subjective description is to share feeling and elicit a response from the reader. But feeling must be kept within bounds so that it does not get out of control. Too much subjectivity can backfire. An essay with a dominant impression has a subjective slant.

In contrast, the tone of *objective* description is literal and factual. The tone is impartial and impersonal. In scientific and business writing, for example, much description is based on unbiased, objective observation. Its aim is to reproduce for the reader exactly what the writer observed without reference to the writer's feelings about the subject. In *Thinking in Pictures*, Temple Grandin objectively describes a demonstration of a machine built by Robert Richardson of Prescott, Arizona, for desensitizing unrideable horses:

> The wild horse was placed in a narrow stall similar to a horse trailer, with two gentle horses in adjacent stalls to keep it company because wild horses will panic when they are alone. The horse's head protruded through a padded opening in the front of the stall, and a rear pusher gate prevented him from backing up and pulling his head inside. Sand slowly filled up the stall so that the horse hardly felt it until he was buried up to his back. . . . It wasn't until the sand came up to his belly that he jerked slightly, but then he appeared to relax. He seldom put his ears back, which is a sign of fear or aggression, and he never tried to bite anybody. He was alert and curious about his surroundings, and he acted like a normal horse in a stall. . . . He was free to move his head, and eventually he allowed people to touch his face and rub his ears and mouth. Touching that had been intolerable was now being tolerated.

Effective Language in Description

Effective word choice is crucial for strong descriptive writing. Modifiers should be chosen with care to express a precise image. E. B. White warns against the use of meaningless modifiers. In *The Elements of Style* he calls *very, rather, little,* and *pretty* "the leeches that infest the pond of prose, sucking the blood of words." Perhaps this graphic metaphor can help you avoid them.

Sometimes writers also err by larding descriptive prose with adjectives. Although the right adjective can convey an idea, an action verb can often convey it better. For example, the two sentences below express the same idea, but the first slows the pace with a *be* verb and a meaningless modifier (*very*). The second, streamlined version substitutes a strong action verb and deletes the adjectives.

The child *was very loud* and defiant.

The child *roared* his defiance.

In drafting and revising descriptive writing, look for words that can convey sharp, clear images—verbs that are vibrant and energetic, nouns that are specific, and modifiers that crackle with meaning. (See chapter 9 for more on the use of effective words.)

WRITING A PAPER OF DESCRIPTION

When you write a descriptive paper, it should have a purpose—to share an impression that lingers in your memory. All details in the paper should contribute to this dominant impression. After you select a topic, you decide on a vantage point from which to view it. Then you prewrite.

Selecting a Topic and Prewriting

Sensory details are the leaven of description. As you look for a topic, watch for details that tantalize the senses. Jot down perceptions of scenes, people, or events that intrigue you. What sights, sounds, smells, tastes, or textures delight or displease you? Bittersweet memories as well as euphoric ones can provide provocative description. Mine your memory by prewriting. Select the event or experience that has the richest impression.

Whether you have toured Ravenna, Italy, looking at mosaics, or viewed the scenic wonders of your home state or visited local neighborhoods, you have stored numerous sensory impressions. Perhaps you remember the aroma from your neighborhood bakery, the cherubic face of the baker, and his friendly pat on your shoulder. And you still cherish the mouth-watering flavor of his big cinnamon rolls. Perhaps you visited a family in Mexico, who made marvelous enchiladas; or the centenarian who lived next door told you fascinating stories. Your father may have passed on a love of woodworking, showing you how to make fine furniture. Flora Kyle recalls her grandfather as he crafted a hope chest for her aunt. To help you capture sensory details, prewriting for Flora's paper appears here:

Sight: What did I notice?

Grandfather was meticulous. Every joint had to be perfect.

chestnut, maple, cedar boards

plane spewing wood curls

alternated woods in a chevron pattern on lid

lined chest with cedar

long hinge connected lid to chest

high luster of the finish

Aunt Lally's tears of happiness

Aunt Lally put a wedding ring quilt she had made in the chest.

Sound: What did I hear?

whine of the saw

groan of the plane

scratch of sandpaper

pounding of hammer

Aunt Lally's appreciation when she received chest on her sixteenth birthday

Smell: What did I smell?

aroma of cedar

smells of glue and shellac

fresh air when he opened the windows to let out fumes

Touch: How did the wood feel?

rough texture of boards

splinter in my finger

crispness of wood curls

satin smoothness of the hand-rubbed finish

Point of Description

Chest is now mine. Reminds me of Aunt Lally and grandfather.

Determining the Dominant Impression

A hodgepodge of details without a central point will lack unity. A paper of description should have a *dominant impression* or overall feeling. If you select a topic you care about, then you will have a reason for writing. To find that reason, ask yourself questions:

- What is the mood of the description?
- Why do I want to share it?
- Why might the reader want to read it?
- Why is it memorable?

If you can convey a dominant impression in an unusual way, then it will involve readers. Try to go beyond surface details; delve into the meaning of your perception. A description does not have to be dramatic or earth-shaking; it has only to be important to you for an identifiable reason. Some of the most interesting writing is based on everyday occurrences presented in a special way.

Perhaps you recall a perfect day when you and your family rode the ferry to Kelly's Island in Lake Erie. The white prow of the ship gleamed as it parted indigo waves. Scrolls of clouds drifted across the azure sky. You lolled on the sun-splashed deck during the hour ride, trolling the cares of the week and losing them among the waves. As you biked around the edge of the lush green island, passing through patches of shade and sun, a light breeze cooled your skin. You stopped to sprawl on the white sand and stare at two fishing boats while gulls swooped over the waves and driftwood bobbed nearby. At the glacial grooves, you gazed at the great stones, pondering the huge natural force that had scored them so long ago. At a tiny village you ate foot-long hot dogs, sitting on a shady park bench. Every family member was amiable and smiling for the entire day. There were no squabbles or schedules, just an air of unblemished peace and companionship. (In case you didn't notice, the last half-sentence summarizes the dominant impression.)

While you prewrite and draft, you may uncover the wisp of a story. At first it may appear unimportant, or it may make you uncomfortable. But before tossing it away, take a second look. Could you merely mention the tale, perhaps at the end of your description? Would the bit add depth and meaning? Paul Allen

Dotson, Jr., drafted a description of a dining room light fixture. As he revised, he speculated about its meaning to him and realized it was more than just a beautiful object. There was a memory, an untold story, behind it—one he did not want to tell. But by referring to this story, he enriched the dominant impression.

The Crystal Chandelier

In the dining room of a house where I once lived hung a crystal chandelier. It was a gorgeous old-fashioned fixture with eight lights and numerous dangling crystals that sparkled with the colors of the rainbow. The chandelier had three settings: High, medium, and low. When it was set on high, my wife and I would entertain friends and relatives, balance our accounts, and write letters. When the chandelier was on medium, I would often lounge in a chair next to the stereo and listen to soft music while staring at the colors emanating from the crystals. Yet my favorite setting was low. There were nights I would arrive home before my wife and would prepare dinner for the two of us. When she would walk into the dining room, the colors from the crystals would shine on her hair; she would smile, and I would see the most beautiful woman in the world. Though we are no longer together, those moments under the crystal chandelier are among my fondest memories.

Rarely is an entire story told. Someone once said that a story is like an iceberg: seven-eighths of it stays beneath the surface. The writer must decide how much to reveal. If you think there might be a story lurking in your prewriting notes, ask yourself these questions:

- Why do I have a special fondness for the object or impression?
- Did something happen, a bit of history, that cast a shadow on or brightened my life?
- How much do I want to say?
- Will that be enough? Will the ending seem complete?

Selecting a Vantage Point and Transition

You might think of a writer as holding a camera, aiming the lens in a certain direction to record an impression or a story. Wherever the writer is viewing the scene from is the *vantage point*. The writer may remain fixed in one spot or move around. A *fixed observer* describes only what can be seen from one position. A *moving observer* describes from more than one position. With each movement, the writer keeps the reader informed with transitional phrases such as "turning at the first country road," "reaching the summit," or "descending a narrow, crooked stairway."

Imagine in your mind's eye the position from which you will view your topic. Will you remain in one spot or will you move? Will you be close or distant? Will you be observing for a few moments or over time? What would be the most interesting vantage point for the reader? What transitions will you need to keep readers informed of your movements?

Drafting an Introduction

Openings can be powerful if a clear sense of the dominant impression starts to emerge. Sometimes a description opens with a specific thesis. For example, Nancy Smathers began a paper describing her father with the sentence "A tall, husky man has long been a special person in my life." Then she described him, giving physical details and aspects of personality to fill in the picture she wished to evoke (see chapter 7).

A vivid comparison can form an unusual opening. Jennifer Ramey opened her paper, "Maintaining a Marriage," this way:

> A good marriage is like a fine-tuned car. Care for it, work on it, and treasure it, and it will run well. Communication is the engine of a marriage. Effective communication goes beyond knowing a partner's favorite foods and activities. Heartfelt communication requires sensitivity—an awareness of the other person's feelings, embarrassments, concerns, and goals. Quality communication requires loyalty and listening with empathy, trying to understand what the other person is experiencing.

Another opening may take readers directly to a scene, where they observe a specific place along with the writer. Present tense may be used to describe a current setting. Or a scene from the past may open with specific details, such as "In 1890 Central City had dusty unpaved streets and 132 inhabitants, not counting 56 horses, 63 dogs, and 75 cats." Or a short phrase such as "three months ago," "several years ago," or "once" may identify the past.

A narrative opening—often an anecdote—may lead into the main idea of the description. For example, Annie Dillard shares an early experience at the start of "Seeing," a descriptive essay which reveals her wonder at the "unwrapped gifts" and "free surprises" of a world that "is fairly studded and strewn with pennies cast from a generous hand."

> When I was six or seven years old, growing up in Pittsburgh, I used to take a precious penny of my own and hide it for someone else to find. It was a curious compulsion; sadly, I've never been seized by it since. For some reason I always "hid" the penny along the same stretch of sidewalk up the street. I would cradle it at the roots of a sycamore, say, or in a hole left by a chipped-off piece of sidewalk. Then I would take a piece of chalk, and, starting at either end of the block, draw huge arrows leading up to the penny from both directions. After I learned to write I labeled the arrows: SURPRISE AHEAD or MONEY THIS WAY. I was greatly excited, during all this arrow-drawing, at the thought of the first lucky passer-by who would receive in this way, regardless of merit, a free gift from the universe. But I never lurked about. I would go straight home and not give the matter another thought, until, some months later, I would be gripped again by the impulse to hide another penny.

Organizing and Developing a Description

To be clear and effective, description requires a logical order for details. The organization of a description often arises quite naturally from a particular topic. If you describe an object, a place, an animal, or a person, then spatial order works well. In spatial order, details are arranged according to space or location. You can use spatial order to show direction: east to west, north to south, left to right, top to bottom, front to back, inside to outside, or vice versa. For instance, to describe an Irish setter, you might go from the head to the tip of the tail. As a moving observer, you might explore a haunted house, going in through the creaking front door, up the spider-webbed staircase, down a dusty hall to a narrow, spiral stairway that leads to an attic filled with who-knows-what.

Chronological order, a sequence of time, might be used to describe the changes in a garden, beginning in spring and continuing through summer, fall, and winter. A street scene might be described from the wee hours of the morning to late at night. Similarly, a person might be described at different stages in his or her life, as Michele Bates does in "How a Computer Changed My Life," later in this chapter.

Another possible order for description is from abstract to concrete or from general to specific (or vice versa). For example, to describe the disorder of a pack rat's nest, you might begin with your general impression of the nest (and the shock of finding this mess in your basement) and move to your surprise at seeing the specific items the rat had taken: an old spoon, a shiny metal button, a marble, and other trifles. Or if a topic requires emphasis, you might go from least to most important or most to least important.

Some topics may benefit from comparison. Comparing two views can give a fresh slant to an ordinary topic. For example, a tarnished silver belt buckle from Great-Great Grandfather's Civil War uniform might be considered worthless by one cousin, but another might view it as a priceless family heirloom. People, too, can be described from more than one vantage point. One student was quite candid when she described a relative from two vantage points. (That is why Lori withheld her last name in the following paper.)

My Fiery Grandma

My grandmother is like a brightly burning fire. She can be warm and welcoming, a "light" ever ready to give aid. However, she can also be cruel and destructive, freely turning emotions into ashes. When controlled, Grandma is a warm, gentle person. She doctors wounds with soft hands and a kindly smile. She can make a person feel safe and protected. She has offered food and shelter to those less fortunate than herself, allowing them to warm themselves at no cost, while still providing all the love her twelve grandchildren could want. She has encouraged hopes and dreams, as if they were dry wood she just needed to spark into life. To enter her presence is like coming into a fire-lit room after being in the cold. The fire is there, warming skin and bones while her welcome fills one with good cheer.

My grandmother is like a fire in less positive ways as well. When she is in one of her fiery moods, her tone and words can blister. The warmth, shelter, and love once freely offered sometimes flare into regret and bitterness, searing what was to an ash. Hopes and dreams she once nurtured can wither under a well-turned phrase. During these times she is like a house fire, destroying and burning everything and everyone in her path. No subject, person, or idea is safe from her at such times. Yet despite these vices, she is still "Gammy," and the entire family would be less joyful without her.

—Lori I.

Unusual comparisons are valuable when describing an emotion, a phenomenon, or other abstract topic. The right comparison allows you to pin down an elusive idea and express it in a novel way. Comparisons using figures of speech such as *similes* and *metaphors* are excellent ways to energize description. Similes and metaphors are unusual comparisons between two basically different items. You can easily identify a simile because it includes *like* or *as*. Lori's first sentence contains a simile: "like a brightly burning fire." Her second sentence contains a metaphor: "She can be . . . a light." What other examples of figurative language do you see?

Writing a Conclusion

Successful endings give a sense of completion and satisfaction. In description, as in narration, the major point often appears at the end. The ending may be a brief summary that explains the point in an interesting way. Perhaps the description ends on an optimistic note that looks to the future. Or it might end on a philosophical note that relates physical details to an abstract thought. Anne Morrow Lindbergh is both optimistic and philosophical at the close of *Gift from the Sea:*

> The waves echo behind me. Patience—Faith—Openness, is what the sea has to teach. Simplify—Solitude—Intermittency . . . But there are other beaches to explore. There are more shells to find. This is only the beginning.

Sometimes a surprise or twist ending is effective. These endings require preparation, however. You cannot simply swoop down and attach an ending that is foreign to the description or story. You need to prepare the reader in small ways. Note that Paul mentions his wife early in "The Crystal Chandelier." He does not suddenly introduce her at the end. In "How a Computer Changed My Life," Michele describes a problem, then surprises the reader with her solution. Effective endings are smooth; they grow out of whatever has preceded them.

Revising a Description

To be clear and interesting, a description must be more than a bundle of details. Each detail must contribute to an overall effect. If a detail seems unnecessary, you may want to put it aside. This does not mean you should trash details; just stow them at the end of your document until you are sure they will not be needed. As you revise your description, try to find the central idea. What is the dominant impression? This checklist will help you to revise.

∼ Checklist for Revising a Description

1. Does the opening line arouse interest for this audience? Could it be improved?

2. Is the vantage point suitable?

3. Is the voice appropriate? Should it be more personal or friendly? More emotional or less?

4. Is the order of details effective? Could it be improved?

5. Have I involved at least three senses? Might I find more sensory details to make four? Are all details effective?

6. Is the imagery sharp and clear? Could it be improved?

7. Are most verbs in the active voice? Are the nouns and adjectives specific enough?

8. Is transition needed to clarify any shifts?

9. Could the sentence structure be varied and improved?

10. Does the ending seem complete?

11. Is the dominant impression clear and effective? Does any detail *not* support the dominant impression?

Two Sample Descriptive Papers

In the first paper, the student writer describes sensory details, creating a dominant impression that reinforces her thesis. She uses a narrative strategy, along with cause and effect, to support the description.

How a Computer Changed My Life

During the past decade, video computer games have been deluging the country, and my home is no exception. After realizing how much money, time, and energy I spent at my favorite arcade, I decided to invest in a computer and numerous games. Then I could play at home for free, still get my household chores done, and relax in comfort after work while I played. These anticipations soon proved to be grave misconceptions.

Countless hours were spent in front of the computer as I tried to maneuver Super Muncher and other heroes away from bombs, monsters, and other dangers. I sharpened my aim so that I could destroy space dice that fell around my hero, spaceship, or whatever. I was hooked on video games. My addiction took me to haunted houses, jungles, and the sea, where I searched for hidden treasures. As the computer games began to possess my time, the laundry began spilling over the edges of the hamper. The shelves of the pantry became bare because there was little time for grocery shopping, not to mention meals. My friends soon learned that calling me on the telephone was fruitless. They knew, being computer owners themselves, that I could have been destroyed by enemy fire if I had stopped to take their calls.

There was never time to chat or enjoy conversation. Practicing, playing, and conquering took every moment of my spare time. During the first few weeks of ownership, the physical exertion I expended on my new toy was incredible. My muscles ached and my neck was stiff from sitting in one position and looking in one direction. My eyes burned; they were red from lack of rest and constant staring at the screen. My fingers, hands, and arms throbbed with pain. I had blisters on my fingers from operating the joystick and my thumb was numb from the pressure I had to apply to maneuver through the mazes.

When I finally came to my senses, I realized that as an adult, I could certainly find better things to do with my money, time, and energy. This video madness had to stop. In order to maintain my home and my sanity, I decided that my computer and the games would make a lovely Christmas gift for my brother and his family.

—Michele Bates

Questions for Discussion

1. How does Michele set the scene?

2. What is the dominant impression?

3. Which details show cause and effect?

4. There is a gap in time between the third and fourth paragraphs. How does Michele span the gap?

5. The last sentence stops suddenly. Yet is it enough to give a sense of completeness and to satisfy the reader?

In the second paper, the student writer presents an impressive number of vivid descriptive details. She employs the technique of comparison and contrast to explore the topic and to make her thesis all the more convincing.

Please, Do Not Forget Me

In England on a barren hillside, stands a long forgotten castle that has given way to centuries of neglect. Fragments of its once stately grey stone walls litter the courtyard. A spire that once stood tall atop a tower now lies upon a heap of rubble. Windows that once gleamed in the sun are darkened with grime. Winged creatures of the night fly through broken windowpanes. The store room is dank and musty; gone are the fine foods and wines. Gone are the people who danced in the ballroom; gone is the grandeur of former years.

So too, can be the life of a person suffering from severe depression. Often the person will go into seclusion, letting time and the world pass. Hiding in the dark recesses of the mind, the victim of depression cringes, hoping others will pass on by, paying no heed to the one that dwells within. Little by little, parts of the person are lost in the rubble of distress. Slowly, bit by bit, the self seems to be less and less. No longer does it feel that anyone might want anything it might be able to give. There is no room left for the food of good thoughts or warm feelings. The dark coldness of lost hope and worthlessness permeates the empty storage room. Unkempt thoughts weaken the body as well as the mind.

One summer day someone wonders how the old castle used to be. How had it looked with sturdy walls, clean windows, and polished floors? Had the steeple, standing tall and straight against the blue sky, seemed inviting to all who passed? Was the store room full, waiting for the banquets that were to come? Finally, someone decides to do something about the neglect. He picks up a stone and places it back into the wall, then another and another. He washes windows and the sunlight once again streams through. He sweeps the dusty floor and dreams of the day the castle can be restored.

Despite protests, the victims of depression, too, need help and caring commitment to pick up the pieces of their lives, to wash their eyes and let in the light. They
need help to discard the dark thoughts that flit about their minds, help to air the
dark musty places that need a caring touch, help to let in a fresh dream of what they
might be. Then one piece at a time, their lives can be restored to become a little
better, day after day.

Not all the castle walls and floors that are polished will shine as brightly as
before. The store room will still have a faint mustiness, and a few stray creatures
may venture in. But the castle can be a wonderful, grand place of peace.

—C. J. Banning

Summary

Effective description has a purpose; it is not just a filler. You can use description as a major or minor writing strategy. Description often undergirds narration,
comparison, persuasion, or another major strategy. The tone may be subjective
or objective.

A paper of description has a dominant impression. Selected sensory details,
referring to sight, sound, smell, touch, or taste, enliven description. Strong verbs
and specific nouns also help description come alive. When planning a description, think about the vantage point or location from which you will observe the
subject. Will you remain stationary or will you move around?

Sometimes there is a story connected with an object, place, or impression.
Depending upon the situation, you might merely mention the story or you might
develop it. Sometimes a story has a lesson or moral that will give depth to the
paper.

You can organize descriptive details in spatial or chronological order, through
comparison, or in another logical way. Devote care to beginnings and endings so
that they are suitable and appealing. Examine word choice to strengthen verbs and
delete meaningless modifiers. Revision is an essential part of effective description.

Key Terms

sensory details	objective tone	simile
dominant impression	vantage point	metaphor
subjective tone	fixed observer	moving observer

Practice

Small Groups: *Devising Similes and Metaphors*

Directions: In groups of three or four, consider the items below. Select those
that appeal to you and devise unusual comparisons that are similes and metaphors. Don't hesitate to have fun! Appoint a recorder to save the best.

1. Fill in the blanks with a *fresh* comparison:
   a. He walked like a . . .   (Avoid clichés such as *duck.*)
   b. She ate like a . . .   (Avoid *horse.*)
   c. Her smile was like . . .   (Not *ray of sunshine*)
   d. His tongue was as sharp as . . .   (Not *knife*)
   e. He dressed like . . .   (Not a *hippie* or *hobo*)
   f. They were as quiet as . . .   (Not *mice*)
   g. She was as proud as . . .   (Not *peacock*)

2. Comparisons of objects: sunflower seed, cocoon of a moth, a pencil without an eraser, an untuned violin, a flattened tin can, dripping faucet, car without tires, cabbage, turnip, grapefruit, burned-out light bulb, acorn, snapdragon, or other objects you choose.

Example

Object: empty corn husk

Simile: My life is like an empty husk.

Metaphor: The empty husk of my life . . . .

3. Comparisons of birds and insects: ladybug, hummingbird, dragonfly, house fly, termite, wasp, bluejay, woodpecker, meadowlark, canary, bobolink, ant, hoot owl, bumble bee, firefly, mosquito, or other birds and insects.

Example

His words bit like the sting of an angry wasp.

Writing a Description

Directions: Select one of the cases below and write a description.

1. Imagine that the person you love most has disappeared. The police have asked you to write a description so that a detective could pick this person out in a crowd. You are to describe any individual characteristics that might aid in recovery: body build; the way the person walks; the attitude he or she projects; typical facial expression; vocal quality; scars, birthmarks, or moles; likes and dislikes; places he or she might go; and any other distinctive characteristics.

2. You have your first car. How did you get it? What does it look like? What will you use it for? How do you feel about it?

3. Imagine that UPS has delivered a large box to your home, addressed to you from your Aunt Agatha. Inside is a present you have dreamed of for years but have been unable to afford. Describe the object and how you feel about it, using sensory details.

4. Your neighbor has found a box of old family photos in the attic of a deceased relative's home. They are jumbled together without dates or names, and she is upset that she does not recognize or know her forebearers.

Now think of your family album. How much will your descendants know about the people pictured there? Select a photo of one relative whom you would particularly like to have remembered. What features, characteristics, and experiences will you describe?

5. Long ago a special relative gave you a music box for your birthday. You were thrilled by the miniature carousel that still moves and plays a tune. Describe the music box, giving sensory details. Try to convey the magic the music box has for you.

Forty Ideas for Descriptive Papers

1. My favorite place to be alone
2. My most beloved pet
3. A frustrating moment
4. The most intimidating person I know
5. The kindest person I know
6. First date
7. First job
8. First performance review
9. My worst boss
10. A Saturday night hangout
11. Riding the rapids in Colorado
12. A ride on the canals of Amsterdam
13. A ride on the Staten Island ferry
14. The first time I . . .
15. My worst spanking
16. Why I chose . . . (your college or university)
17. My happiest moment
18. My high school reunion
19. My . . . heritage
20. A marriage proposal
21. Aunt Lacy's Courtship
22. An unusual wedding
23. A train ride
24. My favorite restaurant
25. My favorite vacation spot
26. A flower garden to attract butterflies

27. My mother's homemade bread
28. Butchering time on the farm
29. Making apple butter
30. My first apartment
31. The best dog I ever had
32. A description of my neighborhood
33. A family heirloom and its significance to me
34. A cedar chest
35. My father's toolbox
36. A shop in Chinatown
37. An incident in Paris
38. German Village in Columbus, Ohio
39. Riding the trolley in San Francisco
40. A family of bald eagles

CHAPTER 12

Process Analysis

Explaining How

> It is far easier to discuss Hamlet's complexes than to write orders which
> ensure that five working parties from five different units arrive at the
> right time equipped with proper tools for the job.
>
> —G. B. Harrison

Analyzing a process or procedure and writing clear, concise directions to describe it is not always easy. In the 1960s, before the public was familiar with photocopiers, Ohio State University placed a coin-operated copier in a campus library. The directions were so complicated that many users needed assistance. To resolve the problem, OSU offered a prize of $100 to whoever could write the best set of instructions. A student won the prize.

In daily life we analyze processes and formulate procedures to simplify tasks and to ensure quality work. You may build or refinish furniture, do crafts, prepare elaborate dishes, write software programs, or complete a variety of other processes. On the job you may follow instructions for running a piece of equipment or performing a task, or you may train new employees, showing step by step how a procedure is performed. Processes such as these require clear explicit directions. Other kinds of processes do not require directions but still take the form of a series of steps or stages. These processes include regular occurrences in the natural world—such as digestion, photosynthesis, or the development of a hurricane—as well as complex procedures that may not be performed by one person—such as the production of steel or the publication of a book.

TWO KINDS OF PROCESS ANALYSIS

Process analysis is the observation and explanation or description of a process. For clarity, *chronological order* is necessary: steps, stages, and events are described

164

in sequence as they normally occur. There are two basic kinds of process analysis: directions (or instructions) and process descriptions.

Directions for Procedures

The simple experiments you conducted in high school science and chemistry labs were procedures. When you assemble shelving or make lasagna you also perform a procedure. To ensure good results, you follow the directions carefully. If any steps are omitted or the order is reversed, the deviation may mar the final result.

Directions for a procedure should be clear and concise. That is why they are generally written in second person with *understood "you."* This way each step begins with an active verb: "*Insert* the tab . . . ," "*Open* the chamber . . . ," "*Lift* the switch. . . ." Some directions contain diagrams or other illustrations to show the steps of the process. Still, certain assumptions are made about the level of knowledge the reader has. Any reader who lacks this basic knowledge may find the directions to be puzzling. Perhaps you have worked with instructions that seemed incomplete or overly complicated. You may have experienced the frustration of trying to decipher steps that were not fully explained. If so, you know that instructions should be more than a brief list.

When directions are inadequate or nonexistent, the result can be a disaster. Without clear directions, for example, one young man began a welding job only to find the equipment was different from that used in his previous job; he ruined $400 worth of equipment the first night. In the graphics department of another company, a young man new on the job was not instructed in the proper procedure for disposing of solvent-soaked rags; he stowed them in a covered metal trash can. During the night combustion occurred, engulfing the room and its contents in flames. The moral is that people providing directions to novices should not assume any particular knowledge or expertise.

To write clear instructions, you might assume the role of a beginner. Try to anticipate the points that may be difficult, unclear, or risky for the novice. Specify the equipment and material needed at the beginning. Then describe the operation in detail so that the reader understands. This role playing can help you to devise a clear explanation or description of a process.

Process Descriptions for Procedures

Just as a set of directions explains a sequence, so too does a process description. Both are written in chronological order. The purpose and style of writing differ, however. Directions are prescriptive; they tell the reader directly what to do. Process descriptions, on the other hand, relate a process as it occurs, often using present tense verbs: "The tab *is inserted* . . . ," "The mollusk *opens* its chamber . . . ," "The switch *is lifted*. . . ." In this way process description is similar to narration. But the story a narrative tells is something that occurred only once, while the subject of a process description must be a procedure—whether natural or of human invention—that occurs in the same way over and over again.

Writers in the sciences often use process description to explain biological functions or the behavior of organisms. Industrial consultants may report on a company's standard operating procedures or on a particular manufacturing process. Technicians may write to explain the workings of a particular mechanical device or software application. In this kind of situation, the goal is to explain a process in such a way that readers understand each stage of the process and how the various stages interact.

TRANSITION IN PROCESS ANALYSIS

A transition is a word, phrase, sentence, or paragraph that connects ideas, informing the reader of what is ahead and pointing out the direction of a piece of writing. Transitions indicate shifts of meaning and of relationships such as time, location, sequence, space, similarity or difference, certainty or uncertainty. *Signpost transitions* are located at the beginning of sentences. *Embedded transitions* appear at various places within a sentence.

For process analysis, use transitions that indicate chronological order (usually signpost transitions). These may be numerical transitions (*first, second, third,* and so forth) or others that indicate time or sequence. Use numerical transitions to indicate the *major steps* in a process or procedure. Use other transitions of time to indicate *substeps.* (Two or three *first*'s and *second*'s would be confusing.) To mark substeps, you can use any of the following signpost transitions that are appropriate:

next	finally
then	later
after that	when
while	last year
during	after
as soon as	earlier
after one hour	meanwhile

WRITING A PROCESS PAPER

As noted earlier, the purpose of a process paper is to provide directions for a procedure or to describe a process. To fulfill either purpose, a writer must know how much readers know about the topic and whether they are likely to have performed or witnessed the procedure or process before. Steps or stages must be placed in chronological order. Precautions and warnings may need to be inserted at strategic points. For clarity and conciseness, second-person with action verbs are most effective:

Warning: *Perform* the steps in the order given. Failure to do so may cause fire.

In process descriptions, adequate use of detail is key to maintaining readers' interest. At the same time, it is important not to burden them with so much detail that the description of the process becomes hard to follow. Be careful to maintain the thread of the action. When possible, use the active voice: "Workers *load* the oranges into large combines, which *squeeze* them to a pulp." Process descriptions are generally written in the third-person present tense. (For more on active and passive verbs, see chapter 8.)

Selecting a Topic and Prewriting

The topic for a process paper should be based on your personal experience or observations and be complex enough that readers won't find it obvious. You may find that narrowing the topic is essential: even a fairly simple process paper can become surprisingly lengthy. The subject should be one you know well. To develop your thinking skills, however, you should probably avoid a recipe or any other process you learned to perform from written instructions.

The quickest way to start is to make a scratch outline listing the steps of a procedure or process. An outline allows you to set up the steps and substeps in the correct order before beginning to draft.

Drafting an Introduction

An introduction to a process paper may be as short as one sentence or as long as a paragraph, depending upon the purpose for writing and the length of the paper assigned. Particularly for directions, the finished product or result of the process should be stated in the introduction so that the reader has a clear sense of purpose. If you simply dive into the first step, you are likely to confuse readers.

The introduction should also include a thesis statement that restricts the idea yet leaves it broad enough to accommodate all the details that are later explained in the body of the paper. The thesis should identify the process, make a claim about it, and specify the result, product, or benefit for the reader:

> White-water rafting can be an enjoyable experience for the beginner who is well prepared. (Claim/result: enjoyable experience)
>
> Setting up a backpacking tent correctly can net a good night's sleep. (Claim/result: good night's sleep)

The following student introductions illustrate only two of many options for an introduction. Others are given in chapter 3.

Generalization Followed by Restriction   An accurate generalization may be used for the beginning of a process analysis. In the following example, Patricia Jones Black opens with a generalization followed by a restriction. Safety is her key idea. Since Patricia's introduction is only two sentences long, she chooses to combine it with the first point.

How to Process Green Beans

Home-grown green beans can be served year round when they are properly processed and stored. By following the twelve steps listed here, you can safely take green beans from the garden to the table several months later. First, pick beans that are round and tender. Three to five pounds of beans will be needed for each quart to be processed.

Historical Opening   Melinda Ham selected an unusual topic that carries a hint of nostalgia. She begins by describing the slow-paced life of pioneer days.

Apple-Head Dolls: A Remnant of Yesteryear

Years ago when life was less complicated and most families lived miles away from their nearest neighbors, family entertainment was more often homespun than manufactured. Children had to invent their own games. Parents frequently made toys for their children out of natural materials because cash was scarce. One popular homemade toy was the apple-head doll. These dolls had wizened faces, like very wrinkled old people, with a variety of expressions. By following these simple instructions, you, too, can make an unusual doll for a child in your family.

Developing a Process Paper

In a process paper, you present the steps in an orderly sequence so that the reader can understand and possibly duplicate the procedure. You should also provide any necessary precautions to prevent problems. In her paper on making apple-head dolls, Melinda explains the process clearly, using numerical transitions and active verbs to indicate major steps. Her transitions are italicized here.

First, gather the necessary materials. An apple and cotton balls are needed for the face, hair, and beard of a male doll. Or you may wish to make a pair of dolls, male and female. The apple should be large because the head will shrink later. The body consists of a fine gauge wire coat hanger, a large paper clip, clean cotton rags (an old sheet, pillow case, or shirt), varnish or shellac, and scraps of fabric for clothing. Other items needed are a sharp paring knife, pliers, a small bowl, a bottle of pure lemon juice, plain table salt (not iodized), and about eighteen inches of heavy thread or fine cord.

Second, make the face of the doll. With the paring knife, thinly peel the apple. *Then* carve out the tiny eye sockets, nose, mouth, and ears. *After the head is carved*, place it in a small bowl. Pour one-fourth cup of lemon juice over the apple. Let set for thirty seconds, *then* rotate so that all sides are covered with juice. Wait one minute. To make the eyes, press two apple seeds horizontally into the carved sockets.

Aging is the *third step*. Unbend the paper clip, leaving the smallest "hook." Push the straight end of the clip into the top of the core down through the apple. *When the wire emerges*, bend it about an inch to make a right angle to support the apple. Loop a length of heavy thread over the top hook and tie a knot. *Next* suspend the thread from a window catch, away from direct sunlight, where the apple can hang for two to four weeks. *When the desired "wrinkling" occurs*, apply a thin coat of clear shellac or varnish to protect from further deterioration. Let dry overnight.

Fourth, add "hair" to the head. For a male, pull apart a cotton ball to form a beard. Glue around the jawline. A narrow strip of cotton around the back will form a fringe of hair around a bald spot. For a female doll, a large cotton ball (or two) will be needed for her hair, which can be arranged as desired.

Making the body is the *fifth step.* Use pliers to twist a thin wire coat hanger into a simple stick figure. Wrap strips of rags around arms and legs to give a rounded effect. Secure the rag strips with rubber bands or adhesive tape or both.

Creating clothing is the *sixth* step. Design simple clothes for the dolls. The male doll might wear a simple dark suit with a white shirt and perhaps a cap or hat. The female doll might wear a tiny apron, shawl or cape, sunbonnet, and long dress.

The final step is attaching the head. Attach the apple head firmly to the neck wire. Twist the clip wire tightly around the body wire so that the apple-head will remain upright. If wire shows, cover with a necktie, shawl, or scarf.

Writing a Conclusion

An effective conclusion to a process analysis provides a sense of completion, often by referring specifically to the result of the process. If possible, end on a positive note. Even if the results of a procedure are negative, you might summarize what was learned, refer to a benefit or emotion, or add a bit of humor. Two examples of satisfying endings are illustrated here.

Summary Ending   In concluding a paper that explains how to take pets to a veterinarian, Janet Edington emphasizes planning and precaution. She summarizes the main idea of her paper in two well-balanced sentences.

> Stress and mistakes can be avoided through care and preparation. By displaying determination, vigilance, and patience, you can transport your pets safely to and from their medical checkups.

Reference to Benefits   Melinda ends by pointing out what makes apple-head dolls special.

> Apple-head dolls are not only easy to make, but unusual. The face and expression of each doll will vary somewhat. The clothing can vary greatly. Apple-head dolls make attractive and distinctive gifts.

Revising a Process Paper

Clarity and completeness are the main qualities you need to check for in a process paper. The following questions should be helpful.

∼ Checklist for Revising a Process Paper

1. Is the thesis clear and specific? Does the introduction establish the purpose and point out the product or result of the process?

2. Is each stage of the process discussed in sufficient detail?

3. Do transitions clearly distinguish major steps as well as substeps?

4. Have precautions been included at appropriate spots if necessary to prevent potential problems in following directions?

5. Does the conclusion seem to complete the paper in a satisfying way?

Two Sample Process Papers

Keith Witzel wrote directions for replacing a defective electrical outlet. His
assignment required him to prepare an outline for an in-class paper. Later, while
writing the paper, he revised his tentative introduction and conclusion. These
changes reveal flexibility—he used his outline as a tool, not as a prescription.

Outline: How to Replace That Defective Electrical Outlet Safely

Thesis statement: To replace a defective electrical outlet correctly, follow these
five main steps: First, assemble the materials; second, shut off the power;
third, remove the cover plate and the receptacle; fourth, replace the receptacle and cover plate; fifth, restore power.

   I. Assemble materials.
      A. 120V–15 amp receptacle
      B. Needle-nosed pliers with cutting edge
      C. Slotted screwdriver

  II. Shut off power: Trip circuit breaker or unscrew fuse if circuits are shown.
      If in doubt, trip main switch.

 III. Remove cover plate and receptacle.
      A. One screw in cover plate
      B. Two screws on receptacle
         1. Pull receptacle from utility box.
         2. Remove wire from each side and bottom.

  IV. Install new receptacle and replace cover plate.
      A. White insulated wire to silver-colored terminals
      B. Black insulated wire to brass-colored terminals
      C. Uninsulated ground wire to utility box
         1. Use ground screw provided with receptacle or grounding clip.
         2. All wires stripped approximately five-eighths inch and looped
            clockwise
      D. Receptacle connected to utility box (two screws)

   V. Restore Power. Put main switch on, flip circuit breaker, or seat fuse.

Conclusion: You will find that following these instructions will ensure a safe
and functional outlet and save the cost of an electrician.

How to Replace That Defective Electrical Outlet Safely

Many people refuse to replace defective electrical connections in the home,
either because of a lack of knowledge concerning the proper procedure or from fear

of creating a fire hazard. By following a few simple guidelines, however, almost anyone can make minor repairs safely.

Most electrical circuits in the home are made up of general lighting circuits of either 15- or 20-amp circuits. These are the circuits used for small appliances, lamps, television, and others. These items are connected into the general lighting circuits by plugging into the wall outlet receptacles. If one of these receptacles becomes defective, it is a safe and simple process to replace it by following five main steps: First, assemble the necessary materials; second, shut off the house current; third, remove the receptacle; fourth, install the new receptacle; fifth, restore power and check the operation of the new receptacle.

First, assemble the necessary materials. These include a pair of needle-nosed pliers with a jaw approximately two inches long, tapering to a pointed end; a slotted screwdriver; a utility knife; and a new receptacle rated at 15 amps or 20 amps as required.

Second, shut off the power to the circuit that contains the defective receptacle. This is done by turning the main switch (marked on handle) to the "off" position on the circuit breaker or fuse box. Check to make certain that the electricity is off by trying to operate appliances in various locations of the house. They should not function.

Third, remove the cover plate from the defective receptacle by turning the screw in a counterclockwise direction. Remove the two screws that hold the receptacle outlet to the utility box (the small metal box mounted in the wall), and pull the receptacle from this box. There will be a white insulated wire, a black insulated wire, and possibly an uninsulated ground wire (depending on the age of the structure) attached to the receptacle. Remove these wires and discard the used receptacle.

Fourth, install the new receptacle and replace the cover. Before installation, inspect the black and white wires to ensure that each end is free of insulation for approximately five-eighths inch and the ends are formed into loops. These loops should be made in a clockwise direction. The purpose is to ensure that the wire is secured around the screw as the screw is tightened.

After that, install the wires to the new receptacle. The white wire is connected to the silver-colored side of the receptacle and the black wire to the brass-colored side. Tighten each screw firmly. Next, connect the uninsulated wire (if used) to the green screw on the bottom of the receptacle. Push the receptacle into the utility box and tighten, using the screws supplied with the new receptacle. Remount the receptacle cover, being careful not to overtighten this screw, which could cause the cover to crack.

Finally, restore power to the house and check the receptacle to see that it is functioning properly. If not, check to see that you have flipped all breaker switches.

If each of these steps is followed closely, you will not only have the satisfaction of doing the job yourself, but also the satisfaction of saving the cost of an electrician.

—**Keith Witzel**

Questions for Discussion

1. Is Keith's paper a set of directions for a procedure or a process description? How do you know?

2. How does Keith's final paper differ from his outline? Why do you think he made the changes he did? Do they seem like improvements?

3. How clear do you find Keith's analysis of the process? Is any step or sub-step unclear? If so, how might it be clarified?

In the next paper, Ann Kemmerley describes a procedure used at her job. Both embedded and signpost transitions (italicized) provide tight links and clarify the steps for the reader.

How to Prepare Books for Sale at the Dorcas Carey Public Library

Many library books are read each year in the village of Carey. Some books, however, fail to be as popular as others and collect dust on the already crowded shelves. To dispose of the less popular works, the Dorcas Carey Public Library uses a *four-step process* to prepare books for sale.

"Weeding" is the term given to the *first step in this process*. Periodically, an assistant librarian looks through every book on a shelf for its last circulation date, found on the pocket inside the back cover. If this date goes back five years or more, the book is weeded from the shelf and placed in a stack beside the shelf. Often books will also be weeded if they are in poor condition because most people do not read books that are falling apart. This step of weeding is completed after the head librarian checks each book and decides whether to try the less popular work in another section or *to sell it*.

The books selected to be sold must then be prepared for sale. *This second step* includes ripping out the back pockets and marking out any identification. The back pocket, which holds the book's circulation card, is torn away from the page or cover where it is glued and thrown away. Any library identification, such as name and address or price, must be covered by a black marker. If this marking out is not done, a reader may confuse books bought at the book sale with those currently in circulation. An important part of this step is the saving of the circulation card, for it will be used in the *following steps*.

The removal or "pulling" of all the books' cards from the library's card catalog is the *third and lengthiest step*. In this step all cards pertaining to a book must be pulled from the drawers by tearing the lower hole. The circulation card saved in step two gives the information needed to complete this step. The circulation card's top line indicates the author, and its second line gives the title. The book's author card is pulled first. On the reverse side of this card may be a list of subjects related to the book. Each subject given is *then* found and the cards pertaining to the book are pulled. The last card to be removed from the main card catalog is the title card. *Before step four*, it is necessary to pull another card for the book from the author file in the main office.

The fourth and final step in preparing books for sale is crossing them off in the accession books. The accession books list every book in a library according to an assigned number given at the time of purchase. This number is found on the circulation card's right side. The number is located in the accession book and "sold" is printed in the margin reserved for such remarks. At this time the circulation, author, subject, and title cards can be discarded, and books are ready for sale to the public.

The four steps for preparing books for sale are not complicated, but they do require some time. The effort put forth, however, is well worth the shelf space that can be used for new books (purchased with funds from the books sold) and the joy a reader receives from buying an inexpensive book to add to his or her own library.

—Ann Kemmerley

Questions for Discussion

1. Is Ann's paper a set of directions for a procedure or a process description? How do you know?

2. How clear do you find Ann's analysis of the process? Is any step or substep unclear? If so, how might it be clarified?

3. Find some instances where Ann has taken time to explain the purpose for various steps and substeps. Do these explanations help you better understand the process? Do they ever make the process hard to follow? Explain your answer.

Summary

Process analysis is often used in daily life and on the job. A process analysis is a logical explanation of a process, either giving directions or a description. The analysis is arranged step by step in chronological order. Numerical transitions can mark major steps; other appropriate transitions can mark minor steps.

To write a process paper, identify the topic and the result in the introduction. Develop the body with adequate details according to how much readers already know. Include precautions and warnings if needed. Possible endings include a summary, a reference to a benefit or emotion, and humor.

Key Terms

process analysis	transition	major step
directions	signpost transition	substep
process description	embedded transition	generalization
chronological order	numerical transition	

Test Yourself

True or False: Guidelines for Process Papers

Directions: Write T (true) or F (false) in the correct blank.

_____ 1. The finished product, result, or benefit of the process should be stated in the introduction.

———— 2. Active verbs are best for explaining a process or procedure.

———— 3. To be clear, steps should be parallel.

———— 4. Numerical transition is recommended for processes with sub-steps.

———— 5. Substeps should not be marked with numerical transition.

———— 6. When a writer uses "first," there should be a "second."

———— 7. Instructions in manuals are prescriptive.

———— 8. Precautions are necessary to forestall possible hazards.

Practice

Writing Ideas

1. How to tie a shoe (as explained to a five-year-old child)
2. How to bake a cake from a mix (as explained to a nine-year-old child)
3. How to make delicious popcorn (not in a microwave oven)
4. How to make your favorite sandwich
5. How to brush a shedding dog or cat with little fuss
6. How to make a paper airplane that will fly
7. How to plant a tea rose
8. How to preserve autumn leaves with wax paper
9. How to plant peas
10. How to clean a bedroom quickly

Test Yourself Answers

All answers are true. This exercise can be used as a reference while writing a process paper.

Fifty Ideas for Process Papers

1. How to have a successful garage sale
2. How to select and eat crawfish Southern style
3. Quilting with little hand-sewing
4. Servicing the printing needs of a company
5. Touchup painting on a car
6. Patching a bicycle tire
7. Teaching a parakeet to talk

8. How to water ski
9. Fishing for bass
10. Racing a sailboat
11. One way to quit smoking that works!
12. Trimming a poodle
13. How to cope with obscene telephone calls
14. Grooming a horse for show
15. How to saddle a horse correctly
16. How to pack a suitcase efficiently
17. Weightlifting for beginners
18. Making a terrarium
19. How to set up a water garden
20. Assembling an aquarium
21. How to shower and dress in five minutes
22. Changing a flat tire safely and efficiently
23. How to wallpaper a room
24. Painting a house the professional way
25. Fireproofing a home
26. Burglar-proofing your home
27. How to build a bird house
28. How to refinish antique furniture
29. How to construct a concrete patio
30. How to make a Christmas wreath
31. How to teach children the value of money
32. Obtaining a small business loan
33. How to make a doll cradle
34. How to bathe a bedridden patient (or an infant)
35. How to explain death to a child
36. How to install an upgrade of a software package
37. How to give an injection with minimum discomfort
38. Organizing a Neighborhood Watch program
39. How to make ceramics
40. How to enjoy white-water rafting
41. How to become a lady wrestler
42. How to curb fat intake when eating out

43. How to be an excellent waitress
44. Piñatas: An easy and affordable way to make your party memorable
45. How to raise big, beautiful roses
46. A family tradition: planting potatoes
47. How to have healthy house plants
48. Preserving the natural beauty of your wood deck
49. How to install landscaping logs for a flower garden
50. Gardening in patio pots or window boxes

CHAPTER 13

Illustration

Showing with Examples

Example moves the world more than doctrine.
—Henry Miller

Whether you talk to your boss, a neighbor, or a child, chances are that you use illustrations, or *examples*. After a trip to Chicago, you might describe your visit to a restaurant atop a tower. As the elevator inched upward, it creaked and groaned. You wondered if the cable might break. You felt like an unwilling extra in a Hitchcock movie. As you were seated at a table beside the glass wall, you glanced down at the twinkling lights of the city, shrouded in black velvet. Your head felt strange and your stomach, storm-tossed. Clenching your teeth, you looked away and politely declined a beverage. As your friends drained their glasses, you whispered "Let's get out of here." When they seemed reluctant, you added, "I feel ill." After hearing this illuminating example, your listener or reader would better understand acrophobia, the abnormal fear of high places.

An example evokes a picture in the mind. Supplying appropriate examples is one of the best ways to explain, convince, and lure a reader on. Whether you compose an employment application letter, a technical report, a college paper, or an essay exam answer, the right examples will demonstrate your knowledge.

USING EXAMPLES

What one person calls illustration, another may call exemplification. To *illustrate* simply means to clarify through example; you include impressions, facts, statistics, or expert opinion to lend substance to your writing. The examples may relate an incident, describe, compare, or explain. *Anecdotes* are brief stories, often humorous. An *analogy* is an extended comparison. *Historical examples* usually concern people or events. *Literary allusions* are examples taken from literature.

Hypothetical examples are conjectures—supposedly true. However, real examples drawn from life are the most interesting and convincing.

An illustration paper may be a personal essay, as is "Envy" at the end of this chapter, or it may be considerably more academic. Examples are valuable for explaining a concept, illustrating a problem, or supporting a reaction for papers in psychology, law enforcement, business management, philosophy, literature, composition, and other fields. On the job you might use illustration to persuade in a proposal, grant application, or other rhetorical situation.

The key in any instance is to choose examples that count, that enable your reader to understand what you mean and to see that you know what you are talking about.

WRITING A PAPER OF ILLUSTRATION

For a paper of illustration, you have a wide range of topic choices and organizational strategies. Select a topic you can develop with interesting examples, perhaps from your own experience or from that of someone you know. Then arrange the examples in an order that reflects your purpose.

Selecting a Topic and Prewriting

The topic may be concrete or abstract, according to the assignment. When something is concrete, it is detectable through at least one of the five senses, often more. You can see, hear, feel, smell, or taste it. If you write about an abstract principle, you can clarify it with concrete examples familiar to the reader. You can cite a variety of examples as long as they all have a central thread.

Excellent illustrations can often be lifted from everyday life. When you describe what you know firsthand, your words sound authentic; they ring true. For instance, if you have a family heirloom, memento, or special gift (possibly a music box), you might find a topic there. Perhaps your great uncle has a set of silver swords hanging over the fireplace. What do these objects represent to your family? Or perhaps your home has an unusual feature: a tower room, a secret room or passage, or something else. What is the story behind it?

Once you have chosen a topic, prewrite to form a pool of details. To start your creative juices flowing, write your topic at the top of a clean sheet of paper. Then jot down every idea that dives into your mind—examples, incidents, events—anything that might be used as support. If you know the topic well, you will soon have a page of examples and details. To start prewriting, the following questions will be helpful:

- Why am I interested in the topic?
- What relevant examples can I recall?
- Who is connected with the topic?

- If the topic is a person, did he or she have a favorite saying, mannerism, or habit that might be relevant?
- How has he or she influenced me? Can I give an example?
- What changes have occurred; how do I feel about the changes?
- What is my main point?

Finally, draft a thesis that makes a point about your topic, ideally one that is unfamiliar to your readers.

Organizing and Developing a Paper of Illustration

To organize and develop your paper, choose an order, select examples, and weave explanation with examples, all the while focusing on your purpose.

Order   To organize a paper of illustration, select an order that suits your purpose and topic. You might organize examples chronologically or according to importance or in any other way that will advance your point (see "Seven Common Orders," chapter 3). As you read the student papers in this chapter, notice the organizational strategies. If your topic is a narrative that spans a period of time or discusses various stages of someone's life, then chronological order is a good way to organize. Dixie O'Rourke uses chronological order for a paper, as shown in this outline:

Envy

  I. Introduction: Example of envy at age ten (very strong).

 II. Body
   A. Age thirteen. Envy had decreased somewhat.
   B. Example: Sudden change in Dixie's perspective.
   C. Today: Envy seldom occurs.

III. Conclusion

Other topics can be organized according to some variation on order of importance. For a paper about exotic pets, you might move from relatively familiar examples to more surprising or outrageous ones. For a paper on natural cures for common ailments, you might move from examples of cures for minor ailments to examples of cures for more life-threatening ones. Such orders have the advantage of holding readers' attention by providing examples that increase in interest.

Relevant, Accurate, and Sufficient Examples   Every example you include should be *relevant* to your thesis, illustrating your main point in some way. Resist the temptation to include an example just because it is odd or funny. Avoid examples that veer from the topic. Illustrations should illuminate a point. Irrelevant examples distract from the thesis.

Check to see that examples are *accurate*. In attempting to be humorous or to dramatize a point, writers sometimes embellish examples but such extravagance can sabotage logic. An example may be dramatic, but it should not be too far-fetched or unusual—the one-in-a-million variety. To palm off an atypical example as typical is dishonest. If you generalize from an example, it should be *representative of its class* (typical). When researching, consider the source of your statistics; is it reliable? When was the study, experiment, or poll conducted? Is the information up to date?

How many examples will be sufficient? The answer depends on the nature of your thesis and the weight of the examples you have to include. The sheer number of examples is less important than their quality. Select impressive examples that will provide concrete support for your thesis. A controversial or debatable thesis will require several high-quality examples to convince a skeptical audience. As a rule, when examples are brief, you need more than when they can be developed in detail.

In a paper entitled "The Talent Within," Nicole Vanderkooi cites several brief examples in each paragraph. Each example is clearly relevant. Her third paragraph appears here:

> Possessing a natural skill can be overpowering, a constant pressure. Children with such talent have expectations already set for them. At age six, Sarah Wells was told she had a promising future in gymnastics and was enrolled in nightly classes. Despite many strained muscles, injured ankles, and missed slumber parties, she persevered and gained confidence. Yet she endured many lows as well as highs; she became critical of herself. Constant pressure from her parents and coaches and a desire to win made her dream a reality. At thirteen, Sarah began her powerful run to the vault. To keep her lead in the meet, she had to score at least a 9.5. As her hands hit the leather, she felt the adrenaline pump, and she scored a perfect 10. A spectator cheered, "That's awesome!" Sarah Wells won the meet. By now her childhood was gone, but in its place was a confidence powered by success. To some people, that is robbery; to Sarah it is a rewarding way of life.

Weaving Examples with Explanation   As you draft, try to find an interesting way to enter your topic. How will you approach it? You might start with a series of short examples, eye-catching details drawn from everyday life. To connect the examples to your thesis, you will need to interlace them with explanation. Bryan Vaughn weaves example with explanation as he describes his perceptions of happiness:

> During my childhood, happiness meant anything from having waffles for breakfast to being able to stay outside after the streetlights came on, catching lightning bugs and playing tag. Early in my adolescence, happiness seemed to take on another meaning. Driving fast was my new source of happiness. I discovered that a motor could be affixed to just about anything. My first few inventions were just this side of lethal. When I consider these vehicles, it's a wonder I'm still alive today. I rode go-carts, three-wheelers, snowmobiles, motorcycles—anything I could put gas in, I drove.
>
> During mid-adolescence, my perception of happiness changed again. Sports became my passion. For me, nothing could compare with the exhilaration of being

part of a winning team. Our football team was the defending state champion. Our basketball team finished third in the state, and our baseball team was the conference champion. Happiness was being one of the main players on every team and having the potential to play college sports and possibly having a career in professional sports.

But those dreams ended during a football game when I received a severe spinal injury. After two months in the hospital, I was sent home—handicapped, but thankful. At this time happiness took on yet a new meaning: I was just glad to be alive and able to walk. . . .

As my life began to return to normal, I saw a new source of happiness. One day I saw, parked in front of a Sunoco station, a red 1969 Pontiac GO Judge. That same day I bought "The Judge" and spent every spare minute working on it. . . . But later an old man drove out in front of me without warning and wrecked my happiness. . . . Although I bought another car, it was not the same as the Judge.

Now that I have matured to a ripe old twenty-two, the word *happiness* means much more than ever before. . . .

Like Bryan, Barb Bronson weaves explanation and example to support her thesis. But she also makes several striking comparisons. The chief one is an *analogy*, or extended comparison, that first appears in the title: "Clipper Ship Mom." This comparison continues throughout the paper. Barb gives her personal observations on a distressing topic. Since the major examples are so powerful, a few provide adequate support. The first two paragraphs appear here:

Clipper Ship Mom

Unique and truly American, the clipper ship is a fast sailing cargo ship whose shipmaster's talents have never been surpassed. My mother reminds me of those early ships and courageous sailors. Whenever the open sea of marriage gave warning of an approaching storm, Clipper Ship Mom would batten down the hatches and set her course in preparation for the rough voyage ahead. As a child, I watched helplessly as Clipper Ship Mom sailed to a hell where my father resided as gatekeeper.

Even when my father was sober, his behavior was unpredictable. Petty, trivial incidents would arouse his raging temper. But whenever he had too many drinks, it was like coming face to face with Satan himself. So many times I wished Mom would take us away to some safe place where we could hide. I also knew Mom had been taught to honor her marriage vows—for better or worse. When I was fourteen I awoke to an argument which led to my father's yanking my mother to the front yard in her night clothes and placing a gun to her temple as her five children watched. He told us to say goodbye to our mother; she was going to "meet her maker." Frozen with fear, we clung to each other as tears streamed down our faces. Looking to the heavens above, I whispered a prayer for God to spare her life. He must have heard the prayer, for after a while Dad calmed down and we all went back to bed.

Writing a Conclusion

As with any essay, the conclusion for a paper of illustration should provide a satisfying close. Ending on a positive note, especially after the recounting of a painful experience, is gratifying for the reader. Barb Bronson ends "Clipper Ship Mom" by continuing the comparison and expressing gratitude:

> My clipper ship, my mom, has endured many rough storms. Every day I thank God that my mother stood fast. Words can never express how lucky I feel to have her. At the present Clipper Ship Mom and crew continue to sail steadfastly on course, but on different seas.

In a paper about a series of failures she faced, Phyllis Parks ends on an optimistic note, providing some specific examples of current successes:

> Despite the failures I have experienced, all phases of my life have not been grim. My daughter from my first marriage has grown into a beautiful, healthy young lady. Fifteen months ago my new husband and I were married. I am also enrolled in college classes. Now I truly feel successful.

Sometimes writers have a tendency simply to repeat their introductions in slightly different words or to summarize their body paragraphs. Try to find a more satisfying conclusion. Consider explaining a particular insight, noting an advantage, offering a suggestion, or expressing an opinion that is supported by your examples. Leave your readers feeling they have learned something from your presentation of examples.

Revising a Paper of Illustration

After your first draft has cooled a bit, go back and read through the examples carefully. Try to distance yourself from each one so that you can evaluate it impartially. As you make revisions, consider the principles you have learned so far. The following checklist will help you revise.

➤ Checklist for Revising a Paper of Illustration

1. What is the main point of the paper? Is the point clear?
2. Is each example relevant, accurate, and valid?
3. Does each example add substance to my claim?
4. Do the examples create interest?
5. Are there enough examples?
6. Are examples arranged in a clear, logical order? Or could the order be improved?

TWO PAPERS OF ILLUSTRATION

The students who wrote the following papers spent many hours and much effort not only in writing but also in revision. First, Anita Ketcham describes her hobby in an unusual way, blending explanation with example.

Bathtub Solitude

An avid tennis player can be found lobbing away on the court; a woodworker may enjoy crafting furniture in a workshop; a gardener may relax by tending flowerbeds. I, too, have an enjoyable hobby—one that is not only relaxing and challenging but also educational. Like tennis, woodworking, and gardening, my hobby is done in the best possible place. That is why I do crossword puzzles in the bathtub.

As a mother of four young children, I rarely find time to sit down. Any time I do take for myself is soon interrupted. Mom sitting down is like a red flag waving, signaling a parade of little feet. This is why the bathtub is the perfect place to relax while working puzzles. There I cannot answer the telephone or pour a glass of milk or dress a Barbie doll. Those tasks have to wait. For a half hour, I escape to my own private retreat. Although it's not like Hawaii or the Bahamas, yet I am totally alone with my book and my bubbles, and it seems like heaven. The toughest problem I have to face is a six-letter word for supplication.

Working crossword puzzles is challenging. My favorites are the large "challenger" puzzles because the clues are difficult, requiring considerable thought. Still, I enjoy matching wits with the puzzlemaker. Some words can have several meanings and the clues can be ambiguous. A good puzzle solver learns to look at clues from different angles. For example, a five-letter word for the clue "drop a line" could be *write* or *angle*, but the answer the puzzlemaker wanted was *erase*. "Iron clothes" could be a clue for *press;* however, *armor* was the answer. A very difficult clue can be frustrating, especially for a puzzle printed in a newspaper because answers are not available until the next day. Although I rarely complete a difficult puzzle, I always try to improve my skills in order to do better with the next one.

Working crossword puzzles is educational. By using a dictionary often, I have expanded my vocabulary. Words such as *hirsute* and *litigious* have been added to my lexicon—as well as the word *lexicon.* And where else but in crossword puzzles could one find such a plethora of insignificant information? I know that Guido's note is an *ela,* but I do not know who Guido is. I know that the answer to "Roman bronze" is *aes* and that Caesar's road is an *iter,* should anyone ask. Not all of the knowledge I have gleaned from crossword puzzles is this trivial; some I have even found useful. Knowing that Siam is the former name of Thailand and that Istanbul was once Constantinople has helped me to defeat my husband during heated games of *Jeopardy.* He thinks he is married to a genius! I will never tell him my secret.

For my soon-to-be birthday, my husband will probably give me a bottle of bubble bath, the latest copy of *Dell Championship Crosswords,* and an hour to myself. Then I can enjoy some peace and quiet, sharpen my wits, and discover words new to me. All knocks on the door will be ignored. I will come out only when my toes are too wrinkled to stay longer.

Questions for Discussion

1. Look at Anita's opening. What expectation does she set up with the first three brief examples? Notice how she surprises the reader with a hobby that is different.

2. What comparisons do you see in paragraph two?

3. How do the examples in paragraphs three and four function? What is their purpose?

4. Look at Anita's ending. How do the examples function there?

Next, Dixie O'Rourke offers a series of extended personal examples to show how she learned to control her emotions.

Envy

One evening without warning, envy crept into my young heart. The year was 1957. The place was a backyard ice rink at the home of my best friend, Sylvia. Although the time was only 5:00 p.m., dusk had already arrived. Sylvia had just gone inside to eat dinner with her family in their comfortable brick home in a pleasant neighborhood.

Outside I continued to cut figure eights and spin on the ice while Sylvia ate dinner. As I paused to catch my breath, I found myself staring through the dining room window. Inside, the brightly lit room appeared warm and friendly as the family gathered around the table. Sylvia's father stood at the head, reading from the family Bible.

As I continued to window peek, I felt an overwhelming surge of envy and ill will. Suddenly, I was resentful not only of Sylvia's many possessions, but also of her intact family. I longed to live like Sylvia. This flood of painful feelings changed not only how I felt toward her, but also how I felt toward myself. The contentment of my childhood had shattered: I was ashamed of my house, my family, and myself.

Only ten years old, I was unable to deal with these new feelings of inferiority and kept them locked tightly within. I feared losing my best friend; I was afraid that if I told Sylvia how I felt, she might not like me anymore. I also feared telling my grandparents (with whom I resided); they might feel hurt and angry. So I told no one.

By junior high school, the feelings of shame and resentment had begun to diminish. Although I still felt pangs of envy when my friends flaunted their possessions, I had learned to control the envy so that it did not overwhelm me. The technique was simple—nothing new. I would count my blessings and thank God for each and every one of them. My grandparents had set a good example for me.

When I was thirteen, a sobering experience brought my perspective into a more realistic focus. During the school lunch hour, a group of students, whom I envied, gathered in front of the malt shop across from the school. This particular day the group welcomed and invited me to go with them to a carnival at a shopping center across town. The plan was to meet after school the next day and walk to the carnival. Knowing my grandfather's second job took him near the area, I offered the group a ride.

When school let out that afternoon, I ran home to plead for a ride and money for the carnival. Smiling, my grandmother lifted the lid of an old blue sugar bowl and gave me several silver coins. The next day grandpa drove his old Chevrolet, freckled with rust, to the school; and five of us piled in. When we reached a large parking lot, my friends hurried off toward the carnival without a word or backward glance to either of us.

Grandpa locked the car doors, bid me goodbye, and started toward the factory. As I watched him fade into the crowd, my eyes watered. Not one person had thanked him for the ride or waited for me. The envy I felt for that group fled. Suddenly, I felt proud of my grandfather even though he wore bib overalls and carried a lunch bucket. I felt fortunate to have both my grandparents.

Although I still feel a twinge of envy now and then, I no longer have the strong feelings of my youth. As my values have changed, I have focused my energies in a positive direction; presently, I'm working full time and attending classes for a nursing degree. Over the years, I have learned to subdue envy and to make the most of what I have.

Questions for Discussion

1. What do you notice about Dixie's opening?
2. How does she set the scene for the reader?
3. What do you notice about Dixie's vantage point? (See the second paragraph: "outside," "inside.")
4. What incident causes a sharp shift in Dixie's perspective?
5. Examine her conclusion. What do you notice?

Summary

An illustration paper uses examples to explain, convince, or persuade. The topic may be concrete or abstract; both kinds need concrete examples for support. Prewriting will help the writer find raw material. The best examples are relevant, accurate, and adequate. The number needed depends not only on the type and quality of the examples but also on the topic and the purpose.

Examples can be organized in various ways, according to the topic and purpose. Chronological order, concrete-to-abstract order, and comparison are often used. Examples woven with explanation are effective. Ending on a positive note can provide a satisfying close.

As you revise your illustrations, weigh their effectiveness. Check the relevance, accuracy, quality, and number. Arrange in a logical order.

Key Terms

illustration	concrete
example	abstract
exemplification	analogy

Practice

Ideas for Writing

1. A pet food company is seeking winsome cats and dogs to be featured in television commercials. Write a letter explaining why your pet should be featured. Include examples of behavior and training.
2. Recently you purchased a home. Near the back fence, on a neighbor's property, stands a large, old apple tree. The tree has not been pruned or sprayed. Several limbs extend over the fence, and rotten apples dot your

lawn. Insects swarm on the apples, and bees have stung your children twice. You would like the tree to be cut back to the fence line. Describe the problem and make the request.

3. Describe a seemingly small incident such as a chance meeting or a sudden impulse that influenced your life.
4. Describe a scary Halloween experience.
5. Write an article for your campus newspaper using humorous examples to spoof a campus condition or a consumer product.

Forty Ideas for Papers of Illustration

1. The most frugal person I know
2. What humor is appropriate in the workplace?
3. Aggressive drivers
4. The courage of a handicapped child
5. My grandmother's perseverance
6. How my parent's divorce affected me
7. Learning from hardship
8. My father's gift: persistence
9. How my view of work has changed
10. How possessions complicate our lives
11. A grandmother/grandfather is . . .
12. My obnoxious neighbor
13. Being a latchkey kid: not for the timid
14. Adversity as an asset
15. Lessons I learned from a groundhog (or what else?)
16. Saving dollars at the supermarket
17. Do you call that a vacation?
18. Internet pests
19. Common sense: in short supply
20. Avoiding common telemarketing scams
21. Common gardening mistakes
22. My favorite teacher
23. . . . : not my favorite television show
24. What is passive aggression?
25. Drunk drivers are getting away with murder

26. Cincinnati's gardens
27. The wonders of West Virginia
28. Does sexual equality set the stage for male exploitation?
29. Should property be confiscated for victimless crimes?
30. Beware the pirates of the road
31. What are good manners?
32. A wonderful neighbor
33. Soothing upset restaurant patrons: an art
34. Optimism pays
35. Puppy love
36. Flea markets can be dangerous
37. Services to ease your business trip
38. Ways to detect bogus currency
39. Ways to attract hummingbirds
40. My Achilles heel

CHAPTER 14

Division and Classification

Taking Apart and Grouping

If people cannot write well, they cannot think well. And if they cannot think well, others will do their thinking for them.

—George Orwell

TWIN METHODS OF THINKING

Division and classification are twin methods of taking apart and grouping items and ideas logically. Division can be as simple as cutting a large pizza into equal portions or as complicated as splitting an atom. Classification is the opposite of division: to classify, you take a hodgepodge of items, and sort and group them into categories or a system. Classification sorts items according to a *principle of selection*. (A principle of selection governs or regulates each category.) For example, Jackie Gleason, whose weight fluctuated greatly, had three wardrobes organized by size: small, medium, and large. You may organize your wardrobe according to season. In one closet you might place clothes for cool weather; in another, clothes for warm weather. And within each closet you might have categories: groups of clothes worn for different occasions. Or you might organize each closet by color or some other principle of selection.

Division and classification allow us to establish order in our lives. The Gregorian calendar divides a year into twelve months, each month into weeks, and each week into days. Each day is divided into hours, each hour into minutes, and each minute into seconds. Our linear measurement follows the U.S. Customary System. Length is divided into miles, furlongs, rods, yards, feet, and inches. These systems of measurement and countless other systems allow us to organize our world and to function effectively.

Every day you divide and classify interchangeably with little or no thought to the method. Division and classification help to clarify your thinking. And so it is with writing. You may find a topic and divide it into three or more points or categories or reasons. Then you prewrite, accumulating a store of ideas, which you later classify. Whether you realize you are dividing or classifying at a particular moment is unimportant as long as the result is logical.

Guidelines for Division and Classification

1. Divide and classify items according to the purpose and audience.
2. Avoid overlapping parts or categories.
3. Make each part or category large enough to contain a significant number of items or details.
4. Make all parts parallel; all items in a category should be similar and equal.
5. Organize all parts or categories to fit into one logical system.
6. Arrange parts or categories in a logical order.

WRITING A PAPER OF DIVISION AND CLASSIFICATION

Whether you emphasize division or classification, you will be considering relationships, either between elements or items. Your topic and your purpose will determine the order.

Selecting a Topic and Prewriting

Many famous writers advise selecting a subject you know and care about. Chances are that you already have a wealth of details just waiting to be mined and classified. What fairly complex topic could you make clearer, using division and classification? If you are a family-history buff, you might describe your dominant impression of a quirky relative by grouping traits into well-defined categories. Perhaps you live near a place with little-known features that might attract tourists. If you were to write a brochure, what features would you describe and how would you classify them? Or you might describe the kinds of people who patronize a store or restaurant.

Observing at a restaurant buffet, Patricia Rush classified the members of "Annoying Eaters of America" as "inspectors, gulpers, and conversationalists." Here is how she described the second group:

> Gulpers are the Indianapolis drivers of the table. To prepare for the race, they
> pile their platters high, thus cutting down on stops for refueling. They are determined

to finish the meal first, even at the cost of indigestion. Stuffing their mouths and chomping, they shovel in the food and wash it down with great gulps of water. When every scrap is gone, they sometimes take a morsel of bread and swab their platters clean. Often their belches can be heard throughout the restaurant. Gulpers are usually males in ragged T-shirts and dingy jeans. For them, these garments may have more than one use; gulpers sometimes finish by wiping their hands across their chests or thighs.

Any topic that brings to mind words such as *types, kinds, features, parts, aspects, components, reasons,* or a similar category is appropriate for division and classification. This paper analyzes and explains, describes and clarifies.

With a topic in mind, you can use any of the various prewriting techniques you learned in chapter 2 to unearth details and ideas quickly. Still another way of prewriting can be helpful for division and classification: the "because" technique. This technique works well for topics that can be divided into advantages, benefits, or reasons. Just ask a question about the topic, then answer "because. . . ." Jot down your answer and ask "What else?" Repeat the sequence until you have enough material. After that, group the details logically into main points.

To show how this technique works, let's assume you have a fourteen-year-old daughter, Kim, who has been invited to go riding with Brad, the sixteen-year-old next door. But you are convinced Brad is a reckless and irresponsible driver. Simply telling Kim this will not carry much weight. Evidence is needed to support the claim. The "because" technique will help you organize relevant facts:

Questions	*Answers*
1. Why does Brad seem irresponsible?	*Because* I have seen him speed by children on bikes, run stop signs and red lights, cross over a double line, and tailgate. I often hear him brake sharply, squealing his tires.
2. Are there any other reasons?	*Because* he backed into his mother's car with a loud bang last week. His car has several dents although he's had it only three months.
3. What else?	*Because* he has had twelve parking violations and two speeding tickets.

Your prewriting could continue until everything you know about Brad's driving has been listed. Then you could analyze the details and divide them into three categories such as: *carelessness, speeding,* and *ignoring traffic rules.*

Organizing a Division and Classification Paper

Perhaps the most common order for a paper of division and classification is some order of degree: simple to complex, least to most important, easy to difficult, and so forth. To make a case against Brad as a driver, you might organize points from the least to the most dangerous aspects of his driving.

Brad is a reckless and irresponsible driver

1. *Because he is careless.*

   Last week he backed into his mother's car.

   His car has several dents in it after only three months.

   He does not slow down for children on bicycles.

2. *Because he speeds.*

   He has had two speeding tickets.

   He drove 50 mph on a street posted at 35 mph

   At high speeds, he drives too close to other cars.

   He turns corners too fast, squealing his tires.

3. *Because he often ignores other traffic rules.*

   He has twelve parking violations.

   He turns quickly without signaling to other drivers.

   He passes when there is a double yellow line.

   He drove through a stop sign last week.

   He sometimes drives through red lights.

The discussion so far has placed classification before division. But some writers reverse the procedure, listing main points before prewriting details. How or where you start does not matter. What is important is that you write in the most comfortable way possible and generate enough material to develop a topic well.

Drafting an Introduction

After you have chosen a topic and prewritten numerous details, the next step is to draft a tentative thesis. As you may recall, a thesis statement not only tells the reader the topic but often suggests an order of presentation and hints at an attitude toward the topic. In a paper of division and classification, the thesis statement frequently sets up a logical order of degree, from least important to most important, for example. In his thesis statement, Mark Newell places three main points first:

> A good location, plenty of patience, and the right ammunition are three advantages I use to achieve successful squirrel hunting.

Not all thesis statements specify points or categories; some simply make a brief claim. For example, the parent might say, "You can't go out with Brad for three reasons."

Developing a Paper of Division and Classification

As you draft, follow the order set up in your tentative thesis or working outline. If you see a problem, revise the order in the most logical way. It is important to establish the larger order of the paper before the internal order of paragraphs so that you can gain a sense of direction or focus for the entire paper. Also look for effective transition from the thesis to body paragraphs. How will you link them?

Using Embedded Transition   Subtle transition is the mark of a proficient writer. Practicing with a three-part thesis statement and devising a link from each part of your thesis to the matching main point will deepen your awareness of how transition works. In the next example, Mark Brady begins by stating an opinion in the first sentence. In the second sentence he gives a fact. In the third sentence, the thesis, he supports opinion with three reasons (italicized):

> Upland bird hunting in Ohio is in a sad condition. Populations of three game birds—the ring-necked pheasant, the blue grouse, and the bobwhite quail—have dwindled. Three main factors for this decline are *the kind of hunters, increased pollution*, and *clearing of woods and underbrush for farming.*

Note how Mark returns to each of the main points of his thesis in the opening sentences of his body paragraphs:

> Along with the good *hunters* in the fields are a number of ignorant *hunters* who shoot every bird they can, despite the fact that they are exceeding the daily bag limit. . . .
>
> The second reason for the dwindling bird population is the *increased pollution* in our environment. . . .
>
> The *farmer* is probably the biggest reason for the declining bird populations. . . .

Again, in his conclusion, Mark reinforces each of his initial main points:

> Frankly, most of those concerned seem to contribute to poor hunting conditions. The *nonsportsman hunter* takes home more birds than allowed. The *manufacturers who make pesticides and weed sprays* sometimes fail to adequately check the long-term effects of products upon birds and their eggs. Many *farmers* clear their land and plow in the fall, not leaving cover or grain for the game birds. Surely we must work to solve this problem before it is too late.

Mark does an excellent job of connecting his thesis to the main points of his paper with the following types of embedded transitions:

1. Repetition of key terms: *hunters, increased pollution*
2. Synonyms: *ignorant hunters, nonsportsman hunters*
3. Pronoun and antecedent: *hunters/they*
4. Natural relationships: *farming/farmers, pollution/manufacturers/pesticides/ sprays, nonsportsman/bag limit*

STUDENT EXAMPLE: AN ESSAY WITH
MAIN POINTS STATED IN THE THESIS

In the following essay, Michele Flahive states three main points in the thesis. She uses embedded transition to establish clear links from the thesis to body paragraphs. These links provide unity and mark the path of the main idea. Note how she repeats a key term (italicized) in the first sentence of each body paragraph:

Diamonds: A Girl's Summer Friend

As the batter walks up to the dusty plate on the diamond, she scans the outfield. Spying a vacancy between left and left center, she knows this is the best area to hit the ball. While the pitcher gets ready to make her move, the batter stands in position. In a slow pitch, the ball sails off into a perfect arc, dropping right where the batter wants it. With her heart pounding, she swings the aluminum bat and cracks the ball. Quickly, she runs three bases, listening to the cheers of teammates and hoping to reach home plate before the ball. For her the *challenge*, the *enjoyment*, and the *camaraderie* make softball a game worth playing.

The first game of the season seems always to pose a special *challenge*. The players often feel a bit rusty and nervous. Just walking onto the field and up to bat that first time takes strength of will. But once the umpire yells, "Play ball," the nervousness melts away and determination flows in. Enthusiasm for the game takes over.

Enjoyment of softball is the heart of the game. After a long day of work or school, it is a pleasure to leave the stress behind and walk out onto the diamond. Since both teammates and crowd are just out for an evening of recreation, there is no great pressure to win. The fun and action provide a refreshing reward at the end of a day.

The challenge and enjoyment would be incomplete without the *camaraderie* of teammates who share the same passion for a rousing game of softball. And when a member is feeling down for missing a ball or for striking out, words of encouragement flow from other members. Then too, there is a sense of unity as everyone plays together in the infield and outfield, backing each other up as needed.

As August slowly winds to an end, so must the summer softball season. It can be a sad time for many die-hard ball players who must leave the diamond and put away their gloves. Yet some players take heart, for not only does autumn bring bright foliage and cool evenings, but it also heralds the fall softball season!

Did you notice how Michele sets the scene and pulls the reader right into the action at the very beginning? With just a few concrete details, she creates an image of the dusty plate, batter with pounding heart, aluminum bat, sound of the bat hitting the ball, perfect arc, and cheers. This vivid description helps the reader to relive what she feels and sees as she walks up to the batter's box.

STUDENT EXAMPLE: AN ESSAY WITHOUT
THE MAIN POINTS STATED IN THE THESIS

In the next essay, Peggy Reeves makes only a brief claim in her thesis, the first sentence. Yet she states principles of selection later: she classifies details according to place ("lying around"), damage, and emotional hazards. All details support her thesis—referring back to the key word, *trying*:

Fore!

Having a golfer for a husband is trying. He has countless golf accessories lying around. I find golf balls beneath furniture, under cushions, and in corners. On the end table, piled high, are stacks of *Golf Digest*, *Golf*, and golf catalogs. When I take freshly washed clothes out of the dryer, I sometimes find tees and ball markers. When I open the hall closet to put the sweeper away, there is barely enough room to squeeze it in among the golf clubs, golf shoes, and golf ball boxes.

At times my husband's hobby leads to physical damage. When he practices in the garage with his driving net, the ball sometimes misses the net and dents the garage door, ceiling, or wall. (I fear the window will be next.) Sometimes he even chips golf balls over the coffee table and scrapes the family room ceiling with his club. And he never thinks to call "Fore!"

Golf presents hazards for the emotions, too. When my husband watches a golf tournament on television, he yells when a player misses a putt by a long shot and grumbles about the player's swing. He may even call him names. Worst of all is his "golfer's withdrawal" after a bad day at the golf course and sometimes during the winter months when he can't play. Then he lapses into grim silences and does not answer when I try to talk to him.

There are times when I envy the wives of workaholics.

For beginning writers, an explicit thesis statement is usually advisable. Even if you prefer to follow Peggy's example, your instructor may recommend starting with a tentative thesis that spells out main points or categories that set up the order of your draft. That way it is easier to avoid confusion and to establish tight transition and unity.

Making Main Points Parallel   When main points are parallel, the resulting balance strengthens transition, sentence structure, and unity. (To review parallelism, see chapter 8.) In the example below, note how Joanne M. Pohlman begins each main point with the same type of structure, a gerund phrase (italicized). Each main point in the body explains the matching point in her thesis:

Thesis: As a volunteer member of the National Ski Patrol, I earn the opportunity to meet many interesting people, learn challenging skills, and spend time with my family.

Parallel points: 1. *Joining the Central Division of the Patrol* has acquainted me with approximately eighty other patrollers. . . .

2. *Becoming a member of this national organization* takes more than being a proficient skier. My training. . . .

3. *Being able to ski with my family* is the main reason I chose to become a patroller.

Writing a Conclusion

A conclusion should flow logically and smoothly from the body of a paper. As a result, the reader should gain a sense of completeness or closure. To provide a satisfying conclusion, writers often allude to the thesis, as Joanne Pohlman does. At the end of the paper about skiing, she repeats the name of the organization and expresses appreciation:

Finally, I feel fortunate to belong to the National Ski Patrol. Although I receive no wages, I do gain new friends, invaluable skills, and a closeness with my family that is priceless.

Revising the Paper

A paper of division and classification is more complex than those discussed in earlier chapters. The guidelines below should help you to organize your paper successfully:

☞ *Checklist for Revising a Paper of Division and Classification*

1. Has the topic been narrowed to one item?
2. Is the introduction focused and interesting?
3. Do the main points follow the order set up in the thesis statement?
4. Are the main points linked with the thesis?
5. Are the main points parallel?
6. Are the main points well supported with specific details and examples?
7. Can clarity be improved?
8. Does the internal order of each paragraph flow well?

TWO SAMPLE PAPERS OF DIVISION AND CLASSIFICATION

In the first paper, Nicole Vanderkooi describes three types of people a tourist might encounter on the streets of New Orleans.

The Melting Pot of New Orleans

The sweet voice of jazz and spicy smell of Cajun cuisine capture Nicole's senses as she walks through the French Quarter of New Orleans. People from every walk of life seem to wander these cobblestone streets. On the corner of Bourbon Street sits a bum, playing his harmonica. In a horse-drawn carriage, a tourist reclines, listening to the clip-clop of hooves and the driver's southern drawl. In an art gallery, a sightseer from New York purchases yet another work for his loft. Carrying a briefcase, a local businessman strides past the shops, bent on another destination.

Draped with tattered overcoats and wearing tennis shoes, the bums of this elusive city wear weathered grins amid week-old whiskers. Their daily hours are spent collecting tips for providing the pleasure of hearing their sultry saxophones. The night brings them home to humid, stagnant alleys. These bumbling creatures walk alone, attended only by their instrument and ever faithful bottle, enclosed in a brown paper bag.

Tourists and sightseers dot the avenues of New Orleans. At daybreak they begin to roam the high-priced novelty shops and spacious old plantations surrounding the area. Often dressed in walking shorts, they sport "I survived New Orleans nightlife" T-shirts and sun visors or sunglasses. Frequently, a wife is escorted by an overburdened husband and a trusty guidebook. By night, infamous nocturnal pleasures entice many to partake in Cajun feasting and boisterous drinking.

Yet another colorful feature of this Louisiana melting pot is the local business-man. Attired in a single-breasted black suit, an ivory silk shirt, and a brilliant tie, this worldly person projects professionalism and sophistication. Finding him in an art gallery or trendy coffee shop, drinking a black brew from small cups is not unusual. Nightly, he often dines at a specialty restaurant and listens to the rhythms of jazz. The entrepreneur's companion may be a colleague or a breathtaking, well-dressed woman.

New Orleans graciously accepts the prize for the most captivating city. There musical vagrants, inquisitive visitors, and quick-witted tradesmen catch the eye and capture the heart.

Questions for Discussion

1. What are Nicole's three categories? How does her way of introducing them differ from a standard thesis statement introduction?
2. What kind of order does she use within each paragraph?
3. Where has Nicole used embedded transition to link body paragraphs to her thesis?
4. What kinds of specific details does Nicole use to describe each of her categories? Are the details comparable in each case? Why do you think so?
5. How does Nicole establish closure in her ending?
6. What else do you notice?

In the next paper, Jane Tinker classifies football fans into three categories. Her tongue-in-cheek tone and adroit use of concrete details enable readers to share her amusement.

Buckeye Fever

Every autumn for the past twelve years, I have witnessed an outbreak of "Buck-eye Fever" in my neighborhood. The ailment seems to hit victims in varying inten-sities. They are the casual, the concerned, and the ardent fans of the Ohio State Buckeyes.

The mildest strain of Buckeye Fever is evident in the casual fans. When time per-mits, they enjoy watching the game on television or listening on radio. But if time is limited or the weather turns sunny and warm, they forsake the game without a sec-ond thought. If given tickets, they will go—they may even buy them occasionally. The casual fans usually know the names and numbers of a few star players. Some casual fans feel that if the Bucks lose the game, an afternoon's viewing time is wasted. Casual fans are not interested in watching the Saturday night replay, for they already know the result.

Buckeye Fever hits concerned fans with moderate severity. They watch or listen to every Buckeye game possible. With buddies they enjoy seeing the Bucks on tele-vision. Enthusiastic, the concerned fans enter into the game, yelling and screaming as excitement mounts. If they have to miss a game, they will tape it on the VCR to watch later. They will purchase tickets to a game if readily available, but they will not stand in line for hours. They know the names and numbers of all starting players and are also aware of the opponent's capabilities. If Ohio State loses, the concerned fans are very disappointed, but not upset if the game was well played.

The ardent fans have contracted a serious case of Buckeye Fever. This strain may be terminal to some relationships. On Friday nights, the ardent fans are planning and preparing their elaborate tailgate lunches for the next day's game. Early Saturday mornings they rise early to proudly display their scarlet and gray flags in a prominent place and to beat the traffic jam to home games or any other within driving distance. Their tickets have been purchased either by waiting long hours in line or by knuckling into scalpers.

Dressed in their red sweaters and gray pants, the ardent fans anticipate the glory of Buckeye victory. They know the names, numbers, and personal statistics of all fifty team players as well as the high school players being recruited for next season. Later the ardent fans watch the replay to relive moments of victory. Depending on the outcome of the game, the Buckeye coach is either a saint or a bum. When the Bucks lose, the ardent fans are furious; then they become depressed. The depression may last until the following Tuesday, when they begin to anticipate the upcoming game.

Despite the degree to which a fan catches the fever, they all agree that football can be a very exciting game to watch. And for them, no team is more exciting than the Ohio State Buckeyes.

Questions for Discussion

1. How does Jane's introduction to her three categories differ from Nicole's?

2. What principle of organization has Jane used for her paper?

3. Where has Jane used embedded transition to link body paragraphs back to her thesis?

4. Why do you think Jane devotes more attention to her final category than her first two?

5. How does Jane's ending differ from Nicole's?

Summary

Division and classification help us to organize our lives. Division is the process of splitting a system (topic) into parallel parts. Classification (the opposite) is the grouping of various items or ideas into categories to form one system. Each category is governed by a principle of selection. Division and classification can be interchanged.

The "because technique" is a method of prewriting, helpful for developing advantages, benefits, reasons, or similar topics. For a paper of division and classification, main points and categories are often organized according to importance.

To write well, a writer should know and care about the topic. For clarity, main points should be tightly linked to the thesis statement. An excellent means of connection is embedded transition. To support the thesis, body paragraphs should be fleshed out with facts, concrete details, and reasons. A reference to the thesis can establish closure at the end of a paper.

Key Terms

division

classification

principle of selection

because technique

embedded transition

Test Yourself

Embedded Transition

Directions: Examine Joanne Pohlman's thesis and main points about skiing (under "Making Main Points Parallel"). Identify each type of transition below: Repetition of key terms (R), synonym (S), pronoun/antecedent (P), or natural relationships (N). (To check your answers, turn to the end of the chapter.)

_____ 1. National Ski *Patrol*/Central Division of the *Patrol*

_____ 2. join/member

_____ 3. meet/become acquainted

_____ 4. interesting people/eighty other skiers

_____ 5. spend time with my *family*/ski with my *family*.

Classification

Directions: Analyze the statements below and classify them according to the listed categories. (Answers appear at the end of the chapter.)

cliché	common belief	myth
old saying	superstition	fad
stereotype	tradition	trend

_____ 1. "Punkers" dye their hair unusual colors such as green, orange, or purple.

_____ 2. Groups of people who ride motorcycles and wear black leather jackets are dangerous.

_____ 3. Red sky at night; sailors' delight
Red sky in morning; sailors take warning.

_____ 4. An unusual custom, hundreds of years old, survives in Olney, England. There, on the day before Lent, housewives bake pancakes and race to the church service, flipping the pancake three times or more during the contest.

_____ 5. When a couple divorce, the mother should receive custody of very young children.

_____ 6. To win at bridge, select a seat that is parallel with the bathtub in the house.

_____ 7. Money is the root of all evil.

_____ 8. According to Greek legend, Cerberus guarded the underworld, the realm of Hades, devouring anyone who tried to leave.

_____ 9. Don't make mountains out of molehills.

_____ 10. The middle class is gradually disappearing.

Practice

Collaborative Learning: Classification

Directions: Select the word in each group that is not in the same category as the other three words. Then compare your selections with other group members. Discuss disagreement. You may use dictionaries.

1. tanning lotion
   shaving cream
   toothpaste
   cleansing cream

2. hickory
   walnut
   elm
   oak

3. pearl
   ruby
   diamond
   emerald

4. lace
   snowflake
   frost
   water

5. crocus
   daffodil
   zinnia
   tulip

6. wolf
   coyote
   prairie dog
   dog

7. squirrel
   rat
   woodchuck
   fox

8. lion
   hyena
   leopard
   tiger

9. daisy
   rose
   chrysanthemum
   violet

10. knife
    tongs
    scissors
    can opener

11. Siamese
    Angora
    Manx
    Silver Tabby

12. bat
    ski
    golf club
    tennis racket

Test Yourself Answers

Embedded Transition

1. *repetition of key term*
2. *natural relationship*
3. *synonym*
4. *natural relationship*
5. *repetition of key term*

Classification

1. *fad*
2. *stereotype*
3. *superstition/old saying*
4. *tradition*
5. *common belief/tradition*
6. *superstition*
7. *old saying, a misquotation of "The love of money is the root of all evil" (1 Timothy 6:10)*
8. *myth*
9. *cliché*
10. *trend*

Fifty Ideas for Division and Classification Papers

1. Why I enjoy river rafting
2. Three unusual features of . . . (novel or short story?)
3. Raising ostriches can be profitable
4. Techniques of bird-watching
5. Wheelchair etiquette
6. Three charming coastal towns in Maine
7. Favorite camping spots in the Rocky Mountains
8. Three good reasons to visit Sanibel Island, Florida
9. Unusual places to visit in California (or any other state)
10. Interesting one-day trips (within your state?)
11. The best caves in the United States
12. Inexpensive ways to show appreciation
13. Advantages to growing older
14. Pitfalls in renting an apartment
15. Factors to consider when buying a computer
16. Hazards in buying a used car (or anything else)
17. Why I enjoy woodworking (or other hobby)
18. Key factors in growing healthy houseplants
19. Basic systems of radio-controlled aircraft models
20. Guidelines for selecting a college (or day care center or ?)
21. Inexpensive ways to burglarproof a home
22. Commercials that irritate
23. Why I like or dislike . . . (hometown, college, fishing, or what?)

24. Why I enjoyed driving a school bus (or any other job)
25. Ethical considerations for an engineer (secretary, nurse, or whom?)
26. Kinds of patients/clients/customers
27. Relatives
28. Neighbors
29. Annoying drivers
30. Bosses
31. Employees
32. Why I quit smoking
33. The joy of my old truck
34. Self-awareness
35. The mystique of my first car
36. Why I like my Buick Regal
37. A snake for a pet?
38. Ways to cope with anger
39. Ways to get better photographs
40. Precautions to take when . . .
41. Perils of babysitting
42. Why shop for resale clothing?
43. Training tips for competitive swimming
44. The most unusual person I know
45. My father's persistence
46. My favorite aunt
47. My wonderful grandfather
48. My courageous mother
49. An uncle that cared
50. A father that made a difference

CHAPTER 15

Comparison and Contrast

Exploring Likenesses and Differences

Both tears and sweat are wet and salty
but they render a different result.
Tears will get you sympathy,
but sweat will get you change.

—Jesse Jackson

Jesse Jackson's powerful comparison uses simple words with vivid connotations to evoke strong images. He suggests that tears represent sorrow and inaction whereas sweat represents work and action. Juxtaposing the two subjects illuminates both in a meaningful and informative way. This is the whole point of comparing and contrasting.

In our personal lives, we use comparison and contrast daily to make informed choices between alternatives, weighing advantages against disadvantages, pros against cons, possibilities against difficulties. Sometimes the process of comparing and contrasting is automatic, as when a customer decides between a fish and a chicken sandwich. At other times the process may be deliberate and complex; for example, a new car buyer makes long lists of comparative features, trying to decide between two attractive models.

Careful comparison and contrast is also essential to success in business. As Nancy Bazelon Goldstone notes in the beginning of *Trading Up*, much of our economy revolves around choices based on comparison and contrast:

> [The time is] 8:29 a.m.: the trading room of a large commercial bank on Wall Street. The room is filled with people. The United States government is about to release key information on the state of the economy. It is deadly quiet.

The head foreign-exchange trader stands nervously behind his desk. He knows this information will move the dollar. If the data are good, the dollar will go up. The head trader will order his traders to telephone their counterparts at other banks and buy. If the numbers are very good, he will buy at least $100 million. If the numbers are bad, the dollar will fall; the head trader will sell. The decision to buy or sell must be made immediately because the price will begin to change the instant the information is released.

The term *comparison* is generally used to include both similarity and difference whereas the term *contrast* refers only to difference. Since difference is usually more interesting than similarity, most writers of comparison and contrast papers select topics that include differences. Regardless, subjects of comparison or contrast should be of the same species, class, or category. When they are, then you can compare points for a logical reason.

THE PURPOSE OF COMPARISON OR CONTRAST

Every paper of comparison or contrast needs a specific purpose. The fact that an instructor assigns the paper is *not* adequate. To determine the specific purpose, you might ask yourself, "Why might readers like to read about this topic?"

Determining a Purpose

When a topic is unfamiliar to readers, your purpose in comparing or contrasting may be to inform them of significant distinctions between two subjects. When the topic is familiar, your purpose might still be informative; but to hold readers' attention, you should present new insights or a fresh perspective. To move beyond trite generalities, ask yourself, "How much do readers already know?"

Or the purpose of comparison or contrast might be to persuade. Then the strategy would be shaped to influence readers toward a certain viewpoint. For example, an employee might write a proposal comparing a present procedure to a proposed new procedure. The purpose would be to convince readers that the new procedure would save time and money. Or a sales representative might compare the superior features and moderate cost of a store's leading microcomputer to that of a competitor. The dual purpose would be to offer quality to the customer as well as to make a sale.

A third purpose of comparison or contrast might be to entertain by presenting the features of two subjects in a humorous way. An outrageous comparison might be the basis of a joke, anecdote, or short story, as in the following anecdote about Sir Winston Churchill.

A reporter once asked Sir Winston: "Doesn't it give you a thrill to see a packed hall every time you give a speech?"

Sir Winston replied, "It is quite flattering, but then I always remember that if instead of making a political speech, I was being hanged, the crowd would be twice as big."

Comparison or contrast may have a dual purpose: to entertain and inform or to entertain and persuade or to inform and persuade. Drafting a purpose statement can help you to clarify the purpose of your comparison or contrast.

Writing a Purpose Statement

A purpose statement enables you to focus stray thoughts and stake out the direction of your paper. The statement can establish both the general and the specific purpose, as the following examples illustrate:

Purpose: To entertain and inform the reader by comparing the behavior of the male and female praying mantis.

Purpose: To inform the reader of the advantages and disadvantages of planting annuals rather than perennials.

Purpose: To inform and persuade the reader that the way medical personnel are portrayed on television is often unrealistic.

TRANSITION IN COMPARISON OR CONTRAST PAPERS

As you move from detail to detail while comparing or contrasting, you will need special transitions to indicate shifts in meaning. For your convenience, here are some transitions that point out likeness or difference:

Similarity		*Dissimilarity*	
also	too	but	yet
and	both	in contrast	on the other hand
again	similarly	however	on the contrary
likewise	in addition	still	although
besides	then too	conversely	nevertheless

Now and then you may need a *transitional sentence* to bridge a gap in thought. For example, after discussing one horse, you might supply a sentence of transition to introduce another horse: "Whereas Rocket looked as if he had been groomed for the Kentucky Derby, Skip had the careless air of a beachcomber." Two other tips you may want to consider: (1) Place *also* or *however* within a sentence rather than at the beginning, where they may sound tacked on or out of place. (2) Substitute *too* or *then too* to avoid overuse of *also*.

PITFALLS TO AVOID IN COMPARISON OR CONTRAST PAPERS

In selecting a topic for a comparison or contrast paper, beware of three common pitfalls: overused topics, trite expressions, and hasty generalizations. Predictable topics such as "winter versus summer" or "a ranch house versus a two-story" can cause instructors to wince. They may groan when they see pointless comparisons between states, children, houses, or the like. The old axiom "Don't tell readers what they already know" still applies. When you select your topic, make it fresh by putting a new spin on an ordinary idea. For example, you might contrast a husband and a wife's views of buying an antique sofa for their home.

Trite expressions often infiltrate papers of comparison or contrast. Experienced writers avoid threadbare expressions and devise original comparisons, using concrete nouns, vivid adjectives, and active verbs to make the description come alive. Sensory language enables the reader to sample the experience vicariously. Few readers enjoy frayed phrases like these:

different as day and night	a different story altogether
like two peas in a pod	are worlds apart
spitting image of his father	looked like twins

Hasty generalizations—exaggerated, unsupported claims—are another frequent pitfall in comparing or contrasting. Unintentionally, writers may repeat misstatements they have heard or think are probably true yet lack evidence to substantiate. Broad, general topics in particular can lead to unsupported generalizations. For example, a student who selected the topic "city life versus country life" generalized from stereotypes. The result was a series of overstatements, such as these:

"City dwellers take little time to enjoy life and nature."

"City dwellers are so concerned with garbage strikes, pollution, and crime that they have no time for raising flowers."

To sidestep hasty generalizations, first narrow your topic. Then check each claim carefully: Do you have adequate evidence to back up your statements? To be safe, avoid pronouncements about what a majority does or does not do. Writing about your own experience decreases the likelihood of blundering into unsupported generalizations.

ANALOGY: A SPECIAL KIND OF COMPARISON

As noted earlier, the subjects of a comparison or contrast should be of the same species, class, or category. Sometimes, however, writers choose to make imaginative comparisons, finding unusual likenesses in things that are of completely different categories. In "The Attic of the Brain," for example, biologist and essayist Lewis Thomas compares the unconscious human mind with the attic of a house. As an attic is filled with "unidentifiable articles too important to be thrown out with the trash but no longer suitable to have at hand," the unconscious mind contains "functionless, untidy, inexplicable notions . . . we'd like to keep but at the same time forget."

In "Snapping the Leash," journalist Murray Kempton compares the darker forces of human nature to "a raging tiger" that each individual "spends [his or her] life building a cage to pen . . . in." Later in this chapter, student writer Hope Bogard compares her mother to a "rosebush" providing "strength, support, and security" to its growing "buds."

Such imaginative, nonliteral comparisons have much in common with the poetic devices of simile and metaphor. (See "Create a Simile or Metaphor" in chapter 4.) When extended over the course of a paragraph or an essay, comparisons like these become *analogies*. To be effective, an analogy should be consistent, apt, and fresh. It should also help readers see the subject in a new light. Note how writer Gretel Ehrlich uses the analogy of "cowboying" to illuminate the work of the writer:

> Both jobs—writing and cowboying—take up the whole mind and heart. . . .
> A good hand on a ranch requires vigilance, acute powers of observation, readiness to anticipate what might go wrong or what's coming next, a taste for recklessness, intuitive skills, patience, and what cowboys look for when they buy a horse: a lot of heart. Aspiring to those qualities as a rancher, I can only hope my writing will benefit as well.
>
> —Gretel Ehrlich, "Life at Close Range"

Analogies are often used to help explain something abstract in terms of something concrete. In this way they can play an important role in scientific and technical writing, as writers try to help readers understand ideas and concepts that are complex or difficult to grasp. John McPhee notes one such analogy to illustrate the scale of geologic time:

> [G]eologists will sometimes use the calendar year as a unit to represent the time scale, and in such terms the Precambrian era runs from New Year's Day until well after Halloween. Dinosaurs appear in the middle of December and are gone the day after Christmas. The last ice sheet melts on December 31st at one minute before midnight, and the Roman Empire lasts five seconds.
>
> —John McPhee, *Basin and Range*

In academic and professional writing, make sure that any analogies you devise have a clear explanatory purpose. Readers may not see the point of an analogy that is used primarily for decoration or entertainment.

WRITING A PAPER OF COMPARISON OR CONTRAST

Writing a paper of comparison or contrast is similar to writing a double paper of division or classification. You examine relationships between elements or unite and organize them in a logical order that reflects your purpose.

Selecting a Topic and Prewriting

If you are at a loss for a topic, you might consider a comparison of two books or two literary characters, or you might describe a prospective purchase that requires evaluation. For example, the purpose of a comparison of two cars might be to determine which one better suits your needs and to inform an interested reader of your findings. To gather information, you might visit showrooms, talk to sales representatives, and drive the two cars. Sources of this sort can be identified in general terms such as "One salesperson said that. . . ." If, however, you were to read *Consumer Reports* or another publication, you would need to supply specific documentation, as explained in chapter 22.

To save time, prewrite details in parallel lists. Simply head two columns with the selected topics, then skip a space and start listing. Each time you write in a detail for one item, add a corresponding detail for the other. Placing the details side by side will make the lists parallel.

	Chevrolet Lumina	*Ford Taurus*
Features:	————	————
	————	————
	————	————
Price:	————	————
MPG:	————	————
Warranty:	————	————
Styling:	————	————
Handling:	————	————
Comfort:	————	————
Maintenance:	————	————

Once you have completed your parallel lists, classify details into categories. These categories can act as main points for clarity and ease of reading. For example, the price, expected cost of maintenance, and cost of operation (mpg) could be grouped under the category of economy. To compare two people, classify details into categories such as background, education, work history, achievements, eccentricities, style of dress, habits, mannerisms, speech, goals, character, or values.

After prewriting and grouping details, you can focus your paper with a thesis statement. After you draft your thesis, check to see that it (1) identifies a specific topic, (2) indicates similarity and/or difference, and (3) sets up an order of main points. Although not all thesis statements are this explicit, many instructors prefer such a clear focus, as in the following examples:

Thesis: Although the Chevrolet Lumina and the Ford Taurus are similar in several respects, they vary in comfort, performance, and cost.

Thesis: Whether I am in the mood for an exhilarating challenge or a leisurely ride through the woods, I have horses for each mood. (Kathy Burton)

Thesis: Despite obvious differences, the two series *Earth's Children* and *The Hitchhiker's Guide to the Galaxy* have much in common. (Melissa Baker)

Organizing a Paper of Comparison or Contrast

The *block* and *alternating* methods are two basic ways to organize parallel points of comparison or contrast. For an easily understood topic, the block method is simple and suitable. This order lists all the pertinent points about the first subject in one block of parallel details, then lists the points about the second subject in corresponding order. This balanced arrangement ensures that the details are easy to follow.

Block Outline of Contrast

I. *Thesis statement:* Mr. Courtney and Mr. Graham, my former neighbors, contrasted greatly in appearance, demeanor, and friendliness.

II. Mr. Courtney (first subject)
   A. Appearance
      1. Meticulous. Clothes perfectly pressed.
      2. Clean-shaven. Hair neatly groomed.
      3. Short, trim, and muscular.
   B. Demeanor
      1. Solemn. Never seemed to smile. Eyes glared.
      2. Never out except to care for lawn. Swore and hurried.
      3. Children afraid of him. He scowled when greeted.
   C. Friendliness
      1. Unfriendly.
      2. Protected his privacy.

III. Mr. Graham (second subject)
   A. Appearance
      1. Clothes never hung quite right.
      2. Hint of a beard. Hair untidy.
      3. Tall and rather heavy.

    B. Demeanor
       1. Always smiling. Kind eyes.
       2. Often outside. Hummed, sang, worked in rose garden.
       3. Charmed children. Pitched ball, played hide-and-seek.
    C. Friendliness
       1. Regarded as grandparent by children.
       2. Concerned, a real neighbor.
IV. Conclusion

For a complex comparison, the alternating method is an effective way to organize. You explain comparable points paired in parallel order. In other words, you alternate the subjects. Because of frequent shifts from subject to subject, the alternating method requires more transition than the block method.

Outline of Contrast (Alternating Subjects)

   I. Introduction

  II. Appearance (first main point)
    A. Mr. Courtney
    B. Mr. Graham

 III. Demeanor (second main point)
    A. Mr. Courtney
    B. Mr. Graham

 IV. Friendliness (third main point)
    A. Mr. Courtney
    B. Mr. Graham

  V. Conclusion

When only similarities are discussed, the pattern can be similar to one of the preceding examples for contrast. When you include both similarities and dissimilarities, however, the structure of the comparison becomes more complicated. Usually, similarities are discussed first, as in the following outline, unless there is a reason for reversal.

Outline of Comparison and Contrast (Alternating Subjects)

  I. Introduction

 II. Similarities
    A. Point 1
       1. Subject one
       2. Subject two
    B. Point 2
       1. Subject one
       2. Subject two

III. Differences
    A. Point 1
        1. Subject one
        2. Subject two
    B. Point 2
        1. Subject one
        2. Subject two
    C. Point 3
        1. Subject one
        2. Subject two

IV. Conclusion

Drafting an Introduction

Introductions of comparison or contrast papers can set the scene for the two subjects by revealing what, where, how, and when. Chuck Chesnut gives these details as he wryly contrasts two neighborhood animals. (His thesis is italicized.)

The Pet and the Pest

In my neighborhood there are several animals, but none quite like "the pet" or "the pest." When I walk out my back door and see or hear the pet, as I call him, I smile. He is a friendly old basset hound that lives in the next yard behind our house. But when I walk out my front door and see or hear the pest, my hackles rise. She is the high-strung miniature poodle that resides across the street. Some days I mutter, "The dog from Hell!" or something unprintable. *These dogs vary greatly not only to the eye and the ear but also to my sense of values.*

An appropriate analogy can lead into an abstract topic. The next example, written by Hope Bogard for her mother for Mother's Day, starts with an unusual comparison.

A Rosebush and My Mother

When many people look at an uncut rose, they see a thorny stem with shiny leaves and a beautiful flower. But when I look at a growing rose, I see beyond the beauty of the buds to the mother plant. *The rose is exquisite, but it could not be this way without the strength, support, and security of the rosebush, just as I could not achieve my goals without the strength, support, and security provided by my mother.*

A narrative opening is an easy and effective way to set the stage for a comparison or contrast. Terri Bloomfield uses narration by presenting a few graphic details to describe a sudden change in her life:

My Life after Dealing with Death

As I pushed my Fiero up to sixty-five miles an hour, the possibility of being killed in an automobile accident was miles of thoughts away. Being young, I felt invincible—why should I worry about an unpleasant subject like death? In a few days, however, I had to confront that topic in an instant. On August 18, 1993, my best friend and my cousin were killed in an automobile accident. The realization of how quickly life can be snatched away changed my life, starting the moment I met death face-to-face.

Developing a Comparison or Contrast Paper

The order in which you develop your parallel points in a comparison or contrast depends upon the purpose and the audience. One technique, level of familiarity, starting with the familiar and going to the unfamiliar, is quite effective, allowing less explanation than the reverse requires. You use analogies, anecdotes, or examples to flesh out ideas. A topic that involves physical description will need numerous concrete details to support the main points. In the next example from "My Two Neighbors," Betty Fetter's precise descriptions enable the reader to visualize two individuals:

> Mr. Courtney was a meticulous person who seemed to reflect this quality in every aspect of his life. His clothes were always perfectly pressed, his face clean-shaven, and his hair neatly groomed. His short frame was trim and muscular despite his age. He seemed always to wear a solemn expression; I never once saw him smile. His glaring eyes echoed his disgust with people and his contempt for life.
>
> Seldom did I see Mr. Courtney outdoors except to care for his lawn. Despite the swearing and hurrying to get the job done, his yard was the best tended in the neighborhood. Local children never went near his house because they knew that the slightest transgression would be met with angry retribution. Mr. Courtney was a private person, and everyone treated him and his property with the respect he so vehemently demanded.
>
> Many times a greeting to Mr. Courtney would be answered with an angry scowl. Mr. Courtney was indeed an island unto himself. Every encounter with him would remind me of another, much more gentle, man—a very dear friend who had taught me the value of friendship and the real definition of the word *neighbor.*

Note that after the first block of details, Betty smoothly introduces the second block with "would remind me of another, much more gentle, man . . . ," leading into a description of Mr. Graham:

> If judged by first appearance, Mr. Graham would not have made a very good impression. His clothes, although neatly pressed, never hung quite right on his tall, rotund body. He seemed always to have a shadow of a beard, and his hair usually looked as if he had started to comb it but had been interrupted. He was, however, always smiling; and his love for people and life was reflected in his eyes.
>
> Many times I would hear Mr. Graham singing or humming while he worked in his garden or trimmed his rosebushes. He always worked with the same patience and deliberation, nurturing and caring for each plant. With this same calm concern, he charmed the children of the neighborhood. It was common to see him pitching a ball, playing hide-and-seek, or sitting on his porch with a group of children at his feet. The children regarded him as a grandparent and treated him with great respect, as did everyone in the neighborhood. He was a real neighbor to all, friend or stranger.

Writing a Conclusion

When the purpose of a comparison is to inform, a brief summary may be in order. In her conclusion, Betty not only summarizes but also shares insights gained from experience:

> Although Mr. Graham died a year ago, his memory will live in the hearts of the people who were lucky enough to have known him. For me, he made it easier to accept the Mr. Courtneys of the world. Mr. Graham knew the secret of happiness, and the values that he taught will remain a part of my life forever.

Sometimes an analogy is continued throughout a piece of writing, giving a sense of completeness and closure. Hope Bogard extends her analogy until the very end:

> Often the rosebush is blamed if its roses are not perfect, and often a mother is judged if her children do wrong. Seldom is the rosebush praised for her prize-winning blooms, and seldom is a mother given credit for her children's successes. But I can reward my mother's achievements, and I can offer my little "buds" the encouragement, endurance, and stability my mother so generously gave.

For a serious topic, a change of perspective can provide just the right note for ending. Terri Bloomfield concluded with this thought:

> After witnessing the death of my cousin and best friend, I cherish life much more. I know firsthand that life is precious and fragile. Now I never take today or tomorrow for granted. I feel as if I must appreciate life not only for myself, but for my cousin and my friend, too.

Revising a Paper of Comparison and Contrast

If you keep your outline handy as you revise, this will help you to maintain the balanced order that comparison and contrast require. The checklist that follows should also be helpful.

➤ Checklist for Revising Comparison and Contrast

1. Is the thesis clear and specific?
2. Is the order of points in the thesis the same as their order in the body?
3. Are main points and paragraph details arranged in parallel form?
4. Does every paragraph have a topic sentence?
5. Does every topic sentence have adequate support?
6. Does the conclusion seem complete?
7. Does anything else need to be said?

THREE PAPERS OF COMPARISON

In the first paper, Rosy Erdy looks at her parents' similarities and, more important, their differences:

Parents through a Child's Eyes

The old axiom "opposites attract" certainly seems true in regard to my parents. Despite a physical resemblance, their differences far outnumber their likenesses. The most distinctive differences are in their childhood backgrounds, political views, and personalities.

Born only a year apart and in their middle seventies, my parents resemble one another. Both have thinning, silver-colored hair. Both are less than average height: Mom refers to herself as "petite"; Dad says he is "not tall." But these similarities are superficial.

The childhood backgrounds of my parents were certainly not alike. Growing up, Mom lived only in the city, whereas Dad knew only the life on a farm. Mom was the first of her family to graduate from high school; Dad went to work immediately after completing the eighth grade at a rural school. A strong religious environment influenced Mom, whereas no visible religious commitments existed in Dad's family. Shortly after their marriage, however, Dad adopted Mom's religion. He still attends church regularly with her, but only half-heartedly.

My parents' political differences became quite apparent when I was very young because Mom is a loyal Democrat and Dad is a proud Republican. Every four years after a presidential election, they return from the polls loudly declaring that it is fruitless to vote. They know that the vote of one cancels out the vote of the other.

My parents' greatest difference is in personality. Mom has always been more friendly and outgoing, whereas Dad tends to be shy. Mom seems to be always laughing, even with tears in her eyes, but Dad seems more serious. Mom demonstrates affection freely; Dad has difficulty in letting his emotions show. Years ago, Mom administered discipline, while Dad stayed in the background. Afterward he gave us emotional support on the sly.

Mom is forthright and open, but Dad is soft-spoken and reserved. Mom seems to have a strong opinion on everything; Dad tends to be quiet and easily swayed. No one in the family needs to worry about anything because Mom does it for us. If Dad ever worries, he keeps it well hidden. Privacy is not a word in Mom's vocabulary; it seems to be her God-given right as a mother to know everything about her family. On the other hand, Dad quietly respects everyone's privacy.

Despite their many contrasts, my parents have been married over forty years. They have been steadfast in their devotion to each other and to the family. As a result, my brother and I have been greatly influenced by the blending of their differences. From our wonderful parents, we have gained a balance and stability that has been transmitted to our own families' lives.

Questions for Discussion

1. What is the effect of including similarities? What would be the effect if Rosy had included only differences?

2. Which method of organization does she use?

3. Notice that she mixes a few first-person references with the third person. Are these necessary and effective? Why or why not?

4. Are her examples convincing support for her claims?

5. How would you describe the tone of the essay?

6. Comment on her conclusion.

The next paper, by Jeff Patten, contrasts two books by the same author:

I, Claudius and *Claudius the God*

In 1934 Robert Graves published a rather lengthy book of historical fiction entitled *I, Claudius.* The novel was written in such a manner as to have the reader believe it was an autobiography of the Roman Emperor Tiberius Claudius Drusus Nero Germanicus. *I, Claudius* takes the reader from the Emperor's earliest childhood remembrances up to the year 41 AD, when he became Emperor of the Roman Empire. It is there, minutes after Claudius's ascent to the throne, that the book ends.

This abrupt ending seemed to demand a sequel, and in 1935 Graves published *Claudius the God.* This second "autobiographical novel" chronicled the life of Claudius from his ascent to the throne to his murder. Although each of the novels was written about the same person, by the same author, there are few similarities. *I, Claudius* and *Claudius the God* seem similar only in the basic form in which they are written. They differ in readability, style, and entertainment value.

The two books resemble each other only in narrative autobiographical form. The reader experiences the life of ancient Rome, narrated through the thoughts and words of the Emperor Claudius. Graves has an almost mystical way of making the reader feel as if the Emperor Claudius had penned the words himself. The novels provide accounts of the seedy, scandalous lives of the ruling Caesars. Greek and Latin phrases reveal careful research. The historical accuracy makes the novels seem authentic.

There the resemblance ends. *I, Claudius* is an easily read, thoroughly engrossing book. Readers receive the impression of a smooth, flowing manuscript. They are led chronologically, with a few pauses for reflection, through the turmoil and pageantry of the Roman Empire and its rulers. *Claudius the God*, however, is a rather choppy, disjointed work. Readers are required to leap from one story line to another with little or no hint of a chronological advance. One can only speculate as to the reason. Yet one thing is certain. The readability and style of *I, Claudius* are far superior to its sequel.

Style is a significant difference between the two novels. Although both manuscripts were thoroughly researched, the historical data are presented in two very different ways. In *I, Claudius* the facts are colorful; the pompous and elegant lives of the ruling class make for fascinating reading. In contrast, the facts presented in *Claudius the God* seem dry and mundane; furthermore, the story line makes for dull reading.

The net result of these differences makes the books unequal in entertainment value. *I, Claudius*, whatever its historical worth, is a very good story. Even readers who ordinarily do not enjoy histories or autobiographies will likely enjoy this novel because it is so entertaining. The sequel, however, is a chore to read—much like reading a history textbook.

If it were not for the many weaknesses of *Claudius the God*, the set would make worthwhile reading. Robert Graves's prowess as a poet and distinguished writer shines brightly in his first novel, but fails miserably in the second.

Questions for Discussion

1. Why do you think Jeff spent two paragraphs on the introduction?
2. How are the two novels alike? How are they different?
3. What method of organization does Jeff use?
4. How would you characterize the tone of Jeff's essay?
5. Comment on the conclusion.

Like Jeff Patten, Melissa Baker looks at works of fiction, but she focuses on similarities:

Journeys with Ayla and Arthur

One good book is a pleasure; two good books are a treasure. Two series of books that are consistently good throughout are a miracle. Yet Jean Auel and Douglas Adams have performed these miracles. Auel's series, *Earth's Children*, set in prehistoric Europe, and Adams's series, *The Hitchhiker's Guide to the Galaxy*, set in outer space, are both interesting and entertaining from the first book to the last. The characters in both series are fascinating even when they have a lesson to impart. Despite obvious differences, the two series have much in common.

Jean Auel's continuing saga is a trilogy: *The Clan of the Cave Bear, The Valley of the Horses*, and *The Mammoth Hunters*. Auel tells the story of Ayla, her heroine, from age five until adulthood. The character is so well drawn that readers empathize with her. Auel's visual details are equally vivid. Readers not only feel what Ayla feels, but also see what she sees. Reading this series is almost like living it. Readers may become so absorbed in the story that they are surprised and disappointed to find themselves in the modern world when they put the book down.

Douglas Adams's science fiction series, containing four books—*The Hitchhiker's Guide to the Galaxy; The Restaurant at the End of the Universe; Life, the Universe, and Everything;* and *Thanks for All the Fish*—may be disconcerting to the uninitiated, but typical of Adams's tongue-in-cheek, absorbing style.

Arthur Dent is Adams's somewhat reluctant hero. Adams begins Arthur's story when the hero is almost thirty years old, but after Arthur and the readers take off on their joy ride through the universe, time has no meaning. The quirky qualities of Adams's main character bring him to life. One of those quirks is his not enjoying the adventures as much as the readers do. Even though some of the characters and situations are bizarre and sometimes outrageously funny, Adams makes them ring true. The reader cannot wait to get to the next planet.

So what can a prehistoric woman and a twentieth-century space traveler have in common? Surprisingly, their stories are alike in many ways. Ayla and Arthur are both homeless. Ayla's home is destroyed by a natural disaster, while Arthur's is destroyed by an unnatural disaster. After losing their homes, both set out on daunting journeys, knowing they can never go back. Ayla's journey takes her into the vast empty spaces of prehistoric Europe; Arthur's takes him into the emptiness of outer space.

During their travels both main characters meet many different people, although the people Ayla meets are not quite as unusual as those Arthur meets. Even though these people are miles and planets apart, they possess many of the same human frailties. Both Ayla and Arthur encounter prejudice, avarice, tyranny, and jealousy. Learning to deal with these problems helps them (and the readers) on their own journeys.

Readers who would like to learn about prehistoric life or to speculate about the future and space travel will be apt to find Auel's or Adams's extraordinary series of novels highly enjoyable.

Questions for Discussion

1. How does the organization of Melissa's essay differ from the organization of the previous two?

2. Melissa uses a question as a transitional device. Can you find it?

3. Can you find an example of rhyme?

4. Can you find an example of alliteration in the description of Arthur Dent?

5. What else do you notice about this essay?

Summary

Comparison and contrast are useful wherever you go. They are used at home and in the workplace, in business and other professional writing as well as literary publications.

Your paper of comparison or contrast should have a specific purpose. Writing a purpose statement will help you to narrow the topic and focus your details. Transitions to indicate similarities and differences are especially important to help readers keep on track. Three common pitfalls to avoid are (1) stating the obvious, (2) trite expressions, and (3) hasty generalizations. Readers prefer fresh comparisons and vivid, accurate details. Using an analogy can help readers understand a difficult concept. Prewriting details in parallel lists will save you time. After that you can classify details into main points and write a thesis.

The block and alternating methods are two basic organizational strategies. The block method is suitable for easily retained material. The alternating method is better for complex material. Physical description requires concrete details for clarity. Transition between groups of details alerts the reader to shifts of meaning.

Take care in organizing and developing your introduction, body, and conclusion. Check your main points to be sure they are parallel. Your conclusion should contribute a sense of completeness.

Key Terms

comparison	analogy
contrast	block method
purpose statement	alternating method
hasty generalization	

Test Yourself

Selecting a Topic for Comparison

Directions: Read the titles below. Judge whether or not the topics would be suitable for a 500-word paper of comparison. In the blanks write "S" for *suitable* or "U" for *unsuitable*.

_____ 1. The courage of my two grandmothers

_____ 2. Two men

_____ 3. Two pets: Dillard Duck and Tom Terrapin

_____ 4. Good and evil

_____ 5. Tipping versus nontipping

Practice

Ideas for Writing

Directions: Select a topic from the list below (or one of your own) to contrast in a paragraph. Prewrite by making parallel lists of details.

1. Two brands of jeans
2. Two kinds of cereal
3. Two hamburgers
4. Two bars of bath soap
5. Two brands of frozen pizza
6. Two kinds of french fries

Test Yourself Answers

1. *S*
2. *U (too broad)*
3. *U (Ducks should not be compared to turtles—different categories.)*
4. *U (To narrow this topic, two literary characters could be specified.)*
5. *U (This topic would result in a paper of argument, not comparison or contrast.)*

Fifty Ideas for Comparison or Contrast Papers

1. Two films with a similar theme
2. Two songs
3. Two short stories with similar plots but interesting differences
4. Two very different poems on the same subject

5. Two books on the same topic
6. Two special people or characters
7. A person compared to a literary character
8. An owner's view of a property and a bank appraiser's view
9. Two presidents
10. Two heirlooms
11. Two unusual restaurants
12. Two microcomputers
13. Two favorite baseball pitchers
14. Two athletes in the same sport
15. Two football teams
16. Two favorite vacation spots
17. Two unusual friends
18. Two neighborhoods
19. Two roller coasters
20. Two cars
21. A baseball team that went from the cellar to the top
22. Life before and after losing weight
23. Life before and after having children
24. Life before and after college
25. Life before and after . . .
26. Opposing views on U.S. military intervention
27. Life before and after an unsettling experience
28. Changes in attitude, thinking, or behavior
29. Two grandparents
30. Two teachers
31. Two television shows
32. Two talk-show hosts
33. Two celebrations of a holiday
34. Two types of commercials
35. Two very different bosses
36. Two news commentators
37. Till versus no-till farming
38. Drivers in the United States and drivers in Italy
39. Two versions of an accident

40. A man's view of incidents of touching in the workplace versus a woman's
41. Writing styles of two science fiction writers
42. Two people who have influenced my life
43. Styles of two comedians
44. Two singers or musicians
45. Expectations of an event as opposed to what actually happened
46. Changes in lifestyle
47. Two ways of coping with manipulative criticism
48. Training procedures at two restaurants
49. Safety procedures at two places I have worked
50. Two dress codes

CHAPTER 16

Definition

Explaining What Something Is

> *The beginning of wisdom is the definition of terms.*
> —Socrates (470–399 BC)

Clarity is crucial in oral and written communication on the job—not only to prevent red ink, but also to protect people's lives. Unfamiliar terms can lead to confusion, error, or harm. Definition at the right time can dissolve misunderstanding and promote safety. Definition is useful in college, too. Clear, specific definitions can improve your grades on exams as well as on papers. An instructor may ask questions such as "Can you define irony?" "What is 'tool steel'?" or "What is the essence of the accounting principle of materiality?"

Yet the answers beginning writers commonly give are vague descriptions, not clear definitions. Learning to write clear definitions will sharpen your thinking and help you be more precise and accurate in your word choice. This chapter explains both formal sentence definition and extended definition.

FORMAL SENTENCE DEFINITION

Providing a formal sentence definition on the spur of the moment is not easy. For example, a writing instructor had just explained formal sentence definitions to his freshman composition class. He turned to a student who seemed half asleep and said, "Brad, will you please define *mammal* for me?"

Suddenly awake, the student stammered, "Er . . . a mammal is hairy; uh . . . it has a hard skeleton and provides milk."

With a twinkle in his eye, the instructor replied, "So far, you have not ruled out the coconut."

220

A formal sentence definition is a complete sentence that classifies something and then differentiates it from other members of its class. A formal sentence definition, which is more complete than a fragmentary dictionary definition, has four parts:

1. The term to be defined
2. A *be* verb—usually *is* or *are*
3. The classification (genus, class, or species)
4. The distinguishing features or characteristics

Below are two illustrations of the parts of a formal sentence definition:

Term	*Verb*	*Classification*	*Distinguishing Features*
A pelican	is	a large, web-footed water bird	with a distensible pouch hanging from its bill for catching and storing fish.
Lynxes	are	a species of wildcat in the Northern Hemisphere	which has a very short tail; tufted, tapering ears; and a ruff on each side of the face.

Although some formal sentence definitions contain more information than others, only enough information to distinguish the object being defined from other members of its class is necessary. For example, there are many water birds with webbed feet, but only the pelican has a distensible pouch hanging beneath its bill. There are several species of wildcat in the Northern Hemisphere, but only the lynx has the slender tufted ears, unusual ruff, and very short tail.

To write a formal sentence definition about any concrete term, you might find these questions helpful:

1. What distinguishing features do all items in the class have?
2. How can similar items be ruled out?
3. What purpose or function does the item serve?

To practice writing formal sentence definitions, start with a familiar object such as an *apple*. First, consider what category an apple belongs to (fruit) and then how apples are unlike other members of the category such as plums, pears, and peaches. Next, think about the characteristics all apples have in common. To be complete, include all four parts of a formal sentence definition:

Term	*Verb*	*Classification*	*Distinguishing Features*
An apple	is	a _____	_____

An apple is a fruit, of course, but you might be more precise by stating the purpose it serves: An apple is an edible fruit. You can be even more specific by giving its taxonomic category, the rose family. At first you may jot down characteristics such as red and round. (Are apples actually round?) After you finish your definition of an apple, see the example at the end of the chapter.

There are two precautions to observe when writing formal sentence definitions. First, avoid defining a term by repeating the term or using a derivation.

Avoid: A keystone is the key stone in an arch.

Instead: A keystone is the central wedge-shaped piece at the top of an arch that holds the other stones in place.

Also avoid using the phrase "is when" or "is where" in a definition, which results in an ungrammatical construction.

Avoid: A greenbelt *is where* a band of parks, farmland, or unused land surrounds a community.

Instead: A greenbelt *is* a band of parks, farmland, or unused land surrounding a community.

EXTENDED DEFINITION

Extended definitions explore the meanings of words or phrases more fully than formal sentence definitions through explanation, description, example, anecdote, comparison, and so forth. In an extended definition, you may discuss physical features, causes, effects, influences, or changes in meaning. The goal of a paper of extended definition is to explain a term or concept clearly in an *original* way.

You can often develop a paper of definition primarily with material drawn from your own experience, although you may wish to consult dictionaries, thesauruses, or books of quotations. These reference books will help you gather ideas and find a focus for your paper. Dictionary definitions are usually unnecessary in extended definitions. *Include a dictionary definition only for a justifiable reason:* if the audience might be unclear about a denotative meaning or if you are contrasting definitions.

As you gather ideas, keep in mind that dictionaries have strict limits on space. Although they can clearly define concrete words in a short entry, they necessarily omit the subtleties of abstract words. And since dictionaries cannot keep pace with the flood of new words, some recently coined words or phrases, although commonly used, are not listed. For example, can you find the much touted term "family values" in your dictionary?

Sources will not give you all the answers. You need to go beyond them, to think about other meanings a word may have acquired and to define concepts in an original way. Talking to others is often a good way to clarify nuances of words.

PITFALLS TO AVOID IN
EXTENDED DEFINITION

Typical pitfalls in definition include use of unnecessary definitions and commonplace information, stereotyping, and overstatement. Any definition should be used for a genuine purpose, not to fill space. Multiple dictionary definitions are necessary only when distinctions in meaning need to be clarified. The writer who presents information readily available to the public risks boring or antagonizing the reader. Readers often become impatient with old information unless it is a favorite story that merits retelling or a universal truth skillfully presented.

Stale: Growing old is a fear of many people. Many people believe they are old when they turn forty.

Fresh: When my fortieth birthday tiptoed in one chilly October morning, I glanced in the bathroom mirror and suddenly felt old.

Stereotypes injure a writer's credibility. Perceptive readers dismiss sweeping generalizations; they want the truth, not distortions. In the student examples below, can you spot stereotypes and problems in logic?

- The elderly lead lonely, secluded lives, crisscrossed with financial worries.
- A mother's desired end is handling her three jobs well: housewife, mother, and career.

In addition to stereotyping, both of these sentences overstate. Not all elderly people fit this pigeonhole. Not all mothers desire a career. Effective writers qualify generalizations and identify opinions, perceptions, and inferences. Common overstatement includes all-or-none claims that lack support, as in the following bloopers:

"Friends are forever." (Question: Do all friends last a lifetime?)

"Success is defined in as many different ways as there are people on earth." (Question: Does no one agree with anyone else?)

Another pitfall of extended definitions is the tendency some students have to become so enamored of the quotations they find that they plaster their papers with them. Keep in mind that the purpose of a paper of extended definition is for *you* to define the concept according to your own experiences and beliefs. Any quotations you use should support your ideas, not the reverse. And when you use quotations, make sure that you don't simply plop them on the page, expecting the reader to somehow bridge the gaps in thought; use transitional phrases carefully to link the quotation to the text.

When using quotations, you are required to (1) indicate that they are quotations by enclosing short quotations with quotation marks or indent long quotations and (2) give proper credit to your sources. Check with your instructor for his or her preferred format for documenting sources. You may also consult chapters 22 and 23.

WRITING A PAPER OF EXTENDED DEFINITION

Selecting a Topic and Prewriting

To learn as much as possible from writing a definition paper, select an abstract term for the subject. What do you feel strongly about? How does this topic relate to you? How does it affect your principles and values? How much support can you provide for your thesis? You will be wise to sidestep Herculean topics such as "time" and "democracy" that are very broad. If you choose a term you have learned in another class, be careful that you do not merely summarize other people's ideas; make the term your own. If you are unable to find a topic, try scanning the suggestions at the end of this chapter. Perhaps they will stimulate an idea or two.

Narrow your topic so that it can be covered adequately in the assignment. For instance, the topic of "discrimination" would be too broad. You would need to limit it to one type, such as "discrimination against short people." One student defined "prejudice against short men." He gave examples of how he copes with shortness through elevator shoes, hairstyles, and dress. Then he explained how these changes have improved his life and gained him respect. If you select a quality such as "professionalism," you might narrow it to professionalism for a paralegal (or whatever field you are in).

Once you have narrowed your topic, do some prewriting to come up with examples, stories, comparisons, cause-and-effect factors, changes in meaning, and so forth. The technique of clustering, discussed in chapter 2, is particularly helpful for prewriting about an abstract concept.

Consulting Sources

Before or after prewriting, consult two or three large dictionaries to discover what they say about your topic. You may find specific details and ideas you can use in your paper. If possible, also consult the unabridged *Oxford English Dictionary*, a set of twelve volumes (with supplements) which traces the history of words introduced into the English language since AD 1150. There you may find an unusual detail to serve as an attention-getter for your introduction. Or you might trace the history of a word whose meaning has changed during your lifetime, your parents', or your grandparents'. Or you might trace a relatively new word, one that originated in the twentieth century. For such papers, you might also interview people of various ages to gain insights about the connotations that have been attached to the word.

Other places to mine ideas are books of quotations. *Bartlett's Familiar Quotations, The Quotable Woman,* a Bible with a concordance, and similar references are quick and easy to use. In copying down material, be sure to set it off with quotation marks. Copy the page number, name of the author, and source to save a frantic search later.

Organizing a Paper of Definition

To organize your paper, first consider the rhetorical situation. Then devise an organizational strategy that is appropriate for your purpose and audience, possibly chronological order, order of importance, level of generality, or another order. (You may want to refer to chapter 3, which explains seven common orders.)

For your reference, here are three sample scratch outlines arranged according to order of importance:

Professionalism at a Golf Club

a. Ethics = respect

b. Customer service

c. Accuracy of records

d. Dress of personnel

Stress in Nursing

a. Too little time

b. Patient pressure

c. Dealing with death

My Procrastination

a. Examples: Cause

b. Effects

c. How I am overcoming

Drafting an Introduction

Opening with a quotation is one of the easiest ways for a beginning writer to achieve a polished introduction. A relevant quotation can set the tone and indicate the direction of a paper. When separated from the introduction, the quotation receives special attention and announces the topic. The quotations that open the chapters of this book show how to format and document a quotation that precedes your main text. Notice that because the quotations are indented and set apart from the text, quotation marks are not needed. The author's name appears beneath the quotation. Inclusion of the source is optional. Include dates of works written *before* the twentieth century. (Dates of works written in the twentieth century are omitted.)

To forge a link from an introductory quotation to the text of your paper, you need embedded transition in the first sentence of the text. Repeating a key term from the quotation or using a synonym or related word in an early sentence will establish a clear link. The objective is to be subtle. A direct reference, unless cleverly done, can mar the opening and stamp the work as that of an amateur. With a little thought, you can avoid a *weak* transition, such as "The quote . . . ," "In this quotation . . . ," "As stated in the quotation above . . . ," or "I think the above quotation means. . . ."

In the following example, the student writer (who prefers to remain anonymous) uses an embedded transition in her first sentence. A synonym (*alcoholism*) echoes a word in the quotation (*drunkenness*). (Note, too, that the first sentence here is a formal sentence definition.)

Living with an Alcoholic

Drunkenness . . . spoils health,
dismounts the mind, and unmans men.
                    —William Penn

Alcoholism is a disease caused by continual heavy drinking of alcoholic beverages. In the acute and chronic stages, alcoholism consists of symptoms ranging from the obvious to the obscure. Usually, it is not difficult to recognize a person who is inebriated; generally, staggering and slurring of speech are apparent. Accompanying neurological disorders such as tremors (shakes), hallucinations, and seizures are easily discerned. Hidden to the naked eye is the damage endured by the liver, stomach, and pancreas. Not only is excessive drinking devastating to the physical and mental health of the alcoholic, but it is also devastating to the alcoholic's family.

Living for eighteen years with my father, who was a severe alcoholic, was much like living with Dr. Jekyll and Mr. Hyde. The alcohol would turn my kindhearted, loving father into a brutal, hateful monster. Because of my father's unpredictable behavior, high anxiety and fear were normal, everyday emotions for me.

Did you notice that the first paragraph is written in *third* person? The writer gives general background information before narrowing the topic to the alcoholic's family. In the second paragraph, she shifts to *first* person because it reveals specific details about her life. See how she eases the jump from third person to first with a gerund phrase ("Living . . . with my father").

Did you note the simile in the second paragraph? The phrase "like living with Dr. Jekyll and Mr. Hyde" not only sets up a striking comparison but also establishes a natural relationship with "unmans the man" in the opening quotation.

Developing an Extended Definition

The heart of any good piece of writing is vivid imagery. Concrete details and action verbs make writing come alive. Depending on the subject and purpose, a paper of extended definition may be developed by almost any strategy or combination of strategies—description, comparison, narration, examples, or explanation, for instance. There are five basic techniques for developing an extended definition.

Operational Definition   To define an operation, the writer tells (a) what the object being defined does, (b) how it works, and (c) the basic principle underlying its performance. For example, a one-sentence operational definition might state that a refrigerator is a mechanized box, powered by electricity or gas, that circulates coolant to a condenser to chill food, medicines, or other items. An expanded operational definition would explain in detail how a refrigerator works. Operational definitions are often used in technical writing.

Defining by Comparison   Comparison is useful for explaining abstractions, such as emotions. If you can find an object to compare an idea or emotion to, then this technique will help to clarify your definition. In the following example, Marjorie Holmes begins with concrete images before going to abstract feelings:

> What feeling is so nice as a child's hand in yours? [It is] so small, so soft and warm like a kitten huddling in the shelter of your clasp. A child's hand in yours— what tenderness it arouses, what power it conjures up. You are instantly the very touchstone of wisdom and strength.

Defining by Synonym   In defining by synonym, a writer provides another word or phrase that has the same meaning. The synonym can be included either in parentheses or as an appositive:

> Rocky Collins will fight F. G. Jones for the bantamweight (112 to 118 pounds) world title.

> At one time many people believed that human intelligence could be judged by phrenology, the study of the shape of the skull.

Defining by Negation   Another effective technique of definition is *negation* (contrast). Using this technique, the writer tells what the term is not. In a paper entitled "Fear of Failure," Phyllis Parks uses negation in her opening sentence:

> Failure is not a pretty word. The very mention of it creates images and feelings of someone who is inept and incompetent.
> The word itself strikes fear in my heart. Sometimes my life has seemed as though it has been one failure after another. But with time has come an appreciation for the value of failure.

In an essay called "Pioneers: A View of Home," poet Nikki Giovanni begins her definition of *home* by explaining what she thinks a home is *not:*

> Home is not the place where our possessions and accomplishments are deposited and displayed. It is this earth that we have explored, the heavens we view with awe, these humans who, despite their flaws, we try to love and those who try to love us.

Weaving Example with Explanation   A lone example without interpretation may be of little use to readers. You cannot assume that every reader will see the connection you intend. You need to link the example to the main idea and comment appropriately. Chris Layman, a student writer, first uses negation. Then he weaves example with explanation in an extended definition of honesty:

> "Do as I say, not as I do," my parents would often say as I was growing up. However, admonitions such as this often fade from the mind, whereas examples form lasting impressions. As children grow they need models to follow. They need to determine how they will live their lives, what their values will be, and how they will treat other people. A father is a model that his children depend on to learn how to act within their society and to form their own set of values.
>
> Recently, my young son and I were in a store when he noticed a $100 bill lying on the floor. I had always told my son to be honest; now I could show him what honesty meant. Together we went to the store manager and put the money in his care, hoping the rightful owner would return to claim it. This incident allowed me to act as a role model for my son, and it set an example I hope he will follow throughout his life.

Weaving in Dictionary Definitions   If a dictionary definition is necessary in your paper, you can easily identify the copied material by using quotations marks and by identifying the source. The three examples that follow will not be suitable for every writing situation, but you can adapt them to fit your paper if appropriate.

> Although *Webster's College Dictionary* defines _____ as the "_____," this definition does not. . . .

> According to *Webster's New World Dictionary*, _____ is "_____," but that definition does not. . . .

> Meanings can change over time. The first edition of *The American Heritage Dictionary* defines _____ as "_____." The third edition, however, has added another meaning: "_____" We might go beyond these to say. . . .

To weave other types of quotations into the text of your paper, see "Weaving Quotations into the Text" in chapter 23.

Writing a Conclusion

A conclusion for a paper of definition should be brief and appropriate. One way to end is with a formal sentence definition. Another is to allude to an opening quotation. A third way is to summarize changes and end on a positive note.

Closing with a Formal Sentence Definition   Debby Ketcham concludes her paper with a formal sentence definition. The definition is followed by a sentence of summary and another of comment:

> Finally, poise is an inner mental balance, the ability to face new situations calmly, to hold one's temper, to cope with stress, and to deal with embarrassment. All these

situations require a control over emotion and the ability to present a calm, tactful, polite manner. Poise is truly a valuable trait.

Alluding to an Opening Quotation   A reference to the beginning creates an "echo ending" and establishes closure. Using this technique, Penny Amrine repeated parts of a quotation by Joseph Conrad in her conclusion. In the last sentence she provides a formal sentence definition:

> My loneliness did indeed wear a "mask." For months I had endured its "naked terror" without being able to identify its misleading appearance. Loneliness for me was life without intimate friends and relatives to lean on for love and companionship.

Another student writer, Nancy O'Hanlon, refers to her opening quotation in a different way. Smoothly, she integrates quoted material into the first sentence of her conclusion:

> Like Emerson, I have learned that "worry is the form of interest you pay on trouble before it comes." Although I have not had many real troubles in my life, I still worry. But through reading and future experience, I hope to learn more about controlling worry.

Ending with a Personal Lesson   Those of us who successfully survive a painful experience often extract a lesson, a bit of wisdom. The student who wrote "Living with an Alcoholic" summarized her insights:

> Over the years I have tried to educate myself on alcoholism. Counseling has helped me to understand how alcoholism victimizes the entire family. Now, at age 33, I realize that despite how it seemed at the time, my father was only a human being who was consumed by a dread disease.

The last line reveals the writer's compassion as well as her intellectual and emotional growth since those early years of torment. The implicit note of forgiveness and the gentle tone provide a positive ending to a wrenching topic.

Revising a Paper of Definition

To revise a paper of extended definitions successfully, you need to examine its many facets. The checklist below will enable you to scrutinize individual aspects.

➤ *Checklist for Revising Extended Definitions*

1. Is the topic narrow enough to be defined in a short paper?
2. Will the introduction entice the interest of readers?
3. Have important terms been defined if they are apt to be unfamiliar to the average reader? Have terms with more than one possible meaning been explained fully?

4. Do formal sentence definitions (if any) conform to the standard four-part format? Do the distinguishing characteristics included apply only to the subject of the definition?

5. Is there any unnecessary definition, particularly too much from dictionaries? Has too much commonplace information already familiar to most readers been provided?

6. Have stereotypes and overstatement been avoided?

7. Has the extended definition been fully developed? Might more examples, comparisons, anecdotes, or other details be included?

8. Have quotations been kept to a minimum? Are all quotations worked smoothly into the text so that their point in the paper is clear? Has proper credit been given to the original source in each case?

9. Does the paper have a clear pattern of organization? If not, would order of importance or some other order be appropriate?

10. Is the closing effective?

TWO SAMPLE PAPERS OF DEFINITION

Jeannine Caudill talked to her friends before she wrote the following paper, which is based on their experience as well as hers. Skillfully, she states several generalizations that are axioms (universal truths). Three questions begin her introduction.

Mother Love

Love cannot be forced, love cannot be
coaxed and teased. It comes out of
Heaven, unasked and unsought.
                    —Pearl Buck

What is mother love? Is it a feeling, an emotion, or the dedication of an entire lifetime? Is it bad or good, imaginary or genuine? One thing is certain; mother love is difficult to define, especially to those who have not experienced it. None of the dictionaries seem to think *mother* and *love* should be combined into the phrase *mother love*. Yet there is motherhood, mother lode, and motherland. Could any of these words be more fitting to combine with *mother* than the word *love*?

Psychiatrists define mother love, doctors prescribe it, lawyers divide it, children bask or drown in it, and fathers observe it. Perhaps even a mother cannot define it, but some still try. Love as only a mother can feel begins for some women with the first knowledge of pregnancy. For others, it comes with beholding the charm of their own soft, sweet-smelling baby. The baby does not have to be beautiful to inspire great love. Perhaps mother love at this stage of life is a myriad of feelings: infant dependency, mother's pride of accomplishment, and primitive emotions that have been basic to the human race since its beginning. Whatever the reasons, loving a baby seems very easy.

The real growth of mother love begins later. Much of the time during a child's life, no one seems to love him or her except the mother. True mother love develops over many years and through many trials. When a toddler throws a fit in a store, shouts a loud "No," or dampens a neighbor's carpet, mother love is put to a test. But even in this stage, the child is very appealing to her. Here a new facet of love begins, pride in the child's independence.

The early school years strain the most patient mother. After the thumb-sucking, leg-hugging, insecure years come the years of grade cards, teacher conferences, show and tell, and four hundred papers to be praised and hung up.

Many older mothers say to younger mothers, "If you think things are bad now, just wait till he's a teenager!" But the young mothers often counter with "Nothing could be worse." This lack of foresight must be a tool of Mother Nature. Otherwise, only the very brave would dare to have a child.

Mother love seems never to end. It usually begins with the birth of a child and continues to encircle and entwine the mother's heart down through the years. Strangely enough, the only person who can appreciate the real meaning of mother love is a mother.

Questions for Discussion

1. What do you notice about Jeannine's introduction?
2. Examine the first sentence of the second paragraph. What do you notice about the sentence structure?
3. Do Jeannine's examples ring true? Why or why not?
4. What does she do before she comments?
5. How would you describe the tone of the essay?

In the following paper, Ron Willetts cites a dictionary definition and parts of speech for *work* for a significant reason: He expands upon its meanings as a noun and as a verb. In the first main point, he uses narration and explanation to illustrate his early view of work. He defines later views by explanation, associations, and examples.

Changes in My View of Work

My friend there is a Hell . . . when a man has a family to support, has his health, and is ready to work, and there is no work to do. When he stands with empty hands and sees his children going hungry, his wife without the things to do with. I hope you never have to try it.

—Louis L'Amour

The *Oxford American Dictionary* defines work as a noun that means "Use of bodily or mental power in order to do or make something, especially as contrasted with play or recreation." Work is also defined as a verb: "to perform work, to be engaged in bodily or mental activity." Over the years I gradually learned to understand these concepts, but only when I became unemployed for an extended period did I understand L'Amour's definition.

When I was very young, work was not a verb, it was a noun, a place to go and a place to leave. My grandfather would come home from work in the evenings, and we would go through a ritual. As he drove his truck into the garage, I would be waiting. He would pick me up, and somewhere between the truck and the house, I would remove the hat from his head and transfer it to mine. Once inside, he would place his dinner bucket on a chair, and I would rummage through it for the leftover cookie, banana, or candy bar that was always there. At that time in my life, I did not have to worry; all my needs were taken care of.

When I became a young adult, the word *work* took on a new meaning. It was not only a noun, but suddenly a verb, a task to be performed for which one received some form of remuneration. This definition began to form when I was in the eleventh grade and began helping the janitors after school during basketball season. For sweeping the classrooms and dusting the teachers' desks, I received a modest sum and attended the home games at no cost. Thus work became associated with money. And money became closely associated with girls, cars, entertainment, and other necessities. At this time, work was a necessary evil, for it took time away from my social life.

When I became older, I found the word *work* had to be redefined once again. Along with being a place to go and an activity to perform, work became a goal. This new meaning became associated with other words such as wife, insurance, children, house, and friends. Between 1965 and 1988, work was no problem for me. If I changed jobs, the longest period of unemployment was two days. Once I quit one job on Friday and started a new one the following Monday.

In 1988, however, the story changed. Due to economic conditions, I became unemployed after working at a company for fifteen years. That company and my coworkers were as much a part of my life as my own family. I felt rejected and depressed. The severance pay ran out. The unemployment benefits were exhausted. The retirement fund vanished, and the bills began to pile up. I was no longer able to provide for my family. But then I thanked God we were living in modern times when it was acceptable for a married woman to work. Although my wife's income did not pay all the bills, it did allow us to feed the family and keep the electricity turned on.

Being unemployed for over two years creates a situation that at times is almost unbearable. Perhaps the worst part is being told that one cannot be hired because he is overqualified and undereducated. Being told that one could perform the task, but would not be satisfied with the job is enough to make a person ill. A man needs to be able to provide for his family.

Yes, my friend, there is a hell—I know, for I have been there. It is my sincere hope that I am the last person that has to define the lack of work as hell.

Questions for Discussion

1. Discuss the use of the dictionary definition in the introduction. Would the paper have been as effective without it? Why or why not?

2. Briefly summarize the changes in Ron's viewpoint.

3. What causes are specified?

4. Discuss the effectiveness of this ending. What device does he use?

Key Terms

formal sentence definition   negation
extended definition   allusion
operational definition

Summary

The general purpose of any definition is to explain and clarify. Clear definition is needed to forestall misunderstanding and mistakes. Formal sentence definitions are one-sentence definitions with four parts: the term, a *be* verb, the classification, and features that distinguish the subject from other members of the class. Extended definitions are explanations that may include description, comparison, anecdotes, reasons, examples, or formal definitions.

There are four common pitfalls in definition: unnecessary definition, repeating common information unnecessarily, stereotyping, and overstatement. Keeping a specific audience in mind will help to dodge these pitfalls.

Writing a paper of extended definition requires that you narrow the topic and draw from personal experience. You may also consult sources for definitions or opening quotations. You can develop the paper by using any of five techniques: operational definition, comparison, synonym, negation, or weaving example with explanation. Arrange the details and examples in a clear, logical order suitable for the purpose and audience.

To conclude a paper of extended definition, you might end with an original formal sentence definition, allude to an opening quotation, or extract a personal lesson or bit of wisdom.

Practice

Collaborative Exercise: Discerning Genuine Definitions

Directions: Identify the satisfactory definitions in the list below and mark with an *S.* Mark the others unsatisfactory with a *U.* Discuss why they are unsatisfactory. (You may consult a dictionary.)

1. A sprinkling can is a utensil that is not a bucket, dishpan, or bowl.
2. A cut is when you slash open the skin.
3. A book is like a little golden door to opportunity.
4. A daffodil is a bulbous cultivated plant that usually has a yellow or white flower with a trumpet.
5. Honey is a sweet gooey substance that is delicious on breakfast cereal.
6. "Monopoly" is a table game that resembles life because you trade, buy, and sell.

7. *Morale* refers to the condition of the spirits of individuals or employees.

8. The ruffed grouse, sometimes called "partridge" or "pheasant," is a North American game bird with spotted brown feathers.

9. Gelatin is a clear quivery substance, made in various colors.

10. A dandelion is a small edible weed with fuzzy yellow flowers and saw-toothed leaves.

11. Dissatisfied means not content.

12. Friendship is that which you experience with a friend.

13. Love is a flame that blazes in the heart.

14. Empathy is as refreshing as pure cold water from a spring.

15. A fruitcake is a cake that contains fruit.

16. The gemsbok of southern Africa is an antelope with long, sharp, straight horns.

17. A suitcase has a handle and is used to carry clothing.

18. Used for timber, the Douglas fir is a tall evergreen tree with short needles and egg-shaped cones.

19. A vacation is where you tire yourself out having fun so that you are glad to go home and go to work.

20. Poetry is the ultimate linguistic expression.

Collaborative Writing: Formal Sentence Definition

1. Appoint a recorder to jot down the comments of the group. Define one of the terms below in a formal sentence definition.

   dog   cow   cucumber   chair   couch

2. Ask each other questions to limit the term and identify the essential features. For example:
   a. How does a dog differ from a wolf or coyote?
   b. What kind of dog? Prairie dog? Wild dog? What?
   c. What is the purpose of the dog?

   (*Note:* You may want to limit the term to watch dog, police dog, Seeing Eye dog, hunting dog, or other kind of dog.)

3. Finally, revise the definition so that it reads smoothly.

4. Repeat the procedure, using another term.

Ideas for Formal Sentence Definition

Directions: Write a formal sentence definition or a paragraph that includes a formal sentence definition. Select a concrete word from the list below or use one of your own.

oranges   ballpoint pen   drum   turnips   plums

Practice Sentence Definition: Possible Answer

An apple is an edible fruit of the rose family that can be red, yellow, green, or multicolored; when mature, the small seeds are encased in a core connected to a flexible stem at the top and the blossom end.

Forty Ideas For Papers of Definition

1. What is marriage?
2. Appreciation
3. Compassion
4. Responsibility
5. Professionalism
6. Enthusiasm
7. Emotional security
8. A family value
9. What is the "positive attitude" that employers seek?
10. Procrastination
11. Honesty
12. Attitude: Victim or winner?
13. Self-discipline
14. Ethics for the nurse (or other professional)
15. Fear of . . .
16. Self-acceptance
17. What is integrity?
18. Jealousy/envy
19. Loyalty
20. What is an education?
21. Satisfaction
22. Ambition
23. Maturity
24. What is customer service?
25. What is patriotism?
26. What is empathy?
27. Discrimination (What kind?)
28. What is a stepmother/stepfather?
29. Anger

30. Harassment on the job
31. Stress on the job
32. Prejudice
33. Embarrassment
34. Optimism
35. What does a college degree really mean?
36. Trust
37. Impulsiveness
38. Forgiveness
39. Wisdom
40. Freedom (What kind or kinds?)

CHAPTER 17

Cause and Effect

Explaining Why

Our least deed, like the young of the land crab,
wends its way to the sea of cause and effect as soon
as born, and makes a drop there to eternity.

—Henry David Thoreau
Journal, March 14, 1838

Thoreau's observation reminds us that a single decision, action, or event can cause far-reaching effects. The relationship between cause and effect can be more intricate and extensive than we may imagine. Sometimes we lack complete information and see only part of an effect. Or we may assume a connection between two events where none exists. Other times we glimpse only *short-term effects* while significant *long-term effects* remain hidden for years. From our limited perspective in the present, we can only peer into the future. There is the ever present risk of blithely underestimating or disregarding the repercussions of certain acts and of making unwise decisions based on ill-founded predictions.

The greater your knowledge and insight, the more accurate your assessments and predictions will be. Causal analysis allows you to reflect on your experience and to learn from the past. With study and practice, you can improve your ability to analyze cause and effect. You can question dubious information and withhold judgment until adequate proof is available.

CAUSE-AND-EFFECT RELATIONSHIPS

The purpose of *causal analysis* is to determine whether or not a cause-and-effect relationship actually exists; and, if it does, precisely what it is. A *cause* influences or changes something or someone else. The resulting change is called

237

the *effect*. A causal analysis is an examination of effects with one or more causes or of conditions that may have contributed to an effect. In this chapter you will find suggestions to help you evaluate possible cause-and-effect relationships and to draft a paper of causal analysis. In a nutshell, you will be searching for answers to these questions:

- Did one event, condition, or situation lead to another?
- Was there more than one cause? More than one effect?
- How did the change occur?
- What was the effect or result?

Logical Principles of Cause-and-Effect Relationships

As you explore possible cause-and-effect connections, examine the logic of your conclusion or inference. Is it reasonable, sensible, and sound? To be valid, an analysis that claims causal relationships must be based on two logical standards:

Two Principles of Logic in Cause and Effect

1. The cause is able to produce the effect.
2. Other causes that might have produced the effect have been ruled out.

To establish that the two principles (standards) have been met, follow these four steps:

Steps in Causal Analysis

Step 1: Assess the conditions that existed.

Step 2: Ask whether or not these conditions could possibly have caused the results that have been assumed.

Step 3: Explore alternative explanations: What else might have happened?

Step 4: Try to determine whether or not there is actual proof that the cause produced the effect. If you cannot exclude all other possibilities, then the explanation remains an assumption.

For example, if you have a problem of quality control in spray painting automatic washers, you then explore all conditions that might have contributed to the effect. Has there been an atmospheric change that could have interfered with drying? Is there a mechanical defect somewhere? Or is the problem a result of human error? Could a combination of causes have produced the problem? Only after you have ruled out all other possibilities will you be able to pinpoint the cause(s).

When starting to analyze cause and effect, lay aside any preconceived notions. You might think of yourself as a detective who is objectively searching out the facts of a case. Adopt an attitude of "I really don't know" or "I'm not sure." If you formulate a theory, test it carefully. All the while, keep in mind the following basic principle: *Complex events, conditions, or situations seldom stem from a single cause*. Therefore, don't halt your search too soon. You may find more than one cause.

Two Fallacies to Avoid in Analyzing Cause and Effect

There are two fallacies of cause and effect: *non sequitur* and *post hoc*. A *non sequitur* is an assumption that is confused with fact. Often non sequiturs occur in predictions. For example, it was once widely said that "a Catholic will never be elected president." But John F. Kennedy became the first Roman Catholic president of the United States. (For a detailed explanation of non sequitur, see chapter 18.)

The *post hoc* fallacy occurs when chronology is mistaken for causation. One event happens soon after another; the first event is thought to have caused the second although it did not. There is no proof for the assumption. For instance, if you felt fine until two hours after you ate Aunt Tessie's crab cakes, you might assume they caused your illness. If several other family members experienced the same symptoms and all ate the crab cakes, then this suggests your theory might be true. But what else might have happened? The condition may have been a case of "stomach flu." Only an analysis by a reputable laboratory could be regarded as conclusive proof. If you wanted to be doubly sure, you could have two laboratories run the same test. If the crab cakes were innocent, then the conjecture was a post hoc fallacy. (See chapter 18.)

If we keep in mind that much of what we "know" is actually inference, value judgment, theory, or myth, we are more likely to pause and seek evidence before leaping to conclusions about why something happened.

WRITING A PAPER ANALYZING CAUSE AND EFFECT

Every time you inquire about *how* or *why* something happened, you begin causal analysis. A paper of causal analysis allows for a wide range of topics to be organized and developed in various ways.

Selecting a Topic and Prewriting

When you are looking for a writing topic, you might begin by thinking about subjects you are truly curious or concerned about, either because they affect you personally or because they affect your community. For example, "How are my new responsibilities at work affecting my home life?" "Why are there so many traffic accidents at the corner of Fifth Street and Delerue Avenue?" You might also consider topics of interest to people generally: "What are the positive and negative effects of fad diets?" Or you might look for topics where there might be disagreement: "Does liquor advertising seriously influence adolescents to start drinking?"

Once you've selected a topic, you take on the role of a detective, looking for clues. Putting yourself into this role should alert you to little details that could be significant and might be overlooked. Asking questions can be a powerful tool in prewriting:

1. What was the overall effect or result?
2. What conditions were present?
3. Did one event (or condition) really influence the event (or condition) that followed?
4. If so, what was the *extent of the influence?*
5. What else might have happened?
6. What was the probable cause?

Note that although these questions are phrased in the past tense, for some topics the *present* tense may be applicable: What *is* the effect or result?

As you think of possible answers, jot them down. Although you may find a wide array of clues, that does not mean you will find all of the evidence. Nor does it ensure that you will determine the extent of each factor's influence. Persist until you have examined all available clues from different angles.

Organizing a Cause-and-Effect Paper

Once you have examined your topic thoroughly, your next decision will be how to organize details. The big question is this: "What does the reader need to know?" Your answer will help you decide where the major emphasis will be and whether to start with the cause or the effect. Then set up a scratch outline in a way that seems logical. It will give you a trail to follow while drafting, and you can always revise if needed. To begin arranging your random notes from prewriting, consider the following questions:

• Was there a single cause and single effect? Or were several factors involved?
• Will the major emphasis be on the specific phenomenon (cause)? Or will it be on the consequence (effect)?
• What kind of order will be best?

Chronological order is often simplest and most efficient. This way you discuss the cause before the effect. Sometimes *reverse chronological order* is used with effect before cause. If you have multiple causes and/or multiple effects, you may need to organize your main points by order of importance. Several possible strategies are presented here. If one seems to fit your topic, adapt it as needed.

Outline A: Single Cause with Multiple Effects (chronological order)

Claim: High consumption of soft drinks containing sugar and caffeine contributes to overweight, health problems, and mild addiction.

 I. Introduction (specifies the cause): high consumption of soft drinks containing sugar and caffeine
 II. Body (order of importance)
   A. Describes/explains effect no. 1: overweight
   B. Describes/explains effect no. 2: health problems
   C. Describes/explains effect no. 3: mild addiction
III. Conclusion

Outline B: A Single Effect Produced by Multiple Causes (reverse chronological)

Claim: Many farmers in the South are diversifying crops to increase profits.

 I. Introduction (specifies the effect): Many farmers in the South are decreasing the acreage they formerly allotted to tobacco in favor of vegetable crops. Fresh produce supplied to urban markets yields more profits than tobacco.
 II. Body (order of importance)
   A. Cause no. 1: Nicotine has been identified as a cause of cancer.
   B. Cause no. 2: Many people have ceased smoking because of possible health hazards.
   C. Cause no. 3: Dim prospects for future tobacco markets.
   D. Cause no. 4: High prices of fresh produce promise lucrative returns.
III. Conclusion

If you discuss both multiple causes and multiple effects, you will need a more complex outline. The block or alternating method might be used, depending on the situation.

CASE STUDY

Lisa was walking within the pedestrian lane at a plant where she worked. A tow-truck driver failed to sound his horn, cut the corner too sharply, and knocked her down. Lisa was rushed to the hospital, where a leg fracture and numerous bruises were treated. A witness to the accident corroborated Lisa's report of what happened. Now you, the supervisor, have to record the accident, your follow-up, and recommendation. You might use the order shown in Outline C.

Outline C: Multiple Causes and Multiple Effects (block method)

I. Introduction: who, what, and where?

II. Body: Explanation of causes and effects (why)
   A. Causes
      1. Failure to sound horn
      2. Cutting corner too short
      3. Driving in the pedestrian lane
   B. Effects
      1. Knocked Lisa down on pavement
      2. Severe physical injuries
      3. Unable to work for several weeks
      4. Tow-truck driver cited for negligence and suspended one week.

III. Recommendations
   A. Transfer offender to line job if available or give further suspension as determined by the committee.
   B. More education and training in plant safety are needed for tow-truck drivers (purchase training videos).

Once in a while you may need to explain a *series* of interrelated events. To emphasize the chronology of each cause and its immediate effect, you could use an alternating method. In other words, cause and effect would alternate in pairs in chronological order.

Outline D: A Series of Events Linked to Each Other (alternating method)

I. Introduction: overview of causal relationship

II. Body (chronological order)
   A. Cause no. 1
   B. Effect no. 1
   C. Cause no. 2
   D. Effect no. 2 (continue as needed)

III. Conclusion

Drafting an Introduction

Your chief considerations in writing an introduction are to establish your topic and attract readers' interest. You might appeal to your readers' needs, possibly with an anecdote or other strategy to show how knowing about this cause-and-effect relationship could benefit them. Or you might suggest that the causes or effects will be surprising. Watch for a hook that will make your analysis of cause-and-effect meaningful for your readers.

As the preceding model outlines suggest, the introduction may take various forms, depending on the emphasis and kind of causal relationships. For example, you might begin with a *narrative*, possibly an eyewitness account of an accident, then go on to describe the cause and effect(s). Your thesis could then link the cause with the specific effects you will focus on.

Or you might open by describing a specific effect, showing why it is important or interesting to consider what caused it. You might explain the effect by classifying *examples* and presenting *illustrations*. Or you might provide an overview of the causal relationship, briefly presenting the links that the rest of your paper will explore. For example, you might *describe* the causes of a problem.

Developing a Paper Analyzing Cause and Effect

Your purpose will help you to devise a suitable writing strategy to develop your paper adequately. Most topics will require a thorough explanation with specific details and examples that reflect the purpose. Usually, the primary purpose of causal analysis is to inform or to persuade. Even when the purpose is informative though, the paper will still have an *argumentative edge*, or element of persuasion. It may range from a hint to much more. In short, whether *implicitly* or *explicitly*, you will argue for your claim that a cause has led or will lead to an effect. (The difference between an informative and a persuasive paper of causal analysis is a matter of degree and strategy, not necessarily content.)

To substantiate any claim, you need convincing proof. For example, you might contend that action should be taken to keep sixteen-year-olds from driving after midnight because of an extremely high rate of accidents for that age group. To make your claim plausible, you would have to produce valid research and possibly expert opinion to indicate that the hours after midnight are a dangerous time for sixteen-year-old drivers to be out on the roads.

Writing a Conclusion

The conclusion of a cause-and-effect paper summarizes the consequence or result. It may mention a repercussion, influence, benefit, or implication for the future. Or there may be an allusion to the title or opening that establishes closure, as in "Silver Lining," later in the chapter. Regardless, the ending should flow from the description of cause and effect and give a sense of completeness.

Revising a Cause-and-Effect Paper

As you start to revise your cause-and-effect paper, look at the larger items first. Pay particular attention to the strategy, logic, and tone. After you are satisfied with these aspects, check the smaller aspects, as explained in chapter 4. The checklist below will also be helpful.

≋ *Checklist for Revising a Cause-and-Effect Paper*

1. Does the strategy emphasize the purpose?
2. Is there adequate evidence for the claim?

3. If not, have I qualified my statements with *seem, appear,* and other words that allow for chance?
4. Could there be another contributing factor?
5. Is the tone impartial and fair?
6. Is the situation clear? Have I explained enough?

TWO SAMPLE PAPERS OF CAUSE AND EFFECT

In the first paper, Jo Rae Sloan begins with the cause and explains the effects. To develop the paper, she combines explanations with examples:

Silver Lining

To a nineteen-year-old girl, owning her own vehicle oftentimes seems alluring. But once the dream becomes a reality, the resulting responsibilities may seem overwhelming at times. Several months ago I had an opportunity to buy a pickup truck with help from my mother. Having my own transportation is convenient, and I do take pride in my Chevy pickup; yet the upkeep and expense can be exasperating.

Before I bought a truck, I had to schedule my activities around the other family members. I had to borrow my mother's car and worry about the possibility of putting a dent in the fender before I returned. Now I can hop in my Chevy and go whenever I need or wish without a care. I am a cautious driver and have insurance. Although I still park in a far row of parking lots, away from other vehicles, I no longer worry about possible dents.

When I drove someone else's car, I did not really care how it looked. Once I owned my own vehicle, however, my feelings changed. I take pride in my Chevy truck. When I first purchased it, I took it to a body shop for a new paint job with stripes and for the windows to be tinted. Now I vacuum my truck every week as well as wash and wax it regularly. All this takes time and effort. The work and expense are much more than I bargained for.

In the "good old days," all of my extra cash went for clothes, cosmetics, and anything else I wanted. Not now—every cent seems to go to my truck. The expected expense is bad enough, but the unexpected expense can be heartbreaking to a full-time student with a part-time job. Insurance takes a big chunk of my earnings. Filling the gas tank is another regular expense, along with the cost of oil and periodic maintenance. The unexpected expense of a new tire, a muffler system, and other repairs has been formidable. Thank goodness, I live at home and don't have to make payments to a car dealer. My mother is willing to wait for a payment when necessary.

As a result of buying my truck, I have been forced to budget—I haven't bought any new clothes since graduation last June. Although I seldom have more than a few dollar bills and silver, lining my pockets, I have a wonderful sense of independence. My Chevy truck has transported me from adolescence to adulthood.

Questions for Discussion

1. What is the single cause of the effects Jo Rae describes?
2. How do her expectations compare with reality?

3. How does she feel about the effects at times? What is her overall feeling?
4. Does Jo Rae use the block or the alternating method of organization?
5. What is the effect of placing advantages before disadvantages?
6. What is the effect of the title? To what old saying does it allude?

In the next paper, Mary Ann Holvick also describes a single cause that produces multiple effects. First she explains her job, then she presents the benefits:

Why I Enjoyed Being a School Bus Driver

Often when two people are introduced, they initiate conversation by inquiring about each other's occupation. For six years my answer to that question produced raised eyebrows and caused my new acquaintances to exclaim, "You couldn't pay me enough to do that job!" Then I would explain that driving a school bus had rewards other than the usual monetary compensation: mastering a machine, enjoying nature, and participating in children's lives.

Achieving control of the school bus was an arduous task. I had to learn a maintenance routine which included checking all oil and fluid levels, inspecting all hoses and belts for signs of wear, and verifying that all lights and warning buzzers were functional. The most difficult aspect was backing the bus, thirty-eight feet long, from a narrow country road into a still narrower driveway. Yet I derived great satisfaction from knowing the children on the bus were safe because it was in top running condition, and I was confidently in control.

Nature rewarded me for my early morning hours with a spectacular array of sunrises, which fired the deep-textured woods and fence rows with iridescent colors. Although I had grown up in the country, I never tired of watching the trees, wildflowers, and farm crops grow, blossom, and display the triumphant colors of a purpose fulfilled. Under the cover of vegetation, animals and birds carried on their daily lives, unabashed by the passing of so many curious eyes. The children and I enjoyed sights such as a buck deer bounding across an open field, a skunk hunting for his insect breakfast, a flock of Canadian geese flying in formation, and a hawk carrying away his prey with victorious cries.

The children, however, were my constant source of delight. The younger ones were always eager to share their concerns with me. I became a doll fashion advisor and new clothes admirer. I sympathized with the losing Little League team and empathized with the disappointed owners of bologna sandwich lunches. I patched dozens of scraped knees and critiqued hundreds of homework papers. Grade cards were presented for approval; and, occasionally, love notes were dropped surreptitiously into my lap by red-faced little boys.

Older students generally remained aloof until desperation brought them to me, seeking advice about dating or dealing with unreasonable parents. For homecoming queens I saved newspaper pictures, and I congratulated teams for their athletic feats and scholastic achievement. And I worried over their safety each weekend when carloads of teenagers jammed the downtown square. Although I do not have any children of my own, I have loved several hundred boys and girls who made me a part of their lives.

If, like my new acquaintances, I had considered only the hard work involved in my job, then I would not have been a school bus driver. Of course, I received a monetary reward, but my real rewards were the physical discipline of driving, intimacy with nature, and the trusting love of the children.

Questions for Discussion

1. What is the cause in Mary Ann's paper?
2. What are the effects?
3. How does Mary Ann use description to convey her feelings about her job? Which examples do you find most vivid? Why?
4. What order is used to organize details relating to children? For organizing main points?
5. How would you describe the voice of the paper?

Summary

Causal analysis is the study of relationships between two events or conditions, one of which is thought to have caused the other. Causal analysis enables you to learn from experience and to predict what will possibly happen. Cause-and-effect relationships can be incredibly complex. We may assume a complex problem has a single cause, when, indeed, there are several causes. Often we see only the short-term effects. The long-term effects may not be apparent until years later.

Two basic principles of logic govern cause and effect: (1) the cause is able to produce the effect and (2) other causes that might have produced the effect have been ruled out.

As you analyze cause and effect, watch for two common fallacies: *non sequitur* and *post hoc*. As you try to determine why something happened, proceed carefully. Avoid making unfounded inferences or hasty generalizations. Proof is needed before you cite a cause.

Prewriting and making a scratch outline will ease the task of drafting. Although several outlines appear here, the one you choose should be adapted to your writing situation. Depending on the purpose, papers of cause-to-effect or effect-to-cause can be developed in various ways. Description and comparison and contrast are often used. Various writing strategies can be combined.

Endings of cause-and-effect papers summarize the consequence or result. They may also mention benefits or implications for the future. The ending may establish closure by referring to the title or opening. When revising your paper, pay particular attention to the strategy, logic, and tone.

Key Terms

cause	long-term effect	post hoc
effect	causal analysis	argumentative edge
short-term effect	non sequitur	

Practice

Writing a Cause-and-Effect Paragraph

Directions: Read the following selection from *Thinking in Pictures*, by Temple Grandin. Note how Grandin, who is autistic, describes her feelings through comparison. Then write a paragraph about the *effects* of touching in a particular instance. Did the touching involve another person or an animal? Was the touching pleasant or unpleasant? Why?

> From as far back as I can remember, I always hated to be hugged. I wanted to experience the good feeling of being hugged, but it was just too overwhelming. It was like a great, all-engulfing tidal wave of stimulation, and I reacted like a wild animal. Being touched triggered flight; it flipped my circuit breaker. I was overloaded and would have to escape, often by jerking away suddenly.
>
> Many autistic children crave pressure stimulation even though they cannot tolerate being touched. It is much easier for a person with autism to tolerate touch if he or she initiates it. When touched unexpectedly, we usually withdraw because our nervous system does not have time to process the sensation.

Collaborative Exercise: Writing "If . . . Then" Statements

Directions: In small groups, work through the items. Discuss each claim and the implications that follow from it. Then write a series of inferences derived from each statement. (The first inference is shown as an example.)

1. *Claim:* Exercise is good for you; therefore, you should exercise regularly. (What conditions are implicit in this statement? *Hint:* How much? For whom?)
   - Exercise in _____ is good for you; therefore, you should _____.
   - If _____ is good and if you have no _____, then _____.
   - If you have _____, then you should obtain _____ before you exercise.

   Can you see any more implications?

2. *Claim:* Since research indicates that classical music played softly for extended periods can increase intelligence in the early years, it should be played during part of the elementary school day.
   - If classical music _____, then it should be _____.
   - If some children find classical music distracting, then _____ it should _____.

   What else?

Fifty Ideas for Papers of Cause and Effect

1. Thirty seconds of success and its effect
2. Grandmother's favorite proverb and its influence on me
3. Three words that changed my life

4. Exchanging a job for a career
5. The effect of a telephone stalker on my life
6. The effects of giving deserved praise
7. The effects of fatherhood on a sports enthusiast
8. How owning a cat affected my life
9. The effects of being raised in a . . . neighborhood
10. Influences of an alcoholic parent on a family
11. How my thinking has changed since attending college
12. Effects of losing my job
13. Being the oldest of five children
14. How cancer changed my life
15. The effects of crime at . . . campus
16. Influence of my stay-at-home mother
17. A father's example
18. Being a golfer (or ?) can be hazardous to your health
19. Effects of winning . . .
20. Effects of living in a motherless home
21. How my parents' divorce changed my life
22. How reading influenced my life
23. How losing . . . pounds influenced my life
24. Effect of college classes on my self-esteem
25. Switching from fast food to healthy home cooking
26. Effects of having seven credit cards
27. Effects of uncensored television viewing on children
28. Legal implications of unmarried couples living together
29. Hugs: touching improved our family's well-being
30. Fear gave me wings
31. Changes in my neighborhood
32. Gaining a Seeing Eye dog
33. Effects of owning my first car
34. Stress on a nursing assistant
35. Peer pressure in high school
36. Effects of being a cheerleader
37. Effects of having a paper route
38. Effects of living near electrical power lines
39. What causes leukemia?

40. What causes Alzheimer's disease?
41. Fertilizer runoff into streams
42. The influence of my favorite teacher
43. A dream can generate power
44. Why I worked at . . . for . . . years
45. Why I . . .
46. Reasons people become homeless
47. How my parents' living through the Great Depression influenced me
48. Effects of importing wolves into Yellowstone Park
49. Why I live on a mountain
50. An act of kindness and its effect on me

PART 3

Critical Thinking and Persuasion

CHAPTER 18

Detecting Fallacies

A most valuable trait is a judicious sense of what not to believe.

—Euripides, *Helen* (412 BC)
Trans. Richmond Lattimore

When you open your local newspaper, do you ever see ads such as "$1000's possible reading books, part-time, no experience required"; "Earn $529 weekly, mailing company letters from home"; or "Lose weight naturally, just take three tablets daily"? Or perhaps you get a phone call and hear you've won a wonderful vacation for two! The trip can be yours—absolutely free—*after* you purchase an expensive television set or similar item. Although there may be a kernel of truth in such claims, all are designed to benefit the claimant, not the susceptible target.

The trigger to any scam or other deception is an overly trusting attitude on the part of the victim. To protect ourselves from ripoffs, deceptive arguments, propaganda, and errors in thinking, two precautions are essential. The first is to develop a healthy sense of skepticism; to realize that any offer that sounds too good to be true invariably has some strings attached. Even legitimate offers can make unexpected and burdensome demands. For example, Ronald Reagan once warned, "Accepting a government grant with its accompanying rules is like marrying a girl and finding out that her entire family is moving in with you before the honeymoon. (A skeptic reads the fine print and asks probing questions.)

The second precaution is to understand logical and emotional fallacies and how they occur. Errors may result from omission, oversimplification, or exaggeration. When an event or situation is appraised, significant factors may be overlooked, ignored, or de-emphasized. Or their significance may be misjudged and overemphasized. When full knowledge is lacking, incorrect assumptions are often made. Accuracy may also suffer as writers hurry to meet deadlines. Critical thinking is an important part of the writing process. To help you think more critically, this chapter explains both logical and emotional fallacies.

LOGICAL FALLACIES

Logical fallacies are errors in reasoning. Although flawed, these errors can seem plausible and persuasive. Logical fallacies may be found in everyday conversation, talk shows, chat rooms, political speeches, advertising, published writing, and student papers. When we read histories, biographies, and other works, we may find distortions and fabrications. The library is not necessarily a hall of truth, nor is what *60 Minutes* says the only view of a story. There are eight common logical fallacies:

Eight Common Logical Fallacies
_____

1. Card stacking
2. Either/or fallacy
3. False analogy
4. Red herring
5. Begging the question
6. Hasty generalization
7. Non sequitur
8. Post hoc fallacy

Card Stacking

Card stacking is the act of slanting, distorting, or fabricating facts to suit the speaker's or writer's purpose. This fallacy involves deception, either intentional or unintentional. Perpetrators of scams intentionally "stack the deck" against truth, deceiving the victim. For example, in recent years many persons have been contacted by telephone and told their credit has been approved. They have been offered loans of $5,000 to $10,000. The only condition is that applicants have to pay a "one-time fee" of $249 to join a club to get a loan. The victims, eager to believe, pay the fee; the telemarketers move on, leaving no forwarding address.

Card stacking is unethical. A speaker or writer has the obligation to tell the truth. Still, scientific researchers have been known to fudge facts in order to support an illogical conclusion. To save time, they may take unethical shortcuts or even fabricate data. Or they may select only the facts that support a theory, omitting support for the other side. Sooner or later, however, such practices are generally discovered and discredited.

Sometimes students unintentionally commit card stacking while doing research. They may have too few sources to provide an objective view. Insignificant details may be exaggerated or significant details underemphasized. Important facts may be omitted through carelessness or insufficient research.

Either/Or Fallacy

The *either/or fallacy* occurs when we assume there are only two sides to an issue or two alternatives for a problem when there are actually more. Sometimes this fallacy is called the "fallacy of false alternatives." It has also been dubbed the "black or white fallacy." Basically, the either/or fallacy presents the writer's view as the only correct alternative. The either/or fallacy is a simplistic judgment that may occur from incomplete consideration of a problem or from jumping to a premature conclusion. On bumper stickers you may have seen this fallacy in slogans such as "Make love, not war" and "America: Love it or leave it."

In the 1992 presidential campaign, candidate Ross Perot oversimplified our country's policy-making process. Despite his good intentions, the either/or fallacy came out in his campaign: "Either elect me and have a truly democratic government or elect one of my opponents and continue as we are." This either/or claim overlooked the possibility of change by other political candidates.

False Analogy

The fallacy of *false analogy* hinges upon an invalid comparison. Just as an invalid check will not clear a bank's requirements, neither will a false analogy clear a test of logic. In this fallacy two cases or items are compared and assumed to be similar although they are basically different. A conclusion that is true for one is assumed to be true for the other. You may have heard someone say, "We tried this before, and it didn't work." But conditions may have changed since the first attempt, or the way the alternative was applied may have counteracted its effectiveness. Two cases are seldom the same.

In other words, a false analogy exaggerates similarity, making the comparison illogical and unsound. The fundamental problem with a false analogy is that it ignores a basic difference in the two cases. For example, a few years ago a group of citizens who lived in an earthquake-prone state argued for underground rail systems, pointing out that such systems have worked well in other states. The analogy was false, however, since the successful systems were located in states with little earthquake activity. A false analogy can be revealed by pointing out a significant difference.

Red Herring

The fallacy called *red herring* drags in a side issue to distract the audience from the main issue. This fallacy is rather like the tactic that burglars in old movies often used, carrying steak along to throw to the watchdog before robbing the mansion. In the red herring fallacy, the writer suddenly tosses the reader a "bone," an irrelevant point, to avoid proving the original claim. In other words, the subject is abruptly changed in order to divert attention from the real issue.

Using the red herring fallacy, a speaker or writer attempts to prove a point by leapfrogging to an irrelevancy: for example, "the mayor is a man of integrity; he is a church member and a fine family man." But the discerning listener or reader knows the mayor's church membership and family status do not necessarily prove he has integrity. No real proof has been submitted.

Begging the Question

In the fallacy of begging the question, the word *question* refers not to sentence structure, but to the subject under discussion. When a question is "begged," it is not discussed. To avoid giving a direct answer, people may hide their beliefs in a thicket of words. *Begging the question* in this case is simply empty talk that sidesteps the issue. Begging the question may also occur through restatement: for example, "Football is entertaining because it is such an enjoyable sport" or "Irrelevant courses such as ancient history are a waste of time." In neither case has proof been offered. The reader is asked to agree with the first part of each statement. The argument moves in a circle by repeating the claim in different words. The issue is dodged, and the proposition is assumed to be true.

Begging the question may also employ phrases such as "everyone knows," "the fact is," or "obviously" when the opposite is true. An example is "Everyone knows it is not safe to swim for an hour after eating." Statements that beg the question can be short and simple or long and complicated. Students sometimes beg the question when writing essay answers on tests and exams. They pile up words in an attempt to screen the fact they lack the answer, or they make a general claim, but neglect to provide support.

Hasty Generalization

A *hasty generalization* is a broad general statement that lacks adequate support. The writer misstates, exaggerates, or minimizes the facts. Hasty generalizations are assumptions that occur in various ways, but three of the most common are (1) presenting inferences as fact, (2) stereotyping, (3) taking a small or atypical sample of a group and generalizing about a larger group or population.

Hasty generalization can be averted by careful, accurate word choice to reflect the facts. You can identify opinions and qualify generalizations so that they are accurate. You can avoid absolute terms unless adequate evidence is available. When conducting research, you can secure a representative sample (see chapter 5). A hasty generalization may resemble the non sequitur somewhat (both contain inferences), but the hasty generalization does not set up a false cause and effect as the non sequitur does. Nor does the hasty generalization refer to specific instances as the non sequitur does.

Non Sequitur

Translated from Latin, the phrase *non sequitur* simply means "it does not follow." Such fallacies contain faulty assumptions about cause-and-effect relationships. In other words, a cause is asserted for some effect, but the effect "does not follow" logically from the cause. Non sequiturs may use words such as *because, therefore,* and *if . . . then,* and they may be attempts to persuade someone to do something. A student may claim, for example, "I should get an A on this paper because I spent thirty hours working on it and handed it in two days early." But the quality of the paper does not necessarily follow from either of the two facts offered as justification for a good grade. An advertisement may urge, "Buy Brand-X frozen dinners because your family deserves the very best." Obviously, no clear cause-and-effect relationship is established in such a claim.

Non sequiturs may appear in predictions: "Because Marilyn vos Savant is listed in the *Guinness Book of World Records* as having the highest IQ, she would make an excellent president." The fallacy here is in assuming that the chief requirement for the presidency is stellar intelligence. Jimmy Carter, for example, is highly intelligent, but many historians do not consider him to be among the best presidents.

CASE STUDY

NON SEQUITUR—A GROCER'S "MISTAKES"

Eddie Cantor credits much of his success as an entertainer to a grocer he once knew. Cantor, who was raised on the lower East Side of New York, would do errands for neighbors. In return, they would give him a hunk of cake, a slice of salami, or another treat. But they insisted he go to a grocery ten blocks away rather than neighborhood stores.

One day Eddie went to a nearby store and bought exactly the same groceries, but the housewives knew and berated him. Baffled, he wondered how they knew. The next time at the distant store, he observed every move of the grocer. Eddie decided the man was near-sighted [a non sequitur]. An order might call for twelve buns, but the grocer put in thirteen. He put in five bananas instead of four. He did not stop at the quart line on the milk jug, but went over. Making another assumption, Eddie pointed out the "mistakes."

The grocer replied that he always put in a little more than was required. Long remembering the grocer's words, Cantor applied them not only to his personal life, but also to his career. After many years he went back, but the little grocery had disappeared. At last on the Upper East Side, he found the grocer. The man had become the head of a large chain of supermarkets.

The Post Hoc Fallacy

One evening in New York City, so the story goes, a small boy kicked a lamppost. At that moment the lights went out all over the city; a power blackout had occurred. Yet the boy thought he had caused the power failure. This kind of thinking illustrates the post hoc fallacy: because one event follows another, the first is thought to have caused the second. But there is no evidence of a connection:

Facts:	Event A: Boy kicked lamppost.
	Event B: Power blackout.
Post hoc fallacy:	A caused B. (Because event B followed event A, A is thought to have caused B.)

The full Latin name of this fallacy is *post hoc ergo propter hoc*, meaning "after this, therefore because of this." Although no proof is offered, this fallacy assumes that one event or condition was caused by another. The truth is that the two events or conditions only *correlate*, meaning they exist together but do not interact upon nor influence one another.

One autumn, for example, a commodities trader who had heard that the tails of beavers were unusually fat reasoned that the sign signaled a severe winter. He thought about buying orange juice futures, but did not. That winter a freeze hit Florida, sending orange juice prices higher. The rumor about beavers originated in Canada. Of course, the size of the beavers' tails in Canada and temperatures in Florida had no connection; they were isolated incidents. Anyone who concluded that the first condition heralded the second stumbled into the post hoc fallacy.

We have all heard similar post hoc fallacies: Bad luck is often attributed to breaking a mirror, walking under a ladder, or stepping on a crack. Supposedly, eating too many strawberries during pregnancy causes a child to be born with a "strawberry mark." And you probably know other fallacies based on superstitions. Hundreds, perhaps thousands, of years ago, these beliefs sprang up because two events happened one after the other. Perhaps someone broke a mirror and cut a foot severely. Someone else may have walked under a ladder and broken a leg soon after. In each case, the first event was blamed for causing the second.

The Pattern of Superstitious Thinking: A Post Hoc Fallacy

Part 1: Superstition: Handling toads causes warts. (A causes B.)

Part 2: Because Shawn handled a toad and the following week a wart appeared on his thumb, the toad caused the wart. (Therefore, A caused B.)

A systems analyst says that his subordinates seldom have trouble with any fallacy except the post hoc. Once in a while a team member will seize on an obvious but incorrect cause for a problem. The member errs in assuming two factors have a cause-and-effect relationship when they merely correlate.

To avoid confusing the fallacies of cause and effect, notice that post hoc involves two events that occur in a sequence whereas the non sequitur has only one. If a statement contains both fallacies, label it post hoc. For your convenience, the following list summarizes the main distinctions between post hoc and non sequitur.

Post hoc	*Non sequitur*
Two sequential events or conditions. (A apparently caused B)	Only one fact or event plus an inference.
No proof that the first event caused (or will cause) the second.	Only an opinion, often a prediction.

EMOTIONAL FALLACIES

Americans are bombarded with emotional fallacies every day. When we drive past a billboard, open a magazine, or turn on a television set, we are exposed to cleverly planned propaganda. Usually, the propaganda contains emotional fallacies designed to arouse strong feelings and impel us to buy products, donate money, or accept ideas. The propagandists know that if they can trigger strong feelings, then logic may be dethroned and emotion may rule.

Understanding how these fallacies work can help you not only to resist them but also to avoid them in your research and writing. This is not to say that all emotional appeals are to be avoided. *Whereas emotional fallacies attempt to manipulate, emotional appeals attempt to persuade honestly and fairly.* Although the difference between the two may be only one of degree, it is significant.

An emotional appeal may be warranted in an argument, for example, but the emotion should be controlled and used ethically. A modicum of emotion may also be appropriate in other kinds of writing. To make these decisions for your writing, you need an ear that is sensitive to word choice as well as an eye that is quick to note the amount of emotion and how it is used. Deception is never acceptable.

In most emotional fallacies, *transfer* plays an important role. Transfer uses the connotations of words and pictures to manipulate our responses. The idea is to carry the positive connotations over to products, ideas, and people. Positive transfer presents products in the most attractive way possible with appealing names and surroundings. Commercials for some products, for instance, portray endearing family scenes—perhaps of children, puppies, or kittens. On the other hand, negative transfer is often used in political campaigns to disparage opponents, as in name-calling. Emotional fallacies can interfere not only with logical thinking but also with fairness and objectivity. Eight common emotional fallacies are discussed here:

Eight Common Emotional Fallacies

1. *Argumentum ad hominem*
2. Bandwagon
3. Plain folk appeal

4. Status appeal

5. Scare tactics

6. Testimonial

7. Improper appeal to authority

8. Glittering generality

Argumentum ad Hominem

During the 1992 presidential campaign, George Bush resorted to name-calling when he repeatedly labeled candidates Clinton and Gore as "bozos." Name-calling, mudslinging, and smear tactics are all forms of *argumentum ad hominem* ("against the man"). This fallacy can be a verbal attack, including a disparagement of character. In an ad hominem argument, a person is assaulted—not the issue. Another form of ad hominem uses derisive humor to discredit. A personal characteristic that is irrelevant to performance becomes the subject of unkind joking. Former President Gerald Ford was ridiculed for his lack of physical coordination and former Vice President Dan Quayle for his misspelling of *potatoes*. Neither characteristic pertained to the ability to perform in office.

The ad hominem fallacy is not only unethical and unkind, but also impractical. Persons who indulge in name-calling or backbiting endanger their credibility and their careers. Students who indulge lose points and credibility as writers.

Bandwagon

Another emotional fallacy urges everyone "to jump on the bandwagon," to go along with the crowd. *Bandwagon* is the fallacy of "everyone's doing it, so you should, too." Peer pressure is exerted to exploit the desire to belong to a group or to do what other people are doing. The fallacy also capitalizes on the belief that the majority knows best.

Ads and commercials using the bandwagon appeal often show large groups of happy people using the same product and enjoying the results. For example, ads for soft drinks feature explicit entreaties like "Join the Pepsi Generation." In McDonald's commercials about "happy meals" for children, bandwagon is implicit. The bandwagon fallacy focuses on common ties of family, nationality, race, age, religion, gender, job, or special interest. Thus the propagandist may call upon us as United States citizens, Polish Americans, Catholics, Protestants, men, women, baby-boomers, truck drivers, or members of another group to do something.

Plain Folk Appeal

Awareness of the plain folk appeal can be helpful in analyzing your reading audience, particularly in setting up an argument and in letter writing. Establishing a common bond ("common ground") can have a positive and powerful influence. As long as the plain folk appeal is not overdone or inaccurate, it is all right to use it or any other emotional appeal. Just ask yourself, "Is the writing honest and fair?"

The *plain folk appeal* stresses similarity to ordinary people or the so-called average citizen. A speaker wears ordinary clothing, adopts similar speech habits, and participates in everyday activities to show that someone of high status is just "a regular guy" at heart. For example, Fiorella La Guardia, who gained renown as mayor of New York City (1935–1945), spoke three languages. When he visited various neighborhoods to campaign, he would vary his speech according to his audience. As a result, the listeners felt he was one of them and truly their representative.

The secret to effectiveness with the plain folk appeal is sincerity. If insincerity is detected, the tactic can backfire. For example, while running for reelection, George Bush tried this appeal. Accompanied by the media, he once went into a supermarket, ostensibly to purchase a few groceries. Enthusiastically, Bush exclaimed over the convenience of scanners, which were new to him. To the public, the event appeared to have been staged. Bush was perceived as a rich man out of touch with ordinary life and was ribbed by the media.

On the other hand, William Clinton, Bush's opponent, mastered the plain folk appeal. Clinton, who had humble beginnings, went by the nickname of Bill and mentioned his early background often during the campaign. As he mixed with citizens in town meetings, he exuded charm and genuine friendliness. But he downplayed his attendance at private schools and his studies at Oxford. None of these three men could be considered "plain folk" or ordinary citizens. Through opportunity, determination, and effort, they became extraordinary.

The plain folk appeal is seldom a problem in student essays, but you may encounter it being misused during your research. Now, however, you should be prepared to recognize abuses and to apply the appeal appropriately.

Status Appeal

The old saying "keeping up with the Joneses" illustrates status appeal, or snob appeal as it is sometimes called. *Status appeal* is a pitch to better oneself by wearing stylish clothes, driving expensive cars, taking exotic vacations, or buying whatever a company sells that requires lavish spending. For example, a commercial for a well-known car uses status appeal: "It's the difference between just getting there and truly arriving." Such commercials feature attractive people, dressed in stylish attire, who purchase top-of-the-line luxuries. The implication is that the viewer can be like them by buying and using the manufacturer's product.

Status appeal is the opposite of plain folk. Whereas plain folk can arouse friendly feelings when appropriately used, status appeal may antagonize, even when used appropriately. The applications for status appeal are limited. Unless you are a marketing major who creates advertising copy or writes sales brochures or a business communications student who writes sales letters, you will probably not use the status appeal in your college writing. Nonetheless, you need to be aware of it so that you can recognize it and deal with it appropriately.

Scare Tactics

Daily we encounter appeals that use *scare tactics*. These appeals attempt to manipulate us into accepting a product, message, or person. Often the danger is exaggerated, and other alternatives do exist. For example, some insurance ads use scare tactics to sell policies. One ad showed a mother holding a young child in her arms with the caption "What will they do when you are gone?"

After the Americans with Disabilities Act was passed July 26, 1992, new scams, using fear tactics, arose. The scams exploit the anxiety of small employers about failure to comply with the act, exaggerating the danger of penalties and lawsuits in order to sell expensive seminars and printed materials. For example, one company sells literature that the federal government provides free. Another ploy is to offer high-priced consulting services to help meet federal guidelines. Scare tactics, based on misinformation, line the pockets of promoters.

But scare tactics can also warn the public of possible hazards. For example, warnings about the dangers of small children drinking household cleaners or the danger of unhooked safety belts are a public service. In some cases, alarming statistics are given and frightening pictures shown (such as an accident caused by a drunk driver) to motivate people to protect themselves and their families.

To determine the legitimacy of an appeal, ask: "Is the claim truthful? Does it have the interest of the audience at heart? Will it really protect or benefit them?" In research papers, scare tactics are best avoided. A calm, objective tone and a logical approach that stresses benefits is the most effective way to persuade. In a process paper, a legitimate warning may be imperative.

Testimonial and Improper Appeal to Authority

Because Bo Jackson gives a testimonial for Nikes, a non-athlete may be convinced to purchase a pair. Other ball players have plugged a variety of goods from shaving lotion to snuff. The fallacy inherent in a *testimonial* is the assumption that something is true or good just because a well-known person says so. Never forget, however, that unless stated otherwise, the person giving the testimony has been paid by the sponsor.

Political testimonials for candidates are often given in election campaigns. Although a well-known public figure may endorse a relatively unknown candidate, we should keep in mind that endorsements are a form of patronage, an exchange of political favors. In student writing, testimonials seldom appear, but a related fallacy sometimes occurs—improper appeal to authority.

An *improper appeal to authority* is the giving of testimony by well-known persons about a particular field in which they are unqualified. The so-called authority, who lacks relevant credentials, goes out on a limb, claiming something is true. Some instances of this fallacy may be harmless; nonetheless, deception is inherent. For example, when physicians, researchers, or other professionals step outside their fields of expertise, their claims become meaningless. In writing papers, consider the qualifications of the researcher as well as the validity of the claim.

Glittering Generalities

Glittering generalities proffer fuzzy phrases that sound good but lack substance. In other words, these vague generalizations "glitter," but have little meaning. A glittering generality contains an undefined term. If people were called upon to define the term, they might respond with different definitions. For instance, what is a "red-blooded American"? The "American way"? "Good government"? "Old-fashioned goodness"? All of these phrases can be stretched to mean whatever a writer wants.

Glittering generalities use positive words to persuade us to accept a product or proposal without thinking. Loaded with positive connotations, these statements stir emotions and cloud thinking. Propagandists often use glittering generalities to appeal to our sense of fair play, brotherhood, or love. They sprinkle their talk with virtuous words like *liberty, loyalty, patriotism, progress, truth, honor,* or *justice.* These words suggest ideals that all "good" people believe in. Glittering generalities play on the emotions, urging us to do something without examining the facts.

DEALING WITH FALLACIES

Fallacies are dishonest arguments that cheat on the facts or use an overdose of emotion to beguile an audience. Although there may be temptations to resort to fallacious persuasion, this path is unwise from both an ethical and a practical standpoint. Ethically, we have the obligation to give readers and listeners the facts. In the long run, deception is invariably impractical. Chances are the truth will eventually emerge, and the reputation of the unethical writer or speaker will be tarnished.

Honesty is still the best policy. Businesses, communities, and families are built on trust. Those who treat employees, customers, and members fairly and who supply their needs will tend to endure. Furthermore, the habits built in the home and in the classroom tend to carry over into the workplace.

You may become fascinated by finding and categorizing fallacies, but if you find it difficult to label a particular case, don't worry. Recognizing deception, manipulation, and misstatement is what is important, not a particular fallacy's name. By learning the characteristics of fallacies, you can develop healthy skepticism as well as thinking skills.

This chapter is much more than an intellectual exercise, however. The most important lesson is to *apply* your learning. Thinking skills can be applied almost anywhere. Critical thinking is valuable in writing and revising papers as well as in protecting yourself against scams. Critical thinking can improve one's self-image and professional image. Critical thinking is a transferable skill that is in demand.

Summary

Critical thinking requires distinguishing facts from fallacies. Logical fallacies contain errors in reasoning. Eight common logical fallacies are card stacking, either/or, false analogy, red herring, begging the question, hasty generalization, non sequitur, and post hoc.

Critical thinking also requires recognizing emotional fallacies, appeals that are overstated and designed to manipulate. Emotional fallacies are propaganda techniques that attempt to overrule logic with a rush of feeling. Yet some emotional *appeals*, not fallacies, can be used with restraint in college speaking and writing. An emotional appeal should be appropriate, honest, and fair.

There are eight common emotional fallacies: *argumentum ad hominem*, bandwagon, plain folk, status appeal, scare tactics, testimonial, improper appeal to authority, and glittering generality. Positive or negative transfer usually appears in emotional fallacies.

It is both unethical and impractical to use fallacies in your writing. Understanding them can help you to avoid them as well as recognize deception and manipulation.

Key Terms

logical fallacy	transfer
emotional fallacy	credibility
card stacking	*argumentum ad hominem*
either/or fallacy	bandwagon
false analogy	plain folk
red herring	status appeal
begging the question	scare tactics
hasty generalization	testimonial
non sequitur	improper appeal to authority
post hoc fallacy	glittering generality
correlation	ethics

Test Yourself

Fallacy Review

_____ 1. A comparison that has more differences than likenesses.

_____ 2. Reasoning that states or assumes only two alternatives exist when there are actually more.

_____ 3. An attack upon a person's character rather than against the issue.

_____ 4. Circular reasoning that assumes something is true and reads as if it were true. Circumvents the issue.

_____ 5. An appeal to follow the majority and do something because "everyone else is doing it."

_____ 6. Appeal based on the premise that the speaker/writer is one of the common people, an average citizen.

_____ 7. An overly broad statement, an inference, based on inadequate evidence.

_____ 8. (After this, because of this.) This fallacy assumes that because one event occurs after another that the first caused the second.

_____ 9. A side issue is presented to distract from the main issue.

_____ 10. How can this chapter help you? State two ways.

Acceptable or Hasty Generalizations?

Directions: Mark "A" for acceptable generalization or "H" for hasty generalization. Then check your answers at the end of the chapter.

1. Pit bulls are killers.
2. Women tend to score higher on vocabulary tests than men.
3. Most teenage drivers today are more reckless than those of other decades.
4. Left-handed folks are better at arithmetic than right-handed.
5. Beef is a versatile and nutritious food.
6. College professors are politically liberal.
7. Football players are less intelligent than other college students.
8. Men don't cry.
9. Childhood is the happiest, most carefree time of life.
10. Heavyset folks have cheerful dispositions.

Practice

Case Problems: Analyzing Logic

Directions: In small groups read the following cases aloud. Then discuss the main points and implications. Decide if the logic is valid or invalid. Give reasons for your decisions.

1. In "Life on the Job," Roy Harris, Jr., tells about Dave Brown of Cerritos, California, an ironworker who has helped build tall luxury condominiums. "Hanging iron" requires that Dave work on steel girders, high above the traffic, bolting columns together. As he finishes each one, he signs it and draws little yellow flowers with a yellow marking pencil. Dave explains

that his job is "really like playing with a big erector set. . . . Here each part is numbered and you just put them where they're supposed to go." Do you agree or disagree? Is his analogy valid? Why or why not? Can you make a distinction between theory and application?

2. A *Wall Street Journal* editorial entitled "Life Imitating Art" related that Congress invited movie and television stars to speak on social questions. For example, Jack Klugman, who played a medical detective in the TV show *Quincy*, has discussed "the issue of approving new drugs." Ed Asner, who depicted a newspaper editor, "has testified on the media." Brooke Shields, actress, "has spoken out against smoking because she doesn't indulge." Do you see any problems with such evidence? What fallacy is illustrated here?

3. In an essay entitled "Blue Jeans Are Here to Stay," a student made the following claims. Discuss their validity.

> The atmosphere at business meetings . . . is more casual when people dress in blue jeans. The fact that everyone feels comfortable eases the tension. Conversation is easily developed; ideas and thoughts flow more freely. The second factor that makes blue jeans popular is their quality. Everyone likes the thought of receiving the best value in clothing for the right price. Blue jeans have this feature. They are purchased for reasonable prices and provide excellent wear. . . .
>
> The most influential factor that causes people to buy blue jeans is their comfort in wearing. Most people like to feel good in the clothing they wear. Blue jeans are made to give this feeling to all who wear them. There is an exact size to provide everyone with a unique fit. Then they are pleased with themselves and present a cheerful attitude toward life.

4. A reader wrote to the editor of *U.S. News and World Report:* "In his conversation, 'Universities Are Turning Out Highly Skilled Barbarians' (November 10) Steven Muller is 100 percent on target. We have lost our sense of values and direction. Our society is similar to our games: As a ball bumping around in a pinball machine, we bump from problem to problem with little or no action to solve them. We as a society lack the gut feeling to stand up for our values and solve our society's problems."

5. According to L. A. Winokur in "You May Have Her to Thank for It When the Boss Bursts into Flames," a customer service representative was having problems with a troublesome coworker. The rep decided to take the advice of a sorceress who had written a book to help women rid themselves of workplace problems. The rep made a paper ship, piled it with "chocolate coins," and sketched the coworker on it. Then the customer service rep "blessed the drawing and chanted, 'I wish you well.'" Soon after, the coworker left for a position in the East.

6. In an election pamphlet, the Ohioans for Wildlife Conservation made the following claims:

If the don't-knows get away with banning trapping, how long before someone starts a crusade to save the fish and worms and hellgrammites from the mean old fishermen? . . . The natural food and fur resources of Ohio have been abundant since Indian times, since explorer and missionary times, since pioneer times, and still are. There are, indeed, fake furs to supplant the natural sources but there's no need to accept the substitutes.

Collaborative Learning: Identify the Fallacies

Directions: Identify the fallacy or propaganda device in each example.

1. As a burglar raised and entered a ground-floor window, a large black cat arched its back, hissed, and dashed across the room to a stairway. Ignoring the cat, the burglar sneaked into the bedroom and opened a wall safe, cleaned out its contents, and continued to look for valuables. Suddenly, he was confronted by two policemen with drawn guns. At that moment he realized the cat was an omen—he should have left immediately. (The safe was wired to an alarm in police headquarters.)

2. Mike wrote an argument paper using information from only two sources: a paid political advertisement and three pamphlets from the National Rifle Association. Discuss any problems you see in his sources and the quality of his evidence.

3. Excerpt from student theme: "The mature person is continuously open, flexible, curious, and active." (*Hint:* See a dictionary for the meaning of *continuously*.)

4. A ninety-year-old grandmother makes her own wine using a mixture of grape juice, skins, seeds, and stems. She says this wine is rich in vitamins and "restorative powers." Recently she had a minor stroke, but is now completely recovered. She attributes her recovery to drinking three small glasses of her homemade wine daily. Do you agree with this reasoning? Why or why not?

5. Four-year-old Jill Smythe has won twenty beauty contests. Her mother has enrolled Jill at a school of dance, for she believes that Jill will become a movie star. Discuss the path of this reasoning and where it leads.

Test Yourself Answers

Fallacy Review

1. *False analogy*
2. *Either/or fallacy*
3. Argumentum ad hominem
4. *Begging the question*
5. *Bandwagon*
6. *Plain folk*
7. *Hasty generalization*

    8. Post hoc ergo propter hoc
    9. Red herring
  10. (a) Increase your learning
      (b) Sharpen your thinking skills
      (c) Improve grades
      (d) Protect yourself against scams

Acceptable or Hasty Generalizations?

    1. H. There are three breeds of dogs classified as pit bulls. Not all are dangerous.
    2. A. Fact. Tend to qualifies the statement, indicating a majority.
    3. H. Opinion, a value judgment.
    4. H. No evidence to substantiate this statement.
    5. A. Fact. Beef can be prepared in many ways; it contains many nutrients.
    6. H. Not all.
    7. H. No evidence to support this claim.
    8. H. Not all men.
    9. H. Not for everyone.
  10. H. Thin people don't? All heavyset people do?

CHAPTER 19

Problem Solving

A problem well stated is a problem half solved.
—Charles F. Kettering

Businesses, industries, and other organizations frequently face major problems of costs, personnel, and service. Prices of materials and wages rise. Competitors cut prices. Inventories "shrink." Equipment malfunctions. Deliveries run late. Personnel make mistakes, and customers complain. Problems of some sort occur in every workplace.

A newly hired bookkeeper at a large family-run automobile dealership in the Midwest, for example, faced a problem that seemed minor at first. The parts manager was given cash to buy parts, for which he did not always turn in sales receipts. When the bookkeeper asked for them, the manager would apologize and promise to bring them in. After two months, however, five receipts were still unaccounted for. The bookkeeper began to wonder if the parts manager were pocketing funds. But because he was a well-respected family man—and a relative of the owner—and had worked at the company for six years, she wasn't certain how to proceed.

After pondering the problem, she realized she could (1) say nothing and hope he would eventually turn in all receipts, (2) report the irregularities to the office manager or the owner immediately, or (3) wait awhile and watch. If she chose the first alternative, she risked never balancing the petty cash account and possibly losing her job for not reporting the problem. If she chose the second and the parts manager produced the missing receipts, she risked embarrassment and a loss of respect for making a fuss over a "simple matter." The bookkeeper selected the third alternative because it carried the least risk. Prodding the parts manager, she received a few old receipts, but he continued to "forget." After six months, when she lacked receipts for $6500 worth of parts and an audit deadline loomed, she went to the owner, explaining she had done her best to correct the problem. He questioned the parts manager, who confessed. The bookkeeper had salvaged her job and gained respect by problem solving.

DEWEY'S METHOD OF PROBLEM SOLVING

Since primeval times, people have been solving problems randomly, trying one plan, and when that did not prove practical, trying another. In the early twentieth century, John Dewey, an American philosopher and educator (famous for his *Studies in Logical Theory*), devised an efficient problem-solving method. Dewey defined a systematic six-step procedure that has been widely adopted and adapted by scientists, business personnel, and others. This basic procedure, known as "the scientific method," is also practical for individual use.

Studying Dewey's method of problem solving can sharpen thinking skills and increase efficiency. At the same time learners can gain skills transferable to college papers and workplace writing. Dewey's method is an effective way to organize research papers and reports that focus upon a concern or problem. A simplified version of his method appears here:

1. *State the problem.* Identify it.
2. *Define the problem.* Limit its scope. Examine its history.
3. *Formulate criteria.* Devise standards to measure the problem.
4. *Propose alternatives.* Consider possible solutions.
5. *Evaluate alternatives.* Apply criteria to solution options.
6. *Recommend action.* Select best possible solution(s).

Dewey knew that a problem must be confronted and clearly identified before it can be solved. Once the shape and identity of a problem are discerned, a plan of attack can be created. Dewey's main criterion for evaluating an alternative was "Will it work?" Finding practical solutions was his primary concern. He welcomed opportunities to test new ideas. He believed no knowledge is ever so certain that it should not be reconsidered in the light of new evidence. Dewey went to great lengths to be objective.

HOW CAN ONE BE OBJECTIVE?

> An adult who ceases after youth to unlearn and relearn his [or her] facts and to reconsider opinions . . . is a menace to a democratic community.
>
> —Edward Thorndike

Before objectivity can be achieved, one must be willing to relinquish old biases and to accept new knowledge. In science, objectivity is an essential part of every experiment and operation, an impartial way of conducting scientific work so that subjectivity is ruled out as much as possible. For the rest of us, the road to objectivity is not so clearly marked.

Basically, there are two general ways to obtain information: firsthand and secondhand. Both ways can present problems in terms of objectivity. Although we observe something firsthand, we may see only part of it and think we saw

100 percent. Or we may misinterpret the meaning of what we observed; we may make incorrect inferences and treat them as fact. Information gained secondhand is often subject to error and distortion. Although we may try very hard to be objective, we may overemphasize details that interest us. Unwittingly, we may engage in card stacking (chapter 18). So how can one be as objective as possible and minimize the chances of error?

First, *we can reserve judgment.* We can hold back our opinions until they are solidly grounded. We can listen to both sides of an issue and consider all facets of a problem. By reserving judgment, we can look for facts and comprehensive coverage before making decisions.

Second, *we can try to be impartial and fair.* We can remain open to new information. The fact that one deduction fits should not lead us to ignore other possibilities or conflicting viewpoints. Often someone with a different perspective can give valuable assistance in solving a problem and in averting mistakes. For example, a manager who was converting her department to a computerized operation invited her secretary to go along to shop for computers although the secretary had never used one. When the manager found a model she liked, she inquired, "What do you think of this keyboard?" Regarding the computer for a moment, the secretary responded, "Wouldn't those recessed keys require extra pressure and cause more errors?" They tried the keyboard and found her assessment to be correct.

Third, *we can qualify generalizations and refrain from embellishing facts.* We can distinguish inference from fact. To be objective, we must seek the truth.

Fourth, *we can keep in mind that no one is immune to mistakes.* To be human means to be susceptible to error. Although we think we understand something, our information may be only partial. When we attempt to explain, we may be able to tell what caused something, what affects it now, and what may affect it in the future. We may even be able to discuss its apparent effect on other things. Nonetheless, our understanding is inferential, incomplete, and inconclusive at some point. This awareness should keep us not only humble, but also alert.

TRANSITION IN A PROBLEM-SOLVING PAPER

In a problem-solving paper, you will need special transitions to signal cause-and-effect relationships. To direct the reader, you place appropriate transitions near reasons why an event happened or a description of how it affected another event or situation. Examples of these transitions are listed for your convenience:

therefore	an outcome	as a result
thus	a consequence	one part
affected	one effect	a by-product
two factors	an offshoot	an outgrowth
three aspects	one influence	one proposal
one difficulty	one complication	

WRITING A PROBLEM-SOLVING PAPER

A problem-solving paper combines various writing strategies into a basic format. This format, more or less, follows Dewey's method of problem solving. Although you and your peers may use the same general pattern of organization, you will make individual decisions that allow for difference and creativity. Examples are presented in this chapter merely to help you find fresh ideas.

Selecting a Topic and Prewriting

To find a topic for a problem-solving paper, you might begin by considering your experience. Perhaps a work-related topic might do. Or perhaps you know about a family, a neighborhood, a community, or a city facing a problem. Any one of these areas might yield an appropriate topic. The problem should be significant, yet not too technical or complex. Although it might be interesting to investigate a widespread social concern or national problem, it is best to steer clear of such topics in a short paper. Problems of this magnitude require extensive research.

The problem you select should be complex enough for the length of paper required. The problem should have at least three alternatives. That does not mean all alternatives must be feasible. Two or more can be ruled out, but one must provide a means to alleviate or to resolve the problem. Sometimes all three may be needed. If the problem cannot be alleviated, look for another topic.

As you search for details to use in a problem-solving paper, watch for changes, increases or decreases, cause and effect, side effects, risks, advantages and disadvantages. Note that changes may be negative or positive and their effects may be simple or complicated. Advantages may be short-term or long-term. Asking questions will speed your search.

Questions to Discover Details for Problem Solving

- What exactly is the problem?
- When was it first noticed?
- What or whom does it affect?
- What are its effects? (Signs, symptoms, characteristics?)
- How far does it extend? (Scope?)
- What were the causes? (History?)
- What, if anything, has been done to alleviate the problem?
- What other alternatives exist?
- What are the advantages and disadvantages of each alternative?
- What is the best alternative? Or will a combination be needed?

Caution: Beware of oversimplification. Complex problems seldom have a single cause.

Making an Outline

Dewey's method of problem solving furnishes an easy and effective way to organize information. You can adapt this method to most problems whether they concern an individual, a group, or a community. Using the six steps, you can start your scratch outline. Steps 1 and 2 will form the introduction of the paper. Steps 3, 4, and 5 form the body. Step 6 forms the conclusion. The diagram below shows how the six steps can be grouped:

Introduction

Step 1:   Identify the problem

Step 2:   Define the problem

Body

Step 3:   Identify criteria

Step 4:   Propose alternatives

Step 5:   Evaluate alternatives

Conclusion

Step 6:   Recommend action

Following the order of the six steps will simplify organizing your paper. The working outline here illustrates how you might convert the six steps into an outline.

    I. Introduction
       A. Attention-getting detail
       B. Description of the problem
       C. History of the problem
       D. Identification of the cause(s)

   II. Body
       A. Specific criteria stated
       B. Alternative 1 and evaluation
       C. Alternative 2 and evaluation
       D. Alternative 3 and evaluation

  III. Conclusion
       A. Recommendation or best alternative
       B. Relevant comment

SAMPLE OUTLINE FOR A PROBLEM-SOLVING PAPER

Engineering student Jack Buroker wrote a problem-solving paper in the form of a proposal. Jack, who is employed as a welder, analyzed a production problem and made a recommendation:

Proposal to Increase Production in the Welding Department

I. Introduction

A recent concern indicated by the management of ———— Structural Steel is the low production in the welding department. This problem seems to stem primarily from having only one overhead crane, which is accessible from only 25% of the floor area. The former building, which was smaller, was equipped with two overhead cranes that were accessible from 100% of the floor area.

II. Criteria to be considered:
   A. Does the cost of the proposal fit the limited budget of $2,000?
   B. Does the proposal conform to safety regulations?
   C. Will the proposal increase production appreciably?

III. Alternatives and evaluation
   A. Equip the building with three additional overhead cranes.
       1. Advantages:
           a. Would increase production to the maximum potential.
           b. The cranes are proven to be safe.
           c. The additional cranes would provide 100% accessibility to the floor area.
       2. Disadvantage: These three cranes would cost $500,000.
   B. Equip the buildings with JIB cranes.
       1. Advantages:
           a. Cost would be within budget: $2,000.
           b. Would increase production
       2. Disadvantages:
           a. Have not been proven safe.
           b. The increase in production would be minimal.
   C. Revise the procedure in the welding department from fabricating one piece to fabricating several pieces. This change would save time by reducing waiting time on the one overhead crane.
       1. Advantages:
           a. Would increase production by 10% to 25%, depending on job.
           b. Cost would be minimal.
           c. Procedure has been proven to be safe.
       2. Disadvantage: Does not increase production to maximum.

IV. Conclusion

Although the present procedure used by the welding department worked well in the former building, this method is not the best for the present building. The procedure could be refined with little expense to increase production safely on a short-term basis. As production increases, funds could be allocated for eventual purchase of more overhead cranes to increase production to maximum potential.

Drafting an Introduction

Problem-solving papers can begin in several ways. You might open with an appropriate quotation or a brief dialogue that illustrates a vital aspect of the problem. Another way is to start with a narrative that describes the problem; then you might describe cause and effect. Keith Zuspan described an incident that happened where he worked:

Preventing an Expensive Problem

One of the most recent crises at ——— State Headquarters in ——— occurred in the executive building. A twenty-five-year-old air-conditioning unit failed to maintain the required cooling level in this large complex. When such an event occurs, it is imperative that the Building Operations Supervisor take action immediately. The supervisor must be able not only to recognize the potential risks, but also to correct the problem in the least amount of time and in the most efficient manner.

The interior climate of these buildings must be maintained within the strict guidelines mandated by the corporate office. The guidelines state that the temperature and humidity in the complex must remain within a specified range to protect all computer and electronic equipment. Damage to the equipment would result in lost information, which could cost the corporation a large sum.

Charles Blaney has a problem, involving his dog and a neighbor's dog, that could prove costly and disrupt neighborly relations if he does not take precautions. In the introduction of this paper, Chuck explains:

Dilemma of a Dog Owner

Bocephus, my male Chesapeake Bay retriever, is of champion stock. Bo is a pure-bred with a bloodline free of genetic defects. He is a well-trained show dog who will normally stay in our yard, even if left unattended. Recently, however, a neighbor has been letting his female rottweiler out for nightly runs. She is in season and has visited Bo; however, the fence of Bo's kennel has kept them separated. Lately when Bo gets an opportunity, he sneaks out of the yard and runs over to the neighbor's property. But if the two should fraternize, this would cause a legal problem.

If these two bloodlines were to be mixed, I could be sued by the neighbor. Legally, I would be responsible for the pregnancy and a ruined bloodline. According to the law, the owner of a male dog is liable unless the dog is on a leash and supervised or confined to the owner's property. Furthermore, Bo would not be allowed to sire champion Chesapeake Bay retrievers.

The introduction of a problem-solving paper sets the stage for the identification of criteria and a discussion of alternatives.

Identifying Criteria

To check decisions and to evaluate possible solutions to problems, we need to develop criteria. By identifying our own specific criteria, we can measure the existing alternatives and make more logical decisions than we might otherwise make.

What Are Criteria?   Instead of criteria, you may be used to talking about "guidelines," "specifications," "company policy," "diplomacy," or similar terms. All of these are criteria, used to weigh decisions and evaluate alternatives. Criteria are simply the factors that influence decision making and problem solving.

Daily life offers many opportunities to apply criteria. For instance, when planning a major purchase, you use criteria to weigh the advantages and disadvantages of comparable products. Before buying a new television set, you might consider some, or perhaps all, of the following criteria:

screen size	warranty on the entire set
kind of cabinet	warranty on picture tube
brand name	quality of sound
price	convenience

A criterion (the singular of criteria) is *one* standard, rule, principle, or test used to evaluate a decision or proposal. For example, *Webster's Collegiate Dictionary, Tenth Edition* defines *criterion* as "a standard on which a judgment or decision may be based."

Dewey's first criterion, "Will it work?" is a factor in solving any problem. Time is another important criterion to consider. Other common criteria are listed here:

Is it cost-effective?	Is it ethical?
Is it safe?	Is it fair?
Is it practical?	Is it appropriate?
Is it legal?	Is it beneficial in the short run? Long run?

Stating Criteria   To identify criteria, ask: "What factors will influence this decision?" Perhaps the simplest way to specify criteria is to pose each criterion as a question. In her paper Nancy Miller stated criteria as questions:

> Making our house more energy-efficient required careful consideration. When the alternatives to this problem were evaluated, three main questions were asked. First, what is the cost? Second, how energy-efficient is the alternative? Third, will the alternative raise the equity in our home?

In the next example, Linda Gubernath identifies the chief influences on her family's decision to buy a pickup truck. Linda begins with her husband's criterion, then her children's, then hers. She ends with the most important factor of cost, which affects all family members:

> My husband, as many men do, preferred another pickup truck. He needed a vehicle which could transport scouting equipment, home improvement supplies, and other cargo. The children, however, decided it was time for the van they had been wanting. They needed a vehicle large enough to ride in comfortably without sitting shoulder to shoulder. I insisted the vehicle have an automatic transmission, room for four or more passengers, and a price that would fit within the family budget.

A third example was written by a mother who had recently lost her job through a layoff. Carol Walkins specified three concerns in her job search: day shift, pay scale, and location:

> A major problem that I faced was the possibility of having to work the evening or midnight shift if I found employment in another factory. With two elementary school children, I needed to be at home in the evenings in order to spend important time with them. Since my family depends on my income, I also had to find a job that would provide a pay scale similar to that of my former job. Location was another factor to be considered. My husband works locally, and we own our home. Therefore, moving was not an option.

For clarity in a problem-solving paper, some instructors like for students to state criteria before alternatives. Regardless, do not confuse criteria with alternatives. Criteria are the factors or considerations that govern decisions. Alternatives are the options for action—possible solutions. In other words, criteria provide a means to weigh the benefits and risks of an alternative.

Proposing and Evaluating Alternatives

Usually, a problem-solving paper presents at least three alternatives. Perhaps two of the choices can be eliminated, leaving one that can best solve the problem. This does not mean that every problem can be solved with one alternative. Perhaps a combination will be needed. Or perhaps the best that can be done is to alleviate the problem.

After alternatives are determined, each possibility is evaluated according to criteria. In this fifth step, advantages and disadvantages become apparent. Upon a first glance, an alternative may seem to be a practical solution to a problem. After research and analysis, however, hidden disadvantages may emerge.

To evaluate alternatives for a paper, research the feasibility of each one. Do not assume there are no disadvantages. To be objective, a paper must specify disadvantages as well as advantages. (An omission of either would constitute card stacking.) Then evaluate the alternatives according to the criteria.

A problem may have a short-term alternative and a long-term solution. When Carol analyzed her problem of unemployment, she found both:

> My first alternative was to collect the nine months of unemployment compensation that I qualified for. I could accomplish my household tasks during the day, leaving the evenings free for my children. Collecting unemployment and saving on babysitting fees would compensate for the weekly paycheck. Although the idea of staying home was appealing, collecting an unemployment check would be temporary and not a real solution to the problem.
>
> A second alternative was to go job hunting. Although it seemed like a logical solution, I knew that a good job would be difficult to find at this time. To secure factory work with daytime hours would be almost impossible. Daytime office jobs were available, but I lacked the training needed to qualify. I realized that it was unrealistic to expect to find a suitable, well-paying job locally.

A third option was available, however. Because I had lost my job due to foreign trade, I was eligible for a new federal program under the Trade Readjustment Act. This program would pay for college tuition for two years as well as books and supplies. I could attend day classes while the children were in school. The plan would also pay a small allowance for living expenses for up to one year if grade and attendance requirements were maintained. Although this option would require a drastically revised family budget, I knew I could manage.

Carol combined steps 4 and 5 of the problem-solving method: she proposed an alternative, applied criteria, and evaluated. This order enabled her to avoid undue repetition. The parallelism of her points helped to make the paper clear and easy to read. The details prepared the reader for the conclusion.

Writing a Conclusion

The end of a problem-solving paper presents the recommendation the writer has prepared the reader to accept. In other words, the selected solution should flow logically from the discussion of alternatives. Some conclusions contain a call for action, perhaps pointing out the consequences of inaction. In his paper about the air-conditioning problem on the job, Keith Zuspan concluded by making a recommendation:

> Repairing the existing air-conditioning unit would, in fact, be the most efficient and economical method of regaining the desired environmental controls required for the complex. It is also the writer's opinion that by utilizing the in-house building mechanics to complete this project, additional money could be saved.

Other conclusions, like the ending of Nancy Miller's paper, summarize the action already taken and explain how a solution fits the criteria:

> After reviewing the three alternatives, we chose the third, which proved to be the most cost-effective as well as energy-efficient. By purchasing the siding and windows together, we received a discount. The new furnace also proved to be energy-efficient, and we saw a sizable reduction in heating expense in the first year after installation. This third option has also increased the home's equity dramatically, although part of the increase is due to inflation. In 1972 we paid just over seven thousand dollars for the house, and now, two decades later, the house is worth over fifty thousand dollars.

Linda Gubernath used a similar conclusion for her paper discussing the purchase of a truck:

> Our family is now the proud owner of a gray General Motors S-15 truck with two jump seats tucked into the rear of the extended cab. My husband can haul his varied cargo. The children appreciate the extra room of this late model truck. I enjoy not having to shift gears. But best of all, the payments fit the family budget.

Revising a Problem-Solving Paper

To produce your best work, allow plenty of time for revising, editing, and proofreading your problem-solving paper. The following checklist will help to ensure that you check strategic points:

⋙ *Checklist for Revision*

1. Is the problem clearly defined in the introduction? Are the causes and pertinent history of the problem explained?

2. Are specific criteria for evaluating alternative solutions identified? Are these criteria reasonable and adequate?

3. Are different alternatives for solving the problem identified and described?

4. Is one particular alternative recommended? Is it clear why this is the best solution available?

5. Is the conclusion effective? Does it flow logically from the discussion of alternatives?

6. Have transitions been used effectively?

THREE SAMPLE PROBLEM-SOLVING PAPERS

In the first example, Rajini Maturu proposes a solution to a problem faced in the workplace:

Unhappy Customers at the Bank of India

The Union Bank of India is a financial institution that has 1,000 branches all over India. In the city of Secunderabad, the Union Bank caters to the financial needs of local customers. There the branch manager has to tackle the problem of customer dissatisfaction toward the check-cashing procedure.

Presently, there are four staff members of the bank taking care of the four steps of the check-cashing routine. During the banking hours between 10 a.m. and 2:30 p.m., there are about seventy customers. The customer first presents the check to a clerk, who enters the check number and amount in a register. The clerk gives the customer a metallic coin, called a token, with a number.

Then the customer goes to another clerk, who debits the customer's account with the amount of the check. Next, an accountant verifies the customer's signature. Finally, the check is taken to the cashier, who identifies the customer by the token number and makes the payment. During this procedure each customer waits for at least thirty minutes to cash a check.

There are two important aspects to the problem of expediting the check-cashing procedure. One aspect is the cost involved in bringing about changes since the branch is allowed a budget of $2,000 dollars. The other aspect to be considered is the amount of time saved by introducing the changes.

A proposed solution is to increase the number of staff members. Three additional clerks could be appointed to handle the check cashing. The cost of this change would mean $500 per clerk. For three more clerks, the total cost would be $1,500, which is within the budget limit. The main drawback to this proposal is that the customers would still have to wait for at least fifteen minutes to cash their checks.

A second proposal is the opening of a teller counter. This would mean creation of a separate cubicle with ledgers containing customer information. The specimen signatures of the customers would be stored at the teller counter. Here the entire check-cashing procedure could be managed by one employee called the teller officer. When a check was presented for payment, the teller officer would scrutinize the customer's signature, enter the check amount in the cash register, and make payment to the customer. This proposal would cost $1900; hence, the expenses would be within the budget. As all the operations would be managed by one employee, the check could be cashed in eight minutes. This would mean a considerable reduction in the customer's wait.

A third proposal is to computerize all the customer's records. With this method the check would be cashed in two minutes. This is the best proposal as far as the time element is concerned. The cost involved in purchasing the computers and training the clerks would be $4,000 dollars, however. The disadvantage to this proposal is that it does not meet the budget requirements.

The second proposal of creating a teller counter appears to be the most suitable action at this time. This proposal reduces the waiting period to cash a check from thirty minutes to eight minutes, and the expenses involved are within the budget specifications.

Janet Burks, a volunteer playground supervisor at her children's school, addresses the problem of how to deal with the number of children to be supervised at recess:

Problem: Playground Supervision

There was an old woman who lived in a shoe;
She had so many children she didn't know what to do.

—Mother Goose

The old lady living in a shoe and a volunteer playground supervisor have a similar problem. Both have so many children they do not know what to do. Although Mother Goose does not tell readers how many children the old woman had, the number was certainly fewer than the 120 or so children for which the playground supervisor is responsible.

What, specifically, can be done to solve this problem? Apparently, there are three possible solutions: soliciting additional volunteers, decreasing the number of children released for recess at any one time, or presenting a tax levy to pay the salaries for full-time supervisors. But any possible solution would be governed by two major constraints: cost and feasibility.

Presently, volunteers come to the playground to supervise during the hour-long midday recess (includes lunch time). The supervisor's responsibility is to circulate among the children and either to help them or to maintain discipline. The job is physically, emotionally, and mentally draining because the supervisor's tasks vary all the way from tying a kindergartner's shoe to helping a child who has fallen off the slide to resolving disputes. During this vigil, children may approach her frequently with problems, complaints, or accident reports. She cannot be everywhere at once. Children can be hurt before she even knows about a fight.

A complication arises when the supervisor must handle an extreme disciplinary situation. She is not allowed to administer discipline, but instead escorts unruly (and often unwilling) children to the principal's office. While she is attending to one child, 119 or so are outside without supervision.

As the volunteer program has continued, more people have been quitting because of difficulties they confront. This factor has made the playground problem even worse. One proposal is to solicit the help of more volunteers. Having more would provide two supervisors each day. Then the child-to-supervisor ratio of 120 to 1 would decrease to 60 to 1. Although this proposal has the advantage of being inexpensive, it also has the disadvantage of being unlikely. Most parents are not volunteering to help (many work) and probably will not volunteer in the future.

A second proposal is to decrease the number of children released for recess at any one time. This proposal would involve shortening the midday recess to thirty minutes and staggering recess times. Only two classes (of the usual five) would be on the playground at once, cutting the number of children to supervise to approximately 40 per session. The others would return to their rooms for quiet play with teacher supervision. But the children would probably object, and teachers would not want to assume additional duties.

The third proposal would be to present a tax levy to pay the salaries of full-time supervisors. The rate per hour would be much less than the rate required to pay teachers to supervise the playground during their lunch break. At the same time, the rate would be high enough to attract people to the job. Full-time volunteers sometimes do not come. Then too, full-time supervisors would have standard rules, which the volunteers do not have. The main disadvantage is voter reluctance to approve higher taxes.

The writer's recommendation is a combination of the first and third proposals. First, information concerning the problem could be distributed to parents. They would know that if enough volunteers cannot be found, then a tax levy would be necessary. The levy would provide the necessary funds for employing full-time supervisors.

Although the old lady in the shoe did not know what to do, let it not be said that the same is true of Sycamore's parents and teachers. Let us solve this problem together.

In the final example, Chris Hafley offers a solution to a problem facing his community:

A Plan for Quality Emergency Care

In the small northwest Ohio city of ———, the city fire department provides emergency medical care for its residents and township residents. In the past decade, a need for more advanced prehospital intervention has developed. To provide better medical care, the city council elected to send ten of twenty Advanced Emergency Medical Technicians to paramedic school at Sandusky Providence Hospital.

Before these ten people graduate and begin to function as paramedics, a dilemma must be resolved as to how the Rescue Squad will respond to possible life-threatening medical and trauma emergencies. With only one paramedic on duty as part of a two-person team, it would be almost impossible for the squad to function properly and respond efficiently to all calls twenty-four hours a day. Therefore, a committee has been organized to investigate four possible solutions.

The criteria set up by the investigational committee for review of the recommendations were availability, training, and cost-effectiveness. The first solution suggested was to respond with an ambulance and two police officers. But the officers' level of medical training is limited to basic first aid and CPR training. They would not be much help with patients needing advanced life support. To upgrade all the officers' training to at least emergency medical technician would involve considerable expense to the city. This method would be the most expensive option of the four, costing initially $30,000 to certify all eighteen officers. There are many times, however, when officers are out on call and thus are unavailable.

The second option would be to arrange for one additional paramedic to be on call at home for twenty-four hours a day. This plan would cost approximately $27,000, but it would be the most effective as far as availability is concerned.

The third option would be to dispatch an additional ambulance as a backup system for the first ambulance. After researching this option, more people favored it than any of the others because of quality of assistance and cost-effectiveness. Personnel on the ambulance already have the necessary training. Availability, however, would be a problem at times since the ambulance personnel make numerous out-of-town transfers.

The fourth option would provide for the fire department pumper to respond along with the ambulance. Research shows that this alternative would be the most cost-effective. The idea is to have two firefighters cross-trained as Basic Emergency Medical Technicians. There would be two firefighter EMTs on each shift. This option would cut down the number of personnel to be trained and would be the least expensive way for the city to provide the additional staff to assist in medical emergencies. The initial cost would be about $12,000 for training. An advantage to using the firefighters would be that they are usually available to respond to medical emergencies with the ambulance.

After all the information was compiled and the alternatives were reviewed again and again, the review committee recommended both options three and four be implemented. Thus if the firefighters were unavailable, the second ambulance might possibly provide a backup.

Questions for Analysis

1. Does each paper provide a clear description of the problem?
2. Are the criteria clear?
3. Does the order of alternatives seem appropriate?
4. Are alternatives evaluated according to the criteria?
5. Does the conclusion seem logical and complete?
6. What are the chief differences in the way the three problems are solved?

Summary

John Dewey's method of problem solving is widely known as "the scientific method." Objectivity is an essential aspect of problem solving. Although no one can be 100 percent objective, we can work to control our biases and mistakes.

Dewey's six steps of problem solving provide an easy and efficient way for you to organize a paper: (1) identify the problem, (2) describe the problem, (3) specify criteria, (4) propose alternatives, (5) evaluate alternatives according to the criteria, and (6) recommend the best alternative(s).

Criteria are standards of measurement—the factors or considerations that influence decision making. You apply criteria so that you can weigh the advantages and disadvantages of alternatives. This way you can evaluate the practicality of possible solutions to a problem.

For a problem-solving paper, you may need special transitions to show cause and effect. Your conclusion should flow logically from the body. The conclusion presents the solution you have prepared the reader to accept.

Key Terms

scientific method	alternative	firsthand information
criteria	objectivity	secondhand information
criterion		

Practice

Collaborative Identification of Criteria

The following introduction to a problem-solving paper was written by Patricia Davis. After you read it, brainstorm possible criteria that would influence the final decision. One group member should record all of these. Finally, examine your list of criteria and decide which are most important in determining a solution.

A Pet for Aunt Emily

My aunt, although eighty-three years old and rather frail, is still able to care for herself. Aunt Emily lives alone in her own home on a limited income. Ordinarily, she is quite independent and self-sufficient, but last week she surprised me. When I dropped by, she asked for advice. Confiding that she was lonely, she explained she needed companionship and was thinking about getting a pet. But she was unsure about what sort of animal would be best for her. She asked me to help in deciding what kind of pet would be the most enjoyable and suitable.

Collaborative Problem Solving

Directions: Select *one* of the following cases. Steps 1 and 2 of Dewey's problem-solving method are given. Supply steps 3, 4, 5, and 6.

1. Your neighbors often stay out until 2:30 a.m. on weekends. They leave their Doberman tied out in the backyard, where he howls—keeping you awake until they take him in. You do not know if he is hungry, lonely, or what. The dog does not recognize you, but from a distance he seems fairly friendly. What are your alternatives? What risks are involved? How will you solve this problem?

2. You are a man who works a forty-hour week, the father of two boys, ages ten and twelve. The boys are active in sports programs after school. After

supper they always have homework. Last month your wife took a full-time job that sometimes requires her to work overtime. Since then the laundry has piled up, and the house has lost its tidy look. Many times there are dirty dishes stacked in the kitchen sink. Dinner during the week is often just sandwiches and canned soup or TV dinners. What factors should be considered? What alternatives exist? What will you do?

3. You, your husband, and child live in a small town. He works nights. One evening you are alone except for your three-year-old child, asleep in her room. About eleven o'clock you hear a scratching noise in the chimney of the fireplace. Terrified, you watch a small dark creature creep out and fly across the living room. It perches in one corner up near the ceiling. What will you do? What are your alternatives? What factors must be considered?

4. You are a sales representative for a store that sells computers and software. While you are running a booth at a trade show, you meet a woman who asks if you still have the same sales manager, J. D. Smith. When you reply "Yes," she says, "That's too bad." Then she tells about her boyfriend buying software out of the sales manager's home.

   For a few days, you mull over the pros and cons of telling the owner, whom you admire and trust. You do not trust the sales manager because of his office pranks and complaints behind the owner's back. What other factors should you consider? Is there any other alternative? What do you decide?

5. You are the assistant manager of a bookstore. As you enter the store from the back, you see the nine-year-old son of your best friend looking at a book. He glances around and inserts it inside his jacket. Then he starts walking rapidly to the front of the store.

   Store policy requires that you alert another employee, stop shoplifters immediately after they leave the store, and retrieve the merchandise. You are to warn them that if they ever reenter, charges will be filed. Parents or guardians of children who shoplift are to be notified. To prevent your friend from hurt and to protect yourself from an awkward situation, you are tempted to ignore what you saw and mention it to no one. What factors should be examined? Is there a third alternative? What do you decide to do?

Case Problem: How Can The Windmill Make a Profit?

Directions: Using the problem-solving method, discuss the following case.

An Amish restaurant, The Windmill, has been in business for twenty-five years. Medium-priced, the food is served family style. Ten years ago the dining rooms were repainted; no other redecorating has been done. The rest rooms are small and drab. The place is always clean; the service, friendly; the food, excellent. Homemade pies, cakes, muffins, and rolls are featured. Fresh vegetables are used. Each day of the week, the dinner menu features smoked sausage and sauerkraut, beef and noodles, fried chicken, turkey and dressing, or some other entree in addition to the regular fare of steak, chops, and ribs. Profits have been very good until recently.

During the past month, two attractive restaurants have opened nearby. The small one offers inexpensive Chinese food of average quality; much of the business is "take out." The large restaurant is spacious and elegant. It specializes in seafood, offering everything from scrod to lobster. The food is good, but expensive.

The owners of The Windmill have called a meeting with their full-time employees. The purpose of the meeting is to (1) pinpoint the causes of the problem, (2) predict whether it is short- or long-term, (3) explore alternatives, and (4) make a recommendation.

Fifty Suggestions for Problem-Solving Papers

1. A problem on the job
2. Stress management for nurses
3. Stress management for police officers
4. More training for emergency medical technicians
5. More training for computer lab assistants
6. Security for twenty-four-hour businesses
7. Automobile security from theft
8. Spotting shoplifters
9. Harassment in the workplace
10. A problem in a community/town/city
11. How can we attract new industries and businesses to the city?
12. How can we attract more tourists?
13. How can we find funds to replace playground equipment in the city park?
14. Staffing athletic programs on a low budget
15. Inadequate child-care facilities for working parents
16. Recycling can be simplified
17. Finding a new city landfill
18. Local litter control
19. Stray animal control
20. Drag racing on city streets
21. Staffing a church nursery
22. Lack of recreation for teens
23. Complaints and the apartment owner
24. Problems for families when women start careers

25. Burglar-proofing a house
26. Adjustment to college after . . . years
27. How can citizens influence the content of television shows?
28. Where to vacation next year?
29. Buying a second vehicle
30. Teaching children the value of money
31. Good nutrition on a low budget?
32. Establishing a regular investment plan
33. Maintaining an exercise plan
34. Weight control
35. Mastering the fear of failure
36. Personal security at night when alone
37. Clearing away a misunderstanding with a friend
38. Coping with a difficult person
39. Coping with a troublesome neighbor
40. Coping with divorce
41. Coping with discrimination
42. Breaking the nicotine habit
43. Alcoholism in the family
44. Adjusting to retirement
45. Finding an excellent nursing home
46. Investigating alternatives for elder care
47. Relocating in a new community
48. Buying a home
49. Making a house more energy-efficient
50. Monitoring children's television programs

CHAPTER 20

Shaping an Effective Argument

Truth is one forever absolute, but
opinion is truth filtered through the moods,
the blood, the disposition of the spectator.

—Wendell Phillips (1859)

Hardly a day passes that you do not need to persuade someone of something. It may be as trivial as convincing a friend to try a new restaurant or as significant as convincing an interviewer you are qualified for a position. You may be required to write a persuasive research paper, a proposal, or an application for a grant. You may use persuasion to sell a product or to obtain payment. Skill in persuasion will enable you to become a more effective writer both in college and in the workplace.

Facts alone may not convince. When a problem arises, you may have a practical solution and all the relevant facts; but unless you can persuade effectively, your suggestion or recommendation may go unheeded. Many people act on perceptions and instincts that are not always logical. And priorities vary. Unless you can tap into your audience's priorities and needs, chances are your proposal will be rejected. Then, too, facts can be interpreted in various ways. Therefore, careful audience analysis is essential to draft an effective persuasive strategy.

In a college class you may be asked to write a persuasive essay, a reaction paper, or a paper of argument. The writing strategy you select will be determined by the purpose of the assignment, the topic, and the amount of resistance to the proposition. Will the audience agree or show reluctance, firm opposition, or hostility? A persuasive essay implies a somewhat informal paper, usually based on experience. A reaction paper is usually written in response to a reading or piece of literature, as discussed in chapter 26. A paper of argument is longest, often requiring research, as explained in this chapter.

The general purpose of any argument is to persuade readers to accept a belief, adopt a policy, or enact a decision, proposal, or law. An argument urges change and often includes a call for action. In this book, the term *argument* is used in a broad sense that overlaps with persuasion. In the strictest sense, *argument* appeals only to logic and perhaps ethics, whereas persuasion includes logical, ethical, and emotional appeals.

THREE PERSUASIVE APPEALS

More than two thousand years ago, the Greek philosopher Aristotle defined three kinds of appeals that make up an argument: *logos* (logic), *ethos* (ethics), and *pathos* (emotion). Logical appeals are based on facts, sound inferences, and working theories (see the discussion of accuracy in Chapter 5). A logical argument appeals to the mind, using evidence, reasons, and examples to support a claim or proposition.

Aristotle recognized, however, that logic alone is not always sufficient to persuade an audience. To be convincing, you must also gain the trust of your readers; and to do so you must be perceived as honest, fair, and responsive to moral obligations. Aristotle called this the appeal to *ethos*, to the trustworthiness and credibility of the person making the argument. This ethical appeal requires you first to demonstrate knowledge of your subject. Second, you must approach the subject in an evenhanded way, presenting differing viewpoints accurately and fairly. Finally, your written voice should seem reasonable, controlled, and concerned.

An ethical appeal is designed to strike a responsive chord in the minds of the readers, entreating them to do what is right, good, fair, and best. Ethics can be broadly defined as a set of moral values—principles of conduct for an individual, group, profession, or society. Sound ethics are fundamental to a well-constructed argument.

Effective arguments are marked not only by appeals to logic and ethics but also by appeals to the emotions. Emotional appeals work best, however, when used in moderation. They stir the feelings of readers with figurative language, connotation, and anecdote. Former president Reagan, a master storyteller, used emotional appeals well, often telling stories to illustrate a point. Such appeals can be powerful, for they bypass the intellect.

The three appeals can be identified by the types of questions they raise with readers:

- Logical appeal: Is the claim or petition factual and reasonable? True or false? Practical or impractical?

- Ethical appeal: Is it just or unjust? Honest or dishonest? Good or bad?

- Emotional appeal: Do the words arouse feelings of empathy, sympathy, or antagonism? Do they make the reader care about the subject?

In an effective argument, all three appeals are intertwined. Ignoring any of the three weakens the chain of persuasion. Effective appeals harmonize. An emotional appeal that conflicts with a logical appeal is unethical. Credible persuasion rests on facts and ethical reasons bonded with appropriate emotion. For example, a presentation to a board of directors might reveal little emotion, whereas a speech for a graduation ceremony, recognition dinner, or farewell party might express considerable feeling.

Used wisely, emotion can motivate. Although logic can point out a path to a goal, unless emotion moves an audience to act, the argument may be in vain.

Guidelines for Using Persuasive Appeals

1. *Alert the listener to a problem by using suitable emotion.*
2. *Use restraint.* Do not overstate. Exaggerated appeals can backfire.
3. *Do not oversimplify.* Guard against either/or alternatives.
4. *Avoid conflicting appeals.* Contradiction undermines arguments.
5. *Show and tell.* Use examples and anecdotes to illustrate and interest.
6. *Do not circumvent an issue.* Focus your argument on the issue.

WRITING AN ARGUMENT PAPER

As you write an argument paper, keep the three types of appeal in mind. Consider how they can help you focus your paper.

Selecting a Topic

The topic for an argument paper should be controversial and significant. A controversial topic has at least two points of view. To be significant, the disagreement would involve more than a definition of terms or a question of fact that could be easily checked. This means the topic would center on more than a simple question of truth or a matter of personal preference. For instance, to argue that computers can be fun would be unsuitable. Or to argue vaguely that R.E.M. is better than the Beatles would be futile since this judgment hinges upon personal taste. But a paper that contains adequate support and criteria to evaluate the characteristics of both musical groups could yield a logical argument.

Claims of judgment involve an opinion or rating that is significant and logical, resting on facts and reasons. Aesthetic judgments evaluate the worth or value of music, art, and literature. Ethical judgments evaluate whether something is beneficial or harmful, humane or inhumane, moral or immoral, right or wrong. Functional judgments evaluate how well something or someone works. Arguments, including judgments, make five types of claims.

Five Basic Claims Made In Arguments

1. *Claim of judgment:* What is the writer's position on the issue? What are the criteria upon which the judgment is based?
2. *Claim of fact:* What is actually true? (Myth as opposed to fact or updates in scientific thinking might be typical examples.)
3. *Claim of interpretation:* What do the facts mean?
4. *Claim of cause:* Why did something happen? Why is it the way it is? (A valid hypothesis provides the simplest and best explanation.)
5. *Claim of policy:* What should be done? What is the best alternative to solve the problem? Or are there several acceptable alternatives?

Before an argument can be resolved, the participants must agree on a *basic premise* or *proposition* upon which the argument rests. For example, two students could agree on the basic premise that a college diploma should signify competency, although they disagree about how competency should be measured. Since they agree on the underlying belief, a logical argument could be constructed.

To write effectively about a value-laden topic, you must be open-minded, fair, and alert. Topics such as gun control, abortion, and religion carry emotional baggage that make them difficult to argue for three reasons: (1) rarely do the opposing views agree on a basic premise, (2) articles and other sources are often slanted toward a particular view, and (3) the research writer must sift the evidence while keeping his or her biases under control. Other topics for argument may have inherent hazards, too. For your consideration, some typical problems that students wade into are listed here:

Common Hazards in Selecting Topics for Argument

1. *The topic is too broad.* Subjects should be narrowed to a proposition that can be supported and discussed well in the allotted length.
2. *The topic is strictly informational.* A paper of argument does more than collect information. The writer strives to convince the reader of a proposition.
3. *The topic is hackneyed.* Sometimes students resurrect old papers or debate notes from high school. An important reason for assigning a paper of argument is to spur you to think and learn.
4. *Inadequate support is available.* If a topic is recent, a researcher may find little data available. If a topic is heavily laden with emotion, the researcher may find bias and fallacies in the sources.

Typically, instructors groan when they see old, overused topics such as capital punishment, legalizing marijuana, and the like. To be significant, a topic does not have to have worldwide or national implications—it may be a campus, community, or neighborhood issue. Such topics can yield fresh material.

Criteria for Selecting an Argument Topic

1. Is there disagreement about the subject or an area of resistance?
2. Is the issue significant and challenging?
3. Can I obtain enough factual information?
4. After research, will I be able to thoroughly understand the issue?
5. Can I write about the topic in a fair, objective tone?

Gathering Information and Prewriting

The more knowledgeable and sophisticated your readers, the more they will insist on adequate proof of a claim. Yet a writer seldom has all the facts needed to attain a comprehensive view of a controversial topic. To be knowledgeable and objective, you need information from a variety of sources and viewpoints. In the workplace, you may talk to personnel at other companies who have resolved a similar question or problem. You may also consult journals, trade magazines, or online services.

In a college class, you may be asked to take a position on a literary work and write a paper of argument. In that case, you examine the work closely, make notes, think, and write (see chapters 26, 27, and 28). Or you may be required to do a research paper with text citations and a list of works cited (chapters 21, 22, and 23). To focus a search for information, you might begin by posing a controlling question.

Drafting a Controlling Question A controlling question narrows the search for information and establishes the direction a paper will take. This question limits the topic and aids in finding appropriate source materials. After you write your controlling question, check to see whether or not it performs these two vital functions:

1. Identifies the *specific* topic and scope
2. Specifies the *direction* of the research

For controversial topics, the wording of the question should receive special attention. The words should be fair and objective. Notice how one word can change the tone of a question:

Biased: Should drivers be *forced* to wear seatbelts?

Neutral: Should drivers be *required* to wear seatbelts?

A neutral controlling question will help you to analyze a controversy fairly. Rereading the question from time to time will aid you in withholding judgment until key facts and implications are clear. The researcher who maintains an open mind is more likely to appraise an issue impartially than is one who leaps to a quick decision.

Searching for Reliable Sources   You need to gain an accurate overview of an issue, not just gather evidence to bolster one point of view. Understanding varying views is necessary to shape a convincing argument. Read from several sources to compare accounts and judge credibility. Not all sources are authoritative or reliable. Some may contain incorrect or outdated information, logical fallacies, or bias.

As you select books, look at the back cover, in the foreword, or in the introduction for the writer's credentials. Is he or she an authority in the field? Then scan a few pages and listen to the tone of the writing. Does it sound objective or biased? Does the coverage seem slanted? Do the significant points of the controversy seem to be covered? If you find inconsistencies or differing interpretations, jot down page numbers and authors. These discrepancies should be mentioned in your paper.

To research a local issue, you might interview the people involved and read newspaper accounts. Reputable newspapers and magazines are good sources of information on current events. On the front page of a newspaper is recent news; on the editorial pages are opinions of columnists, editors, and guest writers.

To research a topic in a specialized field, consult journals or trade publications for technical information and opinions of authorities. Popular magazines may give brief factual overviews of issues, but the treatment may be incomplete. While interviewing and reading, watch for facts, statistics, expert opinion, cause and effect, reasons, and examples that constitute support for either side. Try to spot anything that seems biased, irresponsible, or incompetent. Make careful notes that fairly represent the differing views you encounter.

Making Con/Pro Lists   You can simplify the task of organizing the chief points of a controversy by listing pros and cons while reading. To separate evidence against and for the proposition, just write *con* and *pro* at the top of a sheet of paper. Then as you read, list proof in two vertical columns, placing parallel points side by side. Leave plenty of white space between items to add notes. Follow each item with the name of the author and page number. This identification will save time spent on documentation later. The lists will look like the examples below except that actual points and answers will be listed:

Con	*Pro*
Main point (Barnes 140)	Agrees with facts, then disagrees about implications (Aker 39)
Main point (Barnes 141)	Objection and answer (Berry 149)
Main point (Smith 33)	Objection and answer (Conroy 12)

Stating a Position

After you list the significant points of disagreement for an argument, your next task is to select the viewpoint you think is soundest. Then write a proposition, indicating your position on the issue.

Writing a Proposition   The thesis statement of an argument is called the *proposition*. The tone of this statement is usually serious and much stronger than that of an ordinary thesis. To draft a proposition, you might start by writing a controlling question, then explore its implications:

Controlling question: Since privacy issues are involved, should telemarketing firms be subject to restrictions?

Possible thesis: Telemarketing is an invasion of privacy that should not be permitted.

Possible thesis: Telemarketing is a legal right that should not be abridged.

Taking a Position of Compromise   Sometimes you may not agree wholeheartedly with either view; you see some validity in both views. If you reach an impasse, try a middle-of-the road approach. Can you think of a way to modify your stand with a compromise that is acceptable to you? The examples below may suggest some ideas:

Compromise: Telemarketing should not be permitted after 5:00 p.m.

Compromise: Telemarketing by computerized dialing should not be allowed.

Each time you revise your thesis, check it carefully. Does it say what you mean? Could the terminology be confusing to the reader? Does it need to be revised further? Creating a focused title may also be helpful at this point.

Writing a Focused Title   A focused title acts like a thesis statement, clearly stating the proposition. Focused titles can be quite beneficial. You can glance back at the title from time to time to ensure that the argument is staying on course. A focused title indicates a position.

Focused title: English Should Be Declared the Official Language of the USA

Focused title: The USA Does Not Need an Official Language

When an issue is heated, a writer may pose a question in the title to create a zone of neutrality. This zone allows the writer to present and evaluate the evidence before declaring a position in a *delayed thesis*. This *indirect approach* lowers the temperature of the argument and encourages consideration of differences. Although a neutral question title does not indicate a position, it does indicate a persuasive purpose:

Neutral question title: Should English Be Declared Our Official Language?

Although the neutral question title can be quite effective, your instructor may specify a focused title to simplify the writing of your paper. When misused, the neutral question title can lead to vague, rambling papers. Regardless of which kind of title you use, understanding the opposing view will assist in focusing your persuasive strategy.

Understanding Opposing Views

Two landowners were involved in a boundary dispute that dated back to their grandfathers' time. Years before, a rail fence had been erected by one grandparent and moved by the other. At last one man consulted a lawyer. Relating the history of the argument, the client presented one view of the dispute. The lawyer assured him that the law was on his side and asked when he wanted to sue. The client replied, "Never. I just gave you the other guy's version."

Researching both views provides an opportunity not only to weigh the facts, but also to consider the priorities, values, and attitudes of readers who disagree. Sometimes readers may agree with a proposal, but not act. Then the first task is to discover the *area of resistance* and determine why they are reluctant. The second task is to prepare a persuasive strategy that will overcome their resistance. For example, voters may agree that more money is needed to fund local schools, but they may resist voting for higher taxes. How do you convince them that the benefits justify the expense? That is the question that would control the direction of the argument.

Once you understand the opposing view, you will be more alert to possible evidence. Then you can decide how to shape the argument to emphasize advantages and benefits.

Questions to Help the Writer Analyze Readers

1. How much do readers know about the topic?
2. How strong is their disagreement or resistance?
3. If readers agree on a proposal, why are they reluctant to act?
4. What is important to readers?
5. What is important to me?
6. What change can I reasonably expect?

Planning the Shape of an Argument

There is no "one size fits all" strategy of argument. Arguments come in all shapes and sizes, depending on the rhetorical situation. Thus a writer is left to devise a strategy that will accommodate the situation in the best possible way. The structure of a logical argument consists of four basic parts: (1) making a claim (stating the purpose), (2) anticipating objections from readers, (3) countering objections by supporting the claim with solid evidence, and (4) submitting a conclusion derived from the evidence.

Four Elements of a Logical Argument

Claim: The specific proposition of a writer is the claim. A claim may be made directly or indirectly.

Objections: Knowing the main points of the opponents helps a writer to answer objections effectively.

Evidence: A writer supports a claim with facts, interprets the facts, and explains—giving statistics, reasons, examples, or other evidence. (The most effective arguments contain an appeal designed to satisfy or benefit the reader.)

Conclusion: The end of an argument is often a restatement of the claim. It may be a summary of main points or a logical generalization. It may attempt to motivate the reader to act.

Direct or Indirect Order: Early or Delayed Thesis?   To organize an effective argument, you first consider whether to use direct or indirect order. In other words, will an early or a delayed thesis be most persuasive? How the four parts of the argument are arranged and developed depends on the implications of the topic and the probable impact on the audience. Think: How will the proposition be received by readers?

Direct Approach If your readers are likely to be well-informed and only mildly opposed to a proposition, you may decide to be direct and bring out the proposal early. Then the thesis can be stated in the introduction. Here is an example of a proposition that would probably meet with little resistance from employees who will readily accept change:

Early thesis: A new system of billing will speed up the collection process and save an estimated $50,000 annually in collection costs.

Indirect Approach An indirect plan, on the other hand, allows you to delay your thesis until much later in the paper. A delayed thesis allows you to consider the main points of the other side before mentioning your points. This arrangement sets the stage for a congenial discussion. Often it is wise to treat an argument as a misunderstanding or as a difference in perception. This low-key approach is less likely to be perceived as threatening or combative. Any hint of antagonism, sarcasm, impatience, or superiority will undermine your stand. A reader who is patronized or derided may be offended. Negative undertones can sabotage the flawless logic of an argument.

Readers who are likely to be uninformed or hostile will require more facts and reasons than will readers who are well informed. You need to lay extra groundwork for your recommendation. The stronger the objection, the more time you will need to prepare them to accept the proposition. As long as the path of an argument is clear, the thesis statement may be postponed until the body or conclusion.

Delayed thesis: Genetic engineering within certain limits can be beneficial.

Sometimes, however, a thesis is implicit (unstated). Still, the argument is focused on one unmistakable conclusion. Since arguments with implicit theses require considerable skill, they are best left to experienced writers. Most instructors require an explicit thesis to aid in establishing the direction of an argument. Regardless of the type of argument you write, stress the benefits, advantages, and strengths of your proposal.

Summary: Factors to Consider in Planning an Argument

1. What does the audience believe about the issue?
2. How does the audience feel about the issue?
3. Which order will be most effective: direct or indirect?
4. What kind of title will be most effective?
5. How much transition will be needed to make points of view clear?

Presenting Opposing Viewpoints   To set the tone for a calm, courteous discussion, place the opposing view *before* your own. This method acknowledges the main points of the opposition and shows that you have considered the evidence. This arrangement is akin to listening, indicating a willingness to suspend judgment. This makes your argument stronger, for it emphasizes your answers to the opposing point of view. See Labeling Points of View for advice on keeping viewpoints clear.

When you are *for* an issue, the argument seems simpler for most students to set up. *Then you take the pro side of the issue and place it second.*

(con) Opponents of gambling   (con) Anti-gambling faction

(pro) Proponents of gambling   (pro) Pro-gambling faction

But when you are *against* an issue, setting up the terminology seems to take more thought. Then it may be easier to label the views *first* and *second* in the correct order, remembering to place your view second. To prevent possible confusion in your notes, clearly label points of view and place them at the top of your lists of points.

First view: Advocates of gambling   Supporters of gambling

Second view: Adversaries of gambling   Critics of gambling

After points of view are clearly identified, you consider whether to present the argument in block or alternating (point-by-point) form.

Block or Alternating Organization   There are two basic ways you can set up a controversial topic. The simplest is the block method. This way the main points of the opposing side appear in one chunk before the proponent's arguments. This arrangement has an advantage in tone. Describing the opponent's

LABELING POINTS OF VIEW

If differing points of view go unlabeled, readers may become bewildered. To prevent confusion, identify the side holding each view *every time there is a shift from one to the other*. Familiar transitional pairs appear below:

adversaries	opponents	critics	opposition
advocates	proponents	supporters	sponsors

Select either *one pair* of terms or *two closely related pairs* and repeat them throughout your paper. For example, you might substitute *opponents* for *the opposition* to provide variety. But abrupt shifts to dissimilar pairs would be distracting; the puzzled reader would have to stop and reread. Clarity is more important than variety.

When selecting labels for viewpoints, beware of slanting. For instance, a student writing about sex education called the opposition "right wingers" while labeling the other side "proponents." This mismatch of terms not only lacked parallelism but also revealed bias. Likewise, avoid *liberals* and *conservatives*. These words have been bandied about so much their meanings have blurred. In some contexts, they have also taken on negative connotations.

To maintain an objective tone, try to avoid personal involvement in the argument. Two tips should be helpful: (1) Use third person, not first. (2) Try putting yourself in the role of a reporter writing a news item. This role should help you to distance yourself from the topic and avoid slanting.

view before countering objections not only conveys a sense of fairness but also postpones disagreement.

When an issue is complex, the alternating method is clearer than the block. The alternating pattern pairs one of the opposing points with one of the proponent's, arguing back and forth, emphasizing the answers to points. A possible disadvantage is that disagreement emerges earlier than in the block method. Then too, the alternating method requires extra transition. In fig. 20.1, each box represents a paragraph (others could be added).

In the block method, the opponent's view (con side of the paper) is summarized after the introduction. One paragraph is usually adequate for major con points. In the remaining pro blocks, the writer counters the opponent's points and submits evidence for the pro view.

The alternating method places contrasting points together. To add force to an argument, always *start with a con point and answer with a pro point*. An unanswered

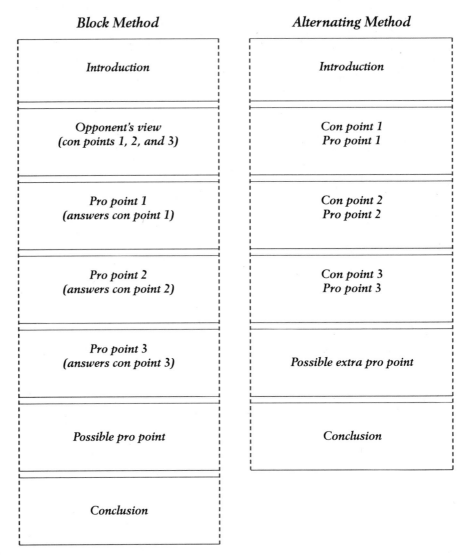

Figure 20.1 Ways to organize an argument.

point would pose a serious flaw in any argument. If you cannot answer a point adequately and should decide to reverse your original position in the argument, that is all right. It shows you have an open, logical mind.

Usually, main points are arranged in least-to-most-important order so that the argument gradually builds. The best point is placed last, where it receives the most emphasis. To plan a paper on a controversy, the following questions will be helpful:

Questions for Shaping a Controversial Topic

1. What is at stake? Is there a hidden agenda?
2. Where is the best spot for the proposition? (Direct or indirect order?)
3. Is a definition needed?
4. How much background information will be needed?
5. Is there a common ground?
6. Can any concessions be made?
7. What are the advantages to accepting the proposition?
8. Are there disadvantages?
9. Will the block or alternating method be more suitable?
10. What is the best way to conclude the argument?

Drafting a Neutral Introduction

The purpose of an introduction is to present a factual overview of the argument. The introduction describes the issue and its origin, cause(s), and history. The introduction tells *when, who, what, how,* and perhaps *why,* defining the area of disagreement. The tone should be neutral. If readers are familiar with a topic, background information may be brief. If a topic is unfamiliar, the introduction should be more detailed. In the first example below, the writer describes a local problem that had been aired extensively by the media:

Curbing Overpopulation of Deer by "Harvesting"

The rapid growth of deer herds in Sharron Woods and Blacklick Park in Central Ohio poses problems. With no predators, the deer have multiplied to the point where they have stripped the woods and run out of food. Samuel B. Randall, attorney for Metro Parks, estimates that in the 700 acres of Sharron Woods, 375 deer live, which is "10 times the number the park can support." The controversy is over the means by which the deer herds will be decreased. One alternative is to let nature resolve the problem. Other alternatives are to use birth control or to move the deer. A fourth alternative, "harvesting," has led to requests for intervention. Recently, a Franklin Court judge declared he had no jurisdiction over the case (Candisky 1).

In the next introduction Norma Caldwell, a student writer, gives a bit of history and summarizes a less controversial topic:

Megadoses of Vitamin C Are Not Safe for Everyone

Many people consider vitamin C, ascorbic acid, to be a "Wonder Drug" (Williams 259). When Linus Pauling, the Nobel Prize chemist, first published his book *Vitamin C and the Common Cold* more than two decades ago, he stirred up considerable interest in this vitamin. Pauling and his followers believe vitamin C can cure everything from the "common cold to cancer." They believe megadoses of vitamin C to be safe and necessary for maintaining good health and recommend taking up to several thousand milligrams daily (Hausman 189). Other researchers, pharmacists, and doctors insist Pauling's tests were inconclusive and are contradicted by more recent research and test results. Many of these specialists believe that megadoses are unnecessary and possibly dangerous (Baringa 374).

When background events stretch out over several years, chronological order is usually the best way to organize details. Rita F. Fleming uses chronological order in the first two paragraphs of her paper:

The Bittersweet Truth about Aspartame

In 1965, a G. D. Searle chemist named James Schetter "synthesized a compound," hoping to find a treatment for ulcers. After splashing his hand with his latest creation, he licked a finger as he moved some lab papers and discovered that the new substance tasted intensely sweet. Thus aspartame was discovered. In 1973 G. D. Searle started the production of NutraSweet in compliance and with the approval of the Food and Drug Administration. But the agency soon questioned the company's studies, and Searle voluntarily suspended marketing (Farber 52).

Over the next seven years, the FDA investigated both Searle and aspartame to answer "basic questions about the product's safety." Court documents gathered by attorney and food safety advocate James Turner and interviews with FDA policy makers and scientists showed that the safety studies were done correctly. Searle went on to conduct "independent studies on the effects of aspartame" on both animals and humans. No evidence of danger was found. In 1981 the FDA approved aspartame as a liquid sugar substitute to be sold under the name of NutraSweet. In 1986 the FDA approved the dry form, called Equal (*Safety* A1).

Finding a Common Ground

Agreement sets the scene for mutual respect. A point of agreement or *common ground* increases the chances that a proposition will receive thoughtful consideration from readers who disagree. Common ground can be a shared interest, a belief, an understanding, or a goal. In the second paragraph of her paper about vitamin C, Norma Caldwell presents a common ground of established fact:

For many years vitamin C has been generally accepted as a vital nutrient required by humans for good health and "prevention of scurvy." Some of the many uses of vitamin C are as follows: to fight infection, heal wounds and fractures, enhance iron absorption, metabolize folic acid and proteins, manufacture collagen, retain capillary wall strength, build not only teeth and bones but also certain brain chemicals (Burtis, Davis, Martin 186). In addition, vitamin C reduces the "risk of blood clot formation" (Mindell 43).

A common ground prepares the reader for a reasonable argument. In her paper about aspartame, Rita Fleming provides facts and advantages before presenting disadvantages:

Nearly "180 times sweeter than sugar," aspartame is the most popular low-calorie sweetener available today. Each year over "100 million Americans consume carbon-ated beverages, iced tea, desserts, presweetened cold cereal and other products" sweetened with aspartame (Farber 52). NutraSweet has been referred to as a "dieter's dream" since it contains few calories, and many products containing aspartame have been labeled "low calorie" (*Sweeteners* 49).

To settle on a common ground, a writer not only presents facts but also listens to the connotations of words. Ill-chosen phrases can inflame feelings. But tactful words create an air of peaceful deliberation.

Acknowledging Points of Agreement

While analyzing the main points of the opposing view, watch for a way to grant a point. Agreeing before disagreeing is not only fair but also tactically sound. Rita Fleming extends the common ground of her argument by conceding a point:

> Many consumers assume that when the FDA approves a product, it is safe for them to use. True, aspartame has been generally accepted as harmless, and many people use it with "no apparent ill effects," but others do "complain of side effects." According to Richard Wurtman, a neuroscientist at the Massachusetts Institute of Technology, aspartame has been linked to "numerous side effects." Some of the most common are "seizures, migraine headaches and mood swings" (*Macleans'* 31, 32).
> Dr. John Olney of Washington University, St. Louis, has found that aspartate, a chemical found in NutraSweet, may have the "potential to cause brain damage" as well as brain tumors in animals. Many questions about the safety of aspartame remain unanswered (Farber 47, 48).

To show agreement with the opposition's point, acknowledge it with a word or phrase such as *certainly, granted, it is true, proponents agree,* or *advocates recognize.* Then present the related pro point. The following phrases or similar ones might be used:

It is true that . . . but. . . .

Proponents realize that . . . , yet they believe. . . .

Supporters recognize . . . ; still they do not acknowledge. . . .

Refuting Opposing Points

To refute a point means you show that it is irrelevant or only partly true or completely false. In answering objections, avoid any hint of disrespect or antagonism; be respectful and friendly. When you show respect for the reader's view, your chances for acceptance of the proposition increase. To be convincing, a writer needs adequate evidence. The opinion of just one authority is inadequate; multiple sources are required. Opinion must be substantiated by facts, reasons, and examples. As a rule, the more evidence, the more convincing the argument, but do not oversell.

Select the most noteworthy points of the argument. Use quality evidence. Weak evidence will not support a claim for very long. Careful readers will be apt to spot distortions, omissions, quotations taken out of context, or other problems. There must be solid proof that the proposition is logical, beneficial, and ethical. Only a sound, ethical argument will stand up under intense scrutiny.

Dodging Fallacies

For an argument to be effective, the logic must be impeccable. A writer who misquotes, transposes statistics, misdiagnoses cause and effect, or trips over hasty generalizations may be perceived as careless, uninformed, biased, or manipulative. Although name-calling, exaggeration, or other blunders may be discounted in conversation, readers are unlikely to be so patient or forgiving. (See chapter 18 for more on fallacies.) Let's consider two fallacies from papers:

> The most annoying thing in the world is to pick up the telephone after a long day at work and find a telemarketer at the other end of the line.
>
> A voluntary national service would solve the United States' problems.

Both claims are hasty generalizations. Certainly there are greater annoyances than a telephone interruption, and no one action could possibly solve the numerous problems faced by the United States. Another common fallacy is assuming that a complex problem results from a single cause. Rarely does a complex problem have only one cause. For example, presidents are often blamed for problems existing long before they took office. The truth is that many factors influence complicated problems.

A final precaution to keep in mind is that an analogy cannot constitute proof. Although valid analogies are useful for explanation, they prove nothing.

Writing a Conclusion

A conclusion is the final nail in the building of an argument. A conclusion should restate the thesis and leave the reader persuaded that the reasoning is valid. If action is advocated, the conclusion should convey a sense of immediacy, a feeling that impels the reader to act. Rita Fleming closes with a reference to risk:

> Although the FDA has allowed aspartame to remain on the market, a look at the history of this chemical raises severe doubts about its long-term safety for everyone. The risks of using this product regularly far outweigh any advantages.

The conclusion of an argument should be sound, appropriate, and complete. It should not stray into irrelevancies, fail to take a stand, or end abruptly. To be forceful and complete, most arguments need a restatement of the thesis. Restatement redirects the reader's attention to the proposition, as in the following example. Kathy Kerchner writes:

Finally, the use of restraints is a prime concern in geriatric facilities. Research on physical or mechanical restraint use is vague, and more is needed. For many confused residents, restraints are harmful in the long run. If a restraint not only denies freedom and dignity for the aged, but also leads to disorientation, then justification for use must outweigh possible consequences. Caregivers should exhaust all other alternatives before applying a restraint and continue to reevaluate its need from time to time.

Kathy's ending is one of compromise. She realizes that there is no one solution for all situations or all patients at all times. Still, she takes a firm stand, pointing out the dangers of long-term use of restraints.

Revising an Argument

Reviewing your outline will help you check the organization of your paper. Could the order be improved? Would any section or subsection fit better in another spot? Reread the paper and check it with the outline as you go. Do you see any discrepancies? This method forces you to look more closely at work that has become familiar. Using a checklist will help you guard against omissions.

 Checklist for Revising an Argument

1. Is the issue clearly defined?
2. Does the introduction have a neutral tone?
3. Has a common ground been established?
4. Are points of view clearly identified?
5. Are main points of the opposition presented fairly?
6. Is adequate evidence presented to refute each con point?
7. Is the logic sound and ethical?
8. Is the language calm and rational?
9. Does the conclusion summarize the position?
10. Is the organization clear to the reader?

In summary, to build an effective argument about a controversial topic, you should (1) define the disagreement, (2) find the area of resistance or dissent, (3) respect the audience, and (4) ensure that evidence is logical and ethical.

Two Sample Papers of Argument

Both papers are presented in MLA format, reduced to show proportional margins for an 8½ × 11" page. Chapter 23 provides specific guidelines for papers in MLA style. The first paper was written by a nursing student who was interested in a medical controversy with ethical concerns. Janet Edington opened with the history of a prescription drug. Then she briefly explained the approval process for prescribed drugs before giving the con and pro views in block order:

Edington 1

Janet Edington

Professor _____

English _____

15 March 1997

Should Terminally Ill Patients Have the Right to Use Preapproved Drugs?

In September 1937 the drug Elixir Sulfanilamide went on the market in the United States. No tests were carried out to check its safety. After taking this prescription drug, more than one hundred people died. This incident proved to be the "catalyst" that plunged the United States government into product safety. The following year Congress passed the Federal Food, Drug, and Cosmetic Act of 1938. As a result the Food and Drug Administration, whose primary purpose is to protect the public from harmful products, was established. The FDA has been given the authority to require drug manufacturers to substantiate the "safety and effectiveness of their products" prior to marketing (Farley 10).

Frustrated by the long waiting period of clinical testing, one thousand AIDS patients were motivated to demonstrate in front of the FDA's headquarters in Rockville, Maryland, in October 1988, hoping to influence the FDA into allowing them to take experimental medication for the treatment of their disease (Gorman 57). The action of these demonstrators illustrates a critical issue: should terminally ill patients have the right to use prescription drugs without the FDA's approval (Lord 26)? The issue can be better understood by examining the procedure a drug goes through to be approved.

The drug approval process begins with the manufacturer "conducting preclinical studies that take the drug from test tube experiments to animal testing." The purpose of this testing is to determine safety and side effects with animal subjects. After the necessary information is compiled, the new drug application (NDA) begins. A five-year clinical study of efficacy is then established with human subjects. From developing to marketing, a drug can take from five to ten years to get into the hands of a patient (Farley 10).

Although the drug approval process is lengthy, adversaries to the application of preapproved drugs feel it is "unethical" to give medication to a patient who might think an improvement or reversal is going to take place. Dr. Paul D. Parkman, the Federal Food and Drug Administrator's AIDS coordinator, commented: "Terminally ill patients need effective drugs not false hope" (McLearn 37). Parkman points out that "toxicity of drugs" can lead not only to needless suffering, but also to hastened death. Then too, lawsuits may arise from patients not understanding possible side effects (38).

Advocates agree that the FDA has the most stringent regulations in the world, assuring the public that only tested products reach the marketplace (Farley 7). But advocates believe that ethics are not compromised by controlled dispensing of preapproved drugs. Ethics are violated when facts are distorted or withheld so that a person is misled into thinking another course is advisable. The more a patient knows about preclinical test results, the greater the ability to make an informed decision regarding acceptable treatment. Advocates suggest clinical research findings can be provided, as well as the pros and cons regarding alternative treatment. Then the patient is better prepared to make "an informed decision" regarding the use of preapproved drugs (Prescription 14).

Advocates believe that even the risk of death may be worth taking, in for example, heart patients whose blocked coronary arteries can mean certain death (Katzman 33). The Heart and Lung Association states, "In the United States alone, approximately 700,000 heart attack patients are hospitalized annually," of whom "9 percent die in-hospital." Advocates calculate that streptokinase, which reopens blocked coronary arteries of heart attack victims, could have saved "as many as 11,000 lives each year" (34). Yet FDA approval of this drug came a full two years after its NDA was filed, which means 22,000 deaths might have been prevented in the interim (21). For a terminally ill person, the potential benefits may far outweigh the possible risks. These patients should be allowed a choice.

As far as lawsuits are concerned, advocates point out that "physicians prescribing preapproved drugs would need good reason under malpractice law for doing so, especially if approved alternatives were available" (Katzman 36). Patients using such drugs would have to acknowledge they were taking a special risk by signing an informed consent document, which would release the doctor and hospital of liability before treatment began (34).

Advocates also emphasize that when a satisfactory treatment for a certain illness is already available, new drugs for the same disease would have to pass even higher standards of proof. After streptokinase was approved, researchers discovered a new drug—TPA, a genetically engineered clot-dissolving agent—that appeared more effective than its predecessor.

Researchers were so convinced of its safety and effectiveness that all research was halted, and TPA's manufacturers filed its NDA immediately. The same FDA advisory committee that approved streptokinase voted against TPA. Why? They required that "any adverse side effects" of TPA be compared with those of streptokinase. The FDA finally approved TPA, but by that time it was available in eight other countries (Katzman 34). What this example illustrates is that the FDA's approval system sometimes unnecessarily delays new drugs to critically ill patients.

Finally, advocates point out that there is no such thing as a guaranteed 100% safe drug. In the end, drug safety can be determined only by its individual effects upon a patient. Many lives are lost that might have been saved while new preapproved drugs sit on shelves for years, waiting for FDA final approval. Restrictive laws should not limit alternative treatment that might save or improve the quality of life for terminally ill patients. These patients should have the right to use preapproved drugs.

Edington 4

Works Cited

"A Prescription for Drugs." Economist 318 (1991): 14.

Farley, Dixie. "How FDA Approves New Drugs." FDA Consumer 21 (1987-1988):
    7-18.

Gorman, Christine. "Cutting Red Tape to Save Lives." Time 31 October 1985:
    57-58.

Katzman, Sam. "The FDA's Deadly Approval Process." Consumers' Research April
    1991: 31-34.

Lord, Nancy. "A Free Market Alternative to the FDA." Consumers' Research July
    1990: 26-28.

McLearn, Don. "Great Expectations: Is the U.S. Doing Its Best to Beat AIDS?"
    FDA Consumer 23 (1989): 37-39.

Questions for Discussion

1. Where is Janet's thesis located?
2. Does she find a common ground?
3. How would you describe the tone of her argument?
4. Would her argument be more effective in alternating order?
5. Janet cites an authority who gives support for the opposing view. Does this example add or detract from her argument? Why?
6. How does she establish the authority's credentials?
7. Is the argument primarily a logical, ethical, or emotional appeal?
8. How convincing is the argument?

The second paper, written by Cheryl Pickering, begins with a description of an unusual sport. Then Cheryl presents the con and pro points in alternating order:

Pickering 1

Cheryl Pickering

Professor _____

English _____

June 7, 1997

Cockfighting Should Be Considered a Felony in Ohio

Cockfighting is a spectator sport that never appears on television or in a public arena. These contests take place in secluded spots, usually at night, indoors or outdoors. In a pit or small arena, two roosters are turned loose to fight each other to the death (Allred 421). Often the spectators bet among themselves as to the outcome of the struggle.

Fighting roosters are fitted with gaffs, which are "thin, razor-sharp spurs" attached to the roosters' legs with "leather cuffs." The gaffs are "usually 1-1/8 to 2-3/4 inches long"; some are up to 4 inches long (Allred 424). When the roosters attack each other with their feet, the gaffs cut the roosters repeatedly until one or both "bleed to death or suffer nerve damage" that leaves one unable to defend itself. Sometimes the gaffs become stuck in the other rooster, and the handlers must pull the gaff out without damaging the injured rooster any further. The fight is then resumed. When one rooster stops fighting or dies, the match is over (427).

Cockfighting is illegal. As reported by Randall Edwards and Jim Woods, staff reporters for the Columbus Dispatch, "Cockfighting is a felony in 16 states. [But] it is [only] a fourth degree misdemeanor in Ohio, with a maximum penalty of 30 days in jail and a $250 fine" (4).

Yet Larry Cantrell, a cockfighting supporter, perceives the activity as "one of man's inherent rights." Cantrell was quoted in the Columbus Dispatch as saying, "I believe that man is a superior being. Everything put on earth is for man's use. . . ." Although Rev. David Couto, pastor of a Baptist church in Athens, Ohio, agrees with this basic premise, he disagrees with the interpretation of it. Rev. Couto points out that "Dominion doesn't mean being cruel. Dominion simply means reigning over. . . . Nowhere [in the Bible] can you find cruelty to animals sanctioned." Opponents generally agree that animal abuse should not be tolerated, regardless of who owns the roosters (Dispatch 1).

The owners of the gamecocks, however, say it is a "natural instinct" for the roosters to fight to the death (Allred 391). Glyde March, a veterinarian and retired professor of poultry science at The Ohio State

University says it is "natural for one chicken to fight another. I don't see cruelty in it" (Blackford and Edwards 1). To cockfighting supporters, this activity is perfectly normal and should be allowed.

Critics of this sport disagree. Sandy Rowland, Director of the Great Lakes office of the Humane Society of the United States, feels that "forcing roosters to cut and slash one another to death is cruel and barbaric" (Associated Press 3). Other opponents of this sport do not believe it is "natural" for roosters to fight with razor-sharp gaffs in a staged confrontation. They believe the fights are cruel and inhumane. They feel that cockfighting should be declared a felony, not just a minor offense, and that fines should be more severe than they are at present for people who engage in this activity.

When there is betting of large sums on a cockfight, a fine of $250 and a sentence of 30 days in jail are inadequate deterrents. According to Fred Bailey, Director of the Ohio Department of Agriculture, "If you want to stop it [cockfighting], you're going to have to make it a felony" (Edwards 2). Rep. Dean Conley, D-Columbus agrees and calls for "stricter penalties" for those convicted of participating in cockfighting (Edwards and Woods 4).

Animal abuse under the guise of recreation should not continue. Citizens should contact their state representatives and speak out. If cockfighting were declared a felony offense and if it carried higher fines and longer periods of incarceration, then more people would be deterred from watching and promoting this inhumane and illegal sport.

Pickering 3

Works Cited

Allred, Kelli. "Cockfighting." Foxfire 8. Ed. Elliot Wigginton and Margie
    Bennett. Garden City: Anchor, 1983.

Associated Press. "Over 300 Arrested in Southern Ohio Cockfighting Raids."
    News Journal [Mansfield, OH] 13 May 1991: A3.

Blackford, Darris C., and Randall Edwards. "Supporters of Cockfighting Say
    It's One of Man's Inherent Rights." Columbus Dispatch 15 May 1991: A1.

Edwards, Randall. "Raids Are Not Expected to End Cockfighting in Ohio."
    Columbus Dispatch 19 May 1991: D2.

Edwards, Randall, and Jim Woods. "Lawmaker Seeks Stricter Penalties for
    Cockfights." Columbus Dispatch 14 May 1991: B4.

Questions for Discussion

1. Why is a detailed description of cockfighting included?
2. How would you describe the tone of Cheryl's argument?
3. Where is her thesis located?
4. Does the argument rely primarily on a logical, ethical, or emotional appeal?
5. How convincing is the argument?

Summary

Formal arguments are based on logical appeals. Most arguments, however, also involve persuasion. They use combinations of three basic appeals: logical, ethical, and emotional. To construct an effective argument, you assess the rhetorical situation. Then you blend an appropriate combination of all three appeals to overcome resistance to the proposition.

An argument has a basic premise or underlying belief called the proposition. This belief is the starting point of the argument. If participants cannot agree on a basic premise, they cannot reach consensus.

Arguments can make any of five basic claims: claims of judgment, fact, interpretation, cause, or policy. Before taking a definite stand, you need to thoroughly research your topic. You might begin by writing a controlling question. This will help to direct your search. Making notes in a con/pro format during research will simplify your analysis of the issue. After your research is completed, you may decide to take a different stand, perhaps a position of compromise.

An effective argument has four basic parts: claim (position), objection, evidence, and conclusion. For mild opposition, the claim (thesis) may be direct and early. But if there is strong opposition, the claim is generally indirect and delayed to prepare the reader. An argument on a controversial topic can be arranged in block or alternating order. Main points are usually placed in least- to most-important order.

The introduction of an argument describes the background of the issue and defines the disagreement. If possible, follow with an area of agreement or common ground. A common ground sets the scene for calm deliberation. In the third section, summarize all the opposing points if you use the block method. For the alternating method, place objections and refutation in pairs. Counter each objection with logical evidence.

For clarity, clearly identify points of view. Use pairs of parallel transitions to distinguish viewpoints. Fallacies of hasty generalization, oversimplification, and overstatement are common culprits in arguments of beginning writers. The conclusion of an argument should be appropriate, complete, and relevant.

To simplify the task of revision, review your outline and check it against the order of your paper. They should be the same. Reread your argument, again checking the order, and ask yourself questions about vague or doubtful points.

Key Terms

persuasion	premise
argument	proposition
logical appeal (*logos*)	controlling question
ethical appeal (*ethos*)	compromise
emotional appeal (*pathos*)	delayed thesis
claim	area of resistance
claim of judgment	objection
claim of fact	direct order
claim of interpretation	indirect order
claim of cause	common ground
claim of policy	refute

Practice

Writing Exercise: Examining Opposing Points of View

Directions: Select a topic. Write two paragraphs from two *contrasting* points of view. Separate the paragraphs and indicate the person speaking. Be biased and emotional if the occasion calls for it.

1. *Dental charge.* A busy dentist has a policy that if a patient misses an appointment without canceling, a minimum charge of $25 is added to the bill. A woman who missed her appointment because she took her injured child (who suffered a broken arm) to the emergency room is protesting the extra charge. Write the dentist's view, then her view.

2. *Deadline.* Your boss is running late on a project report which is due at 8:00 a.m. tomorrow. At 4:30 p.m. he hands you ten pages of his first typed draft with hundreds of red-penciled changes. He says he will have the last six pages revised by the time you have printed out the first ten. You have a dinner date with your fiancé, and you know the job will take at least two hours to complete. Write your boss's view of the situation and your view.

3. *Broken window.* A ten-year-old has just batted a softball through the thermopane window of a neighbor's house. It landed on the dining room table while she was entertaining dinner guests. One guest received a nick on the face from flying glass. Write the batter's version of the event and then the neighbor's.

4. *Persian cat:* Your cat has misbehaved, so you have put it outside on a cold day. It is sitting outside on the porch, meowing. Write your thoughts, then the cat's.

5. *Ball game:* Select a favorite sport. Then imagine you are two reporters writing accounts of the same game. One reporter favors the hometown team; the other does not.

Collaborative Learning: Negative Connotations

Directions: Pretend you have had a mild disagreement with a family member. Later you overhear the person describing the exchange. Which terms below would you dislike? Which would be acceptable? Do your group members agree or disagree? If so, why? (Consult a dictionary if you wish.)

dispute	quarrel	strife	brawl
bicker	scrap	controversy	altercation
squabble	fight	conflict	hassle
quibble	difficulty	dissension	beef
spat	row	argument	feud
tiff	fracas	disagreement	contention

Case Problem: Should John and Sara Have a Child by Surrogacy?

Directions: If possible, select a partner who disagrees with you. Diverse viewpoints should facilitate coverage of the topic.

Stage 1. John and Sara are an upper-middle-class couple who live in a large, comfortable home in an excellent neighborhood. They are childless because Sara had a hysterectomy many years ago. For eleven years they have waited unsuccessfully for a child of similar ancestry to adopt. Now that they are both past age forty, the chance of their receiving a child is slight.

One day Sara proposes that they contact a lawyer to arrange a surrogate birth. Her husband would be the natural father of the child, and she could adopt it. At first John is hesitant; but later he becomes eager to have his own child, one that will continue his family line. Still, he wants to be absolutely sure they are not rushing into something they will later regret. He tells Sara he will play the role of the devil's advocate as they discuss the pros and cons.

*Assignment One: List the advantages and disadvantages John and Sara should consider.

Stage 2. Sara and John contact a lawyer who specializes in surrogacy. He says the cost of a surrogate birth is about the same as adoption—$20,000. He knows a healthy thirty-year-old woman of Irish ancestry (as Sara is) who has had one (successful) surrogate birth and is willing to have another. Since her husband's wages cover only their living expenses, she has started a fund for their children's college education. (Her husband finished high school; she dropped out to marry although she had been an *A* student.) The lawyer writes up a contract.

*Assignment Two: What items should be covered in the contract? List them.

Stage 3. What is your personal opinion about Sara and John's decision? Do you think they are making the right decision? Why or why not?

*Assignment Three: Using the strategy below, formulate an effective argument.

1. Find an area of agreement (common ground).
2. Summarize the con view. List major points.
3. Pro view: Answer the opponent's major points.

Fifty Suggestions for Papers of Argument

1. Should athletic teams be suspended for repeated poor sportsmanship leading to violence?
2. Should classes for gifted students be discontinued?
3. Refusal of insurance: reasonable risk or genetic discrimination?
4. Should fraternities be banned from college campuses?
5. Should English be declared the official language of the United States?
6. Should great books courses be revived in high schools?
7. Should school boards censor school libraries?
8. Are two terms in a congressional office long enough?
9. Should perks for ex-presidents be curbed?
10. Every home should have at least three smoke alarms.
11. Should banks and vendors be allowed to sell customers' personal data?
12. Should random drug testing be permitted in the workplace?
13. Should the legal driving age be raised to seventeen?
14. Human cloning: a race of mirror images?

15. Should drunk-driving penalties be increased?

16. Should indeterminate sentencing be abolished?

17. Has the Supreme Court violated the First Amendment?

18. Should medium-security inmates work on community projects?

19. Should penalties for rape be stiffened?

20. Should a "shoot the burglar" law be enacted?

21. Should perpetrators collect damages for injuries incurred during a crime?

22. Near-death experiences: fact or fiction?

23. Should the growing of tobacco be subsidized?

24. Should women go into combat?

25. Should the police force of . . . be expanded?

26. The city of . . . needs more fire protection.

27. Should households be limited to two dogs?

28. Should license fees be raised for dogs that aren't neutered?

29. Should cats be licensed?

30. Should inmates receive free college tuition?

31. Should surrogate births be legal?

32. Should pornography be banned on the Internet?

33. Should sex education begin in kindergarten?

34. Should throwaway bottles be banned?

35. Should the federal "marriage tax" be eliminated?

36. Should earnings of children under fourteen be taxed at the present rate?

37. Should ceilings on inheritance taxes be raised?

38. Should social security income be taxed?

39. Should caffeine in soft drinks be restricted?

40. Should MSG be banned as a commercial food additive?

41. Should diagnostic X rays for breast cancer be minimized?

42. Should nursing homes be restraint-free?

43. Should organ transplants be allocated to heavy drinkers during a shortage?

44. Should oil-eating bacteria be housed on every tanker?

45. Should power boats be illegal on environmentally threatened waters?

46. Should beverage bottle/can deposits be required to prevent littering?

47. Should "nonalcoholic" beer (0.5 percent) be sold to minors?

48. Should certain species be removed from the endangered list?

49. Should the . . . Act be repealed?

50. Should the federal budget be balanced?

PART 4

Writing from Sources

CHAPTER 21

Planning Research and Locating Sources

> *To be conscious that you are ignorant of the facts is a great step to knowledge.*
>
> —Benjamin Disraeli

The ability to find information readily and to follow established research practices is important not only in college but also in the workplace. Professionals in business, law, engineering, medicine, and other fields have to locate, sort, and analyze large quantities of information. Through college research projects, you can develop skills valued by employers: the ability to plan and manage your time, to locate sources of information, and to analyze and evaluate ideas and viewpoints, as well as to provide appropriate documentation for the sources you use in your written work.

Employers today look for employees who can go beyond the basic task of a job. According to David Mitchell, vice president of the Marion Whirlpool division, "In the old days, you looked for people who could do the work. Now, we're looking for communication skills, math skills, and the ability to function on a team. . . . The most important quality they need . . . is the ability to learn." Employers also pay close attention to an applicant's attitude. The president of Fulfillment Corporation of America, Larry Morse, says, "We want an employee who has fresh ideas, well-honed skills and . . . a positive attitude in our work force." As you research you will increase your ability to learn. You will also develop qualities such as perseverance and patience, elements of the positive attitude employers seek.

SCHEDULING RESEARCH TASKS

Procrastination may be tempting when the deadline for a research paper seems distant—perhaps a month or more away. But dawdling can lead to anxiety and even panic when the deadline suddenly looms. The first step toward alleviating anxiety and initiating action in any major project is to list the tasks involved and make a schedule that includes a tentative deadline as well as the actual deadline. Schedule your paper so that it will be completed two or three days before the date due. That way if a minor emergency occurs, you will not have to worry or beg for more time.

A tentative timetable will help you pace your research project. Estimate the time needed to do a preliminary search, to compile a list of sources, to read, to take notes, to return to the library, to draft, to revise, and to edit and proofread. If you start immediately, then you can build a little flex time into your schedule. This way you can breathe easily, for the worst that can happen will be that you finish a few days early, which rarely occurs.

Plan a minimum of two trips to the library; one is seldom enough. If you have problems locating materials, three or more trips may be required. Reading and note-taking will take big chunks of time. Start your draft as soon as you find a thesis. Writing the draft will take several sittings. For a top-quality paper, you will need several revisions and multiple proofreadings. To help you start planning, a tentative schedule for a three-week research paper appears here. Adapt it to fit your particular assignment.

Tentative Three-Week Research Schedule

	Days	Date
1. Select a topic. Write a controlling question, if possible.	1	_____
2. Go to library, start source cards, obtain materials.	1	_____
3. Read, limit topic, take notes, make scratch outline.	2–3	_____
4. Write thesis and start draft. Return unneeded materials. Get more if needed.	1–2	_____
5. Read, revise outline, work on draft.	3–4	_____
6. Finish and print first draft.	2–3	_____
7. Let paper cool. Type list of works cited. Do further research, if needed.	1–2	_____
8. Revise printed copy and add revisions. Check format. Print out copy.	2–3	_____
9. Revise again, proofread, print out clean copy.	1	_____
10. Edit and proofread several times.	1	_____
11. Tentative deadline: Print final copy. Proof again.	1	_____
12. Final deadline: Submit research paper.		_____

DETERMINING THE PURPOSE

The first step in the research process is to determine the purpose. Is it to inform, to propose a solution to a problem, or to persuade? All three types of research require substantial reading and documentation of sources. An informative research paper explores what is actually known about a topic. In this type of paper, you summarize, define, and quote sources. You also report on areas of consensus or disagreement among authorities in the field and compare opinions fairly. Although the tone of an informative research paper may be somewhat informal, a paper of scholarly inquiry is detached and impersonal. (Ask your instructor which is preferred.)

Many topics for research papers center on problems. For example, you might investigate a business, medical, ethical, legal, social, or environmental problem. The problem might involve your family, your campus, your community, your workplace, or a group to which you belong. Like an informative paper, a problem-solving paper reports existing data and expert opinion. But in it you also evaluate alternatives and make a recommendation for solving or alleviating the problem, based on your findings (see chapter 19).

A persuasive research paper is quite different from either the informative or problem-solving paper. In a persuasive paper you summarize a controversy and argue for a point of view, belief, or course of action. This means selecting a position and supporting it with facts, reasons, and examples. The tone of an argument depends upon the topic and how it is approached (see chapter 20). Nonetheless, the tone should be objective and fair. If your instructor gives you free rein in determining the purpose, consider your topic first.

SELECTING AN APPROPRIATE TOPIC

The subject of research should be provocative and challenging. It should offer the opportunity to learn and to draw a conclusion. Avoid topics that are well-covered in a single source. Nor should a college paper be a rehash of a high school paper. Your topic should be worthwhile—one that you would like to explore. For example, if you have several family members with the same health problem, you might investigate the cause and various methods of treatment. Or if you are interested in soybean production, you might research the genetics of several hybrid varieties, then discuss the advantages and disadvantages of each one. Since a research paper requires many hours of searching, reading, thinking, and writing, you should select a topic you will be comfortable with.

Your topic should be appropriate for your current level of skill. Advanced writers who are familiar with research practices may want to select topics involving extensive research, whereas beginning writers may prefer a topic less complex or technical. Select material that you can comprehend.

Another consideration is whether or not the topic can be researched in the allotted time. By doing a preliminary search, you can determine whether or not you can secure enough material. If a topic is very new or very old, there may have been little written about it. For instance, if you wanted to investigate whether or not George Washington really wrote his farewell address, you might find only one book, written in 1859. Even though the book is comprehensive, it would not be sufficient for a research paper that requires a variety of sources. On the other hand, if you wanted to discover the truth about UFOs, you would find reams of material, but actual evidence would be slim and inconclusive. Start looking for materials early; you may have to change your topic.

LIMITING A TOPIC

Selecting a topic for a research paper can be intimidating, rather like picking up an octopus. The crux of the problem is where and how do you grasp it? First, decide which leg (aspect) of the topic you might like to examine. Let's suppose, for example, that you are interested in knowing more about the Amish. Obviously, this topic itself is much too broad: The numerous facets of Amish life and the range of differences within regional groups would be impossible for you to research. How can you narrow the topic quickly? One way is to ask yourself questions: "What aspect of Amish living interests me? What might most readers not know?" Nudge your brain a bit. You might consider schooling, religion, occupations, or other topics.

Another way to limit this topic is to look up "Amish" in the *Library of Congress Subject Headings*, a multivolume listing of headings used to catalog books. A subject search of your library's card or an online catalog may yield many subtopics. For example, a subject search of one library system's online catalog found 110 subjects with 215 entries (listed alphabetically) under the heading of "Amish." Although only 8 appeared on the first screen, one of those triggered an idea (see fig. 21.1).

Item seven on this screen led to searching "Amish Social Life and Customs," farther down the list, which yielded 30 entries. From these entries, the topic could be narrowed.

For some topics you may need to do preliminary reading before you can determine the direction a paper will take. Reading an overview in an encyclopedia is a quick way to obtain leads, too. Reading abstracts and digests, which give the main points of materials, may also act as a springboard for ideas.

After preliminary reading about rain forests, Flora Kyle found that several rain forests exist around the world. As a result, she narrowed her topic to Amazon rain forests but still found too much information for a 1500- to 1700-word paper. Feeling overwhelmed, she consulted her professor, who suggested thinking about how deforestation of the Amazon rain forests affects residents of the United States. What are the consequences? Why should we be concerned? Thus she was able to limit her focus to three main reasons and to start a scratch outline before returning to the library.

```
You searched for the SUBJECT: amish
110 SUBJECTS found, with 215 entries; SUBJECTS 1-8 are:

    1.   Amish . . . . . . . . . . . . . . . . . . . . . . . . . . . .   14 entries
    2.   Amish   Anecdotes . . . . . . . . . . . . . . . . . . .    1 entry
    3.   Amish   Attitudes . . . . . . . . . . . . . . . . . . . .    1 entry
    4.   Amish   Audio Visual Aides . . . . . . . . . . . . .    1 entry
    5.   Amish   Canada . . . . . . . . . . . . . . . . . . . . . .    1 entry
    6.   Amish   Canada Bibliography . . . . . . . . . . . .    2 entries
    7.   Amish   Canada Social Life And Customs . . . .    3 entries
    8.   Amish   Child Abuse Religious Aspects . . . . .    1 entry
```

Figure 21.1 Sample subject search from an online catalog.

Scratch Outline

Controlling question: Why should U.S. citizens be concerned about deforestation of the Amazon rain forest?

1. Spread of disease from fleas and mites that leave the deforested area
2. Effect on the ozone layer by greenhouse gases produced by burning in the rain forest
3. Worldwide climate changes

SELECTING SUITABLE SOURCES

To refresh your memory on research terminology, remember that firsthand research is primary research, and *primary sources* are original sources, such as letters, diaries, autobiographies, and other original writings. For example, the novel *War and Peace* is a primary source. The term *secondary sources* refers to information that someone else has collected, analyzed, or changed. A commentary on *War and Peace* is a secondary source.

Whether primary or secondary, not all sources are equally suitable for academic research. Most of us are inclined to smile or shrug when headlines of supermarket publications proclaim "Ninety-year-old woman pregnant!" or "Man frozen in block of ice for 500 years recovers!" We dismiss the articles as figments of a copywriter's overactive imagination. But evaluating information for a research paper is not so simple. Three questions should be helpful as you seek out suitable sources:

1. *Is the source reliable?* Certain newspapers, magazines, and books contain shoddy research and are unsuitable for research papers. Beware of books without an author, especially those that promote the views of a group or cult or vendor. If in doubt, consult your instructor.

2. *Is the source written on an adult level?* Reject any material that is overly simplified or directed toward adolescents.

3. *Does the source have depth?* Popular magazines often give an overview of a topic or issue with few details. For example, they may merely say, "It is known" or "A study revealed . . ." with no information about the source, size of study, participants, or researchers. In good research writing, all sources should be identified. For a research paper, you need solid, reliable evidence: statistics, reasons, examples, and expert opinion.

To find suitable sources for a research paper, start your search at the library, not your home bookshelf or that of a friend. Coffee table reading (popular sources) is not what research is about. You will need in-depth, up-to-date material, written by experts in the field.

USING THE LIBRARY

Libraries are not only resources in themselves but also connections to other resources—through loan programs and computer networks. Unless you are doing very advanced research, your college library should provide all you need.

Finding Your Way Around

Many libraries provide a map of the facility and a brochure that describes available services. Look for these materials in a rack near the main entrance or information desk. If you don't find any, inquire. Before you start, you should know there may be several computer areas, each with a different function. You may find computerized indexes, CD-ROMs, regional online networks, and an international online network—all located at different computer terminals. Do not be dismayed; instructions for using all of these sources except the international online network will be posted nearby. For that you will need the assistance of library personnel, unless you are already adept at using the Internet. All of these computerized services are discussed in this chapter.

You should also know that libraries have four excellent sources for beginning a search: general references, indexes, catalogs, and bibliographies. These sources may be in print, on microfilm or microfiche, or online (computerized). General references are mainly dictionaries, encyclopedias, atlases, and almanacs. These references can give you a definition and basic understanding of a topic as well as leads for further research. They will also help you to discover whether or not a topic is feasible.

Indexes and catalogs tell what has been written about a subject. Many specialized indexes list sources of information for science and technology, art, business, nursing, medicine, drama, education, and others. Indexes give specific titles, authors, and publications—including magazines, newspapers, pamphlets, government publications, maps, pictures, records, tapes, films, and videos as well as books. Catalogs also list titles, authors and other bibliographic information, and they may specify location of items.

Bibliographies are similar to indexes and catalogs, but they may be more comprehensive. For example, *Books in Print* lists every book in print in the United States, giving authors, titles, and subject area. *Paperbound Books in Print*, which lists all paperbacks in print, is valuable in locating sources on recent topics. *The Bibliographic Index* is helpful for locating subjects you cannot find in other indexes. Computerized lists of bibliographies are sometimes referred to as directories.

As you search for sources, do not assume a source is unavailable just because you cannot locate it. There may be another copy somewhere else, or the book may have been returned but not yet checked in. Ask at the circulation desk. Then too, your library's central catalog may consist of one complete system or it may be in segments, both printed and computerized. Older books or newspapers

PROCEDURE FOR MAKING A WORKING BIBLIOGRAPHY

1. Start with the *Library of Congress Subject Headings* to determine how the subject may be listed. If the listings are few, copy by hand. If extensive, take to a nearby copier for duplication. You can then do a computer search by subjects if you wish. If you don't find what you need, try a thesaurus.

2. To gain an overview of the subject, do preliminary reading in dictionaries, encyclopedias, and other general references (take brief notes if desired).

3. Use indexes, printed or computerized, to find articles in newspapers, magazines, and journals. Make a source card for any promising title or print out computer listings.

4. Use the card catalog or a computerized catalog to find promising book titles and make appropriate source cards.

Figure 21.2 Sample Library of Congress subject headings.

Abnormalities, Human   *(May Subd Geog)*
            ₍*QM690-QM695 (Human teratology)*₎
            ₍*RG626-RG629 (Obstetrics)*₎
    UF   Abnormalities
            Abnormalities, Congenital
            Birth defects
            Congenital abnormalities
            Defects, Birth
            Deformities
            Developmental abnormalities
            Human abnormalities
            Malformations, Congenital
            Teratology
    BT   Morphology
            Pathology
            Teratogenesis
    SA   *subdivision* Abnormalities *under*
                individual organs and regions of the
                body, e.g. Heart—Abnormalities

may be listed on microfilm or microfiche. Materials may be stored on site or borrowed via an interloan network. A methodical plan and general library knowledge can save you hours of fruitless searching.

Finding Key Subject Headings

To find information easily, first determine how the subject is classified and cataloged. Although a few academic libraries still use the Dewey Decimal System, most are organized according to the Library of Congress system. The Dewey Decimal System uses numbers to designate subject areas: 000–099 for General Works, 100–199 for Philosophy and related disciplines, 200–299 for Religion, and so on. These numbers will guide readers in locating library materials.

In the Library of Congress system, however, materials are cataloged alphabetically: A for General Works; B for Philosophy, Psychology, Religion; C–D for History and Topography (except America); E–F for America; and so forth. The *Library of Congress Subject Headings* (LCSH) is a very large book, usually located adjacent to the card catalog and the computers. By consulting it, you can find the key words under which subject headings for books are listed. For example, in looking up *birth defects* in LCSH, you would be referred to *Abnormalities, Human*, which lists several headings that could be investigated (see fig. 21.2).

Other sources may use the LCSH as a guide, but often they have their own subject headings. Sometimes a thesaurus is handy to find synonyms under which a subject may be listed. For a computer search to be fruitful, the topic should be fairly specific. If you were to search a general topic such as *AIDS*, you would be flooded with entries on screen. Instead, you might limit the topic to *babies born with AIDS*, which would yield a more manageable amount of material.

Preliminary Reading References

To gain a quick overview of a subject, do brief preliminary reading. If the subject is not new, begin with short selections from dictionaries, digests, or encyclopedias. Many encyclopedias also contain bibliographies that you can use to locate additional sources. For topics about North American subjects, *Encyclopedia Americana* is well respected. Even more comprehensive is the *Encyclopeadia Britannica*, which is more scholarly. In addition, many encyclopedias and dictionaries are available on medical, legal, business, or other specialized topics. They range from the *Encyclopedia of Chemistry* to the *Encyclopedia of Advertising* to the *Encyclopedia of Rock, Pop, and Soul.*

Book Review Digest is an index to books that have received three or more reviews in newspapers or popular periodicals. It gives the location of contemporary reviews of books. *Technical Book Review Index* discusses technical and scientific books. On university campuses, there may also be a separate English library which houses reviews of various literary works as well as other works. If a subject is relatively new, information may be available in newspapers, atlases, almanacs, journals, magazines, and electronic media.

Atlases contain not only maps and charts but also historical, political, cultural, and economic information. Almanacs can help you locate statistics, political summaries, and information about advances in science and technology. Almanacs also contain a variety of facts on subjects from sports events to farm prices. *The World Almanac, Reader's Digest Almanac, Information Please*, and others feature reviews of each year's highlights.

Periodical Indexes and Abstracts

You can find recent information in newly published articles in periodicals (newspapers, magazines, journals, newsletters, and bulletins). Periodicals are published daily, weekly, quarterly, or annually. To find these materials, consult indexes and abstracts. Indexes (printed and computerized) list articles alphabetically according to subject. Abstracts not only list subject headings, but also summarize key information in a highly condensed form. For example, you might consult *Psychology Abstracts* (1927 to present) or *Historical Abstracts* (1955 to present).

General indexes list articles designed for a general audience. For example, *The Readers' Guide to Periodical Literature* (1905 to present) lists over 200 popular periodicals. *The Magazine Index*, often found in college libraries, is a microfilm index of over 400 periodicals. Newspaper indexes, such as the *New York Times Index* and the *Wall Street Journal Index*, can also guide you to articles of general interest. All these indexes include scientific, technical, and literary articles, but they are not as extensive as those found in specialized indexes. If you use popular sources, you will need to supplement them with more scholarly sources.

Specialized indexes, abstracts, and yearbooks list technical or scholarly research and government publications. For example, *The Humanities Index* (1974 to present) lists articles on archaeology, history, literature, performing arts, philosophy, and religion. The *Social Sciences Index* (1974 to present) lists articles on economics, geography, government, law, political science, psychology, and sociology. Prospective teachers might consult the *Education Index*. Accounting students might seek out the *Accountant's Index*. Medical technology students might search the *Cumulative Index to Nursing and Allied Health Literature*. The *Public Affairs Information Service* (PAIS) (1915 to present) carries subject listings of material by public and private agencies on economic and social concerns, international relations, and public administration.

Some indexes of periodicals in your library may be on CD-ROM, accessed through a computer terminal. Computerized indexes are updated regularly and available without charge. By doing a title, author, subject, keyword, or other type of search, you can get an on-screen listing of articles. Terminals are often connected to a printer so that you need not copy bibliographic data by hand; by selecting items and pushing a key, you can print out a custom-tailored list. Your library may have a general periodical index (GPI), Info-Trac, or similar system. These systems provide on-screen help, making them easy to use. A nearby pamphlet usually explains the services available.

Government publications are cataloged according to a different system. Although there are indexes to these publications, such as the *Monthly Catalog of United States Publications* and *American Statistics Index*, the help of a librarian may be necessary unless you can tap into "The Reference Room" on the Internet (which is free).

Of course, one library will not carry every periodical listed in every index. To determine which periodicals are available, consult your library's periodical catalog (or periodical list). If your library doesn't have a periodical you need, ask if it is available by courier or fax. Some libraries belong to an interlibrary loan system that shares periodical articles this way. There is usually a charge for the service.

Catalogs of Library Holdings

Some students may be surprised to learn that the familiar old card catalog that helped them all through high school no longer exists in their campus or community library. In many libraries, card catalogs are obsolete, for source information has been transferred to computerized databases. Other libraries are in the process of this transfer, and their card catalogs are incomplete. Acquiring a familiarity with online catalogs, however, should enable anyone to locate listings easily.

Card Catalogs Some libraries may still catalog books that are on the premises by using a traditional alphabetical card catalog on 3- by 5-inch file cards

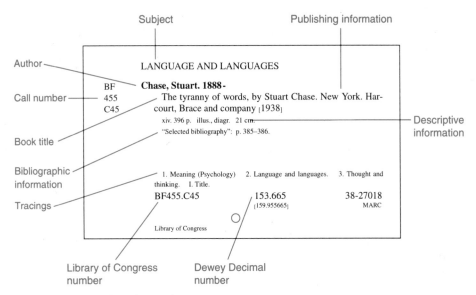

Figure 21.3 Sample index card.

in a bank of small drawers, or on microfiche cards or microfilm. Some libraries have one card catalog; some have two. If two banks of catalogs exist, one is for author and title cards; the other is for subject cards. You might start by scanning the subject cards, looking for titles that seem relevant (see fig. 21.3).

If you find a relevant title, read the description on the card to see if the book contains material you might need. If so, copy *all* the call letters and other necessary data onto your index cards. If you have found book titles and names of authors in bibliographies, look for these in the other card catalog. As you find more possible sources, copy all necessary data onto index cards.

Local Online Central Catalog   Many libraries have transferred their card catalogs to an online central catalog. This means you must use a computer terminal to locate most of the holdings housed on the premises. (There may also be an incomplete card catalog, a print catalog, or files on microfilm or microfiche.) Instructions posted near the terminal or on the screen will explain how to conduct a search by subject, author, title, or keyword. Most systems indicate not only the location of a book but also its availability and date of return if it has been borrowed.

Online Central Catalogs for Regional Networks   You may find that you can access more than one online network from the same computer terminal. A college or university with multiple campuses and libraries may have an online regional network that connects all the sites. This means that you can order materials from the main campus when you are on a branch campus and vice versa.

Or you may be able to access a statewide hookup of colleges and universities. Such networks allow patrons to locate off-site materials and order some of them through an interlibrary loan. A central catalog for each network appears on screen, telling the location of materials (which campus, college, or university) and whether or not they are available.

If you plan to order materials from another site and face a deadline soon, be sure to ask about delivery dates and availability. You also need to inquire about notification. Does the library notify you of arrivals, or must you check a posted list? If you are to check a list, where will it be?

Direct Electronic Sources

More and more libraries and homes will have direct access to information through computers, using CD-ROM and various online information services.

CD-ROM   A CD-ROM is a portable database, a type of compact disc which stores digitized data (print, visual displays, and sound) that is accessed through a personal computer. A variety of reference works—such as encyclopedias and atlases—are now available on CD-ROM. Back issues of *Time* magazine and other periodicals are also available, as well as interactive multimedia sources produced by the National Geographic society and other educational publishers. Subject areas covered on CD-ROM include ecosystems, plant growth, insects, nutrition, ocean life, and space exploration. New products appear every month.

You can purchase CD-ROMs at most computer stores. Or you may be able to use or borrow them at libraries. Reference materials on CD-ROMs, including government documents, must remain on site; but books on CD-ROMs are sometimes available to take home. Check with a librarian to see what is available.

OCLC: An International Online Network   Many public libraries belong to an international online network, called OCLC, that makes difficult-to-obtain materials available through interlibrary loan. This means that if you are unable to locate materials, you may be able to order them there. Since the OCLC network is accessed only by librarians, you will need to request this service.

Internet Services   Many libraries and most private online services offer access to the Internet. You might think of the Internet as a huge brain with millions of cells (a network of individual computers using telephone lines). The Internet is a worldwide network of an estimated 200 million users that allows you to contact any other user in another part of the world. The Internet has an electronic mail system (e-mail) that allows you to leave messages if someone is not online at the same time you are. The "Net" also provides access to electronic journals, newsletters, bulletins, and texts, sometimes for a subscription fee.

Much of the information on the Internet is available without cost to anyone who has the skill and perseverance to find it, although there may be a charge for the telephone call in some areas. (Ask at your campus library lab.) Free services on the Internet include bulletin boards, special interest groups, and software. Bulletin boards permit users to post and read information and requests. Special groups chat informally about various topics, contributing information and opinion.

A major problem with the Internet is its lack of organization. There is no central catalog. The Net is more or less a random series of private collections. Then too, technology changes so rapidly that state-of-the-art products may become obsolete in a year or two. *Search engines* such as Lycos or Webcrawler can ease your search. For example, Webcrawler yields an extensive list of bibliographies and allows viewing of 100 at a time. Most *browsers* (which come with your Internet service) offer search engine pointers.

Ask your library computer lab assistant for a list of electronic addresses. For a private online service, however, the electronic address may be referred to as a "path of access." The address for a Web page or gopher site is called the Uniform Resource Locater (URL). If you are working from a home computer, it is best to purchase a clear easy-to-read instruction book before attempting to use the Internet. There are Internet directories, reference books, users' guides, and special catalogs available.

Private Online Services   From your home computer, you can easily access the Internet through a private online service for a monthly fee. If you use an online service that provides research assistance, check out the extra fees before you begin. Some services may be free, but some research services run from a high of $100 per hour to a low of $2.50 per hour (in two-hour blocks). On the high end are Nexis, Dialog, and Dow Jones News/Retrieval, which offer specialized historical database services. Primarily for individual use, Compuserve, America Online, Microsoft Network, and Prodigy provide more general, low-cost services. These include e-mail, electronic bulletin boards, access to the Internet, and information retrieval.

America Online affords access to extensive financial information as well as general information. For example, three full pages of information on Iowa Beef Packers, Inc. (IBP), were easily obtained, providing an overview of the corporation, top personnel, sales totals of products for the year, key competitors, stock market prices, debt ratio, and dividends.

Prodigy Service offers a database of newspapers, magazines, journals, radio and TV transcripts, medical newsletters, books, photos, and maps for a low fee to members. Prodigy also has an online service designed for students, called "Homework Helper." Although Homework Helper is not as extensive as services designed for professional researchers, it offers access to major newspapers, such as the *Los Angeles Times* and *USA Today*. Prodigy carries over 500 magazines and other publications, including 100 U.S. history books, 700 works of literature, and other sources. Since online services are rapidly expanding their offerings, ask about any you may need. Most have a toll-free number.

Making a Working Bibliography: Source Cards

A working bibliography is a list of possible sources for your research (see Procedure for Making a Working Bibliography on page 323). This bibliography will help you find materials, develop your outline, and give you a head start on a "Works Cited" page (list of references). When you go to the library, take 3- by 5-inch index cards rather than sheets of paper. Cards are best because you can easily sort and alphabetize them. Two sturdy rubber bands will help to prevent loss.

A Warning   When you find promising articles, documents, or books, start your source cards right away. Listings may vanish from newsgroups, academic servers, and the World Wide Web; what you find today may not be there tomorrow. Even listings on regional networks may change, although not nearly as fast. If you duplicate any materials, make source cards on the spot. If you delay and have to retrace your steps, the materials may be gone—borrowed by someone else.

How to Begin   Copy all information for each source onto one card, using only one side. Copy the call numbers from the catalog card or index entry onto the upper right corner of the source card. Underneath that, copy other pertinent information. For any other reference materials, make source cards, too. For computerized listings that can be printed, printouts will suffice temporarily, but make sure the information is complete.

For any item you obtain through the Internet or an online service, write down not only the usual information but also the *electronic address* and *access date*. Take pains to copy the address exactly; add no extra spaces or extra punctuation, which may hinder retrieval. Computerized and nonprint listings vary so much that it is impractical to give examples here. Perhaps the best solution is to take this book with you and consult chapter 22 for unusual entries as you make your source cards.

Making Source Cards

1. For *books*, you need:
   a. Full name(s) of author(s)
   b. Full title (including subtitle, if any)
   c. Editor(s) or translator(s)
   d. Total volumes and specific volume number(s) you will use.
   e. City of publication (if unfamiliar, also include state), name of publisher, date of publication
2. For *periodicals*, you need:
   a. Full name(s) of author(s)
   b. Full title of article (including subtitle, if any)
   c. Name of periodical

    d. Full date of periodical (for academic journals also include the volume and issue number, if listed)

    e. Inclusive page numbers (including section letters for newspapers)

3. *Nonprint material and online sources.* When creating cards for special kinds of sources, you need to jot down various items.* By definition, nonprint sources such as tapes, compact discs, CD-ROMs, television programs, and others have no page numbers. These materials require special documentation.

    Since online material may come from a nonprint source or a printed source, the documentation for these items varies widely, too. In addition, you always need the electronic address and date of access for materials gained from Internet sources, or private online services.

Finding Materials in the Stacks and Other Places

To use materials that are stored on site, the next step is to take your source cards and computerized catalog listings with you to the stacks. The stacks are the rows of shelves where periodicals and books are stored. To find the correct row, look up at the outside ends of the stacks. There the subject listing or the range of call letters for each row is found. (*Note:* The entire code appears only on books, not at the end of the stacks.) Periodicals may be shelved by title and date or by subject, title, and date (alphabetically by title and numerically by year). Periodicals are stored in open containers or in binders on shelves, or they may be stored on microfilm or microfiche in drawers. Books are shelved in numerical order by call numbers as well as alphabetical order by the author's last name. When searching for a book, match the call letters from your source card with those on the spine of the book.

If books or other needed materials are not on a shelf or in a file, computerized listings can tell you if they are available. If materials are out, they can be reserved. If a college library lacks certain materials, try a public library. Most have an interlibrary loan system. Or you might check with bookstores, particularly for recent topics. (If a book is out of stock, ask about ordering it.)

Skimming Materials at the Library

Previewing briefly at the library will save you from copying or lugging home irrelevant materials. Check the copyright date, and skim the introductory pages to discover the author's credentials and what the book covers. Then read a page here and there to sample the depth and tone. To obtain a variety of viewpoints, look for materials by several authors. Although they may all cite classic research, their interpretations may differ somewhat. Each writer should also cite other

---

*Consult chapter 22 (MLA 3–5 or APA sections 3, 4).

research that contributes to the body of knowledge. (You may want to consult these sources, too.)

Guidelines for Evaluating Sources

1. *When was the data collected?* Is it still relevant? Not all early sources are outdated; some are classics. Scientific and technological information may change rapidly whereas material in other disciplines changes more slowly.

2. *What is the writer's professional status?* Look for a brief biography on the dust jacket or in the introduction of a book or at the beginning of a periodical. What other materials has the author written? What is his or her position? Obviously, an article by a well-known physician about a medical discovery would carry more credibility than one by a local reporter.

3. *How credible is the publication?* Journals tend to be more scholarly than most magazines. The *New England Journal of Medicine*, for example, is an excellent source. Yet *Scientific American*, the *New Yorker*, and the *Harvard Business Review* also present in-depth articles.

   To assess the credibility of a nontechnical book, consult *Book Review Digest*. For reviews of technical works, see *Technical Book Review Digest*. Consult the volume of the digest for the year the book appeared or for the year after publication.

4. *How much data is given about research?* What were the characteristics of the sample or study group? How large was it? Was the sample representative of the general population? Have other researchers obtained similar results? If an experiment was controlled in a laboratory, have other qualified personnel been able to replicate the experiment?

5. *If a topic is controversial, do sources examine various points of view?* A balance of viewpoints is necessary to give comprehensive coverage. Does the tone seem impartial or does the author seem biased?

6. *Are enough sources available to give comprehensive coverage?* A few articles, even well-detailed ones, are inadequate for a research paper. To understand the thinking in a field and find adequate coverage of a topic, collect numerous sources written from a variety of viewpoints.

As you find unfamiliar abbreviations in your reading, turn to the reference pages for abbreviations in the handbook section of this book. You may want to mark the section with a paper clip for easy reference.

Photocopying

Since some books, many periodicals, and all material on microfilm or microfiche cannot be removed from the library, it is wise to take adequate change along to photocopy. This way you can eliminate some note-taking at the library.

If you need only a page or two from a periodical, photocopy to eliminate a special trip for returns. Legally, you may make one copy of a periodical or a small part of other material and use it for private study or research. After using a copier, make a source card for each publication to preserve bibliographic data or write the date and other source information at the top of the copy.

A PRECAUTION

Prior to taking notes at the library, refer to chapter 23 so that you know what to look for. Even though you may have written a research paper before, this one may differ considerably. Chances are that your English professor will expect a different kind of paper from those you wrote before.

Chapter 23 explains how to save time by taking preliminary notes. Or if you prefer to summarize and paraphrase, read those sections in chapter 23. *Always insert quotation marks around copied material immediately to avoid confusion.* Attempting to summarize and paraphrase when rushed can lead to your borrowing the author's words without being aware of it. Careful documentation, summarizing, and paraphrasing will help you to avoid unintentional plagiarism (chapter 23).

Summary

Making and following a schedule that lists each task can help you meet a research project deadline. To start a research project, you need to determine your purpose, choose a suitable topic, and limit the topic to a manageable focus.

To discover whether or not adequate sources are available, conduct a preliminary search. Start with *Library of Congress Subject Headings* to find possible listings. To gain an overview of a topic, do preliminary reading in dictionaries, encyclopedias, abstracts, or almanacs. Indexes, card catalogs, and online catalogs can provide convenient access to library materials. On-site periodicals and books are housed in the stacks. Others may be available through an interlibrary loan system or online network. If adequate material cannot be located in libraries, bookstores may provide alternative sources.

You need to make a source card for each potential source, including all pertinent bibliographic information. Or if you have a computer printout, make sure all necessary source data is included. If not, write it on the printout.

You can evaluate potential sources by skimming them in the library. You should also decide whether enough sources are available to give comprehensive coverage of the subject. Photocopying is a convenient way to retain reference materials. To avoid retracing of steps, make a source card or write necessary documentation on each copy immediately.

Key Terms

tentative schedule	central catalog	search engine
primary sources	CD-ROMs	electronic address
secondary sources	online services	access date
periodicals	Internet	
indexes	working bibliography	
abstracts	source cards	
card catalog	call numbers or letters	
online catalog	stacks	

Practice

Preliminary Library Search

Directions: To familiarize yourself with the resources available at a campus library, search the following sources. You can also start a working bibliography for your research paper. The completed search can count as a ten-point quiz.

1. *CD-ROM periodical index.* Type in a subject. Select materials that might be useful. Print out a list. If the library is not computerized, use the *Readers' Guide to Periodical Literature.*

2. *Online central catalog or network.* Select three books that might be useful. Print out (or copy) the bibliographic data.

3. *Card catalog.* Check the card catalog for another book that might be useful. Copy down the information necessary to find it. If the campus library does not have a card catalog, this item is a free point.

4. *Encyclopedia.* Check an encyclopedia to find basic information on a topic. In three sentences, summarize the most important points. If a topic is not listed, try an almanac, atlas, or yearbook. Summarize the information in one sentence.

5. *Indexes.* Consult an index that is not computerized. It might be the *New York Times Index, Applied Science and Technology Index,* or another index. Find and copy an entry that might be relevant.

6. *Determine which system of cataloging the library uses.* Write it here.

7–10. List four sources of information not listed on this quiz that you might consult. Specify the general area of the library where the material is located.

Fifty Ideas For Research

1. Advantages and disadvantages of home schooling
2. Natural pesticides

3. What has happened in countries that have legalized drugs?
4. How well do laws protect abused children?
5. Aerial photography
6. Becoming a pilot of a hot-air balloon
7. What are the chief factors that influence children's academic success?
8. Effective ways to protect oneself when alone
9. Assertiveness
10. Guidelines for selecting quality day care for children (or the elderly)
11. What has happened in countries that have socialized medicine?
12. Nutrition during pregnancy
13. Causes and prevention of burnout in nurses (or anyone else)
14. Pollution of the oceans
15. Handling sexual harassment in the workplace
16. What are the best ways to quit smoking?
17. How could the federal government encourage the family unit?
18. What should everyone know about heart disease?
19. Alzheimer's disease
20. How simple and safe is RU-486?
21. Effects of sleep deprivation
22. Is Lamaze best for every mother-to-be?
23. What should every prospective homeowner know?
24. Is diet important in preventing and treating cancer?
25. Effects of noise on hearing and emotional well-being
26. How has etiquette in the workplace changed since the 1950s?
27. Sources and effects of caffeine
28. What alternatives exist for treating breast cancer?
29. Communication strategies to handle difficult people
30. Weight control through surgery?
31. Building a child's self-esteem
32. PMS: Definition and treatment
33. What is Fragile X syndrome?
34. Is it better to just let forest fires burn?
35. Grounds for and consequences of divorce
36. Techniques for healing a marriage
37. Preventing and treating Lyme disease

38. What are the best investments for working couples on a budget?

39. What is the truth about silicone implants?

40. What is the verdict on no-till farming?

41. What caused the Civil War?

42. Whatever happened to solar energy in home construction?

43. What is gene therapy? Does it pose any dangers?

44. What is the truth about the safety of living near electrical power lines?

45. Opportunities for women in the military today compared with opportunities during World War II

46. Is irradiated food safe?

47. How safe are microwave ovens with long-term use?

48. Are sperm banks super-race banks? Who donates? How are buyers protected?

49. How have child-custody laws changed since the 1950s?

50. Is there a need for legal guards to limit use of fetal tissue transplants?

CHAPTER 22

Documenting Sources Clearly

*Every [person] has a right to [an] opinion, but
no [one] has a right to be wrong in . . . facts.*

—Bernard Baruch

In the workplace, accurate and complete information is essential not only in writing checks and invoices, but also in keeping records. Daily business and legal transactions must be preserved. Problems in safety, personnel, and other areas must be noted and investigated. Medical treatments, lab tests, and drug dosages must be logged. All this documentation constitutes proof. And proof must be provided for daily functioning as well as for cases of complaint, audit, or dispute.

Inaccuracy and inadequate documentation can result in cash imbalances, negative publicity, job loss, medical complications, and legal problems. For example, an engineer from the Florida Department of Transportation described a lawsuit that had extended over three years. It hinged upon the date of the removal of an existing structure; the date was thought to be unimportant and was not recorded. Yet it was the key to winning or losing the case. So it is that lack of documentation can create major problems: things that seem insignificant today may become quite significant tomorrow.

Accurate and adequate documentation enhances credibility not only in the workplace, but also in college writing. Readers feel they can trust someone who supports a claim with evidence and presents facts fairly. Careful, accurate documentation is a hallmark of professionalism.

WHAT IS DOCUMENTATION?

When a researcher provides sources, this process is known as documentation. It gives credit to the author and allows readers to check facts or to search further. On the other hand, taking someone else's work and presenting it as one's

337

own or using large parts without permission is unethical and potentially illegal. Legally, you may use small parts of copyrighted works (less than 10 percent of the entire work) for research if the author does not prohibit such use and if you document clearly what you quote, summarize, or paraphrase. If credit is not given to an author, the offense is *plagiarism*.

Whether intentional or unintentional, plagiarism is risky and impractical. Penalties for plagiarism in colleges and universities range from a failing grade to suspension. Usually, an experienced instructor who is familiar with a student's writing can detect plagiarism. Each writer has his or her own individual voice and style of expression. When plagiarized material from professional writers is added to most undergraduate writing, the additions are readily apparent.

Why take this unnecessary risk when you can easily avoid it? When you are making your source cards and note cards and drafting your paper, just use the three forms of documentation listed below.

1. *Sources provided within the text.* Identify the author's name and other source information either in the text or in a parenthetical citation.

2. *Quotation marks.* Enclose copied words within quotation marks.

3. *List of sources.* Place a works cited list or a reference list (bibliographic data) at the end of a research paper to identify all sources mentioned, summarized, paraphrased, or quoted.

Two commonly used forms of academic documentation are those recommended by the Modern Language Association (MLA) and the American Psychological Association (APA), both of which are covered in this chapter in detail. Models for citations and entries also appear in this chapter; chapter 23 explains how to use them in a research paper.

MLA STYLE OF DOCUMENTATION

The Modern Language Association has over 30,000 members who teach English and other languages. This professional organization has endorsed a style of documentation that has been widely adopted in the United States and many foreign countries for research in the humanities. Although the long MLA style is still used, most English instructors seem to prefer the short MLA style, which has no endnote page.

The short MLA style, explained here, requires brief source references within the text of a research paper. These references are then keyed to entries that list bibliographic data for each work. This page of entries is entitled "Works Cited" and placed at the end of the paper. See Common Questions about Source Information for help on compiling references.

Parenthetical Citations: MLA Style

Source information placed within parentheses is called *parenthetical citation*. You will be using citations throughout your research paper. For easy reading,

COMMON QUESTIONS ABOUT SOURCE INFORMATION

1. Where are the publication date and the place of publication found?

   Answer: Near the beginning of the book, usually on the back of title page.

2. What if there is more than one publication date?

   Answer: Take the latest one.

3. What if more than one city of publication is given?

   Answer: Cite the first one.

4. What if the book has been published by two companies?

   Answer: List both publishers in the order given.

5. What if no date, page, publisher, or place of publication is given?

   Answer: Use *n.d.* to mean no date, *n. pag.* for no page, and *n.p.* for no publisher or no place.

6. What if a model for an entry is not given?

   Answer: Construct a model similar to the one most like it.

7. What title is used for the source page?

   Answer: If the MLA style is used, the page is called "Works Cited." The APA style has a page called "References."

8. Which style of documentation should be used on the job?

   Answer: Some large firms have their own style manuals. If not and if no preference is expressed, use either the MLA or APA style.

keep citations brief. Try to insert the author's name into the text of your paper so that you can limit citations to just a page number. (Page numbers of cited material always appear in parentheses.) Key or match each of your citations to a works cited entry. Several citations may refer to the same entry.

You will need a parenthetical citation each time a source is cited. If the source is from more than a single page, cite all page numbers. Some paragraphs may need several citations; others may need only one. Rarely will you have a paragraph without a citation.

The examples of parenthetical citations that follow are in MLA style. For more detailed information, see the *MLA Handbook for Writers of Research Papers*, Fourth Edition, by Joseph Gibaldi, on which these guidelines are based.

Single Author When the author is identified in the text, put only the page number in parentheses. When the author's name is not mentioned, include the author's last name before the page number in parentheses. Do *not* separate the two with a comma.

> Theodore Bernstein, assistant managing editor of
> The New York Times for seven years, points out that
> the word bandit "has a flavor of heroism." Bernstein
> advises: "Avoid any suggestion of glorifying outlaws"
> (17).

> One editor has advised against the use of the word
> bandit because its "flavor of heroism" has the effect
> "of glorifying outlaws" (Bernstein 17).

> Work Cited
>
> Bernstein, Theodore M. Watch Your Language. Great Neck,
>   New York: Channel, 1958.

Two or More Works by the Same Author   To make citations for two (or more) works by the same author, place a comma after the author's name, followed by a condensed title, then the page references: (Goodman, "Working Marriage" 146) (Goodman, "Reagans" 48).

> Works Cited
>
> Goodman, Ellen. "The Reagans Are Not the Waltons."
>   At Large. New York: Summit, 1981. 48-49.
> ---. "A Working Marriage." Keeping in Touch. New York:
>   Fawcett, 1985. 168-71.

Two or More Authors   For works with two or three authors, include all last names; spell out *and:*

> Four "aims of argument" are identified: "inquiry,
> convincing, persuasion, and negotiation" (Crusius and
> Channell 8).

> Some researchers recommend "rapid-fire questioning"
> during survey interviews (Kinsey, Pomeroy, and
> Martin 54).

For four or more authors, include only the first author's last name and the Latin abbreviation *et al.* ("and others"): (Klein et al. 53).

Works by Two Authors with the Same Last Name   When two authors have the same last name, give their full names in the text (preferred usage) with just the page number in each citation. If names are not given in the text, then include the first initial in the parenthetical citation: (G. Mueller 24), (A. Mueller 36).

Entire Work   When citing an *entire* work, not a specific page, state only the author's name in the text and, if helpful, the title. Be sure the source is on your works cited list.

```
H. W. Fowler's Modern English Usage reflects his
spartan life. Fowler believed in simplicity not only
in living, but also in writing a sentence. Clarity
had top priority.
```

Articles of a Single Page   It is not necessary to include the page number when referring to an article that is a page or less long.

```
According to its secretary, Michael Heyman, "the
story of the Smithsonian is also the story of its
volunteers."

                    Work Cited
Heyman, Michael. "Smithsonian Perspectives."
     Smithsonian Apr. 1996: 16.
```

Source with No Author Given   For unsigned works, shorten long titles. Begin with the word by which the work is alphabetized in works cited: (DJIA)

```
                    Work Cited
"The DJIA through the Century." Wall Street Journal
     28 May 1996: R29.
```

Corporate Author   Although a work by a group or an agency can be cited in parentheses, the preferred usage is to include the name in the text:

```
Stride Rite's beautifully illustrated Annual Report
de-emphasized the dismal trend of lower profits (21).
```

```
Yet many stockholders who follow the Dow know their
shares are worth less than one-half of the original
cost.
```

```
                        Work Cited
Stride Rite Corporation. Annual Report 1995. Cambridge,
     MA: Stride Rite, 1996.
```

Indirect Source   When possible, use an original source rather than a second-hand one which quotes the original. If you are unable to obtain the original source and must use a secondary source, place *qtd. in* ("quoted in"), before the citation for the secondary source.

```
Ralph Waldo Emerson said: "Our best thoughts come from
others" (qtd. in Cohen 9).
```

```
                        Work Cited
Cohen, Herb. You Can Negotiate Anything. New York:
     Bantam, 1980.
```

Quotations by Two or More Authors in One Sentence   Follow each quotation with a separate parenthetical citation.

```
Zinsser says, "The most important sentence in any
article is the first one" (59), and Bernstein suggests
the writer "ask . . . what it is he is writing about"
to find the focus for that sentence (75).
```

Two or More Sources in One Citation   If you cite information from two or more sources, include identifying information for each source in your parenthetical citation, separated by semicolons.

```
All seem to agree that good writing is hard work
(Bernstein 44; Trimble 54; Zinsser 33).
```

Work of More Than One Volume.   If your works cited list includes more than one volume of a multivolume work, include the volume number, separated from the page number by a colon: (Nicolson and Trautman 3: 25).

Literary Works Because classic prose works may appear in different editions, include chapter (*ch.*), book (*bk.*), and part (*pt.*) in addition to page numbers. Place extra information after the page with a semicolon between.

```
In the Republic, Plato has Socrates ask: "What do you

consider to be the greatest blessing which you have

reaped from your wealth?" (221; bk. 1)
```

```
                    Work Cited
Plato. "The Republic." Five Great Dialogues. Trans.

    B. Jowett. Ed. Louise Ropes Loomis. Roslyn, NY:

    Classics Club, 1942.
```

To cite classic verse plays, poems, and other works, leave out page numbers. Instead, give the division—canto, act, scene, book, part—and the line(s). Separate numbers by periods. For example, (*Waste Land* 1.35) refers to canto 1, line 35; (*Electra* 1.60) refers to scene 1, line 60. Note that the word *line* is spelled out in citations:

```
Dickinson ends her poem "Wild Nights--Wild Nights!"

with a prayer: "Might I but moor--Tonight-- / In Thee!"

(lines 11-12).
```

```
Romeo and Juliet provides one of Shakespeare's most

quoted lines: "But soft! What light through yonder

window breaks?" (2.2.2).
```

Nonprint Sources Since most nonprint sources (interviews, television programs, compact discs, CD-ROMs, and others) lack page numbers, a citation is unnecessary if the author's name is stated in the text. Use only a works cited entry. If the author's or performer's name is not cited in the text, place in a citation: (R.E.M.). For sound recordings, the medium (compact disc) is stated in the works cited entry:

```
                    Work Cited
R.E.M. "I Remember California." Green. Compact disc.

    Warner, 1988.
```

Long Quotations Quotations of five lines or more are set off, indented ten spaces. The parenthetical citation is placed one space after the final punctuation.

Charles C. Moskos summarizes the argument well:

> The principal argument raised against linking
> national service and federal educational
> aid is that it would have a regressive
> effect. . . . Students from wealthy families
> who do not need aid would be unaffected,
> while poor students would have to enter
> national service in order to get aid. (380)

Punctuation   For short quotations within the text, place a period or other punctuation *after* the parenthetical citation. For long block quotations, set off from the text, place the period one space *before* the parenthetical citation.

Using Notes with MLA Parenthetical Citations

Content notes and bibliographic notes can be used along with parenthetical citations to provide more information. To insert a note, place a superscript Arabic number at a suitable place in the text. Then at the bottom of the same page, place a matching number before the note. Keep the notes short and informative. Content notes and bibliographic notes can be mingled and numbered in sequence.

Content Notes   When a secondary source is cited, a content note can provide complete publication data on the original source. Or a necessary explanation may be included, as in the example below:

Several months ago when obesity specialist Dr. Frank
Greenway from UCLA revealed that a thigh reduction
cream really worked, several news accounts incorrectly
reported reductions of as much as 1-1/2 inches. The
fact was that the most a woman's thighs shrunk was 1-1/2
centimeters or approximately 1/2 inch. Furthermore, the
safety of the cream has been questioned.[1]

Note

[1] Several news sources have pointed out this
misstatement.

Bibliographic Notes To provide evaluative comments on sources or for references having several citations, use notes.

The <u>Wall Street Journal</u> and other newspapers carried numerous articles questioning President Clinton's role in the Whitewater affair, some even comparing it to Watergate.[1]

Note

[1] For a sample of articles taken from editorial pages, see Gigot and also Radelat.

Works Cited

Gigot, Paul. "What Did He Know, and When Did He Know It?" <u>Wall Street Journal</u>. 7 Jan. 1994: A10.

Radelat, Ana. "Whitewater Dogs Clinton." <u>Marion Star</u>. 14 Jan. 1994: 4.

PREPARING A LIST OF WORKS CITED: MLA STYLE

Use these general guidelines for the format of your works cited page.

- Type *Works Cited*, centered, at the top of the page.
- Alphabetize entries according to the last name of the author. When an author's name is not known, alphabetize by the first word in the title except for *a*, *an*, or *the*.
- Double-space the entire listing of works cited.
- Do not indent the first line of an entry. Indent *five* spaces (or one-half inch on a word processor) for succeeding lines of the entry.
- Place a period after each subdivision of an entry and at the end of each entry.
- Underline the title of an *entire* work such as books, magazines, newspapers, plays, paintings, and others.
- Place quotation marks around titles of short works that appear in longer works, such as articles, chapters, stories, poems, and songs.
- Cite inclusive page numbers (121–28) for specific essays, articles, short stories, and so forth that appear in a book or periodical.

RECOMMENDED ABBREVIATIONS FOR MLA WORKS CITED ENTRIES

PUBLISHERS' NAMES

Shorten the names of publishers, omitting *Inc.*, *Company*, and so forth, and using only the first name when there are more than one. *University Press* is shortened to *UP* (or *U of . . . P*). In some cases, initials are used. Some examples follow:

Appleton-Century-Crofts	Appleton
Beacon Press, Inc.	Beacon
Cambridge University Press	Cambridge UP
Henry Holt and Company	Henry Holt
Holt, Rinehart and Winston	Holt
New American Library	NAL
University of Chicago Press	U of Chicago P

STATES

Use zip code abbreviations without periods: NY, OH, CA.

GOVERNMENT PUBLICATIONS

Use the following abbreviations:

Congressional Record	Cong. Rec.
Government Printing Office	GPO
House of Representatives Report	H. Rept.
House of Representatives Document	H. Doc.
Library of Congress	LC
Senate Resolution	S. Res.
Senate Document	S. Doc.

- Number the works cited page just as the other pages of the paper in Arabic numerals.
- Use shortened forms for the names of publishers and reference sources (see Recommended Abbreviations).

1. SAMPLE MLA ENTRIES FOR BOOKS

Include the author's name as it is printed on the title page. In the works cited entry, reverse the name and place a comma between the last and first part: Bickford, Scott, Jr. Except for Jr. and roman numerals (which are part of a name), leave out titles, affiliations, or degrees.

Underline the titles and subtitles of books. Separate the title and subtitle with a *colon* unless the main title ends with a question mark, an exclamation point, or a dash. An underline can be typed as a solid line under all the words in a title or name even when it contains a colon. Do *not* underline the period at the end of a title.

Specify the city of publication, publisher, and year of publication (or copyright date if publication date isn't listed). If the city is well known, you can omit the state, country, or province if there is no chance of confusion.

1.1. A Book by One Author

The last name of a single author comes first.

```
Powell, Colin. My American Journey. New York: Random,
     1995.
```

1.2. Two or More Books by One Author

List the name once in the first entry (alphabetically by title). For the second entry, type three hyphens and a period instead of the name.

```
Goldberg, Natalie. Wild Mind: Living the Writer's Life.
     New York: Bantam, 1990.
---. Writing Down the Bones: Freeing the Writer Within.
     Boston: Shambhala, 1986.
```

1.3. A Book by Two or Three Authors

When there are two or three authors, reverse only the first name. Spell out *and*.

Musciano, Chuck, and Bill Kennedy. <u>HTML: The Definitive</u>

<u>Guide</u>. Sebastopol, CA: O'Reilly, 1996.

1.4. A Book by Four or More Authors

For a book with four or more authors, you may include only the first author and add *et al.* ("and others"), or you may state all the authors in the order given on the title page.

Taylor, Anita, et al. <u>Communicating</u>. 5th ed. Englewood

Cliffs: Prentice, 1989.

1.5. Corporate Author: A Book by a Group

Boston Women's Health Book Collective. <u>Ourselves and</u>

<u>Our Children</u>. New York: Random, 1978.

1.6. Second or Later Edition of a Book

Specify any edition other than the first by number (2nd ed., 3rd ed.), by name (Rev. ed.), or by year (1990 ed.).

Figler, Howard. <u>The Complete Job-Search Handbook: All</u>

<u>the Skills You Need to Get Any Job and Have a Good</u>

<u>Time Doing It</u>. Rev. ed. New York: Henry Holt,

1988.

1.7. A Work in an Anthology

Enclose in quotation marks the title of an essay, a short story, a poem, or other work in an anthology or other book collection. The anthology title and editor(s) follow. State the inclusive page numbers for the specific piece at the end of the entry. If you are citing a previously published scholarly article, insert *Rpt. in* ("Reprinted in"), the title of the collection, and the new publication data.

Maddox, Jack, and Rosa Maddox. "How We Got Over."

<u>Talk That Talk: An Anthology of African American</u>

<u>Storytelling</u>. Eds. Linda Goss and Marian E.

Barnes. New York: Simon, 1989. 117-25.

1.8. A Book by an Anonymous Author

<u>Go Ask Alice</u>. New York: Prentice, 1971.

1.9. A Book with an Editor or Editors

```
Reed, Ishmael, Kathryn Trueblood, and Shawn Wong, eds.

    The Before Columbus Foundation Fiction Anthology:

    Selections from the American Book Awards,

    1980-1990. New York: Norton, 1992.
```

1.10. A Book with an Author and an Editor

```
Tolkien, J. R. Unfinished Tales. Ed. Christopher

    Tolkien. Boston: Houghton, 1980.
```

1.11. A Book in Volumes

When using just one volume of a multivolume work, give that volume number before the place of publication.

```
Shakespeare, William. "Cymbeline." The Tragedies

    of Shakespeare. Ed. Warren Chappell. Vol. 2.

    New York: Random, 1944.
```

When using two or more volumes of a work, include the total number of volumes after the title.

```
Nicolson, Nigel, and Joanne Trautmann, eds. The

    Letters of Virginia Woolf. 5 vols. New York:

    Harcourt, 1977.
```

1.12. An Article from a Reference Book

The place and publisher can be omitted for encyclopedias, dictionaries, and other well-known reference books. Page numbers can also be omitted if the entries are alphabetical. If the entry is signed, lead with the author's name.

```
"The Civil War." Encyclopedia Americana. 100th

    Anniversary Library Edition. 1995.
```

1.13. An Introduction, Preface, Foreword, or Afterword

Start with the author of the piece, then identify what you are citing—for example, "Preface." If the book is by a different writer, include his or her name as shown in the following example.

```
Ehrlich, Gretel. Introduction. My First Summer in
     the Sierra. By John Muir. New York: Penguin, 1987.
     vii-xvi.
```

1.14. A Translation or Edited Edition

```
Dostoyevsky, Fyodor. The Brothers Karamazov. Trans.
     Constance Garnett. Ed. Manuel Komroff. New York:
     NAL, 1957.
```

1.15. A Pamphlet

Treat a pamphlet as a book, even if very short.

```
Lazear, David G. Teaching for Multiple Intelligences.
     Bloomington: Phi Delta Kappa, 1992.
```

1.16.   Government Publications

When the writer is unknown, list the government agency as author. If two or more works are issued by the same government, place three hyphens in place of the author's name (---.). Repeat if the works are by the same agency (---. ---.). Most congressional documents require the number and session of Congress, the house (S or HR), and the kind and number of publication, (S. Res. 19, H. Res. 49). The *Congressional Record*, however, requires just the date and page.

```
United States. Postal Service. A Consumer's Directory
     of Postal Services and Products. Washington: GPO,
     1991. Publication 201.
---. Dept. of Health and Human Services. Your Medicare
     Handbook. Washington: GPO, 1986.
```

2. SAMPLE MLA ENTRIES FOR ARTICLES

Periodicals comprise journals, magazines, newspapers, newsletters, and similar publications. Scholarly journals, which are usually published quarterly, are not aimed at a general audience. Since these articles often describe original research and give professional opinion, they are valuable sources for research papers.

Works cited entries for articles in periodicals follow the general guidelines for books except that different publication information is provided, and inclusive page numbers (for the entire article) appear. For names of publications beginning with *the*, omit the first word: *Wall Street Journal*. For a daily periodical, put the day before the month and year with no intervening punctuation. As you consult various periodicals in your research, collect the following information on your note cards. Then you will be well prepared to construct works cited entries later.

1. Name of author (if given)
2. Title of article
3. Name of source (periodical)
4. Series (if one)
5. Volume number (scholarly journals only)
6. Issue number (if one)
7. Publication date
8. Edition (if given)
9. Inclusive page numbers of the article

2.1. Article in a Journal with Continuous Paging

Many scholarly journals use continuous paging, starting in January and continuing throughout the year. The volume number and year are sufficient identification.

Keefe, Jack A., and Peter A. Magaro. "Creativity and

Schizophrenia." Journal of Abnormal Psychology 89

(1980): 390-97.

2.2. Article in Journal That Pages Each Issue Separately

Include issue numbers for journals that do *not* number pages continuously. After the volume number, place a period and the issue number together with no space: 10.3 (indicating volume 10, issue 3).

Alsalam, Nabeel. "Interpreting Conditions in the Job

Market for College Graduates." Monthly Labor

Review 116.2 (1993): 51-53.

2.3. Article from a Monthly Magazine

Include the cover date. Abbreviate all months except May, June, and July, using the first three letters. (The first four letters are allowed for September.) When the paging of an article is not consecutive, write only the first page number with a plus sign.

Robertson, David. "When a Biographer's Subject Is Less

Than Perfect." Writer Aug. 1995: 12+.

2.4. Article from a Weekly Magazine or Weekly Newspaper

```
Morrow, Lance. "Childhood's End." Time 9 Mar. 1992:
    22-23.
```

2.5. Article from a Daily Newspaper

When a newspaper has different editions, specify the edition between the date and the page.

```
D'Souza, Dinesh. "Separation of Race and State." Wall
    Street Journal 12 Sept. 1995, Midwest ed.: A22.
```

2.6. An Anonymous Article

When the author of an article is unstated, begin with the title and alphabetize by the first significant word in the title.

```
"Poor Judgment but No Smoking Gun." U.S. News and World
    Report 14 Apr. 1997: 38.
```

2.7. An Editorial

When citing a signed editorial, start with the author's name, then the title. Next, write *Editorial* (no underlining or quotation marks). When the editorial is unsigned, start with the title.

```
Nilsen-Blair, Susan. "We Are the World." Editorial.
    Imprint 40.3 (1993): 4.
```

2.8. A Letter to the Editor

```
Roberts, Clay. Letter. Wall Street Journal 30 June
    1993, Midwest ed.: A15.
```

2.9. Review

```
Applebaum, Herbert A. Rev. of Social Anthropology of
    Work, ed. Sandra Wallman. Current Anthropology 21
    (1980): 307-08.
```

2.10. Sacred Writings

The article, chapter, or "book" (as in books of the Bible) is placed before the verses (if applicable). The title of the entire work follows. (Titles of sacred writing are not underlined nor enclosed with quotations marks.) If the work has more than one version, the abbreviation for the version is placed last.

```
Proverbs 22:1. Bible. KJV.
```

3. SAMPLE MLA ENTRIES FOR CD-ROMS AND OTHER PORTABLE DATABASES

Electronic information may be published in two or more formats. Specify the medium of publication: CD-ROM, videodisc, video CD, laser disc, or diskette. Also give the manufacturer or vendor (distributor). Since some electronic versions of data are leased to vendors in different forms, specify the version (2nd or later) and the date of release. If there is more than one date, give the original date of publication and the date of the version you used. When you cite electronic data from a printed source, include the following items when relevant:

1. Author's name
2. Title of database or product (underline)
3. Title of the part of the work, if relevant (in quotation marks)
4. Other publication information: edition, volume, place, publisher's name, copyright date, and any other relevant data
5. Edition or version (if specified)
6. Medium of publication (CD-ROM) or (diskette) or another
7. Manufacturer or vendor (if leased)
8. Date of electronic publication (year)

3.1. Periodical Published on CD-ROM

Many newspapers, magazines, journals and other periodicals can be accessed from databases. Usually, source information is provided at the beginning of the file.

```
Hansen, Robert W. "Stigma, Conflict, and the Approval
     of AIDs Drugs." Journal of Drugs (Winter 1995):
     129-39. CD-ROM. UMI-ProQuest. 1995.
Mayer, Thomas. "Banking Systems." New Grolier
     Multimedia Encyclopedia. CD-ROM. Novato, CA:
     Software Toolworks. 1992.
Morrow, Lance. Reporting by Tom Curry. "William
     Clinton: The Torch is Passed." New York Times
     4 Jan. 1993. Time Almanac. CD-ROM. 1992.
```

3.2. Nonperiodical Publication on CD-ROM

Some nonperiodical databases are published only once with no revisions or updates. Cite nonperiodical CD-ROMs the way you would cite a book, but include the publication medium. (Usually, there is a publisher, no vendor.)

Hanson, Mervin, Richard Paselk, and John Russell.
"Atomic Orbitals." Chemical Bonding Series:
Visualization of the Abstract in Chemistry.
CD-ROM. Arcada, CA: Redwood Software, 1994.

Quicken. "Making a Will," Family Lawyer. CD-ROM.
Hiawatha, Iowa: Parsons Technology, 1995.

The Presidents: A Picture History of Our Nation.
CD-ROM. Washington: National Geographic Soc.,
1991.

3.3. Publication on a Diskette

Computer programs, languages, and other software on diskettes (floppy disks) may be updated from time to time. For updates specify the edition, version, or other update. Separate publication information from the title of the product with a period.

Bird, Alan. "TimeOut." Quickspell. Diskette. San Diego:
Beagle Bros., 1987.

Schulman, Bob, Joseph Schrader, and Joseph Jacobs.
Quicken. Vers. 7. Diskette. Metro Park, CA:
Intuit, 1997.

Write Now. Vers. 4.0. Diskette. Novato, CA: WordStar,
1993.

3.4. A Work in More Than One Publication Medium

Some stores offer bundles of software in one package. Follow the directions for a nonperiodical CD-ROM (3.2) and state the media in the package.

Davidson, Robin. "Australian Northern Territory." From
Alice to Ocean. CD-ROM, book. Santa Clara: Claris,
1993.

4. SAMPLE MLA ENTRIES FOR ONLINE DATABASES

For material you access through online databases, commercial or public, you will see items that give a printed source and items that do not. In your works cited entry, give information for all previously printed sources as well as the following information:

- *Medium.* Specify the name of the online service or network used to obtain material before the medium of publication (online).
- *Date of access.* The date you get material is the date of access. Place this date at the end of the works cited entry; the original publication date (if there is one) is specified before the medium.
- *Availability statement.* If your instructor requests an availability statement or an electronic address, supply the path of access or URL at the end of the entry. Precede with *Available:*.

4.1. Online Material with a Printed Source

When online material carries a printed source or analog, cite that first according to the previous guidelines for books and periodicals. Follow this with the title of the database, the medium of publication, the online service or network, the date of access. If your instructor requests an availability statement or electronic address, add the path of access or URL at the end of your entry, preceded by *Available:*, as in the first example below.

a. Abstract: Electronic Journal Article to Be Published

```
Wang, Yi-Peng, and Franklin Fuchs. "Length,
     Force, and CA2+-Troponin C Affinity in Cardiac
     and Slow Skeletal Muscle." Scheduled for
     publication in American Physiological Society
     Journal (1997): APSstracts 1:0022C. Online.
     Internet. 8 Sept. 1997. Available: gopher://
     oac.hsc.uth.tmc.edu:3300/00/publications/
     apsstracts
```

b. Electronic Journal with a Print Source

```
"Customer Satisfaction Studies: Implications for
     Job." New Horizons in Adult Education. 6.2 (1992):
     n. pag. Internet. 5 Sept. 1996.
```

c. An Electronic Directory

Striner, Sara, and Mark Sweeney. "Commonly Used
　　　Newspapers on Microfilm." Serial & Government
　　　Publ. Div. Library of Congress. Jan. 1993. Online.
　　　Internet. 6 Mar. 1997.

d. Electronic Texts: An Online Collection and a Document

Frost, Robert. "The Pasture." Imaginative Frost
　　　Poems. n.d. Online. Oxford Text Archive. Internet.
　　　8 Mar. 1997.

"Preamble to the Charter of the United Nations."
　　　n.d. Online. Oxford Text Archive. Internet.
　　　8 Mar. 1997.

4.2. Online Material with No Printed Source

a. Electronic Data Files

"Iran-Contra Affair." CBS News/New York Times National
　　　Surveys, 1986. (15 data files). Online. Internet.
　　　6 Sept. 1995.

"IBP, Inc." 1994. Hoover's Handbook Database. Online.
　　　America Online. 25 Dec. 1994.

b. Electronic Journal with No Printed Source

Karros, Eric. "Eric's Journal." Karros Kronicles.
　　　(11 Sept. 1995). Online. America Online. 11 Sept.
　　　1995.

c. An Electronic Newsletter

"Internships Expose Minority Students to HSPH
　　　Research." Around the School. 28 July. Harvard
　　　School of Public Health. Online. Internet.
　　　25 Aug. 1995.

5. SAMPLE MLA ENTRIES FOR OTHER SOURCES

Note that for broadcast, film, and recorded sources that involve various personnel, you begin the entry with the name or title that is the primary subject of emphasis in your paper as shown below:

```
Stouffer, Marty. "Cutthroat Trout." 2 episodes. Wild
     America. PBS. WOSU-TV, Columbus, OH. 11 Sept.
     1995-12 Sept. 1995.
"Cutthroat Trout." 2 episodes. Marty Stouffer. Wild
     America. PBS. WOSU-TV, Columbus, OH. 11 Sept.
     1995-12 Sept. 1995.
```

5.1. Television or Radio Programs

The items in a works cited entry for a television or radio program generally follow the order below. (Omit any items that are not relevant.) Include any other relevant items such as performers, director, conductor, or number of episodes.

1. Episode or segment title (Enclose in quotation marks. If there are two or more episodes, state the total.)
2. Author's name (in reverse order if it begins the entry)
3. Program title (underlined)
4. Series title
5. Network (for example, CBS)
6. Local call letters and city (for example, WBNS, Columbus, OH)
7. Date of broadcast

```
"John Williams Gala Celebration." Comp. and Cond. John
     Williams. Host: Richard Dreyfuss. Evening at the
     Pops. PBS. WOSU-TV. Columbus, Ohio. 9 July 1993.
"Open Line." Host and prod. Fred Andrel. News 820
     Update. WOSU-AM, Columbus, Ohio. 7 July 1993.
```

For sound recordings of television or radio programs, see 5.2. For a videotape of a performance, see 5.3. For interviews conducted on television or radio, see 5.4.

5.2. Sound Recordings

If the recording is on compact disc, omit the medium. Specify audiocassette tape or LP. Also include manufacturer and date. The name you place first depends on whom you want to emphasize—composer, conductor, or performer. Some sound recordings may include printed material, as in the first example.

The Art of Belly Dancing. Perf. and Cond. George Abdo.
    "Flames of Araby" orchestra. Instruction booklet
    by Vina. Monitor, 1975.

Chant. Perf. Benedictine Monks of Santo Domingo
    de Silos. Dir. Ismael Fernandez de la Cuesta/
    Francisco Lara. Madrid, Spain: Hispavox. Rec.
    1973, 1980, 1981, 1982. Angel Records, compilation
    1994.

Mann, Herbie. "Memphis Underground." The Best of Herbie
    Mann. LP. Atlantic, 1970.

Marley, Bob. "Stir It Up." Legend. Island Records, 1984.

Strauss, Edvard. "The Merry Widow Waltz." Viennese
    Favorites. Cond. Arthur Fiedler. Boston Pops
    Orchestra. Audiocassette. RCA Victrola, 1983.

5.3. Films, Videocassettes, Videodiscs, Video CDs, Laser Discs, Filmstrips, and Slide Programs

Include all pertinent information in an order that reflects your emphasis. For video recordings, include the original date of release as well as the date of the release of the recording.

a. A Film, Video Recording, or Performance

Enchanted April. Dir. Mike Newell. Perf. Miranda
    Richardson, Josie Lawrence, Polly Walker, and Joan
    Plowright. Screenwriter Peter Barnes. Warner
    Brothers, 1992.

If material is not a film, specify the medium. Some materials may include an original release date, perhaps in another form. For example, some laser discs contain films in IMAX. If material has an original release date, include that date before the medium.

b. Videocassettes, Videodiscs, Video CDs, Laser Discs, Filmstrips, and Slide Programs

MacArthur Foundation, J. D. and C. T., National Science
    Foundation, and Jostens Foundation. <u>Tropical</u>
    <u>Rainforest</u>. 1992. Laser disc. Denver: Lumivision.
    1994.

"Those Wonderful Dogs." Narr. Richard Kiley. Writer and
    Prod. Barbara Jampel. Music by Scott Harper.
    National Geographic Society. 1989. Videocassette.
    Columbia Tristar. 1994.

5.4. Interviews

Published interviews are treated as excerpts from anthologies and periodicals. Broadcast interviews are treated as television or radio programs. Personal and telephone interviews are listed as such. In all cases list the name of the person interviewed first.

MacLeish, Archibald. "Archibald MacLeish." Interview
    with Benjamin De Mott. <u>Writers at Work: The Paris</u>
    <u>Review Interviews 5</u>. Ed. George Plimpton. New
    York: Penguin, 1988. 23-48.

Senitko, Melanie. Personal interview. 15 June 1996.

Witzel, Carol. Telephone interview. 17 Apr. 1997.

5.5. Cartoon

Larson, Gary. "Best of the Far Side." Cartoon. <u>Sunday</u>
    [Cleveland] 23 May 1993: 4.

5.6. Legal References

For papers requiring several legal citations, see the most recent edition of *A Uniform System of Citation* (Cambridge: Harvard Law Rev. Assn.). A usual rule is to neither underline nor enclose in quotation marks any laws, acts, or similar documents in the text or in the list of works cited. Works of this sort are generally cited by sections. The year is included when it is significant:

```
14 US Code Sec. 77a. 1964

U.S. Const. Art 2, sec. 1
```

Court cases (*Brown v. Board of Ed.*) are underlined or italicized in text but not in the list of works cited:

```
Brown v. Board of Ed. 347 U.S. 483. 1954.
```

DOCUMENTING YOUR SOURCES
USING APA STYLE

For research papers about the social sciences, many instructors prefer the American Psychological Association style of documentation. Although APA and MLA styles both key parenthetical citations in a text to a list of sources at the end of a paper, the two forms differ in several ways. In APA style, text citations include the year of publication in parentheses immediately after the author's name. The APA list of sources is entitled "References," and the first line of each entry on the list is indented. There are other minor differences such as arrangement, capitalization, and underlining, as explained in the following sections. For the original guidelines, see *Publication Manual of the American Psychological Association*, Fourth Edition, upon which this section is based.

Parenthetical Citations: APA Style

The primary differences between APA and MLA citation styles are the inclusion of the date and the page number in APA style. Ampersands (&) are also used, as is the abbreviation for page.

Single Author   In APA style the author's name is usually mentioned in the text, followed by a parenthetical citation indicating the year of publication. Page numbers follow the cited material, unless the entire work is cited, in which case no page numbers are required. If the author is not identified in the text, his or her last name precedes the year in a parenthetical citation following the cited material.

```
Theodore Bernstein (1958) points out that the
word bandit "has a flavor of heroism" (p. 17).

Research shows that experienced writers seem to have
much stronger revision habits than do student writers
(Sommers, 1980).
```

Note that page is abbreviated *p.*, or *pp.* for pages; likewise, when needed in parenthetical citations, chapter is abbreviated *ch.* and section is abbreviated *sec.*

Two or More Works by the Same Author   Different works by one author are distinguished by their dates. For multiple references in the same year by one author, distinguish with lowercase letters: 1993a for the first title alphabetically, 1993b for the second, and so forth.

Two or More Authors   For a work with two authors, cite both every time. For three to five authors, include all at the first mention; for subsequent mentions, cite the first author's name followed by *et al.* For six or more, cite the first followed by *et al.* for all citations. Use the word *and* in text but the ampersand symbol for parenthetical citations.

```
Rivers, Moss, and Wang (1995) claim . . .

These findings have been labeled "ridiculous, perhaps

fraudulent" (King & Alberti, 1989, p. 322).
```

Works by Two Authors with the Same Last Name   Distinguish by initials: "J. Neff (1993) and C. A. Neff (1988) also found. . . ."

Source with No Author Name Given   For unsigned sources, use an abbreviated version of the title. Place article titles in quotation marks, and underline book and pamphlet titles: ("Jim Crow," 1996), (*Recycling*, 1991).

Corporate Author   In general, give the name in full each time you cite it. However, if the name is long, it may be abbreviated in subsequent citations.

```
First reference: (American Association of Retired People

[AARP], 1986)

Later references: (AARP, 1986)
```

Indirect Source   Precede the indirect source with the phrase *as cited in.*

```
Jameson's findings (as cited in Baure & Dinks,

1992) . . .
```

Two or More Sources in One Citation   List alphabetically by authors' last names, separated by semicolons: (Adams, 1993; Coates & Tan, 1989; Martiniu, 1975). If citations are two works by the same author, include the dates, separated by commas: (Wiggins, 1989, 1991).

Personal Communications   Personal interviews, letters, and the like are cited only in the text; they are not included on the reference list.

```
According to the hospital's chief administrator, the

procedure is no longer performed there (J. A. Wells,

personal communication, July 12, 1996).
```

Long Quotations   Quotations of forty words or more are set off, indented five spaces (or the same indentation as a paragraph for word processing). The parenthetical citation is placed one space after the final punctuation.

```
Moskos (1988) summarizes the argument well:

     The principal argument raised against linking

     national service and federal educational aid is

     that it would have a regressive effect. . . .

     Students from wealthy families who do not need

     aid would be unaffected, while poor students would

     have to enter national service in order to get

     aid. (p. 380)
```

PREPARING A LIST OF REFERENCES: APA STYLE

Use these guidelines for the format of your references page:

- Type *References*, centered, at the top of the page.
- Alphabetize entries according to authors' last names or, when no author is listed, the first major word of the title.
- Double-space all entries, and indent the first line of each entry five spaces.
- Arrange multiple works of one author by dates of publication, earliest first. Give the author's name in *each* entry, followed by the publication date.
- Use an ampersand (&) instead of *and* when listing two or more authors.
- Put publication dates in parentheses after the author's name. Place a period after the parentheses.
- Capitalize only the first word of a book or article title and the first word of any subtitle. Proper nouns in the title, however, should be capitalized. Book titles are underlined, but article titles are not enclosed in quotation marks.

- For books that have more than one volume, cite volume numbers in parentheses, following the title: (Vols. 1–5).

1. SAMPLE APA ENTRIES FOR BOOKS

Entries for books include author, date, title, place of publication, and publisher. Use all the names in a publishing company (Simon & Schuster, not just Simon), but don't include "Publishing Company," "Inc.," and other nonessential words.

1.1 A Book by One Author

Powell, C. (1995). <u>My American journey</u>. New York: Random House.

1.2 Two or More Books by One Author

Books by the same author are listed according to date, from least to most recent.

Goldberg, N. (1986). <u>Writing down the bones: Freeing the writer within</u>. Boston: Shambhala.

Goldberg, N. (1990). <u>Wild mind: Living the writer's life</u>. New York: Random House.

1.3 A Book by Two or More Authors

List all authors, last name first.

Musciano, C. & Kennedy, B. (1996). <u>HTML: The definitive guide</u>. Sebastopol, CA: O'Reilly.

1.4 A Book by an Unknown Author

<u>Go ask Alice</u>. (1971). New York: Prentice-Hall.

1.5 Book, Revised Edition

Figler, Howard. (1988). <u>The complete job-search handbook: All the skills you need to get any job and have a good time doing it</u> (Rev. ed.). New York: Henry Holt.

1.6 A Work in an Anthology

> Maddox, J., & Maddox, R. (1989). How we got over.
> In L. Goss & M. E. Barnes (Eds.), <u>Talk that talk:</u> An
> <u>anthology of African American storytelling</u> (pp.
> 117-125). New York: Random House.

Note that for an edited work the designation "Ed(s)." is included parenthetically. Inclusive page numbers in APA style include all digits.

1.7 Encyclopedia or Dictionary

If a major reference work has a large editorial board, you may cite only the name of the executive editor and follow it with "et al." If the work has more than one volume, include the number of volumes after the edition in parentheses: (4th ed., Vols. 1–30.)

> Soukhanov, S. H., et al. (Eds.). (1992). <u>The</u>
> <u>American heritage dictionary</u> (3rd ed.). Boston:
> Houghton Mifflin.

If the author of the entry is not given, start with the title of the article. Include in parentheses the volume number and page numbers for the article. End with the place of publication and the publisher.

> The Civil War. (1995). In <u>Encyclopedia Americana</u>
> (Vol. 6, pp. 782-819). Danbury, CT: Grolier.

1.8 A Brochure

When a brochure has no author given, start with the segment title, then give the title of the brochure, underlined.

> Lesson 1: Setting up your first account. (1992).
> <u>The official audio guide to Quicken for Macintosh</u>.
> [Brochure]. San Jose, CA: Personal Training Systems.

2. SAMPLE APA ENTRIES FOR ARTICLES

Note that article titles are not enclosed in quotation marks, and only their first words (and proper nouns) are capitalized. Titles of journals and magazines are underlined and capitalized normally. For a journal give the volume number, underlined, in arabic numbers, but do not write *vol.* Do not abbreviate months. In listing page numbers of newspapers, abbreviate to p. or pp.; *omit* p. or pp. for references to journal and magazine articles.

2.1 Article in a Journal with Continuous Paging

Keefe, J.A., & Magaro, P.A. (1980). Creativity and schizophrenia. Journal of Abnormal Psychology, 89, 390-397.

2.2 Article in a Journal That Pages Each Issue Separately

Issue numbers are included in parentheses after the volume number.

Alsalam, N. (1993). Interpreting conditions in the job market for college graduates. Monthly Labor Review, 116(2), 51-53.

2.3 Magazine Article

Robertson, David. (1995, August). When a biographer's subject is less than perfect. Writer, 12-14.

2.4 Newspaper Article

D'Souza, D. (1995, September 12). Separation of race and state. Wall Street Journal, p. A22.

2.5 Anonymous Article

Poor judgment but no smoking gun. (1997, April 14). U.S. News and World Report, p. 38.

3. SAMPLE APA ENTRIES FOR COMPUTERIZED SOURCES

The fourth edition of the APA *Publication Manual*, published in 1994, offers general guidelines for documenting material retrieved electronically. The following sample entries are based on those guidelines. Note that author, date, title, and other standard information are generally listed as for books and periodicals.

Include date of original issue if possible; for electronic databases, also include the exact date of retrieval. Following the title, indicate the electronic source; conclude the entry by providing retrieval information.

3.1 CD-ROMs and Other Portable Databases

Hansen, R. W. S. (1995, Winter). Stigma, conflict, and the approval of AIDS drugs [CD-ROM]. Journal of Drugs, 129-139. UMI-ProQuest.

Mayer, T. (1992). Banking systems. New Grolier multimedia encyclopedia [CD-ROM]. Novato, CA: Software Toolworks.

3.2 Computer Software and Computer Programs

Schulman, R., Schrader, J., & Jacobs, J. (1994). Quicken (Version 5.0) [Computer program]. Metro Park, CA: Intuit.

Write Now 4.0 [Computer software]. (1993). Novato, CA: Wordstar.

3.3 Material Accessed through Online Databases

Stiner, S., & Sweeny, M. (1993, January). Commonly used newspapers on microfilm [Online]. Serial & Government Publication Division. Library of Congress. 1995, September 6. Available: gopher:// marvel.loc.gov:70/00research/reading rooms/newspaper/ bibguides/common.nesps

Internships expose minority students to HSPH research [6 paragraphs]. (1995, July 28-August 25). Around the School [Online newsletter]. 1995, September 5. Available: gopher://hsph.harvard.edu:70/00/around

4. SAMPLE APA ENTRIES FOR OTHER SOURCES

For broadcast, film, and recorded sources, enclose in parentheses any information needed to identify contributing personnel.

4.1 Television and Radio Programs

Include the broadcast date and the broadcasting network or station.

```
Stouffer, M. (Writer, Director, & Producer).
(1995, September 11). Cutthroat trout. Wild America.
Columbus, OH: WOSU-TV.
```

4.2 Films, Video Recordings, and Other Visual Media

Indicate the specific medium in brackets. Include the city and producing organization, if available. For video recordings, include date of original release or production at the beginning of the citation; include date of video release at the end.

```
Newel, M. (Director), & Barnes, P. (Screenwriter).
(1992). Enchanted April. [Film]. Burbank, CA: Warner
Brothers.

Kiley, R. (Narrator), & Jampel, B. (Writer &
Producer). (1989). Those wonderful dogs. National
Geographic Society. [Videocassette]. Culver City, CA:
Columbia Tristar. 1994.
```

4.3 Audio Recordings

When referring to specific lyrics or compositions, begin with the lyricist/composer followed by the original copyright date; then provide recording information, including date, if different from copyright. In some cases, it may be appropriate to begin with the performer or conductor or with the title. Include the medium in brackets. For nonmusical recordings, lead with the original writer's name, if provided, or with the title.

```
Blitzstein, M. (1941). In the clear. [Recorded by
Dawn Upshaw]. On I wish it so [CD]. New York: Elektra
Entertainment. (1994).
```

<u>Official audio guide to Quicken</u>. (1992). (Cassette recording No. IQU4.00M-1-A). San Jose, CA: Personal Training Systems.

4.4 Published Interview

Begin with the name of the person interviewed and the date of the interview, then the title, if any, and identifying information in brackets. Conclude by identifying the source according to the guidelines for books or periodicals.

MacLeish, A. (1974, summer). "Archibald MacLeish." [Interview with Benjamin De Mott]. In George Plimpton (Ed.), <u>Writers at work: The Paris Review interviews</u> 5 (pp. 23-48). New York: Penguin. (1988).

Summary

Accurate and complete documentation is essential both in the workplace and in college. The primary purpose of documentation is to supply source information for the reader and to give credit to the author. When material is borrowed without providing documentation, the offense is plagiarism.

Different styles of documentation are used for research papers. MLA documentation style requires a list of works cited that provides complete bibliographic information for each source used. Within the paper, sufficient identifying information is provided—in parentheses as well as in the text itself—to key each source to its works cited entry. Formats for entries vary according to the works: books, articles, electronic, or other forms.

APA documentation style differs in several significant ways from MLA style. For example, APA parenthetical citations always refer to publication date, and the list of sources is titled "References."

To present accurate and complete documentation, follow a style guide carefully, using the correct model for each entry.

Key Terms

documentation	parenthetical citation
document (v.)	content note
plagiarism	bibliographic note
MLA style	APA style
works cited	list of references

Practice

Recognizing Items That Need to Be Documented

Directions: Go to a library or use your own materials to make examples of entries for an MLA style list of works cited or an APA style references list. Follow the textbook models carefully, checking format and punctuation.

1. Book by one author
2. Book by two or three authors
3. Book with an editor or editors
4. Work in an anthology by several authors
5. Book with several volumes
6. Article in an encyclopedia
7. Article from a daily newspaper
8. Article from a monthly magazine
9. Article from a journal with continuous paging
10. Videotape
11. One author quoting another author

CHAPTER 23

Using Sources and Writing a Research Paper

I have lived in this world just long enough
to look carefully the second time into things
that I am the most certain of the first time.

—Josh Billings (Henry Wheeler Shaw)

As an employee was leaving a manufacturing plant, security guards stopped him and searched his tote bag. Inside they found a $35 telephone. Assuming he had stolen the telephone, the company fired him six days later. Then they placed notices on eleven bulletin boards and the company's electronic mail system, saying the telephone was company property and the employee had violated work rule #12 about theft. The employee filed suit against the company for libel.

At the trial two years later, a coworker testified to accompanying the defendant to a mall where he had purchased the telephone. The defendant explained that his company telephone had been damaged by a flood. But he had lost the sales slip (for reimbursement) for the new telephone. His boss had said to just keep the telephone. After the firing, the man had applied for 100 jobs, but was rejected each time it was learned why he had been fired. The jury awarded the defendant $1.3 million in damages. The moral of this story is that an open mind is a prerequisite to tracking the truth.

RESEARCHING WITH AN OPEN MIND

Research, which can be scholarly inquiry or scientific investigation, implies a fair and thorough consideration of existing facts before reaching a conclusion. When doing any kind of research, be open to new evidence even though it conflicts with what you "know" or believe. Withhold judgment until you have thoroughly reviewed the facts, noted inferences, and identified theories.

As you read reputable accounts of polls, experiments, and studies, notice the tentative, or provisional, words used to qualify discussions of results. These *uncertain* words indicate that evidence is *not* conclusive even though a growing body of research may indicate that a conclusion or theory is probably true. Look at how the journal *Science* uses tentative words (italicized here) to discuss results of several studies about the cause of perfect pitch:

> A research team from Dusseldorf, Germany, *may* have located the physical basis of one exceptional form of mental performance: perfect pitch—the ability to identify any musical note without comparison to a reference note. . . .
>
> A team led by neurologists Gottfried Schlaug and Helmuth Steinmetz of Dusseldorf's Heinrich Heine University *reports* that the planum temporale, a region of the brain cortex that processes sound signals, is far larger on the left side than on the right in professional musicians—and especially in those who have perfect pitch.

Using Tentative Words to Discuss Theories

Overstatement undermines the credibility of research. Yet beginning writers sometimes assume that because a study or experiment *suggests* that something is true, that it is indeed true. By the time they summarize their research notes, they have catapulted theory into the realm of fact. Often one word, *prove*, is what launches this assault upon truth. To discuss uncertain research findings competently, qualify your statements with tentative words. Use accurate terminology, as shown below.

Common Research Terms

Verbs	Nouns
indicates	indication
found	findings
may	possibility
detected	detection
identified	identification
discovered	discovery
reported	report
studied	study
observed	observation
suggests	suggestion
reinforce	reinforcement
resulted in	results
influence	influence
theorize	theory

SHORTCUTS TO READING AND NOTE-TAKING

Reading for a research paper can be a pleasant experience when the topic is challenging, the material absorbing, and the reading selective. To save time and prevent frustration, skim materials first; then read only the relevant sections. When time is limited, it is better to read widely and mull over ideas than to spend hours reading remotely related material and copying details that may never be used.

To avoid undue interruption while reading books, make abbreviated references on cards rather than full-fledged notes. Whenever a note-worthy passage appears, jot down the subject, last name of the author, the first few words of the passage, and the page number. Then slip the card into the book, with the subject notation visible, and continue reading. On photocopied articles, notes can be made along the way. React in the margins, jotting summary words, posing questions, and underlining topic sentences. Then you will have more time to ponder and relate ideas.

RESEARCH READING

Reading for research, if you are absorbed in your topic, can be just as interesting as the latest bestseller. Research reading, however, requires an organized, critical approach.

Examining Credentials and Dates

As you read, it is important to examine the credentials of writers and researchers as well as dates of surveys, studies, and other research materials whenever you can. (To find this background information, scan the preface, introduction, or any footnotes that accompany the research.) As new knowledge is discovered, previous knowledge may become dated. For example, rapid advances in biotechnology continue to yield new products, medicines, and environmental practices, causing some previous developments to become obsolete. By reading widely, you can find out what other researchers in the field regard as the latest discoveries.

≈ Checklist for Examining Credentials and Sources

1. Does the author/researcher have advanced degrees, licenses or certification, and a fine reputation in the field?

2. When was the study or poll taken? Where? Size of sample?

3. Has there been other research that reports similar or conflicting results? What do authorities in the field generally accept?

4. Does the interpretation of results seem logical? Does the language seem objective? Or does the writer seem to have a hidden agenda? For example, a nutritionist on a radio talk show recommended a vitamin preparation that he had invented.

Recognizing Information That Must Be Acknowledged

The very nature of a research assignment requires that the majority of what you write will be based on outside sources. Therefore you will need to gather carefully all of the source information required for parenthetical citations and works cited entries (see Tips for Compiling a List of Sources). Carelessness can result in unintentional plagiarism. Perhaps knowing that the Latin *plagiarius* means "kidnapper" will remind you not to kidnap absentmindedly any original words. For a discussion of this offense, including its risks and penalties, see chapter 22.

Restating Common Knowledge   Factual information that is familiar to the general public is considered common knowledge. For example, it is common knowledge that orange juice is high in vitamin C, that Thomas A. Edison perfected the incandescent light bulb, and that Alfred Hitchcock directed suspense films. So if you came across such facts in your research, you would not be expected to acknowledge the source for them—*unless you decided to quote the source directly.* In your early efforts at research, however, it is best to cite the source of any piece of information that you were unaware of before reading a source.

Acknowledging Everything Else   Practically all other information gathered in research requires documentation, including the following:

- Historical information that is not commonly known
- Current information based on a writer's direct observation or reporting
- Statistics

TIPS FOR COMPILING A LIST OF SOURCES

- *Alphabetize* source cards before typing entries.
- Start making entries early. They do take time and care.
- Double-space entries.
- In making entries, follow the correct format model (see chapter 22). Check the form and punctuation of each entry.
- As you add more citations to the paper, make a new entry for each one unless the source already has an entry.

- Surveys and opinion poll results. Give the researcher, date, place, size of sample, and any other pertinent information in the text of the paper if possible.
- Research results and interpretations. Give names of researchers, date.
- Expert opinion, estimates, predictions
- Theories. Identify the person who originated the theory, if possible.
- Artistic interpretations or criticisms
- Tables, charts, graphs, and other visual material
- Any statement that is subject to debate
- Footnote from printed material

As you take notes—and while drafting your paper—make sure that you provide proper documentation. Promptly noting the author, publication, date, and page number for all such information will preclude a frantic search and possibly a return trip to the library. When you are filling in note cards, you can jot down information any way you wish as long as it is accurate and complete (see chapter 22).

Stating Your Own Ideas and Conclusions   Since you will not have an outside source for your own ideas and conclusions based on your direct observation, no documentation is required for those. Yet you need to acknowledge all sources that lead to your conclusions. For example, it would be highly improper to omit documentation just because you agree with another author. Even if you restate his or her ideas in your own words, documentation is needed. The next section should help to answer further questions as they arise.

NOTE-TAKING: PARAPHRASING, SUMMARIZING, AND QUOTING

No matter how you take notes, accuracy is essential. As you paraphrase, summarize, and quote sources, take care to preserve the meaning of the original passage. Distinguish fact from opinion, and transcribe numbers and other figures accurately. Two common problems in research papers are (1) pulling ideas out of context and (2) omitting significant information. Both distort meaning. Make sure to identify the source of each note clearly, including the specific page number or numbers.

When paraphrasing and summarizing, you also need to be careful to use your own phrasing, not the words and sentence structures of the original source. Otherwise, the result might be plagiarism. The following sections show you how to paraphrase, summarize, and quote competently.

Paraphrasing

A paraphrase is a restatement of an original passage. As you paraphrase, take care to select accurate synonyms, not variations of the same words to replace major words. For example, if an author uses the word *defend*, do not write *defending*. Find a different word such as *protect*. Just because you may not think of another synonym does *not* mean you can use the original without quotation marks. When stumped, consult a dictionary or thesaurus.

Although *minor* words (articles, prepositions, and conjunctions) may be included in a paraphrase without quotation marks, try to vary your word choice and sentence structure. Enclose borrowed *major* words (nouns, adjectives, adverbs, and verbs) in quotation marks as well as any *phrases* you copy from the original. For specialized or technical terms, enclose in quotation marks only the first time; after that, you may use the term as needed without quotation marks.

Since generic words (names of a general category, such as *cat*) have no synonym, they can be used without quotation marks. They require only a citation to indicate borrowing of ideas and information, as illustrated in the following examples of paraphrase and summary. First is the original passage from *Nonverbal Communication in Human Interaction*, by Mark Knapp, about the subject of nonverbal communication and an unusual horse:

Original

Herr von Osten purchased a horse in Berlin, Germany, in 1900. When von Osten began training his horse, Hans, to count by tapping his front hoof, he had no idea that Hans was soon to become one of the most celebrated horses in history. Hans was a rapid learner and soon progressed from counting to addition, multiplication, division, subtraction, and eventually the solution of problems involving factors and fractions. As if this were not enough, von Osten exhibited Hans to public audiences where he counted the number in the audience or simply the number of people wearing eye glasses. Still responding only with taps, Hans could tell time, use a calendar, display an ability to recall musical pitch, and perform numerous other seemingly fantastic feats. After von Osten taught Hans an alphabet which could be coded into hoof beats, the horse could answer virtually any question—oral or written. It seemed that Hans, a common horse, had complete comprehension of the German language, the ability to produce the equivalent of words and numerals, and an intelligence beyond that of many human beings.

Paraphrase

To explain how animals "read" nonverbal signals, Mark L. Knapp tells a strange story of a horse bought by Herr von Osten in Berlin, Germany. While teaching the horse, Hans, to rap out numbers with a forehoof, von Osten did not suspect that the animal would ever become famous. But Hans learned so fast that he could soon do arithmetic. When von Osten showed Hans in public, the horse "counted the number of people wearing eyeglasses." He could even "tell time," read a calendar, remember musical pitch, and do other tricks. When von Osten drilled the horse in the alphabet, tapped out with a hoof, Hans responded to almost any query. He appeared not only to understand German well, but also to know more than many people (1).

Note that in the paraphrase, *generic* words such as horse, musical pitch, and alphabet are included without quotation marks. Synonyms have been substituted for all major words that were not generic. Two phrases have been quoted, for a paraphrase would have been a bit awkward and wordy there. As this example suggests, a paraphrase is often a little shorter than the original, but it may be as long or even a bit longer if necessary. If you are paraphrasing complex material, you may need to include more explanatory words, using your own vocabulary to help clarify difficult ideas.

In the next example, however, major words that are not generic and variations of major words (italicized) have been copied; the result is unacceptable:

Plagiarized Paraphrase

According to Mark L. Knapp, in 1900 in Berlin, Germany, Herr von Osten *purchased* a horse. *When von Osten trained* the horse to *count* by rapping his hoof, he did not know that Hans would *become one* of the most famous horses *in history*. Hans was a *rapid learner* and *soon* could do arithmetic. When von Osten showed the horse, Hans *counted the audience* and those *wearing eyeglasses*. By *tapping* his hoof, Hans *told time*, *used a calendar*, and *displayed* musical ability. *After Herr von Osten taught Hans a coded* alphabet, *it seemed* Hans, a horse, understood German well and knew more than many people (1).

Summarizing

A summary is more condensed than a paraphrase. Rather than restating every point of a relatively brief passage, a summary reduces a long passage—perhaps several paragraphs or even several pages—by 50 to 75 percent, focusing only on the original's main ideas. In the summary below, Mark Knapp's original passage has been restated and condensed:

Summary

Mark L. Knapp tells an amazing story of a horse owned by Herr von Osten of Germany in the early 1900s. His owner taught Hans to do arithmetic, drummed out with a front hoof. Then von Osten began showing the horse in public, where Hans computed the total of persons with spectacles and did other tricks. He seemed to have learned the alphabet, for he could tap out a response to most queries. Many people were convinced Hans knew German well. In fact, he appeared brighter than many people (1).

Note that the summary is less than half as long as the original. Synonyms replace the major words that are not generic. Although some supporting details have been eliminated, the summary still makes essentially the same points as the original. The source is clearly identified, and the page number is placed in parentheses *before* the final period.

Guidelines for Writing Paraphrases and Summaries

1. *Read the entire original carefully several times so that you are sure you understand it completely.* If you can mark the original, underline the topic sentences and key points for ease of reference.

2. *Rewrite, retaining the order of the original.* Changes in order may distort meaning.

3. *Reread the original.* Check to see that you have not changed the order or unwittingly copied material that should be paraphrased.

4. *If you are unable to paraphrase difficult phrases,* copy and enclose in quotation marks.

5. *Reduce material by 50 percent or more for a summary.* Retain main ideas. Combine related ideas.

6. *Cite source and pages.*

7. *Checkpoint.* Is the paraphrase or summary clear? Has all important information been included? Are all spellings correct?

Using Quotations

Quotation is a respected practice used by educators, researchers, and other writers. Appropriate quotation in a research paper indicates responsible writing. Here are five reasons you might include quotations:

1. To present *technical* words for which there is no accurate paraphrase. Quoting the exact words prevents misunderstanding.

2. *To allay any doubt* about the accuracy of a surprising statement or evidence. By giving the exact words, you avert a reader's suspicion.

3. *To avoid an awkward or wordy paraphrase.* Do not abuse this privilege, however. Keep such quotations brief.

4. *To capture the flavor of the original.* Paraphrase will often not do justice to a passage that is vivid, unusual, and interesting, phrased in a *unique* way.

5. *To enhance your credibility as a writer.* By including quotations appropriately, you demonstrate that you know the basics of documentation.

Do not, however, overload your paper with a string of quotations. Unless your instructor specifies otherwise, use brief quotations at intervals, along with an occasional long quotation.

Making Changes in Quotations

Your readers expect that what you enclose in quotation marks will be the exact words of the original source. There are, however, some accepted conventions for indicating any changes you make in the original. To shorten a long quotation, you may omit unnecessary words and replace them with an ellipsis.

Ellipsis   An ellipsis (a set of three spaced dots) can replace wordy or irrelevant material you wish to omit at the beginning, middle, or end of a sentence. The result should still be a complete sentence. The example below, an excerpt from a *Wall Street Journal* article entitled "Chemicals Bad for Ozone Are Declining," by Amal Kumar Naj, shows an ellipsis:

> "Dr. Montzka said the measurements . . . make it possible to predict when the ozone layer will recover. He said the rate of recovery will depend on stratospheric temperature and chemical emissions from volcanoes" (B4).

To omit an entire sentence or more, use four dots. (The fourth dot is the period.) If you omit material and use an ellipsis, take care not to distort the meaning.

Brackets   If you need to add something to a quotation for clarity or logic, you can insert the explanatory words within brackets [ ]. Originally, the paragraph below used *he*, which has been replaced with the name of the researcher:

> "Barring unusual changes in temperature and emissions, [Dr. Montzka] estimated that it will take 50 to 60 years before the Earth's ozone layer is restored to the levels before 1970."

When the verb tense of a quotation differs from the text of your paper, you can resolve this inconsistency by substituting another tense in brackets. In the example below, the original was written in the present tense. For the sake of logic, two changes to the past tense (in brackets) replace the original wording.

> Farley Mowat describes the clothes of the Ihalmiut, a tribe that became extinct in the 1950s, as "two suits of fur, worn one over the other. . . . The inner suit [was] worn with the hair of the hides facing inward and touching the skin while the outer suit [had] its hair turned out to the weather" (422).

Once in a while, you may find an error in grammar or spelling in one of your sources. To indicate that you are reproducing the original error rather than creating one of your own, you may insert the Latin word *sic* ("thus") in brackets after the error, as shown after this grammatical mishap:

> An example of the radical nature of the organization is this advice from a pamphlet it published: "Thieves should be punished by having there [sic] hands cut off."

Keep in mind, however, that some words have two or more correct spellings. It is always a good idea to check two dictionaries to be sure a word is actually misspelled or misused.

Quotation within a Quotation When your source contains a quotation, change the double quotation marks in the original to single marks (' '). Then enclose the full quotation in double quotation marks, as shown below:

In *Strictly Speaking* Edwin Newman writes: "Most conversation these days is as pleasing to the ear as a Flash-Frozen Dinner is to the palate, consisting largely of 'You've got to be kidding,' 'It's a bad scene,' 'How does that grab you?' 'Just for openers . . .'" (16).

MAKING A WORKING OUTLINE

Once you have completed the bulk of your research and note-taking, you can use your note cards to start a working outline. Without an outline, ideas for a research paper tend to intermingle. To establish order and avoid confusion, take a few minutes to draft a working outline. This chore will simplify and shorten the twin tasks of drafting and revising.

A simple way to start is to classify your note cards. Sort through the cards according to subject and place related items in piles. Then examine each pile and label it with a category under which all items will fit. After that, organize the categories into a possible order. If you become puzzled, ask yourself questions as you draft your outline.

Questions for Developing a Thesis and an Outline

1. *What is the purpose of the paper?* How can I make the purpose clear?
2. *What are the main points of my research?*
3. *What thesis can serve as an umbrella for all the main points?* Do I have irrelevant material? Do I need to narrow the topic?
4. *Is chronological order visible anywhere?* Are there historical items to place in chronological order? Might they make an interesting introduction or should they come later? Will the overall order be chronological or just the introduction?
5. *How should the body of the paper be organized?* Should main points be arranged according to importance? Or should they go from concrete to abstract? Or would some other order, possibly problem solving, work best?
6. *Does the material seem comprehensive?* Are there significant gaps? Do I need more information to be complete?

When you are comfortable with a tentative order, number your note cards and copy the categories and subcategories into outline form. Leave spaces for adding items. By the end of the writing process, your working outline will have become a formal outline, ready for submission along with your paper, if required. (An example of an outline submitted with a student paper appears near the end of this chapter.)

DRAFTING A RESEARCH PAPER

As you begin to draft, keep in mind that your working outline is subject to change. In the course of getting your thoughts on paper, you may make slight changes or even find a different organization emerging. If so, take the time to rethink your working outline before continuing to draft.

Drafting a Thesis and Introduction

The sooner you can state a clear thesis, the sooner you can begin to organize and draft your research paper. If uncertain, reexamine your controlling question and rewrite it as a thesis statement. Or you might prefer to draft the introduction as a whole unit rather than in pieces. You may even find that your thesis has mushroomed out over several sentences as in Wilma Dunnington's introduction. Although her purpose is clearly informative, there is no one thesis sentence:

The Genome Project

Possible effects
Probably few readers can imagine a time when genetic profiles would be used as a basis for marriage or divorce, a time when genetic testing would be required by employers to screen applicants. It is easier to envision a world where children "diagnosed with cystic fibrosis would be spared their fate by a gene transplant," a world where cancers would be revealed and treated before a single cancer cell could grow (Bishop and Waldholz 22). These are the "threats and promises" of what could be the "most ambitious scientific research project ever undertaken" (22). The Human

Definition
Genome Project is an effort to identify all of the genes in the human body.

In *Principles of Anatomy and Physiology,* Tortora and Anagnostakos report that the Human Genome Project will take an estimated fifteen years and cost three bil-

Main goal
lion dollars. The over-riding goal of the project is to "conquer genetic disease" (953). Marwick points out that in the human body are more than 100 thousand genes. Occasionally, a gene is injured, resulting in "abnormal features or disorders." Some-

Explanation
times an embryo will not grow; other times children are born with defects. Some conditions caused by a damaged gene may not be apparent until a person becomes aged (3247).

A second way to begin the introduction is with a generalization, followed by a refutation of a common misperception. John King applies this strategy in his opening:

Computer Security: How Secure Is It?

Generalization
Computer security has become a major concern in all aspects of business, government, and personal life. People who think breaches in computer security do not

Refutation begins
involve them are seriously mistaken. Most people's names pass through a computer

several times a day, whether through "direct mailing lists, credit checking, or financial transactions" (U.S. Dept. 141, 145). These uses make it extremely difficult for us not to be affected somehow by someone tampering with information stored in computer files.

With access to a valid social security number and the right computers, hackers can wreak havoc in almost anyone's life. They can find out essential data such as bank balances, credit card numbers, income, and speeding tickets. They can even determine the amount of education a person has. A hacker can quickly type a few changes, and very quickly the victim will not have any money left (U.S. Dept. 142, 143).

A third way to open your research paper might be with an analogy to give a new slant to an old topic. In the next example, note how Sharon M. Abood links her title to the text in the second paragraph. Note, too, that she uses no citations because her introduction is based on common knowledge:

The Beast Can Be Brought to His Knees

When given the diagnosis of cancer, tough, brawny men and vigorous, spirited women are often terror struck at the words *cancer* and *pain*. Thoughts of death, disfigurement, and agonizing pain flash through their minds, causing confusion and anguish. Many times it has been pain that spurred them to the doctor's office initially.

True, cancer pain can affect a patient from head to toe, from headache pain to deep muscle and bone pain. But there is a wide variety of medication and treatment available. Pain treatment can be a combination of medical procedures, medication, and diversional activities, individualized for each patient—the beast can be humbled. And every patient has the right to expect an alleviation of pain as a result of cancer treatment.

For other kinds of openings, see chapter 3.

Weaving Quotations into the Text

Every quotation you use requires transition to weave it into your text. Usually, an introductory phrase precedes the quotation. To keep your transitional phrases strong and responsible, give the full name of the researcher, team, organization, study, or poll whenever possible. To identify a person, give degrees, position, or other credentials. The examples below illustrate transitional phrases for introducing quotations:

According to Dr. Sheila S. Smith, a psychologist at Blake University,

A study by an Ohio State University medical team found ". . ."

In March 1997, the American Medical Association reported:

ames A. Bell, a scientist at Jones Laboratories of New York City, stated:

Others like Dr. H. R. Smythe believe that ". . ."

Unwise shortcuts can lead to weak, fuzzy transitions. Instead of giving source information, some beginning writers substitute personal opinion, a vague phrase, or that wishy-washy word *it*. All of the following phrases are inappropriate.

Weak Phrases

"In my opinion" or "I feel"	(So what?)
A study revealed . . .	(What study? Who did it?)
Experts/researchers/authorities say . . .	(All?)
It is believed . . .	(Who believes?)
It is estimated . . .	(Who estimated?)
It is predicted . . .	(Who predicted?)

Short Quotations   Quotations of four lines or fewer (three for poetry) are considered short. You can use short quotations to identify special terms or include vivid words and difficult-to-paraphrase segments. Short quotations, too, require transition to link them to the text.

Sometimes you may lack the name of a researcher to use as a transition to a quotation. Often popular magazines summarize research, giving only a minimum of details about several studies. When April Rausch was confronted with this problem, she presented the vital information that was available, using two short quotations:

> In 1991, as reported by *USA Today*, thirty-seven babies in the United States died "while sleeping in bean-bag infant cushions." Although some of the babies were thought to have died of Sudden Infant Death Syndrome, others apparently smothered. After a research team headed by James S. Kemp and Bradley T. Thach tested bean-bag cushions from two makers, using rabbits, the Consumer Product Safety Commission cited the cushions as a potential "asphyxiation hazard." In late 1991 infant bean-bag cushions were removed from the market (*USA Today* 5).

Block Quotations   A block quotation is a long quotation of five lines or more (four for poetry). For a research paper (MLA style), double-space and indent block quotations *ten* spaces on the left margin, none on the right. Do *not* use quotation marks for a block quotation because the indentation and parenthetical citation alert the reader that the material has been borrowed. Careful writers use long quotations for a valid reason; overuse signals a hastily written paper. In the example below notice that (1) the source and author are identified in the text of the paper *before* the long quotation, (2) a *colon* is placed after the verb, (3) the period appears one space *before* the citation.

```
In The Managerial Woman, management consultants

Margaret Hennig and Anne Jardim state:

          Studies of women who enroll in continuing

          college education programs show that many of

          the women who fail in these programs . . .
```

```
have never discussed their goals with

their husbands. The husbands never really

understood why their wives had gone back

to school, and the wives on their own had

attempted to maintain the same level of

housework they had been accustomed to. (212)
```

Inserting Explanatory Notes

Once in a great while you may have material that is useful in discussing your subject but that seems to interrupt the text. In such cases you have the option of including the information in an explanatory note. To do so, insert a superscript numeral at an appropriate point in your text. Then you can place the note either at the bottom of the same page or on a separate page, headed "Note" or "Notes." Begin the note with a matching superscript number (see "Content Notes" in chapter 22).

Writing a Conclusion

The conclusion of a research paper may be longer than those of the other papers you have been writing. A graceful ending of three to five (or more) sentences is usually expected. Although new information is not introduced in the conclusion, a writer may leave the reader with a new thought. A brief summary or reference to the future may be appropriate. Peggy Bean combines these three techniques in her closing:

> Although the fetal alcohol syndrome is a tragic disorder, it is also a preventable one. Therefore, it is important that the general public become aware of the risks ethanol poses to the developing fetus, especially to the fetus of a chronic alcoholic. Once families know the cause of this disorder, they can assist the alcoholic mother-to-be in securing professional help.

Bonnie L. Rice ends her research paper with a reference to the future and to what a reader might do to help in a similar situation:

> Efforts toward education, intervention, and prevention of adolescent suicide are being made. They must continue and expand. But can the individual do something to help? Yes, the greatest problem for the unhappy adolescent is isolation from close relationships; one person can be that caring friend who is missing from someone's lonely life.

Sometimes beginning writers tack on a quotation at the end without transition. Although the quotation may be appropriate, the abyss between the body and the quotation halts the smooth flow of thought. To link a quotation to a conclusion, use a transitional segment, as italicized in the following example:

Child abuse is an ancient problem, but it is an occurrence that concerns us all, a problem that needs to be solved. For as James Agee wrote, "In every child who is born, under no matter what circumstances, and of no matter what parents, the potentiality of the human race is born again; and in him, too once more, and of each of us, our terrific responsibility towards human life. . . ."

REVISING, EDITING, AND FORMATTING

When you finish the rough draft of your research paper, heave a sigh of relief, and take a break if possible. If not, perhaps you might alphabetize the entry cards for your works cited list and start typing that or do some other related chore. Before you start to revise your paper, however, you need to gain distance so that you can come back and examine it objectively.

Revising

Persistence, time, and care are the keys to successful revision and proofreading. Yet you may be so preoccupied with content that order, documentation, and mechanics receive low priority. Several revisions spaced over several days will catch more errors than one intensive session the night before a deadline. The checklist below will prove helpful in assisting a tired brain to focus during this all-important stage:

 Checklist for Revision

1. Compare your outline and paper. Is the order the same? Is it sound?
2. Now read the paper aloud. Is the introduction interesting and complete?
3. Are the main ideas clear?
4. Is there sufficient transition? Is each quotation linked to the text?
5. Are there too many direct quotations? Should some be paraphrased or summarized instead?
6. Could the order of details within paragraphs be improved?
7. Is the conclusion logical and complete?

Checking Documentation

Every source you use in your research paper must be acknowledged according to a standard documentation style. Two of the most common—Modern Language Association (MLA) style and American Psychological Association (APA) style—are described in detail in Chapter 22. Both use parenthetical citations within the text that are keyed to a complete bibliographical list.

In the course of drafting and revising, even the most conscientious writer may omit, misplace, or lose a text citation while rearranging sentences or paragraphs. If a problem occurs, don't panic! Remember you have your earlier drafts and note cards (if you followed the tips in chapters 3 and 21). Also check to see that every paragraph in your research paper has at least one text citation unless there is a reason for not including one. Remember, too, that if you split a paragraph you will probably have to make another citation.

Checklist for Parenthetical Citations

1. Is there a citation for every source used?
2. Does every parenthetical citation for a printed source include a page number (except for single-page sources and entire works)?
3. Is the name of the author/researcher/group included either in the parenthetical citation or in an introductory phrase?
4. If there is more than one source by the same author, does a short form of the title appear in parenthetical citations?

Editing and Proofreading

To catch errors in a research paper, proofread when you are alert. Go over your paper several times—one sitting is seldom enough. For example, watch to see that you have the correct spelling of prefixes, as in words beginning with per- and pre-. To attain the high grades that most students desire, revise and proofread several times. If you follow the editing guidelines outlined in chapter 4 and provide the necessary effort, your paper should be a success.

Using an Appropriate Format

Some instructors may give few or no instructions for formatting a research paper; others may give precise instructions. Most expect good quality white, 8½- by 11-inch paper. If you plan to use erasable paper or to submit a photocopy, check with your instructor first. A title (cover) page may or may not be required. Some instructors like the title page format commonly used in the workplace (see the research paper at the end of this chapter). The MLA style does not require a title page whereas the APA style does. Both styles require that you double-space the entire manuscript, including quotations and list of sources. Some instructors also prefer that you staple or use a paper clip rather than a binder to keep pages together.

Margins and Indentation   Standard specifications for research papers call for one-inch margins (top, bottom, and sides). Page numbers are placed one-half inch from the top right and flush with the right margin. Indent the first line of paragraphs one-half inch (five spaces on a typewriter). For long quotations, the MLA style indents one inch (*ten* spaces) from the left margin. The APA style, however, indents long quotations one-half inch (*five* spaces).

MLA Style Heading, Title, and Page Numbering   If you decide not to have a title page, MLA style advises starting the first page of the manuscript with your name, your instructor's name, the course number, and the date on consecutive lines one inch from the top left margin. Next, center the title. Capitalize the first and last words and major words of the title. Do not underline any words unless you mention a book title or use a foreign phrase or other wording that requires underlining. (Never underline your own title.) Page numbers, in the upper right corner, are preceded by the writer's last name. The top of the first page of a research paper, MLA style, looks like this:

```
                                                              Bellows 1

     Susan N. Bellows
     Professor Raintree
     English Composition 112
     1 March 1997
                          New Sources of Antibiotics
          Many of the wonder drugs of former decades are losing their effectiveness
     as bacteria acquire immunity to certain antibiotics. Thus there is a
     never-ending search for new medicines to replace older ones that have become
     obsolete.
```

APA Style Headings, Title, and Page Numbering   The APA style requires a title page with a "running head" (abbreviated title) of the first two or three words of the title, the full title, and the byline. The full title should summarize the main idea of the manuscript briefly and simply. The byline contains the writer's name and the institutional affiliation (college, university, or other site). In the byline use no extra words such as *by* or *from*. The preferred form of an author's name is first name, middle initial, and last name.

First, type the running head (the first two or three words of the title) and the page number one-half inch from the top right margin in lowercase with capitals. Skip down about one-third of the page and type the full title, centered in lowercase with capitals (if needed, on two lines, double-spaced). Double-space, then center the writer's name. Double-space again and center the name of the institution. The top of a title page, APA style, looks like this:

```
                                    New Sources Of Antibiotics 1




                    New Sources of Antibiotics from Land and Sea
                              Susan N. Bellows
                             Professor Raintree
                               Psychology 101
                               May 15, 199-
```

Page numbers in APA style are preceded by the running head from the title page on succeeding pages. This means that the first two or three words are taken from the title. Note that the page number appears five spaces after the head.

Sample Student Research Paper: MLA Style

A complete student research paper using the Modern Language Association style follows in the next section. The outline appears before the paper. For clarification, a final section has been added, entitled "Annotation of Works Cited," which categorizes each source that Kathy Rummer has used. For specific guidelines regarding the parenthetical citations in this paper, see chapter 22.

Dr. Nightingale: Nurse Practitioners in Primary Medical Care

by

Kathy Rummer

CM 112 English Composition

Mrs. Juanita Gordon

March 10, 199-

Thesis: The nurse practitioner can address three problems within the United States health care system: the shortage of primary care physicians and physician's assistants, escalating costs, and quality routine medical care at affordable prices.

    I. The Nurse Practitioner

        A. Definition: education and training

        B. Origin of the program

   II. Description of Nurse Practitioners and Physician's Assistants

        A. Similarities: Routine duties. High performance ratings in long-term care. Education. Both cut costs of health care.

        B. Chief difference: Amount of supervision.

  III. Nurse Practitioners' Contributions to Alleviate Health Care Problems

        A. Shortage of physicians and physician's assistants; NPs can alleviate

        B. Rising costs; NPs can cut costs

        C. NPs provide quality primary care at affordable prices

   IV. Obstacles for Nurse Practitioners

        A. Physicians' fears

        B. Increased risks and liabilities

        C. Improving: Reimbursement by Medicaid and Medicare

    V. Conclusion

Although the use of nurse practitioners is not widespread, this career field offers an opportunity not only for health care professionals, but also for the United States health care system to meet primary medical needs with quality care at affordable prices.

Dr. Nightingale: Using Nurse Practitioners
in Primary Medical Care

"Good nursing does not grow of itself; it is the result of study, teaching, training, practice, ending in sound tradition which can be transferred elsewhere."

Florence Nightingale
(qtd. in Kelly 33)

The role of the "nurse practitioner" has evolved over several decades in response to a shortage of physicians and physician's assistants, escalating costs, and a shortage of affordable health care. A nurse practitioner (NP) is a registered nurse who has completed an "accredited two-year program of study and clinical practice," earned a master's degree in nursing, and passed a national exam for a "particular specialty" ("Nurse Practitioners"). In California, for example, NPs are certified to provide "routine medical care, prenatal care, and family planning services" ("Need a" 4). They must pass a course in pharmacology and work for six months in a "preceptorship," receiving intense training, before they can write prescriptions.

The nurse practitioner program has evolved as a result of the short supply of physician's assistants (PAs). In 1965 the physician's assistant program was created to relieve the shortage of physicians. Using a physician's assistant for routine medical care freed physicians to concentrate on more complex medical problems (Sidel and Sidel 203, 204). But for some reason the program attracted relatively few medical students. In 1970 the American Medical Association asked the American Nurses Association (ANA) to supply nurses to be trained as physician's assistants. Instead of complying with the request, the ANA created its own alternative to the physician's assistant--the nurse practitioner (Sidel and Sidel 204).

The intent of the American Nurses Association was that this new health care professional's "training and philosophy [would reflect] nursing and not medicine" (Sidel and Sidel 204). Dock and Stewart point out that this philosophy is based on the "Nightingale concept" of nursing in which there is "neither independence nor subordination but interdependence and cooperation." According to the Nightingale philosophy, nursing is not a "subcaste of medicine." A nurse is not a "handmaid," but a "helpmate and partner" (367).

Both the nurse practitioner and physician's assistant handle routine medical care. NPs and PAs can give approximately 80% of the treatment of adult primary care (Larkin 9). Both must be licensed to practice. As of July 1995, forty-six states had granted nurse practitioners limited authority to prescribe medications (Donegan).

Both nurse practitioners and physician's assistants received high praise from long-term-care administrators in 1990. A poll of administrators who were involved in a study in Massachusetts elicited enthusiastic responses concerning the effectiveness of NPs and PAs:

* More than 90% said they thought that residents under the care of an NP or PA got more medical attention than those under the care of a physician alone.
* More than 80% said the NP or PA had a faster response time than the physician.
* More than 90% said that the NPs or PAs had a positive impact on nursing staff and nursing practices ("LTC").

The costs of training physician's assistants and nurse practitioners are much less than those of training physicians, resulting in savings to patients (Sidel and Sidel 213). Then too, both the PA and the NP earn less than the physicians. For example, a salaried nurse practitioner in a long-term-care facility is more "cost effective" than a physician who is paid for each patient seen ("Though Cost-Effective"). Hiring a nurse practitioner or a physician's assistant for a family practice is less costly than going into practice with another physician.

Although the roles of nurse practitioner and physician's assistant are similar in many respects, there are significant differences. The nurse practitioner has more independence. Nurse practitioners can work alone with the supervision of a consulting physician. In fact, many nurse practitioners supervise clinics and practice in rural areas with only telephone contact with a physician (Kelly 337, 340). Some NPs with special training even give anesthesia (Adelman 19). A physician's assistant, however, must always "function under the supervision of a physician and cannot function independently" (Kelly 169).

Education and training needed to practice as a nurse practitioner or as a physician's assistant have many similarities. Both programs now require a college degree plus medical training. In former years there were both certificate and non-degree programs for NPs and PAs, but these "option[s] [have been] closed off. In the future, the only way to be certified will be to graduate from an approved [medical] school" (Sidel and Sidel 210). NPs are usually trained in long-term care, obstetrics, family practice, and rural general practice whereas many physician's assistants select specialty areas (Kelly 337-43; Stimmel 2060).

There are many reasons for the shortage of primary care physicians certified in "general pediatrics," "general internal medicine," and "family practice" for which NPs fill a gap (Mullan 1481). Many medical schools do not emphasize the importance of primary care (Stimmel 2060). Many older general practitioners are retiring and are not being replaced due to a lack of interest by new graduates (Report 1092). Large patient loads, inadequate equipment, lack of trained assistants, low income, and few opportunities for continuing education make primary care unattractive to many physicians (Dunne 103-07). Dr. T. Reginald Harris, former president of the American Society of Internal Medicine, says that "regulatory intrusions" have lowered the morale of many internists (Gorman 56). Some obstetricians have given up their practices because of the high cost of liability insurance (Adelman 19).

A 1990 survey by the U.S. Department of Health and Human Services revealed that "45 of the 50 states were experiencing serious shortages in primary care" (Mullan 1481). American Medical News estimated an additional 35,000 physicians are needed to meet America's primary care needs (Little 4). In 1992, the National Residency Matching Program filled only "64% of the positions in pediatrics, and 60% of the positions in internal medicine . . . with U.S. seniors." A follow-up revealed that of those entering, 60% left internal medicine and 40% left pediatrics to "pursue subspecialty training" (Report 1092). Nurse practitioners could help to alleviate this shortage.

A second factor in the health care problem is the cost. In the past few years, health care costs have exploded for a number of reasons. Hospitals have overexpanded, leading to empty beds. Many physicians order additional and unnecessary diagnostic tests in a cautious effort to avoid malpractice suits (Clark 40). Then too, physicians are often faced with large debts from education and increased expense to practice; both affect patients' costs (45). Lack of preventive medicine can increase health costs as well. A disease that could have been prevented in childhood may develop into a severe problem that requires expensive care (Sidel and Sidel 213). NPs provide education in preventive measures to promote health (Kelly 189, 454).

A nurse practitioner can offer many of the services of the physician at a lower cost (Sidel and Sidel 203). For example, nurse practitioners are providing many pregnant women with affordable care during pregnancy and

childbirth in regions where physicians are not easily available (Adelman 19).
A study by the National Birth Center in 1989 revealed that "of 11,814 women
admitted for labor and delivery at 84 freestanding birth centers" the low
rate of cesarean section was unusual--although the national average for
C-sections was 24%, the average for the birth centers was only 4.4% (Nurse-
Midwives 6). Reducing the number of surgical births results in lower costs to
patients. In addition, nurse practitioners tend to order fewer "inappropriate
expensive tests" than physicians do (Sidel and Sidel 213). Yet the quality of
care provided by NPs is comparable.

      According to the Congressional Budget Office, which reviewed the results
of a variety of studies, "Nurse practitioners have performed as well as
physicians with respect to patient outcomes, proper diagnosis, management of
specified medical conditions and frequency of patient satisfaction" ("Nurse
Practitioners" 4). During two studies in long-term geriatric-care settings,
one in western states and the other in New England, "researchers observed no
statistically significant changes in residents' functional status or use of
medications" where PAs and NPs performed "additive care" with physicians or
served as "surrogates" for the physicians ("Though Cost-Effective" 3). The
investigators also agreed that the use of nurse practitioners was economical.

      Yet the role of nurse practitioner has met with considerable resistance.
Many physicians perceive nurse practitioners as encroaching "upon their turf."
Although nurse practitioners are qualified, these physicians fear "more
mistakes" because NPs "are not fully trained." And, of course, as NPs assume
more responsibility, they also assume more "risks and liabilities" (Hinkle).

      However, the greatest obstacle, lack of reimbursement from Medicaid and
Medicare, has been alleviated somewhat. In 1989 a federal mandate ordered
"direct payment of primary care and pediatric nurse practitioners under
Medicaid." Medicaid reimburses for NPs in "nursing homes, skilled nursing
facilities and rural health settings. All third-party payers pay nurse
anesthetists" (Adelman 19). Since October 1990 Medicare has reimbursed
geriatric nurse practitioners for every other visit at "85% of the physician
rate" (Medicare 2).

      The health care problem in the United States is serious. While citizens
and lawmakers frantically search for a cure, a valuable resource--the nurse
practitioner--may be overlooked. Although the use of NPs is not widespread,
this program offers an opportunity to meet U.S. primary health care needs
with professionals who can provide quality care at affordable prices.

Rummer 5

Works Cited

Adelman, Susan Hirshberg. "Let's Not Hand Over Primary Care to Nurses."
American Medical News 29 July 1991: 19-20. Infotrac: Health
Reference. CD-ROM. Information Access. Feb. 1993.

Clark, Matt, et al. "Health-Cost Crisis." 9 May 1977. Medical Care
in the United States: The Reference Shelf. Ed. Eric F. Oatman.
Vol. 50. New York: Wilson, 1978. 38-44.

Dock, Lavina L., and Isabel M. Stewart. A Short History of Nursing.
4th ed. New York: Putnam's, 1938.

Donegan, J. Brenda. "Bill Would Allow Nurses To Prescribe, Says Perr."
Star [Marion] 9 Aug. 1995: 3A.

Dunne, John B. "Why Rural Doctors Are Missing." Apr. 1976. Medical Care
in the United States: The Reference Shelf. Ed. Eric F. Oatman.
Vol. 50. New York: Wilson, 1978. 103-08.

Gorman, Christina. "Is Health Care Too Specialized?" Time 14 Sept. 1992:
56. Infotrac: Magazine Plus Index. CD-ROM. Information Access.
Feb. 1993.

Hinkle, Janice, Dean of Nursing, Marion Technical College. Personal
interview. 1 Mar. 1995.

Kelly, Lucie Young. Dimensions of Professional Nursing. 5th ed. New
York: Macmillan, 1985.

Larkin, Howard. "Physician's Assistants: Rx for Stress: PAs Can Help
Lift Burden on Busy Physicians." American Medical News 25 Mar.
1991: 9-10. Infotrac: Health Reference. CD-ROM. Information Access.
Feb. 1993.

Little, Linda. "More Emphasis on Family Practice Urged." American
Medical News 26 Oct. 1990: 4. Infotrac: Health Reference. CD-ROM.
Information Access. Feb. 1993.

"LTC Administrators Give High Marks to NPs, PAs." Brown University
Long-Term Care Letter 8 Dec. 1990: 2. Infotrac: Health Reference.
CD-ROM. Information Access. Feb. 1993.

"Medicare Expands Payments for Nurse Practitioners." Brown University
Long-Term Care Letter 8 Dec. 1990: 2. Infotrac: Health Reference.
CD-ROM. Information Access. Feb. 1993.

Mullan, Fitzhugh. "The Future of Primary Care in America." American
Family Physician 44 (1991): 1481-83. Infotrac: Health Reference.
CD-ROM. Information Access. Feb. 1993.

Rummer 6

"Need a Prescription? Ask a Nurse." People's Medical Society Newsletter
    June 1992: 4-5. Infotrac: Health Reference. CD-ROM. Information
    Access. Feb. 1993.

"Nurse-Midwives and Birth Centers: A Team That Lowers the Cesarean
    Rate." People's Medical Society Newsletter June 1992: 6. Infotrac:
    Health Reference. CD-ROM. Information Access. Feb. 1993.

"Nurse Practitioners Can Provide 75% of Primary Care in Nursing Homes."
    Brown University Long-Term Care Letter 23 Dec. 1990: 4. Infotrac:
    Health Reference. CD-ROM. Information Access. Feb. 1993.

"Report of the Medical Schools Section Primary Care Task Force." Journal
    of the American Medical Association 268 (1992): 1092-94. Infotrac:
    Health Reference. CD-ROM. Information Access. Jan. 1993.

Sidel, Victor W., and Ruth Sidel, eds. Reforming Medicine. New York:
    Random, 1984.

Stimmel, Barry. "The Crisis in Primary Care and the Role of Medical
    Schools: Defining the Issues." Journal of the American Medical
    Association 268 (1992): 2060-66. Infotrac: Health Reference.
    CD-ROM. Information Access. Jan. 1993.

"Though Cost-Effective, NPs May Not Affect Outcomes." Brown University
    Long-Term Care Letter 8 Dec. 1990: 3. Infotrac: Health Reference.
    CD-ROM. Information Access. Jan. 1993.

WORKS CITED, BY CATEGORY

The sources that Kathy Rummer used in her research paper are categorized in the list that follows. This list should be helpful when you make your works cited list. For more information on the Modern Language Association style of documentation, see chapter 22.

A Book with One Author

Kelly, Lucie Young. Dimensions of Professional Nursing. 5th ed. New York: Macmillan, 1985.

A Book with Two Authors

Dock, Lavina L., and Isabel M. Stewart. A Short History of Nursing. 4th ed. New York: Putnam, 1938.

Work by One Author in a Compilation with One Editor

Dunne, John B. "Why Rural Doctors Are Missing." Apr. 1976. Medical Care in the United States: The Reference Shelf. Ed. Eric F. Oatman. Vol. 50. New York: Wilson, 1978. 103-08.

Work by Several Authors in a Compilation with One Editor

Clark, Matt, et al. "Health-Cost Crisis." 9 May 1977. Medical Care in the United States: The Reference Shelf. Ed. Eric F. Oatman. Vol. 50. New York: Wilson, 1978. 38-44.

Anonymous Work in a Compilation with Two Editors

Sidel, Victor W., and Ruth Sidel, eds. Reforming Medicine. New York: Random, 1984.

Article from a Newspaper

Donegan, J. Brenda. "Bill Would Allow Nurses to
Prescribe, Says Perr." Star [Marion] 9 Aug.
1995: 3A.

Signed Material Accessed from a Periodically Published Database on CD-ROM

Adelman, Susan Hirshberg. "Let's Not Hand Over Primary
Care to Nurses." American Medical News 29 July
1991: 19-20. Infotrac: Health Reference. CD-ROM.
Information Access. Feb. 1996.

Gorman, Christina. "Is Health Care Too Specialized?"
Time 14 Sept. 1996: 56. Infotrac: Magazine
Plus Index. CD-ROM. Information Access. Feb.
1993.

Larkin, Howard. "Physician's Assistants: Rx for Stress:
PAs Can Help Lift Burden on Busy Physicians."
American Medical News 25 Mar. 1991: 9-10.
Infotrac: Health Reference. CD-ROM. Information
Access. Jan. 1996.

Little, Linda. "More Emphasis on Family Practice
Urged." American Medical News 26 Oct. 1990: 4.
Infotrac: Health Reference. CD-ROM. Information
Access. Feb. 1996.

Mullan, Fitzhugh. "The Future of Primary Care in
America." American Family Physician 44 (1991):
1481-83. Infotrac: Health Reference. CD-ROM.
Information Access. Feb. 1993.

Stimmel, Barry. "The Crisis in Primary Care and the
Role of Medical Schools: Defining the Issues."

Journal of the American Medical Association 268
(1992): 2060-66. Infotrac: Health Reference.
CD-ROM. Information Access. Jan. 1996.

Anonymous Articles Accessed from a Periodically Published Database on CD-ROM

"LTC Administrators Give High Marks to NPs, PAs." Brown
University Long-Term Care Letter 8 Dec. 1990: 2.
Infotrac: Health Reference. CD-ROM. Information
Access. Feb. 1996.

"Medicare Expands Payments for Nurse Practitioners."
Brown University Long-Term Care Letter 8 Dec 1990:
2. Infotrac: Health Reference. CD-ROM. Information
Access. Feb. 1996.

"Need a Prescription? Ask a Nurse." People's Medical
Society Newsletter June 1992: 4-5. Infotrac:
Health Reference. CD-ROM. Information Access.
Feb. 1996.

"Nurse-Midwives and Birth Centers: A Team That Lowers
the Cesarean Rate." People's Medical Society
Newsletter June 1992: 6. Infotrac: Health
Reference. CD-ROM. Information Access. Feb. 1996.

"Nurse Practitioners Can Provide 75% of Primary Care
in Nursing Homes." Brown University Long-Term Care
Letter 23 Dec. 1990: 4. Infotrac: Health
Reference. CD-ROM. Information Access. Feb. 1996.

"Report of the Medical Schools Section Primary Care
Task Force." Journal of the American Medical
Association 268(1992): 1092-94. Infotrac: Health
Reference. CD-ROM. Information Access. Jan. 1996.

"Though Cost-Effective, NPs May Not Affect Outcomes."

<u>Brown University Long-Term Care Letter</u> 8 Dec.

1990: 3. <u>Infotrac: Health Reference</u>. CD-ROM.

Information Access. Jan. 1996.

Interview

Hinkle, Janice, Dean of Nursing, Marion Technical

College. Personal interview. 1 Mar. 1996.

Summary

Effective research requires an open mind and a thorough consideration of available evidence. In reporting research findings, you should use provisional words, such as *suggests* and *indicates*.

If you borrow from a source, enclose any original words in quotation marks. While taking notes, be careful to use your own language when possible. Although generic words and minor words can be used without documentation, try to paraphrase and summarize most of the time. Quotations, used for good reasons and introduced appropriately, enhance a research paper, but excesses should be avoided.

If necessary, you can make minor changes to quotations using ellipses to indicate omissions. Brackets can indicate substitutions or additions.

A working outline, based on your sorted note cards, is quite helpful when you begin drafting. The sooner you can state a thesis, the sooner you can begin to organize and draft. Use clear transitional phrases as you weave quotations, paraphrases, and summaries into your draft. Both short and long quotations require parenthetical citation. Use quotation marks to set off short quotations. Block quotations do *not* require quotation marks because they are indented on the left.

For every parenthetical citation, make a corresponding entry for your works cited or list of references, giving full bibliographic data as explained in chapter 22. Observing the guidelines for documentation and for good writing will help to make your research paper a success.

Key Terms

provisional	generic term
paraphrase	summary
minor words	short quotation
major words	block quotation

Test Yourself

What Are the Facts about Documentation?

Directions: Fill in the blank with true (T) or false (F). To check your answers, turn to the end of this chapter.

_____ 1. Minor words such as *a, an, the, but, of, on* may be copied without documentation.

_____ 2. Plagiarism may be unethical, but it is legal.

_____ 3. Plagiarism refers only to copying from published works.

_____ 4. A general word that has no accurate synonym can be copied without documentation.

_____ 5. If an author's unique idea is used but not his or her words, the source must be identified.

_____ 6. All special terms should be set off with quotation marks the first time they are used.

_____ 7. A selection from an author's work may be copied if placed in quotation marks and if the source is identified.

_____ 8. If even a few of an author's major words are copied, they must have both quotation marks and a citation.

_____ 9. Quotation marks and documentation are both needed for copied material that is not indented.

_____ 10. If only statistics are copied, quotation marks are not used, but a source is supplied.

Practice

Transitional Phrases to Introduce Quotations

Directions: For the following items, write a transitional phrase to introduce the quotation. For help, see "Weaving Quotations into the Text," in this chapter. (*Source for this exercise:* Siebert, Al. *The Survivor Personality.* New York: Berkeley, 1996. Both quotations appear on page 64 of Siebert's book.)

1. Quotation: "The most direct access to the subconscious mind is through dreams. When we fall asleep, our rational, logical thinking relaxes."

2. Quotation: "Our dreams contain information about what is happening in our lives, our bodies, and the world around us."

Practice

Writing a Summary

Directions: Write a summary following "Guidelines for Writing Summaries" in this chapter. Your tasks are as listed:

1. Find a one- or two-page article (three pages if much space is taken by pictures) in a popular magazine. Or if you prefer, select a short article from a journal to be used for your research paper.

2. Duplicate the article on a copier. This copy will be turned in to the instructor along with the summary.

3. Reread the article. Underline each topic sentence and essential supporting data. Number each topic sentence for convenience in writing your summary.

4. To begin your summary, write an introductory sentence that gives the author's name and the source. (Turn back to "Transition for Quotations.")

5. Make one entry for a works cited list. Place at the bottom of your paper.

6. Staple the copy of the article to your completed summary.

Test Yourself Answers

1. *true*
2. *false*
3. *false*
4. *true*
5. *true*
6. *true*
7. *true*
8. *true*
9. *true*
10. *true*

PART 5

Writing to Find Employment

CHAPTER 24

Writing an Effective Résumé

*Good communication is as stimulating
as black coffee. . . .*

—Anne Morrow Lindbergh

As interviewers thumb through stacks of résumés, all directed toward the same position, they select not only those that are neat and accurate but also those that are distinctive and stimulating. To obtain an interview in these competitive times, you need to set forth your qualifications in the best possible way. Yet there is no one résumé style, and new styles continue to evolve.

Years ago the *chronological* résumé, which emphasizes education and experience, was the popular choice. Although this style may still work adequately for applicants with regular employment and promotions, it is not the best choice for others, for it does not specify skills. For someone who is out of the workforce or who is switching careers, the chronological résumé may actually be detrimental, for it reveals inexperience and gaps in employment. In the 1980s the *functional* résumé became popular. This résumé style presents specific skills and de-emphasizes irregular employment. The chief disadvantage is that the paragraph format takes longer to read.

Today the leading style is the *combination* résumé, a hybrid that combines the best features of earlier styles. A combination résumé enables employers to match quickly an applicant's qualifications to job requirements. A combination résumé offers *optimal flexibility* for both the applicant who has related work experience and the one who does not. Combination résumés come in several versions, which can be individualized to fit the applicant.

RESEARCHING AND PREWRITING FOR A COMBINATION RÉSUMÉ

An effective combination résumé reveals careful planning, specific skills, positive qualities, and specialized knowledge. The emphasis is on qualifications—not when, where, or how you obtained them. The suggestions in this chapter focus on providing dates when necessary and listing specific skills directly related to a service-oriented job objective. Many employers have said résumés of this type rank among the best they have seen.

Identifying Employers' Needs and Requirements

The more you know about what employers in your field are looking for, the better you can tailor your résumé to an employer's specific needs. To begin, research the following questions:

1. What positions are available that I'm qualified for?
2. What are the job duties of the positions?
3. What skills, qualities, and habits do potential employers seek?
4. Which kind of position is likely to be most appropriate for me?

The best place to secure career information quickly and inexpensively is your campus library. In an hour or less, you can gain an overview of your career field and identify possible positions for you. The *Occupational Outlook Handbook* and the *Dictionary of Occupational Titles* define conventional jobs as well as many not commonly known. Special software packages provide profiles of career fields on state and national levels. A computerized index or the *Readers' Guide to Periodicals* will assist you in locating articles in journals and magazines (see chapter 21).

Help wanted ads, particularly those in specialized journals and the business pages of metropolitan newspapers, can assist you in your search. There you can learn about qualities and skills desired, salary ranges, and terminology for your field. Unless there is a shortage in your field, however, an estimated 80 percent of the jobs open at any one time are never advertised. You can search for these hidden jobs by talking to acquaintances and others working in the field, conducting information interviews with potential employers, and reading.

Identifying Qualifications

A giant first step toward compiling an effective résumé is the identification of *transferable skills*, skills that can be applied on another job. A skill is an "art, trade, or technique, particularly one requiring the use of the hands or body," developed through practice. Thinking tasks are also skills—analytical tasks such as problem solving, decision making, designing, and the like. After identifying skills, you can devise ways to attest to positive personal qualities and work habits.

Transferable skills will become the heart of your combination résumé. To look for skills, examine your experience in the workplace, in college, and during leisure hours. You can start by brainstorming. Take three sheets of paper and write three headings: "Workplace Skills," "Academic Skills," and "Leisure Skills." On the "Workplace Skills" page, jot down duties and tasks performed from both paid and unpaid jobs. (Include military service and volunteer work.) Leave an inch or so of space between items to add more details later. On the second sheet, list tasks performed during academic training. On the third sheet, list hobbies and any skills you may have developed during leisure hours. To prod a sluggish memory, you might ask yourself the questions in the following sections.

Workplace Skills   As the questions listed below indicate, workplace skills include many abilities and responsibilities that may not have been specified in your job descriptions but may be additional tasks you took on.

- What equipment can I operate, maintain, or repair? Include everything from oscilloscopes to cash registers to tractors.
- What tasks can I perform effectively? Include record keeping, accounting, and other procedures such as specific software applications.
- What systems, layouts, or operations have I designed or executed?
- What problems have I helped to solve or alleviate? Include cost control, procedural changes, security, troubleshooting, and the like.
- Have I ever taken an inventory, conducted an audit, or done research? Include online research, lab or legal research, surveys, or other.
- What oral communication skills have I developed? Have I conducted meetings? Given public presentations? Taught or trained? Screened applicants? Greeted clients? Do I speak a second language well?
- What tasks have required interpersonal skills? Handling difficult clients or patients? Resolving problems? Negotiating? Making collections?
- What have I done that demonstrated responsibility? Have I supervised or managed? Reorganized a department? Expanded? Resolved disputes? Budgeted? (State amount if large.) Hired? Fired? Scheduled? Coordinated projects?
- What writing did I do on the job? Minutes or memos? Letters or newsletters? Procedures or manuals? Reports or proposals? Patient charts?
- How else have I contributed to the success of projects and operations? Have I decreased costs? Increased profits? Improved client or community relations?
- Did I receive training in the military or in special courses on the job?
- Do I have any special licenses or certifications?

Academic Skills   In your courses you have been *trained* to perform certain tasks, but do *not* list courses. Ask yourself what *skills* you gained from the courses—that's what employers want to know. Also consider skills gained from internships, clinics, or other educational outside work. You might start by asking yourself questions such as these:

- What equipment have I learned to operate? Repair? Maintain? Improve?

- What procedures have I performed? Medical, legal, accounting, or others?

- How have I used management skills? What projects have I completed? (Include work with campus organizations, fund-raising, events planning, tutoring, counseling, case work, and others.)

- What oral communication skills and interpersonal skills have I honed? Giving presentations? Empathetic listening, questioning, or nonverbal communication? Recognition of communication barriers? Business etiquette or telephoning? Group dynamics? Instructing clients, handling complaints, crisis intervention, or others?

- What research and writing skills have I demonstrated? Include online research, paralegal and other specialized research, research papers, business report writing, independent study projects, published work in campus newspapers or magazines, and the like.

- What other specialized training do I have? Include skills such as "calculate depreciation," "compile federal tax returns," "build prototypes," "diagnose electrical failures." Include knowledge from courses in business ethics, law, CPR, and others relevant to your field.

Leisure Skills   You may have acquired leadership, financial, teaching, human relations, or other skills during leisure hours. Consider activities and memberships in high school, college, or community organizations as well as hobbies. To start a train of thought, review the previous questions about work and academic skills. You may have developed some of these skills during your leisure. Then ask yourself other questions such as these:

- What projects have I completed for my family and home? You might list compiling a family genealogy, remodeling a kitchen, or building a patio. Or perhaps you transferred all your household accounts to a computer file.

- What community projects have I participated in? Planning? Serving on committees? Managing a scout troop or other youth group? Coaching a team? Assisting in a day care center? Counseling on a hotline? Judging contests? Writing a newsletter? Conducting meetings? Organizing?

- Have I developed special skills in photography, music, computers, drawing, designing, writing, cooking, sewing, woodworking, or others?

- What special training have I received? Have I worked as a volunteer firefighter, librarian, pianist, or in another position? Do I have CPR or EMT training? Do I have certification or special licenses as a pilot, chauffeur, or other?

- Do I have other knowledge gained from adult education courses, seminars, workshops, conferences, or special projects that helped to develop skills?

Compiling a comprehensive skills list will require more than one session. Time is needed to mull over your work, academic, and leisure experience. When you finish, you may have at least twenty specific, transferable skills (some students identify more than fifty). Then you may be able to identify some items that indicate positive qualities and work habits.

Personal Qualities and Work Habits Employers also look for positive personal qualities such as reliability, honesty, confidentiality, and flexibility. However, you won't claim these directly on your résumé. Avoid trite, unsubstantiated claims such as "work well with people," "honest," and "hard-working." Instead, you can give specific examples that imply or indicate these intangible qualities and sound work habits. You might list items such as the following:

- Never missed a day's work in five years
- Met all deadlines for reports and projects
- Collected cash receipts and made bank deposits
- Entrusted with keys to open and close business
- Maintained and monitored confidential client files
- Received two promotions within one year
- Acted as supervisor during boss's two-month leave

Or perhaps you had a security clearance or bonding. You may have had independent access to computer codes, valuable merchandise, confidential formulas, procedures, or other private information. One applicant identified flexibility as a quality that had served her well in all the positions she had held. After pondering how to present this item effectively, she wrote the following summary and placed it directly before "References upon request":

FLEXIBILITY:

During 22 years' experience, have performed backup work, acting in various capacities. At ———, handled major "touchy" accounts. At ——— Corp., substituted for accounts payable and payroll clerks. At ———, filled in for manager's secretary. All these jobs, as well as the present job of production coordinator at ———, require flexibility, tact, and maturity.

DRAFTING THE RÉSUMÉ

The major parts of a combination résumé are the *job objective*, *skills*, *work experience*, *education*, and, in some cases, *achievements*. The job objective always comes first, with other major parts following in most- to least-important order.

This means you organize your qualifications to your best advantage. Other information, such as military service, memberships, and personal data, follows the major parts. You can draft each of the major parts separately. In fact, it is not uncommon for the job objective to be drafted last. For clarity and ease of reference, let's start with the job objective.

The Service-Oriented Job Objective

In the past a job objective was very brief, perhaps just a word or two, stating the position applied for. Today experts recommend beginning with a service-oriented objective that states types of skills the applicant can bring to the position. The focus is on one position or one branch of an occupational field. If you are qualified for two distinct positions or occupational areas, then compile two résumés.

A service-oriented job objective acts as a thesis statement, providing a *focus* for the résumé. The major skills are then explained in the body of the résumé. Such objectives have three parts: (1) position desired, (2) the type of facility, company, or industry which the applicant prefers (optional), (3) major skill areas of the applicant. Here are some examples:

- Junior accounting position with a health care facility that needs someone versed in medical terminology as well as computer and corporate accounting applications.

- System specialist position. Can install and support MACOLA, Windows 95, and other software. Interested in training and in performing related services.

- Position as medical laboratory technician where superior accuracy, dependability, and interpersonal skills are sought.

- Assistant managerial position with retail business that requires accounting, computer, and writing experience.

- Paralegal position that offers an opportunity to interview clients, conduct research, and apply computer skills.

The best job objectives steer away from personal needs. They use fragments and do *not* refer to *I* or *me*. Words are selected with care. Note that a phrase such as "desire to work for a company that is a leader in the field" may suggest the candidate's aim is to start at the top. A vague phrase such as "job in the nursing field, either late afternoon or midnight shift" focuses too much on the writer. The best job objectives specify a position and focus on service:

> Pediatric nurse at a hospital needing help on second or third shift. Skilled in caring for young children, including postsurgical and terminal care.

Prewriting can speed the narrowing and drafting of your job objective. Just start by asking yourself questions, such as those following, and jotting down your answers.

1. What position do I want? Should my objective be specific or general?
2. What kind of facility, business, or industry do I want to work for?
3. What are the major skill areas that employers need for this position?
4. Do my qualifications fit the objective? ·
5. Is the wording correct for the field? (Use the right terminology.)

Then draft your service-oriented objective, giving the three parts explained earlier. (To save time, complete the practice exercise at the end of the chapter.)

CASE STUDY

MARK'S CASE

Mark, a young graduate with a bachelor's degree but little work experience, saw an ad for a position that sounded interesting. The employer was seeking someone with three strengths: initiative, computer skills, and writing skills. Since Mark was strong in all three areas, he used these terms in his job objective and as section headings to organize transferable skills on his combination résumé.

Under *initiative* Mark listed the following items: Arose at 3 a.m. as disk jockey during college. During high school, managed paper route for two years, worked Saturdays as a bookkeeper, won $6,000 scholarship. Under *computer skills* Mark listed skills gained from management information systems courses. Under *writing skills* he grouped research, documentation, and other writing skills, listing a 90-page marketing research paper.

Mark's effort won an interview and a job offer. He had tailored his qualifications to the employer's needs.

Grouping and Sharpening Skills

Your transferable work, academic, and leisure skills will make up the body of your résumé. If you are fortunate enough to have considerable work experience in your field, group your work skills, using action verbs for emphasis, underneath the name of the employer. But for most students, this is the exception, not the rule. If you have little or no work experience in your chosen field, your next task is to revise your prewritten skills lists. For clarity, this task has been broken into four possible steps.

1. Sort skills into categories according to the needs and requirements of potential employers. (This means that work, academic, and leisure skills will be mixed.)

2. Strategically arrange the skills into a neat column, with general category headings. To improve readability and impact, place a bullet (large dot) or a hyphen before each skill entry. Put important details at the beginning of each category.

3. Begin each skill entry with an appropriate *action* verb.

4. If you have five or more impressive skills or honors, you may be able to group them in a section titled "Achievements," or "Accomplishments," or something equally appropriate.

You can impress interviewers by labeling groups of skills with an eye to potential employers' needs. For example, headings might read "Computer Skills," "Communication Skills," "Public Relations Skills," "Technical Skills," or whatever is best for you. To see how groups of skills will look on a résumé, take a moment to examine the examples at the end of the chapter.

Combining Skills   If a group of skills looks rather skimpy, combine it with a related group. Then add a dual heading such as those in the following examples:

Accounting/Computer Skills

• Post accounts receivable and payable
• Compile daily sales record
• Bill customers and answer questions
• File social security and annuity payments
• Make out payroll
• Compile weekly, quarterly, and annual reports
• Know basic business laws and regulations
• Write documentation and footnotes for balance sheets
• Operate Macintosh and IBM desktop computers
• Use TaxCut and TurboTax software
• Use Quicken, Lotus 1-2-3, and WordPerfect

Systems/Report-Writing Skills

• Operate AS 400
• Use IBM-PC compatibles on Novell network daily
• Use Market Force Plus
• Create data for demonstration copies of software
• Operate Lotus 1-2-3, Windows 95, WordPerfect, Quattro Pro, and others
• Produce user-defined lead generation reports
• Compile various computer graphics and charts

- Write weekly, monthly, quarterly reports
- Assist in writing the annual report

Adding Action Verbs   Action verbs can make skills interesting, parallel, and convincing. Notice that skill entries are actions you *do*, not vague claims. "Fast typist" is a vague claim, but "type 70 wpm" is a skill. "Excellent manager" is a claim, but "managed 15 employees" indicates a skill. (Skills are written in the present tense if you still have them.) Select accurate, positive verbs. Careless word choice can paint an applicant as naïve, unqualified, or arrogant. To avoid undue repetition, consult a thesaurus. For your convenience, a sample list of action verbs appears here:

calculate	establish	maintain	record
compute	expand	operate	refine
conduct	implement	organize	reorganize
coordinate	increase	originate	repair
create	initiate	plan	research
decrease (costs)	innovate	prepare	schedule
develop	install	produce	support
devise	interpret	provide	test
direct	investigate	recommend	train

Citing Accomplishments   Employers seek to hire people who can cut costs, solve problems, and perform quality work. If you have five or more such distinctive achievements, you may list these immediately after the job objective. The manager of mail services for a large corporation labeled her accomplishments a "Record of Productivity," which she placed before work experience.

Record of Productivity

- Streamlined entire mail services operation for corporate headquarters of ———, Inc. This changeover included reorganizing job duties of all mail room personnel, developing new procedures, and reorganizing the physical layout for greater efficiency.
- Despite a 25% increase in mail flow, maintained quality service with no additional personnel. Increased number of in-house mail services for employees.
- Wrote and justified proposal for $80,000 for new equipment through equivalent savings in one year's time.
- As benefits approver at ———, maintained 97% accuracy and production criteria.

- At ——— Corporation, changed all accounts receivable functions from manual to computerized system.

To identify potential achievements on your skills lists, search for superior work, particularly any regarding finances or saving of resources, personnel, or time. Then *add a second part that provides specific data*. This addition can sometimes expand a skill to an accomplishment:

- *Skill:* Decreased costs; *add:* 20% through selective bulk buying
- *Skill:* Generated sales; *add:* of $850,000 during 199- to 199- fiscal year
- *Skill:* Computerized outdated inventory system; *add:* cutting storage time by one-third

You may also include honors, awards, and other distinctions you've received to fill out a list of accomplishments.

Discovery Questions for Finding Accomplishments

1. Have I received recognition at work for distinguished service, perfect attendance, highest sales, or exceeding production quotas?
2. Did I earn distinction in high school, in college, or in the community? (Consult your old newspaper clippings, certificates, trophies, scholarship awards, and the like.)
3. What difficult or long-term projects have I completed?
4. What significant problems have I solved?
5. Have I done anything else noteworthy?

Education

For higher education, provide names and addresses (optional) of institutions, dates, degrees, and major(s). Also state your minor concentration if relevant. Specify grade point average (GPA) if B+ or higher. GPA is usually stated in decimals such as "3.35/4.0," the second figure indicating the scale. If the GPA of your major is higher, you can cite it: "Major GPA 3.6/4.0."

Place teaching certification, nursing licensure and other professional certification with education. Listing a high school degree is optional, depending on the applicant's age, qualifications, and available space. If included, it might be accompanied by notes such as "Took college preparatory courses," "Wrote for school newspaper," "Trained in debate." High school honors can also go here. (GEDs should not be noted.)

Work Experience

Experience in your targeted field should be emphasized by allotting more space than for other jobs and by listing specific skills. Still, minor job experience

COMMON QUESTIONS AND ANSWERS ABOUT WORK EXPERIENCE

- *How far back should I go on work experience?* Your last three jobs are usually enough unless you have earlier work in your targeted field. Or you might go back ten years.

- *Should any work experience ever be omitted?* Employment of one month or less can be omitted. Lengthy gaps in employment can be a cause for concern, especially if you are not currently working.

- *How can I make a job title sound better?* Some jobs such as dishwasher, cleaning person, gardener, and bartender can be retitled with euphemisms: kitchen assistant, housekeeper, greens keeper, and server. (If the job had no formal title, give it a suitable one.)

- *What if I have no work experience?* Your best bet may be to head for the campus placement service or an employment agency to inquire about temporary or part-time work. If possible, obtain a position in your targeted field.

is better than none. It points to the desire to work and familiarity with the work world. If you have served in the military, include that under work experience. State term of service, branch, and rank upon leaving. List travel or training relevant to your job objective.

Always state promotions (for example, "Hired as crew member. In six months, promoted to assistant manager"). If you have had steady employment, include the employers' names and dates, preferably with months (Jan. 1995 – March 1997). List dates in reverse chronological order (beginning with the most recent). If you have held a succession of minor, unrelated jobs, or have large gaps in employment, a short summary with a *range of dates* without employers' names can save space as well as conceal gaps and de-emphasize frequent job changes. At the end of this summary, insert a sentence *telling what you have learned*. See Common Questions and Answers about Work Experience for more suggestions.

1991 to 1997	**SUMMARY OF WORK EXPERIENCE**

During high school and college, held part-time and temporary employment at fast food restaurants, a service station, car wash, and campus library. Developed initiative and a concern for accuracy. Learned to budget, schedule time, and provide courteous customer service.

Other Information on a Combination Résumé

If you can find space on your résumé for other minor, but significant, information, it can give a sense of the kind of person you are. Employers look for well-rounded applicants who can interact with other personnel well; any extra information on a résumé is considered. Possible items to list include the following (in this order):

- *Honors or awards*. If not listed with "Accomplishments," group honors such as "Employee of the Month," "Top Salesperson of the Year," civic awards, dean's list and other academic distinctions under "Honors."

- *Memberships*. Memberships in service clubs and professional organizations imply commitment to a community and a career. Do *not* list lodges, religious affiliations, or any membership that might arouse prejudice.

- *Activities and interests*. Concentrate on intellectual and physical pursuits. Do *not* list computer games, shopping, television, collecting comic books, and the like.

- *Personal data*. Keep to a minimum. Some applicants include "married with children" to suggest personal stability. Birth date, height, and weight are *not* advisable unless relevant to the job.

- *Availability*. Graduating students often indicate their final term. Otherwise, date of availability is unnecessary. If you are not working, do *not* emphasize that fact by stating "Available immediately."

- *Relocation*. If you are willing to relocate, this can be an advantage for some jobs. But don't limit yourself by identifying a specific state.

- *References*. At the end of the résumé, type "References upon request." (Chapter 25 provides information about reference lists.)

Your résumé should contain only positive information that will benefit you. Layoffs can be labeled as "downsizing" or "cutbacks." Do not mention anything that might arouse bias such as firings, demotions, ethnicity, handicaps, or medical disabilities. (Note, however, that a handicap or medical condition *which might interfere with performance* must be disclosed before a position is accepted.) Although employers often request salary history or desired salary, the routine advice of career consultants is to withhold this information until the interview.

ORGANIZING SECTIONS

After the job objective comes the section on accomplishments (if there is one). The major sections of work experience, education, and skills follow but *not* necessarily in that order. Use most- to least-important order, arranged according to the *needs of the employer*. The order is also influenced by requirements of the field (and possibly the state) as well as the competition. To decide the order best for you, start by asking yourself, "Which section will be most important to potential employers?"

Extensive work experience in the desired field usually comes first; the order is *work experience, skills, and education.* But if a degree and licensing or certification is required, then education takes precedence. In that case, the order would be *education, work experience, skills.* For example, a registered nurse who has three years' hospital experience would use this order.

If you are close to graduation and have little work experience, you can emphasize your academic achievement by using this order: *education, skills, work experience.* Degreed applicants who are *switching career fields* might also use this order, particularly if their educational record matches well with the new career field.

For college students who are *not* close to graduation and who have little work experience in their chosen field, skills can come first. Usually, these inexperienced applicants will organize this way: *skills, education, work experience.* Or if you will be competing with applicants who have higher degrees than you, you might use that same order, depending on the amount of work experience.

There is no one, correct order of presenting your record. After careful consideration, use the combination that will satisfy best the needs of the employer and bring the greatest benefit to you.

REVISING, EDITING, AND PROOFREADING A RÉSUMÉ

To appraise your work critically, imagine you are an employer, scanning the résumé of an unknown applicant. How would the document appear then? Is the layout balanced? Well-organized? Well-developed? Neat and attractive? Are sections arranged in an appropriate order? Are words specific and positive? Does each skill start with an action verb?

Chances are that a superficial résumé, hastily compiled, will not bring in interviews. Employers assume a résumé reflects the intellectual ability, competency, and attitude of the applicant. Take time to revise as much as necessary so that your résumé will outclass the competition and net you the opportunities you deserve.

Checking Layout, Order, and Emphasis

Layout does make a difference. The *white space* throughout the résumé, not just the margins, influences appearance, readability, and credibility. Neat, aligned columns provide a balanced look. A crowded résumé is more difficult to read than a well-spaced one. To be easily read, dates of education and work experience should appear on the left in reverse chronological order.

If your résumé runs more than one page, put a brief heading at the top of the second page and any succeeding pages to prevent loss or confusion when the interviewer is comparing applicants' qualifications. Specify your name and the page number. If possible, reduce the type one or two sizes to ensure that it won't be mistaken for the first page, should it get separated.

The order of sections on a résumé determines the emphasis. Examine the order: Does your job objective come right after the heading? Do major sections occupy more space than minor sections? Are the sections ranked from most to least important? Have you included as many minor sections as space allows? Are they appropriate?

➤ Checklist for Revising the Layout and Order of a Résumé

1. Is the résumé attractive and well balanced? How might it be improved?
2. Is there enough white space for easy reading?
3. Is every column aligned?
4. Is reverse chronological order used for items with dates?
5. Are sections arranged in most- to least-important order?
6. Are skills grouped strategically? Could the order within lists be improved?
7. Are all major sections well developed and accurate?

Puffery and Pitfalls

There is a big difference between presenting qualifications in the best light and inflating the truth. Yet misstatement and overstatement in résumés are common. Estimates of inaccurate résumés run as high as one out of three. Although many of the discrepancies are due to carelessness, some are not.

Interviewers are wary of puffed phrases, particularly in education and employment sections. Possibly you have heard of instructors who listed fake degrees and taught college courses, physicians who falsified credentials and performed surgery, or other cases of deception. As reports of such trickery have increased, employers have begun checking references much more thoroughly than a decade or two ago.

To a potential employer, even small discrepancies may imply that an applicant is careless, unqualified, or untrustworthy. A woman who was applying for an accounting position accidentally misstated her college graduation date by one year on her résumé. The error was discovered when the company received her college transcript. She was not hired. An inaccurate entry on a résumé or application can also result in dismissal after hiring. Accuracy is essential. All information should be triple-checked.

Scrutinizing Word Choice

Extra words dilute meaning. To interviewers, vague wordy phrases may imply that the applicant lacks confidence and competence. When reviewing the skills lists on your résumé, weigh every word. Does each one start with an action verb? Delete unnecessary words and qualifiers, such as *very* and unneeded prepositional phrases.

Weak and Wordy Phrases

have a knowledge of	know about	familiar with
provided assistance	exposed to	very good with
acquainted with	had exposure to	worked on

Instead of the first phrase above, say *know*. Instead of "provided assistance," say *assisted*. Instead of "had exposure to," say *used* or *operated:* if you do not actually feel capable, avoid the item altogether. *Tip:* Watch for *of, to, on, with,* and other prepositions that often indicate unnecessary words.

Adjusting Length

"How long should a résumé be?" is a common question with no definite answer. Although many employers prefer one-page résumés for *entry-level* employees, this preference does not rule out longer résumés for applicants with extensive qualifications. Two-page résumés are increasingly common for newly graduated applicants who use the combination format. If you plan a second page, however, the page should have sufficient information. A fraction of a page may appear to be the result of poor planning. When expanding your résumé to fill a second page, be careful not to indulge in puffery. A concise one-page résumé is far better than a puffed two-page one.

Résumés should be concise except for those prepared for the federal government, where a dozen or more pages may be expected. Since requirements vary among federal agencies, obtain an agency's criteria before starting to prepare. For other employers, prepare an additional one-page summary when your résumé will run three pages or more. (Place the summary first.)

Ways to Expand a Résumé

1. Review the suggestions for identifying skills to find more. Also consider adding more minor categories if appropriate.
2. Add white space. Have you triple spaced between sections? Have you centered your headings? A centered heading takes more space than one aligned on the left. (Refer to figs. 24.1, 24.2, and 24.3 for examples of headings and use of white space.)
3. If you have summarized minor work experience, you might expand that paragraph by listing employers unless doing so will be a disadvantage.
4. If you are *not* working, you can supply the names, addresses, and telephone numbers of previous employers. If working, reserve for a sheet of references (chapter 25).

When you cut the length, start with suggestion 1 below. Then go only as far as needed; don't toss out good material unnecessarily. To adjust the length of your résumé, you have several options:

Ways to Cut the Length of a Résumé

1. *Group similar skills on one line.* This technique is simple and quick. (See résumé examples in figs. 24.1, 24.2, and 24.3.)

2. *Narrow the margins and place major headings to the far left.* If you have centered the first heading with "Résumé of" above your name, you can conserve space by placing it on the same line as your name. To the far right, you can place your telephone number on the same line (see figs. 24.1 and 24.3).

3. *Omit some minor items.* Personal data, high school data, availability, ability to relocate, and activities are optional.

4. *Summarize unrelated work experiences.* Beware of cutting too much; work experience of any kind can be an asset.

5. *Reduce size of type.* Many software packages allow you to change the size of fonts. To save space, you might list skills in ten-point type with skill headings in twelve-point.

6. *Last resort:* Double-space between sections. The résumé will not be as attractive or clear as when triple-spaced.

Eagle-Eyed Proofreading

You know and I know that errors can creep into a draft for a multitude of reasons. But serious applicants take the time and expend the effort to proofread the finished résumé several times when they are fresh. Otherwise, they are unlikely to nab every error. And employers expect polished, error-free résumés.

Spelling Errors   Misspelled and misused words have disqualified many an applicant. In fact, some résumés are never read because of errors in the cover letter. Although a spelling checker can catch misspellings, it cannot monitor usage. An eagle eye is needed to detect misused words and inappropriate ones. (Common offenders, such as *principal/principle* and *appraise/apprise*, are explained in the Handbook.) If you have the slightest doubt about spelling or usage, consult a dictionary at once. And run a spelling check before every printout.

Consistent Punctuation   To ensure clarity and readability, set off fragments that are in paragraphs with periods. Fragments listed in columns do *not* require periods. Be consistent in punctuation and concentrate on clarity.

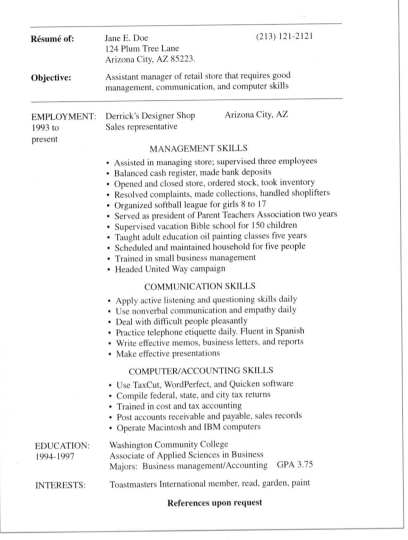

Résumé of: Jane E. Doe   (213) 121-2121
                 124 Plum Tree Lane
                 Arizona City, AZ 85223.

Objective: Assistant manager of retail store that requires good
                 management, communication, and computer skills

EMPLOYMENT: Derrick's Designer Shop   Arizona City, AZ
1993 to   Sales representative
present

MANAGEMENT SKILLS

- Assisted in managing store; supervised three employees
- Balanced cash register, made bank deposits
- Opened and closed store, ordered stock, took inventory
- Resolved complaints, made collections, handled shoplifters
- Organized softball league for girls 8 to 17
- Served as president of Parent Teachers Association two years
- Supervised vacation Bible school for 150 children
- Taught adult education oil painting classes five years
- Scheduled and maintained household for five people
- Trained in small business management
- Headed United Way campaign

COMMUNICATION SKILLS

- Apply active listening and questioning skills daily
- Use nonverbal communication and empathy daily
- Deal with difficult people pleasantly
- Practice telephone etiquette daily. Fluent in Spanish
- Write effective memos, business letters, and reports
- Make effective presentations

COMPUTER/ACCOUNTING SKILLS

- Use TaxCut, WordPerfect, and Quicken software
- Compile federal, state, and city tax returns
- Trained in cost and tax accounting
- Post accounts receivable and payable, sales records
- Operate Macintosh and IBM computers

EDUCATION: Washington Community College
1994-1997   Associate of Applied Sciences in Business
              Majors: Business management/Accounting   GPA 3.75

INTERESTS: Toastmasters International member, read, garden, paint

References upon request

Figure 24.1 Résumé of applicant with strong part-time experience.

Other Problems   Notice that some software packages have strange spellings with capital letters in the middle of the name. Check the packages to be sure you are correct. But do not overuse capital letters, which can imply weak writing skills and/or arrogance. The spelling of compound words is a slippery slope; some are hyphenated—others are not. (Consult an up-to-date dictionary.) Finally, check to see that colloquial words and slang have not slipped in.

MELODY A. SMITH
612 Greenlawn Drive
Marion, Ohio 43302
(614) 587-0755

OBJECTIVE: Paralegal or related position requiring training and skills in
paralegal duties, communications, and computer applications

EDUCATION: **Marion Technical College,** Marion, Ohio 43302
Associate of Applied Business Degree
June 1997   Major in paralegal studies, GPA 3.6/4.0

PARALEGAL TRAINING
- Investigated legal problems
- Drafted Contracts
- Prepared memorandas
- Applied problems in tort law
- Practiced basic accounting principles
- Attended legal education seminar
- Increased knowledge of criminal law
- Drafted complaints and responses
- Drafted and executed wills in accordance with Ohio law
- Researched and wrote argument paper
- Prepared partnership agreements
- Implemented debt collection practices

COMMUNICATION SKILLS
- Gave presentations successfully
- Wrote collection letters
- Coordinated workers' compensation presentation
- Conducted survey of opportunities for paralegals
- Trained in questioning and active listening
- Received practice in accepting criticism

COMPUTER SKILLS
- Conducted legal research using LEXIS COonline
- Operate IBM and Macintosh computers
- Use WordPerfect, Lotus 1-2-3, dBase III Plus
- Solved tax problems on PC/Taxcut

Figure 24.2 Résumé of applicant with no paid work experience in desired field.

➤ *Checklist for Editing and Proofreading*

1. Are all dates accurate?

2. Are months as well as years specified for education and related work experience?

3. Is there any duplication of skills? (If so, cut.)

Résumé of Melody A. Smith   page 2

EXPERIENCE: **Smith and Jones**
Attorneys at law, Marysville, Ohio

Nov. 1996 to   <u>Paralegal intern</u>
April 1997   • Researched legal problems and observed in court
                 • Filed documents in appropriate courts
                 • Performed title examinations (real estate)
                 • Assisted in updating office filing system
                 • Prepared various probate documents
                 • Obtained notary public commission
                 • Observed and witnessed real estate closings
                 • Served as witness to powers-of-attorneys
                 • Proofread legal descriptions of property
                 • Wrote and typed letters; contacted clients
                 • Prepared corporation sales reports of securities

June 1992 to   **A. O. Smith (Westinghouse),** Upper Sandusky, Ohio
April 1995   <u>Promoted to quality control inspector</u> from other jobs
                 • Supervised quality control of 10 workers
                 • Trained employees
                 • Supplied building line with parts
                 • Assembled small motors
                 • Connected stators and other tasks

May 1990 to   **American Legion, Club 162,** Marion, Ohio 43302
June 1992   <u>Maintenance supervisor</u>
                 • Ordered supplies, cleaned facility, opened/closed building

1989–1990   **Abbot & Company,** Prospect, Ohio 43342
                 • Assembled, inspected, and packed electrical harnesses

1988–1989   **Howard Swink Advertising,** Marion, Ohio 43302
                 • Typed letters, filed, answered telephone, presented ad
                   campaign for school project

HONORS: Dean's List; National Honor Society

ACTIVITIES: Reading, puzzles, crafts, swimming, walking

References upon request

4. Does every skill start with an action verb?
5. Is every word positive or neutral?
6. Is every word spelled correctly?
7. Are punctuation and capitalization consistent and correct?

Résumé	JOHN J. TRULANE 8941 East Center Street Denver, CO 80200	Telephone: (111) 222-3333
Objective	Assistant systems manager for company requiring experience in management of information systems, communication, problem solving	

ACCOMPLISHMENTS

- Adapted accounting software for XYZ Electronics
- Provided training for XYZ employees
- Created motivational plan that led to increased sales of 20%
- Graduated summa cum laude
- Won *The Wall Street Journal* award for student achievement
- Awarded "Best Persuasive Speaker" in oral communications class
- Selected to serve on university student advisory panel
- Won first prize in regional essay contest
- Awarded Crissinger Scholarship ($6,000)

COMPUTER SKILLS

- Operate systems AS 400 and UNIX
- Use Microsoft NT, Word, Excel, WordPerfect for Windows,
  and MACOLA accounting software
- Design flow charts and document programs
- Program in SQL, C++, and dBase
- Make minor repairs on IBM computers
- Quick to detect problems in security of software and systems
- Assist potential users in defining system needs
- Answer application and support questions for clients
- Use online and Internet services, electronic mail

COMMUNICATION SKILLS

- Give oral reports, informative and persuasive presentations
- Write brochures and training literature
- Write proposals for potential users
- Trained in logic and detection of propaganda
- Write business letters; short and long reports with graphics
- Designed questionnaire, conducted survey, compiled results,
  and wrote report for research project

Figure 24.3 Résumé of applicant with strong work experience in desired field.

A FINAL NOTE ON APPEARANCE

Your résumé is your ambassador. An immaculate appearance is imperative. Purchase high-quality twenty-pound bond paper. Buy enough so that you have matching paper for cover and follow-up letters. White is best for résumés that will be duplicated by a campus placement office, an employment agency, or other agency. Otherwise, ivory or soft grey is suitable.

John J. Trulane   8941 East Center Street   2

PROBLEM-SOLVING SKILLS

- Detected computer security problem at XYZ Electronics and secured evidence to identify offender
- Set up improved method of systems security
- Revised performance evaluation procedure to permit input from employees
- Answer questions from suppliers and end users
- Customize software for company and client needs
- Handle complaints and work out compromises

Education   OLYMPIA UNIVERSITY

June 1995   Bachelor of Computer Science in Business, GPA 3.6/4.0
                 Majors: Management of information systems & marketing

Experience   XYZ ELECTRONICS COMPANY

July 1993   Promoted to sales manager
to   - Supervise five employees. Hire, fire, and train.
present   - Order, track, and report inventory
                 - Monitor cash register. Make nightly bank deposits
                 - Sell, install, and provide support for systems/software

                 MC BURGER'S

May 1991   Promoted to assistant manager after six months
to   - Supervised eight employees
June 1992   - Kept sales records, ordered supplies, made bank deposits
                 - Opened and closed store

Member   Small Business Association

Activities   Swimming, bowling, camping, and reading

Availability Two weeks' notice. Will consider relocation.

References upon request

You can vary the format by using capital letters, oversize letters, boldface, or underlining for headings. You can lead into each skill entry with a hyphen, an asterisk, or an oversize dot (best), followed by one space. Some software packages may offer more capabilities.

To give a picture frame look, use one-inch margins all around. Triple-space between sections, if possible, and double-space between subsections. You can center major headings or locate them at the side or mix the two arrangements.

Work with your résumé until you have an effective layout that enhances your qualifications.

Never send pale or smudged copies to an interviewer. An electric typewriter, letter-quality printer, or laser printer is an absolute necessity. Select a font that is neat and clear. Avoid script and other informal or difficult-to-read fonts. After that, duplicate your résumé, using the high-quality paper, on a first-class copier. If you do not have access to a quality printer or an excellent copier, then have your résumé printed at a local shop.

You should be aware that some companies prefer résumés that can be scanned or faxed. (This requirement rules out light type, fancy fonts, and some colored paper.) Others may want to receive your résumé on a disk. Some companies even encourage applicants to send résumés by e-mail. There may be special formatting requirements to follow. Adapting your résumé to these special needs may make the difference between serious consideration or none.

Companies, institutions, and government agencies have varying expectations for acceptable résumés. If your résumé is to work efficiently for you, you should determine what each employer expects and do your best to meet those expectations.

Summary

A combination résumé combines the best features of the chronological and functional résumé styles. This hybrid emphasizes skills and abilities and de-emphasizes dates of employment.

You have accumulated many transferable skills, but unless you clearly link them to job requirements in your chosen field, your résumé may be ineffective. Research your career field to discover the correct terminology and to discover which skills are in demand.

Identify your workplace, academic, and leisure skills. Start each skills entry with an action verb.

A service-oriented job objective should be linked to your skills headings. This job objective focuses on serving an employer.

Revision, editing, and proofreading are essential for an excellent résumé. The layout should be attractive with plenty of white space for easy reading. Neat columns, not long solid paragraphs, improve readability. Do not use first person. Proofread carefully. Every word must be spelled correctly.

Print out your résumé on twenty-pound bond paper. Use a quality printer with a clear, conventional font and new ink cartridge or a laser printer. Your résumé is your ambassador.

Key Terms

combination résumé   service-oriented objective

transferable skills   accomplishments

workplace skills   reverse chronological order

academic skills   puffery

leisure skills

Practice

Writing a Service-Oriented Job Objective

Directions: Fill in the blanks below. Then draft your objective from this exercise, adding minor words such as *that, which, with,* and others when appropriate. Revise and edit until the objective reads smoothly. See job objectives in figs. 24.1, 24.2 and 24.3.

Position: _____

Where: _____ (type of company, facility, industry or business—optional)

Verb or participle: _____

Examples: needs/needing, require/requiring, seeks/seeking, offers/offering, affords/affording, desires/desiring

Skills headings: _____, _____, _____

Collaborative Exercise: Revising Skills Lists

Directions: Working with a partner, check each other's drafts of skills. Questioning each other will help you to find more transferable skills and an action verb for each skill.

1. Is the item a claim or a skill? (*Note:* A skill tells what one can *do:* "type 60 wpm" and "monitored cash drawer" are skills. But "work well with others" and "honest" are vague claims. Instead, cite specific duties that point to a skill or an ability. Example of an interpersonal skill: "Resolved customer complaints.")

2. Does each item begin with an action verb?

3. What else did you do that required accuracy, responsibility, communication skills, tact, problem solving, or trustworthiness?

4. How can that task be reworded for your skills list?

5. Is there anything else that you did at work, in class, or during leisure hours that might be transferable?

Collaborative Exercise: Revising a Job Objective

Directions: Using the criteria below, critique the job objectives of your group members. Place a question mark after any word or phrase that does not sound appropriate. Make suggestions.

1. Is the objective limited to *one* position or area?
2. Does the objective focus on service to an employer?
3. Is the objective written in third person?
4. Is the objective written as a fragment, not a sentence?
5. Are the skills in the objective the same as those in the skills headings?
6. Is the wording correct and appropriate?

CHAPTER 25

Writing Letters for Employment

*I hope I shall possess firmness and virtue enough
to maintain what I consider the most enviable of all
titles, the character of an honest man.*

—George Washington

Effective business letters can be crucial to getting the job you want. Unquestionably, a neat professional format; well-organized content; and correct grammar, punctuation, and spelling are essential. But the tone and attitude, revealed in your written voice, will also determine whether or not you are considered for a position. For jobs involving handwritten numbers or other data (accounting, finance, medicine, sales, and others), neat handwriting is essential. In fact, some employers may even request a handwritten cover letter. Even if you are looking for another type of job, take extra pains to write your signature neatly. Employers draw inferences from incidentals, even messy, illegible signatures. Always take the time to produce your best work when corresponding with potential employers.

WRITING AN EFFECTIVE COVER LETTER FOR A RÉSUMÉ

When hundreds of people vie for a single position, a cover letter may be the only document in a job packet that an interviewer reads. If a cover letter contains even a whiff of incompetence or dishonesty the résumé may well be tossed aside, unread. Regardless of whether a résumé is mailed, faxed, or delivered in person, a cover letter is usually expected.

As you write your cover letter, keep in mind that the primary purpose is to motivate the interviewer to read your résumé. Express interest in the position, present an overview of your credentials, and make a courteous request for an interview. The tone of a well-written cover letter is professional and confident, never desperate, half-hearted, or arrogant. A confident letter may spark confidence in its reader—exactly the effect you wish to achieve.

Like other business letters, cover letters have three basic parts: introduction, body, and closing.

Effective Introductions

A pet peeve of interviewers is triteness in cover letters. Imagine having to read dozens of letters that begin with "I saw your ad in . . ." or some other predictable phrase. To make a cover letter stand out, hook the reader's interest with your very first words. Select them judiciously: the wrong words may steer you into a low-paying position. If you have experience in your desired field, shy away from "entry-level" or "trainee." These words peg you as having minimal skills and lacking experience. For inexperienced applicants, however, an entry-level position in your chosen field affords an opportunity to gain practical knowledge and skill.

To create a distinctive opening that will work for you, adapt one of the four basic openings for cover letters. (Note that when a definite position is available, you can specify it in the introduction of your cover letter. Otherwise, you may want to be less specific, for you may be qualified for several related positions.)

The Name Opening   You are fortunate, indeed, if you can begin with the name of a person the employer knows, one who has referred you or who will recommend you. Often a referral will open doors that might otherwise remain closed. If you learn of an available position from an executive or from someone else the employer respects, seize the opportunity! First, state the name of the person making the referral. Then mention the position and give the main areas of your qualifications:

> Jason Blank, systems manager of Incatech, advised me of an opening in your company for a junior accountant. He recommended I apply, for he is familiar with my accounting background and computer experience.

> Cynthia Jones, vice president of Blink's Advertising, has suggested I apply for the position of copywriter at your company. The requirements she mentioned match my training and experience in advertising.

The Creative Opening   To find just the right detail for an unusual opening, search your résumé and memory. Watch local papers for news items about potential employers, possibly the arrival of a new business or the expansion of a

124 Plumtree Lane
Arizona City, AZ 85223
May 1, 199–

Sally Chen, President
Sally's Tall and Short Shop
332 Main Street
Anywhere, U.S.A. 00000

Dear President Chen:

As an artist, I have developed a keen eye for detail, line, and color. This ability, along with my academic training and work experience, should qualify me for the position of manager of Sally's Tall and Short Shop.

At Washington Community College, I earned an Associate of Applied Business degree with a major in business management. There I received training in small business management, business law, cost and corporate accounting, computing and filing of tax returns. I operate IBM and Macintosh computers and use PC Taxcut, WordPerfect, and Lotus 1-2-3 software. Training in interpersonal communication, including active listening and questioning, has helped prepare me to serve customers well.

For four years at Derrick's Designer Shop, I arranged window displays weekly, assisted customers, assisted in shop security, balanced the cash drawer, opened and closed the store, and made bank deposits. Whenever the owner was away, I managed the shop, supervising eight employees. Other experience is explained on the enclosed résumé.

May I have an appointment to discuss my qualifications and salary history? My telephone number is (000) 121-1212. I am available Mondays, Tuesdays, and Thursdays 4:30 to 9:30 p.m. or anytime Friday or Saturday morning.

Sincerely,

Jane A. Doe

Jane A. Doe

Figure 25.1 Cover letter with creative opening and reference to salary history.

local company. Then match your experience, activities, and talent so as to spark the interest of an interviewer:

Perseverance does pay off. After five years of attending night classes, working as a restaurant manager, and providing for a family, I am graduating magna cum laude with a B.S. degree in restaurant management. Would these qualifications plus confirmed workaholic tendencies equip me for the position of manager of your hotel's dining room?

After Hastings, Holby, and Haberman move to the new downtown location, they may need more personnel. If so, please consider my legal training and work experience, which should qualify me for a paralegal position.

An unusual example of a creative opening was written by an elementary schoolteacher who had been out of the job market for several years to raise six children. She explained how her skills, interests, and talent could serve the publisher. And she landed the position of editorial assistant in the children's literature division. Here is the opening of the letter that won the interview:

Over the years, I have taught children, produced children, and raised children. I am familiar with their desires, delights, and dreams. You might say I am an expert on children. Surely, this experience as well as my academic training should make me a valuable member of your editorial staff.

The Summary Opening   Although traditional, the summary opening can be quite workable when your strongest qualifications are linked to the desired position. You might give two or three main points taken from the headings of your résumé. But be sure the points are clearly connected to the current needs of potential employers (see fig. 25.2).

A simple way to get up-to-date information about employers' needs is to clip job descriptions and ads. Underline the skills and abilities required for positions you would like. After that, draft an introduction that suggests how your training and experience meet those needs. Be sure that your description truly reflects your qualifications. In the following summary openings, notice that the focus is upon *how the applicant can serve the employer:*

Training in social work, an internship in student admissions, and a bachelor's degree in psychology should help me fulfill the responsibilities of human services coordinator for Blinhard University.

Because City Hospital needs a clinical dietitian with expertise in implementing nutritional care plans and counseling patients, my training and work experience should make me a promising candidate.

My management skills in nursing have been honed by supervision of nursing personnel, development of nursing policies and procedures, and preparation of six-figure budgets. This background, along with a recently acquired M.S.N. degree, should qualify me for director of nursing at Memorial Hospital.

The Question Opening   Opening with a question is a popular method, but a word of caution is advisable. Some personnel directors say that question openings are "overused" and frequently "filled with clichés." One interviewer even went so far as to say he tossed letters that opened with stereotypic questions into the wastebasket unread. Still, an original question opening can serve as an attention-getter if it is fresh, appealing, and relevant.

331 Cherry Lane
Wintoska, Oregon 47000
April 20, 199-

Ms. Cheryl Withers
Office Manager
Baywood and Goldberg
1221 North Main Street
Wintoska, Oregon 47000

Dear Ms. Withers:

When an old and respected law firm like Baywood and Goldberg advertises for a junior accountant, I am interested. My three years' work experience and my training in accounting and information systems should enable me to perform successfully for you.

As the only accountant for a hardware store, I assume many responsibilities. During my first year, I streamlined bookkeeping operations by converting a manual arrangement to a computer system. At that time I also wrote a proposal for a federally funded small business loan that won the owner a low-interest loan. Daily I handle accounts receivable and accounts payable. I write collection letters and call customers who are behind in their payments. Weekly I make out the payroll and handle insurance payments. Weekly and monthly balance sheets are also compiled. Quarterly, I write reports and file tax returns.

On June 10, 199–, I will graduate from Franklin University with a bachelor's degree in accounting. There I have received training not only in cost and corporate accounting, but also in finance and business law. Since my minor is in data processing, I am familiar with a wide range of computers and accounting software, as explained on the enclosed résumé.

At your convenience, would it be possible to set up an appointment to discuss how I can serve your firm? Salary is open. Will you please call (000) 389-4689 between 5:30 and 9:00 p.m. Monday through Wednesday or weekends?

Sincerely,

Rosalind Caton-Green

Rosalind Caton-Green

Figure 25.2 Cover letter with summary opening.

Whatever opening you use, avoid any hint of overconfidence or presumption. Note, for example, that the sample introductions use phrases such as "*should* qualify me for the position" rather than "*will* qualify me." At the same time, an opening that seems doubtful or anxious is not likely to open many doors. Striking the proper balance can be tricky, so thoughtful applicants evaluate and revise their openings carefully, using their own words and avoiding trite phrases.

The Body of the Letter

The body of a cover letter explains the qualifications mentioned in the introduction. When you develop these points, retain the order set forth in your opening. After summarizing the highlights from the résumé, conclude the body with
an *indirect* reference to the résumé. A direct reference, such as "Please see the
enclosed résumé," is awkward. An indirect reference is worked smoothly into
a sentence in a dependent clause or phrase. The indirect references below are
italicized:

> Since age fifteen, I have been working. During these years I have dealt with
> the public and gained significant insights into providing customer service.
> For me, the customer is really number one. Supervision of eight employees
> has also offered opportunities to polish my interpersonal skills, *as indicated
> on the enclosed résumé.*

> On June 12, 1995, I will graduate summa cum laude from Buckeye Univer-
> sity with a bachelor of arts degree in education. There I majored in English,
> specifically the teaching of high school literature and composition. In my
> senior year, I won first prize in the National Arts and Letters contest involv-
> ing five area colleges. Seven poems have been published in magazines, *as
> explained in the enclosed résumé.*

Effective Conclusions

The end of a cover letter is rather like a good-bye. As such, it should be brief,
cordial, and courteous. Courtesy is integral to good business relations, yet many
applicants fail to include courtesy words in cover letters. Instead, they border on
arrogance without realizing it, sounding presumptuous or overly forceful. One
applicant concluded with "I will be in town Tuesday and will stop by," presuming
that he would be welcomed. Others thank in advance, assuming they will gain an
interview, unaware that busy interviewers may take offense.

You can transform a demand into a polite request with just a few courtesy
words and a question mark:

> Demand: "Call me at . . ."
> Polite request: "Will you please call me at . . . ?"

A question with a question mark is more polite than a statement. A question
is a request whereas a statement often sounds like a demand. You can set an
appropriate tone in your letters by using questions with courtesy words such
as *may, please, appreciate, appreciation,* and *your convenience.* Let consideration
shine through your words as in the following examples:

> May I have an appointment at a convenient time to further explain how I
> might serve your company as a junior accountant? Please dial (611) 121-2121
> anytime Saturday or Monday through Thursday at 4:30 to 9:30 p.m.

If you think there might be a place for me in your firm, will you please call (402) 269-2626? I can be reached in person after 4 p.m. weekdays and 8–11:30 a.m. Saturdays, or you may leave a message and I will promptly return your call.

≫ Checklist for an Effective Conclusion

1. *A courteous request for an interview.*
2. *Home telephone number.* Protect your privacy and your job. Giving a work number poses hazards.
3. *Availability.* Specify the hours you can be reached at home or the possibility of leaving a message.

How to Handle the Salary Question

Sooner or later, all applicants will confront the question of salary. Rather than be unprepared, begin to research salaries in your field; then you'll know what to expect locally, statewide, or nationally. Information about salary ranges can be gained from libraries, friends, employment agencies, information interviews, and temporary employment.

Although an ad may request "desired salary" or "salary history," you are not obligated to divulge your answers. Yet you should respond. In a cover letter, you can specify a salary range, such as "$26,000 to $29,000" or "upper 20s." But before you do, consider that your answer may jeopardize your chances of being hired. The risk is twofold: If your figure is too high, employers may conclude you are overqualified or overpriced; if too low, they may think you underqualified. Even if you are aware of current salary ranges, a small business may not be able to comply. Then the question you must decide is "Will I work for less?"

In a telephone conversation, you might say that salary is "open" or sidestep questions about salary history (another can of worms) until the interview. In the conclusion of a cover letter, you can postpone your answer tactfully.

At your convenience, may I set up an interview to discuss my qualifications, including expected salary [or salary history if requested]? My telephone number is (000) 910-6721, and I'm available after 6:30 p.m.

Other Considerations

A job search may entail dozens of mailings and many interviews before the right position is found. The wisest course may be to write two basic cover letters and see which elicits more responses. Each time you contact a potential employer, customize the basic letter with the current date and correct inside address and salutation as well as any other suitable changes. A cover letter should be limited to one uncrowded page with "picture frame" margins and plenty of white space. Before mailing, proofread your letter carefully, and check to see that it is signed.

When contacting several employers, be sure each letter is inside the correct envelope and signed.

Five Guidelines for an Effective Cover Letter

1. *Secure the name of the interviewer.* If unknown, call the company. If impossible to secure a name, send to "Human Resources Director." "Dear Director" can serve as your salutation.
2. *Write in a confident, courteous tone.*
3. *Individualize the letter.* Avoid trite phrases or examples from books. Be original.
4. *Type an individualized letter for each company.* Although a résumé may be duplicated, a cover letter may not. Form letters without an inside name and address are inappropriate and ineffective.
5. *Sign each letter in black ink to match the type.* Never leave a letter unsigned. Employers tend to view the omission as carelessness and a disregard for detail.

Revising a Cover Letter

Rarely is an excellent cover letter dashed off in a few minutes. Examine, revise, and proofread your draft several times. Whether or not you are granted an interview may hinge upon how effective your cover letter is.

Checklist for Revising a Cover Letter

1. Does the introduction focus on the employer's needs?
2. Does the introduction set up the main points of the body?
3. Does each paragraph center on one main idea?
4. Is the material well organized?
5. Are qualifications linked to job requirements?
6. Is the résumé referred to indirectly at the end of the *body?*
7. Is the tone confident without sounding overly confident?
8. Is an interview *requested* in the closing?
9. Has a telephone number been included? A time to call?
10. Are the words polite and appreciative? Do they conform to standard usage?

FORMAT FOR A BUSINESS LETTER

All business letters contain similar elements, but the positioning of the elements differs slightly. The *modified block format* (shown in figs. 25.1 and 25.2) is most common for letters that are *not* typed on letterhead stationery. Letters typed with letterheads often follow the *block format*, with the date and all other typed elements aligned at the left margin. Then the typed signature may be followed by a line of type indicating the writer's title.

Modified Block Form

Heading: At the top right-hand corner of the margin, place your address and the date.

Inside address: Type the recipient's name and address—just as they appear on the envelope—several spaces below the heading at the left-hand margin.

Salutation: "Dear ————" or other salutation comes two spaces below the inside address, also at the left margin. The salutation is always followed by a colon.

Body: Body paragraphs are single-spaced, with double-spacing between paragraphs. Indentation is optional.

Complimentary close: A close such as "Sincerely" or "Yours truly" is separate and double-spaced after the final body paragraph. The close is aligned with the heading and followed by a comma.

Signature: Leave four lines after the complimentary close for the handwritten signature. Below this space, place the typed signature.

PACKAGING JOB SEARCH DOCUMENTS

A positive first impression is important not only for applicants but also for their job search packet. Chances are the applicant will never meet the interviewer unless the documents in the packet are immaculate. Erasures, strikeovers, and smudges are verboten. The résumé, cover letter, and other items should be perfectly printed by a laser printer (if possible) or by an up-to-date electric typewriter, preferably on *white* twenty-pound bond paper. White paper transfers more clearly than colored when duplicated or scanned or faxed. Use a clear, conventional type style. Italics or unusual fonts are difficult for a scanner to read.

When finally satisfied with the quality of your résumé and cover letter, place them inside a 10- by 13-inch manila envelope, unfolded. This precaution will protect against weather, wrinkling, fingerprints, or dropping. If you are employed, do *not* enclose a sheet of references, lest your employer be contacted prematurely. One applicant made this unfortunate mistake, only to find he had no job with either firm. The interviewer had telephoned the employer immediately, and the man was fired upon his return an hour later.

If unemployed, you can enclose references along with the résumé and cover letter; yet this is unnecessary since most employers wait until after an interview to run a reference check. If you enclose letters of recommendation, do *not* send the originals, which could disappear into an employer's file. When an employer wants a grade transcript, order one and arrange to have it mailed directly to the company. Because oversized envelopes require extra postage, you can conserve by using standard envelopes for mailings to companies that seem less desirable.

PROVIDING A LIST OF REFERENCES

When you walk into an interview with a up-to-date, well-organized sheet of references, you have a definite advantage. This preparation not only boosts your confidence, but also indicates to the interviewer your ability to plan ahead and organize. Yet relatively few job seekers are aware of the full significance of this important job search tool, nor do they think to add financial references to the usual list of former employers, teachers, and the like. However, financial references are significant. From the employer's point of view, someone who is financially stable seems more likely to be trustworthy and reliable.

Guidelines for Compiling a List of References

1. *Request permission before using names.* With teachers and others you have not seen for many years, try to meet in person, to make sure you're remembered. Otherwise, telephone. If you must write, enclose a stamped, self-addressed envelope and politely request an early reply. (Employers expect to be contacted; it is unnecessary to ask for their permission, although you may.)

2. *Be sure the person is willing to give you a reference.* If you sense reluctance or a lack of enthusiasm, ask someone else. A lukewarm response can do you harm.

3. *Employment references.* From your last two positions, list supervisors. If you know employees at the company to which you are applying who would give favorable references, include their names, too.

4. *Other references.* Include coworkers, teachers, coaches, scout leaders, or anyone else who can attest to your good qualities—except relatives and the clergy. For financial references, list banks, charge accounts, or paid-up loans.

5. *Indicate in parenthesis your relationship to the reference.*

6. *Organize the list of references in most- to least-important order.* Put employers first, character references second, and financial references third.

7. *Include complete addresses and telephone numbers.*

8. *Include your name, address, and telephone number.* Place this information at the top of the sheet in a centered heading like the one on a résumé.

9. *If working, take precautions.* Across the top, before the heading with your name, type in capital letters: PLEASE DO NOT CONTACT MY CURRENT EMPLOYER UNTIL THE FINAL STAGES OF INTERVIEWING. If using a computerized résumé service, ask that neither your résumé nor reference list be sent to your present employer. Posting a résumé on a web site is *not* advisable for applicants who are presently working.

WRITING A LETTER OF APPRECIATION

Several applicants had interviewed for the position of Financial Aid Director at Marion Technical College, but the search committee could not agree. Then a letter of appreciation for the interview arrived from Andrew Harper, who was the only applicant to send a thank you. The committee reevaluated his credentials and called him for a second interview. Andy got the job. That one brief letter tipped the scales in his favor. Why? What is significant about a letter of appreciation?

First, a letter of appreciation reveals a sincere interest in a position. Since most applicants interview for several positions and seldom send follow-up notes, an employer does not know whether or not they are genuinely interested. Second, a thank you conveys an implicit message, implying the sender is considerate and appreciative. It also suggests motivation, perseverance, and a positive attitude. Third, the letter indicates good human relations skills. See fig. 25.3 for an example.

There is no standard format for a letter of appreciation, but *timing* and *tone* are important. Mail your letter either the day of the interview or the next day. But keep your priorities straight: accuracy is more important than same-day mailing. Edit and proofread several times. Read the letter aloud to gauge the tone. Be sure the tone mirrors *enthusiasm*, not the image of a forlorn applicant sitting by a silent telephone. Avoid phrases such as "I'll be waiting to hear from you," "If you are interested, please call me," or "I eagerly look forward to hearing from you," which may suggest doubt or anxiety.

To write a successful letter of appreciation quickly, follow the outline below, including any of the six parts that are relevant to your situation.

Outline: Letter of Appreciation

1. Thank you
2. I'm interested
3. I enjoyed . . . (or was impressed by . . .)
4. I'm available (give date)
5. Another item you might like to know (optional)
6. If you need more information (give telephone number and time to call)

1122 Valley Road
Clearview, Washington 98222
February 6, 199-

Dr. Margaret Berman
Mad River Medical Association
1555 Main Street
Wenatchee, Washington 98555

Dear Dr. Berman:

Thank you for the opportunity to discuss the possibility of working at Mad River Medical Association. I enjoyed meeting with you and your staff and was impressed with the organization and friendly atmosphere. After interviewing with you, I am even more eager to become a part of your medical team.

Once my program at Bellevue Technical College is complete on March 19, 199–, I will be available for employment. If accepted for the position of medical secretary, I am prepared to put all my efforts into achieving the goals set by your practice and to serving your patients accordingly.

If you should need any further information concerning my credentials, please contact me at (000) 365-1111 any time convenient for you.

Sincerely,

Trena M. Craig

Trena M. Craig

Figure 25.3 Letter of appreciation.

WRITING A LETTER OF ACCEPTANCE

Often employers notify successful applicants by telephone. If you should be called, be sure the terms of the job offer are clear before accepting. Acceptance over the telephone is an oral contract. If you have other offers pending, ask for more time to decide.

Dear Ms. Hendricks:

Thank you for the job offer. The staff nurse position, evening shift, on the surgical floor will not only be challenging, but will also offer numerous opportunities to learn. The salary of $_____ per hour with $_____ on weekends is more than acceptable.

On June 12, I will arrive early to fill out the insurance forms, receive instructions, and begin.

I am looking forward to working with you and the other members of the staff at Belvedere General Hospital.

Cordially,

Jonathan Jones

Jonathan Jones

Figure 25.4 Abbreviated letter of acceptance.

After making a decision, call in your acceptance *and* send a letter accepting the job offer and the terms (see fig. 25.4). Specify the primary provisions of the offer and keep a copy. This letter not only protects the employer but also protects you by forestalling misunderstanding or friction later.

Outline: Letter of Acceptance

1. Thank you or an expression of appreciation
2. Acceptance of the offer (sound pleased)
3. Main points of the job offer
4. Date and time to begin work
5. Courtesy closing

WRITING A LETTER OF REFUSAL

Never let the door slam on a job offer. Courtesy is important even in a refusal, for some day you may wish to reapply at the company. A refusal should be made promptly so that the company can continue the search. The refusal can be made over the telephone, but unless you are adept at speaking off the cuff, it is wiser to mail a decision.

Begin by tactfully expressing appreciation for the offer. But avoid an overly enthusiastic tone that might mislead the reader into thinking the letter is an acceptance. Provide a general reason for the refusal, without mentioning anything that

Dear Ms. Plymale:

Thank you for the informative tour of Tucker & Taylor's downtown facility and the attractive offer of the junior accounting position.

I have, however, accepted another offer that is more consistent with my career goals.

Your time, consideration, and courtesy are appreciated.

Sincerely,

Rafael Perez

Rafael Perez

Figure 25.5 Abbreviated letter of refusal.

might seem negative about the company or the offer. Close with a positive comment. See fig. 25.5 for an example.

Outline: Refusal of a Job Offer

1. Expression of appreciation for the job offer
2. Brief refusal
3. Reason for the refusal (optional)
4. Courtesy closing

WRITING A LETTER OF RESIGNATION

Business etiquette requires that when an applicant accepts another position, the present employer be notified in writing. Appreciation should be expressed, and the date of leaving specified. A letter of resignation should be sent to the head of the department. If you are asked to go within the hour, don't be surprised or take offense. Many companies require that personnel working with computer records or other data requiring security depart immediately. Sometimes, however, when there is no immediate replacement, the employee will be asked to stay longer.

Try to leave on a friendly footing. Even if your employer does not take your resignation well, retain your dignity. If you are treated unprofessionally, be very careful that bitterness does not seep into your letter of resignation. Later you will be glad you retained your professional demeanor.

Sometimes an employee is fired and given the opportunity to write a letter of resignation. Although this event is disheartening, the employee should take advantage of the offer unless prepared to contest the termination in court. A letter of resignation is a protection not only for the employer but also for the discharged employee. It gives the appearance of leaving of one's own accord, which will be an advantage in future employment interviews.

Outline: Letter of Resignation

1. Express appreciation (possibly regret).
2. State the exact date of leaving.
3. If another job has been accepted, give a reason for leaving. State in general terms such as "opportunity" or "generous offer."
4. If you want to take accrued vacation time or holidays, specify.
5. Keep the letter positive and end on an upbeat note.

The letter shown in fig. 25.6 was written by a company's star sales representative who had been asked to tender his resignation. A powerful client had complained over a refusal to be given a large discount and had arranged a deal with the sales manager. Then the client demanded the sales representative be fired,

Mr. James Jones
Sales Manager
Mazdex, Incorporated
111 East Main Street
Anywhere, USA

Dear Jim:

My five years with Mazdex have been challenging and rewarding. This association has provided an opportunity for applying and developing my skills as well as gaining practical knowledge of the business world. It is with reluctance that I tender my resignation, effective immediately.

I have decided it is time to turn my career in a slightly different direction as an accounting software trainer/sales consultant. My experience with Mazdex has provided me with valuable skills and contacts.

Finally, Jim, I appreciate your assistance and training. You have helped to make our association pleasant and productive. I look forward to dealing with Mazdex in a different capacity.

Sincerely,

John R. Smith

Figure 25.6 Abbreviated letter of resignation.

and the manager complied. Although filled with indignation, the discharged employee knew his future career depended upon subordinating feelings and conducting himself in a professional manner. To gain control, he waited a day to write the letter.

Summary

The purpose of a cover letter is to motivate an employer to read the résumé. Word the introduction of your cover letter carefully to avoid trite phrasing. To be effective, use one of four basic openings: name, summary, creative, or question. Your introduction should indicate interest in the position and set up the main points you will develop.

Develop each main section of the résumé into a paragraph in the body of the letter. The last body paragraph should contain an indirect reference to your résumé. In the conclusion *ask* for an interview courteously. Specify a home telephone number and times of availability. When an employer requests a salary history or required salary, you can postpone the request by indicating a willingness to discuss the topic in an interview.

If a letter and résumé are to be mailed in a standard envelope, fold them correctly. Mail or hand-deliver your cover letter and résumé. After that, update your list of references. Before using the references, secure permission to ensure all referrals are positive.

After an interview, send a letter of appreciation to the potential employer. When a job is offered, send a letter of acceptance or refusal. Notify your present employer of your decision to leave with a letter of resignation. If firing has occurred, an upbeat letter of resignation can facilitate a future job search.

Key Terms

cover letter	question opening	letter of appreciation
name opening	courtesy closing	letter of acceptance
creative opening	list of references	letter of refusal
summary opening	financial references	letter of resignation

PART 6

Writing in Response to Essays, Fiction, and Poetry

CHAPTER 26

Reading and Responding to Essays

. . . the unexamined life is not worth living.

—Socrates, 5th century BC

Essays have long been a popular form of exposition. The precursors of this tradition were ancient Roman writers, including Seneca and Plutarch. In the sixteenth century, Michel de Montaigne refined the tradition with his famous essays, which included self-appraisal as well as responses to reading and religion. Later, English essayists such as Samuel Johnson, George Orwell, and Virginia Woolf continued the informal style Montaigne had created. Today you read informal essays on the editorial pages of daily newspapers, columns by journalists that discuss politics, cultural trends, or other news. You write informal essays in college composition classes that call for writing based on experience.

READING ESSAYS

Essays are short literary compositions that focus on one major idea. Essays may run from one page to several pages. Usually, the perspective of the writer dominates, although other viewpoints may be considered. Sometimes essays include a reaction or response to an idea, event, or trend. The reaction is a commentary that explains the basis for the opinion or position. Essays range all the way from lighthearted spoof to political commentary to serious argument.

Three Types of Essays

Generally, essays are classified as *informal* or *formal*, although the degree of formality varies within each category. You can easily identify informal essays by their conversational tone, self-disclosure, humor, freshness, and loose structure. Informal essays, often written in first person, tend to be subjective and frank. Formal essays, on the other hand, are characterized by a more dignified, reticent tone; logical reasoning; and tight structure. Formal essays, usually written in third person, tend to be more objective.

The *personal essay* is a subcategory of the informal essay. The personal essay brings the reader closer to the writer, who shares opinions and biases, revealing a perspective on daily life. In the introduction to *The Art of the Personal Essay*, Phillip Lopate explains, "The hallmark of the personal essay is its intimacy. The writer seems to be speaking directly into your ear, confiding everything from gossip to wisdom. . . . At the core . . . is the supposition that there is a certain unity to human experience."

Point of View and Voice

In nonfiction the point of view or perspective of the *author* affects the voice the reader hears. How the speaker (author or narrator) views a topic and feels about it is reflected in the sound of the writing; the voice may be objective or highly subjective or somewhere in between. To analyze point of view and voice, you might consider the following questions:

- How friendly or formal, close or distant does the speaker sound?
- How is the subject treated? Seriously? With amused detachment? How?
- How does the speaker seem to feel about the subject?
- Does the voice seem objective? Somewhat partial? Biased?
- If the topic is controversial, do you agree or disagree? Why?

In "A Ride through Spain," a descriptive essay by Truman Capote, the reader hears a light, conversational voice like that of a friend. Capote writes from the point of view of a passenger on the train. His voice reveals his enjoyment of the experience. The opening and ending of this informal essay appear here:

A Ride through Spain

Certainly the train was old. The seats sagged like the jowls of a bulldog, windows were out and strips of adhesive held together those that were left; in the corridor a prowling cat appeared to be hunting mice, and it was not unreasonable to assume his search would be rewarded.

Slowly, as though the engine were harnessed to elderly coolies, we crept out of Granada. The southern sky was as white and burning as a desert; there was one cloud, and it drifted like a traveling oasis. . . .

It was like a party, and we all drifted back to the train as though each of us wished to be the last to leave. The old man, with my shirt like a grand turban on his head, was put into a first-class carriage. . . .

The train moved away so slowly butterflies blew in and out the windows.

Imagery

In the excerpt from "A Ride through Spain," Capote uses concrete images and figurative language, which enable the reader to share the train ride vicariously. Frequent similes ("sagged like the jowls of a bulldog") and other devices enable the reader to visualize the trip and to sense the camaraderie of fellow travelers. Assonance and other devices of sound contribute to the images and movement. For example, the last sentence reflects the movement of the train: the long *o* in *so* and *slowly* slows the rate of speech as do the three syllables of *butterflies* and the phrase *in and out the windows*. In fact, the language is rather like that of a lyric poem. Figurative language and concrete images as well as symbols are often used in essays and other nonfiction writing.

The next essay, "A Very Human Search for Security," by Ellen Goodman, opens with imagery, which catches the reader's interest and emphasizes the main idea. Goodman is a Pulitzer Prize–winning journalist whose syndicated column appears in hundreds of newspapers across the country. "A Very Human Search for Security" was written in 1978 and reprinted in *Close to Home* in 1979.

A Very Human Search for Security

There is usually a steady flurry of mail in drifts along the edges of my desk. But a recent column on Sen. Edward Brooke's divorce seemed to seed one of those abrupt changes in weather: Suddenly, there was a blizzard.

Some of it was predictable fallout: the letters in defense of the senator or in sympathy with the wife, the letters deploring the state of politics and those worrying about public knowledge of private lives.

But the bulk—and I mean the *bulk*—contained long, personal tales by or about other older women who were also divorce statistics. They bore testimony to the syndrome that Tom Wolfe once described as "wife-shucking," or what others more politely label "the plight of the displaced homemaker."

There was depressing sameness to the stories—new variations of old themes. "My mother was one of the women who grew up obeying all the rules of the game," wrote a 30-year-old daughter of a newly "shucked" wife from Indiana. "When she was 56, the rules were changed. Life really isn't fair."

"I am a member of that [Mrs. Brooke's] generation of women," wrote a Houstonite. "I call us discards. It's like being a skilled worker when automation takes over. I have all the old skills and nobody wants them anymore."

Those portraits, testimonials of a generation's worst pain, had a cumulative effect on me, as a reader. In fact, I think that it is impossible to overestimate the impact of this massive role model of despair—the bereft older homemaker—on younger women and on the general society. It seems to determine many of the anxieties we live with, and the decisions we make every day.

The most widespread and dramatic of these decisions can be read in black and white, in numbers and percentages. Sometime this summer, for instance, the Census Bureau, clicking away like that old population clock, will register a new American reality. On that day, half of all the adult women in the country will be holding jobs. The largest increases in this figure have come from the younger women. The biggest percentage jump in any category has been among mothers of pre-school children.

The reasons behind the figures are, I know, largely those of economic need. But there is an emotional component to the 50 percent—a very human search for security.

Psychologist Abraham Maslow once suggested that there is a hierarchy of human needs. At the most basic level, along with the necessity of food and shelter, is the need for safety: sameness. But what has happened is that, slowly, women have relocated their sense of security. Once it was firmly lodged in marriage. Now it seems to rest increasingly outside the home—in jobs or, at least, job potential.

I don't know exactly how much of this shift in perspective is due to divorce—the experience or the specter—but I know how vivid our fearful image is of the homemaker without a husband. The widow, or the 60-year-old divorcée sent from court (unlike Mrs. Brooke) into the "independence" of poverty and loneliness, is haunting.

Faced with this sort of image, some younger women can hide their anxiety and even don the costume of the Total Woman as a security blanket. But more of us seek this thing, this security, in the one realistic way offered by society: employment.

It's not that we are naive. We know that jobs, like marriages, can also collapse. And we know that work doesn't immunize people from personal pain.

But it is a hedge against the risks of life. Even at its worst, work seems to be an immense addition to the arsenal of self-protection. It offers a shield of paychecks and friends and identity.

Questions for Discussion

1. From whose point of view is the essay written?

2. What figurative language do you notice in the first paragraph? What is the effect? (Clue: What is being compared?)

3. How does the author's voice sound?

4. What are the connotations of "wife-shucking" as opposed to "plight of the displaced homemaker"? How do these terms influence the reader?

5. What is the prime fear of older, unskilled women who have been "shucked"?

6. Goodman points out that this fear has both economic and emotional components. What does she mean?

7. In Goodman's eyes, what are the advantages work provides?

8. Would you categorize the essay as formal, informal, or personal?

9. Although the essay was written two decades ago, do you think it applies today? Why or why not?

10. Do you have any other comments?

The next essay, "Were Dinosaurs Dumb?" was written by Stephen Jay Gould, a paleontologist at Harvard University. Gould has published over one hundred scholarly articles in scientific journals and several full-length works. "Were Dinosaurs Dumb?" was first published in 1978 in *Natural History* magazine and was reprinted in *The Panda's Thumb*. Gould disputes the theory that dinosaurs were of low intelligence and argues that there is a valid alternative explanation for the size of dinosaurs' brains. See whether or not you agree with his line of reasoning.

Were Dinosaurs Dumb?

When Mohammed Ali flunked his army intelligence test, he quipped (with a wit that belied his performance on the exam): "I only said I was the greatest; I never said I was the smartest." In our metaphors and fairy tales, size and power are almost always balanced by a want of intelligence. Cunning is the refuge of the little guy. Think of Br'er Rabbit and Br'er Bear; David smiting Goliath with a sling shot; Jack chopping down the beanstalk. Slow wit is the tragic flaw of a giant.

The discovery of dinosaurs in the nineteenth century provided, or so it appeared, a quintessential case for the negative correlation of size and smarts. With their pea brains and giant bodies, dinosaurs became a symbol of lumbering stupidity. Their extinction seemed only to confirm their flawed design.

Dinosaurs were not even granted the usual solace of a giant—great physical prowess. God maintained a discreet silence about the brains of behemoth, but he certainly marveled at its strength: "Lo, now, his strength is in his loins, and his force is in the navel of his belly. He moveth his tail like a cedar. . . . His bones are as strong pieces of brass; his bones are like bars of iron [Job 40:16–18]." Dinosaurs, on the other hand, have usually been reconstructed as slow and clumsy. In the standard illustration, *Brontosaurus* wades in a murky pond because he cannot hold up his own weight on land.

Popularizations for grade school curricula provide a good illustration of prevailing orthodoxy. I still have my third grade copy (1948 edition) of Bertha Morris Parker's *Animals of Yesterday*, stolen, I am forced to suppose, from P.S. 26, Queens (sorry Mrs. McInerney). In it, boy (teleported back to the Jurassic) meets brontosaur:

> It is huge, and you can tell from the size of its head that it must be stupid. . . . This giant animal moves about very slowly as it eats. No wonder it moves slowly! Its huge feet are very heavy, and its great tail is not easy to pull around. You are not surprised that the thunder lizard likes to stay in the water so that the water will help it hold up its huge body. . . . Giant dinosaurs were once the lords of the earth. Why did they disappear? You can probably guess part of the answer— their bodies were too large for their brains. If their bodies had been smaller, and their brains larger, they might have lived on.

Dinosaurs have been making a strong comeback of late, in this age of "I'm OK, you're OK." Most paleontologists are now willing to view them as energetic, active, and capable animals. The *Brontosaurus* that wallowed in its pond a generation ago is now running the land, while pairs of males have been seen twining their necks about each other in elaborate sexual combat for access to females (much like the neck wrestling of giraffes). Modern anatomical reconstructions indicate strength and agility, and many paleontologists now believe that dinosaurs were warmblooded.

The idea of warmblooded dinosaurs has captured the public imagination and received a torrent of press coverage. Yet another vindication of dinosaurian capability has received very little attention, although I regard it as equally significant. I refer to the issue of stupidity and its correlation with size. The revisionist interpretation, which I support in this column, does not enshrine dinosaurs as paragons of intellect, but it does maintain that they were not small brained after all. They had the "right-sized" brains for reptiles of their body size.

I don't wish to deny that the flattened, minuscule head of large bodied *Stegosaurus* houses little brain from our subjective, top-heavy perspective, but I do wish to assert that we should not expect more of the beast. First of all, large animals have relatively smaller brains than related, small animals. The correlation of brain size with body size among kindred animals (all reptiles, all mammals, for example) is remarkably regular. As we move from small to large animals, from mice to elephants or small lizards to Komodo dragons, brain size increases, but not so fast as body size. In other words, bodies grow faster than brains, and large animals have low ratios of brain weight to body weight. In fact, brains grow only about two-thirds as fast as bodies. Since we have no reason to believe that large animals are consistently stupider than their smaller relatives, we must conclude that large animals require relatively less brain to do as well as smaller animals. If we do not recognize this relationship, we are likely to underestimate the mental power of very large animals, dinosaurs in particular.

Second, the relationship between brain and body size is not identical in all groups of vertebrates. All share the same rate of relative decrease in brain size, but small mammals have much larger brains than small reptiles of the same body weight. This discrepancy is maintained at all larger body weights, since brain size increases at the same rate in both groups—two-thirds as fast as body size.

Put these two facts together—all large animals have relatively small brains, and reptiles have much smaller brains than mammals at any common body weight—and what should we expect from a normal, large reptile? The answer, of course, is a brain of very modest size. No living reptile even approaches a middle-sized dinosaur in bulk, so we have no modern standard to serve as a model for dinosaurs.

Fortunately, our imperfect fossil record has, for once, not severely disappointed us in providing data about fossil brains. Superbly preserved skulls have been found for many species of dinosaurs, and cranial capacities can be measured. (Since brains do not fill craniums in reptiles, some creative, although not unreasonable, manipulation must be applied to estimate brain size from the hole within a skull.) With these data, we have a clear test for the conventional hypothesis of dinosaurian stupidity. We should agree, at the outset, that a reptilian standard is the only proper one—it is surely irrelevant that dinosaurs had smaller brains than people or whales. We have abundant data on the relationship of brain and body size in modern reptiles. Since we know that brains increase two-thirds as fast as bodies as we move from small to large living species, we can extrapolate this rate to dinosaurian sizes and ask whether dinosaur brains match what we would expect of living reptiles if they grew so large.

Harry Jerison studied the brain sizes of ten dinosaurs and found that they fell right on the extrapolated reptilian curve. Dinosaurs did not have small brains; they maintained just the right-sized brains for reptiles of their dimensions. So much for Ms. Parker's explanation of their demise.

Jerison made no attempt to distinguish among various kinds of dinosaurs; ten species distributed over six major groups scarcely provide a proper basis for comparison. Recently, James A. Hopson of the University of Chicago gathered more data and made a remarkable and satisfying discovery.

Hopson needed a common scale for all dinosaurs. He therefore compared each dinosaur brain with the average reptilian brain we would expect at its body weight. If the dinosaur falls on the standard reptilian curve, its brain receives a value of 1.0 (called an encephalization quotient, or EQ—the ratio of actual brain to expected brain for a standard reptile of the same body weight). Dinosaurs lying above the curve (more brain than expected in a standard reptile of the same body weight) receive values in excess of 1.0, while those below the curve measure less than 1.0.

Hopson found that the major groups of dinosaurs can be ranked by increasing values of average EQ. This ranking corresponds perfectly with inferred speed, agility and behavioral complexity in feeding (or avoiding the prospect of becoming a meal). The giant sauropods, *Brontosaurus* and its allies, have the lowest EQ's—0.20 to 0.35. They must have moved fairly slowly and without great maneuverability. They probably escaped predation by virtue of their bulk alone, much as elephants do today. The armored ankylosaurs and stegosaurs come next with EQ's of 0.52 to 0.56. These animals, with their heavy armor, probably relied largely upon passive defense, but the clubbed tail of ankylosaurs and the spiked tail of stegosaurs imply some active fighting and increased behavioral complexity.

The ceratopsians rank next at about 0.7 to 0.9. Hopson remarks: "The larger ceratopsians, with their great horned heads, relied on active defensive strategies and presumably required somewhat greater agility than the tail-weaponed forms, both in fending off predators and in intraspecific combat bouts. The smaller ceratopsians, lacking true horns, would have relied on sensory acuity and speed to escape from predators." The ornithopods (duckbills and their allies) were the brainiest herbivores, with EQ's from 0.85 to 1.5. They relied upon "acute senses and relatively fast speeds" to elude carnivores. Flight seems to require more acuity and agility than standing defense. Among ceratopsians, small, hornless, and presumably fleeing *Protoceratops* had a higher EQ than great three-horned *Triceratops*.

Carnivores have higher EQ's than herbivores, as in modern vertebrates. Catching a rapidly moving or stoutly fighting prey demands a good deal more upstairs than plucking the right kind of plant. The giant theropods (*Tyrannosaurus* and its allies) vary from 1.0 to nearly 2.0. Atop the heap, quite appropriately at its small size, rests the little coelurosaur *Stenonychosaurus* with an EQ well above 5.0. Its actively moving quarry, small mammals and birds perhaps, probably posed a greater challenge in discovery and capture than *Triceratops* afforded *Tyrannosaurus*.

I do not wish to make a naive claim that brain size equals intelligence or, in this case, behavioral range and agility (I don't know what intelligence means in humans, much less in a group of extinct reptiles). Variation in brain size within a species has precious little to do with brain power (humans do equally well with 900 or 2,500 cubic centimeters of brain). But comparison across species, when the differences are large, seems reasonable. I do not regard it as irrelevant to our achievements that we so greatly exceed koala bears—much as I love them—in EQ. The sensible ordering among dinosaurs also indicates that even so coarse a measure as brain size counts for something.

If behavioral complexity is one consequence of mental power, then we might expect to uncover among dinosaurs some signs of social behavior that demand coordination, cohesiveness, and recognition. Indeed we do, and it cannot be accidental that these signs were overlooked when dinosaurs labored under the burden of a falsely imposed obtuseness. Multiple trackways have been uncovered, with evidence for more than twenty animals traveling together in parallel movement. Did some dinosaurs live in herds? At the Davenport Ranch sauropod trackway, small footprints lie in the center and larger ones at the periphery. Could it be that some dinosaurs traveled much as some advanced herbivorous mammals do today, with large adults at the borders sheltering juveniles in the center?

In addition, the very structures that seemed most bizarre and useless to older paleontologists—the elaborate crests of hadrosaurs, the frills and horns of ceratopsians, and the nine inches of solid bone above the brain of *Pachycephalosaurus*—now appear to gain a coordinated explanation as devices for sexual display and combat. Pachycephalosaurs may have engaged in head-butting contests much as mountain sheep do today. The crests of some hadrosaurs are well designed as resonating chambers; did they engage in bellowing matches? The ceratopsian horn and frill may have acted as sword and shield in the battle for mates. Since such behavior is not only intrinsically complex, but also implies an elaborate social system, we would scarcely expect to find it in a group of animals barely muddling through at a moronic level.

But the best illustration of dinosaurian capability may well be the fact most often cited against them—their demise. Extinction, for most people, carries many of the connotations attributed to sex not so long ago—a rather disreputable business, frequent in occurrence, but not to anyone's credit, and certainly not to be discussed in proper circles. But, like sex, extinction is an ineluctable part of life. It is the ultimate fate of all species, not the lot of unfortunate and ill-designed creatures. It is no sign of failure.

The remarkable thing about dinosaurs is not that they became extinct, but that they dominated the earth for so long. Dinosaurs held sway for 100 million years while mammals, all the while, lived as small animals in the interstices of their world. After 70 million years on top, we mammals have an excellent track record and good prospects for the future, but we have yet to display the staying power of dinosaurs.

People, on this criterion, are scarcely worth mentioning—5 million years perhaps since *Australopithecus*, a mere 50,000 for our own species, *Homo sapiens*. Try the ultimate test within our system of values: Do you know anyone who would wager a substantial sum, even at favorable odds, on the proposition that *Homo sapiens* will last longer than *Brontosaurus*?

Questions for Discussion

1. What stereotype does Gould topple (first paragraph)?
2. How has the thinking of many paleontologists changed concerning dinosaurs?
3. What does Gould point out about the ratio of body size to intelligence in large and small animals?
4. How do brain sizes of mammals and reptiles differ?
5. Summarize the research of Harry Jerison and Hopson. What does Gould conclude about variation in brain size from these findings?
6. What evidence of behavioral complexity in dinosaurs does Gould point out?

7. What challenge does Gould issue at the end?

8. Since this essay was written in 1978, there has been considerable written discussion about possible reasons for the demise of dinosaurs. Are you aware of any other theories?

9. How do the voices of Goodman and Gould differ in these essays?

10. On the whole, would you say Gould's essay is less or more formal than Goodman's? Why?

WRITING A RESPONSE TO AN ESSAY

When you are asked to react in writing to a question, an event, or an essay, more than a visceral response is required. A reaction is a short thoughtful commentary that considers the facts, their meaning, and possible consequences of an action. Responding to an essay or other literary work requires that you consider the main idea, the writer's point of view, logic, and accuracy.

A paper of reaction is similar to other expository papers in many respects; but reactions differ in purpose, length, and formality. The purpose is to present a point of view and persuade the reader that the response is sound and reasonable. A reaction paper is an analysis, complete with examples that are usually drawn from the writer's experience. Sometimes references to historical figures or literary characters are made. Ideally, a reaction paper reviews and interprets the facts, then presents an opinion and discusses possible implications—although not necessarily in that order.

Papers of reaction tend to be brief, one or two pages. The level of formality may vary according to the subject and the assignment. For example, some assignments may ask for an example of how the idea might be applied to a field of study. Reaction papers for college classes are usually expected to be serious and focused. Although a bit of humor may be appropriate, beware of too much. Humor could distract and conflict with the intent of the assignment.

Although a paper of reaction does not require research, it does require a study of the original source, careful consideration of the main points, and a well-reasoned opinion, based on fact.

Prewriting

Copying and enlarging an essay will allow you more space to make prewriting notes. First, read the essay quickly to gain a general impression. Then reread more slowly, underlining key points. Write brief comments as they occur to you. Jot brief questions in the margin, and then watch to see if the author answers them. Place a question mark beside any statement that seems doubtful or inconsistent. Circle unfamiliar words and look them up after you reread. Write any definitions near the word, at the bottom, or on a separate sheet. The following questions will also be helpful as you prewrite:

1. What is the main point of the essay?
2. What support does the author offer?
3. Is the support convincing? Why or why not?
4. Do you see any logical inconsistencies?
5. Are there implications, side effects, or other possible consequences that should be discussed?
6. Has the writer omitted any significant facts that you are aware of?
7. Is there anything you would like to know more about?
8. What do you find especially interesting or challenging?
9. Is there any aspect you particularly like or dislike?
10. How might the ideas in the essay be applied to your field of study?
11. How would you describe the author's voice?
12. Does the philosophy behind the essay remind you of another writer or source? If so, how?

Drafting

To be sure you clearly understand the writer's point of view and reasoning, begin by drafting a brief summary of the thesis and significant points. Writing a short summary is a vital step not only to clarify but also to use later in the introduction. Next, formulate your thesis, reacting to (agreeing or disagreeing) the writer's major point or position on the issue. After that, look over your prewriting notes to gather material for discussion.

At this point you might start a working outline: just copy your thesis at the top of a clean sheet and list the writer's significant points in the order presented. Leave several spaces between points to insert your thoughts and comments, which will become the body of your paper. Often these can be arranged according to importance.

If you are responding in the affirmative, you might develop your paper in several ways, depending on what is appropriate. If the topic is relevant to your life, you might discuss the implications for you. Just ask yourself: "How might this apply to me?" "What suggestions might I use?" Your answers may help to develop your prewriting notes. Or if the essay discusses a social problem, you might propose a possible alternative to alleviate the problem. Whatever the subject, just remember that a reaction goes beyond summarizing the source; you contribute an informed opinion, using facts, reasons, and examples.

If you disagree with the writer, then your task is more complex. Then you will need to construct a reasonable argument with adequate support. In your discussion, you will be evaluating the opposing view and citing logical reasons to support your point of view. Although you may refer to other works previously read, the assignment rarely requires research. You draw upon your values and experience for support and examples. If you do consult outside sources, however, you will need to document them properly (see chapters 22 and 23). If you will be constructing an argument, see chapter 20, which explains the basics of argument.

Whether you agree or disagree with the original source, it is essential to maintain control of your written voice. A reaction paper is expected to be controlled, objective, and appropriate. The ending may be brief, merely a sentence or two that gives a sense of closure. If you are writing an argument, you will need to restate your position.

 Checklist for Revising a Reaction

As you revise your reaction, you will need to give extra care to checking the organization, development, logic, and voice. Accuracy and appropriateness are vital. The questions below should be helpful:

1. Do I have a clear thesis?

2. Have I actually contributed to the discussion, gone beyond a summary?

3. Is my written voice appropriate?

4. If I am disagreeing, have I responded to the writer's significant points objectively?

5. Does my reaction have a clear logical order?

6. Is each of my points supported adequately?

7. Are facts correctly stated?

8. Are inferences logical and identifiable?

9. If I have alluded to other writers' works, have I given credit to them? If I consulted outside sources, are they properly documented?

10. Is there anything else that should be said?

A SAMPLE PAPER OF REACTION

The student writer whose paper follows plans to become a teacher. Reacting to a reading on the philosophy of Martin Buber, Scott Allen relates the main principles to classroom teachers by presenting impressions, drawing comparisons, and pointing out implications:

A Reaction to Martin Buber's Philosophy

[SUMMARY/COMPARISON]

Martin Buber's philosophy, which seems similar to Plato's in many respects, has important applications for classroom teachers. Although the philosophers disagree about the source of goodness, they both believe that goodness is an absolute, quite distinct from people. They believe we strive to attain goodness by making wise choices.

Buber feels that the formal teaching of values is worthless. Nonetheless, he believes that the teacher presents a selection from the real world and acts as a model to the pupil (indirect teaching). Buber develops the concept of "inclusiveness," which is the complete realization of the submissive person (i.e., the student).

To develop the mental powers to make good choices, Plato suggests the (direct) study of mathematics, philosophy, and other disciplines. Plato attempts to outline an ideal society where everyone can live peacefully and develop to the fullest capacity.

[REACTION AND IMPLICATIONS]

In the educational situation, this inclusiveness means that educators must beware of the dangers of such a relationship. They must refrain from arbitrariness and must exercise responsibility in interpreting the real world to the pupil. I agree: Teachers should consider the needs and rights of their pupils and try to respond in a way that will benefit. This goal requires not only responsibility in the selection of classroom material but also fairness in grading, settling disputes, and other situations which arise. I concur with Buber's theory about the teaching of values: values are caught, not taught. A teacher should be of good character and should act as a role model for students.

How can educators accomplish this responsibility? Buber says they can do it by conscious and willed selection. In other words, educators should know what they want to achieve and select the proper means to achieve it. They should examine their basic principles and understand what is happening—not merely what they think they are doing. They must be objective as well as responsible.

Finally, Buber points out that "Life lived in freedom is personal responsibility or it is a pathetic farce" (27). Rousseau writes in a similar vein when he says that pupils are obliged to develop their intellectual powers to learn a vocation and provide for themselves. Like Buber, Rousseau is greatly concerned about the educator's responsibility of keeping evil away from the pupil. This idea of personal responsibility involves intellectual self-discipline as well as physical self-discipline, but it helps us to gain self-respect and stature in the eyes of others. It helps us to find a purpose beyond ourselves—and perhaps that is what life is really all about.

In short, although Buber's traditional Judeo-Christian philosophy will not appeal to Ayn Rand fans or existentialists with leanings toward Nietzsche or Sartre, I believe it provides an excellent set of principles for undergirding education.

Summary

An essay is a short literary composition, a nonfiction work, on one topic. An essay reveals the author's (and perhaps another's) point of view on one subject. Essays range from formal to informal, from serious to humorous. The personal essay, a subcategory of the informal essay, deals with everyday experience in a confidential manner, using a conversational tone.

In college courses you may be required to write reactions, short papers that respond to ideas in a work. A reaction paper presents a perspective based on logical reasoning. The paper is primarily an informed opinion—a commentary, not just a summary, that analyzes the facts and their implications. Reaction papers require careful reading of the original source. If outside sources are consulted, they must be properly documented.

Key Terms

informal essay   personal essay   implications
formal essay   reaction

Practice

Ideas for Writing Reactions

1. Do you agree or disagree with Goodman's perspective on divorce? Why or why not?

2. React to the changing of social rules as discussed by Goodman or another author.

3. How plausible is Gould's theory about dinosaurs? Why do you think so?

4. Disagree with Gould's belief that *Homo sapiens* will not outlast *Brontosaurus*. Supply facts, reasons, and examples for your argument.

5. Listen to a television or radio talk show host and react to a view about a significant issue.

6. Scan newspapers, magazines, or electronic bulletin boards for positions on issues, and react to one.

7. React to an unusual news item.

8. Turn to the opinion page of a newspaper. Read the columns and letters there. Then write a reaction to an opinion.

9. Has a poem, story, or other piece of literature caused you to ponder an aspect of your life? Might you find a topic there?

10. What other idea might you react to?

CHAPTER 27

Reading and Responding to Fiction

Great literature is simply language charged
with meaning to the utmost possible degree.

—Ezra Pound, "How to Read,"
The ABC of Reading

Why do we read literature? The written word can be far more alluring than a video or movie screen. Literature challenges us to create a world on the screen of the mind. There we can meet intriguing characters, participate in an exciting plot, explore new ideas and sensations. We can watch and wonder about the unfamiliar and untried without undergoing the risks of reality. More than this, we can share moments of human experience that help us reflect on the shape and direction of our own lives.

Literature encourages us to consider large questions of existence: "Do we really have choices, or is life one great predestined plan?" "What is the purpose of living?" "What is worthwhile?" "What responsibilities do we have?" "What is happiness?" Literature allows us to explore common dilemmas such as "Is it wise to stand up for personal beliefs that differ from those of the mainstream?" "What causes conflict between people who love each other?" Literature enables us to laugh at the foolishness and smile at the cleverness of human behavior and thought.

Literature often strips away layers that disguise intentions, motives, and values; it distinguishes the insignificant from the significant. Reading literature helps us to encounter diverse cultures and viewpoints—to confront and interpret reality in a new light. But for literature to affect us deeply, we need to be engaged mentally as well as emotionally.

WHAT IS THE ROLE OF THE READER?

The reader plays an active role while reading literature. Meaning is not limited to the text of a work. As we read, we view ideas through our own window of experience—interpreting, inferring, evaluating—creating meaning. Our view is colored by our individual perception of the world, the topic, the treatment of the text, and the voice of the narrator. Many people assume a literary work has a single meaning or interpretation. The truth is that there is no one right answer about what a work means. Often a piece of literature is subtle, containing meanings of which the author is unaware.

Although readers create meaning to some extent, this privilege is not an invitation to pull a passage out of context and distort it. Evidence found in the work must support any interpretation. To achieve a valid interpretation of a work, the perceptive reader looks for a series of clues, a chain of evidence, upon which to base an interpretation so that it is consistent with the total context. The best interpretations consider the entire work, not just isolated parts, and offer an explanation of passages that may seem contradictory or inconsistent.

Whether you read and write about fiction, drama, or poetry, you may be assured that all three have much in common despite obvious differences in literary form. All have unity—one central idea and a pattern of development. All use figurative language and concrete images in varying degrees. All have rhythm, although rhythm is less marked in prose than in poetry. And all may consider universal questions as well as contemporary issues. This chapter focuses on analyzing fiction, but you can use many of the strategies presented here to analyze drama and poetry as well.

READING AND ANALYZING FICTION

When you read a short story or novel, do you curl up in a comfortable chair and enjoy the tale? Or do you anxiously pore over every word and take elaborate notes that may never be used? For a short work, starting at the story level is not only more fun but also more sensible. Note-taking during a first reading can be annoying and impractical. Once you gain a sense of the entire story, you can quickly reread and look more closely at individual elements. (For convenience, make a copy to take notes on.)

When assigned a novel, however, you can save time by making brief notations, writing questions in the margins and marking noteworthy passages with brackets during the first reading. If you do not own the book, list page numbers of significant items on file cards with an identifying phrase. Then insert them with one edge (your subject note) protruding from the top of the book. That way you can find passages quickly. Since many instructors require page numbers of citations, start keeping track of them early. Once you have finished, you will want to think about individual elements in terms of the whole.

Elements of Fiction

When analyzing fiction, you will be focusing on seven basic elements: point of view, setting, plot, character, symbolism, irony, and theme. Point of view is revealed through the narrator's voice.

Point of View   An author usually selects either a first-person or third-person point of view for the narrator. This means that the narrator's voice is *not* the voice of the author. The narrator may be one of the characters or someone outside the work. When the story is presented through the eyes of *one* character, you have access to only one person's thoughts and observations. F. Scott Fitzgerald's *The Great Gatsby* opens with the narrator reminiscing:

> In my younger and more vulnerable years my father gave me some advice that I've been turning over in my mind ever since.
> "Whenever you feel like criticizing any one," he told me, "just remember that all the people in this world haven't had the advantages that you've had."
> He didn't say any more, but we've always been unusually communicative in a reserved way, and I understood that he meant a great deal more than that. In consequence, I'm inclined to reserve all judgments, a habit that has opened up many curious natures to me and also made me the victim of not a few veteran bores.

The narrator of a story written in the third person, however, is outside the action. Usually, a third-person narrator enters the mind of just one character. But a third-person narrator with *limited omniscience* enters the minds of several characters. Sometimes a third-person narrator is *omniscient* or all-knowing. You might think of an omniscient narrator as standing on a hill, looking down into the lives and minds of the characters.

Sometimes a story is told from *multiple viewpoints*. Two or more characters act as narrators, each giving a different version. In William Faulkner's novel, *The Sound and the Fury*, four narrators give four points of view, each presenting bits and pieces of the same story. In addition, an appendix presents more details of the fictional family's history from an omniscient point of view. To discern the "truth" of this puzzling tale, the reader must filter the points of view and reconcile them with the history. Gauging the truthfulness and accuracy of a narrator, particularly one who is a character, is not always simple. Like human beings, characters may misjudge, understate, overstate, or deceive.

Setting   The time, place, weather, and culture of the characters make up the *setting*. Included in setting, too, are the objects and articles the characters have and use. Symbolism is often intermingled with setting to create a mood. For example, Thomas Hardy's novels take place on wild and stormy moors, which set the scene for passion and outbursts of temper. As you read, note the setting of each action. What is the mood? What objects are present? What familial, social, political, or religious obligations or conditions exist? How do they influence the plot and characters?

Plot   The series of actions or events that occur in a narrative is called the *plot*. Broadly defined, plot includes not only physical action, but also words and thoughts. The action arises from circumstance as well as from human motivation. The characters face a problem or a conflict. How they respond depends on the circumstances, their emotional makeup, and their values. Thus plot and character are intertwined. The physical action in *Romeo and Juliet*, for example, would have had little meaning without the thoughts and feelings of the hero and heroine. Although a narrator may explain part of a plot, readers should watch for clues to interpret meaning.

Plots generally take the form of straightforward narratives. Sometimes, however, they may be structured as letters, diaries, or other "found" writings. For example, in Daniel Keyes's *Flowers for Algernon*, the diary form springs from the plot. The main character, a mentally handicapped man named Charlie, is asked by his doctor to prepare progress reports during the course of an experimental treatment. Early entries begin on a rudimentary level:

progris riport 2—martch 6

Dr. Strauss says I shud rite down what I think and evrey thing that happins to me from now on. I dont know why but he says its importint so they will see if they will use me. I hope they use me. Miss Kinnian says maybe they can make me smart. I want to be smart. My name is Charlie Gordon. I am 37 years old and 2 weeks ago was my birthday. I have nuthing more to rite now so I will close for today.

This early entry reveals not only Charlie's low level of understanding and education but also his desire to learn. Although Charlie is unable to explain what is happening, the phrase "use me" suggests to the alert reader that Dr. Strauss's purpose may not be in Charlie's best interest. After surgery and intensive training, Charlie's intelligence and learning escalate—a process revealed by later diary entries that are longer and more explicit. Toward the end, as Charlie deteriorates, the concluding entries parallel his condition.

When authors use *foreshadowing* in a plot, they scatter clues that hint of events to come. For example, in *Flowers for Algernon*, when Algernon the mouse begins to deteriorate, the alert reader suspects that Charlie will experience the same symptoms; for both have had the same operation. The drastic changes in Algernon foreshadow the plot's irrevocable conclusion.

Characters   The people in a narrative are the characters. To seem realistic, they are endowed with certain qualities and quirks. They may be portrayed as primarily good or evil, weak or strong, serious or fun-loving—or as having some other trait. Major characters are usually revealed indirectly through behavior whereas minor characters tend to be revealed directly through explanation. *Round characters* change and mature; they learn from events and circumstances. *Flat characters*, usually minor characters, do not change or grow. They may lack insight, remaining unaware and insensitive.

Symbolism   A symbol is something material that represents something else, usually an abstraction. A symbol may be a person, a place, an object, an action, or a situation. *Universal symbols* are recognized worldwide, regardless of culture. One common example is ordinary water. Long used in the sacrament of baptism, water is universally regarded as a symbol both of purification and of life. More specifically, a bubbling fountain may represent youth and optimism. A stagnant pond may symbolize contamination or ebbing of life. Water may also signify sexuality. For example, lovers may meet by a placid lake, a river with rapids, or aboard ship on a storm-tossed sea. The condition of the water symbolizes the status of their relationship. When you think something might be a symbol, place a question mark beside it; or if you understand the symbol, make a note.

Irony   Irony refers to an inconsistency or incongruity between what is believed or expected and what is real. An event that is ironic is painfully contrary to what is expected. This means that simple unexpected events are not necessarily ironic. Sometimes irony takes the form of an unexpected twist of the plot; such *situational irony* is sometimes found in the stories of Edgar Allan Poe or the films of Alfred Hitchcock. Using *dramatic irony*, a writer reveals to readers something that one or more characters do not know, which creates suspense. *Verbal irony* involves saying something that is the opposite of what one means. Sarcasm is a form of verbal irony that is fairly easy to detect, but much verbal irony is more subtle.

Writers often use irony to suggest human fallibility—the vanities, unwise judgments, and other limitations that keep us from recognizing the truth around us. Such susceptibility to error is at its most extreme in *cosmic irony*, or irony of fate. Cosmic irony is prevalent in Greek tragedies and other writings; the gods or destiny seem to control events so as to test and frustrate the protagonist.

Theme   The theme or themes are the main ideas embodied in a work. Theme is a universal belief about human life or "the human condition," those experiences that are basic to the human race. Theme may concern good or evil, love or hate, modesty or pride, or some other virtue or vice. Theme may be stated as an observation, insight, doctrine, or general principle. More often than not, theme is implicit. Theme can be implied through a series of events, actions, or dialogue. And sometimes there is more than one theme. In much modern fiction, themes are complex and cannot be reduced to a simple moral as in John Updike's "Still of Some Use," the story that follows.

A Short Story: "Still of Some Use," by John Updike

The short story is an economical way to look at elements of fiction. Good short stories reveal artistry in structure and in form: every word counts. John

Updike, a master of the short story form, graduated from Harvard University and worked on the staff of the *New Yorker* for two years. A prolific writer, his books include eleven collections of short stories, seventeen novels, six volumes of poetry, and a play. "Still of Some Use" was first printed in the *New Yorker* (1980) and later in *Trust Me: Short Stories* (1987):

Still of Some Use

When Foster helped his ex-wife clean out the attic of the house where they had once lived and which she was now selling, they came across dozens of forgotten, broken games. Parcheesi, Monopoly, Lotto; games aping the strategies of the stock market, of crime detection, of real-estate speculation, of international diplomacy and war; games with spinners, dice, lettered tiles, cardboard spacemen, and plastic battleships; games bought in five-and-tens and department stores feverish and musical with Christmas expectations; games enjoyed on the afternoon of a birthday and for a few afternoons thereafter and then allowed, shy of one or two pieces, to drift into closets and toward the attic. Yet, discovered in their bright flat boxes between trunks of outgrown clothes and defunct appliances, the games presented a forceful semblance of value: the springs of their miniature launchers still reacted, the logic of their instructions would still generate suspense, given a chance. "What shall we do with all these games?" Foster shouted, in a kind of agony, to his scattered family as they moved up and down the attic stairs.

"Trash 'em," his younger son, a strapping nineteen, urged.

"Would the Goodwill want them?" asked his ex-wife, still wife enough to think that all of his questions deserved answers. "You used to be able to give things like that to orphanages. But they don't call them orphanages anymore, do they?"

"They call them normal American homes," Foster said.

His older son, now twenty-two, with a cinnamon-colored beard, offered, "They wouldn't work anyhow; they all have something missing. That's how they got to the attic."

"Well, why didn't we throw them away at the time?" Foster asked, and had to answer himself. Cowardice, the answer was. Inertia. Clinging to the past.

His sons, with a shadow of old obedience, came and looked over his shoulder at the sad wealth of abandoned playthings, silently groping with him for the particular happy day connected to this and that pattern of colored squares and arrows. Their lives had touched these tokens and counters once; excitement had flowed along the paths of these stylized landscapes. But the day was gone, and scarcely a memory remained.

"Toss 'em," the younger decreed, in his manly voice. For these days of cleaning out, the boy had borrowed a pickup truck from a friend and parked it on the lawn beneath the attic window, so the smaller items of discard could be tossed directly into it. The bigger items were lugged down the stairs and through the front hall; already the truck was loaded with old mattresses, broken clock-radios, obsolete skis and boots. It was a game of sorts to hit the truck bed with objects dropped from the height of the house. Foster flipped game after game at the target two stories below. When the boxes hit, they exploded, throwing a spray of dice, tokens, counters, and cards into the air and across the lawn. A box called Mousetrap, its lid showing laughing children gathered around a Rube Goldberg device, drifted sideways, struck one side wall of the truck, and spilled its plastic components into a flower bed. A set of something called Drag Race! floated gently as a snowflake before coming to rest, much diminished, on a stained mattress. Foster saw in the depth of downward space the cause of his melancholy: he had not played enough with these games. Now no one wanted to play.

Had he and his wife avoided divorce, of course, these boxes would have continued to gather dust in an undisturbed attic, their sorrow unexposed. The toys of his own childhood still rested in his mother's attic. At his last visit, he had crept up there and wound the spring of a tin Donald Duck; it had responded with an angry clack of its bill and a few stiff strokes on its drum. A tilted board with concentric grooves for marbles still waited in a bushel basket with his alphabet blocks and lead airplanes—waited for his childhood to return.

His ex-wife paused where he squatted at the attic window and asked him, "What's the matter?"

"Nothing. These games weren't used much."

"I know. It happens fast. You better stop now; it's making you too sad."

Behind him, his family had cleaned out the attic; the slant-ceilinged rooms stood empty, with drooping insulation.

"How can you bear it?" he asked, of the emptiness.

"Oh, it's fun," she said, "once you get into it. Off with the old, on with the new. The new people seem nice. They have *little* children."

He looked at her and wondered whether she was being brave or truly hard-hearted. The attic trembled slightly. "That's Ted," she said.

She had acquired a boy friend, a big athletic accountant fleeing from domestic embarrassments in a neighboring town. When Ted slammed the kitchen door two stories below, the glass shade of a kerosene lamp that, though long unused, Foster hadn't had the heart to throw out of the window vibrated in its copper clips, emitting a thin note like a trapped wasp's song. Time for Foster to go. His dusty knees creaked when he stood. His ex-wife's eager steps raced ahead of him down through the emptied house. He followed, carrying the lamp, and set it finally on the bare top of a bookcase he had once built, on the first-floor landing. He remembered screwing the top board, a prize piece of knot-free pine, into place from underneath, so not a nailhead marred its smoothness.

After all the vacant rooms and halls, the kitchen seemed indecently full of heat and life. "Dad, want a beer?" the bearded son asked. "Ted brought some." The back of the boy's hand, holding forth the dewy can, blazed with fine ginger hairs. His girl friend, wearing gypsy earrings and a NO NUKES sweatshirt, leaned against the disconnected stove, her hair in a bandanna and a black smirch becomingly placed on one temple. From the kind way she smiled at Foster, he felt this party was making room for him.

"No, I better go."

Ted shook Foster's hand, as he always did. He had a thin pink skin and silver hair whose fluffy waves seemed mechanically induced. Foster could look him in the eye no longer than he could gaze at the sun. He wondered how such a radiant brute had got into such a tame line of work. Ted had not helped with the attic today because he had been off in his old town, visiting his teen-aged twins. "I hear you did a splendid job today," he announced.

"They did," Foster said. "I wasn't much use. I just sat there stunned. All these things I had forgotten buying."

"Some were presents," his son reminded him. He passed the can his father had snubbed to his mother, who took it and tore up the tab with that defiant-sounding *pssff*. She had never liked beer, yet tipped the can to her mouth.

"Give me one sip," Foster begged, and took the can from her and drank a long swallow. When he opened his eyes, Ted's big hand was cupped under Mrs. Foster's chin while his thumb rubbed away a smudge of dirt along her jaw which Foster had not noticed. This protective gesture made her face look small, pouty, and frail. Ted, Foster noticed now, was dressed with a certain comical perfection in a banker's Saturday outfit—softened blue jeans, crisp tennis sneakers, lumberjack shirt with cuffs folded back. The youthful outfit accented his age, his hypertensive flush. Foster saw them suddenly as a touching, aging couple, and this perception seemed permission to go.

He handed back the can.

"Thanks for your help," his former wife said.

"Yes, we do thank you," Ted said.

"Talk to Tommy," she unexpectedly added, in a lowered voice. She was still sending out trip wires to slow Foster's departures. "This is harder on him than he shows."

Ted looked at his watch, a fat, black-faced thing he could swim under water with. "I said to him coming in, 'Don't dawdle till the dump closes.'"

"He loafed all day," his brother complained, "mooning over old stuff, and now he's going to screw up getting to the dump."

"He's very sensi-tive," the visiting gypsy said, with a strange chiming brightness, as if repeating something she had heard.

Outside, the boy was picking up litter that had fallen wide of the truck. Foster helped him. In the grass there were dozens of tokens and dice. Some were engraved with curious little faces—Olive Oyl, Snuffy Smith, Dagwood—and others with hieroglyphs—numbers, diamonds, spades, hexagons—whose code was lost. He held out a handful for Tommy to see. "Can you remember what these were for?"

"Comic-Strip Lotto," the boy said without hesitation. "And a game called Gambling Fools there was a kind of slot machine for." The light of old payoffs flickered in his eyes as he gazed down at the rubble in his father's hand. Though Foster was taller, the boy was broader in the shoulders, and growing. "Want to ride with me to the dump?" Tommy asked.

"I would, but I better go." He, too, had a new life to lead. By being on this forsaken property at all, Foster was in a sense on the wrong square, if not *en prise*. He remembered how once he had begun to teach this boy chess, but in the sadness of watching him lose—the little furry bowed head frowning above his trapped king— the lessons had stopped.

Foster tossed the tokens into the truck; they rattled to rest on the metal. "This depresses you?" he asked his son.

"Naa." The boy amended, "Kind of."

"You'll feel great," Foster promised him, "coming back with a clean truck. I used to love it at the dump, all that old happiness heaped up, and the seagulls."

"It's changed since you left. They have all these new rules. The lady there yelled at me last time, for putting stuff in the wrong place."

"She did?"

"Yeah, it was scary." Seeing his father waver, he added, "It'll only take twenty minutes." Though broad of build, Tommy had beardless cheeks and, between thickening eyebrows, a trace of that rounded, faintly baffled blankness babies have, that wrinkles before they cry.

"O.K.," Foster said. "You win. I'll come along. I'll protect you."

"Still of Some Use" is a puzzling work because so much that is important is left unsaid. The reader must watch for clues and connections and ponder their meaning. As you make inferences, be sure to base each one on evidence. Qualify your statements to make them tentative.

Questions to Analyze "Still of Some Use"

1. How was Foster's former marriage like the items in the attic? (One clue: Examine paragraph one. Which words might also apply to the marriage?)
2. When Foster shouts, "What shall we do with all these games?" what does he reveal?
3. What does Foster discover as he flips the games down to the truck?
4. What might be the significance of the bookcase and Foster's old toys? (Clues: Workmanship on bookcase and condition of toys. How do they compare to the condition of the marriage?)
5. How does Foster feel about his ex-wife? What makes you think so?
6. Why might Foster's wife drink beer when she does not like it? (Note "parched face.") Why might she share it with him?
7. Only one of Foster's family members is named. What does the lack of names imply?
8. What change does Foster show in his conversation with Tommy?
9. What else do you notice?
10. What themes do you see in the story?

PREPARING AN ANALYSIS OF FICTION

A paper of analysis or "paper of explication" examines the form of a work and explains how the elements contribute to meaning. It is not enough to discuss separate parts; you also need to consider how they affect the entire work. You might discuss the influence of point of view, setting, plot, characterization, symbolism, irony, theme, or a combination of these.

Before you start, a few precautions are in order. First, avoid giving the impression that there is only one valid interpretation of a work. Shun phrases such as "obviously" and "it is evident that." Second, be serious and professional in analyzing the work; avoid harsh criticism or sweet adoration. Third, don't second-guess an author's intent or give the impression of reading his or her mind. Instead, explain your perception of the work.

Writing about Point of View

A narrator may describe the story from inside or outside the action. The following example from a student paper focuses on the perspective of the lonely narrator who is outside the family circle and other groups, looking in. Gradually, the perspective of *The Grass Harp* changes, and the development of the central character, Collin, changes, too:

> *The Grass Harp* by Truman Capote is a beautifully written and sensitive account of a young boy, Collin, who becomes an orphan at age eleven. Collin goes to live with two aged cousins until he is eighteen. The novelette chronicles the changes that occur in his life and the lives of people close to him. Written in first person with Collin as the narrator, the perspective of the book is cleverly done.
>
> Collin is a shy boy who does not make friends easily and who remains on the outer fringes of most groups. He literally stays outside the action, a spectator most of the time. In the Talbo household, he lives with his cousins, Dolly and Verena, and the black maid, Catherine. Collin spends much of his time up in the attic, peering down through a knothole and cracks at the activities going on below. When the story opens, Collin is outside the action not only physically but also emotionally.
>
> Collin is again a spectator when Riley Henderson, whom Collin greatly admires, confesses he is miserable. Riley would have killed himself if it were not for the responsibility of caring for his younger sisters. . . .
>
> When Sister Ida invites the Judge and Dolly to go away with her, Collin feels left out, just as he has many times before; again he is on the outside of a circle, peering in. Again he is a spectator as he peers through a window at Riley, who is now his best friend and who is kissing a girl.
>
> But later there are moments when Collin is accepted and moments when he is able to become an active participant. . . .

❧ *Prewriting Checklist: Point of View*

1. Who is telling the story?
2. Is the voice of the narrator consistent or does it change? If it changes, how?
3. How reliable is the narrator?
4. Should the narrator be taken literally? Or is the piece a satire, a tall tale, legend, myth, fable, or parable?
5. What is the effect of the narrator's voice?
6. Where is the narrator? Inside or outside the action? How does this perspective influence the plot, character, or theme?

Writing about Setting

To write about setting, take notes on the chief features of the place and time (era). Look for changes and contrasts in setting and wonder about their meaning. For example, if you were writing about *The Old Man and the Sea*, by Ernest

Hemingway, you might examine how setting isolates the main character. You could explain how the old man copes with isolation and achieves a qualified success. Although you would also refer to plot, character, and symbolism, the focus would be on setting. Now let's take a look at how Hemingway sets the scene, introducing the main character and preparing for the dramatic action of the novel all in one paragraph:

> He was an old man who fished alone in a skiff in the Gulf Stream, and he had gone eighty-four days now without taking a fish. In the first forty days a boy had been with him. But after forty days without a fish the boy's parents had told him that the man was now definitely and finally *salao*, which is the worst form of unlucky, and the boy had gone at their orders in another boat which caught three good fish the first week. It made the boy sad to see the old man come in each day with his skiff empty and he always went down to help him carry either the coiled lines or the gaff and harpoon and the sail that was furled around the mast. The sail was patched with flour sacks and, furled, it looked like the flag of permanent defeat.

After you have taken notes on setting, you might reread them and write a quick draft, commenting on cause and effect and emphasizing your main idea. This exercise will spur thinking and should yield an overview of your forthcoming paper. See Example of A Quick Draft for one student's draft and notes.

➤ Prewriting Checklist: Setting

1. What in the setting is particularly significant? Features of the landscape? Time of year? Weather? What?
2. Do any parts of the setting seem to be symbolic?
3. How does setting contribute to the tone or mood?
4. Does the setting change? How does this influence the plot and the characters?
5. Is there any foreshadowing (hints of what is to come)?

Writing about Plot

An analysis of plot is usually combined with one or more of the other elements of fiction. The examples that follow are from an analysis of a novel. The student writer discusses plot, character, and theme. The title alludes to a nursery rhyme character, as explained in the opening sentence. The ending also hints at the analogy:

Men, Chicks, and Eggshells

[INTRODUCTION]

Willie Stark, the main character of *All the King's Men*, by Robert Penn Warren, is the Humpty Dumpty who sits on top of the wall, the governorship of Louisiana.

EXAMPLE OF A QUICK DRAFT

Hemingway's *The Old Man and the Sea* begins in a poor fishing village off the Gulf Stream. There, superstition influences the thought and behavior of many residents, but not the old man. Their belief in *salao*, or bad luck, has isolated him. Because he has had bad luck in fishing, going eighty-four days without a good fish, he is shunned. The old man has even been separated from his former companion, the boy.

Alone on his skiff, the old man sits with his tattered flag and patched sail, which seem to be symbols—"looked like a flag of permanent defeat." Two similarities between the boat and the old man stand out: both are old and both appear dysfunctional. Yet these appearances are deceiving. Despite the isolation and hardships imposed by weather, sea, and sharks, both endure. The old man continues his quest for a huge fish. Determined to succeed at any cost, he will not accept defeat.

NOTES:

1. Need to discuss changes in setting at sea and effects on old man and the skiff.
2. Are sharks part of the setting? Not characters; must be setting.
3. Describe condition of the skiff, big fish, and old man when he returns to the harbor.
4. Is irony a significant element here?
5. What else should be mentioned?

Here he reigns in his own anthropocentric world until he falls. The book has an epic quality in plot, character, and theme.

Willie is a farm boy with little education, but one who works hard and long to become a lawyer and achieve admittance to the bar. He believes in God, in honor, and in goodness. And at first he believes what people tell him. But Sadie Burke wises him up. He forsakes orange soda pop and a wholesome view of the world to embrace Scotch whiskey, a realistic view, and Sadie (as well as other mistresses).

[*Note:* a major section of the paper, which appears later, emphasizes character although plot is mentioned throughout the paper. In the conclusion the student writer reacts to the novel, giving her response to plot and character.]

[CONCLUSION]

All the King's Men, like a mighty river, snatches up the reader and thunders to the inexorable finish. When released, the reader is purged and saddened by the tragic mess which some characters have made of their lives, yet gladdened by the few who retain integrity and develop responsibility.

Prewriting Checklist: Plot

1. What is the major conflict, dilemma, or problem?
2. What aspects of the plot create tension? How is it developed?
3. Who is involved and why?
4. Must the chief character make a difficult decision? What is it?
5. Does the chief character lose or triumph? Why or why not?

Organizing and rereading your notes will help you trace the development of the plot and changes in characters. Be alert for cause and effect. Consider character flaws, impulses, values, goals, issues, or coincidences that influence the outcome of the plot. Then try drafting a quick overview of your thoughts and comments.

Writing about Character

Analyzing character takes time and thought. Consider whether or not the character seems true to life. Start with the external aspects and go to the internal qualities. To discover personality traits, notice how the character treats other people. How does he or she speak and act? Modestly or arrogantly? Kindly or rudely? Thoughtfully or impulsively? What motivates the character? Motivation is a strong determinant of behavior. What does he or she seek? For example, Willie Stark in *All the King's Men*, thirsts for political power; but attaining that power has a hidden price, an undesirable consequence:

> Willie Stark is a complex character, a curious blend of good and evil, with Nietzsche-like overtones. As Stark gains power, he becomes a superman whose reign is based on *argumentum ad hominem*, blackmail, and the premise that all men have erred. Yet Stark has a curious code of honor: he never frames anybody. He believes framing is unnecessary; all he does is dig deeply until he finds something.
>
> Although Stark manipulates people and abuses power, he does work for the ultimate good of the people as he conceives it. He provides social services and allocates funds for a lavish hospital, which will be free to the poor.
>
> Stark has an unusual philosophy: "Goodness. . . . You got to make it. . . . And you got to make it out of badness. . . . Because there isn't anything else to make it out of" (257). Although this idea is reminiscent of Romans 8:28 ("And we know that all things work together for good to them that love God, to them who are the called according to *His* purpose"), there is an essential difference that illustrates this character: Stark was a pragmatist who acted independently; he did not rely on his creator for direction.

To discuss character, make an assertion or claim about the character's role or personality. Look for changes in the character and for learning that occurs. Then support this thesis with adequate examples and proof. You might examine how the character functions in the story. Is he the hero? Is she the heroine? Or does the character act as a foil or contrast for a major character?

Prewriting Checklist: Character

1. How and where does the character live?
2. What is significant about his or her appearance? Attire?
3. What does the character say that makes an impression?
4. What motivates the main character? How are these motives revealed?
5. How does the character achieve desires and goals? What values are revealed here?
6. What do you notice about the characters and their relationships with each other? Do they change?
7. What similarities and differences do you see in characters?
8. What do these things imply?
9. Do the characters seem convincing and realistic? Why or why not?
10. What else do you notice?

Writing about Symbols

Uncovering symbols can lead the reader to look beneath a surface meaning for a deeper abstract meaning. The names of characters and places are often symbolic: they represent some aspect of plot, characterization, or theme. In *Jane Eyre*, the mansion of Edward Rochester, Thornfield Hall, is the site of much trouble and pain. Besides the obvious meaning (field of thorns), Rochester's mad first wife, who is imprisoned on the top floor, is a thorn in his life.

You may recall another symbol Charlotte Brontë used in this novel—the giant horse chestnut tree, which stood in the orchard at Thornfield for many years. Near this tree Rochester proposed marriage to Jane without telling her he already had a wife. After Jane accepted his proposal, a storm arose and the huge tree "writhed and groaned." That night the tree, which symbolized Rochester, was struck by lightning and split, foreshadowing the impending tragedy.

A paper on symbolism alone could be difficult and inappropriate for some works. Unless you are adept at interpreting symbols, you may want to widen the scope of your analysis to include other elements.

Prewriting Checklist: Interpreting Symbols

1. What features, objects, or persons might be symbols?
2. Where and how do they appear?
3. Do any of the symbols change? How?
4. Are there any connections between symbols? If so, what?
5. Are the symbols universal or individual? How are they related to the theme of the work?

Writing about Irony

Usually, an analysis of irony is combined with other elements, unless irony is dominant in a work. If irony is a significant part of a story, you may want to analyze and categorize the types of irony embedded in the work. In Jane Austen's *Pride and Prejudice*, for example, verbal irony and situational irony appear throughout the novel. Verbal irony is habitual for the narrator as well as for Elizabeth Bennet and her father. The novel opens with the narrator speaking:

> It is a truth universally acknowledged, that a single man in possession of a good fortune, must be in want of a wife.
> However little known the feelings or views of such a man may be on his first entering a neighbourhood, this truth is so well fixed in the minds of the surrounding families, that he is considered as the rightful property of some one or other of their daughters.

Later Mr. Bennet, who assumes the role of an ironic spectator, says, "For what do we live, but to make sport for our neighbours, and laugh at them in our turn?" Elizabeth, like her father, categorizes people into the simple and the complex, finding amusement in the follies of the simple. Situational irony appears in minor incidents such as Lydia's repeating much of her mother's behavior. The major example revolves around Elizabeth, who begins by detesting Mr. Darcy but who finally loves and marries him.

Hemingway uses cosmic irony in *The Old Man and the Sea*. Even though the old man succeeds in catching the great fish and in taking it home, fate extracts an exorbitant price for success: the sharks not only eat all the flesh off his prize but the old man dies soon after as well.

Prewriting Checklist: Detecting Irony

1. Are there any inconsistencies between expectations and outcomes in the plot that create situational irony?
2. Does the reader or a character know something that another does not?
3. Do any of the characters say the opposite of what they mean?
4. Does fate or cosmic irony play a role in the plot?
5. How does irony influence the work?

Writing about Theme

Theme is a continuing thread, the central meaning that winds through a work. A theme contains an observation about human life or the conditions that prevail.

Usually, the theme is implicit and unstated, but you may find a theme directly stated, perhaps tucked into an obscure turn of the plot. In *All the King's Men*, an explicit statement of the theme reposes in a journal entry of a man long deceased:

... the world is like an enormous spider web and if you touch it, however lightly, ... the vibration ripples to the remotest perimeter and the drowsy spider feels the tingle ... springs out to fling the gossamer coils about you ... then injects the black, numbing poison under your hide. It does not matter whether you meant to brush the web of things ... what happens always happens.

Briefly summarized, the theme is that even small unintentional acts and events can have consequences that reverberate, setting up a chain of cause and effect in our lives and the lives of others. (Willie Stark and others touch the web of circumstance.)

To write about theme, consider that it results from other elements. Look for a series of events and ideas that seem to be connected. Are there sets of circumstances that seem significant? What do they say about human life or values? Also keep in mind that there is not just one way to set forth a theme; readers' statements of theme from the same work will vary.

≫ *Prewriting Checklist: Clues to Theme*

1. Does a set of related events, decisions, behavior, or symbols seem noteworthy? What might they mean?
2. What do characters feel strongly about? What is important to them?
3. What values are revealed by their responses?
4. What happens that strengthens or weakens human character? Could a universal statement be made about this?
5. What other aspects of plot and character challenge, entertain, or disgust readers? What do all these aspects seem to say about human life?

Revising

Accuracy, reasonableness, and fairness are key qualities to aim for in revising the draft of an analytical paper. Scrutinize your draft and add tentative words, qualifying phrases, and textual evidence to support claims and inferences. The following checklist will help you to avoid going out on the proverbial limb:

≫ *Checklist for Revising an Analysis of Fiction*

1. Is the thesis of my analysis clear? What elements will be discussed in the paper?
2. Is there enough evidence to support my thesis?
3. Are my main points clearly related to the thesis?
4. Is the discussion organized in a clear, logical order?
5. How familiar will the audience be with the work? How much do I need to explain?

6. How does the tone of the analysis sound? Is it serious? Is it overly critical or overly favorable?

7. Do I include at least one significant example (preferably more) to support each inference?

8. Are examples labeled correctly? (To check, see "Elements of Fiction," near the beginning of this chapter.)

9. Has each inference been identified by a qualifier such as *indicates*, *suggests*, or another tentative term?

10. Do I explain how elements contribute to meaning?

11. Might I have overlooked any symbols or irony?

12. Have I identified the theme of the work?

A SAMPLE PAPER OF ANALYSIS

The writer of the next paper had difficulty in limiting her topic because Updike's story has such splendid unity. She wanted to focus on symbolism but found that impossible to discuss without also mentioning plot and character. And since much of the symbolism of the games and the empty house was unclear, she selected only the most apparent symbols:

Breaking Up Is Hard to Do

To go beneath the bland surface of "Still of Some Use," by John Updike, and glimpse conflicting emotions, the reader must peel back layers of plot, characterization, and symbolism. Double meanings and other clues must also be detected and examined to identify themes. The story is revealed through Foster's eyes, although the omniscient narrator occasionally interposes a helpful comment.

The plot opens with Foster, his ex-wife, and their two grown sons cleaning out the attic of the vacant house they once shared so that she can sell it. Also helping is the older son's girlfriend. After they finish, Ted, the ex-wife's boyfriend, arrives. Implicit in the plot is an analogy between the contents of the attic and the former marriage: both are obsolete—the last tangible remnants of their lives together as a family are being hauled to the dump.

The characters' responses to this event vary. The older son seems unmoved, but the younger son is visibly upset. Although the older son and his girlfriend notice, neither seems empathetic: he remarks that Tommy has been "mooning over old stuff"; she says Tommy is "very sensi-tive." The boys' mother is concerned, however, and asks their father to "talk to Tommy," adding, "This is harder on him than he shows."

Although Foster has kept a tight rein on his emotions, his inner conflict becomes evident when, "in a kind of agony," he shouts, "What shall we do with all these games?" When his sons respond, "Trash 'em" and "Toss 'em," Foster is "stunned." He stares at the "sad wealth of abandoned playthings," thinking "their lives had touched these tokens and counters once."

Foster's ex-wife also seems reluctant to discard the games ("Would Goodwill want them?") and does not seem altogether happy about severing the marital ties.

Emotional conflict can be sensed in small clues: "her eager steps raced" to meet Ted, yet she readily shares her drink with Foster. When Ted "cupped her jaw," she does not pull away, but she does not smile; her face appears "pouty and frail." Earlier when Foster asks how she can bear to leave the house, she seems to reply just a bit too quickly and flippantly to be convincing. ("Oh, it's fun once you get into it. Off with the old, on with the new.") This response seems defiant, like her drinking beer even though she does not like it. She seems to still care for Foster. For example, when he sits staring out the attic window, she asks, "What's the matter?" After listening a moment, she says, "You better stop now; it's making you too sad."

When Foster and his ex-wife are alone in the attic, his regret about the divorce overwhelms him. He looks at her, and the "attic tremble[s] slightly." Later he seems almost desperate as he begs, "Give me one sip [of her beer]." Since only minutes before he had refused a can, he seems only to want to place his lips where hers have been. As he sips, he shuts his eyes.

Clearly, Foster is reluctant to part with the past—and his former wife. He wonders: What if they had "avoided divorce"? Then all the games would have stayed in the attic, their "sorrow [imperfections] unexposed." This symbolism suggests that Foster would have preferred to remain in a marriage with his imperfections as a husband and father unexposed (to him). As to what those faults are, the reader can only speculate.

So what does the reader actually learn about the cause of the marital breakup? Not much, although the use of symbols is lavish. The most vivid is the image of the games plummeting from the upstairs window to the truck bed: they "exploded," scattering "laughing children," "curious little faces," "hieroglyphs . . . whose code was lost." Like the games, the marriage undoubtedly started out with high expectations, but somehow the code to an enduring relationship was lost (or never found), and the marriage "exploded" in divorce, scattering family members. Now the house is empty and the stove disconnected, signifying the forsaking of the marriage and the disconnecting of relationships.

Readers are led to believe the games—"aping the strategies of the stock market, of crime detection, of real estate speculation, of international diplomacy and war"—somehow represent elements that marred the marriage, but the connection remains hazy and unclear. For instance, the word *token* appears several times, perhaps symbolizing perfunctory or minimal participation in the marriage. There are hints that Foster may have spent little time interacting with his family members: he says "he had not played enough with these games," and "now no one wanted to play." Yet he had spent many hours building a bookcase "so not a nailhead marred its smoothness." And Foster's old toys in his mother's attic are in good condition, unlike the games. Did he devote more attention to objects than to family relationships? Was he given to solitary pursuits?

A stronger hint is Foster's omission of his ex-wife's and older son's names. This omission suggests that his relationships with them were not close. Foster seems to view them in roles in relation to himself rather than as individuals.

In contrast, Ted is a "radiant brute," an extrovert, full of vitality and confidence, friendly even to Foster (Ted always shook Foster's hand). Ted seems to prize time with his children, visiting them instead of helping with the attic. He is charming and complimentary to Foster ("I hear you did a splendid job today"). Unlike Foster, Ted takes the initiative. Already he seems to have made himself a member of the family group: he gives fatherly advice to Tommy ("Don't dawdle till the dump closes"), wipes away "a smudge of dirt along her [Mrs. Foster's] jaw," and thanks Foster for helping (which is rather unusual under the circumstances).

Foster realizes Ted and his ex-wife are a "couple" now. Like the "cardboard spacemen" in the discarded games, Foster seems to feel as if he is a cardboard man, taking up space in a house no longer his (he's "on the wrong square"). Foster feels discarded—of no use as a husband or as a father. But as he is leaving, Tommy asks him to ride along to the dump. Foster declines, then asks, "This depresses you?"

Tommy admits, "Kind of," then adds, "It's changed since you left. They have all these new rules." Although Tommy is apparently talking about the dump, his face is clouded as if he's about to cry. His words seem to mirror a double meaning: Ted and his mother have new rules, and Tommy misses his father.

Foster senses these undercurrents, for he suddenly changes his mind and his mood. He jokes, "You win. I'll come along. I'll protect you." Foster seems pleased—as if he is "still of some use." This desire to be needed and useful is a major theme in Updike's complex work. Closely allied is the theme that divorce even under amicable circumstances is never easy.

—**Mae Mattix**

Summary

By reading literature, we can gain a different perspective on the world and our own lives. A paper of analysis is often assigned after students read fiction. A literary analysis discusses elements of a work and explains how they influence meaning. Such a paper cites portions of the original text and interprets their function. The analysis is an informed opinion, based on parts of the work in regard to the total content.

The form of a work affects the meaning. Fiction may be written as a novel, short story, diary, letters, or some other form. The narrator of a fictional work is not the voice of the author. The narrator may be a character or an omniscient observer who knows all and who stands outside the action. Or the narrator may have limited omniscience. There may be more than one narrator. The alert reader watches for clues to the "truth" of a story. Fiction often reveals meaning indirectly through symbols, irony, and other devices.

A paper of analysis, discusses significant elements of a work such as setting, plot, characters, or theme. Writing a paper of analysis requires several readings of the original source and adequate evidence from the source to support inferences and interpretation. The tone should be serious and professional.

Key Terms

point of view	limited omniscience	plot
narrator's voice	multiple viewpoints	foreshadowing
omniscient observer	setting	character

round character   irony   cosmic irony
flat character   situational irony   theme
symbolism   dramatic irony   paper of analysis
universal symbolism   verbal irony   foil

Practice

Ideas for Papers of Analysis

1. Analyze your favorite short story and give reasons for your preference. Cite examples.

2. Contrast two characters in a short story.

3. Compare two characters from different works.

4. Discuss the characterization in a novel. Are the characters flat or round? Do they seem realistic and convincing?

5. Discuss the irony of a work and how it influences plot and character.

6. Analyze the symbolism in a work and explain how it is related to theme.

7. Discuss the motivation of a central character and explain how it affects his or her life (and possibly other characters).

8. Discuss the influence of setting on plot and character in a work.

9. Select your favorite author and explain why you enjoy his or her writing. Cite examples from specific works.

10. Compare two works with similar themes.

CHAPTER 28

Reading and Responding to Poetry

*The poet is the stained glass window
that transmits sunlight just as
ordinary windows do, but colors it
as it passes through.*

—Robert Hillyer, *In Pursuit of Poetry*

Poetry has taken a backseat in an age of electronic gadgets and cyberspace. We whiz from our homes to our jobs to other places in a whirlwind of activity. At night we tap away at a computer keyboard or collapse in front of the tube. If we read, it's often the headline news or the comics or self-help books, which poet Tess Gallagher calls "hamburger stands of the soul." Gone are the leisurely evenings and Sunday afternoons spent reading and staring into a wood-burning fire. Now there just doesn't seem to be time to read poetry and ponder tendrils of meaning.

Yet poetry can help us discover a hidden dimension of ourselves. Poetry can connect us more closely to nature and to the human race. Through a poem we can peer through a new window on our existence, savoring beauty taken for granted, sharing the warmth of unselfish love or the frigid chill left by death. Poetry acts as a link to the past by recapturing the pleasures and the pains of an earlier age. A poem can reach into the future, kindling desires, fueling dreams—providing the spark that transforms a wish into reality. A poem can fill the present with delight, appreciation, and anticipation. Poetry can yield contentment and acceptance of things we cannot change.

Here the purpose of reading poetry is *not* to classify dozens of literary devices or to analyze meter or to hunt for a message. The purpose is to enter a poem, to experience it, to look at its parts, and to marvel at its artistry. Despite careful analysis, any such knowledge is always incomplete. We can never comprehend all there is to know about a work of art—not that all poems are art. But if we approach each one as if it were, then we are more apt to give it a fair hearing.

HOW CAN A READER GET HOLD OF A POEM?

Great poetry has an essence that is elusive. Unlike expository writing, which is primarily concerned with fact and explanation, poetry is primarily feeling. With a few words poets may sketch scenes or wisps of ideas, leaving the reader to fill in the rest. For the most part, poets show rather than tell. And the more passionate their feelings, the simpler their statements. Consider the closing couplet of Countee Cullen's "Yet do I marvel":

> Yet do I marvel at this curious thing:
> To make a poet black and bid him sing.

Readers familiar with the history of the black experience in the United States will immediately recognize the paradox posed in this poem, which was written about 1920. But someone unfamiliar with this period would be unable to fill in the gaps or appreciate the economy and balance of Cullen's lines. Every word counts; every word is in perfect alignment and tension. The poet has said just enough in a unique and thoughtful way, balancing expectation with surprise.

When readers are required to analyze a poem, they often begin with the question "What does the poem mean?" In the title of his famous textbook, John Ciardi suggests a more effective starting point: "*How* does a poem mean?" For the meaning of a poem is derived not only from its words, but also from its structure. Ciardi also suggests that to study a poem, the reader adopt a playful attitude—for much poetry, like dance, is "a performance" to be appreciated for the pleasure it brings. Ciardi believes the "best any analysis can do is to prepare the reader to enter the poem more perceptively."

To apprehend and appreciate poetry, we need a sense of curiosity, of wonder, and of play. For poets often frolic with words, pairing them in unexpected ways. A sense of play permeates the next poem:

On the Vanity of Earthly Greatness

by Arthur Guiterman

> The tusks that clashed in mighty brawls
> Of mastodons, are billiard balls.
>
> The sword of Charlemagne the Just
> Is ferric oxide, known as rust.
>
> The grizzly bear whose potent hug
> Was feared by all, is now a rug.
>
> Great Caesar's bust is on the shelf,
> And I don't feel so well myself.

To understand and appreciate the structure and sound of this poem, read it aloud. Notice that there are four sets of rhyming couplets. (A couplet is a set of two successive lines.) Listen to the pace of the words, their slowness or quickness. The first line of each couplet tends to be slow and ponderous whereas the second is quick, especially the last phrase. Hear the sound and movement of certain words: "tusks that clashed," "billiard balls," and "grizzly bear whose potent hug." Note that other words suggest a lack of motion: "rust," "now a rug," and "bust is on the shelf."

Each couplet contains surprises not only in sound but also in meaning. The biggest surprise occurs in the last line. What is it? Does the poem seem to have a purpose other than to provoke amusement? Filling in the spaces of meaning in poetry is somewhat like doing a crossword puzzle. You may feel frustrated as you grope for the right word to fit the spaces or as you try to unlock the layers of meaning in an apparently simple poem. But if you approach the poem as a work of art with form, sound, movement, and meaning and if you examine its parts with care, then you will begin to see its fusion and unity.

READING NARRATIVE POEMS

Narrative poems are like miniature stories. They begin with a place and a situation. Often the scene is set very simply with a sparseness of detail. Characters are briefly introduced, and the action begins. The movement is usually from specific to general. Concrete details or symbols often hint of a greater meaning, a *universal truth*, at the end. The length of a narrative poem may vary from an anecdote such as Countée Cullen's "Incident" to a very long ballad such as "The Rime of the Ancient Mariner."

Cullen was born in Louisville, Kentucky, in 1903. By 1925 he had become the most renowned Black writer in North America. Cullen completed theological study at Morgan State College in Baltimore. There he was a Methodist pastor for two years. Then he moved to New York City, where he formed a storefront mission and became politically active. His poem "Incident" deserves several readings.

As you examine this poem, keep in mind that understatement provides a wellspring of power for English poetry. Understatement, however, requires the reader to look beneath the surface of a poem to glimpse its essence. To assist in detecting understatement, keep a dictionary handy. Look up any unfamiliar words or any that might have more than one meaning. Consider all meanings of a word; poets often select ambiguous words that create layers of meanings. Also consider the historical period and the cultural norms that existed then:

Incident
by Countée Cullen

Once riding in old Baltimore,
  Heart-filled, head-filled with glee,

I saw a Baltimorean
  Keep looking straight at me.

Now I was eight and very small,
  And he was no whit bigger,
And so I smiled, but he poked out
  His tongue, and called me, "Nigger."

I saw the whole of Baltimore
  From May until December;
Of all the things that happened there
  That's all that I remember.

Questions to Analyze "Incident"

1. Vocabulary: *glee, incident.* (Also see *incidental.*)
2. How would you describe the tone of verse one?
3. What line in verse one conveys strong feeling?
4. Where does Cullen pair expectation with surprise? What is the effect?
5. Comment on the movement of the poem. (Hint: Examine the changes in tone from verse to verse.)
6. Ordinarily, a rollicking rhyme structure is not used in a serious poem. Why does it work well here? (Clue: Children's poems often use rhyme.)
7. Is this a child's poem? Why or why not?

READING LYRIC POEMS

Originally, lyric poems were sung by the Greeks to the accompaniment of a lyre, a stringed instrument. Lyric poetry, which includes the majority of poems, covers a broad array of subjects and forms. Rather than telling a story as narrative poetry does, lyric poetry expresses a state of mind, revealing thought and feeling. Since there is no plot, word choice and imagery must be unique to distinguish a lyric poem.

Special Effects with Words

Poets select words not only for meaning but also for sound, movement, and color. All four aspects are inseparable. Alliteration (repeated consonant sounds), assonance (repeated vowel sounds), and rhyme are the most common devices of sound. Another device is *onomatopoeia*, whereby the sound of the word mimics its denotation. Listen to *hum, buzz,* and *crack* as you say them. These words sound like the actions they represent. Onomatopoeia supplies vitality to any poem.

Action verbs also give vitality to poetry, enhancing the image and varying the pace. Words may skip or skitter, slink or slither, sprint or stroll across a page. Let's pause for a moment and consider the verb pairs in the previous sentence. First, visualize the difference in movement between *skip* and *skitter.* A child might skip down a sidewalk, but an autumn leaf skitters across a lawn, blown by the wind in quick irregular spurts. Next listen to the sounds of the verb pairs. Notice the repetition of *sli* in *slink* and *slither,* which adds smoothness to their sound. Similarly, *ski* is repeated in *skip* and *skitter* (alliteration). But the third pair sets up a little surprise. Instead of exact repetition at the beginning of the words, the *t* sound comes at a different place in each word: *sprint, stroll.* Finally, listen to the differences in pace. The first word in each verb pair quickens the pace whereas the second slows it. For example, *sprint* with its short *i* is much quicker to say than *stroll* with the long *o* and *ll* sounds.

When you consider adjectives such as *red* and *ruby* or *green* and *emerald,* you can note contrasts in color as well as sound and pace. The eye easily detects that red and green offer an array of shades whereas ruby and emerald are each a specific shade. As you listen to the sounds, you can detect the quickness of *red* and *green. Ruby* and *emerald* sound slower and richer.

Imagery

Our cave-dwelling ancestors drew primitive sketches to represent activities and events in their lives. Similarly, poets sketch images with words to represent significant occurrences, ideas, and emotions. In a poem with a single image, all words contribute. Haiku, an ancient Japanese form of lyric verse, always focuses on a single image. The form generally consists of three lines of seventeen syllables, based on a metaphor. Implicit in the image is a comparison. Typical haiku describe nature or the seasons, much like the following examples:

The Barley Field	**The Barley Field**
by Joso	*by Sora*
Bent down by the rain,	Up the barley rows,
the ripe barley makes this	stitching, stitching them together
such a narrow lane!	a butterfly goes.

If you have seen wheat or oats growing in a field, then you can easily visualize the field of barley, which also grows in willowy stalks. To compare the two poems, jot down differences in the spaces below, beginning with concrete details. Then ask: How do the details influence the effect of each poem?

	(Joso)	**(Sora)**
Angle of stalks	_____	_____
Width of Rows	_____	_____
Image (metaphor)	_____	_____
Punctuation	_____	_____
Connotations	_____	_____
	_____	_____

Repetition   _____   _____
Literary devices   _____   _____
                    _____   _____
Tone   _____   _____

Poems with more than one image lack the splendid unity of poems with a single image. Yet multiple images can be skillfully unified by a central theme. All connotative meanings must, as Ciardi points out, "combine the overtone themes of the words and the images into a single unity." Otherwise, utter confusion could result. To better understand this fusion of multiple images, you might think of a sunburst: all points are separate, but they fuse at the core. So too, multiple images are separate, yet they meet in a central idea.

Emily Dickinson, famous for short lyric poems, was born in 1830 in Amherst, Massachusetts. She was educated at Amherst Academy and Mount Holyoke Seminary. Her innovative style, characterized by whimsical daring and nimble skill, became a strong influence on twentieth-century poets. Yet Emily Dickinson was practically unknown at the time of her death; only a few of her poems had been published in a local newspaper:

[I taste a liquor never brewed]

by Emily Dickinson

I taste a liquor never brewed,
From tankards scooped in pearl;
Not all the vats upon the Rhine
Yield such an alcohol!

Inebriate of air am I,
And debauchee of dew,
Reeling, through endless summer days,
From inns of molten blue.

When landlords turn the drunken bee
Out of the foxglove's door,
When butterflies renounce their drams,
I shall but drink the more!

Till seraphs swing their snowy hats,
And saints to windows run,
To see the little tippler
Leaning against the sun!

Questions to Analyze [I Taste a Liquor Never Brewed]

1. Vocabulary: *tankard, debauchee, foxglove, seraphs, tippler.*
2. What does verse one reveal about the "liquor"?
3. What literary devices do you see?

4. Verse two sets the scene and indicates the central theme of the poem. How would you state it? (You may want to skip on, then answer later.)

5. How does the poet use signs of intoxication to indicate her mood? How does this influence the tone of verses one and two? How do the images in verses three and four differ? (Clue: places)

6. What attitude is shown in verse four?

7. What is the central idea that unifies the series of images?

8. Why might this poem have seemed daring in the late 1800s?

Although a spirit of play is less apparent in the poetry of Archibald MacLeish, still it is there. MacLeish won the Pulitzer Prize for poetry in both 1933 and 1953. He was not only a distinguished poet but also an author and statesman, working for UNESCO and other organizations. Born in Glencoe, Illinois, Mac-Leish graduated from Yale University and obtained a law degree from Harvard, where he became a professor. His most famous poem, "Ars Poetica" (Latin for *poetics*, the theory of writing poetry), written in 1926, contains a series of images. These involve sight, sound (or the lack of it), movement, and touch as well as meaning. Think about the texture of the images. What qualities do they have in common?

Ars Poetica

by Archibald MacLeish

A poem should be palpable and mute
As a globed fruit,

Dumb
As old medallions to the thumb,

Silent as the sleeve-worn stone
Of casement ledges where the moss has grown—

A poem should be wordless
As the flight of birds.
                                    *

A poem should be motionless in time
As the moon climbs,

Leaving, as the moon releases
Twig by twig the night-entangled trees,

Leaving, as the moon behind the winter leaves,
Memory by memory the mind—

A poem should be motionless in time
As the moon climbs
                                    *

A poem should be equal to:
Not true.

For all the history of grief
An empty doorway and a maple leaf.

For love
The leaning grasses and the two lights above the sea—

A poem should not mean
But be

Questions to Analyze "Ars Poetica"

1. Vocabulary: *palpable, mute, medallion, casement, be* ("to have life or reality")
2. Why is *palpable* an excellent word for this poem? (Consider the medical meaning of the word as well as the old Latin.)
3. Consider the sound and imagery of "globed fruit," "sleeve-worn stone," "moon climbs," and "poem." What do you notice?
4. What do you notice about the pace of the pair of lines below?
     A poem should be wordless
     As the flight of birds.
5. What words convey the idea of silence?
6. The final line has no period. What is the effect? (Clues: What does a period do? What idea is conveyed through "motionless in time" and "history" that is similar to ending without a period?)
7. What else do you notice?
8. Each couplet specifies a quality that a poem should have. What are the qualities?
9. The final verse summarizes the meaning of the poem. How would you paraphrase it?

Poets who achieve long-lasting success excel in their ability to create fresh images, for metaphor is the heart of poetry. At the same time, they create a unified work, using not only words but also form to reinforce meaning. The result is a poem that is a treat for the reader each time it is read.

Tips for Analyzing a Poem

1. *Make a copy of the poem, enlarging it, but leaving 1½-inch margins.* The copy will provide a convenient way to take notes and gain an overview of the poem.
2. *Hold off on interpretation.* Going into a poem with preset ideas can close the mind. Withhold judgment; be open to newness.

3. *Look up unfamiliar words.* Read all definitions of a word. Poets sometimes select words with double or triple meanings to enrich a poem. Jot definitions near the example. If space between lines is lacking, write at the side and draw an arrow to the example.

4. *Examine the words.* What is the level of language? Is dialect, jargon, or other special terminology used?

5. *Listen to the feeling behind the words.* How does the voice of the writer sound? From what point of view or perspective is the writer speaking? Listen to the nuances of the words. What emotion do you sense?

6. *Listen for devices of sound and movement.* Do you notice rhyme? Alliteration? Assonance? Onomatopoeia? Any other device? How does the rhythm (a pattern of sound) of the poem reinforce the meaning?

7. *Look for figurative language.* Are there similes, metaphors, personification, symbolism, or other devices that contribute to an image?

8. *Notice punctuation.* Poetry, like prose, is punctuated for a reason. Consider the effect of punctuation—or the lack of it—upon meaning.

9. *Keep the context of the poem in mind while looking at its parts.* Try to discover how each part is linked to the whole.

10. *Consider possible meanings.* Reread the poem and your notes. What does the imagery suggest? What do the words say? Might there be more than one interpretation? If so, which one fits best and why?

11. *Read biographical sketches.* Gaining insight into an author's background and the times is often helpful in understanding a work. Encyclopedias offer easy access to brief biographies. Some poetry books include abstracts of poets' lives. Or you may find a book-length biography.

12. *What is the total effect of the poem?* What is your response to it?

PREPARING AN ANALYSIS OF A POEM

As you browse through poems, choose one you like that offers possibilities for serious discussion. A fairly short poem is usually preferable to a long one, for even a short poem can be complex. You may find different versions of the same poem or possibly different titles. For example, one of William Wordsworth's poems has been widely printed under two different titles: [Daffodils] or [I wandered lonely as a cloud.] (Sometimes brackets are placed around the title of a poem to indicate it was originally untitled.)

Developing Your Analysis

To analyze a poem, first read it silently. Then reread it aloud and listen to the sound and movement. Who is speaking? Watch for clues to how the speaker feels about the subject. If the poem has rhyme, is there a pattern to the rhyme? Next, count the number of syllables in each line and write them at the side to determine how the lines compare. Do any have the same number of syllables? Is there a pattern to the arrangement of the lines?

After that, study the definitions and connotations of key words to see how they contribute to the meaning. Write the definitions and connotations near each word. Next, look for similes, metaphors, analogies, personification, symbols—or any other device that links one part of the poem with another. For more about figurative language, see chapter 27. Jot brief notes as you go. Write any questions you have at the bottom of the page or on the reverse side. You may find the answers later, or you might discuss the questions with someone else. By the time you have finished, you should have accumulated a page of notes to serve as raw material for a rough draft.

Finally, reread the poem aloud to reassemble the parts in your mind and focus on the effect of the entire work. As you do, chances are that you will begin to see how the parts fuse into a central image or theme.

Organizing the Paper

Although there are many aspects to poetry, first-year college students are usually not expected to cover all them. Often an analytical paper on a poem is only one or two pages long. If your instructor allows a choice, select major elements that interest you. Then explain your impression of the way various elements contribute to the unity of the poem.

Guidelines for Organizing and Developing a Poetic Analysis

1. Identify the poem as narrative or lyric. If a special type, specify.
2. Follow the order of the poem as nearly as possible.
3. Explain how the word choice, symbolism, or other elements contribute to the overall effect of the poem.
4. Cite examples of elements.
5. State your perception of the central idea.
6. Describe your response to the poem.

If the poem is short, include the entire text in your paper. If the poem is over half a page, attach a copy to your paper unless the poem is in your textbook. To quote fewer than four lines, use quotation marks and indicate line breaks by a slash mark: "Inebriate of air am I / And debauchee of dew." (*Note:* One space is placed before and after each slash.) If you quote four lines or more of poetry, indent and treat as a long direct quotation (with no quotation marks).

Revising an Analysis of a Poem

Even though your paper of analysis is only a page or two, check the organization and revise carefully. The following questions will help you revise your draft. Select the items that pertain to your subject.

⟩ *Checklist for Revising*

1. Do I have a clear thesis?
2. Do I follow a logical order?
3. Have I discussed the central image (or series of images)?
4. Are any symbols present? Have I explained how they contribute?
5. Have I discussed the devices of sound in the poem?
6. Are there any similes, metaphors, or personification not yet discussed?
7. Have I pointed out connections between related ideas?
8. Have I considered how the poem appears on the page? How many stanzas there are? Their length and any other significant aspects?
9. Have I explained the central idea of the poem?

A SAMPLE ANALYSIS OF A POEM

The following example shows one way to organize a paper that analyzes a poem. A poem of this length usually appears on a separate page, preceding the analysis. (Wordsworth's poem was written about 1800.)

[I wandered lonely as a cloud]
by William Wordsworth

I wandered lonely as a cloud
That floats on high o'er vales and hills,
When all at once I saw a crowd,
A host of golden daffodils,
Beside the lake, beneath the trees
Fluttering and dancing in the breeze.

Continuous as the stars that shine
And twinkle on the milky way,
They stretched in never-ending line
Along the margin of a bay;
Ten thousand saw I at a glance,
Tossing their heads in sprightly dance.

The waves beside them danced, but they
Outdid the sparkling waves in glee;
A poet could not but be gay,
In such a jocund company;
I gazed—and gazed—but little thought
What wealth the show to me had brought:

For oft, when on my couch I lie
In vacant or in pensive mood,
They flash upon that inward eye

Which is the bliss of solitude;
And then my heart with pleasure fills,
And dances with the daffodils.

Form and Meaning in [I wandered lonely as a cloud]

Every time I read William Wordsworth's poem "I wandered lonely as a cloud," it is a source of pleasure. The dazzling beauty of the daffodils is one that any reader can readily conceive and enjoy. But this lyric poem is much more than a vivid description, with contrasts of sight and sound. The poem is alive with motion.

In the first line the narrator compares himself to the cloud that "floats high." The tone of this line and the next differs greatly from that of other lines. The narrator's loneliness is juxtaposed to the happy sight of a "host of golden daffodils" . . . Tossing their heads in sprightly dance."

Light radiates throughout the poem in the words *golden, stars, shine, twinkle, milky way, sparkling waves,* and *flash.* Alliteration in *stars, shine, stretched, saw, sprightly* and in *Ten thousand . . . Tossing* focuses on this glorious sight.

Assonance contributes not only to the unity of the poem but also to the sound, varying the pace. The repetition of the long *o* in *lonely, floats, o'er,* and other examples slows the lines and suggests aloneness. The long *a* in *gazed* and its repetition reflect the narrator's reluctance to leave. In contrast is the short, quick *e,* in "Beside the lake, beneath the trees."

Personification and movement are major features of the poem. The daffodils toss their heads, dance, and laugh with *glee.* Movements of dance are conveyed by the words. *Fluttering* suggests short spurts of movement; *dancing,* a smooth glide. The rhyme scheme and the length of lines mimic the dance of the daffodils. Although the end rhyme is exact, the pattern of rhyming varies in the third stanza. No stanza has the same pattern, although some have the same number of syllables per line. These lines suggest the movement of dancers to music.

If there is a theme to the poem, it might be stated as "Beauty can nourish the spirit" or "Drink in every drop of beauty and store it to cheer the soul."

—**Bettina Dietrich**

Summary

Perhaps the best way to approach a poem is to regard it as a work of art until evidence to the contrary is found. Poems may be narrative or lyric. Poetry tends to be indirect, showing more than telling. Form and meaning are intertwined. Concrete language, imagery, figures of speech, and devices of sound and movement contribute to the meaning of a poem.

To write an analysis of poetry, select a fairly short poem that you like. As you read it aloud, listen to the sound and movement. Watch for clues to the speaker's attitude toward the subject. Count the syllables in each line. Is there rhyme? A rhyme scheme? Figures of speech? What else do you notice? To organize your paper, follow the order of the poem as much as possible. Take examples from the poem and explain how they contribute to the meaning. You might end by describing your response to the poem.

Key Terms

couplet	lyric poetry
narrative poetry	onomatopoeia
universal truth	pace
understatement	haiku

Practice

Ideas for Writing

1. React to the two haiku entitled "The Barley Field." Which do you prefer? Why? Write a short essay giving your response. (See chapter 26.)
2. Analyze Emily Dickinson's poem "I taste a liquor never brewed."
3. Analyze another poem in this chapter and explain how some elements contribute to meaning.
4. Read and analyze another poem of your choice.
5. Research the life of your favorite poet and select one poem that reveals his or her philosophy. Write a short paper that summarizes his life and philosophy. Relate the poem to the philosophy.

Reader

The Going-Out-of-Business Sale

Joyce Maynard

Here is a funny, real-life experience story for those readers who have gone to a huge sale, madly tossed stuff into a cart, and lugged home enough supplies for the next umpteen years. Joyce Maynard has a gift for keeping an amused eye on our complicated lives. This gift has served her well, resulting in several books. Her first was an autobiography, Looking Back, *written when she was only nineteen.*

One of the biggest discount stores in our area was going out of business— every item marked down 50 percent. Now I bet I've made about five hundred trips to this particular store over the last ten years—handed over a couple of thousand dollars, for probably a ton of bobby pins, curtain rods, beach balls, and jumper cables. So it seemed necessary to pay (literally) my last respects.

The place had been pretty well stripped by the time I got there, with half of what was left broken or dirty, and heaped on the floor. The snack bar, where I had hoped to purchase Charlie's tranquility with a bag of popcorn, was closed down, looking like Pompeii at the moment the volcano erupted, with grape soda still percolating in a cooler and coffee cups on the counter. No time for coffee anyway. Shoppers were racing ahead of us, cleaning out all the most popular bra sizes, stripping the shelves of shampoo and vacuum-cleaner bags and batteries. The speakers that used to pipe gentle organ music in my ears were transmitting urgent messages, meanwhile—like an emergency broadcast system during a war-time air raid, notifying shoppers of additional markdowns ("hurry, hurry!") and reminding us that soon the doors would close forever. I picked up my pace and flung a pair of crew socks into my cart for my husband, hitting Charlie on the head by mistake. We were off and running.

There is a danger, at an event like this one, of confusing the end of this particular store with the end of civilization in general. You begin to feel as if this were your last chance ever to buy anything. So you get four lipsticks, and enough photograph albums to see your infant son through high school gradua- tion. I bought sneakers for my three children's next three sizes, and, for Steve, five packages of underwear and (an impulse from somewhere out in left field) a set of car seat covers.

Charlie was pretty quick to pick up the tone of the event. Having rejected the seat in my shopping cart designed for children in favor of the deep basket section of the cart, he stood, as if at the prow of the ship, facing out to survey the ocean of merchandise before him. Sometimes he'd reel in a string of Christmas lights or grab a stuffed animal by the tail. In the shoe department he hauled in a whole clump of tangled together fuzzy bedroom slippers. His diaper had come undone and was hanging down one pant leg; he had appropriated a hat, and he was waving to people as if he were running for office. I had never seen the particular crazed look that appeared on his face when, after I let him down from the cart for a moment, he clutched a bag of sponges and began to spin in circles, singing "Beat It." Even after I picked him up and was walking briskly down the aisle with my son under my arm like a rolled-up newspaper, to regain my cart, he still kept reaching out hopefully for kitchen spatulas and panty hose. And of course I know where he acquired the tendency. As I loaded my bags into the trunk of our car, I couldn't even remember, anymore, what it was I'd bought.

The morning after our excursion to the going-out-of-business sale I spread 5 my purchases out on the bed to show Steve. The crew socks were terrific, he said, but they were women's socks. The top of the blender was great, and so was the bottom. They did not, unfortunately, go together. Boxer shorts, when taken out of the package, turned out to be the kind of underwear that certain very corny comedians are discovered to wear when their pants fall down on stage. Steve informed me that he does not wear this type of shorts, but if he ever decides to join the circus he's all set, with nine pair. By the time I brought out the car seat covers we were both expecting the worst. The covers were intended, of course, for bucket seats. But who knows, someday we may buy a car like that.

Though the store had announced a policy of Positively No Returns or Exchanges (and did not seem at all touched to hear of what a devoted longtime customer I had been), a few days later I was able, after making the thirty-mile trip once more, to replace my two half-blenders with a fancy reel for Steve's fishing rod. When I got home, he looked at it with interest and said he has been meaning to learn how to fly cast, and maybe in a few years he'd get the hang of it.

This morning Steve stopped at our local clothing store—just for a minute—and bought a complete wardrobe of underwear. He said he would've looked for a sale, but he didn't think we could afford one.

Reflecting and Interpreting

1. This story can be read on one level as simply an amusing anecdote about a mother with a baby in a shopping cart, or it can be analyzed in various ways. What do you notice that intrigues you?

2. Maynard starts by using overstatement to create humor. What other devices do you see in paragraph two?

3. Motivation is an important element in this story. What images convey a sense of urgency and influence both Joyce and Charlie to join the melee?

4. What is the danger the author speaks of? Do you think this statement is more than just a witty remark? Why or why not?

5. The mood of the next morning sharply contrasts with the frantic activity during the sale. How?

6. Did the ending surprise you? What device is this?

7. Do you think there might be a moral to this story? If so, how would you state it?

A Writer's Response

1. Brainstorm with your group to produce some guidelines for shopping at huge sales. How can you resist the urge to buy more than you need? Is it best to go alone or with someone? What can you do beforehand as well as during the sale?

2. Have you ever had a purchasing disaster? What did you do? Write an essay using overstatement, understatement, and any other devices that seem suitable. You might try imitating Maynard's style.

Forget the Ford—Try Driving a Winton

Thom Geier

Americans have long had a special fondness for automobiles, sometimes the older, the better. In this essay Thom Geier describes how Alexander Winton contrived a horseless carriage in the late nineteenth century and drove it from Cleveland to New York City— a distance of 700 miles! When Winton arrived, the feat went unacclaimed because reporters refused to believe his tale.

In the 1890s, a Scottish-born bicycle maker named Alexander Winton began tinkering with a contraption that was the latest rage in Europe: the horseless carriage. He soon had a working model of his own, and in 1897, he incorporated the Winton Motor Carriage Co. Not content merely to tootle around town, however, Winton also concocted the long-distance American road trip—driving his buggy 700-some miles, from Cleveland to New York City. The feat went unheralded by disbelieving New Yorkers.

A century later, the Winton name is largely forgotten. But on Father's Day this month, owners of more than a dozen vintage Winton cars, dating from 1899 to 1921, will attempt to repeat the historic trip. "Alexander Winton was one of the first to suggest that motor cars are more than just play toys," says Charles Wake of Sarasota, Fla., Winton's great-grandson, who hatched the idea for the centennial drive.

Following the same basic route taken by his great-grandfather, Wake will lead the caravan in an 1899 Winton. Once out of Cleveland, though, the cars will fan out and proceed at their own pace. Newer Winton cars can cruise comfortably at 40 miles per hour, but the 1899 model peaks at around 20, with barely the power of the eight horses it helped render obsolete. The early one-cylinder car must be crank started and steered by a tiller—Winton did not introduce steering wheels until 1901.

Winton was not the only American to experiment with the motorized carriage, but he quickly recognized its potential for becoming standard transportation. The New York trip served to test and promote his invention. Finding gasoline, then a common cleaning fluid and stove fuel, wasn't a problem: He used just 15 gallons for the entire trip. The real hitch was oil, which needed replenishment about every 15 minutes to prime the components of the engine, transmission, and cylinder.

Unnoticed. After 11 days of driving through dirt and mud—actual travel time 78 hours, 43 minutes—Winton chugged into New York City amid gawking

5

pedestrians and unnerved horses. "As I came down Broadway, I regretted the daylight," Winton later recalled, "for I was literally clad in dust and sadly in need of a bath." Much to his dismay, the trip went largely unnoticed by the press, which didn't believe his account. "The friendlessness of New York sank into my spirit and left no place for elation," he wrote. So he drove directly to the freight yards and took his vehicle and himself home on the next available train.

Still, Winton had proven his machine's durability and was soon in the buggy business. In 1898, he became the first American to sell a gasoline-powered horseless carriage. That year, he sold more than 20 cars for $1,000 each, including one to electrical-wire manufacturer James Packard. Unfortunately, Packard's car suffered mechanical problems and required frequent servicing by Winton's men. When Packard offered some suggestions for improvement, an exasperated Winton reportedly exploded: "If you think you can make a better machine, go and do it." Packard did, founding a rival company that produced luxury cars through the late 1950s.

Winton was more a tinkerer than a tycoon, with a Scottish stubbornness that could cloud his business judgment. When a young Henry Ford applied for a job, Winton booted him from his office, convinced that Ford lacked the mechanical skills to make it in the nascent industry.

Media event. Two years after his first New York trip, Winton decided to return. This time, he brought along Cleveland reporter Charles Shanks, who filed dispatches on every leg of the journey and helped popularize the French word *automobile*. The expedition became a media event, with crowds lining the route. Shanks milked each day's progress for drama, especially after a collision with a boulder near Fairport, N.Y., snapped the buggy's front axle and sent the two flying. "After shooting through space for 25 or 30 feet," he wrote, "we were permitted, by the law of gravity, to bump the ground with a force sufficient to jar the healthiest of nervous systems." Winton cabled for a new axle to be delivered by train so the two could depart the following day. They arrived in New York amid cheering throngs after less than 48 hours of road travel.

As sales boomed, Winton kept breaking records. In 1903, a Winton "Bullet" outfitted with two four-cylinder engines zoomed to 70 miles per hour. That year, another Winton car became the first to complete a transcontinental journey from San Francisco to New York. By this time, Winton was operating the largest automobile factory in the country, a Cleveland plant whose 1,500 workers rolled out 300 cars per month.

Winton continued producing high-quality autos through the early 1920s, but   10
his resistance to mass production proved to be a fatal business mistake. The holder of dozens of patents, Winton developed the first American-made diesel engine, for both manufacturing and marine use, and was experimenting with engines for aviation at the time of his death in 1932.

Winton's legacy is a small fleet of at least 100 surviving automobiles, including three that Cleveland's Crawford Auto-Aviation Museum is lending for this month's journey. "People will wait on street corners in the pouring rain to see vintage cars go by," says curator David Holcombe. "In the museum, they just walk past without taking a second glance." Preserving the pricey buggies is a top priority, though the greatest threat typically comes from rubbernecking drivers in modern cars. For many, it's worth the risk to see Winton's handiwork back on the road—where it belongs.

Reflecting and Interpreting

1. How does Geier set the scene in the first paragraph? What words lend lightness to his tone?

2. What, to you, is the most surprising detail about Alexander Winton's original long distance trip in 1897?

3. The author recounts some interesting interactions between Winton and two men who later became famous. Which anecdote is ironic? Why?

4. Although Winton continued producing cars through the early 1920s, one decision doomed his business. What was it?

5. After developing and marketing successful automobiles, Alexander Winton achieved another "first." What was it?

6. What does Winton's grandson plan to do to honor his grandfather's achievement? How old are the cars that will participate? How fast will they go?

7. What basic order does the author use? Yet there is a flash-forward—can you find it? What transition does the author provide to span the gap in time?

A Writer's Response

1. Have you ever owned an old car or truck that you adored? Write an essay, using concrete words to describe the vehicle. Explain how it influenced you, and why you parted with it.

2. Perhaps as a youngster you had a scooter, bicycle, or other mode of transportation you were particularly fond of. Write an essay that describes the vehicle and conveys your feelings. (For help, see chapter 11.)

The Sound of a Silent Bell

Eric Burns

A reporter observes a book burning in a small town and makes some interesting visual connections—such as cat's eyes and stolen bell clappers. There is much to think about in this piece about fear, silence, and protest in an attempt to preserve goodness. When Eric Burns witnessed this event, he was an NBC news correspondent, appearing regularly on the Today *show and* NBC Nightly News.

A decade and a half ago, as a correspondent for NBC News, I reported on a fundamentalist bookburning in a small town in the Midwest. A local church sponsored the event, but had little support from other churches or neighboring communities or even, it seemed to me, from the majority of people in the town itself. Most of them went along with the idea of a literary exorcism by fire, but few seemed ardent about it, and fewer still provided me with the kind of damnation-and-brimstone sound bites I was expecting.

It had been 2,400 years since the various works of Protagoras were ignited in the heart of Athens.

The story took two days to shoot, my crew and I taping the actual bookburning, for which a zoning variance had to be granted; interviews with a dozen or more people on both sides of the issue; and scenes of daily life in the town, context for the conflagration. We shot farmers working their fields, salesclerks tending their counters, mechanics fixing cars, barbers giving haircuts and slapping on bay rum by the palmful, and old-timers on the stone bench in front of City Hall, spitting tobacco juice onto the sidewalk and resolving matters both momentous and trivial as they spoke to one another so desultorily that they might have been using code.

In the course of it all, I got to know some of the fundamentalists reasonably well. I forgave them their reputation; they forgave me my affiliation with the Eastern liberal media establishment. One man, the vice president of the local bank, for which he had begun to work as a part-time teller almost a quarter of a century earlier, told me that life was good in his town and he hoped my piece would show it. The unemployment rate was below the national average, the number of alcoholics small, the air clean. The kids, he said, did not use drugs or copulate promiscuously. "They're fine young people, Mr. Burns. You'll see."

The next night, the crew and I taped one of the families that had organized   5
the bookburning as they got dressed for the big do: sweaters and sweatshirts to protect themselves from the evening chill, T-shirts and jerseys underneath so they could take off the outer garments if the flames got too hot. "We think we've got something special here," said the sister-in-law of the bank vice president; she

was shooing her husband and kids out the door, into the station wagon, bound for duty. "Not flashy, but special."

I nodded.

"We're just trying to hang on."

It was one of those station wagons with faux wooden panels on the sides and a name like Suburbanite or Country Squire. It eased out the driveway and down the street and, before it disappeared around the stop sign on the corner, one of the kids rolled down a back window and waved.

I waved back.

Within two hours the fire in the church parking lot was raging like the blast   10
furnaces of Protestant hell. Blue-orange flames shot into the night, plastering themselves against an almost starless sky, as volume upon volume of incinerated literature snapped, crackled, and hissed below. Two teenage boys did their best to keep up with the demand for tinder, but it was no easy task. They loaded their wheelbarrows with books in the church basement and pushed them across the parking lot with the wheels squeaking and the huge mounds of cargo constantly shifting, threatening to topple. Sometimes a novel or a biography or an anthology of poems would fall and the boys would kick it aside, picking it up on their next trip and adding it to the mountain of condemned tomes they were erecting about twenty feet from the inferno's outer edge.

As for those who actually threw the books into the blaze, several of them had to be restrained; they wanted to make the flames soar so high that they might have gotten out of control, endangering nearby buildings and eliminating forever the possibility of a future zoning variance. A few small children, the spirit willing but the forearms weak, stood on the perimeter of the fire and flung books so far short that they had to be pushed the rest of the way by an old man with a rake, who seemed to be playing a peculiarly listless version of shuffleboard.

"How tight can you get with that lens?" I said to my cameraman.

"How tight do you want me to get?"

I held one hand parallel to the ground halfway up my nose and the other parallel to the ground at the mid-point of my forehead. "The frame like this."

He shook his head. "I'd have to be right up in their faces."   15

I told him to do it.

"It bugs people sometimes, I move in like that."

"I don't think they'll even notice."

He shrugged.

I wanted their eyes. What I saw in them that night, and was determined to   20
capture on tape, was something at once primitive and reverential. They were wide, unblinking, either focused on something deep within the flames or not focused at all; either as intense as lasers or as blank as television screens when the sets are turned off. So many pairs of eyes, so many tentacles of fire, so much crackling of burnt books in the air.

I tried to decide what the eyes reminded me of, who they seemed to belong to. Was it cave dwellers, their awe inspired by the blaze's violent majesty? Was it

Ku Klux Klanners, the full depths of their hatred unleashed by the heat and frantic flickering? Was it pyromaniacs, their aesthetic impulses triggered by the perversely poetic dance of fire and sparks in the breeze?

No, I decided after a few minutes; it was none of these. What the people at the bookburning in the small midwestern town reminded me of was not other human beings at all. It was animals. Small animals. Cats. Maybe kittens. Attractive creatures: cute, cuddly, fun to play with. I could imagine myself living next door to them and getting along just fine when we happened across one another on the street: a nod and a stroke from me, from them a flick of the tail and a rumbling purr.

But kittens are too insecure to behave sensibly when threatened, and too unsophisticated to understand what really constitutes a threat. At perceived danger they bare teeth, scratch, and claw. Backs arch, eyes gleam with malignant light. They are afraid of whatever is out of their direct ken, and when you are a small animal in a large cosmos, so very much is. They were drawn to the fire, terrified of the fire, kin to the fire; it seemed to fill them with longing as it drained them of reason.

I watched. The cameraman shot them in extreme closeup. Overhead, a shooting star drew a white line under the moon.

I wanted to say something to the men and women feeding the flames. I've 25
read some of the books you're cremating, is how I might have begun, and there's no point. They won't hurt you. The guy who wrote *Slaughter-House Five* has as good a heart as you do, is just as sentimental in his way. The guy who wrote the *Rabbit* novels is lamenting the rootlessness of his character's life, not advocating it. Sure, the woman who wrote *The Women's Room* is angrier than you, but does that mean you reject her reasons without a hearing, consign her arguments, like her prose, to flames of oblivion?

I wanted to say: Read *Catch-22* more slowly; it celebrates the human spirit in times of adversity no less than you do with your faith. Read *Native Son* more openly; it lashes out at injustice precisely as you would if you had been its victims. Read *Lord of the Flies* more carefully and *One Flew Over the Cuckoo's Nest* less defensively and *Ordinary People* without taking it as some kind of personal indictment. Get to know the people who populate the books. Walk the roads they walk and smell the air they breathe and, if you can, feel the pains inflicted on them, or the pains they inflict on others. You don't have to agree with the characters or with the authors who sired them, but you should try to understand their worlds. It is better that possibilities be raised and rejected than that they never be raised at all.

I wanted to say: I know that a lot of these books are not appropriate for your children, but keep your children away from them until they're older. Don't burn them. Don't teach violence against ideas. Teach the testing of ideas, the competition among them, the struggle to find the viable ones and put them into practice. Teach your disagreement with the ideas you do not find viable, and explain your reasons. But don't teach fire. "The great threat to the young and pure in heart," said Heywood Broun in his biography of Anthony Comstock, "is not what they read, but what they don't read."

I wanted to say to the men and women in the church parking lot: Be parents, not arsonists. I wanted to say: Nice kitty. I opened my mouth a time or two, closed it as quickly, spoke not a word.

Then I turned away from the bookburning that I was covering for NBC News, but I could not escape the flames. They were reflected in the windows of a small restaurant across the street, the panes of ebony glass shimmering like a sheet of liquid metal. I could still hear the books sizzling, and as the wind shifted I smelled a particularly acrid kind of smoke.

I stuffed my notebook into my pocket and closed my eyes for a moment. In the   30
next instant I heard a pitchpipe. My eyes snapped open; I turned around again.

The bookburners had begun to sing "What a Friend We Have in Jesus." The words rang through the night in tones piercing and clear, everyone believing in the lyrics, selling the song, and continuing to look at the fire through those small-animal eyes. Humane Inquisitors, they were—scarring no flesh, drawing no blood, breaking no bones; their crimes were against reasonable judgment, not humanity. Yet the sky seemed to darken a little as the music began, the eventual dawn to slip a few minutes further away.

> What a friend we have in Jesus,
> All our sins and griefs to bear.
> What a privilege to carry
> Everything to God in prayer.

The concert lasted almost an hour, hymn after hymn after hymn, voices growing stronger as the night wore on and the fire kept snapping, as if through volume alone could the singers convince themselves of the justice of literature made ash.

The first song I heard was the only one I recognized. There was nothing on the bill from Woody Guthrie.

Several books by Mark Twain were extinguished on that forlorn occasion: *The Prince and the Pauper*, *A Connecticut Yankee in King Arthur's Court*, *Adventures of Tom Sawyer*, and of course that old standby at uprisings against the excesses of the printed word, *The Adventures of Huckleberry Finn*. At least three copies of the latter went up in smoke, one so old it may have been valuable.

The author would not have been surprised. He might even have expressed   35
satisfaction. The first people who objected to his story of Huck and Jim and their life on the Mississippi were the officials of a library in a small but historic Massachusetts town, who found the book "trash and suitable only for the slums."

"Those idiots in Concord are not a court of last resort," Twain fumed when he learned of the controversy, "and I am not disturbed by their moral gymnastics. No other book of mine has sold so many copies within 2 months after issue as this one. . . . They have given us a rattling tip-top puff which will go into every paper in the country. . . . That will sell 25,000 copies for us sure."

He was wrong. Within two months of the prediction, *The Adventures of Huckleberry Finn* had sold fifty thousand copies. It has not stopped selling since. Twain had underestimated the number, but knew full well the paradox that is censorship's very core.

In colonial times, it was the custom to ring bells and fire cannon to announce public celebrations. To those who voted for him, Thomas Jefferson provided a reason for such festivity by being elected the third president of the United States in 1800. To those who preferred the incumbent John Adams, the election was the end of the Federalist dream. Jefferson and Aaron Burr each received seventy-three electoral votes, Adams sixty-five; Jefferson was awarded the presidency by the House of Representatives.

The night before the new president was to be inaugurated, a man who had cast his ballot for Adams, "an aristocrat," decided to make his frustration known. He stole the clapper from the bell in his local church so that triumphant Jeffersonians would not have the pleasure of hearing it clang the next morning. "A protesting witness saw a lesson" in the theft, writes Dumas Malone in the fourth of his six volumes on Jefferson's life. The witness knew that the newspapers would report the incident, and thus commented to a friend "that the man who removed the clapper was defeating his own ends, for now the bell would be heard all over the continent, instead of merely in that one single town."

And so it was. So it still is when a clapper is secreted away, or an attempt made to do so. Readers, after all, are by definition a curious lot. We are sure to start at the sound of a silent bell. In all likelihood, we will find something irresistible in its melody.   40

Reflecting and Interpreting

1. Comment on the title of the essay. This paradox establishes a thread of continuity (one word) that is present in the very first paragraph. What is it?

2. Examine the description of the book burning. How did it affect several of the participants?

3. What similarities does the author see between the participants and kittens?

4. Summarize what Burns wanted to say during the book burning but did not. What may have caused him to remain quiet?

5. Mark Twain knew the paradox that lies at the heart of censorship. What is it?

6. Is the anecdote about Thomas Jefferson's election and the stolen bell clapper off the subject? Why or why not?

A Writer's Response

1. With your group, list the images in this essay that function as symbols. Then analyze how each one functions. (For help with symbolism, see chapter 27.)

2. In a group discuss the implications of Burns's allusion to an earlier book burning. (Protagoras was a teacher who developed principles of debate in early Greece. At the time there were many lawsuits brought by former exiles unable to reclaim their property. Those who could speak well debated in court and in public.) Or you might consider another famous book burning, such as Hitler's, and its effect.

3. Has there ever been a time in your life when you wish you had spoken out against something that was wrong or unjust? For example, imagine you refrained from defending an odd boy that a small tyrant teased on the school bus. What held you back? Or describe a similar incident, explaining the cause and effect.

The Art of Acknowledgement

Jean Houston

Life is like a roller coaster that can take us from the depths of despair to the apex of joy—if we can just hang on. Clinging precariously, some hardy souls survive alone; others derive strength from the support of a family member, friend, or teacher. In this excerpt from The Possible Human *(1982), Jean Houston, a social scientist, describes the visiting professor who enabled her to surmount a devastating experience during her college years. This timeless tale reminds us that we all have the ability to give a priceless gift.*

I was eighteen years old and I was the golden girl. A junior in college, I was president of the college drama society, a member of the student senate, winner of two off-Broadway critics' awards for acting and directing, director of the class play, and had just turned down an offer to train for the next Olympics (fencing). In class my mind raced and dazzled, spinning off facile but "wowing" analogies to the kudos of teachers and classmates. Socially, I was on top of the heap. My advice was sought, my phone rang constantly, and it seemed that nothing could stop me.

I was the envy of all my friends and I was in a state of galloping chutzpah.

The old Greek tragedies warn us that when hubris rises, nemesis falls. I was no exception to this ancient rule. My universe crashed with great suddenness. It began when three members of my immediate family died. Then a friend whom I loved very much died suddenly of a burst appendix while camping alone in the woods. The scenery of the off-Broadway production fell on my head and I was left almost blind for the next four months. My friends and I parted from each other, they out of embarrassment and I because I didn't think I was worthy. My marks went from being rather good to a D-plus average.

I had so lost confidence in my abilities that I couldn't concentrate on anything or see the connections between things. My memory was a shambles, and within a few months I was placed on probation. All my offices were taken away; public elections were called to fill them. I was asked into the advisor's office and told that I would have to leave the college at the end of the spring term since, clearly, I didn't have the "necessary intelligence to do academic work." When I protested that I had had the "necessary intelligence" during my freshman and sophomore years, I was assured with a sympathetic smile that intellectual decline such as this often happened to young women when "they became interested in other things; it's a matter of hormones, my dear."

Where once I had been vocal and high-spirited in the classroom, I now huddled   5
in my oversized camel's-hair coat in the back of classes, trying to be as nonexistent as possible. At lunch I would lock myself in the green room of the college

theater, scene of my former triumphs, eating a sandwich in despondent isolation. Every day brought its defeat and disacknowledgments, and after my previous career I was too proud to ask for help. I felt like Job and called out to God, "Where are the boils?" since that was about all I was missing.

These Jobian fulminations led me to take one last course. It was taught by a young Swiss professor of religion, Dr. Jacob Taubes, and was supposed to be a study of selected books of the Old Testament. It turned out to be largely a discussion of the dialectic between St. Paul and Nietzsche.

Taubes was the most brilliant and exciting teacher I had ever experienced, displaying European academic wizardry such as I had never known. Hegel, gnosticism, structuralism, phenomenology, and the intellectual passions of the Sorbonne cracked the ice of my self-noughting and I began to raise a tentative hand from my huddle in the back of the room and ask an occasional hesitant question.

Dr. Taubes would answer with great intensity, and soon I found myself asking more questions. One day I was making my way across campus to the bus, when I heard Dr. Taubes addressing me:

"Miss Houston, let me walk with you. You know, you have a most interesting mind."

"Me? I have a *mind*?"   10

"Yes, your questions are luminous. Now what do you think is the nature of the transvaluation of values in Paul and Nietzsche?"

I felt my mind fall into its usual painful dullness and stammered, "I d-don't know."

"Of course you do!" he insisted. "You couldn't ask the kinds of questions you do without having an unusual grasp of these issues. Now please, once again, what do you think of the transvaluation of values in Paul and Nietzsche? It is important for my reflections that I have your reactions."

Well," I said, waking up, "if you put it that way, I think . . ."

I was off and running and haven't shut up since.   15

Dr. Taubes continued to walk me to the bus throughout that term, always challenging me with intellectually vigorous questions. He attended to me. I existed for him in the "realest" of senses, and because I existed for him I began to exist for myself. Within several weeks my eyesight came back, my spirit bloomed, and I became a fairly serious student, whereas before I had been, at best, a bright show-off.

What I acquired from this whole experience was a tragic sense of life, which balanced my previous enthusiasms. I remain deeply grateful for the attention shown me by Dr. Taubes. He acknowledged me when I most needed it. I was empowered in the midst of personal erosion, and my life has been very different for it. I swore to myself then that whenever I came across someone "going under" or in the throes of disacknowledgment, I would try to reach and acknowledge that person as I had been acknowledged.

I would go so far as to say that the greatest of human potentials is the potential of each one of us to empower and acknowledge the other. We all do this throughout our lives, but rarely do we appreciate the power of the empowering that we give to others. To be acknowledged by another, especially during times of confusion, loss, disorientation, disheartenment, is to be given time and place in the sunshine and is, in the metaphor of psychological reality, the solar stimulus for transformation.

The process of healing and growth is immensely quickened when the sun of another's belief is freely given. This gift can be as simple as "Hot Dog Thou Art!" Or it can be as total as "I know you. You are God in hiding." Or it can be a look that goes straight to the soul and charges it with meaning.

I have been fortunate to have known several of those the world deems   20 "saints": Teilhard de Chardin, Mother Teresa of Calcutta, Clemie, an old black woman in Mississippi. To be looked at by these people is to be gifted with the look that engenders. You feel yourself primed at the depths by such seeing. Something so tremendous and yet so subtle wakes up inside that you are able to release the defeats and denigrations of years. If I were to describe it further, I would have to speak of unconditional love joined to a whimsical regarding of you as the cluttered house that hides the holy one.

Saints, you say, but the miracle is that anybody can do it for anybody! Our greatest genius may be the ability to prime the healing and evolutionary circuits of one another.

It is an art form that has yet to be learned, for it is based on something never before fully recognized—deep psychological reciprocity, the art and science of mutual transformation. And all the gurus and masters, all the prophets, profs, and professionals, can do little for us compared to what we could do for each other if we would but be present to the fullness of each other. For there is no answer to anyone's anguished cry of "Why am I here, why am I at all?" except the reply, "Because I am here, because I am."

Reflecting and Interpreting

1. In the second paragraph, Houston says she was "the golden girl" and was in a state of "galloping chutzpah." What does she mean?

2. Houston says, "I felt like Job and called out to God, 'Where are the boils?'" (See Job 2:1–10.) What do Houston's comparison and question reveal?

3. In the fourth paragraph, Houston's account of her experience with the university's administration suggests that the school had no record of Houston's recent loss of four loved ones—or her own accident in the theater. What do you make of these events being ignored?

4. What does Houston mean when she describes herself, while conversing with Dr. Taubes, as "waking up"?

5. What do you think she means when she says, "I existed for him in the 'realest' of senses, and because I existed for him I began to exist for myself"? How does Dr. Taubes's attention affect Houston?

6. What is the theme of this essay? What basic belief has Houston derived from this experience? Do you think the belief has universal applications? Why or why not?

A Writer's Response

1. **Small groups:** Notice Houston's alternating of colloquialisms with literary allusions. For example, what is the effect of "wowing" and "on top of the heap" in one paragraph and "hubris" and "nemesis" in another? What other unusual alternations of levels of formality do you see?

2. **Small groups:** How would you describe Houston's attitude as she looks back on this troubling experience? Does she retain a sense of humor? Find examples to support your claims.

3. Have you ever undergone a distressing experience and been helped by someone? Or perhaps you have been able to "prime the healing and evolutionary circuits" of someone? Describe what happened.

4. Do you see any other topic in this essay that you might like to write about? Suggestions: Describe someone you know who might be considered a "saint"? How to discern fair weather from foul weather friends? Houston's use of irony? The similarities and differences of Paul's experience on the road to Damascus (Acts 22) and of Houston's?

 *Igloo*

James Houston

Although James Houston has been an artist, soldier, and glass designer, he can best be described as an adventurer. For a while he lived in the Arctic—a time reflected in several books, including Confessions of an Igloo Dweller, *from which this excerpt is taken. His straightforward descriptions have the air of a secret sharer—one who tells us privileged information. His surprising fall through an old woman's roof turns a descriptive essay into a rich, rare story.*

One of the most difficult tasks for any Arctic archaeologist to determine is anything about the origins and early use of igloos built of snow. We know that ice igloos were occasionally built and used by Inuit as meat caches, for dogs found them impenetrable. Ice igloos were never favored as human dwellings—they are cold! Igloos used by humans were made of relatively dry, hard, wind-packed snow.

Since an igloo by the very nature of the elements will reduce itself to a few pails of water, the best clue we could have of the early existence and source of igloos would be, for example, an engraving of one scratched into walrus or mammoth ivory. No such discovery has been made in Alaska, Canada, or Greenland. Most experts believe that igloos were first conceived somewhere in the vastness of the Canadian Arctic where man was faced with a treeless expanse and was forced to invent and dwell with his family in that small monument to human genius in the face of adversity, the household dome of snow.

I believe these east coast Inuit in what is now Arctic Quebec were among the best snowhouse builders in the world. Toward the end of winter there in 1950, I saw not a single family (except the Hudson's Bay interpreter and the Royal Canadian Mounted Police special) living in anything but an igloo throughout the winter.

An igloo built as an overnight structure for one human traveler alone will sometimes be no bigger than a dog house. Yet igloos can be very large—*ugas*, dance houses, are made to accommodate up to forty persons. I remember their curved domes in Igloolik were so high that the ingenious builders, who did not yet have the invention of the ladder, had to climb the cross pieces on their long sleds to complete the dome from the interior.

When used as family dwellings, igloos need not have only one room under a central dome. The older ones used to bristle with long, complicated entrance passageways and blocks of snow set up and adjusted as a baffle against the prevailing

5

wind. Often there were side apartments used to house in-laws or visiting relatives, or simple meat caches where the family could protect their fortune against the ravages of a wandering bear or their own dogs.

The entrance to the igloo's interior was built with care. It was fully realized that heat rises and cold falls. The entrance to the snowhouse was built well above floor level, thereby preventing the coldest dead air from penetrating into the house. If it did, the parents would inform you that the coldness inside had been created by children playing, running in and out of the house, drawing in behind them freezing drafts of air.

The igloo usually had an air vent over the entrance called the nostril, which was stuffed with a mitten at night. Beneath it was traditionally the only window, made of a clear or almost clear slab of four- to six-inch-thick lake ice. Salty sea ice is too murky. The whole dome of a snowhouse lets in light, important during winter when there is so little natural light. However, in the lower part of the dome around the sleeping bench, the snow wall is doubled on the outside to prevent unwanted drafts.

Inuit also recognized that eating enough food and getting exercise were the best methods of driving out the cold. Of course, they did not mean bending or stretching exercises, or walking on a treadmill. They meant useful work.

The whole family slept side by side, heads toward the entrance passage, on a wide sleeping platform that reached from wall to wall. It was about knee-high above the floor. This platform was made of solid snow. In Arctic Quebec they covered this bed with stunted willows each as slender as a child's finger, loosely shaped into thin mats. Inuit gathered these small branches growing close to the ground during their caribou hunts on the sub-Arctic inland plains. The only other household articles in an igloo were one or, better, two stone seal-oil lamps in which caribou back fat was also burned, and a squarish stone pot suspended from a tennis racketlike drying rack for boots and mittens. Meat for more immediate use was kept in the entrance tunnels to protect it from the dogs.

These houses intended as more or less permanent dwellings were built in the   10
deepest snowbank one could find. And during the course of the winter some of them were partly drifted in by snow. I know this because once, while walking along the bank of a frozen river admiring the opposite side, I fell through the roof of an igloo and landed hard on an icy floor. I could not imagine what had happened until I sat up, trying to feel my coccyx bone, to see if it was broken. Before me was a sleeping platform and on it sat a very old woman, whom I had never seen before.

"*Itiriit,*" she said to me. "Enter." In the circumstances it was a very polite thing to say.

I looked up at her and wondered if I still could rise.

"*Teetilauvit,*" she said, inviting me to have some tea.

I struggled to my feet and sat down in the only place I could, beside her on the bed. She was small and frail, with sunken cheeks, and thin wisps of hair protruding from her parka hood. Her legs were thrust straight out before her in a way impossible for our old folks who sit on chairs at tables. Her sealskin boots were large, stuffed with long caribou stockings and probably several pairs of seal-skin slippers.

I looked up through the hole I'd made in her snowhouse roof and wondered   15
who I'd send to mend it. She lit her pipe and offered me tobacco and the only little book she had. I pulled out a page and rolled it clumsily into a cigarette. We sipped our tea and smoked together for a while. She explained that one son and his wife took care of her.

She showed me a package of tea, nodded at the tobacco, and, feeling around in her sealskin bag, pulled out a small box of fifty .22 cartridges given to her by the trader.

"I give all of these to a young hunter, and tell him to bring me *akikigik kolit*, ten ptarmigan," she explained, spreading the fingers of both hands. "I tell him that he can eat or give away all the other birds he gets as long as he brings me my ten."

"What if he doesn't get that many birds?" I asked her.

"Oh, he'd better get them or I'll give these *sekoapiks*, little bullets, to some-one else who is a better hunter."

Reflecting and Interpreting

1. What two kinds of igloos were in existence? What else do Arctic archaeologists know about igloos? Why don't they know more? What do they theorize?

2. What surprising facts did you learn about the construction, furnishings, and functions of igloos?

3. Were you surprised by the old woman's poise and politeness at Houston's un-invited and unorthodox entry? (Consider how you might have responded if a motorcycle rider had burst through your front window into your living room.)

4. What effect does the chance encounter with a woman whose roof the author falls through have on our understanding of igloo life?

5. Near the end of the story, the old woman replies, "Oh, he'd better get them or I'll give these *sekoapiks*, little bullets, to someone else who is a better hunter." What do you think she means, considering that the first hunter already has the first handful of bullets?

A Writer's Response

1. In everyone's past there seems to be an unusual place to hang out—an uncle's old barn, the inside of a silo, a corner of your grandmother's basement, or the roof of an apartment building. Write a paragraph describing your special place.

2. Research an unusual type of dwelling, perhaps a fort, a historic home, or the home of an indigenous culture. Or you might describe a home you once vis-ited that was very different from your own. Or you might describe an old mill, covered bridge, or other historic structure. What is the story behind the structure? (A descriptive essay should have a central point—explained in chapter 11.)

~ *One Writer's Beginnings*

Eudora Welty

Eudora Welty published her first piece, a short story, in 1936. After writing short fiction for ten years, she then published a novel, Delta Wedding, *in 1946. Since then she has written several books, receiving a Pulitzer Prize in 1971. In 1980 she received the National Medal for Literature and the Presidential Medal of Freedom. In this excerpt from* One Writer's Beginnings *(1984), she explores the connection between reality and the imagination in an attempt to trace her origin as a writer.*

I had the window seat. Beside me, my father checked the progress of our train by moving his finger down the timetable and springing open his pocket watch. He explained to me what the position of the arms of the semaphore meant; before we were to pass through a switch we would watch the signal lights change. Along our track, the mileposts could be read; he read them. Right on time by Daddy's watch, the next town sprang into view, and just as quickly was gone.

Side by side and separately, we each lost ourselves in the experience of not missing anything, of seeing everything, of knowing each time what the blows of the whistle meant. But of course it was not the same experience: what was new to me, not older than ten, was a landmark to him. My father knew our way mile by mile; by day or by night, he knew where we were. Everything that changed under our eyes, in the flying countryside, was the known world to him, the imagination to me. Each in our own way, we hungered for all of this: my father and I were in no other respect or situation so congenial.

In Daddy's leather grip was his traveler's drinking cup, collapsible; a lid to fit over it had a ring to carry it by; it traveled in a round leather box. This treasure would be brought out at my request, for me to bear to the water cooler at the end of the Pullman car, fill to the brim, and bear back to my seat, to drink water over its smooth lip. The taste of silver could almost be relied on to shock your teeth.

After dinner in the sparkling dining car, my father and I walked back to the open-air observation platform at the end of the train and sat on the folding chairs placed at the railing. We watched the sparks we made fly behind us into the night. Fast as our speed was, it gave us time enough to see the rose-red cinders turn to ash, each one, and disappear from sight. Sometimes a house far back in the empty hills showed a light no bigger than a star. The sleeping countryside seemed itself to open a way through for our passage, then close again behind us.

The swaying porter would be making ready our berths for the night, pulling the shade down just so, drawing the green fishnet hammock across the window so the clothes you took off could ride along beside you, turning down the tight- 5 made bed, standing up the two snowy pillows as high as they were wide, switching on the eye of the reading lamp, starting the tiny electric fan—you suddenly saw its blades turn into gauze and heard its insect murmur; and drawing across it all the pair of thick green theaterlike curtains—billowing, smelling of cigar smoke—between which you would crawl or dive headfirst to button them together with yourself inside, to be seen no more that night.

When you lay enclosed and enwrapped, your head on a pillow parallel to the track, the rhythm of the rail clicks pressed closer to your body as if it might be your heart beating, but the sound of the engine seemed to come from farther away than when it carried you in daylight. The whistle was almost too far away to be heard, its sound wavering back from the engine over the roofs of the cars. What you listened for was the different sound that ran under you when your own car crossed on a trestle, then another sound on an iron bridge; a low or a high bridge—each had its pitch, or drumbeat, for your car.

Riding in the sleeper rhythmically lulled me and waked me. From time to time, waked suddenly, I raised my window shade and looked out at my own strip of the night. Sometimes there was unexpected moonlight out there. Sometimes the perfect shadow of our train, with our car, with me invisibly included, ran deep below, crossing a river with us by the light of the moon. Sometimes the encroaching walls of mountains woke me by clapping at my ears. The tunnels made the train's passage resound like the "loud" pedal of a piano, a roar that seemed to last as long as a giant's temper tantrum.

But my father put it all into the frame of regularity, predictability, that was his fatherly gift in the course of our journey. I saw it going by, the outside world, in a flash. I dreamed over what I could see as it passed, as well as over what I couldn't. Part of the dream was what lay beyond, where the path wandered off through the pasture, the red clay road climbed and went over the hill or made a turn and was hidden in trees, or toward a river whose bridge I could see but whose name I'd never know. A house back at its distance at night showing a light from an open doorway, the morning faces of the children who stopped still in what they were doing, perhaps picking blackberries or wild plums, and watched us go by—I never saw with the thought of their continuing to be there just the same after we were out of sight. For now, and for a long while to come, I was proceeding in fantasy.

Reflecting and Interpreting

1. What do we learn about Welty and her father in the first and second paragraphs? Do they seem similar or different? How?

2. In describing the scene on the observation platform in the evening, Welty's imagination becomes active. Can you find the sentence? What is the effect?

3. The description of the porter making up the berths is filled with similes and metaphors. Which ones do you especially like?

4. Welty spends a paragraph describing the sounds of the engine, rails, whistle, and structures that vary the "pitch, or drumbeat, for your car." What device is used here? What do these details reveal about her, even as a child?

5. Note the alternating of images when she describes riding in the sleeper. How do these images and sounds reflect the rhythm of the train?

6. Is the essay written, for the most part, from the point of view of a ten-year-old or from an adult in retrospect? Where does a shift occur? What was "his fatherly gift"? Why does Welty seem to need that?

A Writer's Response

1. Describe a trip you took as a child that was memorable. Use vivid images and sensory language to recapture the experience and your feelings at the time.

2. Welty opens with "I had the window seat." Later she says, "I saw it going by, the outside world, in a flash." You might say we all have a window seat from which we view life as it flashes by. Can you select one vivid "flash" from your window on life to describe in an essay?

Dawn Watch

John Ciardi

John Ciardi was a renowned poet who taught at Rutgers, spent twenty years as poetry editor for the Saturday Review *magazine, and wrote children's books, poetry textbooks, and a translation of* The Divine Comedy. *In the following essay from his book* Manner of Speaking, *Ciardi uses prose to praise a magical time of day.*

Unless a man is up for the dawn and for the half hour or so of first light, he has missed the best of the day.

The traffic has just started, not yet a roar and a stink. One car at a time goes by, the tires humming almost like the sound of a brook a half mile down in the crease of a mountain I know—a sound that carries not because it is loud but because everything else is still.

It isn't exactly a mist that hangs in the thickets but more nearly the ghost of a mist—a phenomenon like side vision. Look hard and it isn't there, but glance without focusing and something registers, an exhalation that will be gone three minutes after the sun comes over the treetops.

The lawns shine with a dew not exactly dew. There is a rabbit bobbing about on the lawn and then freezing. If it were truly a dew, his tracks would shine black on the grass, and he leaves no visible track. Yet, there is something on the grass that makes it glow a depth of green it will not show again all day. Or is that something in the dawn air?

Our cardinals know what time it is. They drop pure tones from the hemlock   5
tops. The gang of grackles that makes a slum of the pin oak also knows the time but can only grate at it. They sound like a convention of broken universal joints grating uphill. The grackles creak and squeak, and the cardinals form tones that only occasionally sound through the noise. I scatter sunflower seeds by the birdbaths for the cardinals and hope the grackles won't find them.

My neighbor's tomcat comes across the lawn, probably on his way home from passion, or only acting as if he had had a big night. I suspect him of being one of those poolroom braggarts who can't get next to a girl but who likes to let on that he is a hot stud. This one is too can-fed and too lazy to hunt for anything. Here he comes now, ignoring the rabbit. And there he goes.

As soon as he has hopped the fence, I let my dog out. The dog charges the rabbit, watches it jump the fence, shakes himself in a self-satisfied way, then trots dutifully into the thicket for his morning service, stopping to sniff everything on the way back.

There is an old mountain laurel on the island of the driveway turnaround. From somewhere on the wind a white morning-glory rooted next to it and has climbed it. Now the laurel is woven full of white bells tinged pink by the first rays through the not quite mist. Only in earliest morning can they be seen. Come out two hours from now and there will be no morning-glories.

Dawn, too, is the hour of a weed I know only as day flower—a bright blue button that closes in full sunlight. I have weeded bales of it out of my flower beds, its one daytime virtue being the shallowness of its root system that allows it to be pulled out effortlessly in great handfuls. Yet, now it shines. Had it a few more hours of such shining in its cycle, I would cultivate it as a ground cover, but dawn is its one hour, and a garden is for whole days.

There is another blue morning weed whose name I do not know. This one   10
grows from a bulb to pulpy stems and a bedraggled daytime sprawl. Only a shovel will dig it out. Try weeding it by hand and the stems will break off to be replaced by new ones and to sprawl over the chosen plants in the flower bed. Yet, now and for another hour it outshines its betters, its flowers about the size of a quarter and paler than those of the day flower but somehow more brilliant, perhaps because of the contrast of its paler foliage.

And now the sun is slanting in full. It is bright enough to make the leaves of the Japanese red maple seem a transparent red bronze when the tree is between me and the light. There must be others, but this is the only tree I know whose leaves let the sun through in this way—except, that is, when the fall colors start. Aspen leaves, when they first yellow and before they dry, are transparent in this way. I tell myself it must have something to do with the red-yellow range of the spectrum. Green takes sunlight and holds it, but red and yellow let it through.

The damned crabgrass is wrestling with the zinnias, and I stop to weed it out. The stuff weaves too close to the zinnias to make the iron claw usable. And it won't do to pull at the stalks. Crabgrass (at least in a mulched bed) can be weeded only with dirty fingers. Thumb and forefinger have to pincer into the dirt and grab the root-center. Weeding, of course, is an illusion of hope. Pulling out the root only stirs the soil and brings new crabgrass seeds into germinating position. Take a walk around the block and a new clump will have sprouted by the time you get back. But I am not ready to walk around the block. I fill a small basket with the plucked clumps, and for the instant I look at them, the zinnias are weedless.

Don't look back. I dump the weeds in the thicket where they will be smothered by the grass clippings I will pile on at the next cutting. On the way back I see the cardinals come down for the sunflower seeds, and the jays join them, and then the grackles start ganging in, gatecrashing the buffet and clattering all over it. The dog stops chewing his rawhide and makes a dash into the puddle of birds, which splashes away from him.

I hear a brake-squeak I have been waiting for and know the paper has arrived. As usual, the news turns out to be another disaster count. The function of the wire services is to bring us tragedies faster than we can pity. In the end we shall all be inured, numb, and ready for emotionless programming. I sit on the patio and read until the sun grows too bright on the page. The cardinals have stopped singing, and the grackles have flown off. It's the end of birdsong again.

Then suddenly—better than song for its instant—a hummingbird the color 15
of green crushed velvet hovers in the throat of my favorite lily, a lovely high-
bloomer I got the bulbs for but not the name. The lily is a crest of white horns
with red dots and red velvet tongues along the insides of the petals and with an
odor that drowns the patio. The hummingbird darts in and out of each horn in
turn, then hovers an instant, and disappears.

Even without the sun, I have had enough of the paper. I'll take that hummingbird as my news for this dawn. It is over now. I smoke one more cigarette
too many and decide that, if I go to bed now, no one in the family need know I
have stayed up for it again. Why do they insist on shaking their heads when they
find me still up for breakfast, after having scribbled through the dark hours?
They always do. They seem compelled to express pity for an old loony who can't
find his own way to bed. Why won't they understand that this is the one hour of
any day that must not be missed, as it is the one hour I couldn't imagine getting
up for, though I can still get to it by staying up? It makes sense to me. There
comes a time when the windows lighten and the twittering starts. I look up and
know it's time to leave the papers in their mess. I could slip quietly into bed and
avoid the family's headshakes, but this stroll-around first hour is too good to
miss. Even my dog, still sniffing and circling, knows what hour this is.

Come on, boy. It's time to go in. The rabbit won't come back till tomorrow,
and the birds have work to do. The dawn's over. It's time to call it a day.

Reflecting and Interpreting

1. Ciardi's essay has an argumentative edge, which is apparent in his thesis statement. Where is it?

2. Ciardi has an eye for minute details, which he highlights with similes and
   metaphors. What is the effect of these comparisons?

3. Instead of presenting only beautiful images of the morning, Ciardi pairs negative images with positive ones and presents other unusual contrasts. What are
   the effects?

4. Throughout the essay, Ciardi's carefully chosen words create sensory descriptions that convey an essence of the scene. How many types of appeals to the
   senses can you find?

5. Does Ciardi make his reversed schedule seem logical? Has he supplied enough
   support for his claim to be convincing? Give reasons for your answer.

A Writer's Response

1. Glance at Garrison Keillor's essay, "How to Write a Personal Letter." Now recast a portion of "Dawn Watch," mimicking Keillor's style, into an essay called
   "How to Begin a Day (or an Evening)." How does this contrast with Ciardi's
   style?

2. List favorite spots where you can be alone. Focus on one and freewrite about the atmosphere there, incorporating as many sights, sounds, and other sensory images as possible. Next add a chronological structure, similar to Ciardi's, describing the "events" of a typical visit from beginning to end. How does the passing of time affect what happens there? What time of day is best? Rewrite your draft into a revised essay.

Pedestrian Students and High-Flying Squirrels

Liane Ellison Norman

So what do high-flying squirrels and many college students have in common? What is a significant difference? Liane Ellison Norman creates this unique analogy to illustrate a common view of freshman college students, intent on obtaining the necessary skills to land a good job. Thought-provoking, the essay examines certain traditional beliefs and questions their practicality.

The squirrel is curious. He darts and edges, profile first, one bright black eye on me, the other alert for his enemies on the other side. Like a fencer, he faces both ways, for every impulse toward me an impulse away. His tail is airy. He flicks and flourishes it, taking readings of some subtle kind.

I am enjoying a reprieve of warm sun in a season of rain and impending frost. Around me today is the wine of the garden's final ripening. On the zucchini, planted late, the flagrant blossoms flare and decline in a day's time.

I am sitting on the front porch thinking about my students. Many of them earnestly and ardently want me to teach them to be hacks. Give us ten tricks, they plead, ten nifty fail-safe ways to write a news story. Don't make us think our way through these problems, they storm (and when I am insistent that thinking *is* the trick, "You never listen to us," they complain.) Who cares about the First Amendment? they sneer. What are John Peter Zenger and Hugo Black to us? Teach us how to earn a living. They will be content, they explain, with know-how and jobs, satisfied to do no more than cover the tedium of school board and weather.

Under the rebellion, there is a plaintive panic. What if, on the job—assuming there is a job to be on—they fearlessly defend the free press against government, grand jury, and media monopoly, but don't know how to write an obituary. Shouldn't obituaries come first?

I hope not, but even obituaries need good information and firm prose, and both, I say, require clear thought.

The squirrel does not share my meditation. He grows tired of inquiring into me. His dismissive tail floats out behind as he takes a running leap into the tree. Up the bark he goes and onto a branch, where he crashes through the leaves. He soars from slender perch to slender perch, shaking up the trees as if he were the west wind. What a madcap he is, to go racing from one twig that dips under him to another at those heights!

5

His acrobatic clamor loosens buckeyes in their prickly armor. They drop, break open, and he is down the tree in a twinkling, picking, choosing. He finds what he wants and carries it, an outsize nut which is burnished like a fine cello, across the lawn, up a pole, and across the tightrope telephone line to the other side, where he disappears in maple foliage.

Some inner clock or calendar tells him to stock his larder against the deep snows and hard times that are coming. I have heard that squirrels are fuzzy-minded, that they collect their winter groceries and store them, and then forget where they are cached. But this squirrel is purposeful; he appears to know he'd better look ahead. Faced with necessity, he is prudent, but not fearful. He prances and flies as he goes about his task of preparation, and he never fails to look into whatever startles his attention.

Though he is not an ordinary pedestrian, crossing the street far above, I sometimes see the mangled fur of a squirrel on the street, with no flirtation left. Even a high-flying squirrel may zap himself on an aerial live wire. His days are dangerous and his winters are lean, but still he lays in provisions the way a trapeze artist goes about his work, with daring and dash.

For the squirrel, there is no work but living. He gathers food, reproduces, tends the children for a while, and stays out of danger. Doing these things with style is what distinguishes him. But for my students, unemployment looms as large as the horizon itself. Their anxiety has cause. And yet, what good is it? Ten tricks or no ten tricks, there are not enough jobs. The well-trained, well-educated stand in line for unemployment checks with the unfortunates and the drifters. Neither skill nor virtue holds certain promise. This being so, I wonder, why should these students not demand, for the well-being of their souls, the liberation of their minds?

It grieves me that they want to be pedestrians, earthbound and always careful. You ask too much, they say. What you want is painful and unfair. There are a multitude of pressures that instruct them to train, not free, themselves.

Many of them are the first generation to go to college; family aspirations are in their trust. Advisers and models tell them to be doctors, lawyers, engineers, cops, and public-relations people; no one ever tells them they can be poets, philosophers, farmers, inventors, or wizards. Their elders are anxious too; they reject the eccentric and the novel. And, realism notwithstanding, they cling to talismanic determination; play it safe and do things right and I, each one thinks, will get a job even though others won't.

I tell them fondly of my college days, which were a dizzy time (as I think the squirrel's time must be), as I let loose and pitched from fairly firm stands into the space of intellect and imagination, never quite sure what solid branch I would light on. That was the most useful thing I learned, the practical advantage (not to mention the exhilaration) of launching out to find where my propellant mind could take me.

A luxury? one student ponders, a little wistfully.

Yes, luxury, and yet necessity, and it aroused that flight, a fierce unappeas- 15
able appetite to know and to essay. The luxury I speak of is not like other privi-
leges of wealth and power that must be hoarded to be had. If jobs are scarce, the
heady regions of treetop adventure are not. Flight and gaiety cost nothing,
though of course they may cost everything.

The squirrel, my frisky analogue, is not perfectly free. He must go on all
fours, however nimbly he does it. Dogs are always after him, and when he barely
escapes, they rant up the tree as he dodges among the branches that give under
his small weight. He feeds on summer's plenty and pays the price of strontium in
his bones. He is no freer of industrial ordure than I am. He lives, mates, and dies
(no obituary, first or last, for him), but still he plunges and balances, risking his
neck because it is his nature.

I like the little squirrel for his simplicity and bravery. He will never get ahead
in life, never find a good job, never settle down, never be safe. There are no sure-
fire tricks to make it as a squirrel.

Reflecting and Interpreting

1. Examine the first sentence of the essay. Is this sentence significant, or is it
   merely specifying a characteristic of a squirrel? Give a reason for your answer.

2. Why is the second paragraph relevant? Would some other season have done
   just as well to set the scene? Why or why not?

3. What is the fear that Norman senses in many of her students? What do they assume they should be learning about writing? (What does *obituary* symbolize?)

4. How are the squirrel's activities that Norman observes similar to those of college students?

5. Is Norman advising students not to listen to advisers' and parents' advice
   about an occupation? What is she recommending?

6. Why is Norman sad? What does she mean when she says they "want to be
   pedestrians"? (Check the adjective meaning of this word.) What does she say
   was the most practical advantage she gained in college?

7. Norman says she had "a fierce unappeasable appetite to know and to essay."
   What does she mean? (Check the verb meaning of *essay*.) How are these
   qualities related to finding and keeping a job? Or are they?

8. What qualities does Norman admire in the squirrel? She ends with "There are
   no sure-fire tricks to make it as a squirrel." Is she just being flippant, or is there
   a deeper meaning here? Why or why not?

A Writer's Response

1. With your group, discuss whether or not most jobs are entirely "safe." Once
   you get the necessary skills in your field, will you be immune to job turn-

over? Before answering, list major factors that affect the job market. What are they?

2. What personal qualities are necessary to survive fluctuations in the job market? How will the qualities that Norman mentions help us to regain our equilibrium after a downsizing?

3. Write a descriptive essay that uses an image, as Norman does, to represent your main point. Before you start, list similarities and differences to see if the analogy will work. Check your draft to be sure the meaning of the symbol is clear but not too obvious.

How to Write a Personal Letter

Garrison Keillor

Forget your fear of the white sheet of paper! You don't "owe" anyone a letter—a letter is a gift! So says Garrison Keillor, radio personality and writer, well known for his home-spun philosophy and tales of Lake Woebegon. Keillor takes the dread out of an activity that should just be a time to relax and be yourself.

We shy persons need to write a letter now and then, or else we'll dry up and blow away. It's true. And I speak as one who loves to reach for the phone and talk. The telephone is to shyness what Hawaii is to February, it's a way out of the woods. *And yet:* a letter is better.

Such a sweet gift—a piece of handmade writing, in an envelope that is not a bill, sitting in our friend's path when she trudges home from a long day spent among wahoos and savages, a day our words will help repair. They don't need to be immortal, just sincere. She can read them twice and again tomorrow: *You're someone I care about, Corinne, and think of often, and every time I do, you make me smile.*

We need to write, otherwise nobody will know who we are. They will have only a vague impression of us as A Nice Person, because, frankly, we don't shine at conversation, we lack the confidence to thrust our faces forward and say, "Hi, I'm Heather Hooten, let me tell you about my week." Mostly we say "Uh-huh" and "Oh really." People smile and look over our shoulder, looking for someone else to talk to.

So a shy person sits down and writes a letter. To be known by another person—to meet and talk freely on the page—to be close despite distance. To escape from anonymity and be our own sweet selves and express the music of our souls.

We want our dear Aunt Eleanor to know that we have fallen in love, that we   5
quit our job, that we're moving to New York, and we want to say a few things that might not get said in casual conversation: *Thank you for what you've meant to me. I am very happy right now.*

The first step in writing letters is to get over the guilt of *not* writing. You don't "owe" anybody a letter. Letters are a gift. The burning shame you feel when you see unanswered mail makes it harder to pick up a pen and makes for a cheer-less letter when you finally do. *I feel bad about not writing, but I've been so busy,* etc. Skip this. Few letters are obligatory, and they are *Thanks for the wonderful gift* and *I am terribly sorry to hear about George's death.* Write these promptly if you want to keep your friends. Don't worry about the others, except love letters, of course. When your true love writes *Dear Light of My Life, Joy of My Heart*, some response is called for.

Some of the best letters are tossed off in a burst of inspiration, so keep your writing stuff in one place where you can sit down for a few minutes and—*Dear Roy, I am in the middle of an essay but thought I'd drop you a line. Hi to your sweetie too*—dash off a note to a pal. Envelopes, stamps, address book, everything in a drawer so you can write fast when the pen is hot.

A blank white 8″ × 11″ sheet can look as big as Montana if the pen's not so hot—try a smaller page and write boldly. Get a pen that makes a sensuous line, get a comfortable typewriter, a friendly word processor—whichever feels easy to the hand.

Sit for a few minutes with the blank sheet of paper in front of you, and let your friend come to mind. Remember the last time you saw each other and how your friend looked and what you said and what perhaps was unsaid between you; when your friend becomes real to you, start to write.

Write the salutation—*Dear You*—and take a deep breath and plunge in. A   10
simple declarative sentence will do, followed by another and another. As if you were talking to us. Don't think about grammar, don't think about style, just give us your news. Where did you go, who did you see, what did they say, what do you think?

If you don't know where to begin, start with the present: *I'm sitting at the kitchen table on a rainy Saturday morning. Everyone is gone and the house is quiet.* Let the letter drift along. The toughest letter to crank out is one that is meant to impress, as we all know from writing job applications; if it's hard work to slip off a letter to a friend, maybe you're trying too hard to be terrific. A letter is only a report to someone who already likes you for reasons other than your brilliance. Take it easy.

Don't worry about form. It's not a term paper. When you come to the end of one episode, just start a new paragraph. You can go from a few lines about the sad state of rock 'n' roll to the fight with your mother to your fond memories of Mexico to the kitchen sink and what's in it. The more you write, the easier it gets, and when you have a True True Friend to write to, a soul sibling, then it's like driving a car; you just press on the gas.

Don't tear up the page and start over when you write a bad line—try to write your way out of it. Make mistakes and plunge on. Let the letter cook along and let yourself be bold. Outrage, confusion, love—whatever is in your mind, let it find a way to the page. Writing is a means of discovery, always, and when you come to the end and write *Yours ever* or *Hugs and Kisses*, you'll know something you didn't when you wrote *Dear Pal*.

Probably your friend will put your letter away, and it'll be read again a few years from now—and it will improve with age.

And forty years from now, your friend's grandkids will dig it out of the attic   15
and read it, a sweet and precious relic of the ancient Eighties that gives them a
sudden clear glimpse of the world we old-timers knew. You will have then created an object of art. Your simple lines about where you went, who you saw,
what they said, will speak to those children and they will feel in their hearts the
humanity of our times.

You can't pick up a phone and call the future and tell them about our times.
You have to pick up a piece of paper.

Reflecting and Interpreting

1. Who is Keillor's intended audience? Might other people also benefit from his presentation of the benefits of letter writing? Who?

2. What does Keillor mean when he says that "writing is a means of discovery"? Does this apply to any other kinds of writing besides personal letters? Explain. When does writing work as a means of discovery for you?

3. Examine the last two paragraphs of Keillor's essay. What universal truths can you find?

4. In this essay Keillor mixes developmental strategies. What strategies do you see besides process analysis?

A Writer's Response

1. Alone or with your group members, write a step-by-step analysis of something you do. For example, you might consider a morning or evening "ritual" such as caring for a pet or a Sunday afternoon activity. Create a list of the main points you will cover and in what order. Then discuss ways in which you can use point of view and humor to make the essay more accessible and engaging.

2. Try rewriting some of Keillor's paragraphs using third person only. For instance, rewrite paragraph 3 or 5, deleting all first-person pronouns (*we, I,* etc.). Then try rewriting paragraph 6, 11, 12, or 13, this time eliminating all second-person pronouns (*you, your*). How difficult is this rewriting? How does the third-person point of view change those paragraphs?

⌇ *Falling for Apples*

Noel Perrin

Noel Perrin has served as an associate editor for the Medical Economics *journal. Since 1959 he has taught English at Dartmouth College in New Hampshire. Twice a Guggenheim Fellow, Perrin also received a Fulbright Fellowship to teach one year at the University of Warsaw. His writings include articles, essays, novels, and a history of Japan. In the essay that follows, excerpted from* Second Person Rural, *Perrin describes an early way of making apple cider.*

The number of children who eagerly help around a farm is rather small. Willing helpers do exist, but many more of them are five years old than fifteen. In fact, there seems to be a general law that says as long as a kid is too little to help effectively, he or she is dying to. Then, just as they reach the age when they really could drive a fence post or empty a sap bucket without spilling half of it, they lose interest. Now it's cars they want to drive, or else they want to stay in the house and listen for four straight hours to The Who. That sort of thing.

There is one exception to this rule. Almost no kid that I have ever met outgrows an interest in cidering. In consequence, cider making remains a family time on our farm, even though it's been years since any daughter trudged along a fencerow with me, dragging a new post too heavy for her to carry, or begged for lessons in chainsawing.

It's not too hard to figure out why. In the first place, cidering gives the child instant gratification. There's no immediate reward for weeding a garden (unless the parents break down and offer cash), still less for loading a couple of hundred hay bales in the barn. But the minute you've ground and pressed the first bushel of apples, you can break out the glasses and start drinking. Good stuff, too. Cider has a wonderful fresh sweetness as it runs from the press.

In the second place, making cider on a small scale is simple enough so that even fairly young children—say, a pair of nine-year-olds—can do the whole operation by themselves. Yet it's also picturesque enough to tempt people of any age. When my old college roommate was up last fall—and we've been out of college a long time—he and his wife did four pressings in the course of the weekend. They only quit then because I ran out of apples.

Finally, cider making appeals to a deep human instinct. It's the same one that   5
makes a housewife feel so good when she takes a bunch of leftovers and produces a memorable casserole. At no cost, and using what would otherwise be wasted, she has created something. In fact, she has just about reversed entropy.

Cidering is like that. You take apples that have been lying on the ground for a week, apples with blotches and cankers and bad spots, apples that would make a supermarket manager turn pale if you merely brought them in the store, and out of this unpromising material you produce not one but two delicious drinks. Sweet cider now. Hard cider later.

The first step is to have a press. At the turn of the century, almost every farm family did. They ordered them from the Sears or Montgomery Ward catalogue as routinely as one might now order a toaster. Then about 1930 little presses ceased to be made. Pasteurized apple juice had joined the list of American food-processing triumphs. It had no particular flavor (still hasn't), but it would keep almost indefinitely. Even more appealing, it was totally sterile. That was the era when the proudest boast that, let's say, a bakery could make was that its bread was untouched by human hands. Was touched only by stainless-steel beaters and stainless-steel wrapping machines.

Eras end, though, and the human hand came back into favor. One result: in the 1970s home cider presses returned to the market. They have not yet returned to the Sears catalogue, but they are readily available. I know of two companies in Vermont that make them, another in East Aurora, New York, and one out in Washington state. If there isn't someone making them in Michigan or Wisconsin, there soon will be. Prices range from about 175 to 250 dollars.

Then you get a couple of bushels of apples. There *may* be people in the country who buy cider apples, but I don't know any of them. Old apple trees are too common. I get mine by the simple process of picking up windfalls in a derelict orchard that came with our place. I am not choosy. Anything that doesn't actually squish goes in the basket.

With two kids to help, collecting takes maybe twenty minutes. Kids tend to   10 be less interested in gathering the apples than in running the press, but a quiet threat of no-pickee, no-pressee works wonders. Kids also worry about worms sometimes, as they scoop apples from the ground—apples that may be wet with dew, spiked with stubble, surrounded by hungry wasps. Occasionally I have countered with a short lecture on how much safer our unsprayed apples are than the shiny, worthless, but heavily sprayed apples one finds in stores. But usually I just say that I have yet to see a worm in our cider press. That's true, too. Whether it's because there has never been one, or whether it's because in the excitement and bustle of grinding you just wouldn't notice one little worm, I don't dare to say.

As soon as you get back with the apples, it's time to make cider. Presses come in two sizes: one-bushel and a-third-of-a-bushel. We have tried both. If I lived in a suburb and had to buy apples, I would use the very efficient third-of-a-bushel press and make just under a gallon at a time. Living where I do, I use the bigger press and make two gallons per pressing, occasionally a little more.

The process has two parts. First you set your pressing tub under the grinder, line it with a pressing cloth, and start grinding. Or, better, your children do. One feeds apples into the hopper, the other turns the crank. If there are three children present, the third can hold the wooden hopper plate, and thus keep the apples from bouncing around. If there are four, the fourth can spell off on cranking. Five or more is too many, and any surplus over four is best made into a separate crew for the second pressing. I once had two three-child crews present, plus a seventh child whom my wife appointed the official timer. We did two pressings and had 4 ¼ gallons of cider in 43 minutes and 12 seconds. (Who won? The second crew, by more than a minute. Each crew had one of our practiced daughters on it, but the second also had the advantage of watching the first.)

As soon as the apples are ground, you put the big pressing plate on and start to turn the press down. If it's a child crew, and adult meddling is nevertheless tolerated, it's desirable to have the kids turn the press in order of their age, starting with the youngest: at the end it takes a fair amount of strength (though it's not beyond two nine-year-olds working together), and a little kid coming after a big one may fail to produce a single drop.

The pressing is where all the thrills come. As the plate begins to move down and compact the ground apples, you hear a kind of sighing, bubbling noise. Then a trickle of cider begins to run out. Within five or ten seconds the trickle turns into a stream, and the stream into a ciderfall. Even kids who've done it a dozen times look down in awe at what their labor has wrought.

A couple of minutes later the press is down as far as it will go, and the con- 15 tainer you remembered to put below the spout is full of rich, brown cider. Someone has broken out the glasses, and everybody's having a drink.

This pleasure goes on and on. In an average year we start making cider the second week of September, and we continue until early November. We make all we can drink ourselves, and quite a lot to give away. We have supplied whole church suppers. One year the girls sold about ten gallons to the village store, which made them some pocket money they were prouder of than any they ever earned by baby-sitting. Best of all, there are two months each year when all of us are running the farm together, just like a pioneer family.

Reflecting and Interpreting

1. How would you describe the tone of the first paragraph?
2. Where is the thesis statement located?
3. What are the advantages of cider making, according to Perrin?
4. What piece of equipment is needed to make apple cider? Comment on Perrin's style as opposed to that of an instruction manual. How do the tone and explanations differ?
5. What part of the process seems to intrigue the participants? Why? How does it change the usual behavior of children?
6. At the end of the essay, Perrin cites his favorite reason for cider making. What is it?
7. Notice the title. Normally, we speak of "fallen apples," but what is happening here?

A Writer's Response

1. To be successful, a writer must be competent and knowledgeable about his topic. How would you rate Perrin's expertise on cider making? As a writer? Give reasons for your answers.

2. Have you ever watched or helped in making apple butter, butchering a hog, smoking hams, drying string beans, making quilts, or another activity that was done in a traditional way? Write a paper explaining the process. Include interesting related details as Perrin does. Try to toss in a bit of humor.

❧ *My Daily Dives in the Dumpster*

Lars Eighner

During times of duress Lars Eighner has existed on food and other necessities sal-vaged from dumpsters. Nonetheless, he is not a beaten man; he is a man who is aware of what matters to him. Eighner is the author of Travels with Lizbeth, *published in 1993. The following essay was first published in 1991 in* Harper's *magazine.*

Eating from Dumpsters is the thing that separates the dilettanti from the professionals. Eating safely involves three principles: using the senses and common sense to evaluate the condition of the found materials; knowing the Dumpsters of a given area and checking them regularly; and seeking always to answer the question, Why was this discarded?

Perhaps everyone who has a kitchen and a regular supply of groceries has, at one time or another, eaten half a sandwich before discovering mold on the bread, or has gotten a mouthful of milk before realizing the milk had turned. Nothing of the sort is likely to happen to a Dumpster diver because he is constantly reminded that most food is discarded for a reason.

Yet perfectly good food can be found in Dumpsters. Canned goods, for example, turn up fairly often in the Dumpsters I frequent. All except the most phobic people would be willing to eat from a can even if it came from a Dumpster. I have few qualms about dry food such as crackers, cookies, cereal, chips, and pasta if they are free of visible contaminates and still dry and crisp. Raw fruits and vegetables with intact skins seem perfectly safe to me, excluding, of course, the obviously rotten. Many are discarded for minor imperfections that can be pared away. Chocolate is often discarded only because it has become discolored as the cocoa butter de-emulsified.

I began scavenging by pulling pizzas out of the Dumpster behind a pizza delivery shop. In general, prepared food required caution, but in this case I knew what time the shop closed and went to the Dumpster as the last of the help left.

Because the workers at these places are usually inexperienced, pizzas are often made with the wrong topping, baked incorrectly, or refused on delivery for being cold. The products to be discarded are boxed up because inventory is kept by counting boxes: A boxed pizza can be written off; an unboxed pizza does not exist. So I had a steady supply of fresh, sometimes warm pizza.

The area I frequent is inhabited by many affluent college students. I am not here by chance; the Dumpsters are very rich. Students throw out many good things, including food, particularly at the end of the semester and before and after breaks. I find it advantageous to keep an eye on the academic calendar.

A typical discard is a half jar of peanut butter—though non-organic peanut butter does not require refrigeration and is unlikely to spoil in any reasonable time. Occasionally I find a cheese with a spot of mold, which, of course, I just pare off, and because it is obvious why the cheese was discarded, I treat it with less suspicion than an apparently perfect cheese found in similar circumstances. One of my favorite finds is yogurt—often discarded, still sealed, when the expiration date has passed—because it often will keep several days, even in warm weather.

I avoid ethnic food I am unfamiliar with. If I do not know what it is supposed to look or smell like when it is good, I cannot be certain I will be able to tell if it is bad.

No matter how careful I am I still get dysentery at least once a month, oftener in warm weather. I do not want to paint too romantic a picture. Dumpster diving has serious drawbacks as a way of life.

Though I have a proprietary feeling about my Dumpsters, I don't mind my   10
direct competitors, other scavengers, as much as I hate the soda-can scroungers.

I have tried scrounging aluminum cans with an able-bodied companion, and afoot we could make no more than a few dollars a day. I can extract the necessities of life from the Dumpsters directly with far less effort than would be required to accumulate the equivalent value in aluminum. Can scroungers, then, are people who must have small amounts of cash—mostly drug addicts and winos.

I do not begrudge them the cans, but can scroungers tend to tear up the Dumpsters, littering the area and mixing the contents. There are precious few courtesies among scavengers, but it is common practice to set aside surplus items: pairs of shoes, clothing, canned goods, and such. A true scavenger hates to see good stuff go to waste, and what he cannot use he leaves in good condition in plain sight. Can scroungers lay waste to everything in their path and will stir one of a pair of good shoes to the bottom of a Dumpster to be lost or ruined in the muck. They become so specialized that they can see only cans and earn my contempt by passing up change, canned goods, and readily hockable items.

Can scroungers will even go through individual garbage cans, something I have never seen a scavenger do. Going through individual garbage cans without spreading litter is almost impossible, and litter is likely to reduce the public's tolerance of scavenging. But my strong reservation about going through individual garbage cans is that this seems to me a very personal kind of invasion, one to which I would object if I were a homeowner.

Though Dumpsters seem somehow less personal than garbage cans, they still contain bank statements, bills, correspondence, pill bottles, and other sensitive information. I avoid trying to draw conclusions about the people who dump in the Dumpsters I frequent. I think it would be unethical to do so, although I know many people will find the idea of scavenger ethics too funny for words.

Occasionally a find tells a story. I once found a small paper bag containing   15
some unused condoms, several partial tubes of flavored sexual lubricant, a partially used compact of birth control pills, and the torn pieces of a picture of a

young man. Clearly, the woman was through with him and planning to give up sex altogether.

Dumpster things are often sad—abandoned teddy bears, shredded wedding albums, despaired-of sales kits. I find diaries and journals. College students also discard their papers; I am horrified to discover the kind of paper that now merits an A in an undergraduate course.

Dumpster diving is outdoor work, often surprisingly pleasant. It is not entirely predictable; things of interest turn up every day, and some days there are finds of great value. I am always very pleased when I can turn up exactly the thing I most wanted to find. Yet in spite of the element of chance, scavenging, more than most other pursuits, tends to yield returns in some proportion to the effort and intelligence brought to bear.

I think of scavenging as a modern form of self-reliance. After ten years of government service, where everything is geared to the lowest common denominator, I find work that rewards initiative and effort refreshing. Certainly I would be happy to have a sinecure again, but I am not heartbroken to be without one.

I find from the experience of scavenging two rather deep lessons. The first is to take what I can use and let the rest go. I have come to think that there is no value in the abstract. A thing I cannot use or make useful, perhaps by trading, has no value, however fine or rare it may be. (I mean useful in a broad sense—some art, for example, I would think valuable.)

The second lesson is the transience of material being. I do not suppose that ideas are immortal, but certainly they are longer-lived than material objects.

The things I find in Dumpsters, the love letters and rag dolls of so many lives, remind me of this lesson. Many times in my travels I have lost everything but the clothes on my back. Now I hardly pick up a thing without envisioning the time I will cast it away. This, I think, is a healthy state of mind. Almost everything I have now has already been cast out at least once, proving that what I own is valueless to someone.

I find that my desire to grab for the gaudy bauble has been largely sated. I think this is an attitude I share with the very wealthy—we both know there is plenty more where whatever we have came from. Between us are the rat-race millions who have confounded their selves with the objects they grasp and who nightly scavenge the cable channels looking for they know not what.

I am sorry for them.

Reflecting and Interpreting

1. What three guidelines does Eighner give for eating from dumpsters safely?

2. What drawbacks to dumpster diving does he cite?

3. Through discarded objects in dumpsters, Eighner gains glimpses of people's private lives. Does he abuse this privilege in any way? How does Eighner feel about some of the information that he gains?

4. How does Eighner regard scavenging in dumpsters? Why does he like it better than his former government job?

5. What are the two important lessons of life he has learned? Can you understand why he feels that way? Do you agree with him?

6. Examine the last two paragraphs. Why does he feel sorry for the "rat-race millions"? What does he have that they do not?

A Writer's Response

1. Have you ever endured a time when you were broke and between jobs? How did you survive? Or perhaps you were challenged by a serious illness or other setback. What survival techniques did you develop to get through the difficult time? What small things made a difference? What lessons did you learn? Did the experience change you forever, or did you revert to old patterns when life was once again normal?

2. Consider that Eighner is now working as a writer—a job he obviously likes, even if the financial rewards are (usually) much less than those of a government job. Have you carefully considered the demands of your chosen career and the lifestyle that goes with it? How do the expected job and lifestyle fit your philosophy of life?

How to Get Out of a Locked Trunk

Philip Weiss

Metaphor plays a prominent role in this essay, in which the author ostensibly sets out to discover how to get out of a locked car trunk. By the end, the astute reader knows there is a deeper meaning to the experience. Weiss blends humor, suspense, and romance—all the while explaining a process (in fact, several versions of it). In this clever piece, originally published in Harper's *magazine and later in* The Best American Essays 1993, *Philip Weiss begins with an investigation of one process of escape and uses it to reflect on another.*

On a hot Sunday last summer my friend Tony and I drove my rental car, a '91 Buick, from St. Paul to the small town of Waconia, Minnesota, forty miles southwest. We each had a project. Waconia is Tony's boyhood home, and his sister had recently given him a panoramic postcard of Lake Waconia as seen from a high point in the town early in the century. He wanted to duplicate the photograph's vantage point, then hang the two pictures together in his house in Frogtown. I was hoping to see Tony's father, Emmett, a retired mechanic, in order to settle a question that had been nagging me: Is it possible to get out of a locked car trunk?

We tried to call ahead to Emmett twice, but he wasn't home. Tony thought he was probably golfing but that there was a good chance he'd be back by the time we got there. So we set out.

I parked the Buick, which was a silver sedan with a red interior, by the grave-yard near where Tony thought the picture had been taken. He took his picture and I wandered among the headstones, reading the epitaphs. One of them was chillingly anti-individualist. It said, "Not to do my will, but thine."

Trunk lockings had been on my mind for a few weeks. It seemed to me that the fear of being locked in a car trunk had a particular hold on the American imagination. Trunk lockings occur in many movies and books—from *Goodfellas* to *Thelma and Louise* to *Humboldt's Gift*. And while the highbrow national news-papers generally shy away from trunk lockings, the attention they receive in local papers suggests a widespread anxiety surrounding the subject. In an afternoon at the New York Public Library I found numerous stories about trunk lockings. A Los Angeles man is discovered, bloodshot, banging the trunk of his white Eldo-rado following a night and a day trapped inside; he says his captors went on joyrides and picked up women. A forty-eight-year-old Houston doctor is forced into her trunk at a bank ATM and then the car is abandoned, parked near the As-trodome. A New Orleans woman tells police she gave birth in a trunk while being abducted to Texas. Tests undermine her story, the police drop the investigation. But so what if it's a fantasy? That only shows the idea's hold on us.

Every culture comes up with tests of a person's ability to get out of a sticky   5
situation. The English plant mazes. Tropical resorts market those straw finger-
grabbers that tighten their grip the harder you pull on them, and Viennese in-
tellectuals gave us the concept of childhood sexuality—figure it out, or remain
neurotic for life.

At least you could puzzle your way out of those predicaments. When they
slam the trunk, though, you're helpless unless someone finds you. You would think
that such a common worry should have a ready fix, and that the secret of getting
out of a locked trunk is something we should all know about.

I phoned experts but they were very discouraging.

"You cannot get out. If you got a pair of pliers and bat's eyes, yes. But you
have to have a lot of knowledge of the lock," said James Foote at Automotive
Locksmiths in New York City.

Jim Frens, whom I reached at the technical section of *Car and Driver* in De-
troit, told me the magazine had not dealt with this question. But he echoed the
opinion of experts elsewhere when he said that the best hope for escape would
be to try and kick out the panel between the trunk and the backseat. That angle
didn't seem worth pursuing. What if your enemies were in the car, crumpling
beer cans and laughing at your fate? It didn't make sense to join them.

The people who deal with rules on auto design were uncomfortable with my   10
scenarios. Debra Barclay of the Center for Auto Safety, an organization founded
by Ralph Nader, had certainly heard of cases, but she was not aware of any regulations on the matter. "Now, if there was a defect involved—" she said, her voice
trailing off, implying that trunk locking was all phobia. This must be one of the
few issues on which she and the auto industry agree. Ann Carlson of the Motor
Vehicle Manufacturing Association became alarmed at the thought that I was going to play up a nonproblem: "In reality this very rarely happens. As you say, in
the movies it's a wonderful plot device," she said. "But in reality apparently this
is not that frequent an occurrence. So they have not designed that feature into
vehicles in a specific way."

When we got to Emmett's one-story house it was full of people. Tony's sister,
Carol, was on the floor with her two small children. Her husband, Charlie, had
one eye on the golf tournament on TV, and Emmett was at the kitchen counter,
trimming fat from meat for lunch. I have known Emmett for fifteen years. He
looked better than ever. In his retirement he had sharply changed his diet and
lost a lot of weight. He had on shorts. His legs were tanned and muscular. As always, his manner was humorous, if opaque.

Tony told his family my news: I was getting married in three weeks. Charlie
wanted to know where my fiancée was. Back East, getting everything ready. A
big-time hatter was fitting her for a new hat.

Emmett sat on the couch, watching me. "Do you want my advice?"

"Sure."

He just grinned. A gold tooth glinted. Carol and Charlie pressed him to yield   15
his wisdom.

Finally he said, "Once you get to be thirty, you make your own mistakes."

He got out several cans of beer, and then I brought up what was on my mind.

Emmett nodded and took off his glasses, then cleaned them and put them
back on.

We went out to his car, a Mercury Grand Marquis, and Emmett opened the
trunk. His golf clubs were sitting on top of the spare tire in a green golf bag. Next
to them was a toolbox and what he called his "burglar tools," a set of elbowed
rods with red plastic handles he used to open door locks when people locked
their keys inside.

Tony and Charlie stood watching. Charlie is a banker in Minneapolis. He   20
enjoys gizmos and is extremely practical. I would describe him as unflappable.
That's a word I always wanted to apply to myself, but my fiancée had recently
informed me that I am high-strung. Though that surprised me, I didn't quarrel
with her.

For a while we studied the latch assembly. The lock closed in much the same
way that a lobster might clamp on to a pencil. The claw portion, the jaws of the
lock, was mounted inside the trunk lid. When you shut the lid, the jaws locked on
to the bend of a U-shaped piece of metal mounted on the body of the car. Emmett
said my best bet would be to unscrew the bolts. That way the U-shaped piece
would come loose and the lock's jaws would swing up with it still in their grasp.

"But you'd need a wrench," he said.

It was already getting too technical. Emmett had an air of endless patience,
but I felt defeated. I could only imagine bloodied fingers, cracked teeth. I had
hoped for a simple trick.

Charlie stepped forward. He reached out and squeezed the lock's jaw. They
clicked shut in the air, bound together by heavy springs. Charlie now prodded
the upper part of the left-hand jaw, the thicker part. With a rough flick of his
thumb, he was able to force the jaws to snap open. Great.

Unfortunately, the jaws were mounted behind a steel plate the size of your   25
palm in such a way that while they were accessible to us, standing outside the
car, had we been inside the trunk the plate would be in our way, blocking the jaws.

This time Emmett saw the way out. He fingered a hole in the plate. It was no
bigger than the tip of your little finger. But the hole was close enough to the latch
itself that it might be possible to angle something through the hole from inside the trunk and nudge the jaws apart. We tried with one of my keys. The lock
jumped open.

It was time for a full-dress test. Emmett swung the clubs out of the trunk,
and I set my can of Schmidt's on the rear bumper and climbed in. Everyone gathered around, and Emmett lowered the trunk on me, then pressed it shut with his
meaty hands. Total darkness. I couldn't hear the people outside. I thought I was
going to panic. But the big trunk felt comfortable. I was pressed against a sort of
black carpet that softened the angles against my back.

I could almost stretch out in the trunk, and it seemed to me I could make them sweat if I took my time. Even Emmett, that sphinx, would give way to curiosity. Once I was out he'd ask how it had been and I'd just grin. There were some things you could only learn by doing.

It took a while to find the hole. I slipped the key in and angled it to one side. The trunk gasped open.

Emmett motioned the others away, then levered me out with his big right   30
forearm. Though I'd only been inside for a minute, I was disoriented—as much as anything because someone had moved my beer while I was gone, setting it down on the cement floor of the garage. It was just a little thing, but I could not be entirely sure I had gotten my own beer back.

Charlie was now raring to try other cars. We examined the latch on his Toyota, which was entirely shielded to the trunk occupant (i.e., no hole in the plate), and on the neighbor's Honda (ditto). But a 1991 Dodge Dynasty was doable. The trunk was tight, but its lock had a feature one of the mechanics I'd phoned described as a "tailpiece": a finger-like extension of the lock mechanism itself that stuck out a half inch into the trunk cavity: simply by twisting the tailpiece I could free the lock. I was even faster on a 1984 Subaru that had a little lever device on the latch.

We went out to my rental on Oak Street. The Skylark was in direct sun and the trunk was hot to the touch, but when we got it open we could see that its latch plate had a perfect hole, a square in which the edge of the lock's jaw appeared like a face in a window.

The trunk was shallow and hot. Emmett had to push my knees down before he could close the lid. This one was a little suffocating. I imagined being trapped for hours, and even before he had got it closed I regretted the decision with a slightly nauseous feeling. I thought of Edgar Allan Poe's live burials, and then about something my fiancée had said more than a year and a half before. I had been on her case to get married. She was divorced, and at every opportunity I would reissue my proposal—even during a commercial. She'd interrupted one of these chirps to tell me, in a cold, throaty voice, that she had no intention of ever going through another divorce: "This time, it's death out." I'd carried those words around like a lump of wet clay.

As it happened, the Skylark trunk was the easiest of all. The hole was right where it was supposed to be. The trunk popped open, and I felt great satisfaction that we'd been able to figure out a rule that seemed to apply about 60 percent of the time. If we publicized our success, it might get the attention it deserved. All trunks would be fitted with such a hole. Kids would learn about it in school. The grip of the fear would relax. Before long a successful trunk-locking scene would date a movie like a fedora dates one today.

When I got back East I was caught up in wedding preparations. I live in New   35
York, and the wedding was to take place in Philadelphia. We set up camp there with five days to go. A friend had lent my fiancée her BMW, and we drove it

south with all our things. I unloaded the car in my parents' driveway. The last thing I pulled out of the trunk was my fiancée's hat in its heavy cardboard shipping box. She'd warned me I was not allowed to look. The lid was free but I didn't open it. I was willing to be surprised.

When the trunk was empty it occurred to me I might hop in and give it a try. First I looked over the mechanism. The jaws of the BMW's lock were shielded, but there seemed to be some kind of cable coming off it that you might be able to manipulate so as to cause the lock to open. The same cable that allowed the driver to open the trunk remotely . . .

I fingered it for a moment or two but decided I didn't need to test out the theory.

Reflecting and Interpreting

1. At the beginning of the story, notice where the narrator parks the Buick. How does this detail contribute to the setting of the story? (Hint: Think about what the narrator's fiancée said when she kept refusing his marriage proposal.)

2. Can you see a link between the epitaph on the tombstone and Emmett's bit of wisdom? If so, what is it?

3. At one point Weiss says, "You would think that such a common worry should have a ready fix . . . something we should all know about." What does he mean by this? Can you find a second meaning to apply? (Hint: Consider the implicit analogy that extends throughout the story.)

4. Why do you think the author tells us so much about Emmett and his family? Does it seem off the subject at first? By the end of the essay, however, does the material seem relevant? Why? (Hint: What quality does the narrator see in Charlie and Emmett that he would like to develop?)

5. By the end of the story, do you see any change in the narrator? If so, what?

6. The ambiguous ending of the story is open to more than one interpretation. What does it seem to mean to you?

A Writer's Response

1. Brainstorm with a writing partner or group. List other kinds of traps and entrapment besides car trunks.

2. Freewrite about physical states that mimic social or emotional entrapment.

3. Write two different conclusions to come right after the last sentence of the story. In your opinion, does elaborating enhance or diminish the story's ending?

Notes on Punctuation

Lewis Thomas

Lewis Thomas—physician, educator, and author—has not only published widely in scientific and medical journals but also written science books for the lay reader. In fact, his Lives of a Cell *(1979) won the National Book Award. In the following essay from* Medusa and the Snail, *he treats the topic of punctuation in a unique and amusing manner.*

There are no precise rules about punctuation (Fowler lays out some general advice (as best as he can under the complex circumstances of English prose (he points out, for example, that we possess only four stops (the comma, the semicolon, the colon and the period (the question mark and exclamation point are not, strictly speaking, stops; they are indicators of tone (oddly enough, the Greeks employed the semicolon for their question mark (it produces a strange sensation to read a Greek sentence which is a straightforward question: Why weepest thou; (instead of Why weepest thou? (and, of course, there are parentheses (which are surely a kind of punctuation making this whole matter much more complicated by having to count up the left-handed parentheses in order to be sure of closing with the right number (but if the parentheses were left out, with nothing to work with but the stops, we would have considerably more flexibility in the deploying of layers of meaning than if we tried to separate all the clauses by physical barriers (and in the latter case, while we might have more precision and exactitude for our meaning, we would lose the essential flavor of language, which is its wonderful ambiguity)))))))))))).

The commas are the most useful and usable of all the stops. It is highly important to put them in place as you go along. If you try to come back after doing a paragraph and stick them in the various spots that tempt you you will discover that they tend to swarm like minnows into all sorts of crevices whose existence you hadn't realized and before you know it the whole long sentence becomes immobilized and lashed up squirming in commas. Better to use them sparingly, and with affection, precisely when the need for each one arises, nicely, by itself.

I have grown fond of semicolons in recent years. The semicolon tells you that there is still some question about the preceding full sentence; something needs to be added; it reminds you sometimes of the Greek usage. It is almost always a greater pleasure to come across a semicolon than a period. The period tells you that that is that; if you didn't get all the meaning you wanted or expected, anyway you got all the writer intended to parcel out and now you have to move along. But with a semicolon there you get a pleasant little feeling of expectancy; there is more to come; read on; it will get clearer.

Colons are a lot less attractive, for several reasons: firstly, they give you the feeling of being rather ordered around, or at least having your nose pointed in a direction you might not be inclined to take if left to yourself, and, secondly, you suspect you're in for one of those sentences that will be labeling the points to be made: firstly, secondly and so forth, with the implication that you haven't sense enough to keep track of a sequence of notions without having them numbered. Also, many writers use this system loosely and incompletely, starting out with number one and number two as though counting off on their fingers but then going on and on without the succession of labels you've been led to expect, leaving you floundering about searching for the ninethly or seventeenthly that ought to be there but isn't.

Exclamation points are the most irritating of all. Look! they say, look at what   5
I just said! How amazing is my thought! It is like being forced to watch someone else's small child jumping up and down crazily in the center of the living room shouting to attract attention. If a sentence really has something of importance to say, something quite remarkable, it doesn't need a mark to point it out. And if it is really, after all, a banal sentence needing more zing, the exclamation point simply emphasizes its banality!

Quotation marks should be used honestly and sparingly, when there is a genuine quotation at hand, and it is necessary to be very rigorous about the words enclosed by the marks. If something is to be quoted, the *exact* words must be used. If part of it must be left out because of space limitations, it is good manners to insert three dots to indicate the omission, but it is unethical to do this if it means connecting two thoughts which the original author did not intend to have tied together. Above all, quotation marks should not be used for ideas that you'd like to disown, things in the air so to speak. Nor should they be put in place around clichés; if you want to use a cliché you must take full responsibility for it yourself and not try to fob it off on anon., or on society. The most objectionable misuse of quotation marks, but one which illustrates the dangers of misuse in ordinary prose, is seen in advertising, especially in advertisements for small restaurants, for example "just around the corner," or "a good place to eat." No single, identifiable, citable person ever really said, for the record, "just around the corner," much less "a good place to eat," least likely of all for restaurants of the type that use this type of prose.

The dash is a handy device, informal and essentially playful, telling you that you're about to take off on a different tack but still in some way connected with the present course—only you have to remember that the dash is there, and either put a second dash at the end of the notion to let the reader know that he's back on course, or else end the sentence, as here, with a period.

The greatest danger in punctuation is for poetry. Here it is necessary to be as economical and parsimonious with commas and periods as with the words themselves, and any marks that seem to carry their own subtle meanings, like dashes and little rows of periods, even semicolons and question marks, should be left out altogether rather than inserted to clog up the thing with ambiguity. A single exclamation point in a poem, no matter what else the poem has to say, is enough to destroy the whole work.

The things I like best in T. S. Eliot's poetry, especially in the *Four Quartets*, are the semicolons. You cannot hear them, but they are there, laying out the connections between the images and the ideas. Sometimes you get a glimpse of a semicolon coming, a few lines farther on, and it is like climbing a steep path through woods and seeing a wooden bench just at a bend in the road ahead, a place where you can expect to sit for a moment, catching your breath.

Commas can't do this sort of thing; they can only tell you how the different   10
parts of a complicated thought are to be fitted together, but you can't sit, not even take a breath, just because of a comma,

Reflecting and Interpreting

1. What are the effects of the first paragraph? Do you feel Lewis's strange usage detracts from or enhances his main point? Why? How does the paragraph lead into the rest of the essay?

2. In paragraph 2 on commas, contrast sentence 3 with 4. What is ironic here?

3. What is Lewis's favorite mark of punctuation? Why does he like it better than the period?

4. What mark of punctuation does he find most irritating? Why? What is the effect of the last sentence of paragraph 5?

5. What does he warn against when using quotation marks? How is responsibility involved?

6. Review the unusual comparisons that Lewis makes. How does this imagery contribute to the effectiveness of the essay?

7. What seems to be the purpose of Lewis's essay? What is his thesis? Could the essay be considered a mnemonic device? Why or why not?

A Writer's Response

1. Write a short essay about your favorite mark of punctuation. Or perhaps you might like to recall your difficulties as a child in learning to use certain marks. (For ideas, see "I. Punctuation" in the handbook.)

2. Select three or four related words with the same root—such as human, humanism, humanize, and humanoid. Develop an essay that explains and comments on the words. When suitable, use imagery and irony to illustrate.

Introduction of
Mothers of Invention

Ethlie Ann Vare and Greg Ptacek

Sometimes an author's best fuel is a powerful load of examples and dry wit—especially when those examples loudly decry the opposition's assertions. In this excerpt from Mothers of Invention, *Vare and Ptacek effectively shoot down an unjust stereotype, presenting impressive facts. Ethlie Ann Vare, a free-lance journalist, writes "Video Beat," a syndicated newspaper column. She has also written biographies of Stevie Nicks, Ozzy Osbourne, and Harrison Ford. Greg Ptacek is senior features editor of* CitySports *and has written for a wide range of other publications. He has also consulted on a feature film and written scripts for fitness videos.*

The first inventor introduced in every grammar-school primer is Eli Whitney, the genius who invented the cotton gin in 1793. Fact is, Mr. Whitney *didn't* invent the cotton "engine" in 1793—or any other year. Eli Whitney built a device conceived, perfected, and marketed by Mrs. Catherine Littlefield Green, a Georgia belle who, unlike her Massachusetts-born houseguest, was quite familiar with the cotton boll.

Some accounts have it that Mrs. Greene handed Whitney a virtual set of plans for the cotton gin; others believe she "merely" suggested the idea and financed the work. Either way, Catherine Littlefield Greene somehow got lost on her way to those sixth-grade history texts.

Women have been inventing in America before there was a United States, and in other parts of the world before there was an America. Catherine Littlefield Greene is not the only innovative lady whose accomplishments have slipped through the cracks. Western society has decreed that women do not invent despite facts to the contrary, and makes it a self-fulfilling prophecy by overlooking a few of those facts.

Even in our Smithsonian Museum, the painting honoring America's great inventors—"Men of Progress" by John Lawrence Mott, c. 1856—depicts exactly that: men, all white, and all over the age of forty. By 1856 a young widow named Martha Coston had already patented the Navy's signal flare; Ada Lovelace had designed the prototype computer; Mary Montagu had introduced smallpox inoculation; Nicole Clicquot had invented pink champagne and Elizabeth Flanagan the cocktail; and a Madame Lefebre synthesized the first nitrate fertilizer.

Nor can we look back and laugh at nineteenth-century male chauvinism. In his 1957 book *Inventors and Inventions*, C. D. Tuska, then director of RCA patent operations, said: "I shall write little about female inventors . . . most of our in-   5 ventors are of the male sex. Why is the percentage [of women] so low? I am sure I don't know, unless the good Lord intended them to be mothers. I, being old-fashioned, hold that they are creative enough without also being 'inventive.' They produce the inventors and help rear them, and that should be sufficient."

By 1957 Eleanor Raymond and Maria Telkes had perfected solar heating; Grace Murray Hopper created the basis of computer software; Melitta Bentz invented the modern coffeepot; Mary Engle Pennington developed refrigeration; Margaret Knight invented the square-bottomed bag; Katherine Burr Blodgett patented invisible glass; Gladys Hobby produced the first usable penicillin; Kate Gleason designed the first tract housing; and Hattie Alexander had cured meningitis.

The National Inventors' Hall of Fame in Washington, D.C., boasted a total of fifty-two inductees in 1984; none was a woman. William Coolidge, the inventor of the vacuum tube, is mentioned . . . but not Marie Curie, who invented what we now call the "Geiger" counter and discovered radioactivity. Enrico Fermi makes the grade for building the first atomic reactor . . . but not Lise Meitner, who first created—and named—nuclear fission. Leo Bakeland is honored for inventing Bakelite . . . but not Madame Dutillet, who created cultured marble a century before. . . .

Since 1880, the U.S. Patent Office has officially recognized not only mechanical devices as inventions per se, but also substances, techniques, and processes. . . .

In this volume, we expand the definition of Inventor to include the Discoverers, those who advanced humankind by recognizing the value of things that were in front of everyone else all along.

The list of female inventors includes dancers, farmers, nuns, secretaries, actresses, shopkeepers, housewives, military officers, corporate executives, schoolteachers, writers, seamstresses, refugees, royalty, and little kids. All kinds of people can and do invent. The idea that one's gender somehow precludes the possibility of pursuing any technological endeavor is not only outdated but also dangerous. In the words of 1977 Nobel Prize winner Rosalyn Yalow: "The world cannot afford the loss of the talents of half of its people if we are to solve the many problems which beset us."

Reflecting and Interpreting

1. What do you note about the pairing of facts in the first paragraph? Read the last two lines and the second paragraph aloud. How would you describe the tone?

2. Can you find a thesis statement in this essay? How does the delay affect the effectiveness of the opening?

3. Look at each place where the authors list women inventors. Note how assertions about male inventors contrast with lists of women whose lives disprove

the assertions. Do the contrasts always follow the same structure? Map the examples to show two ways they are presented.

4. Although twentieth-century history books recognize the work of Marie Curie, what is the honor she has never received that the authors think she deserves?

5. What is the stereotype that long governed the recognition of inventors and discoverers? By 1977 this assumption had run aground. How do you know?

A Writer's Response

1. Discrimination appears in many shapes and forms. Have you ever been a victim? How did you cope? Write an essay, giving at least three examples.

2. Since the equal rights movement began, many changes have occurred. Has your life been affected by this movement? If so, how? Write an essay based on examples. (You might contrast your opportunities with those of a parent.)

~ *Road Rage*

Jason Vest, Warren Cohen, and Mike Tharp

Have you ever been crowded onto a shoulder of the road, insulted, or assaulted by an angry driver? If so, you have been a victim of "road rage," an ever-increasing phenomenon that sometimes results in fatalities. Vest, Cohen, and Tharp researched this problem for U.S. News & World Report *and reported their findings in an article, first published June 2, 1997.*

Some of the incidents are so ludicrous you can't help but laugh—albeit nervously. There was the case in Salt Lake City, where 75-year-old J. C. King—peeved that 41-year-old Larry Remm Jr. honked at him for blocking traffic—followed Remm when he pulled off the road, hurled his prescription bottle at him, and then, in a display of geriatric resolve, smashed Remm's knees with his '92 Mercury. In tony Potomac, Md., Robin Ficker—an attorney and ex-state legislator—knocked the glasses off a pregnant woman after she had the temerity to ask him why he bumped her Jeep with his.

Other incidents lack even the element of black humor. In Colorado Springs, 55-year-old Vern Smalley persuaded a 17-year-old boy who had been tailgating him to pull over; Smalley decided that, rather than merely scold the lad, he would shoot him. (And he did. Fatally—after the youth had threatened him.) And last year, on Virginia's George Washington Parkway, a dispute over a lane change was settled with a high-speed duel that ended when both drivers lost control and crossed the center line, killing two innocent motorists.

Anyone who spent the Memorial Day weekend on the road probably won't be too surprised to learn the results of a major study to be released this week by the American Automobile Association. The rate of "aggressive driving" incidents—defined as events in which an angry or impatient driver tries to kill or injure another driver after a traffic dispute—has risen by 51 percent since 1990. In those cases studied, 37 percent of offenders used "firearms" against other drivers, an additional 28 percent used other weapons, and 35 percent used their cars.

Fear of (and participation in) aggressive driving has grown so much that in a poll last year residents of Maryland, Washington, D.C. and Virginia listed it as a bigger concern than drunk driving. The Maryland highway department is running a campaign called "The End of the Road for Aggressive Drivers," which, among other things, flashes anti-road-rage messages on electronic billboards on the interstates. Delaware, Pennsylvania, and New Jersey have initiated special highway patrols targeting aggressive drivers. A small but busy community of therapists and scholars has arisen to study the phenomenon and counsel drivers on how to cope. And several members of Congress are now trying to figure out ways to legislate away road rage.

Lest one get unduly alarmed, it helps to put the AAA study's numbers in context: Approximately 250,000 people have been killed in traffic since 1990. While the U.S. Department of Transportation estimates that two thirds of fatalities are at least partially caused by aggressive driving, the AAA study found only 218 that could be directly attributable to enraged drivers. Of the more than 20 million motorists injured, the survey identified 12,610 injuries attributable to aggressive driving. While the study is the first American attempt to quantify aggressive driving, it is not rigorously scientific. The authors drew on reports from 30 newspapers—supplemented by insurance claims and police reports from 16 cities—involving 10,037 occurrences. Moreover, the overall trendlines for car accidents have continued downward for several decades, thanks in part to increases in the drinking age and improvements in car technology like high-mounted brake lights.

But researchers believe there is a growing trend of simple aggressive behavior—road rage—in which a driver reacts angrily to other drivers. Cutting them off, tailgating, giving the finger, waving a fist—experts believe these forms of nonviolent fury are increasing. "Aggressive driving is now the most common way of driving," says Sandra Ball-Rokeach, who codirects the Media and Injury Prevention Program at the University of Southern California. "It's not just a few crazies—it's a subculture of driving."

In focus groups set up by her organization, two-thirds of drivers said they reacted to frustrating situations aggressively. Almost half admitted to deliberately braking suddenly, pulling close to the other car, or taking some other potentially dangerous step. Another third said they retaliated with a hostile gesture. Drivers show great creativity in devising hostile responses. Doug Erber of Los Angeles keeps his windshield-wiper-fluid tank full. If someone tailgates, he turns on the wipers, sending fluid over his roof onto the car behind him. "It works better than hitting the brakes," he says, "and you can act totally innocent."

Mad Max. While the AAA authors note there is a profile of the lethally inclined aggressive driver—"relatively young, poorly educated males who have criminal records, histories of violence, and drug or alcohol problems"—road-rage scholars (and regular drivers) believe other groups are equally represented in the less violent forms of aggressive driving. To some, it's tempting to look at this as a psychologically mysterious Jekyll-and-Hyde phenomenon; for others, it's simply attributable to "jerk drivers." In reality, there's a confluence of emotional and demographic factors that changes the average citizen from mere motorist to Mad Max.

First, it isn't just your imagination that traffic is getting worse. Since 1987, the number of miles of roads has increased just 1 percent while the miles *driven* have shot up by 35 percent. According to a recent Federal Highway Administration study of 50 metropolitan areas, almost 70 percent of urban freeways today—as opposed to 55 percent in 1983—are clogged during rush hour. The study notes that congestion is likely to spread to currently unspoiled locations. Forty

percent of the currently gridlock-free Milwaukee County highway system, for example, is predicted to be jammed up more than five hours a day by the year 2000.
A study by the Texas Transportation Institute last year found that commuters in
one-third of the largest cities spent well over 40 hours a year in traffic jams.

Part of the problem is that jobs have shifted from cities to suburbs. Commu-   10
nities designed as residential suburbs with narrow roads have grown into "edge
cities," with bustling commercial traffic. Suburb-to-suburb commutes now account for 44 percent of all metropolitan traffic versus 20 percent for suburb-to-
downtown travel. Demographer and *Edge City* author Joel Garreau says workers
breaking for lunch are essentially causing a third rush hour. He notes that in
Tysons Corner, Va., it takes an average of four traffic signal cycles to get through
a typical intersection at lunchtime. And because most mass transit systems are of
a spoke-and-hub design, centering on cities and branching out to suburbs, they're
not really useful in getting from point A to point B in an edge city or from one
edge city to another. Not surprisingly, fewer people are relying on mass transit
and more on cars. In 1969, 82.7 percent drove to work; in 1990, 91.4 percent
did. Despite the fact that the Washington, D.C., area has an exemplary com-
muter subway system, it accounts for only 2 percent of all trips made.

Demographic changes have helped put more drivers on the road. Until the
1970s, the percentage of women driving was relatively low, and many families
had only one car. But women entered the work force and bought cars, something
developers and highway planners hadn't foreseen. From 1969 to 1990 the number of women licensed to drive increased 84 percent. Between 1970 and 1987,
the number of cars on the road more than doubled. In the past decade, the number of cars grew faster (17 percent) than the number of people (10 percent).
Even carpooling is down despite HOV lanes and other preferential devices. The
cumulative effect, says University of Hawaii traffic psychology professor Leon
James, is a sort of sensory overload. "There are simply more cars—and more
behaviors—to deal with," says James.

As if the United States couldn't produce enough home-grown lousy drivers, it
seems to be importing them as well. Experts believe that many immigrants come
from countries that have bad roads and aggressive styles. It's not just drivers from
Third World countries, though. British drivers are considered among the safest in
Europe, yet recent surveys show that nearly 90 percent of British motorists have
experienced threats or abuse from other drivers. Of Brits who drive for a living,
about 21 percent report having been run off the road. In Australia, one study estimates that about half of all traffic accidents there may be due to road rage.
"There are different cultures of driving all over the world—quite clearly, if we
mix new cultures in the melting pot, what we get is a culture clash on the road-
way," says John Palmer, a professor in the Health Education and Safety Department at Minnesota's St. Cloud University.

The peak moment for aggressive driving comes not during impenetrable
gridlocks but just before, when traffic density is high but cars are still moving
briskly. That's when cutting someone off or forcing someone out of a lane can

make the difference (or so it seems) between being on time and being late, according to Palmer.

Unfortunately, roads are getting more congested just as Americans feel even more pressed for time. "People get on a time line for their car trips," says Palmer. "When they perceive that someone is impeding their progress or invading their agenda, they respond with what they consider to be 'instructive' behavior, which might be as simple as flashing their lights to something more combative."

Suburban assault vehicles. This, uh, "instruction" has become more common,   15
Palmer and others speculate, in part because of modern automotive design. With hyperadjustable seats, soundproof interiors, CD players, and cellular phones, cars are virtually comfortable enough to live in. Students of traffic can't help but wonder if the popularity of pickup trucks and sport utility vehicles has contributed to the problem. Sales have approximately doubled since 1990. These big metal shells loom over everything else, fueling feelings of power and drawing out a driver's more primal instincts. "A lot of the anecdotal evidence about aggressive driving incidents tends to involve people driving sport utility vehicles," says Julie Rochman of the Insurance Institute for Highway Safety. "When people get these larger, heavier vehicles, they feel more invulnerable." While Chrysler spokesman Chris Preuss discounts the notion of suburban assault vehicles being behind the aggressive-driving phenomenon, he does say women feel more secure in the jumbo-size vehicles.

In much of life, people feel they don't have full control of their destiny. But a car—unlike, say, a career or a spouse—responds reliably to one's wish. In automobiles, we have an increased (but false) sense of invincibility. Other drivers become dehumanized, mere appendages to a competing machine. "You have the illusion you're alone and master, dislocated from other drivers," says Hawaii's James.

Los Angeles psychologist Arnold Nerenberg describes how one of his recent patients got into an angry road confrontation with another motorist. "They pulled off the road and started running toward each other to fight, but then they recognized each other as neighbors," he says. "When it's just somebody else in a car, it's more two-dimensional; the other person's identity boils down to, 'You're someone who did something bad to me.'"

How can aggressive driving be minimized? Some believe that better driver's education might help. Driver's ed was a high school staple by the 1950s, thanks to federal highway dollars given to states. But a 1978 government study in De Kalb County, Ga., found no reduction in crashes or traffic violations by students who took a driver's ed course compared with those who didn't. Rather than use these results to design better driver's ed programs, the feds essentially gave up on them and diverted money to seat belt and anti-drunk-driving programs. Today, only 40 percent of new drivers complete a formal training course, which may be one reason 20 percent to 35 percent of applicants fail their initial driving test.

The inner driver. But governments are looking anew at the value of driver's education. In April, Michigan passed sweeping rules that grant levels of privilege depending on one's age and driving record. States with similar systems, like California, Maryland, and Oregon, have seen teen accident rates drop.

Those who lose their licenses often have to return to traffic school. But some 20 states have generous standards for these schools. To wit: California's theme schools. There, errant drivers can attend the "Humor's My Name, Traffic's My Game," school, in which a mock jury led by a stand-up comic decides who the worst drivers are; the "Traffic School for Chocoholics," which plies errant drivers with chocolate and ice cream; and the gay and lesbian "Pink Triangle Traffic School."

But the real key to reducing road rage probably lies deep within each of us. Professor James of the University of Hawaii suggests that instead of emphasizing defensive driving—which implies that the other driver is the enemy—we should focus on "supportive driving" or "driving with the aloha spirit." Of course that's hard to do if a) someone has just cut you off at 60 mph or b) you live in Los Angeles instead of Hawaii. Nerenberg, the Los Angeles psychologist, has published an 18-page booklet called "Overcoming Road Rage: The 10-Step Compassion Program." He recommends examining what sets off road rage and to "visualize overcoming it." Other tips: Imagine you might be seeing that person at a party soon. And remembering that other drivers "are people with feelings. Let us not humiliate them with our aggression." In the chapter titled, "Peace," he suggests, "Take a deep breath and just let it go." And if that doesn't work, the windshield-wiper trick is pretty clever.

Reflecting and Interpreting

1. Comment on the incidents described in the opening. Do you think such conflicts are common or isolated? Do they seem to occur more often in certain areas? If so, where?

2. Were you surprised by the findings of the AAA about the rate of "aggressive driving" incidents? Why or why not?

3. When does the peak moment for aggressive driving occur?

4. What do the authors cite as major causes of the increase in aggressive driving?

5. Does the type of vehicle a person drives seem to make a difference in driving habits? How? What types of vehicles seem to predominate in such incidents? Might aggressive people select these types of vehicles?

6. What can states do to alleviate this problem? What have some states already done that seems to be helping? Can you think of anything else that might help?

A Writer's Response

1. In a group discuss what tends to set off road rage. What can a driver do to forestall arousing his or her own impatience and irritating other drivers?

2. With your group discuss possible ways of self-preservation when risky on-the-road situations occur. How can you diffuse an angry driver? What should you do if that person signals you to stop?

3. Have you ever witnessed an incident of road rage? If so, write an essay describing what happened. Is there a moral to the tale?

Rock Threat Subsides

Calvin Trillin

Calvin Trillin, a syndicated columnist and staff writer for The New Yorker, *is known for his humorous depictions of peculiarly American issues and obsessions—particularly those that affect American families. Here he responds to a long-running issue: Does listening to rock music pose a threat to teens? In so doing, Trillin slyly points to a greater danger.*

May 20, 1991

Parents who have been worried about their children being turned into mindless layabouts by rock-music lyrics will be relieved to hear that, according to the latest scientific studies, teenagers pay virtually no attention to the lyrics of rock songs. In other words, just what is turning these teenagers into mindless layabouts is still open to question.

I should also say, in the spirit of generational fairness, that there have been no studies so far to see what is turning so many parents into mindless layabouts. That is probably a much longer story.

According to an article I read in the *Washington Post*, one of the most thorough studies ever done on the impact of rock lyrics was recently completed by two psychologists from California State University at Fullerton, Jill Rosenbaum and Lorraine Prinsky. They found that most teenagers don't listen closely to the words of rock songs, don't catch a lot of what they do hear, and don't much care one way or the other. When the teenagers in the survey were asked why they listen to a rock song, "I want to listen to the words" finished dead last.

This information should change one of the standard discussions that parents and teenagers have about rock music—a discussion traditionally carried on in the family automobile at a time when the music blaring from a boom box in the back seat is loud enough to turn the windshield wipers on and off.

Parent (in a patient and mature tone): I can't imagine why you listen to that 5 moronic garbage.

Teenager: Uhnnn.

Parent: It's just a lot of thugs making as much noise as they can.

Teenager: Nghh.

Parent: Half the time, you can't even make out the words to the song anyway.

Teenager: Actually, much more than half the time. But the latest study indi- 10 cates that this makes no difference whatsoever in my enjoyment of this art form.

That's right. Teenagers don't care about the words. They listen to the lyrics of rock songs about as carefully as their parents listen to the lyrics of "The Star-Spangled Banner."

The California study found that the messages supposedly encoded in some rock songs—exhortations to become dope fiends and burn down cities and worship Satan and engage in hideous sexual excesses and leave the dinner table without being asked to be excused and that sort of thing—were lost on teenagers, even when the researchers furnished printouts of the lyrics for the teenagers to peruse. This is, of course, good news for parents and discouraging news for anybody who has put a lot of effort into trying to use rock lyrics to encourage teenagers to do wicked things.

Since teenagers don't listen carefully to the lyrics, they tend to form their opinion of what the song is about from the title. For instance, the Bruce Springsteen hit "Born in the USA" is described by the *Post* as having "in every verse explicit references to despair and disillusionment." But kids from fourth grade through college who were tested by researchers from the University of California at Los Angeles were mostly under the impression that "Born in the USA" was a patriotic song.

These results shouldn't surprise anybody. Most grownups don't get much past the title of anything, which is why title-writing is such an art. The military is particularly adept at titles. The invasion of Panama, for instance, was called Operation Just Cause. Think of what the public impression of that episode would have been if the Pentagon had chosen a name that would have been, in fact, much less subject to differences of opinion: Operation Tiny Country. Think of how the public view of the war in the Persian Gulf might have differed if our military effort to drive Iraqis from Kuwait had been called not Operation Desert Storm but Operation Restore Despot.

The results of these rock-lyrics studies seem to indicate that putting warning   15
labels on rock records would only draw teenagers' attention to something they might otherwise ignore—sort of like marking the spines of innocent-looking novels, "Warning: This Book Has Some Good Parts."

The results also mean that concerned citizens would be wasting their time mounting a campaign to encourage songwriters to compose more uplifting lyrics. That's a shame. I was sort of looking forward to the forces of good coming up with a song that featured endless repetition of some lyric like "I wanna clean my room" or "I appreciate the great burden of responsibility my father carries and the sacrifices he's made on behalf of me and my siblings, and I have only the greatest respect for him." With the right tune, we now know, that might have made the charts, but nobody would have been listening anyway.

Reflecting and Interpreting

1. What words in the first paragraph surprise you? What happens in the second paragraph that brings a bigger surprise? How would you describe the author's tone? (Look up *humor, overstatement, irony, sarcasm,* and *parody.*)

2. Comment on Trillin's version of the California study: "exhortations to become dope fiends . . . leave the dinner table without being asked to be excused."

Do you think the report actually said this? What is he doing here? What is the effect?

3. What purpose does the dialogue between parent and teenager serve? How does it advance Trillin's main point?

4. What *actually* is Trillin's main point? Can you find his delayed thesis?

5. What humorous device does he use to emphasize the public's tendency to take a title at face value? What are the implications for teenagers?

6. Examine the title of this article. What does it indicate the article will be about? Then reread the paragraph about title writing. What has Trillin done?

7. Examine the last paragraph. Despite his derision, how does Trillin really feel about this issue? (Notice the last half of the final line.)

A Writer's Response

1. Some readers may be offended by Trillin's biting humor and blanket indictment of parents. In a group discuss your feelings about the treatment of the topic. Then identify examples of irony, sarcasm, overstatement, and parody.

2. Write a reaction to this essay. Defend or refute Trillin's treatment of the topic and the issue. Give reasons for your view. (For help see chapters 26, 27.)

DIVISION AND CLASSIFICATION
Taking Apart and Grouping

Where Do We Stand?

Lisa Davis

Have you noticed any slight differences in behavior or conversational style among students of varying cultures on your campus? In this essay, first published in In Health *magazine, Lisa Davis discusses how different spatial needs and eye contact can cause hasty judgments and misunderstanding.*

Call it the dance of the jet set, the diplomat's tango: A man from the Middle East, say, falls into conversation with an American, becomes animated, takes a step forward. The American makes a slight postural adjustment, shifts his feet, edges backward. A little more talk and the Arab advances; a little more talk and the American retreats.

"By the end of the cocktail party," says Middle East expert Peter Bechtold of the State Department's Foreign Service Institute, "you have an American in each corner of the room, because that's as far as they can back up."

What do you do when an amiable chat leaves one person feeling vaguely bullied, the other unaccountably chilled? Things would be simpler if these jetsetters were speaking different languages—they'd just get themselves a translator. But the problem's a little tougher, because they're using different languages of space.

Everyone who's ever felt cramped in a crowd knows that the skin is not the body's only boundary. We each wear a zone of privacy like a hoop skirt, inviting others in or keeping them out with body language—by how closely we approach, the angle at which we face them, the speed with which we break a gaze. It's a subtle code, but one we use and interpret easily, indeed automatically, having absorbed the vocabulary from infancy.

At least, we *assume* we're reading it right. But from culture to culture, from group to group within a single country, even between the sexes, the language of space has distinctive accents, confusing umlauts. That leaves a lot of room for misinterpretations, and the stakes have gotten higher as business has become increasingly international and populations multicultural. So a new breed of consultants has appeared in the last few years, interpreting for globe-trotters of all nationalities the meaning and use of personal space.

5

For instance, says international business consultant Sondra Snowdon, Saudi Arabians like to conduct business discussions from within spitting distance—literally. They bathe in each other's breath as part of building the relationship. "Americans back up," says Snowdon, "but they're harming their chances of winning the contracts." In seminars, Snowdon discusses the close quarters common in Middle Eastern conversations and has her students practice talking with each other at very chummy distances.

Still, her clients had better be careful where they take their shrunken "space bubble," because cultures are idiosyncratic in their spatial needs. Japanese subways bring people about as close together as humanly possible, for instance, yet even a handshake can be offensively physical in a Japanese office. And, says researcher and writer Mildred Reed Hall, Americans can even make their business counterparts in Japan uncomfortable with the kind of direct eye contact that's normal here.

"Not only do most Japanese businessmen not look at you, they keep their eyes down," Hall says. "We look at people for hours, and they feel like they're under a searchlight."

The study of personal space got under way in the early 1950s, when anthropologist Edward Hall described a sort of cultural continuum of personal space. (Hall has frequently collaborated with his wife, Mildred.) According to Hall, on the "high-contact" side of the continuum—in Mediterranean and South American societies, for example—social conversations include much eye contact, touching and smiling, typically while standing at a distance of about a foot. On the other end of the scale, say in Northern European cultures, a lingering gaze may feel invasive, manipulative or disrespectful; a social chat takes place at a remove of about 2½ feet.

In the middle-of-the-road United States, people usually stand about 18 inches   10 apart for this sort of conversation—unless we want to win foreign friends and influence people, in which case, research shows, we'd better adjust our posture. In one study, when British graduate students were trained to adopt Arab patterns of behavior (facing their partners straight on, with lots of eye contact and smiling), Middle Eastern exchange students found them more likable and trustworthy than typical British students.

In contrast, the misuse of space can call whole personalities into suspicion: When researchers seated pairs of women for conversation, those forced to talk at an uncomfortably large distance were more likely to describe their partners as cold and rejecting.

Don't snuggle up too fast, though. Men in that study were more irritated by their partners when they were forced to talk at close range. Spatially speaking, it seems men and women are subtly foreign to each other. No matter whether a society operates at arm's length or cheek-to-jowl, the women look at each other more and stand a bit closer than do the men.

Anthropologist Hall suggests that a culture's use of space is evidence of a reliance on one sense over another: Middle Easterners get much of their information through their senses of smell and touch, he says, which require a close approach; Americans rely primarily on visual information, backing up in order to see an intelligible picture.

Conversational distances also tend to reflect the standard greeting distance in each culture, says State Department expert Bechtold. Americans shake hands, and then talk at arm's length. Arabs do a Hollywood-style, cheek-to-cheek social kiss, and their conversation is similarly up close and personal. And, at a distance great enough to keep heads from knocking together—about two feet—the Japanese bow and talk to each other. On the other hand, the need for more or less space may reflect something of a cultural temperament. "There's no word for privacy in Arab cultures," says Bechtold. "They think it means loneliness."

Whatever their origin, spatial styles are very real. In fact, even those who set out to transgress find it uncomfortable to intrude on the space of strangers, says psychologist John Aiello at Rutgers University. "I've had students say, 'Boy, that was the hardest thing I ever had to do—to stand six inches away when I was asking those questions.'"   15

Luckily, given coaching and time, it seems to get easier to acculturate to foreign habits of contact. Says Bechtold, "You often see men holding hands in the Middle East and walking down the street together. It's just that they're concerned and don't want you to cross the street unescorted, but I've had American pilots come in here and say, 'I don't want some SOB holding my hand.' Then I see them there, holding the hand of a Saudi."

"Personal space isn't so hard for people to learn," Bechtold adds. "What is really much harder is the business of dinner being served at midnight."

Reflecting and Interpreting

1. How does Davis's opening differ from merely giving an example? What device do you see here? How does it influence the tone?

2. How does Davis establish credibility in the second paragraph and again later?

3. What function does paragraph 3 serve? What happens here? (Notice that she asks a question that is not answered until paragraph 10.)

4. Davis makes unusual comparisons. Identify the literary device in "a zone of privacy like a hoop skirt"; "bathe in each other's breath"; "they feel like they're under a searchlight."

5. How do the personal space needs of Americans and those of Middle Eastern people generally differ? What American habits make Japanese uncomfortable?

6. Who was the anthropologist that first studied the use of personal space? When? What is the average distance for Americans to converse? Does this distance vary with gender? How?

7. How do greetings and other habits influence personal space? How does this vary from culture to culture? Is it difficult to learn about this topic? To adapt?

A Writer's Response

1. Have you ever encountered a situation where you were uncomfortable, and you moved forward or backward? Share your experiences with a group. Tell what happened and how it influenced the conversation.

2. In your future career, will it be beneficial for you to be keenly aware of cultural diversity? Why or why not? Write an essay explaining your point of view.

❧ *Three Kinds of Dirt*

Judith Williamson

A neighbor once had a little boy who comforted himself to sleep by repeating "ground-in dirt" and other expressions picked up from television commercials. In this excerpt from Consuming Passions: The Dynamics of Popular Culture, *British author Judith Williamson analyzes how marketing helps us to define the world by differentiating new categories of thought and experience. At the same time consumerism presents more than one paradox.*

How many kinds of dirt are there?

This question might seem to belong in the realm of linguistics, along with the Eskimos' eighteen words for "white," which are often used to show how language arbitrarily divides the continuum of the colour spectrum in ways that vary from culture to culture. Some languages have no word for "brown," others distinguish several kinds of blue; and these divisions form the grid which patterns experience itself, since it is hard to perceive and describe something you have no words for. . . . The language of each culture does not so much name the world, as define its possibilities. Lacking the Eskimos' graded scale of whiteness, so appropriate in their snowy surroundings, we find it hard actually to *see* "white" as anything other than one colour. . . .

This brings us back to dirt. A scientific answer to the question above is found in the *Hoover Book of Home Management,* under the caption *What is Carpet Dirt?:* "Day to day soiling can be divided into five groups but the first three are the most important." These turn out to be, *(1) Surface Litter, (2) Light, Clinging Dust* and *(3) Heavy Dirt and Grit.* Besides lists of their ingredients, we are given warnings of the particular dangers posed by each type of dirt. *Surface Litter* clings recriminatingly to the surface of the pile, making the carpet look uncared for, while although *Light, Clinging Dust* penetrates the pile, some of it always remains on the surface to give a dull, dingy look. In extreme cases it *could* cause carpet rot. *Heavy Dirt and Grit* hold a different kind of menace, for they may lurk undetected: *"a carpet is able to hold its own weight in grit, and yet look fairly normal."*

In case these varied threats should seem like the figment of someone's imagination, a scientific diagram reveals, through a cross-section of a typical carpet, precisely the *three kinds of dirt.* Beneath this diagram is another, demonstrating, logically enough, the *three cleaning principles* which can banish them.

The following section is called *Choosing a Vacuum Cleaner.* "It is wise to select one which will remove all three kinds of dirt." You bet, after hearing what those three can do! And of course, this is the *Hoover* book of home management. Each attachment of your Hoover corresponds to some natural function dictated by the very nature of dirt itself! The two *other* types of carpet soiling, which are less important, are, revealingly, those which cannot be treated by vacuuming

5

since they are *(4) Sticky, Greasy Substances* (although there is a Hoover sham-pooer to deal with this) and finally, *(5) Marks and Stains.*

Generously, the *Hoover Book of Home Management* recommends various other brand names when it comes to aspects of homecare outside its own province. But in every case, the product, whether a cleanser or a kitchen suite, is wheeled on as the "answer" to a "problem," while in fact the product itself defines the problem it claims to solve. Carpet dirt is dealt with, only to give way to the problems of the *absorbed stain*, the *built-up stain* and the *compound stain.* Twenty years later, we are more familiar with different categories, such as the *biological* stain and the *"biological" washing powder* which is required to combat it. No matter that the washing powder is in fact a *chemical* substance, it must be named to match the stain. The product must distinguish itself from its rivals.

And it does this by defining the world around it, creating new categories out of previously undifferentiated areas of experience. Different kinds of smell require different kinds of deodorant, *"intimate"* and otherwise. (Can a deodorant *be un*intimate?). A short while ago we had a new kind of stain, the *"under stain"* which now seems to have disappeared. . . . there are not only different kinds of dirt, there are different kinds of clean: squeaky clean, . . . and the peculiar expanding [clean of] towels and woollens which have to be pressed down into drawers and will hardly lie still after being treated with fabric softener.

If it is language that channels our physical perceptions, it is the language of consumer products which defines our daily life. Whether we feel consciously "for" or "against" consumer society, the terms of our experience, the language of our delight or protest, are the same. I may hold out against buying a conditioner as well as a shampoo—but I cannot wish it out of existence, or ignore the fact that it is associated with healthy, shining hair and that this is desirable. The world of consumerism is the one we live in—it is too late to opt out: but there are two important questions—one, what we say in the language available, the other, what that language itself means.

For the meanings and uses of products cannot be entirely controlled; they can be appropriated and turned around on the society which produces them. Fashion is perhaps the area where the products of consumerism are most obviously rearranged to spell rebellion: in a curious paradox, the more fashionable (in street terms, that is)—the more rebellious. Those who are comfortable within society may like to go around looking like that, but there is a kind of sharpness in dress which is an act of aggression against the "normal." Of course, the rapid turnover which is such an essential part of fashion is also ideally suited to the profit-making industries which supply the young and stylish. It is hard to separate the two things: in many aspects the "anti-social" is patterned in the same form as the social.

Products map out the social world, defining, not what we do, but the ways in which we can conceive of doing things—rather as a building maps out space. Not that products are the originators of any ideology, rather they embody possibilities whose boundaries are more revealing than any one possible use. The most telling thing about a product is usually what you *can't* do with it. It is, broadly speaking, the same form of society which two hundred years ago initiated the *cell* system in prisons and asylums, that has today produced the *one-way TV:* a commodity which is limited to individual reception, when TV technology could equally easily be used for two-way and multiple transmission. The limitation on the use of this particular product simply measures the extent to which individualism and passivity are taken for granted in our society generally. This is also built into the form of, for example, the lecture theatre; which makes discussion among the "audience" almost physically impossible.

Buildings and technology clearly divide up our social space and vision into shapes which are much more permanent than their content. But all products are part of this material landscape, whose contours chart our very vision of life and its possibilities, and whose boundaries mark out our channels of thought. These are not fixed, but they cannot be shifted by an opposition which fits the same slots. Every society has some kind of map, a grid of the terms available to think in at any given time. In ours, consumer goods are just some of the chief landmarks which define the "natural" categories we are accustomed to. It takes the law to define "crime"; it takes medicine to define "sickness"; it takes science to define "nature"; and it takes *Hoover* to define the *three kinds of dirt.*

Reflecting and Interpreting

1. How does paragraph 2 function? (Find the topic sentence.)
2. How does the style of paragraph 2 differ from that of paragraph 6? Why is paragraph 2 so much clearer? (Notice the treatment and development of the categories.)
3. How do most marketers try to distinguish a product from its rivals? What happens in the fashion industry?
4. What does Williamson mean by the sentence "If it is language that channels our physical perceptions, it is the language of consumer products which defines our daily life"? To what extent do you agree?
5. Although marketing expands our conceptual ranges, at the same time it limits our thinking. How? (See "two important questions" and "Products map out the social world. . . .")
6. Although the author gives snatches of her thesis at more than one point in the essay, the most succinct version appears in the last paragraph. Can you find it?
7. Think about the title. Does it seem strange and limiting for an essay that discusses so much more? Why or why not?

A Writer's Response

1. Sometimes an extended example is an effective opening to establish a topic. Try applying this technique to another topic with categories.
2. The more you know about a topic, the better you can classify various parts of it into categories. What specialized knowledge do you have that you might use in writing an essay of division or classification? (For help, see chapter 14.)

How Do We Find the Student
in a World of Academic Gymnasts
and Worker Ants?

James T. Baker

Categorizing individuals is risky business, especially if you are not a member of the group you are classifying. Study carefully how James Baker delineates types of college students he has known and think about the implications. This essay, in which Professor Baker reveals as much about himself as about his students, was first published in The Chronicle of Higher Education.

Anatole France once wrote that "the whole art of teaching is only the art of awakening the natural curiosity of young minds." I fully agree, except I have to wonder if, by using the word "only," he thought that the art of awakening such natural curiosity was an easy job. For me, it never has been—sometimes exciting, always challenging, but definitely not easy.

Robert M. Hutchins used to say that a good education prepares students to go on educating themselves throughout their lives. A fine definition, to be sure, but it has at times made me doubt that my own students, who seem only too eager to graduate so they can lay down their books forever, are receiving a good education.

But then maybe these are merely the pessimistic musings of someone suffering from battle fatigue. I have almost qualified for my second sabbatical leave, and I am scratching a severe case of the seven-year itch. About the only power my malaise has not impaired is my eye for spotting certain "types" of students. In fact, as the rest of me declines, my eye seems to grow more acute.

Has anyone else noticed that the very same students people college classrooms year after year? Has anyone else found the same bodies, faces, personalities returning semester after semester? Forgive me for violating my students' individual "personhoods," but reality makes it so tempting to see them as types. Doubtless you will recognize at least some of them. They have twins, or perhaps clones, on your campus, too.

There is the eternal Good Time Charlie (or Charlene), who makes every   5
party on and off the campus, who by November of his freshman year has worked his face into a case of terminal acne, who misses every set of examinations because of "mono," who finally burns himself out physically and mentally by the age of 19 and drops out to go home and recuperate, and who returns at 20 after a long talk with Dad to major in accounting.

There is the Young General Patton, the one who comes to college on an R.O.T.C. scholarship and for a year twirls his rifle at basketball games while loudly sniffing out pinko professors, who at midpoint takes a sudden but predictable, radical swing from far right to far left, who grows a beard and moves in with a girl who refuses to shave her legs, who then makes the just as predictable, radical swing back to the right and ends up preaching fundamentalist sermons on the steps of the student union while the Good Time Charlies and Charlenes jeer.

There is the Egghead, the campus intellectual who shakes up his fellow students—and even a professor or two—with references to esoteric formulas and obscure Bulgarian poets, who is recognized by friend and foe alike as a promising young academic, someday to be a professional scholar, who disappears every summer for six weeks ostensibly to search for primeval human remains in Colorado caves, and who at 37 is shot dead by Arab terrorists while on a mission for the C.I.A.

There is the Performer—the music or theater major, the rock or folk singer— who spends all of his or her time working up an act, who gives barely a nod to mundane subjects like history, sociology, or physics, who dreams only of the day he or she will be on stage full time, praised by critics, cheered by audiences, who ends up either pregnant or responsible for a pregnancy and at 30 is either an insurance salesman or a housewife with a very lush garden.

There is the Jock, of course—the every-afternoon intramural champ, smelling of liniment and Brut, with bulging calves and a blue-eyed twinkle, the subject of untold numbers of female fantasies, the walking personification of he-manism—who upon graduation is granted managerial rank by a California bank because of his golden tan and low golf score, who is seen five years later buying the drinks at a San Francisco gay bar.

There is the Academic Gymnast—the guy or gal who sees college as an obstacle course, as so many stumbling blocks in the way of a great career or a perfect marriage—who strains every moment to finish and be done with "this place" forever, who toward the end of the junior year begins to slow down, to grow quieter and less eager to leave, who attends summer school, but never quite finishes those last six hours, who never leaves "this place," and who at 40 is still working at the campus laundry, still here, still a student.   10

There is the Medal Hound, the student who comes to college not to learn or expand any intellectual horizons but simply to win honors—medals, cups, plates, ribbons, scrolls—who is here because this is the best place to win the most the fastest, who plasticizes and mounts on his wall every certificate of excellence he wins, who at 39 will be a colonel in the U.S. Army and at 55 Secretary of something or other in a conservative Administration in Washington.

There is the Worker Ant, the student (loosely rendered) who takes 21 hours a semester and works 49 hours a week at the local car wash, who sleeps only on Sundays and during classes, who will somehow graduate on time and be the owner of his own vending-machine company at 30 and be dead of a heart attack at 40, and who will be remembered for the words chiseled on his tombstone:

All This Was Accomplished Without Ever Having So Much as Darkened The Door Of A Library

There is the Lost Soul, the sad kid who is in college only because teachers, parents, and society at large said so, who hasn't a career in mind or a dream to follow, who hasn't a clue, who heads home every Friday afternoon to spend the weekend cruising the local Dairee-Freeze, who at 50 will have done all his teachers, parents, and society said to do, still without a career in mind or a dream to follow or a clue.

There is also the Saved Soul—the young woman who has received, through   15
the ministry of one Gospel freak or another, a Holy Calling to save the world, or at least some special part of it—who majors in Russian studies so that she can be caught smuggling Bibles into the Soviet Union and be sent to Siberia where she can preach to souls imprisoned by the Agents of Satan in the Gulag Archipelago.

Then, finally, there is the Happy Child, who comes to college to find a husband or wife—and finds one—and there is the Determined Child, who comes to get a degree—and gets one.

Enough said.

All of which, I suppose, should make me throw up my hands in despair and say that education, like youth and love, is wasted on the young. Not quite.

For there does come along, on occasion, that one of a hundred or so who is maybe at first a bit lost, certainly puzzled; who may well start out a Good Timer, an Egghead, a Performer, a Jock, a Medal Hound, a Gymnast, a Worker Ant; who may indeed have trouble settling on a major, who will be distressed by what sometimes passes for education, who might even be a temporary dropout; but who has a vital capacity for growth and is able to fall in love with learning, who acquires a taste for intellectual pleasure, who becomes in the finest sense of the word a Student.

This is the one who keeps the most jaded of us going back to class after class,   20
and he or she must be oh-so-carefully cultivated. He or she must be artfully awakened, given the tools needed to continue learning for a lifetime, and let grow at whatever pace and in whatever direction nature dictates.

For I try always to remember that this student is me, my continuing self, my immortality. This person is my only hope that my own search for Truth will continue after me, on and on, forever.

Reflecting and Interpreting

1. What is the question behind the opening paragraph? In paragraph 2?

2. The third paragraph is self-deprecating. How does he feel? Yet he makes a claim. What is it?

3. Paragraphs 5 to 16 set forth categories of students. Are all categories equally well done? Are any underdeveloped? Do any overlap or lack clarity?

4. Can you recognize yourself or your peers in any of these categories? What are the categories? What does this say about Baker's essay?

5. In using humor there is always the risk of offending someone. How did you feel when you read his classifications? Who is Baker's intended audience? Would the humor be suitable for it? (See the publication note above.)

6. Did your response change when you came to the last four paragraphs? Why or why not? What does the author reveal about himself and his values?

A Writer's Response

1. With a group discuss how you decide when someone is crossing the line on humor in writing or in conversation. Can you devise some guidelines?

2. Would you have liked a different ending for Baker's essay? Perhaps you could allude to the title in some way or write an ending that has universal appeal.

3. Turn the tables on Baker! Sort professors into categories similar to his categories for students. Add a final, positive example, called "The Teacher." (For help in writing the essay, see chapter 14.)

The Rival Conceptions of God

C. S. Lewis

C. S. Lewis was a scholar, novelist, and author of many books explaining Christianity, which he embraced after abandoning atheism. In this short essay, excerpted from his book, Mere Christianity, *Lewis clearly distinguishes between two major conceptions of God and explains why he changed his mind about important theological questions. Lewis's argument is unusual, for it is based strictly on logic.*

I have been asked to tell you what Christians believe, and I am going to begin by telling you one thing that Christians do not need to believe. If you are a Christian you do not have to believe that all the other religions are simply wrong all through. If you are an atheist you do have to believe that the main point in all the religions of the whole world is simply one huge mistake. If you are a Christian, you are free to think that all these religions, even the queerest ones, contain at least some hint of the truth. When I was an atheist I had to try to persuade myself that most of the human race have always been wrong about the question that mattered to them most; when I became a Christian I was able to take a more liberal view. But, of course, being a Christian does mean thinking that where Christianity differs from other religions, Christianity is right and they are wrong. As in arithmetic—there is only one right answer to a sum, and all other answers are wrong: but some of the wrong answers are much nearer being right than others.

The first big division of humanity is into the majority, who believe in some kind of God or gods, and the minority who do not. On this point, Christianity lines up with the majority—lines up with ancient Greeks and Romans, modern savages, Stoics, Platonists, Hindus, Mohammedans, etc., against the modern Western European materialist.

Now I go on to the next big division. People who all believe in God can be divided according to the sort of God they believe in. There are two very different ideas on this subject. One of them is the idea that He is beyond good and evil. We humans call one thing good and another thing bad. But according to some people that is merely our human point of view. These people would say that the wiser you become the less you would want to call anything good or bad, and the more clearly you would see that everything is good in one way and bad in another, and that nothing could have been different. Consequently, these people think that long before you got anywhere near the divine point of view the distinction would have disappeared altogether. We call a cancer bad, they would say, because it kills a man; but you might just as well call a successful surgeon bad because he kills a cancer. It all depends on the point of view. The other and opposite idea is that God is quite definitely "good" or "righteous," a God who takes sides, who loves love and hates hatred, who wants us to behave in one way and not in another. The first of these views—the one that thinks God beyond good and evil—is called Pantheism. It was held by the great Prussian philosopher Hegel and, as far as I can understand them, by the Hindus. The other view is held by Jews, Mohammedans and Christians.

And with this big difference between Pantheism and the Christian idea of God, there usually goes another. Pantheists usually believe that God, so to speak, animates the universe as you animate your body: that the universe almost *is* God, so that if it did not exist He would not exist either, and anything you find in the universe is a part of God. The Christian idea is quite different. They think God invented and made the universe—like a man making a picture or composing a tune. A painter is not a picture, and he does not die if his picture is destroyed. You may say, "He's put a lot of himself into it," but you only mean that all its beauty and interest has come out of his head. His skill is not in the picture in the same way that it is in his head, or even in his hands. I expect you see how this difference between Pantheists and Christians hangs together with the other one. If you do not take the distinction between good and bad very seriously, then it is easy to say that anything you find in this world is a part of God. But, of course, if you think some things really bad, and God really good, then you cannot talk like that. You must believe that God is separate from the world and that some of the things we see in it are contrary to His will. Confronted with a cancer or a slum the Pantheist can say, "If you could only see it from the divine point of view, you would realize that this also is God." The Christian replies, "Don't talk damned nonsense."* For Christianity is a fighting religion. It thinks God made the world—that space and time, heat and cold, and all the colours and tastes, and all the animals and vegetables, are things that God "made up out of His head" as a man makes up a story. But it also thinks that a great many things have gone wrong with the world that God made and that God insists, and insists very loudly, on our putting them right again.

And, of course, that raises a very big question. If a good God made the world why has it gone wrong? And for many years I simply refused to listen to the Christian answers to this question, because I kept on feeling "whatever you say, and however clever your arguments are, isn't it much simpler and easier to say that the world was not made by any intelligent power? Aren't all your arguments simply a complicated attempt to avoid the obvious?" But then that threw me back into another difficulty.   5

My argument against God was that the universe seemed so cruel and unjust. But how had I got this idea of *just* and *unjust*? A man does not call a line crooked unless he has some idea of a straight line. What was I comparing this universe

---

*One listener complained of the word *damned* as frivolous swearing. But I mean exactly what I say—nonsense that is *damned* is under God's curse, and will (apart from God's grace) lead those who believe it to eternal death.

with when I called it unjust? If the whole show was bad and senseless from A to Z, so to speak, why did I, who was supposed to be part of the show, find myself in such violent reaction against it? A man feels wet when he falls into water, because man is not a water animal: a fish would not feel wet. Of course I could have given up my idea of justice by saying it was nothing but a private idea of my own. But if I did that, then my argument against God collapsed too—for the argument depended on saying that the world was really unjust, not simply that it did not happen to please my private fancies. Thus in the very act of trying to prove that God did not exist—in other words, that the whole of reality was senseless—I found I was forced to assume that one part of reality—namely my idea of justice—was full of sense. Consequently atheism turns out to be too simple. If the whole universe has no meaning, we should never have found out that it has no meaning: just as, if there were no light in the universe and therefore no creature with eyes, we should never know it was dark. *Dark* would be without meaning.

Reflecting and Interpreting

1. Lewis begins by stating what he does not believe. Does this obscure or clarify what he does believe? Why?

2. In what two basic ways does atheism differ from a belief in God?

3. What are the two broad conceptions of God that Lewis describes? How do they regard good and evil? Which religious groups hold these views?

4. Notice that even though Lewis names three religions that hold the second view, he explains only the Christian view and how it differs from Pantheism. What are some serious questions that these two groups disagree about?

5. What was the "big question" that for years forestalled Lewis's belief in God? How did Lewis resolve this important question? What did he conclude about atheism?

6. What is the effect of the comparison that Lewis makes at the end? Can you explain it further?

A Writer's Response

1. As a child, did you ever do anything that caused you to have an ethical conflict? Did you resolve the conflict yourself or were you found out? What happened? Write an essay describing the incident and commenting on the cause and effect.

2. Write an essay that describes the origin and history of your religious beliefs. Have they changed since you were a child? If so, how? Mention any doubts you may have had as well as any decisions or changes you have made as a result of your beliefs.

A Nonsmoker with a Smoker

Phillip Lopate

Phillip Lopate, a well-known essayist, is the author of Against Joie De Vivre: Personal Essays *(1989), from which this essay is taken. Lopate, a nonsmoker, ponders his thoughts on smoking, contrasting the feelings and views of smokers and nonsmokers. He creates a kaleidoscope of images that causes us to feel—not merely see—clearly first one side of smoking and then the other. The result? A remarkably balanced viewpoint.*

Last Saturday night my girlfriend, Helen, and I went to a dinner party in the Houston suburbs. We did not know our hosts, but were invited on account of Helen's chum Barry, whose birthday party it was. We had barely stepped into the house and met the other guests, seated on a U-shaped couch under an A-framed ceiling, when Helen lit a cigarette. The hostess froze. "Uh, could you please not smoke in here? If you have to, we'd appreciate your using the terrace. We're both sort of allergic."

Helen smiled understandingly and moved toward the glass doors leading to the backyard in a typically ladylike way, as though merely wanting to get a better look at the garden. But I knew from that gracious "Southern" smile of hers that she was miffed.

As soon as Helen had stepped outside, the hostess explained that they had just moved into this house, and that it had taken weeks to air out because of the previous owner's tenacious cigar smoke. A paradigmatically awkward conversation about tobacco ensued: like testifying sinners, two people came forward with confessions about kicking the nasty weed; our scientist-host cited a recent study of indoor air pollution levels; a woman lawyer brought up the latest California legislation protecting nonsmokers; a roly-poly real estate agent admitted that, though he had given up smokes, he still sat in the smoking section of airplanes because "you meet a more interesting type of person there"—a remark his wife did not find amusing. Helen's friend Barry gallantly joined her outside. I did not, as I should have; I felt paralyzed.

For one thing, I wasn't sure which side I was on. I have never been a smoker. My parents both chain-smoked, so I grew up accustomed to cloudy interiors and ever since have been tolerant of other people's nicotine urges. To be perfectly honest, I'm not crazy about inhaling smoke, particularly when I've got a cold, but that irritating inconvenience pales beside the damage that would be done to my pluralistic worldview if I did not defend smokers' rights.

On the other hand, a part of me wished Helen *would* stop smoking. That part   5
seemed to get a satisfaction out of the group's "banishing" her: they were doing the dirty work of expressing my disapproval.

As soon as I realized this, I joined her in the garden. Presently a second guest strolled out to share a forbidden toke, then a third. Our hostess ultimately had to collect the mutineers with an announcement that dinner was served.

At the table, Helen appeared to be having such a good time, joking with our hosts and everyone else, that I was unprepared for the change that came over her as soon as we were alone in the car afterward. "I will never go back to that house!" she declared. "Those people have no concept of manners or hospitality, humiliating me the moment I stepped in the door. And that phony line about 'sort of allergic'!"

Normally, Helen is forbearance personified. Say anything that touches her about smoking, however, and you touch the rawest of nerves. I remembered the last time I foolishly suggested that she "think seriously" about stopping. I had just read one of those newspaper articles about the increased possibility of heart attacks, lung cancer, and birth deformities among women smokers, and I was worried for her. My concern must have been maladroitly expressed, because she burst into tears.

"Can't we even talk about this without your getting so sensitive?" I had asked.

"You don't understand. Nonsmokers never understand that it's a real addic-   10
tion. I've tried quitting, and it was hell. Do you want me to go around for months mean and cranky outside and angry inside? You're right, I'm sensitive, because I'm threatened with having taken away from me the thing that gives me the most pleasure in life, day in, day out," she said. I shot her a look: careful, now. "Well, practically the most pleasure. You know what I mean." I didn't. But I knew enough to drop it.

I love Helen, and if she wants to smoke, knowing the risks involved, that remains her choice. Besides, she wouldn't quit just because I wanted her to; she's not that docile, and that's part of what I love about her. Sometimes I wonder why I even keep thinking about her quitting. What's it to me personally? Certainly I feel protective of her health, but I also have selfish motives. I don't like the way her lips taste when she's smoked a lot. I associate her smoking with nervousness, and when she lights up several cigarettes in a row, I get jittery watching her. Crazy as this may sound, I also find myself becoming jealous of her cigarettes. Occasionally, when I go to her house and we're sitting on the couch together, if I see Helen eyeing the pack I make her kiss me first, so that my lips can engage hers (still fresh) before the competition's. It's almost as though there were another lover in the room—a lover who was around long before I entered the picture, and who pleases her in mysterious ways I cannot.

A lit cigarette puts a distance between us: it's like a weapon in her hand, awakening in me a primitive fear of being burnt. The memory is not so primitive, actually. My father used to smoke absentmindedly, letting the ash grow like a caterpillar eating every leaf in its path, until gravity finally toppled it. Once, when I was about nine, my father and I were standing in line at a bakery, and he accidentally dropped a lit ash down my back. Ever since, I've inwardly winced and been on guard around these little waving torches, which epitomize to me the dangers of intimacy.

I've worked hard to understand from the outside the satisfaction of smoking. I've even smoked "sympathetic" cigarettes, just to see what the other person was experiencing. But it's not the same as being hooked. How can I really empathize with the frightened but stubborn look Helen gets in her eyes when, despite the fact we're a little late going somewhere, she turns to me in the car and says, "I need to buy a pack of cigarettes first"? I feel a wave of pity for her. We are both embarrassed by this forced recognition of her frailty—the "indignity," as she herself puts it, of being controlled by something outside her will.

I try to imagine myself in that position, but a certain smugness keeps getting in the way (I don't have that problem and *am I glad*). We pay a price for our smugness. So often it flip-flops into envy: the outsiders wish to be included in the sufferings and highs of others, as if to say that only by relinquishing control and surrendering to some dangerous habit, some vice or dependency, would one be able to experience "real life."

Over the years I have become a sucker for cigarette romanticism. Few Hollywood gestures move me as much as the one in *Now Voyager*, when Paul Henreid lights two cigarettes, one for himself, the other for Bette Davis: these form a beautiful fatalistic bridge between them, a complicitous understanding like the realization that their love is based on the inevitability of separation. I am all the more admiring of this worldly cigarette gallantry because its experiential basis escapes me.

The same sort of fascination occurs when I come across a literary description of nicotine addiction, like this passage in Mailer's *Tough Guys Don't Dance*: "Over and over again I gave them up, a hundred times over the years, but I always went back. For in my dreams, sooner or later, I struck a match, brought flame to the tip, then took in all my hunger for existence with the first puff. I felt impaled on desire itself—those fiends trapped in my chest and screaming for one drag."

"Impaled on desire itself"! Such writing evokes a longing in me for the centering of self that tobacco seems to bestow on its faithful. Clearly, there is something attractive about having this umbilical relation to the universe—this curling pillar, this spiral staircase, this prayer of smoke that mediates between the smoker's inner substance and the alien ether. Inwardness of the nicotine trance, sad wisdom ("every pleasure has its price"), beauty of ritual, squandered health—all those romantic meanings we read into the famous photographic icons of fifties saints, Albert Camus or James Agee or James Dean or Carson McCullers puffing away, in a sense they're true. Like all people who return from a brush with death,

15

smokers have gained a certain power. They know their "coffin nails." With Helen, each cigarette is a measuring of the perishable, an enactment of her mortality, from filter to end-tip in fewer than five minutes. I could not stand to be reminded of my own death so often.

Reflecting and Interpreting

1. What is the effect of the anecdote as an opening to the essay?

2. Why does the narrator feel "paralyzed"? How does he feel about an issue on which most people have clear-cut opinions? What is the effect on the tone?

3. After pondering his feelings, Lopate admits what? As a result of this admission, his loyalty to Helen causes him to do what?

4. Comment on the contrast between Helen's behavior and her feelings.

5. Lopate admits that he has selfish reasons for wanting Helen to quit smoking. What are they? Comment on the image near the end of paragraph 11.

6. What feeling and memory does a lit cigarette rekindle for Lopate?

7. What is the "cigarette romanticism" that Lopate mentions? Do you think it is still prevalent? Why or why not?

8. Despite Lopate's attraction to a smoker and smoking, he does not smoke. Why?

9. Comment on his treatment of the topic. Do you think his honesty and objectivity are unusual? As a result, how do you feel about the narrator?

A Writer's Response

1. Lopate's essay reveals conflicting views on good manners. With your group identify the implicit question and tell how you resolve it in your homes.

2. Using some of Lopate's techniques, write an essay comparing and contrasting two views. For example, you might discuss a habit you disapprove of but, nonetheless, tolerate in someone you love.

A Tale of Two Proms, One Black, One White

Isabel Wilkerson

This article, first published in the New York Times, *describes how students at a college preparatory school couldn't agree on important prom decisions, so they decided to have two proms, one black, one white. Wilkerson compares the proms and the students' views. They raise an interesting question about what is fair. Even more significant is a broader question the episode raises about legalized integration.*

The rented limousines carrying young men in tuxedoes and young women in taffeta began arriving at a Gold Coast hotel shortly after dusk on Friday, May 3. It was the official Brother Rice High School prom, and it was virtually all white.

Three miles away at a South Side hotel, about 30 of their classmates—tuxedoed young men in kinte cloth cummerbunds—and their dates dressed in satin alighted from borrowed Cadillacs and BMWs for the school's first all-black prom.

It was a turning point that has torn at the heart of the predominantly white boys' Catholic school here and, sociologists say, is a telling allegory of race relations in this country 20 years after the civil rights movement brought an end to legalized segregation.

"For 20 years we have had a kind of token integration," said Dr. Aldon Morris, an associate professor of sociology at Northwestern University. "Now what we're getting is a real debate. What does integration mean and when has it really occurred? It is one of the most fundamental questions facing America right now."

Sociologists say that as society is forced to redefine integration and the forms it may take, it has become apparent that putting the races under the same roof does not guarantee integration.   5

Across the country, college campuses that have been desegregated for decades are witnessing growing racial tension and a disenchantment among blacks who have sought out separate cafeterias and dormitories. The situation at Brother Rice appears to be little different.

The college preparatory school is in a virtually all-white, middle-class neighborhood on Chicago's Southwest Side and has 1,330 students, 12 percent of them black, and no black teachers.

And while blacks and whites participate in classes and clubs and sports together, and many consider each other great friends, they sit at separate tables at lunchtime and go their separate ways after school is over.

On a subtler level, black students express a resentment that their culture does not get the attention that white culture does. They say that while they spend the school year learning mostly about the contributions of whites, black culture is relegated to a few seconds each morning during black history month when a student reads a brief sketch about a black inventor or abolitionist over the loudspeaker.

"We've been experiencing their culture for four years," said Edward Jones, a   10
black senior. "But they don't seem ready to experience ours."

The prom, with all its ritual and mythic significance, appeared to bring an underlying tension to a head. The trouble began when the prom committee, virtually all white, hired a rock band and a disc jockey and announced that the playlist for the music at the prom would be based on the suggestions of the senior class.

They devised what they saw as an objective means of gauging what the class wanted to hear: Each student would list three favorite songs, and the songs mentioned most would be the ones played.

Black seniors began to complain that their preferences would be effectively shut out, that Marvin Gaye would be squeezed out by Bon Jovi. "For every vote we had, there were eight votes for what they wanted," said Hosea Hill, a black senior.

"If you're paying tuition to the school, you should have some input. But with us being in the minority we're always outvoted. It's as if we don't count."

Music became a metaphor for culture and race, and black students consid-   15
ered the gap too wide to close. "They want to dance to that hard-rocking, bang-your-head-against-the-wall kind of stuff," said Sean Young, a black senior.

And others said that even if they could choose half the songs, which they figured was not going to happen, they would probably still be unhappy. "We would have sat down during their songs and they would have sat down during ours," Jones said.

So the black students decided to put together their own prom, with their own site, menu, theme and decorations. When school administrators got wind of the plans, they called a prom committee meeting to discuss grievances, but black students, figuring they would be outvoted, did not show up.

School administrators have refused to discuss the situation. Several of the black prom organizers, including honor students headed for prestigious universities, said they were threatened with suspension and expulsion if they went ahead with an alternative prom. They did it anyway.

And so while about 200 white couples danced to rock music in two adjoining ballrooms at the Marriott Hotel, about 30 black couples listened to the Isley Brothers and Roy Ayers, danced the Electric Slide and crowned their own prom king and queen, James Warren and Devona Rogers, in Ballroom 15 at the McCormick Hotel.

Several hours into the evening, there were bursts of applause as several of   20
the six black couples who went to the main prom to spend time with their white friends showed up at the black prom.

The organizers for the black prom, who said they had nothing against their white classmates, said that white students were welcome to their prom. But by midnight, none had shown up.

Many of the white students have taken the situation personally. Some said they were hurt and felt rejected. Others were angry and embittered.

"Now you find out what they really think of you," said Jerry Ficaro, a white student at the main prom.

He said the black students should have gone along with the majority. "The majority makes a decision," he said. "That's the way it works."

Mike Kane, another white student, said: "I think the whole thing got out of   25 hand. They should have found some way to compromise. We might as well have separate graduations."

Some said they just missed their friends and felt like the class was not whole without the black students. "It's too bad," said Jack Scott, another white senior, "because it's our senior year, and we should be together."

Brother Rice administrators would not allow reporters into the main prom. They have disavowed the black prom, saying the school has nothing to do with it and barring the black students from using the Brother Rice name in their program, napkins and banner.

The principal, Brother Michael Segvich, told the Chicago Tribune days before the proms, "There is only one prom this year at Brother Rice." The black prom "is something we don't want," he said, adding, "I think it has to do with racism. We felt we went out of our way to accommodate. They seemed to have their minds made up to go along with this other party all along."

Morris, the sociologist, said that the situation is symbolic of the misunderstanding that can occur between a majority and minority culture. "What integration has meant for many whites is that blacks had to interact with them on their terms," Morris said.

"It is a kind of cultural arrogance. Not only do many not want to participate   30 in other cultures, but they feel theirs is the culture, that theirs is very much American and what America is."

For many of the black students, a black prom became something of a crusade, a chance to show that they could do something on their own, that they did not have to rely on whites.

And so Edward Jones, an honor student and one of the main organizers, was beaming as he looked across the small ballroom at his impeccably clad black classmates, helping their dates with their chairs or fetching punch or practicing dance steps to black music.

"I haven't felt this way for four years," Jones said. "We love being black. This makes me proud to be black. If at our 20th year reunion, the white students want to sit and point fingers at us, that's OK. We know we did something meaningful."

Reflecting and Interpreting

1. What is an allegory? How do the first two paragraphs fit with the third?
2. What do the black students resent about their four years at Brother Rice school? How does the planning of the prom cause underlying tensions to erupt?

3. What do you think of the "objective means of gauging" which songs would be played at the Brother Rice prom? Consider the views of both sides.

4. Were you surprised that many students really wanted all students to attend and took the other side's lack of attendance personally? What does this indicate?

5. Note Mike Kane's comment. Do you agree or disagree? Can you think of an alternative that might have placated the students and resulted in one prom?

6. How would you define "token integration"? What does Dr. Morris say is "one of the most fundamental questions facing America right now"? Does this conflict of views hinge upon a question of power as well as philosophy? How?

7. How would you state the implicit thesis? What do your peers think?

A Writer's Response

1. With a group, discuss these questions: How much more can government do to facilitate integration? How much should be left to individuals to decide?

2. Wilkerson takes a journalistic approach in organizing and developing this essay. How does the essay differ from a classic argument? Mimicking her style, create a brief rough draft about an issue that can be illustrated by an incident. (Suggestions: pornography seen by children on the Internet, ease of marriage and divorce, the income tax marriage penalty, or some other social problem.)

Two Views of the River

Mark Twain

Our first impression of a wondrous sight often overwhelms us with its beauty and magnetism. But as we become more familiar and more involved with the phenomenon, our focus tends to shift from appreciation to practicality. So it was with Samuel Clemens (who later adopted the pen name of Mark Twain) as he went from apprentice to river pilot of steamships on the Mississippi. This excerpt is taken from Life on the Mississippi, *one of the many books that have placed Twain among the foremost American authors.*

Now when I had mastered the language of this water, and had come to know every trifling feature that bordered the great river as familiarly as I knew the letters of the alphabet, I had made a valuable acquisition. But I had lost something, too. I had lost something which could never be restored to me while I lived. All the grace, the beauty, the poetry, had gone out of the majestic river! I still kept in mind a certain wonderful sunset which I witnessed when steamboating was new to me. A broad expanse of the river was turned to blood; in the middle distance the red hue brightened into gold, through which a solitary log came floating, black and conspicuous; in one place a long, slanting mark lay sparkling upon the water; in another the surface was broken by boiling, tumbling rings, that were as many-tinted as an opal; where the ruddy flush was faintest, was a smooth spot that was covered with graceful circles and radiating lines, ever so delicately traced; the shore on our left was densely wooded, and the somber shadow that fell from this forest was broken in one place by a long, ruffled trail that shone like silver; and high above the forest wall a clean-stemmed dead tree waved a single leafy bough that glowed like a flame in the unobstructed splendor that was flowing from the sun. There were graceful curves, reflected images, woody heights, soft distances; and over the whole scene, far and near, the dissolving lights drifted steadily, enriching it every passing moment with new marvels of coloring.

I stood like one bewitched. I drank it in, in a speechless rapture. The world was new to me, and I had never seen anything like this at home. But as I have said, a day came when I began to cease from noting the glories and the charms which the moon and the sun and the twilight wrought upon the river's face; another day came when I ceased altogether to note them. Then, if that sunset scene had been repeated, I should have looked upon it without rapture, and should have commented upon it, inwardly, after this fashion: "This sun means that we are going to have wind to-morrow; that floating log means that the river is rising, small thanks to it; that slanting mark on the water refers to a bluff reef which is going to kill somebody's steamboat one of these nights, if it keeps on stretching out like that; those tumbling 'boils' show a dissolving bar and a changing channel there; the lines and circles in the slick water over yonder are a warning that that troublesome place is shoaling up dangerously; that silver streak in the shadow of the forest is the 'break' from a new snag, and he has located himself in the very best place he could have found to fish for steamboats; that tall dead tree, with a single living branch, is not going to last long, and then how is a body ever going to get through this blind place at night without the friendly old landmark?"

No, the romance and beauty were all gone from the river. All the value any feature of it had for me now was the amount of usefulness it could furnish toward compassing the safe piloting of a steamboat. Since those days, I have pitied doctors from my heart. What does the lovely flush in a beauty's cheek mean to a doctor but a "break" that ripples above some deadly disease? Are not all her visible charms sown thick with what are to him the signs and symbols of hidden decay? Does he ever see her beauty at all, or doesn't he simply view her professionally and comment upon her unwholesome condition all to himself? And doesn't he sometimes wonder whether he has gained most or lost most by learning his trade?

Reflecting and Interpreting

1. What poetic device does Twain use in the first sentence to refer to his acquisition of practical knowledge?

2. Although he says "all the grace, the beauty, the poetry," has been lost for him, he gives an example that seems to blunt this statement. How do you explain the seeming contradiction?

3. Can you find the passage that serves as a transition from his first view of the river to his later view?

4. Note the language that Twain uses to describe how the river impressed him before and after he became a river pilot. What differences do you notice?

5. Examine the ending. What is the effect of the comparison with a doctor learning his trade?

A Writer's Response

1. **Small groups:** How does Twain establish his credibility as a writer? Does he use block or alternating style to arrange his points of comparison? What is the significance of the verbs in the second view? How does the tone of the first view differ from the second view?

2. Have you ever experienced a sense of awe and wonder when viewing a spectacular sight for the first time? Describe the sight and tell why it was especially memorable to you.

3. Have you ever experienced a sense of acquisition and loss similar to Twain's? Write an essay comparing your two views.

Opposing Principles Help Balance Society

Sydney J. Harris

Liberal, conservative, and radical—what images and reactions does each of these labels bring to mind? Those who use the labels may not really understand what the words they choose mean. In this essay, first published in his column for the Chicago Daily News, *Sydney J. Harris stresses how we need a variety of all three types of people to make a well-balanced society.*

I devoutly wish we could get rid of two words in the popular lexicon: *liberal* and *conservative*. Both are beautiful and useful words in their origins, but now each is used (and misused) as an epithet by its political enemies.

Liberal means liberating—it implies more freedom, more openness, more flexibility, more humaneness, more willingness to change when change is called for.

Conservative means conserving—it implies preserving what is best and most valuable from the past, a decent respect for tradition, a reluctance to change merely for its own sake.

Both attributes, in a fruitful tension, are necessary for the welfare of any social order. Liberalism alone can degenerate into mere permissiveness and anarchy. Conservatism alone is prone to harden into reaction and repression. As Lord Acton brilliantly put it: "Every institution tends to fail by an excess of its own basic principle."

Yet, in the rhetoric of their opponents, both *liberal* and *conservative* have turned into dirty words. Liberals become "bleeding hearts"; conservatives want "to turn the clock back." But sometimes hearts *should* bleed; sometimes it would profit us to run the clock back if it is spinning too fast.

Radical, of course, has become the dirtiest of words, flung around carelessly and sometimes maliciously. Today it is usually applied to the left by the right—but the right is often as "radical" in its own way.

The word originally meant "going to the roots" and was a metaphor drawn from the radish, which grows underground. We still speak of "radical surgery," which is undertaken when lesser measures seem futile. The American Revolution, indeed, was a radical step taken to ensure a conservative government, when every other effort had failed.

Dorothy Thompson was right on target when she remarked that her ideal was to be "a radical as a thinker, a conservative as to program, and a liberal as to temper." In this way she hoped to combine the best and most productive in each attitude, while avoiding the pitfalls of each.

Society is like a pot of soup: It needs different, and contrasting, ingredients to give it body and flavor and lasting nourishment. It is compound, not simple; not like wine that drugs us, or caffeine that agitates us, but a blend to satisfy the most divergent palates.

Of course, this is an ideal, an impossible vision never to be fully realized in   10 any given society. But it is what we should aim at, rather than promoting some brew that is to one taste alone. It may take another thousand years to get the recipe just right. The question is: Do we have the time?

Reflecting and Interpreting

1. In the opening paragraph, notice the contrast of "devoutly wish" with "epithet." Note the tone of each word. What function does this pairing serve?

2. Give some examples of how the meanings of *liberal* and *conservative* have changed over the years. Can you think of any that Harris does not mention?

3. What is Harris's thesis? How many times does he state it (in different ways)?

4. Although the simile of "society is like a pot of soup" is apt, similar comparisons have long been used. Can you think of a fresh one that would serve?

5. This is a very short essay about a very big topic. After reading Harris's explanation, what questions do you have that are left unanswered? How would you expand or develop the essay to incorporate some of those questions and answers?

A Writer's Response

1. The author's closing question—"Do we have the time?"—could almost be a lead-in to a much larger essay. Freewrite on what you think Harris means here.

2. Poll people you meet daily, asking them to define *liberal, conservative,* and *radical* and to give an example of each. (Try to obtain a cross-section of ages and occupations—at least two dozen.) Do any of their definitions match those of Harris? How do they differ? Did the age of respondents seem to influence their replies? Did you notice any other factors that might be an influence? On the basis of your limited research, write an essay on what these words mean. Give examples, including how they are often used during election campaigns.

DEFINITION
Explaining What Something Is

On Being 17, Bright, and Unable to Read

David Raymond

Someone who has experienced a disability can give an insider's view, providing insights that increase an outsider's understanding in a way that a technical definition cannot. David Raymond was a junior in high school when his essay on dyslexia was published in the New York Times.

One day a substitute teacher picked me to read aloud from the textbook. When I told her "No, thank you," she came unhinged. She thought I was acting smart, and told me so. I kept calm, and that got her madder and madder. We must have spent 10 minutes trying to solve the problem, and finally she got so red in the face I thought she'd blow up. She told me she'd see me after class.

Maybe someone like me was a new thing for that teacher. But she wasn't new to me. I've been through scenes like that all my life. You see, even though I'm 17 and a junior in high school, I can't read because I have dyslexia. I'm told I read "at a fourth-grade level," but from where I sit, that's not reading. You can't know what that means unless you've been there. It's not easy to tell how it feels when you can't read your homework assignments or the newspaper or a menu in a restaurant or even notes from your own friends.

My family began to suspect I was having problems almost from the first day I started school. My father says my early years in school were the worst years of his life. They weren't so good for me, either. As I look back on it now, I can't find the words to express how bad it really was. I wanted to die. I'd come home from school screaming, "I'm dumb. I'm dumb—I wish I were dead!"

I guess I couldn't read anything at all then—not even my own name—and they tell me I didn't talk as good as other kids. But what I remember about those days is that I couldn't throw a ball where it was supposed to go, I couldn't learn to swim, and I wouldn't learn to ride a bike, because no matter what anyone told me, I knew I'd fail.

Sometimes my teachers would try to be encouraging. When I couldn't read the words on the board they'd say, "Come on, David, you know that word." Only I didn't. And it was embarrassing. I just felt dumb. And dumb was how the kids

5

treated me. They'd make fun of me every chance they got, asking me to spell "cat" or something like that. Even if I knew how to spell it, I wouldn't; they'd only give me another word. Anyway, it was awful, because more than anything I wanted friends. On my birthday when I blew out the candles I didn't wish I could learn to read; what I wished for was that the kids would like me.

With the bad reports coming from school, and with me moaning about wanting to die and how everybody hated me, my parents began looking for help. That's when the testing started. The school tested me, the child-guidance center tested me, private psychiatrists tested me. Everybody knew something was wrong— especially me.

It didn't help much when they stuck a fancy name onto it. I couldn't pronounce it then—I was only in second grade—and I was ashamed to talk about it. Now it rolls off my tongue, because I've been living with it for a lot of years— dyslexia.

All through elementary school it wasn't easy. I was always having to do things that were "different," things the other kids didn't have to do. I had to go to a child psychiatrist, for instance.

One summer my family forced me to go to a camp for children with reading problems. I hated the idea, but the camp turned out pretty good, and I had a good time. I met a lot of kids who couldn't read and somehow that helped. The director of the camp said I had a higher I.Q. than 90 percent of the population. I didn't believe him.

About the worst thing I had to do in fifth and sixth grade was go to a special   10 education class in another school in our town. A bus picked me up, and I didn't like that at all. The bus also picked up emotionally disturbed kids and retarded kids. It was like going to a school for the retarded. I always worried that someone I knew would see me on that bus. It was a relief to go to the regular junior high school.

Life began to change a little for me then, because I began to feel better about myself. I found the teachers cared; they had meetings about me and I worked harder for them for a while. I began to work on the potter's wheel, making vases and pots that the teachers said were pretty good. Also, I got a letter for being on the track team. I could always run pretty fast.

At high school the teachers are good and everyone is trying to help me. I've gotten honors some marking periods and I've won a letter on the cross-country team. Next quarter I think the school might hold a show of my pottery. I've got some friends. But there are still some embarrassing times. For instance, every time there is writing in the class, I get up and go to the special education room. Kids ask me where I go all the time. Sometimes I say, "to Mars."

Homework is a real problem. During free periods in school I go into the special ed room and staff members read assignments to me. When I get home my mother reads to me. Sometimes she reads an assignment into a tape recorder, and then I go into my room and listen to it. If we have a novel or something like that to read, she reads it out loud to me. Then I sit down with her and we do the assignment. She'll write, while I talk my answers to her. Lately I've taken to dictating into a tape recorder, and then someone—my father, a private tutor or my mother—types up what I've dictated. Whatever homework I do takes someone else's time, too. That makes me feel bad.

We had a big meeting in school the other day—eight of us, four from the guidance department, my private tutor, my parents and me. The subject was me. I said I wanted to go to college, and they told me about colleges that have facilities and staff to handle people like me. That's nice to hear.

As for what happens after college, I don't know and I'm worried about that. 15 How can I make a living if I can't read? Who will hire me? How will I fill out the application form? The only thing that gives me any courage is the fact that I've learned about well-known people who couldn't read or had other problems and still made it. Like Albert Einstein, who didn't talk until he was 4 and flunked math. Like Leonardo da Vinci, who everyone seems to think had dyslexia.

I've told this story because maybe some teacher will read it and go easy on a kid in the classroom who has what I've got. Or, maybe some parent will stop nagging his kid, and stop calling him lazy. Maybe he's not lazy or dumb. Maybe he just can't read and doesn't know what's wrong. Maybe he's scared, like I was.

Reflecting and Interpreting

1. At no point does the author give the technical definition of dyslexia. Should he? What is the effect of this omission?

2. What aspects of Raymond's disability were hardest for him in elementary school? What did he wish for on his birthday? What experience was a turning point for Raymond? How did it help?

3. Why were junior high and high school better than the elementary grades?

4. Were you surprised to learn about the author's IQ? Why does the article mention Albert Einstein and Leonardo da Vinci?

5. Raymond includes many colloquialisms in the essay. How do "blow up" and "didn't talk as good as other kids" affect the tone? Can you find more examples?

6. What is the author's purpose in writing the essay?

A Writer's Response

1. Even though David Raymond was only seventeen when he wrote this essay, his intimacy with dyslexia made him something of an expert in defining it. Have you had a long, difficult experience that makes you somewhat of an expert? Write an essay that gives an insider's view of a problem.

2. If you haven't endured such an experience, perhaps a close family member has. Could you give your view and feelings about the problem? How did it affect you and other family members? (Or you might write about a serious disease or disability or a habit that has strained family relations.)

Defining Success

Michael Korda

America's ongoing romance with the concept of success has in recent years—more than ever before—led to a plethora of how-to books. Michael Korda's first book, Power!, *topped the nation's best-seller list in its first year. In this first chapter from a subsequent book,* Success!, *he begins by telling exactly what he thinks success is.*

Others may ask how you define success. This is more difficult. Success is relative; not everybody wants to put together a four-billion-dollar conglomerate, or become President of the United States, or win the Nobel Peace Prize. It is usually a mistake to begin with such grandiose ambitions, which tend to degenerate into lazy daydreams. The best way to succeed is to begin with a reasonably realistic goal and attain it, rather than aiming at something so far beyond your reach that you are bound to fail. It's also important to make a habit of succeeding, and the easiest way to start is to succeed at something, however small, every day, gradually increasing the level of your ambitions and achievements like a runner in training, who begins with short distances and works up to Olympic levels.

Try to think of success as a journey, an adventure, not a specific destination. Your goals may change during the course of that journey, and your original ambitions may be superseded by different, larger ones. Success will certainly bring you the material things you want, and a good, healthy appetite for the comforts and luxuries of life is an excellent road to success, but basically you'll know you have reached your goal when you have gone that one step further, in wealth, fame or achievement, than you ever dreamed was possible.

How you become a success is, of course, your business. Morality has very little to do with success. I do not personally think it is necessary to be dishonest, brutal or unethical in order to succeed, but a great many dishonest, brutal or unethical people in fact do succeed. You'd better be prepared for the fact that success is seldom won without some tough infighting along the way. A lot depends on your profession, of course. There is a great deal of difference between setting out to become a success in a Mafia family and trying to become vice president of a bank, but the differences simply consist of contrasting social customs and of what is the appropriate way to get ahead in a given profession or business. Whether you're hoping to take over a numbers game or an executive desk, you have to make the right moves for your circumstances. In the former example, you might have to kill someone; in the latter, you might only have to find ways of making your rivals look foolish or inefficient. In either case, you have to accept the rules of the game and play to win, or find some other game. This is a book about success, after all, not morality. The field you go into is your choice, but whatever it is, you're better off at the top of it than at the bottom.

Reflecting and Interpreting

1. In the opening paragraph, what does Korda suggest as the best way to begin succeeding? Do you agree or disagree? Why?

2. First, the author says, "Success is relative," but in the next paragraph he says, "Success will certainly bring you the material things you want." Do the two necessarily go hand in hand? If you disagree, can you give some examples to support your contention?

3. Even if you disagree with Korda on some points, do you see any suggestions for attaining success that might be relevant and helpful to you?

4. Korda says that morality has very little to do with success. Is this true for all occupations? Most? Analyze the examples that he gives to support this claim. For example, would the vice president of a bank who lacks morality be apt to last very long?

5. What about Korda's advice to make one's rivals look foolish or inefficient? React to this statement and any others you question.

6. This is chapter 1 of Korda's book *Success!* How does his definition affect your interest in buying or reading this book? List statements or examples that influenced this decision.

A Writer's Response

1. List some small, realistic daily goals you would like to attain. What can you begin doing to attain them?

2. Write a draft that defines your idea of success. What conditions are necessary to achieve success? What beliefs and values influence your idea of success? Try to be as specific as possible. Give concrete examples. (For help, see chapter 16.)

It's Failure, Not Success

Ellen Goodman

If you were incensed by Michael Korda's essay, so was Ellen Goodman, Pulitzer Prize–winning columnist for the Boston Globe *and author of several books. Compare Goodman's response to the philosophy touted by Korda. Then consider their writing styles. Who, do you think, is the better writer?*

I knew a man who went into therapy about three years ago because, as he put it, he couldn't live with himself any longer. I didn't blame him. The guy was a bigot, a tyrant and a creep.

In any case, I ran into him again after he'd finished therapy. He was still a bigot, a tyrant and a creep, *but* . . . he had learned to live with himself.

Now, I suppose this was an accomplishment of sorts. I mean, nobody else could live with him. But it seems to me that there are an awful lot of people running around and writing around these days encouraging us to feel good about what we should feel terrible about, and to accept in ourselves what we should change.

The only thing they seem to disapprove of is disapproval. The only judgment they make is against being judgmental, and they assure us that we have nothing to feel guilty about except guilt itself. It seems to me that they are all intent on proving that I'm OK and You're OK, when in fact, I may be perfectly dreadful and you may be unforgivably dreary, and it may be—gasp!—*wrong*.

What brings on my sudden attack of judgmentitis is success, or rather, *Success!*—the latest in a series of exclamation-point books all concerned with How to Make It.   5

In this one, Michael Korda is writing a recipe book for success. Like the other authors, he leapfrogs right over the "Shoulds" and into the "Hows." He eliminates value judgments and edits out moral questions as if he were Fanny Farmer and the subject was the making of a blueberry pie.

It's not that I have any reason to doubt Mr. Korda's advice on the way to achieve success. It may very well be that successful men wear handkerchiefs stuffed neatly in their breast pockets, and that successful single women should carry suitcases to the office on Fridays whether or not they are going away for the weekend.

He may be realistic when he says that "successful people generally have very low expectations of others." And he may be only slightly cynical when he writes: "One of the best ways to ensure success is to develop expensive tastes or marry someone who has them."

And he may be helpful with his handy hints on how to sit next to someone you are about to overpower.

But he simply finesses the issues of right and wrong—silly words, embarrass-   10
ing words that have been excised like warts from the shiny surface of the new
how-to books. To Korda, guilt is not a prod, but an enemy that he slays on page
four. Right off the bat, he tells the would-be successful reader that:

- It's OK to be greedy.
- It's OK to look out for Number One.
- It's OK to be Machiavellian (if you can get away with it).
- It's OK to recognize that honesty is not always the best policy (provided you don't go around saying so).
- And it's always OK to be rich.

Well, in fact, it's not OK. It's not OK to be greedy, Machiavellian, dishonest.
It's not always OK to be rich. There is a qualitative difference between succeeding
by making napalm or by making penicillin. There is a difference between climbing the ladder of success, and machete-ing a path to the top.

Only someone with the moral perspective of a mushroom could assure us
that this was all OK. It seems to me that most Americans harbor ambivalence toward success, not for neurotic reasons, but out of a realistic perception of what it
demands.

Success is expensive in terms of time and energy and altered behavior—the
sort of behavior he describes in the grossest of terms: "If you can undermine your
boss and replace him, fine, do so, but never express anything but respect and loyalty for him while you're doing it."

This author—whose *Power!* topped the best-seller list last year—is intent on
helping rid us of that ambivalence which is a signal from our conscience. He is
like the other "Win!" "Me First!" writers, who try to make us comfortable when
we should be uncomfortable.

They are all Doctor Feelgoods, offering us placebo prescriptions instead of   15
strong medicine. They give us a way to live with ourselves, perhaps, but not a way
to live with each other. They teach us a whole lot more about "Failure!" than
about success.

Reflecting and Interpreting

1. Goodman's opening reads rather like stand-up comedy. Does it pique your in-terest? Do you find it inviting or distracting? Why?

2. Where does a general statement of her thesis first appear? Later she makes a more specific claim in regard to Korda. Can you find it?

3. What does Korda omit in his book on success? Comment on the imagery that Goodman uses to make this point. How effective is it?

4. Repetition is an important tool in Goodman's essay. Find and list examples of this technique. How does it contribute to the overall purpose and effectiveness?

5. Goodman says, "There is a qualitative difference between succeeding by making napalm or by making penicillin." Do you agree? Why or why not?

6. Goodman says, "It seems to me that most Americans harbor ambivalence toward success, not for neurotic reasons, but out of a realistic perception of what it demands." What does she mean by that?

7. Note Goodman's ending. Here she echoes two ideas that were expressed earlier. What are they?

A Writer's Response

1. In paragraphs 10 and 11, Goodman sets up an interesting counterbalance by answering a series of Korda's "It's OK" assertions. With a group, can you use this technique to refute a common perception?

2. Whom do you most agree with—Korda or Goodman? Why? Jot down your reasons and revise your draft on success, using any notes that seem suitable.

❧ *What Is Poverty?*

Jo Goodwin Parker

A mystery surrounds the next essay. In 1971 George Henderson, a professor at the University of Oklahoma, was working on a book, America's Other Children: Public Schools Outside Suburbia, *when he received this essay in the mail. The letter's postmark was from West Virginia. Yet when he inquired, no one had ever heard of Jo Goodwin Parker. Was she a real person who, hearing of Henderson's work, had the courage to step forward briefly? Or was she a persona taken by a compassionate writer? To this day, the author's identity remains a mystery.*

You ask me what is poverty? Listen to me. Here I am, dirty, smelly, and with no "proper" underwear on and with the stench of my rotting teeth near you. I will tell you. Listen to me. Listen without pity. I cannot use your pity. Listen with understanding. Put yourself in my dirty, worn out, ill-fitting shoes, and hear me.

Poverty is getting up every morning from a dirt- and illness-stained mattress. The sheets have long since been used for diapers. Poverty is living with a smell that never leaves. This is a smell of urine, sour milk, and spoiling food sometimes joined with the strong smell of long-cooked onions. Onions are cheap. If you have smelled this smell, you did not know how it came. It is the smell of the outdoor privy. It is the smell of young children who cannot walk the long dark way in the night. It is the smell of the mattresses where years of "accidents" have happened. It is the smell of the milk which has gone sour because the refrigerator long has not worked, and it costs money to get it fixed. It is the smell of rotting garbage. I could bury it, but where is the shovel? Shovels cost money.

Poverty is being tired. I have always been tired. They told me at the hospital when the last baby came that I had chronic anemia caused from poor diet, a bad case of worms, and that I needed a corrective operation. I listened politely—the poor are always polite. The poor always listen. They don't say that there is no money for iron pills, or better food, or worm medicine. The idea of an operation is frightening and costs so much that, if I had dared, I would have laughed. Who takes care of my children? Recovery from an operation takes a long time. I have three children. When I left them with "Granny" the last time I had a job, I came home to find the baby covered with fly specks, and a diaper that had not been changed since I left. When the dried diaper came off, bits of my baby's flesh came with it. My other child was playing with a sharp bit of broken glass, and my oldest was playing alone at the edge of a lake. I made twenty-two dollars a week, and a good nursery school costs twenty dollars a week for three children. I quit my job.

Poverty is dirt. You say in your clean clothes coming from your clean house, "Anybody can be clean." Let me explain about housekeeping with no money. For breakfast I give my children grits with no oleo or cornbread without eggs and oleo. This does not use up many dishes. What dishes there are, I wash in cold water and with no soap. Even the cheapest soap has to be saved for the baby's diapers. Look at my hands, so cracked and red. Once I saved for two months to buy a jar of Vaseline for my hands and the baby's diaper rash. When I had saved enough, I went to buy it and the price had gone up two cents. The baby and I suffered on. I have to decide every day if I can bear to put my cracked, sore hands into the cold water and strong soap. But you ask, why not hot water? Fuel costs money. If you have a wood fire it costs money. If you burn electricity, it costs money. Hot water is a luxury. I do not have luxuries. I know you will be surprised when I tell you how young I am. I look so much older. My back has been bent over the wash tubs for so long, I cannot remember when I ever did anything else. Every night I wash every stitch my school age child has on and just hope her clothes will be dry by morning.

Poverty is staying up all night on cold nights to watch the fire, knowing one   5 spark on the newspaper covering the walls means your sleeping children die in flames. In summer poverty is watching gnats and flies devour your baby's tears when he cries. The screens are torn and you pay so little rent you know they will never be fixed. Poverty means insects in your food, in your nose, in your eyes, and crawling over you when you sleep. Poverty is hoping it never rains because diapers won't dry when it rains and soon you are using newspapers. Poverty is seeing your children forever with runny noses. Paper handkerchiefs cost money and all your rags you need for other things. Even more costly are antihistamines. Poverty is cooking without food and cleaning without soap.

Poverty is asking for help. Have you ever had to ask for help, knowing your children will suffer unless you get it? Think about asking for a loan from a relative, if this is the only way you can imagine asking for help. I will tell you how it feels. You find out where the office is that you are supposed to visit. You circle that block four or five times. Thinking of your children, you go in. Everyone is very busy. Finally, someone comes out and you tell her that you need help. That never is the person you need to see. You go see another person, and after spilling the whole shame of your poverty all over the desk between you, you find that this isn't the right office after all—you must repeat the whole process, and it never is any easier at the next place.

You have asked for help, and after all it has a cost. You are again told to wait. You are told why, but you don't really hear because of the red cloud of shame and the rising black cloud of despair.

Poverty is remembering. It is remembering quitting school in junior high because "nice" children had been so cruel about my clothes and my smell. The attendance officer came. My mother told him I was pregnant. I wasn't but she thought that I could get a job and help out. I had jobs off and on, but never long enough to learn anything. Mostly I remember being married. I was so young then. I am still young. For a time, we had all the things you have. There was a little house in another town, with hot water and everything. Then my husband lost his job. There was unemployment insurance for a while and what few jobs I could get.

Soon, all our nice things were repossessed and we moved back here. I was pregnant then. This house didn't look so bad when we first moved in. Every week it gets worse. Nothing is ever fixed. We now had no money. There were a few odd jobs for my husband, but everything went for food then, as it does now. I don't know how we lived through three years and three babies, but we did. I'll tell you something, after the last baby I destroyed my marriage. It had been a good one, but could you keep on bringing children in this dirt? Did you ever think how much it costs for any kind of birth control? I knew my husband was leaving the day he left, but there were no good-byes between us. I hope he has been able to climb out of this mess somewhere. He never could hope with us to drag him down.

That's when I asked for help. When I got it, you know how much it was? It was, and is, seventy-eight dollars a month for the four of us; that is all I ever can get. Now you know why there is no soap, no needles and thread, no hot water, no aspirin, no worm medicine, no hand cream, no shampoo. None of these things forever and ever and ever. So that you can see clearly, I pay twenty dollars a month rent, and most of the rest goes for food. For grits and cornmeal, and rice and milk and beans. I try my best to use only the minimum electricity. If I use more, there is that much less for food.

Poverty is looking into a black future. Your children won't play with my 10 boys. They will turn to other boys who steal to get what they want. I can already see them behind the bars of their prison instead of behind the bars of my poverty. Or they will turn to the freedom of alcohol or drugs, and find themselves enslaved. And my daughter? At best, there is for her a life like mine.

But you say to me, there are schools. Yes, there are schools. My children have no extra books, no magazines, no extra pencils, or crayons, or paper and the most important of all, they do not have health. They have worms, they have infections, they have pinkeye all summer. They do not sleep well on the floor, or with me in my one bed. They do not suffer from hunger, my seventy-eight dollars keeps us alive, but they do suffer from malnutrition. Oh yes, I do remember what I was taught about health in school. It doesn't do much good. In some places there is a surplus commodities program. Not here. The county said it cost too much. There is a school lunch program. But I have two children who will already be damaged by the time they get to school.

But, you say to me, there are health clinics. Yes, there are health clinics and they are in the towns. I live out here eight miles from town. I can walk that far (even if it is sixteen miles both ways), but can my little children? My neighbor will take me when he goes; but he expects to get paid, *one way or another*. I bet you know my neighbor. He is that large man who spends his time at the gas station, the barbershop, and the corner store complaining about the government spending money on the immoral mothers of illegitimate children.

Poverty is an acid that drips on pride until all pride is worn away. Poverty is a chisel that chips on honor until honor is worn away. Some of you say that you would do *something* in my situation, and maybe you would, for the first week or the first month, but for year after year after year?

Even the poor can dream. A dream of a time when there is money. Money for the right kinds of food, for worm medicine, for iron pills, for toothbrushes, for hand cream, for a hammer and nails and a bit of screening, for a shovel, for a bit of paint, for some sheeting, for needles and thread. Money to pay *in money* for a trip to town. And, oh, money for hot water and money for soap. A dream of when asking for help does not eat away the last bit of pride. When the office you visit is as nice as the offices of other governmental agencies, when there are enough workers to help you quickly, when workers do not quit in defeat and despair. When you have to tell your story to only one person, and that person can send you for other help and you don't have to prove your poverty over and over and over again.

I have come out of my despair to tell you this. Remember I did not come 15 from another place or another time. Others like me are all around you. Look at us with an angry heart, anger that will help you help me. Anger that will let you tell of me. The poor are always silent. Can you be silent too?

Reflecting and Interpreting

1. The author opens with a rhetorical question, which she answers in the rest of the essay. Note that eight paragraphs begin with "Poverty is." Do you find this much repetition effective? Why or why not?

2. Parker dismisses the stereotype that "anybody can be clean." What assumptions does this stereotype carry?

3. Does Parker have any hope of circumstances ever improving for her or her children? Why or why not?

4. Can you think of any source from which Parker might have secured help? Might she have contacted some local churches? Individuals?

5. Consider these (and other) statements: "I cannot use your pity" and "Every night I wash every stitch my school age child has on and just hope her clothes will be dry by morning." What do these statements reveal about Goodwin?

A Writer's Response

1. In the nearly thirty years that have elapsed since this essay was written, many federal, state, and local programs have been implemented to help the poor and the homeless. With a group, make a list of available services.

2. Despite the many agencies and individuals who are willing to help the poor, do you think many do not seek available help? Why? What influences are present that were practically nonexistent several decades ago? (Discuss in a group.)

3. Have you or anyone in your family (or acquaintances) lived through hard times—for example, the Great Depression? You might interview someone about what poverty is. How did people "make do" long ago with no government assistance at all? Write an essay defining poverty according to the interviewee.

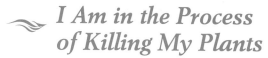

I Am in the Process of Killing My Plants

Linda Weltner

*Perhaps you have rebelled against a popular pastime that was considered not only so-
cially desirable but also "good for you." In this essay from her book* No Place Like Home,
*Linda Weltner lets us laugh at what could possibly be one of the greatest sources of Amer-
ican sheepishness—the inability to keep houseplants alive and well.*

I am in the process of killing my plants.

The philodendron in the living room is getting jaundiced and the English ivy
in the kitchen window is growing limp. I had to move the spider plant from my
study to a hallway so its death throes wouldn't interfere with my concentration. I
have been taking care of these plants for years, but I now wish to make it a matter of public record:

I am cutting off their plant food.

I'm through feeling guilty because I don't mist. I'm tired of feeling ashamed
of dry soil and dusty leaves. And I'm sick of being intimidated by deciduous thugs.
It's time my split-leaved friends figured out that even when it's liquid, there's no
such thing as a free lunch.

Good-natured soul that I am, I fell under their botanical influence during
the environmental seventies. The experts assured me that plants would bring
life and natural beauty into my house. Life! I envisioned growth and change
within my own four walls. Beauty! I imagined the glossy green of a well-turned
leaf and the pleasing arch of a stem. So I brought plants home by the armful,
turned the living room into a greenhouse, and hung plants for curtains in our
bedroom.

Then I discovered one small fact no one had brought to my attention. I had
to take care of them for the rest of my life.

Any old care wouldn't do, either, for each plant turned out to have its own
special needs. One had an aversion to standing in water; another thrived only in
filtered light. Some had cravings for vermiculite, demanded more humidity, or ex-

5

pressed a strong desire for privacy. I once put my Christmas cactus in a closet during its dormancy period and left it there so long I'm surprised it never slipped a ransom note under the door. I bought books on plant-rearing, endured the stink of seaweed fertilizer, and hired sitters to check on my foundlings when my husband and I went away on trips.

But what did I get in return?

Plants brought life to our house, all right, but it wasn't all growth and exciting change. Life amid the foliage is a lot of rotting and dying, drying out and withering. It is turning brown and molting, mealybugs, aphids, and fine particles of poison spray. Plant life, it turns out, is all too often the slime growing on the white pebbles under the pots.

Personally, I prefer living things that are *giving* things: cats who purr when   10
you feed them, dogs that lick your face in return for a treat. When I place myself in servitude to some nonhuman dependent, I want it to wag its tail when I come in the door, to chirp, at the very least to look me in the eye. I tried talking to my plants. I confided in them. I even varied the music they had to listen to, but they never stirred a leaf.

Plants, says expert Thalassa Cruso, have "rather special requirements." Unfortunately, so do I. Without any noticeable response, my nurturing behavior stops dead in its tracks.

Still, if my plants were objects of great beauty, I might not mind their personal shortcomings, but at the moment ugliness is the stem of a four-foot-long rubber plant with two yellow leaves at the end. It's the black circles on the hardwood floor in the living room, and the milky-white ring on the floor in the hall where an avocado plant once leaked. Ugliness is the collection of plant droppings scattered like dandruff around the base of every pot in my house.

Let's face it. Plants have disgusting habits no one wants to talk about. Philodendrons send out repulsive air roots that have to be clipped like toenails; spider plants have never heard of birth control. No matter how old they get, plants wet the floor and whine for bigger pots. Even after years of devoted care, they won't give you leeway for a neglectful week or two. That is why I intend to post this notice where all my overindulged leaf-shedders can see it: The right-to-life movement stops here.

I admit it was unnerving to see the ivy vines desperately clinging to the window at my approach. I had to harden my heart before I could uncurl the tendrils from the macramé ropes, but I managed to dump two plants on the compost heap before I noticed the brand-new shoot on the rubber tree and the great, ruffled philodendron leaf unfurling over there by the couch. At the moment, a tiny white flower on the asparagus fern is begging me to reconsider.

That's why my resolve is crumbling. I may relent, but only if these potted   15
freeloaders agree to meet me halfway. I'm writing this to give them fair warning:

They'd better turn over a new leaf if they want to make this Second Chance City.

Reflecting and Interpreting

1. In the first paragraph, comment on the effect of "death throes," and "make it a matter of public record: I am cutting off their plant food." How would you describe the tone?

2. Why did the author decide to raise plants in the first place? What was it that no one brought to her attention? What did she discover about the needs of plants?

3. What literary device do the following passages illustrate: "I'm surprised it never slipped a ransom note under the door," "hired sitters," and "foundlings"? (Hint: See page 491.)

4. What devices contribute humor in paragraph 12? (Hint: Note the comparisons and verbs.)

5. How did the author's attitude and behavior change as the condition of her plants changed? At what point does she feel remorse and have second thoughts?

A Writer's Response

1. Can you think of some activity or hobby you have tried but have never been able to master—no matter how small and insignificant or how big and embarrassing this shortcoming may seem? Try to imitate Weltner's style as you recount your experience.

2. Perhaps you have been manipulated into assuming a role—for example, family photographer, even though you hate taking pictures, can't remember how to operate the cameras, and often take mediocre pictures that others laugh at. Now freewrite quickly, rebelling against this role and telling what you plan to do with the cameras—or the next batch of pictures. Feel free to exaggerate, personify, or use any other of the techniques that Weltner does.

By Any Other Name

Santha Rama Rau

> *Santha Rama Rau (1923–   ), travel writer, essayist, and novelist, has long shared her experience in India with Western audiences. Her best-known books are* Home to India *(1949),* Remember the House *(1955), and* Gifts of Passage *(1961). The following essay reveals her perception of British rule in India and the clash in cultures in her childhood.*

At the Anglo-Indian day school in Zorinabad to which my sister and I were sent when she was eight and I was five and a half, they changed our names. On the first day of school, a hot, windless morning of a north Indian September, we stood in the headmistress's study and she said, "Now you're the *new* girls. What are your names?"

My sister answered for us. "I am Premila, and she"—nodding in my direction—"is Santha."

The headmistress had been in India, I suppose, fifteen years or so, but she still smiled her helpless inability to cope with Indian names. Her rimless half-glasses glittered, and the precarious bun on top of her head trembled as she shook her head. "Oh, my dears, those are much too hard for me. Suppose we give you pretty English names. Wouldn't that be more jolly? Let's see, now—Pamela for you, I think." She shrugged in a baffled way at my sister. "That's as close as I can get. And for *you*," she said to me, "how about Cynthia? Isn't that nice?"

My sister was always less easily intimidated than I was, and while she kept a stubborn silence, I said, "Thank you," in a very tiny voice.

We had been sent to that school because my father, among his responsibilities as an officer of the civil service, had a tour of duty to perform in the villages around that steamy little provincial town, where he had his headquarters at that time. He used to make his shorter inspection tours on horseback, and a week before, in the stale heat of a typically postmonsoon day, we had waved good-by to him and a little procession—an assistant, a secretary, two bearers, and the man to look after the bedding rolls and luggage. They rode away through our large garden, still bright green from the rains, and we turned back into the twilight of the house and the sound of fans whispering in every room.

Up to then, my mother had refused to send Premila to school in the British-run establishments of that time, because, she used to say, "you can bury a dog's tail for seven years and it still comes out curly, and you can take a Britisher away from his home for a lifetime, and he still remains insular." The examinations and degrees from entirely Indian schools were not, in those days, considered valid. In my case, the question had never come up, and probably never would have come

5

up if Mother's extraordinary good health had not broken down. For the first time in my life, she was not able to continue the lessons she had been giving us every morning. So our Hindi books were put away, the stories of the Lord Krishna as a little boy were left in midair, and we were sent to the Anglo-Indian school.

That first day at school is still, when I think of it, a remarkable one. At that age, if one's name is changed, one develops a curious form of dual personality. I remember having a certain detached and disbelieving concern in the actions of "Cynthia," but certainly no responsibility. Accordingly, I followed the thin, erect back of the headmistress down the veranda to my classroom feeling, at most, a passing interest in what was going to happen to me in this strange, new atmosphere of School.

The building was Indian in design, with wide verandas opening onto a central courtyard, but Indian verandas are usually whitewashed, with stone floors. These, in the tradition of British schools, were painted dark brown and had matting on the floors. It gave a feeling of extra intensity to the heat.

I suppose there were about a dozen Indian children in the school—which contained perhaps forty children in all—and four of them were in my class. They were all sitting at the back of the room, and I went to join them. I sat next to a small, solemn girl who didn't smile at me. She had long, glossy-black braids and wore a cotton dress, but she still kept on her Indian jewelry—a gold chain around her neck, thin gold bracelets, and tiny ruby studs in her ears. Like most Indian children, she had a rim of black kohl around her eyes. The cotton dress should have looked strange, but all I could think of was that I should ask my mother if I couldn't wear a dress to school, too, instead of my Indian clothes.

I can't remember too much about the proceedings in class that day, except   10
for the beginning. The teacher pointed to me and asked me to stand up. "Now, dear tell the class your name."

I said nothing.

"Come along," she said frowning slightly. "What's your name, dear?"

"I don't know," I said, finally.

The English children in the front of the class—there were about eight or ten of them—giggled and twisted around in their chairs to look at me. I sat down quickly and opened my eyes very wide, hoping in that way to dry them off. The little girl with the braids put out her hand and very lightly touched my arm. She still didn't smile.

Most of that morning I was rather bored. I looked briefly at the children's   15
drawings pinned to the wall, and then concentrated on a lizard clinging to the ledge of the high, barred window behind the teacher's head. Occasionally it would shoot out its long yellow tongue for a fly, and then it would rest, with its eyes closed and its belly palpitating, as though it were swallowing several times quickly. The lessons were mostly concerned with reading and writing and simple numbers—things that my mother had already taught me—and I paid very little attention. The teacher wrote on the easel blackboard words like "bat" and "cat," which seemed babyish to me; only "apple" was new and incomprehensible.

When it was time for the lunch recess, I followed the girl with braids out onto the veranda. There the children from the other classes were assembled. I saw Premila at once and ran over to her, as she had charge of our lunchbox. The children were all opening packages and sitting down to eat sandwiches. Premila and I were the only ones who had Indian food—thin wheat chapatties, some vegetable curry, and a bottle of buttermilk. Premila thrust half of it into my hand and whispered fiercely that I should go and sit with my class, because that was what the others seemed to be doing.

The enormous black eyes of the little Indian girl from my class looked at my food longingly, so I offered her some. But she only shook her head and plowed her way solemnly through her sandwiches.

I was very sleepy after lunch, because at home we always took a siesta. It was usually a pleasant time of day, with the bedroom darkened against the harsh afternoon sun, the drifting off into sleep with the sound of Mother's voice reading a story in one's mind, and, finally, the shrill, fussy voice of the ayah waking one for tea.

At school, we rested for a short time on low, folding cots on the veranda, and then we were expected to play games. During the hot part of the afternoon we played indoors, and after the shadows had begun to lengthen and the slight breeze of the evening had come up we moved outside to the wide courtyard.

I had never really grasped the system of competitive games. At home, when- 20 ever we played tag or guessing games, I was always allowed to "win"—"because," Mother used to tell Premila, "she is the youngest, and we have to allow for that." I had often heard her say it, and it seemed quite reasonable to me, but the result was that I had no clear idea of what "winning" meant.

When we played twos-and-threes that afternoon at school, in accordance with my training, I let one of the small English boys catch me, but was naturally rather puzzled when the other children did not return the courtesy. I ran about for what seemed like hours without ever catching anyone, until it was time for school to close. Much later I learned that my attitude was called "not being a good sport," and I stopped allowing myself to be caught, but it was not for years that I really learned the spirit of the thing.

When I saw our car come up to the school gate, I broke away from my classmates and rushed toward it yelling, "Ayah! Ayah!" It seemed like an eternity since I had seen her that morning—a wizened, affectionate figure in her white cotton sari, giving me dozens of urgent and useless instructions on how to be a good girl at school. Premila followed more sedately, and she told me on the way home never to do that again in front of the other children.

When we got home we went straight to Mother's high, white room to have tea with her, and I immediately climbed onto the bed and bounced gently up and down on the springs. Mother asked how we had liked our first day in school. I was so pleased to be home and to have left that peculiar Cynthia behind that I had nothing whatever to say about school, except to ask what "apple" meant. But Premila told Mother about the classes, and added that in her class they had weekly tests to see if they learned their lessons well.

I asked, "What's a test?"

Premila said, "You're too small to have them. You won't have them in your class for donkey's years." She had learned the expression that day and was using it for the first time. We all laughed enormously at her wit. She also told Mother, in an aside, that we should take sandwiches to school the next day. Not, she said, that *she* minded. But they would be simpler for me to handle.

That whole lovely evening I didn't think about school at all. I sprinted barefoot across the lawns with my favorite playmate, the cook's son, to the stream at the end of the garden. We quarreled in our usual way, waded in the tepid water under the lime trees, and waited for the night to bring out the smell of the jasmine. I listened with fascination to his stories of ghosts and demons, until I was too frightened to cross the garden alone in the semidarkness. The ayah found me, shouted at the cook's son, scolded me, hurried me into supper—it was an entirely usual, wonderful evening.

It was a week later, the day of Premila's first test, that our lives changed rather abruptly. I was sitting at the back of my class, in my usual inattentive way, only half listening to the teacher. I had started a rather guarded friendship with the girl with the braids, whose name turned out to be Nalini (Nancy, in school). The three other Indian children were already fast friends. Even at that age it was apparent to all of us that friendship with the English or Anglo-Indian children was out of the question. Occasionally, during the class, my new friend and I would draw pictures and show them to each other secretly.

The door opened sharply and Premila marched in. At first, the teacher smiled at her in a kindly and encouraging way and said, "Now, you're little Cynthia's sister?"

Premila didn't even look at her. She stood with her feet planted firmly apart and her shoulders rigid, and addressed herself directly to me. "Get up," she said. "We're going home."

I didn't know what had happened, but I was aware that it was a crisis of some sort. I rose obediently and started to walk toward my sister.

"Bring your pencils and your notebook," she said.

I went back for them, and together we left the room. The teacher started to say something just as Premila closed the door, but we didn't wait to hear what it was.

In complete silence we left the school grounds and started to walk home. Then I asked Premila what the matter was. All she would say was "We're going home for good."

It was a very tiring walk for a child of five and a half, and I dragged along behind Premila with my pencils growing sticky in my hand. I can still remember looking at the dusty hedges, and the tangles of thorns in the ditches by the side of the road, smelling the faint fragrance from the eucalyptus trees and wondering whether we would ever reach home. Occasionally a horse-drawn tonga passed us, and the women, in their pink or green silks, stared at Premila and me trudging along on the side of the road. A few coolies and a line of women carrying baskets of vegetables on their heads smiled at us. But it was nearing the hottest time of day, and the road was almost deserted. I walked more and more slowly, and shouted to Premila, from time to time, "Wait for me!" with increasing peevishness. She spoke to me only once, and that was to tell me to carry my notebook on my head, because of the sun.

When we got to our house the ayah was just taking a tray of lunch into Mother's room. She immediately started a long, worried questioning about what are you children doing back here at this hour of the day.

Mother looked very startled and very concerned, and asked Premila what had happened.

Premila said, "We had our test today, and she made me and the other Indians sit at the back of the room, with a desk between each one."

Mother said, "Why was that, darling?"

"She said it was because Indians cheat," Premila added. "So I don't think we should go back to that school."

Mother looked very distant, and was silent a long time. At last she said, "Of course not, darling." She sounded displeased.

We all shared the curry she was having for lunch, and afterward I was sent off to the beautifully familiar bedroom for my siesta. I could hear Mother and Premila talking through the open door.

Mother said, "Do you suppose she understood all that?"

Premila said, "I shouldn't think so. She's a baby."

Mother said, "Well, I hope it won't bother her."

Of course, they were both wrong. I understood it perfectly, and I remember it all very clearly. But I put it happily away, because it had all happened to a girl called Cynthia, and I never was really particularly interested in her.

Reflecting and Interpreting

1. Who is the narrator? How does this affect the story? How is dialogue used?

2. Why had the sisters changed from home schooling to the Anglo-Indian school?

3. Why was the first day at school remarkable to Santha? How did it affect her?

4. Identify four more incidents on the first day that made Santha feel out of place at school. What does her sister request their mother do to eliminate one cause?

5. Which sister seems to feel more keenly the pressure at school to conform? Why?

6. What kind of life and status were the girls accustomed to at home? How did that change at school? Cite examples of concrete imagery.

7. Comment on eight-year-old Premila's take-charge attitude on the day of the test. Does this seem unusual in light of her age and prior behavior? Why or why not?

8. Contrast Premila's and Santha's reactions to the test-day incident. Why did they react so differently?

9. How would you state the theme of this story? Compare your statement with that of some of your peers.

A Writer's Response

1. Have you ever been called by different names? Derogatory names? In a group discuss the effect of a name upon one's self-esteem and sense of identity.

2. **For a group:** What period in United States history is reminiscent of this period of British rule in India? Which regime was harsher? Why do you think so?

3. Have you ever felt left out or strange in a new school or neighborhood? Write a narrative, using dialogue, to convey your sense of alienation. (See chapter 10.)

The Emotional Quadrant

Elisabeth Kübler-Ross

"Big boys don't cry!" We've all heard it, and perhaps some of us have said it without an inkling of the possible effects on a child who has a vital need to cry. The following essay by Elisabeth Kübler-Ross, one of the world's foremost authorities on death and dying, traces the effect of a parent's death on a young child. Kübler-Ross, born in Zurich, Switzerland in 1926, received her M.D. from Zurich University in 1957. Four years later she became a naturalized American citizen. A physician, educator, and writer, she published her watershed work, On Death and Dying, *in 1969. Since then she has written several other books and conducted five-day workshops on "Life, Death, and Transition."*

Very young children have no fear of death, although they have the two innate fears of sudden loud noises and of falling from high places. Later on children are naturally afraid of separation, since the fear of abandonment and the absence of a loving caretaker is very basic and meaningful. Children are aware of their dependency, and those who have been exposed to early traumas in life are scarred. They will need to relive the trauma and learn to let go of the panic, pain, anxiety and rage of the abandonment.

These violent feelings arise often, not solely when a member of the family dies. Abandonments of all sorts happen thousands of times over in our society, and if the loss is not associated with the death of a loved one, few people will recognize this. The emergency support systems or shoulders to lean on will not be called into action, and there will be no sympathy visits by neighbors. So the child who feels abandoned in some manner is left vulnerable; his future mind-set could include a general mistrust, a fear of ever allowing a close relationship, an alienation from the person who is blamed for the separation, and a deep grief over the absence of love.

Rene was such a child, and he needed thirty years to heal. He was only five years old when his father told him to get into the car, because they were going somewhere together. Rene was very excited. His father had been drinking for many years; his mom had been in and out of mental hospitals, and there had been very little laughter and happiness in his life. And now his dad was going to take him somewhere. He did not dare to ask him where they were going. To the zoo? To the park? To a football game? He could not understand why Dad had come home in the middle of the week, but he knew that his mom was very sick again, because she had slept all day and never came down even to fix him a sandwich.

In the car, Rene and his father approached a huge building and parked. His father silently opened the car door and let Rene out. The father was very quiet; he did not even smile once. Rene wondered if his father was mad at him. He remembered he had fixed his own breakfast. He had even put the dishes in the sink. He was never noisy when his mom and dad had their fights, and he stayed in the den and out of the way. He had not heard them fighting today, and therefore Rene had hoped it would be a good day.

His dad took him by the hand and led him into a strange room with a funny   5
smell. A Catholic sister came and talked to his father, but no one talked to him. Then his father left the room, and a short time later the sister left also. Rene sat very quietly and waited, but no one came. Maybe his dad had to go to the bathroom. Finally he got up, and out the window he saw his dad walking out of the house toward the car. He ran as fast as he could: "Dad, Dad, don't leave me!" But the car door shut, and he saw the old familiar car turn the corner—out of sight.

Rene never saw his mother again. She returned to the mental hospital, where two years later she killed herself. He didn't see his father again for many years. It was much later that a strange woman came to visit him one day; she told him that his dad had married her and that they had planned to take him out of the home of the sisters to see if it could "work out."

Rene tried to please his dad in every way he could. He painted the new house and worked every free moment he had to get a nod of approval from him. But his dad remained as silent as he had always been. This silence always brought back to Rene the memory of that nightmarish day when he had been taken away from home without so much as an explanation, much less a good-bye or last hug from his mom.

His father never said "thank you" or "I am pleased with you," just as he never brought up the reasons for Rene's placement in the home and the lack of warning. So Rene grew up trying to please, not knowing that the fear of rejection and abandonment was still with him in adulthood. But Rene was afraid of alcoholism, afraid of mental illness, afraid of getting close to anyone. His whole life consisted of work and more work to please his father. He never allowed himself to get angry, to speak up, to express displeasure. The only time his face lit up was at the sight of a parent playing with a child in the park or swinging on a swing in a schoolyard. He spent his free time in those places, vicariously enjoying the laughter of these children, unaware of why he could not experience love and laughter in his own life.

As a mature adult he took an opportunity to look at his pain, anguish, despair, and incomprehension of this totally unexpected abandonment in early childhood, and he emerged a free man. It took him only one week, touched by others who shared their agonies in a safe place where it was regarded as a blessing to get rid of old tears and anger. During that week, Rene felt loved unconditionally. This man has just resolved his conflicts and has begun to understand his inability to trust and relate.

If someone—preferably his parents—had talked with this little boy and   10
made an effort to understand his play, his drawings, his sullen withdrawal and isolation, much pain and unresolved conflict, carried within for decades, could

have easily been avoided. You think those things happened in the last century? No, they still happen every day in our society.

Many, many adults suffer from never having resolved the hurts of their childhood. So children need to be allowed to grieve without being labeled crybaby or sissy, or hearing the ridiculous statement "Big boys don't cry." If children of both sexes are not allowed to express their natural emotions in childhood, they will have problems later on in the form of self-pity and many psychosomatic symptoms. Grief and fear, when allowed to be expressed and shared in childhood, can prevent much future heartache.

Reflecting and Interpreting

1. In the anecdote about five-year-old Rene, from whose point of view is the story told? What is the effect?

2. What is the thesis statement? Where is it stated?

3. Describe Rene's early home life and his relationship with his father. Did the relationship improve when his father remarried? What effect did all this have upon Rene? How effective is this extended example in supporting the thesis?

4. Although the essay devotes only one paragraph to the startling change in Rene, what can we surmise?

5. What danger does Kübler-Ross point to in the conclusion of her essay?

A Writer's Response

1. Years ago in certain cultures in the United States, it was not the custom to give praise lest a child develop a "swelled head." Does this practice still exist? With a group, share experiences and describe the effects as well as any turnarounds.

2. Has something ever happened to you that you felt you could not tell anyone? What was the effect on your peace of mind and behavior? What finally happened? Write an essay describing the event and your reaction to it.

3. Perhaps you have survived a traumatic event with the support of kind friends and family. Write an essay describing the experience and its effect on you.

The Teacher Who Changed My Life

Nicholas Gage

When nine-year-old Nicholas Gage arrived in the United States to live with his fa-
ther, whom he did not remember, he did not expect to be placed in a class for the mentally
retarded. Non-English-speaking, he and his sister somehow learned English. Four years
later Gage met a teacher who changed his life. Now Gage is a well-respected journalist,
the author of Eleni, *a best-selling book that was later produced as a film. The following ex-*
cerpt is from his second book, A Place for Us.

The person who set the course of my life in the new land I entered as a young war refugee—who, in fact, nearly dragged me onto the path that would bring all the blessings I've received in America—was a salty-tongued, no-nonsense school-teacher named Marjorie Hurd. When I entered her classroom in 1953, I had been to six schools in five years, starting in the Greek village where I was born in 1939.

When I stepped off a ship in New York Harbor on a gray March day in 1949, I was an undersized 9-year-old in short pants who had lost his mother and was coming to live with the father he didn't know. My mother, Eleni Gatzoyiannis, had been imprisoned, tortured and shot by Communist guerrillas for sending me and three of my four sisters to freedom. She died so that her children could go to their father in the United States.

The portly, bald, well-dressed man who met me and my sisters seemed a foreign, authoritarian figure. I secretly resented him for not getting the whole family out of Greece early enough to save my mother. Ultimately, I would grow to love him and appreciate how he dealt with becoming a single parent at the age of 56, but at first our relationship was prickly, full of hostility.

As Father drove us to our new home—a tenement in Worcester, Mass.—and pointed out the huge brick building that would be our first school in America, I clutched my Greek notebooks from the refugee camp, hoping that my few years of schooling would impress my teachers in this cold, crowded country. They didn't. When my father led me and my 11-year-old sister to Greendale Elementary School, the grim-faced Yankee principal put the two of us in a class for the mentally retarded. There was no facility in those days for non-English-speaking children.

By the time I met Marjorie Hurd four years later, I had learned English, been   5 placed in a normal, graded class and had even been chosen for the college preparatory track in the Worcester public school system. I was 13 years old when our father moved us yet again, and I entered Chandler Junior High shortly after the beginning of seventh grade. I found myself surrounded by richer, smarter and better-dressed classmates who looked askance at my strange clothes and heavy accent. Shortly after I arrived, we were told to select a hobby to pursue during "club hour" on Fridays. The idea of hobbies and clubs made no sense to my immigrant ears, but I decided to follow the prettiest girl in my class—the blue-eyed daughter of the local Lutheran minister. She led me through the door marked "Newspaper Club" and into the presence of Miss Hurd, the newspaper adviser and English teacher who would become my mentor and my muse.

A formidable, solidly built woman with salt-and-pepper hair, a steely eye and a flat Boston accent, Miss Hurd had no patience with layabouts. "What are all you goof-offs doing here?" she bellowed at the would-be journalists. "This is the Newspaper Club! We're going to put out a *newspaper*. So if there's anybody in this room who doesn't like work, I suggest you go across to the Glee Club now, because you're going to work your tails off here!"

I was soon under Miss Hurd's spell. She did indeed teach us to put out a newspaper, skills I honed during my next 25 years as a journalist. Soon I asked the principal to transfer me to her English class as well. There, she drilled us on grammar until I finally began to understand the logic and structure of the English language. She assigned stories for us to read and discuss; not tales of heroes, like the Greek myths I knew, but stories of underdogs—poor people, even immigrants, who seemed ordinary until a crisis drove them to do something extraordinary. She also introduced us to the literary wealth of Greece—giving me a new perspective on my war-ravaged, impoverished homeland. I began to be proud of my origins.

One day, after discussing how writers should write about what they know, she assigned us to compose an essay from our own experience. Fixing me with a stern look, she added, "Nick, I want you to write about what happened to your family in Greece." I had been trying to put those painful memories behind me and left the assignment until the last moment. Then, on a warm spring afternoon, I sat in my room with a yellow pad and pencil and stared out the window at the buds on the trees. I wrote that the coming of spring always reminded me of the last time I said goodbye to my mother on a green and gold day in 1948.

I kept writing, one line after another, telling how the Communist guerrillas occupied our village, took our home and food, how my mother started planning our escape when she learned that the children were to be sent to re-education camps behind the Iron Curtain and how, at the last moment, she couldn't escape with us because the guerrillas sent her with a group of women to thresh wheat in a distant village. She promised she would try to get away on her own, she told me to be brave and hung a silver cross around my neck, and then she kissed me. I watched the line of women being led down into the ravine and up the other side, until they disappeared around the bend—my mother a tiny brown figure at the end who stopped for an instant to raise her hand in one last farewell.

I wrote about our nighttime escape down the mountain, across the mine- 10
fields and into the lines of the Nationalist soldiers, who sent us to a refugee camp. It was there that we learned of our mother's execution. I felt very lucky to have

come to America, I concluded, but every year, the coming of spring made me feel sad because it reminded me of the last time I saw my mother.

I handed in the essay, hoping never to see it again, but Miss Hurd had it published in the school paper. This mortified me at first, until I saw that my classmates reacted with sympathy and tact to my family's story. Without telling me, Miss Hurd also submitted the essay to a contest sponsored by the Freedoms Foundation at Valley Forge, Pa., and it won a medal. The Worcester paper wrote about the award and quoted my essay at length. My father, by then a "five-and-dime-store chef," as the paper described him, was ecstatic with pride, and the Worcester Greek community celebrated the honor to one of its own.

For the first time I began to understand the power of the written word. A secret ambition took root in me. One day, I vowed, I would go back to Greece, find out the details of my mother's death and write about her life, so her grandchildren would know of her courage. Perhaps I would even track down the men who killed her and write of their crimes. Fulfilling that ambition would take me 30 years.

Meanwhile, I followed the literary path that Miss Hurd had so forcefully set me on. After junior high, I became the editor of my school paper at Classical High School and got a part-time job at the Worcester *Telegram and Gazette*. Although my father could only give me $50 and encouragement toward a college education, I managed to finance four years at Boston University with scholarships and part-time jobs in journalism. During my last year of college, an article I wrote about a friend who had died in the Philippines—the first person to lose his life working for the Peace Corps—led to my winning the Hearst Award for College Journalism. And the plaque was given to me in the White House by President John F. Kennedy.

For a refugee who had never seen a motorized vehicle or indoor plumbing until he was 9, this was an unimaginable honor. When the Worcester paper ran a picture of me standing next to President Kennedy, my father rushed out to buy a new suit in order to be properly dressed to receive the congratulations of the Worcester Greeks. He clipped out the photograph, had it laminated in plastic and carried it in his breast pocket for the rest of his life to show everyone he met. I found the much-worn photo in his pocket on the day he died 20 years later.

In our isolated Greek village, my mother had bribed a cousin to teach her to   15
read, for girls were not supposed to attend school beyond a certain age. She had always dreamed of her children receiving an education. She couldn't be there when I graduated from Boston University, but the person who came with my father and shared our joy was my former teacher, Marjorie Hurd. We celebrated not only my bachelor's degree but also the scholarships that paid my way to Columbia's Graduate School of Journalism. There, I met the woman who would eventually become my wife. At our wedding and at the baptisms of our three children, Marjorie Hurd was always there, dancing alongside the Greeks.

By then, she was Mrs. Rabidou, for she had married a widower when she was in her early 40s. That didn't distract her from her vocation of introducing young minds to English literature, however. She taught for a total of 41 years and continually would make a "project" of some balky student in whom she spied a spark of potential. Often these were students from the most troubled homes, yet she would alternately bully and charm each one with her own special brand of tough love until the spark caught fire. She retired in 1981 at the age of 62 but still avidly follows the lives and careers of former students while overseeing her adult stepchildren and driving her husband on camping trips to New Hampshire.

Miss Hurd was one of the first to call me on Dec. 10, 1987, when President Reagan, in his television address after the summit meeting with Gorbachev, told the nation that Eleni Gatzoyiannis' dying cry, "My children!" had helped inspire him to seek an arms agreement "for all the children of the world."

"I can't imagine a better monument for your mother," Miss Hurd said with an uncharacteristic catch in her voice.

Although a bad hip makes it impossible for her to join in the Greek dancing, Marjorie Hurd Rabidou is still an honored and enthusiastic guest at all family celebrations, including my 50th birthday picnic last summer, where the shish ke-bab was cooked on spits, clarinets and *bouzoukis* wailed, and costumed dancers led the guests in a serpentine line around our Colonial farmhouse, only 20 minutes from my first home in Worcester.

My sisters and I felt an aching void because my father was not there to lead   20
the line, balancing a glass of wine on his head while he danced, the way he did at every celebration during his 92 years. But Miss Hurd was there, surveying the scene with quiet satisfaction. Although my parents are gone, her presence was a consolation, because I owe her so much.

This is truly the land of opportunity, and I would have enjoyed its bounty even if I hadn't walked into Miss Hurd's classroom in 1953. But she was the one who directed my grief and pain into writing, and if it weren't for her I wouldn't have become an investigative reporter and foreign correspondent, recorded the story of my mother's life and death in *Eleni* and now my father's story in *A Place for Us*, which is also a testament to the country that took us in. She was the cata-lyst that sent me into journalism and indirectly caused all the good things that came after. But Miss Hurd would probably deny this emphatically.

A few years ago, I answered the telephone and heard my former teacher's voice telling me, in that won't-take-no-for-an-answer tone of hers, that she had decided I was to write and deliver the eulogy at her funeral. I agreed (she didn't leave me any choice), but that's one assignment I never want to do. I hope, Miss Hurd, that you'll accept this remembrance instead.

Reflecting and Interpreting

1. Although this essay is primarily about a teacher that Gage had the year he was thirteen, he talks about virtually his entire life. Why?

2. What order does Gage use to present the events of so many years? At times he uses what device to weave in past events? How does he accomplish these shifts so that readers can easily follow?

3. What skills did Gage develop as a result of Miss Hurd's instruction? Why did the readings she assign seem particularly relevant to him? How did one of her assignments change his life?

4. Trace Miss Hurd's influence on Gage after he left her junior high class.

5. When Gage uses "salty-tongued, no-nonsense" to describe Miss Hurd, what do you think he means? What other glimpses of her personality do you gain from her interaction not only with Gage but also with other students?

6. Gage weaves in description that gives the reader a portrait of his father and the influence he had on Gage's life. How would you describe the father?

7. In this narrative, Gage reveals much about himself. He has much to be proud of. How would you describe his attitude and the tone of the essay?

A Writer's Response

1. Have you ever changed schools and felt uncomfortable among students who seemed quite different? Describe the experience and how you adjusted. Was any particular person helpful in making you feel comfortable?

2. Consider the people who have influenced your life. Write an essay identifying the incidents that were particularly significant to you. Explain why.

Down with the Forests

Charles Kuralt

During his sojourn with the television series Dateline America (CBS), *Charles Kuralt traveled around the United States in a mobile home, writing unique, offbeat human interest stories. Some of these were character sketches of unusual or vanishing ways of life. In this essay he not only talks about the problem of our vanishing forests but also points out some incongruities.*

Baltimore, Maryland. I was waiting for breakfast in a coffee shop the other morning and reading the paper. The paper had sixty-six pages. The waitress brought a paper place mat and a paper napkin and took my order, and I paged through the pager.

The headline said, "House Panel Studies a Bill Allowing Clear-Cutting in U.S. Forests."

I put the paper napkin in my lap, spread the paper out on the paper place mat, and read on: "The House Agriculture Committee," it said, "is looking over legislation that would once again open national forests to the clear-cutting of trees by private companies under government permits."

The waitress brought the coffee. I opened a paper sugar envelope and tore open a little paper cup of cream and went on reading the paper: "The Senate voted without dissent yesterday to allow clear-cutting," the paper said. "Critics have said clear-cutting in the national forests can lead to erosion and destruction of wildlife habitats. Forest Service and industry spokesmen said a flat ban on clear-cutting would bring paralysis to the lumber industry." And to the paper industry, I thought. Clear-cutting a forest is one way to get a lot of paper, and we sure seem to need a lot of paper.

The waitress brought the toast. I looked for the butter. It came on a little paper tray with a covering of paper. I opened a paper package of marmalade and read on: "Senator Jennings Randolph, Democrat of West Virginia, urged his colleagues to take a more restrictive view and permit clear-cutting only under specific guidelines for certain types of forest. But neither he nor anyone else voted against the bill, which was sent to the House on a 90 to 0 vote." 5

The eggs came, with little paper packages of salt and pepper. I finished breakfast, put the paper under my arm, and left the table with its used and useless paper napkin, paper place mat, paper salt and pepper packages, paper butter and marmalade wrappings, paper sugar envelope, and paper cream holder, and I walked out into the morning wondering how our national forests can ever survive our breakfasts.

Reflecting and Interpreting

1. Kuralt's anecdote is deceptively simple. In the first paragraph, he describes an ordinary scene, but he sets up an expectation. What is it? How does he do it?

2. The second paragraph is only one sentence. He could have put that sentence at the end of the first paragraph. What does placing the sentence apart do?

3. Note how Kuralt alternates the details of an ordinary breakfast with unordinary details of legislation. What is the effect? (Consider that he might have told about the breakfast, then about clear-cutting in a block arrangement.)

4. Usually, heavy repetition is discouraged in writing. But what is the effect of his repetition throughout this piece?

5. Although Senator Randolph urged a compromise bill to "permit clear-cutting only under specific guidelines for certain types of forest," the Senate voted to approve the original bill 90 to 0. Does this seem strange? Why or why not?

6. What is the basic irony that underlies this argument? (Note the title.)

7. Is the argument implicit or does Kuralt declare his position?

A Writer's Response

1. With your group, outline the form of Kuralt's argument. List pros and cons of clear-cutting that you can glean from the newspaper article. How do details of the breakfast contribute?

2. Write an essay using glimpses of an everyday activity to argue an issue. Some suggested topics: the lack of highway courtesy, the sad shape of United States highways or bridges, building stadiums while school buildings deteriorate, waste in a land of plenty, or some other issue that interests you.

Is Saving Legal?

Robert L. Rose

For folks who have grown up hearing "A penny saved is a penny earned"—and even those who haven't—the irony of the following essay will be striking. Rose, staff writer for The Wall Street Journal, *describes a young mother on welfare whose frugality caused her to be charged with fraud. The paper published the news story on February 6, 1990.*

A penny saved is a penny earned. Usually.

Take the case of Grace Capetillo, a 36-year-old single mother with a true talent for parsimony. To save on clothing, Ms. Capetillo dresses herself plainly in thrift-store finds. To cut her grocery bill, she stocks up on 67-cent boxes of saltines and 39-cent cans of chicken soup.

When Ms. Capetillo's five-year-old daughter, Michelle, asked for "Li'l Miss Makeup" for Christmas, her mother bypassed Toys "R" Us, where the doll retails for $19.99. Instead, she found one at Goodwill—for $1.89. She cleaned it up and tied a pink ribbon in its hair before giving the doll to Michelle. Ms. Capetillo found the popular Mr. Potato Head at Goodwill, too, assembling the plastic toy one piece at a time from the used toy bin. It cost her 79 cents, and saved $3.18.

Whose Money?

Ms. Capetillo's stingy strategies helped her build a savings account of more than $3,000 in the last four years. Her goal was to put away enough to buy a new washing machine and maybe one day help send Michelle to college. To some, this might make her an example of virtue in her gritty North Side neighborhood, known more for boarded-up houses than high aspirations. But there was just one catch: Ms. Capetillo is on welfare—$440 a month, plus $60 in food stamps—and saving that much money on public aid is against the law. When welfare officials found out about it, they were quick to act. Ms. Capetillo, they charged, was saving at the expense of taxpayers.

Last month, the Milwaukee County Department of Social Services took her   5
to court, charged her with fraud and demanded she return the savings—and thousands more for a total of $15,545. Ms. Capetillo says she didn't know it, but under the federal program Aid to Families with Dependent Children, she was ineligible for assistance after the day in 1985 when her savings eclipsed $1,000.

Under Sam wanted the money back.

"Tax dollars are going to support a person's basic needs on the AFDC program," says Robert Davis, associate director of the Milwaukee social services department. Federal rules, and the spirit of the program, don't intend for "people to take the money and put it in a savings account."

Welfare's Role

Ms. Capetillo's troubles began in 1988, when the social services department discovered the savings account she had opened in 1984. The tipoff: The department had matched its records with those supplied by her bank to the Internal Revenue Service.

Next, the sheriff department's welfare fraud squad went into action. Investigators contacted the M&I Bank two blocks from Ms. Capetillo's apartment and found she had "maintained $1,000 consistently" in her savings account from Aug. 1, 1985 through May 31, 1988.

In an interview that May with investigators, Ms. Capetillo admitted she hadn't   10
reported the savings account to the department. After doing a little arithmetic, welfare officials figured she should repay $15,545—the amount of monthly aid she received after her bank balance passed $1,000. (The assistant district attorney later considered that harsh; he lowered the figure to $3,000.)

But the judge who got her case found it hard to believe Ms. Capetillo was motivated by fraud. Indeed, for Ms. Capetillo, thriftiness had been a way of life. Her father instilled the lessons of economizing, supporting his nine children on his modest income from a local tannery.

After Michelle was born, Ms. Capetillo began drawing aid—and saving in earnest. She says she rents the second floor of her father's duplex for $300 a month (though the welfare department says it suspects she was able to save so much by skipping at least some rent payments). In the summer, she looks for second-hand winter clothes and in the winter shops for warm-weather outfits to snare out-of-season bargains. When Michelle's T-shirts grew tight, her mother snipped them below the underarm so they'd last longer.

"She cared for her daughter well, but simply," says Donna Paul, the court-appointed attorney who defended Ms. Capetillo. "With inflation, all Grace could expect was for government aid to become more inadequate."

Now that Michelle is getting ready to enter the first grade, Ms. Capetillo says she will no longer have to stay home to care for the child. She says she plans to look for full-time work or go back to school to train to be a nurse's aide.

But her round face, framed by shoulder-length black hair, still brightens at   15
the prospect of bargain-hunting. At her favorite supermarket, her eyes dart from item to item. She spots the display of generic saltine crackers. "See that? That's cheap," she pronounces, dropping a box in her grocery cart.

The total bill comes to $5.98, but Ms. Capetillo forgot the coupon that entitles her to free bacon for spending more than $5. She pockets the receipt, and vows to return for the bacon.

After the law caught up with her, Ms. Capetillo reduced her savings to avoid having her welfare checks cut off. She bought her new washing machine, a used stove to replace her hotplate, a $40 refrigerator and a new bedroom set for Michelle. But that didn't resolve the charge of fraud.

Finally, her day in court arrived. At first, Circuit Court Judge Charles B. Schudson had trouble figuring out Ms. Capetillo's crime. To him, welfare fraud meant double dipping: collecting full benefits and holding a job at the same time.

After the lawyers explained the rules about saving money, he made it clear he didn't think much of the rules. "I don't know how much more powerfully we could say it to the poor in our society: Don't try to save," he said. Judge Schudson said it was "ironic" that the case came as President Bush promotes his plan for Family Savings Accounts. "Apparently, that's an incentive that this country would only give to the rich."

The Limits of Aid

Others differ. County welfare worker Sophia Partipilo says Ms. Capetillo's 20 savings raise the question of whether she needed a welfare check at all. "We're not a savings and loan," says Ms. Partipilo, who handled the case. "We don't hand out toasters at the end of the month. We're here to get you over the rough times."

Ms. Capetillo could have fought the charge. Her lawyer and even the judge said later that there was a good chance a jury would have sided with the welfare mother. Even the prosecutor admits that had she simply spent the money, rather than saving it, she could have avoided a run-in with the law.

But for Ms. Capetillo, going to court once was enough. She was so frightened and her throat was so dry that the judge could barely hear her speak. She pleaded guilty to "failure to report change in circumstance." The judge sentenced her to one-year probation and ordered her to repay $1,000.

A few days later, Ms. Capetillo, who remains on welfare, returns from a shopping trip and is met by Michelle. Banana in hand, Michelle greets her mother with a smile and a gingerbread man she made at half-day kindergarten.

"Now you can see why I do what I do," says Ms. Capetillo.

Reflecting and Interpreting

1. Think about the opening anecdote. Do you think it is effective? Why or why not?

2. Note every expenditure Ms. Capetillo makes in the course of this story. What is the effect of giving the price of every item down to the penny?

3. Laws must be interpreted to cover a broad range of situations. State Ms. Capetillo's view of using her welfare check properly and then the view of the welfare officials.

4. To what did Ms. Capetillo plead guilty? Why? Do you think she was guilty? Why or why not?

5. Comment on the effectiveness of the title. Why do you think so?

A Writer's Response

1. With a group, discuss the inherent flaw in a welfare system that allows a person to be fined for saving money. What changes in welfare have since been legislated? How well do these changes seem to be working?

2. Does the attitude of the welfare officials reflect the policy of governmental officials toward overspending? How do you feel about the proposed amendment to balance the budget? Why do you think this proposal has been defeated?

3. Have you ever been punished or fined when you thought you were innocent? Do you know of someone else who has? Write a description of the incident and then state the two views. Would any of Rose's stylistic techniques work for you?

~ *TV Causes Violence? Says Who?*

Patrick Cooke

The author takes an unusual tack on this controversial topic, claiming that television may well provide young people with more acts of kindness than of violence. This essay was first printed in the New York Times, *August 14, 1993.*

As the Beverly Hills conference on violence on television showed this month, academia's dire warnings about the dangers of watching the tube have always been an easy sell. But with Senator Paul Simon hinting darkly at Government censorship unless the industry does a better job of policing itself, the ante has been raised. The question is: do TV researchers know what they're talking about?

Since the late 1940's, there have been more than 3,000 reports on the effect on viewers of watching television, and TV research itself has become a cottage industry. Most of the conclusions have been grim; many have been baffling. Here are some of the findings of the past few decades: TV leads to hyperactivity in children; TV makes children passive. TV isolates viewers; TV comforts the lonely. TV drives families apart; TV brings families together.

Not even the Public Broadcasting Service has been spared. In 1975, when researchers noticed 2-year-old children obsessively reciting numbers and letters, one study cautioned parents about a new disorder called the "Sesame Street Hazard."

Four years ago, the Department of Education financed the most extensive survey to date of the research on childhood development and TV. It concluded that a disturbing amount of scholarship had been slipshod or influenced by a prevailing attitude that TV is harmful.

Despite the difficulty of obtaining reliable information on how television influences people, some beliefs, particularly about violence, are as persistent as "Cheers" reruns. The National Coalition on Television Violence, for example, has for years asserted that murders and rapes are more likely to occur because of TV violence. According to the organization, "It increases the chances that you will be mugged in the street or have your belongings stolen."

Many Americans agree with this conclusion; the link between mayhem on TV and a real-life violent society, after all, seems to make sense. But consider this possible area for research: Why doesn't anyone ever talk about the many occasions when people are nice to one another on TV? What effect has that had?

Much of the hand-wringing at the Beverly Hills conference centered on the sheer volume of brutality young people witness on TV and how, at the very least, such incidents desensitize them to real violence. But if teenagers have seen 18,000 TV murders by the age of 16, as one study estimated, isn't it possible, given the popularity of shows like "Fresh Prince of Bel Air," "Brooklyn Bridge" and "Beverly Hills 90210," that they also have seen many more incidents of kindness?

From "Little House on the Prairie" to "The Golden Girls" there is no end of people discovering their love for one another. Singles, marrieds, siblings, punks and homeboys share so much peace, tolerance and understanding that you might even call it gratuitous harmony.

It is tempting to conclude that a young person bombarded with hours of dramas in which characters are good-hearted becomes more sensitized to niceness. The conclusion might be wrong, but it's just as plausible as arguing that TV encourages evil.

These issues have been around longer than television has, of course. In the 1930's and 40's, studies warned of the harmful effects radio was having on children's school performance and their ability to distinguish fantasy from reality. "This new invader of the privacy of the home has brought many a disturbing influence in its wake," a psychologist wrote in 1936. "Parents have become aware of a puzzling change in the behavior of their children."

Socrates cautioned that writing would destroy people's memories. Plato's *Republic* warned about the danger of storytellers: "Children cannot distinguish between what is allegory and what isn't, and opinions formed at that age are difficult to change." Comic books were once blamed for young people's poor reading ability, and the early days of film prompted books like *Movies, Delinquency, and Crime.*

Today, of course, we lament that no one writes anymore. And whatever happened to those old-time storytellers? Comic books? Films? Those comics and films are classics now. And it's a shame many of us weren't around to hear those wonderful shoot-'em-up "Gangbusters" in the golden days of radio.

It is possible that today's kids will survive the effects of new technology as well as earlier generations did—provided they aren't forced to watch panel discussions by the TV experts.

Reflecting and Interpreting

1. Look at the conclusions that Cooke presents in paragraph 2. Have any been proven false or true? Why is it difficult to link such causes and effects?

2. Is repetition atypical for tots? What is your reaction to "Sesame Street Hazard," "disorder," and "obsessively"? How do these words influence tone in the essay?

3. Is it just as plausible to argue that as a result of watching television, young people become more sensitized to niceness than to evil? When young viewers see both kind acts and violent acts, which type is more apt to make the deeper impression and more likely to be remembered? Why?

4. How would you assess the quality and quantity of Cooke's examples? Are "Little House on the Prairie," a series that originated nearly thirty years ago,

and "The Golden Girls," an adult comedy first aired in the eighties, relevant? Why or why not? Do other examples lend support to his point? Why or why not?

5. In the final four paragraphs, Cooke gives his opinion indirectly. What does he seem to be saying? Do you agree? Why or why not?

6. Do you think the humor in the final sentence is effective in supporting his argument? Why or why not?

A Writer's Response

1. Keep a journal of television programs for several days, sampling a wide variety for at least fifteen minutes each, more if possible. Log the name of the program, length of time watched, and acts of violence and kindness. (You might also note the type of act.) After your brief survey is finished, summarize the results and share them with a group. Have you changed your mind about the issue?

2. In a group, discuss the methods Cooke uses to try to make the opposition look foolish. Does he succeed or fail? Why do you think so?

Rock Lyrics and Violence against Women

Caryl Rivers

Should the public take a stand against songs that contain lyrics supporting violent acts, such as rape and murder? Caryl Rivers takes a firm position in this essay, which was first printed in The Boston Globe. *Professor Rivers, who teaches journalism at Boston University, has published not only magazine and newspaper articles but also novels.*

After a grisly series of murders in California, possibly inspired by the lyrics of a rock song, we are hearing a familiar chorus: Don't blame rock and roll. Kids will be kids. They love to rebel, and the more shocking the stuff, the better they like it.

There's some truth in this, of course. I loved to watch Elvis shake his torso when I was a teenager, and it was even more fun when Ed Sullivan wouldn't let the cameras show him below the waist. I snickered at the forbidden "Rock with Me, Annie" lyrics by a black Rhythm and Blues group, which were deliciously naughty. But I am sorry, rock fans, that is not the same thing as hearing lyrics about how a man is going to force a woman to perform oral sex on him at gunpoint in a little number called "Eat Me Alive." It is not in the same league with a song about the delights of slipping into a woman's room while she is sleeping and murdering her, the theme of an AC/DC ballad that allegedly inspired the California slayer.

Make no mistake, it is not sex we are talking about here, but violence. Violence against women. Most rock songs are not violent—they are funky, sexy, rebellious, and sometimes witty. Please do not mistake me for a Mrs. Grundy. If Prince wants to leap about wearing only a purple jock strap, fine. Let Mick Jagger unzip his fly as he gyrates, if he wants to. But when either one of them starts garroting, beating, or sodomizing a woman in their number, that is another story.

I always find myself annoyed when "intellectual" men dismiss violence against women with a yawn, as if it were beneath their dignity to notice. I wonder if the reaction would be the same if the violence were directed against someone other than women. How many people would yawn and say, "Oh, kids will be kids," if a rock group did a nifty little number called "Lynchin," in which stringing up and stomping on black people were set to music? Who would chuckle and say, "Oh, just a little adolescent rebellion" if a group of rockers went on MTV dressed as Nazis, desecrating synagogues and beating up Jews to the beat of twanging guitars?

I'll tell you what would happen. Prestigious dailies would thunder on editorial pages; senators would fall over each other to get denunciations into the *Con-*   5 *gressional Record.* The president would appoint a commission to clean up the music business.

But violence against women is greeted by silence. It shouldn't be.

This does not mean censorship, or book (or record) burning. In a society that protects free expression, we understand a lot of stuff will float up out of the sewer. Usually, we recognize the ugly stuff that advocates violence against any group as the garbage it is, and we consider its purveyors as moral lepers. We hold our nose and tolerate it, but we speak out against the values it proffers.

But images of violence against women are not staying on the fringes of society. No longer are they found only in tattered, paper-covered books or in movie houses where winos snooze and the scent of urine fills the air. They are entering the mainstream at a rapid rate. This is happening at a time when the media, more and more, set the agenda for the public debate. It is a powerful legitimizing force—especially television. Many people regard what they see on TV as the truth; Walter Cronkite once topped a poll as the most trusted man in America.

Now, with the advent of rock videos and all-music channels, rock music has grabbed a big chunk of legitimacy. American teenagers have instant access, in their living rooms, to the messages of rock, on the same vehicle that brought them Sesame Street. Who can blame them if they believe that the images they see are accurate reflections of adult reality, approved by adults? After all, Big Bird used to give them lessons on the same little box. Adults, by their silence, sanction the images. Do we really want our kids to think that rape and violence are what sexuality is all about?

This is not a trivial issue. Violence against women is a major social problem,   10
one that's more than a cerebral issue to me. I teach at Boston University, and one of my most promising young journalism students was raped and murdered. Two others told me of being raped. Recently, one female student was assaulted and beaten so badly she had $5,000 worth of medical bills and permanent damage to her back and eyes.

It's nearly impossible, of course, to make a cause-and-effect link between lyrics and images and acts of violence. But images have a tremendous power to create an atmosphere in which violence against certain people is sanctioned. Nazi propagandists knew that full well when they portrayed Jews as ugly, greedy, and powerful.

The outcry over violence against women, particularly in a sexual context, is being legitimized in two ways: by the increasing movement of these images into the mainstream of the media in TV, films, magazines, albums, videos, and by the silence about it.

Violence, of course, is rampant in the media. But it is usually set in some kind of moral context. It's usually only the bad guys who commit violent acts against the innocent. When the good guys get violent, its against those who deserve it. Dirty Harry blows away the scum, he doesn't walk up to a toddler and say, "Make my day." The A Team does not shoot up suburban shopping malls.

But in some rock songs, it's the "heroes" who commit the acts. The people we are programmed to identify with are the ones being violent, with women on the receiving end. In a society where rape and assaults on women are endemic, this is no small problem, with millions of young boys watching on their TV screens and listening on their Walkmans.

I think something needs to be done. I'd like to see people in the industry respond to the problem. I'd love to see some women rock stars speak out against violence against women. I would like to see disc jockeys refuse air play to records and videos that contain such violence. At the very least, I want to see the end of the silence. I want journalists and parents and critics and performing artists to keep this issue alive in the public forum. I don't want people who are concerned about this issue labeled as bluenoses and bookburners and ignored.   15

And I wish it wasn't always just women who were speaking out. Men have as large a stake in the quality of our civilization as women do in the long run. Violence is a contagion that infects at random. Let's hear something, please, from the men.

Reflecting and Interpreting

1. How does Rivers establish a common ground between the two viewpoints?
2. What distinction does she make between the early days of rock and roll and now?
3. Do you agree or disagree with Rivers's belief that "it is not sex we are talking about here, but violence"? Why?
4. Where does Rivers use analogy to emphasize her point? Is the analogy effective?
5. Rivers believes that violence against women is being legitimized in two ways. Do you agree or disagree? Why?
6. What challenges does the author make? What alternatives does she offer? Can you offer any others?

A Writer's Response

1. List each of the points Rivers makes. Can you plot her organizational strategy? How does she respond to her opponents' points? Has she omitted any? What would you add, if anything? Would you make any changes in the order of her points? If so, why?
2. Rivers mentions some ways she believes violence against women is legitimized. Brainstorm on topics you think are legitimized by popular culture. What kinds of challenges would you like to make?
3. Compare Trillin's belief ("Rock Threat Subsides") about the effect of rock lyrics on teens with that of Rivers. Who has the more convincing argument? Why?

Why Not Take Away Sex Offender's Weapon?

Kathleen Parker

Kathleen Parker, syndicated columnist, offers a rationale for granting a pedophile's request to be castrated before leaving prison. Although Larry Don McQuay feared he would eventually murder a child, the state of Texas denied his request in April 1996.

I love a man who knows how to fix things. Larry Don McQuay is such a man.

To the 240 children he molested, McQuay is probably just a perverted monster. But to me, he's a genius.

That's because McQuay, who understands that his pedophilia is incurable, has come up with a way to fix his problem. He wants to be castrated.

Last week he asked the state of Texas, where he has been incarcerated the past six years on sexual assault charges, to castrate him before releasing him. McQuay had earned "good behavior" time on his eight-year sentence, and was scheduled this week for release to a halfway house.

McQuay's reasoning was unassailable: 5

"I am doomed to eventually rape then murder my poor little victims to keep them from telling on me," he said in a message to Justice for All, a Houston-based victims rights group.

Alas, the state of Texas denied McQuay's request, claiming that castration is—guess what?—elective surgery.

Granted, castration wouldn't save McQuay's life and therefore may be considered "elective." But there's another way to look at it. What if castrating McQuay were to save someone else's life? Would that make the operation more necessary, less elective?

McQuay apparently thinks so. The sad fact is, McQuay knows himself better than his captors. He has begged for help with the torment he is compelled to impose on others.

"I have been busting my butt to do everything possible to keep me from re-   10
offending, but everyone seems to be dead set against that," McQuay said. "I got away with molesting over 240 children before getting caught for molesting just one little boy.

"With all that I have coldheartedly learned while in prison, there is no way that I will ever be caught again. Will your children be my next victims?"

There's a chance that sexual offenders, who have the highest recidivism rate of any criminal, may not wish to continue their behavior. There's a chance that some might wish to take whatever measures necessary to stop themselves from hurting others.

Sex offenders, especially pedophiles, apparently do not respond well to therapy and rehabilitation. Meanwhile, there's growing support for castration as a "cure" for pedophiles.

Wisconsin legislators are considering a bill that would offer chemical castration to pedophiles in exchange for parole. Texas last year killed a bill allowing voluntary castrations.

What exactly is our hang-up with castration, anyway? If someone were found   15
guilty of pistol-whipping people, we'd take away his pistol, wouldn't we? It seems to me that a man guilty of sexually assaulting 200 children is wielding a weapon of which he should be divested.

Yet, the idea of castration somehow offends our national sense of manhood. You can imagine how discussions must go within our country's male-dominated legislative chambers. You can hear the awkward chuckles, the playful grimaces, the jock-room banter: "Kill the poor fellow, but don't castrate him for heaven's sake!"

It's just . . . unnatural.

Agreed. It's unnatural to castrate a healthy man. It's also unnatural to sexually assault a child. Who gets priority treatment here?

McQuay may just be trying to get attention, it's true. He may not have sexually molested 240 children as he claims. He only got caught once, after all, with a 6-year-old boy in San Antonio. But isn't the sexual assault of just one 6-year-old boy sufficient justification for any punishment we might conjure? Voluntary castration seems a peace offering by comparison.

Besides, who's worse off if Larry Don McQuay is castrated? McQuay will be   20
happier if he doesn't hurt anyone else. Other 6-year-old boys destined to be his next victims will be happier. So give the man what he wants. Let Larry fix his problem.

And change the law while you're at it. Think of castration not as an appalling, elective surgery, but as a brilliant idea whose time has come.

Reflecting and Interpreting

1. What is the effect of Parker's first two paragraphs?

2. Summarize McQuay's reasoning for making the request. What is his premise? Do authorities in the field tend to agree or disagree?

3. Why did the state of Texas refuse the request? How does Parker respond to this point?

4. What alternative to surgery have legislators in other states proposed? How would this alternative work? Would you be for or against such legislation in your state? Why?

5. Parker offers one possible reason that many people oppose castration of convicted pedophiles about to be released from incarceration. Do you agree or disagree? Can you think of any other possible reasons?

6. Outline the main points in Parker's argument. How does it vary from the classic argument format? (See chapter 20 for further information and outlines.)

A Writer's Response

1. Early in the argument Parker hints at the conflict between the rights of potential victims and the rights of convicted pedophiles. Can you find it? Does society have an obligation to protect the public from predators? Or does the right of the individual supersede this obligation? In a group, discuss this point. Consider relatively recent legislation that has dealt with this obligation.

2. Do some research to discover what, if anything, has been done since 1996 concerning castration of convicted pedophiles about to be released. Then write an essay, taking a position on this—or another—issue. (For help in shaping an argument, see chapter 20.)

Cloning: "The Whole Idea Scares Me Silly"

William Raspberry

In 1978 William Raspberry, journalist and college instructor, reacted to ideas voiced in a book on cloning—an idea regarded by many people as mere fantasy then. Using flippancy, Raspberry described the view of scientists who favored cloning human beings, but he went on to raise ethical questions. Now, after the successful cloning of a sheep and other animals, the questions Raspberry raised twenty years ago have become urgent. In 1997 President Clinton recommended legislation to ban human cloning but to permit embryo research that stops short of producing a baby.

The scientists who are able to talk dispassionately about these things can think of a thousand ways in which clones could be a boon for mankind.

They paint pictures of unprotesting (and unpaid) humanoids doing such unpleasant work as collecting garbage and cleaning septic tanks, fighting wars and providing organ transplants for those of us who might need them.

Cloning would take the randomness out of plant and animal reproduction and even put an end to world hunger.

Those who can discuss these things calmly make them sound like Al Capp's "shmoos," those cuddly little gourd-shaped creatures who would do anything, be anything, or taste like anything you wanted.

"Shmoos" I could handle, since they existed only in the "Li'l Abner" comic strip. Clones give me a problem. Truth to tell, the whole idea scares me silly. I wouldn't hesitate to support a law forbidding cloning or to jail people who insisted on defying that law.   5

Cloning, as every schoolchild knows by now, is the asexual, single-parent reproduction of organisms. It has already been accomplished with plants; and scientists are agreed that the cloning of animals, including human ones, is only a matter of a few technological breakthroughs. David Rorvik ("In His Image: The Cloning of a Man") claims it has already been done.

What brings all this to mind now is a piece in the October issue of Gallery magazine—a long interview with Ted Howard and Jeremy Rifkin, anti-war radicals of the '60s and co-authors of the book "Who Should Play God?: The Artificial Creation of Life and What It Means for the Future of the Human Race."

"One has to look at genetic engineering as an engineering technique," Howard says at one point. "It's a technique that encourages efficiency, weeds out diversity and chance. It moves us away from normal sexual reproduction, which is a lot of fun, maybe, but not efficient. . . . A genetic blueprint is efficient."

Adds Rifkin: "Many scientists have speculated about the possibility of clone banks, where you house and feed your clone. In other words, in this possible future system, you'd have a clone born right after your own birth. Then you use spare parts from that clone when your body needs them. . . . If you need a kidney, you just take it out of him."

Elsewhere, they suggest the possibility of using clones for work involving radiation or dangerous chemicals, or for fighting wars. Always calmly.   10

There are obvious problems, quite apart from the technological ones. For instance, since you and your clone would be physical duplicates, you (rather than the duplicate) might just as well be the clone. And in that case, how calmly would *you* accept the idea of working around leaky reactors, or being converted to cannon fodder, or waiting around to be used for spare parts?

Would you have no rights as a human being? Would you be a free person? And, if not, who would own you?

Also: Who gets cloned? Mindless cretins who are willing to do our dangerous or degrading work? Or "superior" human beings, our brightest and best? And who decides who our best happen to be?

As Howard observes. "The so-called beneficial possibilities will be reserved for those who can pay for them. The others would not benefit. Rather, they would be eliminated. . . . We're going to have to decide who is suitable."

And to whom would you entrust that sort of decision? Who gets to play God?   15

That's one source of my fear. The other is technical. If scientists learn to do this thing, some scientists will in fact do it. And whether you're cloning people or plants, or combining species into wholly new ones, accidents will happen.

I don't like the idea of some careless laboratory assistant forgetting to shut off the incubator and unleashing a few million clones on us—even if they are all exactly like me.

For some things, one is plenty.

Reflecting and Interpreting

1. Examine the wording in paragraphs 1, 2, 4. What words create a sense of calmness and detachment from the issue?

2. Where does Raspberry's thesis statement appear? What is the effect of delaying it rather than presenting it in the first sentence?

3. Why do you think the definition is included in paragraph 6?

4. Rather than summarizing the views of opponents, Raspberry uses another technique. What is it? Do you think this is more or less effective than a summary would be?

5. Does Raspberry use the block or alternating method to present his argument?

6. At the end Raspberry explains his two fears of cloning. What are they?

7. Now we have an additional fear. We know that cloning is not a simple process; it can result in birth defects and deformities. How does this knowledge affect your position on cloning, or does it?

A Writer's Response

1. A traditional view of some scientists has been that if man has the knowledge to do something, then it can or should be done. Do you agree or disagree? Do you see any dangers or complications that are not discussed here? Draft a statement of your position and list reasons for your view.

2. Revise your draft. Do you need to limit the thesis? Do you agree or disagree with the president's position? How? What would you propose?

I Listen to My Parents and I Wonder What They Believe

Robert Coles

Perhaps you have heard the phrase "and a little child shall lead them," which illustrates a theme of this essay by Robert Coles. Here he comments on the insights of children from both wealthy and poor families as they wrestle with "questions of right and wrong . . . taking place in their worlds." His multivolume work, Children of Crisis, *earned Coles, a psychologist, the Pulitzer Prize.*

Not so long ago children were looked upon in a sentimental fashion as "angels" or as "innocents." Today, thanks to Freud and his followers, boys and girls are understood to have complicated inner lives; to feel love, hate, envy and rivalry in various and subtle mixtures; to be eager participants in the sexual and emotional politics of the home, neighborhood and school. Yet some of us parents still cling to the notion of childhood innocence in another way. We do not see that our children also make ethical decisions every day in their own lives, or realize how attuned they may be to moral currents and issues in the larger society.

In Appalachia I heard a girl of eight whose father owns coal fields (and gas stations, a department store and much timberland) wonder about "life" one day: "I'll be walking to the school bus, and I'll ask myself why there's some who are poor and their daddies can't find a job, and there's some who are lucky like me. Last month there was an explosion in a mine my daddy owns, and everyone became upset. Two miners got killed. My daddy said it was their own fault, because they'll be working and they get careless. When my mother asked if there was anything wrong with the safety down in the mine, he told her no and she shouldn't ask questions like that. Then the Government people came and they said it was the owner's fault—Daddy's. But he has a lawyer and the lawyer is fighting the Government and the union. In school, kids ask me what I think, and I sure do feel sorry for the two miners and so does my mother—I know that. She told me it's just not a fair world and you have to remember that. Of course, there's no one who can be sure there won't be trouble; like my daddy says, the rain falls on the just and the unjust. My brother is only six and he asked Daddy awhile back who are the 'just' and the 'unjust,' and Daddy said there are people who work hard and they live good lives, and there are lazy people and they're always trying to sponge off others. But I guess you have to feel sorry for anyone who has a lot of trouble, because it's poured-down, heavy rain."

Listening, one begins to realize that an elementary-school child is no stranger to moral reflection—and to ethical conflict. This girl was torn between her loyalty to her particular background, its values and assumptions, and to a larger affiliation—her membership in the nation, the world. As a human being whose parents were kind and decent to her, she was inclined to be thoughtful and sensitive with respect to others, no matter what their work or position in society. But her father was among other things a mineowner, and she had already learned to shape her concerns to suit that fact of life. The result: a moral oscillation of sorts, first toward nameless others all over the world and then toward her own family. As the girl put it later, when she was a year older: "You should try to have 'good thoughts' about everyone, the minister says, and our teacher says that too. But you should honor your father and mother most of all; that's why you should find out what they think and then sort of copy them. But sometimes you're not sure if you're on the right track."

Sort of copy them. There could be worse descriptions of how children acquire moral values. In fact, the girl understood how girls and boys all over the world "sort of" develop attitudes of what is right and wrong, ideas of who the just and the unjust are. And they also struggle hard and long, and not always with success, to find out where the "right track" starts and ends. Children need encouragement or assistance as they wage that struggle.

In home after home that I have visited, and in many classrooms, I have met   5
children who not only are growing emotionally and intellectually but also are trying to make sense of the world morally. That is to say, they are asking themselves and others about issues of fair play, justice, liberty, equality. Those last words are abstractions, of course—the stuff of college term papers. And there are, one has to repeat, those in psychology and psychiatry who would deny elementary-school children access to that "higher level" of moral reflection. But any parent who has listened closely to his or her child knows that girls and boys are capable of wondering about matters of morality, and knows too that often it is their grown-up protectors (parents, relatives, teachers, neighbors) who are made uncomfortable by the so-called "innocent" nature of the questions children may ask or the statements they may make. Often enough the issue is not the moral capacity of children but the default of us parents who fail to respond to inquiries put to us by our daughters and sons—and fail to set moral standards for both ourselves and our children.

Do's and don't's are, of course, pressed upon many of our girls and boys. But a moral education is something more than a series of rules handed down, and in our time one cannot assume that every parent feels able—sure enough of her own or his own actual beliefs and values—to make even an initial explanatory and disciplinary effort toward a moral education. Furthermore, for many of us parents these days it is a child's emotional life that preoccupies us.

In 1963, when I was studying school desegregation in the South, I had extended conversations with Black and white elementary-school children caught up in a dramatic moment of historical change. For longer than I care to remember, I concentrated on possible psychiatric troubles, on how a given child was managing under circumstances of extreme stress, on how I could be of help—with "support," with reassurance, with a helpful psychological observation or interpretation. In many instances I was off the mark. These children weren't "patients"; they weren't even complaining. They were worried, all right, and often enough they had things to say that were substantive—that had to do not so much with troubled emotions as with questions of right and wrong in the real-life dramas taking place in their worlds.

Here is a nine-year-old white boy, the son of ardent segregationists, telling me about his sense of what desegregation meant to Louisiana in the 1960s: "They told us it wouldn't happen—never. My daddy said none of us white people would go into schools with the colored. But then it did happen, and when I went to school the first day I didn't know what would go on. Would the school stay open or would it close up? We didn't know what to do; the teacher kept telling us that we should be good and obey the law, but my daddy said the law was wrong. Then my mother said she wanted me in school even if there were some colored kids there. She said if we all stayed home she'd be a 'nervous wreck.' So I went.

"After a while I saw that the colored weren't so bad. I saw that there are different kinds of colored people, just like with us whites. There was one of the colored who was nice, a boy who smiled, and he played real good. There was another one, a boy, who wouldn't talk with anyone. I don't know if it's right that we all be in the same school. Maybe it isn't right. My sister is starting school next year, and she says she doesn't care if there's 'mixing of the races.' She says they told her in Sunday school that everyone is a child of God, and then a kid asked if that goes for the colored too and the teacher said yes, she thought so. My daddy said that it's true, God made everyone—but that doesn't mean we all have to be living together under the same roof in the home or the school. But my mother said we'll never know what God wants of us but we have to try to read His mind, and that's why we pray. So when I say my prayers I ask God to tell me what's the right thing to do. In school I try to say hello to the colored, because they're kids, and you can't be mean or you'll be 'doing wrong,' like my grandmother says."

Children aren't usually long-winded in the moral discussions they have with   10
one another or with adults, and in quoting this boy I have pulled together comments he made to me in the course of several days. But everything he said was of interest to me. I was interested in the boy's changing racial attitudes. It was clear he was trying to find a coherent, sensible moral position too. It was also borne in on me that if one spends days, weeks in a given home, it is hard to escape a particular moral climate just as significant as the psychological one.

In many homes parents establish moral assumptions, mandates, priorities. They teach children what to believe in, what not to believe in. They teach children what is permissible or not permissible—and why. They may summon up the Bible, the flag, history, novels, aphorisms, philosophical or political sayings, personal memories—all in an effort to teach children how to behave, what and whom to respect and for which reasons. Or they may neglect to do so, and in so doing teach their children *that*—a moral abdication, of sorts—and in this way fail their children. Children need and long for words of moral advice, instruction, warning, as much as they need words of affirmation or criticism from their parents about other matters. They must learn how to dress and what to wear, how to eat and what to eat; and they must also learn how to behave under X or Y or Z conditions, and why.

All the time, in 20 years of working with poor children and rich children, Black children and white children, children from rural areas and urban areas and every region of this country, I have heard questions—thoroughly intelligent and discerning questions—about social and historical matters, about personal behavior, and so on. But most striking is the fact that almost all those questions, in one way or another, are moral in nature: Why did the Pilgrims leave England? Why didn't they just stay and agree to do what the king wanted them to do? . . . Should you try to share all you've got or should you save a lot for yourself? . . . What do you do when you see others fighting—do you try to break up the fight, do you stand by and watch or do you leave as fast as you can? . . . Is it right that some people haven't got enough to eat? . . . I see other kids cheating and I wish I could copy the answers too; but I won't cheat, though sometimes I feel I'd like to and I get all mixed up. I go home and talk with my parents, and I ask them what should you do if you see kids cheating—pay no attention, or report the kids or do the same thing they are doing?

Those are examples of children's concerns—and surely millions of American parents have heard versions of them. Have the various "experts" on childhood stressed strongly enough the importance of such questions—and the importance of the hunger we all have no matter what our age or background, to examine what we believe in, are willing to stand up for, and what we are determined to ask, likewise, of our children?

Children not only need our understanding of their complicated emotional lives; they also need a constant regard for the moral issues that come their way as soon as they are old enough to play with others and take part in the politics of the nursery, the back yard and the schoolroom. They need to be told what they must do and what they must not do. They need control over themselves and a sense of what others are entitled to from them—co-operation, thoughtfulness, an attentive ear and eye. They need discipline not only to tame their excesses of emotion but discipline also connected to stated and clarified moral values. They need, in other words, something to believe in that is larger than their own appetites and urges and, yes, bigger than their "psychological drives." They need a larger view of the world, a moral context, as it were—a faith that addresses itself to the meaning of this life we all live and, soon enough, let go of.

Yes, it is time for us parents to begin to look more closely at what ideas our children have about the world; and it would be well to do so before they become teen-agers and young adults and begin to remind us, as often happens, of how little attention we did pay to their moral development. Perhaps a nine-year-old girl from a well-off suburban home in Texas put it better than anyone else I've met: 15

I listen to my parents, and I wonder what they believe in more than anything else. I asked my mom and my daddy once: What's the thing that means most to you? They said they didn't know but I shouldn't worry my head too hard with questions like that. So I asked my best friend, and she said she wonders if there's a God and how do you know Him and what does He want you to do—I mean, when you're in school or out playing with your friends. They talk about God in church, but is it only in church that He's there and keeping an eye on you? I saw a kid steal in a store, and I know her father has a lot of money—because I hear my daddy talk. But stealing's wrong. My mother said she's a 'sick girl,' but it's still wrong what she did. Don't you think?

There was more—much more—in the course of the months I came to know that child and her parents and their neighbors. But those observations and questions—a "mere child's"—reminded me unforgettably of the aching hunger for firm ethical principles that so many of us feel. Ought we not begin thinking about this need? Ought we not all be asking ourselves more intently what standards we live by—and how we can satisfy our children's hunger for moral values?

Reflecting and Interpreting

1. Look at the opening paragraph. What is Coles's thesis?
2. React to the father's response to his six-year-old son's question. Do you see any complexities that might make the question difficult to answer?
3. Coles levels two charges that parents oftentimes "default." What does he say? Do you agree or disagree?
4. Much of the counseling for children, professional and otherwise, is directed to "psychiatric troubles, . . . with 'support,' with reassurance, with a helpful psychological observation or interpretation." What did Coles, a psychologist who had long used this approach, discover?
5. What does Coles point out about the parental role and the teaching of values, regardless of whether or not parents provide moral instruction? What does he recommend? When?
6. What universal "hunger" does Coles speak of? What challenge does he issue in the conclusion?

A Writer's Response

1. In a group, react to "it's just not a fair world" and "the rain falls on the just and the unjust." Contrast this view with a contemporary view, described by Dr. James Dobson: "We have been taught to anticipate the finest and best from our existence on this earth. We feel almost entitled, by divine decree, to at least 72 years of bliss, and anything less than that is a cause for great agitation."
2. Many people are concerned over the government's role in "values clarification," discipline, and other public school issues. In an essay explore a concern of yours.

Handbook

A Guide to Usage

CONTENTS

I. PUNCTUATION

I.A. COMMA (,)

The primary task of the comma is to clarify by indicating sentence structure. Commas should be used for a reason. (The old general rule to insert a comma for a pause does not always work.) In fact, many comma errors are due to unnecessary commas. To guide you, here are three don'ts:

Do not place a comma before a parenthesis.

Do not place a comma between a verb and a direct object.

Do not insert a comma if you lack a reason.

I.A.1. Use a comma to separate coordinate words, phrases, or clauses in a series.

(For more information on coordination, see "Parallelism with Items in a Series," chapter 8.)

The Delany children were named *Lemuel, Sarah, Elizabeth, Julia, Henry, Lucius, Manross, Hubert, Laura, and Samuel.* [a series of nouns]

A 1994 book by Sadie and Bessie Delany *made the best-selling nonfiction list, ran as a successful play*, and *won several awards.* [a series of verb phrases]

Sarah "Sadie" Delany, *by completing high school, graduating from Columbia University's Teachers College,* and *circumventing prejudice*, gained a teaching position in an all-white New York City school during the Depression. [a series of participial phrases]

If Sadie had accepted the stereotypes of the time, if she had succumbed to the racial barriers, if she had rejected the long hours of work and study, she would have remained in the South, uneducated and unknown. [a series of adverb clauses]

I.A.2. Use a comma to separate addresses, dates, and titles.

In the late 1890's Henry and Nanny Delany lived with their ten children in a small house on the campus of *Saint Augustine's School, Raleigh, North Carolina.*

Elizabeth "Bessie" Delany was born on *September 3, 1891.*

In 1918 Henry Beard Delany, *Jr.,* encouraged his sister to become a dentist, too.

Bessie Delany, *D.D.S.,* became the second black woman licensed in New York City to practice dentistry.

I.A.3. Place a comma before a coordinating conjunction that joins independent clauses (clauses that could be complete sentences).

The coordinating conjunctions are *for, and, nor, but, or, yet, so.* (See chapter 8 for more on joining independent clauses.)

In 1869 the territory of Wyoming granted women the right to vote, *but* Amendment 19 to the Constitution did not become law until August 1920.

I.A.4. **Use a comma to separate an introductory subordinate clause from the main part of the sentence.**

When the introductory clause is short and will not be misread, the comma may be omitted. (See chapter 8 for more on subordinate clauses.)

After Victoria Claflin Woodhull became one of the first two female stockbrokers in the United States, she became in 1872 the first woman to run for the presidency.

I.A.5. **Use a comma after an introductory participial phrase or infinitive phrase.**

Living in Tasmania and southern Australia, wombats are marsupials that feed on roots, leaves, and vegetables.

To see a wombat, you must look at night.

I.A.6. **Use a comma after two or more introductory prepositional phrases or a long introductory prepositional phrase (a good rule of thumb is four words or more).**

In the icy waters of the North Atlantic, the savage wolf fish grows up to three feet long.

Along the sea bottom, the sea robin walks on its breast fin rays, looking for food.

I.A.7. **Use commas to set off transitional expressions and conjunctive adverbs.**

Transitional expressions include phrases such as *in fact* and *for example.* Conjunctive adverbs include words such as *however, consequently,* and *therefore.*

Finally, the flood waters receded after ten days of rain.

It was, *in fact,* the worst flooding on record in the region.

Flooding is common in the area; *consequently,* people are being discouraged from rebuilding homes there.

I.A.8. **Use commas to set off nonessential (nonrestrictive) elements.**

Use a comma to set off tag words such as *well, yes,* and *isn't it* at the beginning or end of a sentence.

Yes, you really did win a new Lexus.

You are a very lucky fellow, *aren't you?*

Use a pair of commas to set off nonessential phrases that interrupt the flow of a sentence.

One department head, *working late,* inadvertently erased the weekly sales report.

Nonessential appositive

Ricardo Alvarez, *a business owner,* joined our Toastmasters' Club last week. [Essential: Business owner *Ricardo Alvarez* joined our Toastmasters' Club last week.]

Nonessential clause

Our students, *who come from surrounding counties,* usually commute daily. [Essential: Students *who earn a 3.5 cumulative average* graduate cum laude.]

I.A.9. Use a comma to set off a contrasting expression.

My billfold is lying on the dresser, *not the chair.*

I.A.10. Use a comma to prevent misreading.

Sometimes a comma is needed for clarity.

Inside, the stereo was going full blast.

Outside, the children were roaring around the house on their motorbikes.

I.A.11. Use commas to set off a speaker tag or source tag from a direct quotation.

A speaker tag or source tag identifies the speaker or writer and includes a verb of saying, such as *said, called, asked,* or *wrote.*

Derek yelled, "Get out! The rear tire is on fire!"

"The law must be stable," *wrote Roscoe Pound,* "but it must not stand still."

Note that when the speaker tag follows a quotation or part of a quotation, the comma preceding it is placed inside the quotation marks.

I.B. SEMICOLON (;)

Basically, the semicolon has only two uses. If you understand the rules governing it, you should be able to use the semicolon with confidence. Remember that the semicolon is a stronger mark of punctuation than the comma and that it is used for the *larger* divisions within a sentence.

I.B.1. Use a semicolon to connect two closely related independent clauses not joined by a comma and a coordinating conjunction (*and, but, or, nor, for, so,* and *yet*).

(See chapter 8 for more on joining independent clauses.)

Representatives from every state attended the Democratic Convention; the majority voted against "open rule."

I.B.2. Use a semicolon between two independent clauses joined by a conjunctive adverb or other transitional expression.

Sue is an accounting major; *however,* she plans to switch to data processing.

Kevin was not feeling well; *nonetheless,* he went to the dance.

Note that using a comma instead of a semicolon before a conjunctive adverb such as *nevertheless, however,* or *therefore* at the junction of two independent clauses results in an error called a comma splice. For more on comma splices, see section V.B. in this handbook.

I.B.3. **Replace commas with semicolons for clarity when items in a series contain commas.**

Here is our new slate of officers: *Jean Henson, president; Mike Henry, vice president; Scott Trainor, treasurer; and Mary Wiley, secretary.*

I.B.4. **If there are commas within the independent clauses of a sentence, use a semicolon rather than a comma before the coordinating conjunction.**

The Harvest House, a new restaurant on Center Street, features ethnic foods; and the crowds, surprisingly large for a small town, flock in.

I.C. COLON (:)

A colon is used after an independent clause to signal that something will follow.

I.C.1. **Use a colon to precede a list or series that does not fit smoothly into a sentence.**

Sue ordered the following items: *one pair of scissors, two yards of denim, one thimble, and one tape measure.*

Nanette will need these tools: *needle-nose pliers, a monkey wrench, a claw hammer, and a hacksaw.*

However, do not use a colon after a verb or preposition.

Incorrect

My grocery list included: zucchini, papaya, mangoes, and sunflower seeds. [The colon is not needed.]

I.C.2. **Use a colon to formally introduce a quotation.**

My point can be summarized in the words of Edward Haines: "With every civil right there has to be a corresponding civil obligation."

I.C.3. **Use a colon between independent clauses when the second explains the first.**

Jim has a real problem: his hair started falling out last month.

"Let the world slip: we shall ne'er be younger." (William Shakespeare, *The Taming of the Shrew*)

I.C.4. Use a colon in biblical references, expressions of time, and after salutations in business letters.

Use a colon between chapter and verse numbers of the Bible.

Psalm 27:3

Use a colon between the hour and the minute in referring to time.

6:05 P.M.

Use a colon after the salutation of a business letter.

Dear Ms. Brown:

I.D. APOSTROPHE (')

The apostrophe has three basic uses: to form possessives, to form a few plurals, and to indicate omissions.

I.D.1. Use an apostrophe with -s to form the possessive of singular nouns and irregular plural nouns not ending in -s.

today's fashions	my mother's life	the city's attractions
men's clothing	children's toys	mice's lifespans

Note that when adding -s to form the possessive sounds awkward in speech, some writers add only an apostrophe in writing: *Mr. Rogers' neighborhood, Charles' sons.* But it is never incorrect to add both an apostrophe and -s for such words. Whichever practice you adopt, be consistent.

I.D.2. Add only an apostrophe to form the possessive of a plural noun ending in -s.

boys' jeans   horses' manes   butterflies' wings

I.D.3. Indefinite pronouns (*anyone, everyone, everybody, nobody, one,* and so forth) in the possessive case are treated like singular nouns and require an apostrophe before -s.

Everyone's invitation was mailed.	Each one's jacket was labeled.
Anybody's guess is as good as mine.	No one's car was ticketed.

I.D.4. To show joint possession and to show possession with hyphenated terms and names of organizations, make only the last word possessive.

Bill and Thad's boat

father-in-law's car

Cutter and Holt's Welding Company

I.D.5. To show individual possession, use an apostrophe with each name.

Sue's and Joan's themes are late.

I.D.6. Use an apostrophe to form the possessive of words referring to time or to amounts of money.

a minute's rest	a week's wages	one cent's worth
two hours' work	one month's rent	two cents' worth
three days' pay	two years' time	a dime's worth

I.D.7. Use an apostrophe to form the plurals of numbers, letters, symbols, and words referred to as words. (Sometimes the apostrophe is omitted if there is no problem of clarity.)

My house number is simply three 7's, or 777.

Occasionally is spelled with two *c*'s and one *s*.

How many ='s should there be in this equation?

Ashley had three *and*'s in one sentence.

I.D.8. Use an apostrophe to replace omitted letters or numbers in a contraction.

They don't know when they'll be called back to work. [*do not; they will*]

Terry can't go until tomorrow. [*cannot*]

It's his turn. [*It is*]

The class of '89 is planning a reunion. [*1989*]

Note: Do not confuse *it's* with the possessive pronoun *its*, which does not require an apostrophe: "The cat lost its catnip mouse." (*Its*, like *his* and *hers*, is in the possessive case.)

I.E. DASH (—)

Dashes, parentheses, and brackets share a basic function: to set off information from the rest of the sentence. But these marks of punctuation differ in effect. Dashes emphasize material whereas parentheses de-emphasize. Brackets are generally used to enclose clarifying information in direct quotations.

The dash is informal punctuation that indicates an interruption of a sentence. A dash can signal a break in thought or provide special emphasis. Often used in pairs, dashes are bold and dramatic—as long as they are used sparingly. (In typing, use two hyphens without spacing to make a dash.)

I.E.1. Use a dash or a pair of dashes to emphasize appositives or other explanatory material.

"Soon members of the PMAC—referred to as the Derg—were dispatching their 'enemies' without trials."

"There was not—and never had been—a Communist Party in Ethiopia: the country was linked to the West and dependent on free-world aid."

"Soon he realized that his one hope was to make contact with two notorious smugglers who might guide him out—an idea fraught with risk."

"He had to do this—regardless of the consequences."

Note: The preceding examples of dashes are taken from "Escape from Ethiopia," by Trevor Armbrister.

I.E.2. For clarity, use a dash or a pair of dashes to set off nonrestrictive (nonessential) elements containing commas.

The Kincaid triplets—Jane, Janice, and Jeanette—enrolled in Miss Hickman's first-grade class.

I.E.3. Use a dash or a pair of dashes to set off interrupters or to indicate a pause.

Sarah has twenty—yes, twenty—Angora cats!

He's a nuisance—just a big, fat freeloader.

I.F. PARENTHESES ( )

For a discussion of the basic functions and different effects of parentheses and dashes, see the first paragraph of section I.E in this handbook.

I.F.1. Use parentheses to enclose (and de-emphasize) nonessential material.

The United States two-cent piece (issued in 1864) was the first coin with the motto "In God We Trust."

I.F.2. Use parentheses to enclose explanations or definitions.

The *New York Times* and five other metropolitan daily newspapers have joined in a WWW (World Wide Web) site called CareerPath, featuring employment advertisements.

Since the World Wide Web has no central organization, you need a "search engine" (a special site that locates other sites) to surf the Web.

Semicolons have two basic uses (see section I.B.).

I.F.3. In some documentation styles, use parentheses to enclose reference information such as page numbers or dates.

(For more information on documentation styles, see chapters 22 and 23.)

In *The Laughter Prescription*, Dr. Lawrence J. Peter advises making "yourself the target of your own quips" (146).

I.F.4. Occasionally an entire sentence or more is enclosed in parentheses as a kind of aside.

In a Pullman berth, a man can truly be alone with himself. (The nearest approach to this condition is to be found in a hotel bedroom, but a hotel room can be mighty depressing sometimes, it stands so still.)*

I.G. BRACKETS [ ]

I.G.1. Use brackets to insert explanatory material in quotations.

(For more information on using brackets in quoted material, see chapter 23.)

"In a Pullman berth [a curtained bunk on a sleeping car of a train], a man can truly be alone with himself. . . ."*

I.G.2. For clarity, use brackets instead of parentheses to enclose material already within parentheses.

We should be sure to give Emanuel Foose (and his brother Emilio [1812–1882] as well) credit for his role in founding the institute.

I.H. HYPHEN (-)

I.H.1. Use a hyphen to divide a word at the end of a line.

At least one syllable of three or more letters should be before the division: *con-sequently*.

I.H.2. Use a hyphen in spelled-out compound numbers from twenty-one through ninety-nine.

I.H.3. Use a hyphen in spelled-out fractions.

one-fourth   five-eighths
two-thirds   four and one-third

I.H.4. Use a hyphen between two or more words used together as a modifier before a noun (unless the first word ends in *-ly*).

thought-provoking speech   all-out effort
problem-solving quiz   on-the-job training
rosy-cheeked baby   up-to-date data
lightly salted peanuts   highly rated programs

---

*From E. B. White, "Progress and Change."

However, do not hyphenate such modifiers when they do not precede the noun they modify.

The quiz was on problem solving.

The baby was rosy cheeked.

Training was conducted on the job.

The data were up to date.

I.H.5. Use a hyphen with certain prefixes.

These include *ex-* and *self-* with the exceptions of *selfless, selfsame*. There is no hard-and-fast rule about other prefixes such as *anti-, co-, ex-, pre-, pro-, re-*, and *well-*. Check an up-to-date dictionary, and, if given a choice, be consistent.

anti-intellectual	pre-election
co-owner	self-denial
ex-president	well-being

Note: Always use a hyphen when the word to be prefixed begins with a capital as in *pro-American, non-British*, or *mid-July*.

I.H.6. Use a hyphen to avoid doubling a letter and to avoid confusion.

semi-invalid [avoids *semiinvalid*]

re-enlist [avoids *reenlist*]

re-form [avoids confusion with *reform*]

I.I. SLASH (/)

I.I.1. In certain situations, such as highly informal writing or technical papers, use a slash to replace *or,* which is ordinarily required to show alternatives.

all ready/already   radio/television   to/too/two

Note: Many readers object to the use of *and/or.* Often *and* or *or* is sufficient.

I.I.2. Use a slash to separate elements in certain expressions.

Dates: 1996/97

Fractions: 1/4

Places: Dallas/Fort Worth

I.I.3. Use slashes (with a space on each side of the slash) in prose to indicate divisions between lines of poetry.

(See "Preparing an Analysis of a Poem," chapter 28.)

Shakespeare writes: "Like as the waves make towards the pebbled shore, / So do our minutes hasten to their end. . . ."

I.J. QUOTATION MARKS (" ")

Although quotation marks have more than one use, they usually indicate the beginning and end of someone's exact words. Dialogue requires quotation marks. Citations require quotation marks (see chapter 23). Quotation marks may also be used to indicate words used in special ways. Titles of short written works or parts of works are enclosed with quotation marks.

I.J.1. Use quotation marks in dialogue to enclose the exact words of a speaker.

Phoebe called, "Sparky, bring that shoe back here!"

"Come on, Sparky," she cajoled, "bring the shoe back; and I'll give you some Teeny Bits."

I.J.2. Use quotation marks to enclose short direct quotations.

Short is defined differently in different documentation styles. The most commonly used style in English, that of the Modern Language Association (MLA), defines *short* as four lines or less. (Long quotations are indented. For more on quoting sources, see chapter 23.)

In *The Conduct of Life*, Emerson wrote as follows: "The art of conversation, or the qualification for a good companion, is a certain self-control, which now holds the subject, now lets it go, with a respect for the emergencies of the moment."

I.J.3. Use quotation marks to enclose the titles of parts of books and periodicals.

Because this rule is often confused, I'll share an informal guideline that helps me easily remember the principle: Underline (italicize) the title or name of a whole item; use quotation marks around the title of a part. The lists below indicate how the guideline applies:

Underline "Whole" Items	*Use Quotation Marks for "Parts"*
book title	chapter or story title
songbook title	song title
poetry book title	poem title
title of a very long poem [e.g., *Paradise Lost*]	
name of a newspaper	comic, article, or feature title
name of a magazine	article, feature, or story title
pamphlet title	speech, short report
name of a plane, ship, or train	
title of a film, painting, record album, television or radio program	title of an episode of a radio or television series

Finally, a writer does not underline or use quotation marks with his or her own title at the beginning of a work. (See also section I.K. on italics [underlining].)

I.J.4. Use quotation marks to enclose a quotation within a quotation.

If a quotation occurs within a quotation already marked with double quotation marks, the inside quotation is enclosed in single quotation marks, sometimes resulting in three quotation marks at the end of the quotation.

"You must have read Eiseley's 'The Real Secret of Piltdown,'" Bill's friend observed.

Note: In ordinary U.S. usage, the only exceptions to the use of double quotation marks for main, or outside, quotations are long quotations (block quotations), which are not placed within quotation marks because they are indented. (For more information on quoting sources, see chapter 23.)

I.J.5. Traditionally, quotation marks were used to enclose words discussed as words. However, many writers now prefer italics for this purpose (see also section I.K., Italics).

"Computer" is derived from the Latin verb "computare."

I.J.6. Use quotation marks to enclose words used in a special or ironic sense.

What chain of events caused the sinking of an "unsinkable" ship such as the *Titanic?*

Note: Do not use quotation marks for emphasis. The effect can be unintentionally ironic and humorous: Jordan Bailey, "President"; "I'm sure your 'wife' will enjoy the ring you bought at our store."

I.J.7. Use other punctuation with quotation marks correctly.

Commas and (except in one documentation situation) periods always go *inside* closing quotation marks. Colons and semicolons always go *outside* closing quotation marks. The rule for all other punctuation is that if the punctuation is part of the quotation, it goes inside, and if it is not part of the quotation, it goes outside.

"Reading *Space Technology* gives me the insider's view," he says, adding, "It's like having all the top officials sitting in my office for a discussion."

He said, "I will pay the full amount"; this certainly surprised us.

She has two favorite "sports": eating and sleeping.

I.K. *ITALICS* (UNDERLINING)

Italics is a typeface that slants to the right (*Moby Dick*). Since ordinary typewriters do not have italics, underlining is substituted. Italics and underlining can indicate foreign words; special names of vehicles, vessels, or artworks; words used as words; and titles of long works. Since many foreign words have been adopted into English, check a dictionary to see whether or not they should be italicized. Direct quotations in another language are not italicized.

I.K.1. Use italics (underlining) for titles of long works.

For a discussion of when to use italics and when to use quotation marks in titles, see section I.J.3. of this handbook. The treatment of titles differs from one documentation style to another. (For more information on titles of sources in research papers, see chapter 23.) Listed here are the most common kinds of works whose titles are italicized:

books: *A Tale of Two Cities*
Exception: Do not use italics (or underlining) for the names of sacred books: the Bible (or the Holy Bible), the New Testament, the Koran, and so forth.

long poems: *Paradise Lost, The Iliad, The Wasteland*

newspapers and magazines: the *New York Times; National Geographic*

pamphlets: *Letters from an American Farmer*

vessels (planes, trains, ships, spacecraft): the *Titanic;* the *Burlington Zephyr; Challenger*

plays: *Hamlet; The Music Man*

comic strips: *Doonesbury*

films and television and radio programs: *Aladdin; The X-Files; A Prairie Home Companion*

albums and long musical works: *Thriller;* Mahler's *Symphony No. 9*

paintings and sculpture: da Vinci's *Mona Lisa;* Michelangelo's *David*

software: *Windows 95; PageMaker 6.5*

I.K.2. For clarity, use italics for words discussed as words, particularly when quotation marks are used in the same sentence for another purpose.

The word *boudoir* comes from an Old French verb, meaning "to pout or sulk."

I.K.3. Use italics for emphasis, but do so sparingly.

Trust me—take Route 315, *not* Route 23.
What is the *evidence* for that position?

I.L. ELLIPSES (. . .)

An ellipsis is a set of three spaced dots that indicate an omission. When an omission occurs at the beginning of a quotation, an ellipsis is *not* necessary; but an omission in the middle or at the end requires an ellipsis. To shorten a quotation, you can use an ellipsis as long as you do not distort the meaning. When omitting a word, phrase, sentence, or more, be guided by integrity: Is the result fair to the author? Is it grammatically correct? The examples that follow reflect the style of the Modern Language Association. The first two examples are based on an excerpt from Linda Ryberg's "The Midwest Salutes its Swedish Roots" in *Midwest Living*.

Original:

> A harsh first winter on the windswept Illinois prairie in 1846 couldn't stop a tiny group of Swedish immigrants from prospering in the town they founded and named Bishop Hill. After all, they'd crossed the Atlantic, sailed the Great Lakes, and walked 160 miles southwest from Chicago to get there.

I.L.1. Use an ellipsis to show an omission in the middle of a quotation.

> Tracing the history of an Illinois town, Linda Ryberg writes: "A harsh first winter . . . in 1846 couldn't stop a tiny group of Swedish immigrants from prospering in the town they founded and named Bishop Hill."

I.L.2. Use an ellipsis to show an omission at the end of a quotation.

> Linda Ryberg, tracing the history of Bishop Hill, Illinois, explains that in 1846 a small band of Swedish settlers "crossed the Atlantic, sailed the Great Lakes, and walked 160 miles southwest from Chicago. . . ."

> Linda Ryberg, tracing the history of Bishop Hill, Illinois, explains that in 1846 a small band of Swedish settlers "crossed the Atlantic, sailed the Great Lakes, and walked 160 miles southwest from Chicago . . ." (40).

Note: Since there is no parenthetical reference in the first example, the sentence period is placed flush against the last word within the quotation marks. In the second example, however, the sentence period is placed after the parenthetical reference of this short quotation. (For information on using ellipses in long quotations, see chapter 23.)

I.L.3. Use a whole line of ellipsis points to indicate omission of a line or more in quoted poetry.

William Wordsworth was a poet of the city as well as the countryside. While crossing Westminster Bridge, in London, he wrote:

> Earth has not anything to show more fair:
> Dull would he be of soul who could pass by
> A sight so touching in its majesty:
> . . . .
> Ne'er saw I, never felt, a calm so deep!

I.L.4. Use an ellipsis to indicate a pause or hesitation, but use this device sparingly.

Don't swim in this water . . . unless you're fond of sharks.

I.M. PERIOD (.)

I.M.1. **Use a period at the end of statements, mild commands, and indirect questions.**

The temperature in the cave is a constant 58 degrees.

As you tour the cave, please stay on the marked trail.

Many people have asked how the cave was first discovered.

I.M.2. **Use a period (or periods) with some abbreviations.**

If an abbreviation comes at the end of a sentence, use only one period. For more on abbreviations, see section III of this handbook.)

I.M.3. **Use a period as a decimal in numbers.**

1.06   0.910 $149.95

I.N. QUESTION MARK (?)

I.N.1. **Use a question mark at the end of a direct question or request.**

Will you please pick up a roll of stamps on your way?

A group of citizens discussed the question, "Does our town need a city manager instead of a mayor?"

I.N.2. **Use a question mark after each elliptical question in a series.**

Should obscenity be controlled on the Internet? If so, by whom? How?

I.N.3. **Use a question mark in parentheses after an item that is of doubtful accuracy.**

The tunnel from his cell, disguised by a huge poster, was started in 1990(?) but was discovered only after he had fled.

I.O. EXCLAMATION POINT (!)

An exclamation point indicates strong emotion: pain, fear, surprise, indignation, or excitement. An exclamation point cannot bolster a weak statement nor make an argument more convincing. Use exclamation points sparingly; otherwise, they lose their power.

I.O.1. Use an exclamation point to add force to a command or expression of emotion.

"Ouch!"

"Help!" Jimmy screamed. "The horse is standing on my foot."

WATCH OUT! Deer Crossing

II. CAPITALIZATION

If you become lost in the thicket of capitalization, first consult an up-to-date dictionary. If you should find more than one way to capitalize, then let your audience be your guide. In other words, when you are writing for an employer, follow conventional business and technical usage. When writing a college research paper, follow the style manual your instructor recommends.

You may be surprised at certain variations in capitalization. One of the most striking differences concerns the names of software. Business and technical personnel generally follow the spelling of the manufacturer, even if it means placing a capital in the middle of a brand or trade name: for example, *InfoTrac*. Fortunately, the capitalization of most words is standard and can usually be found in a good desk dictionary.

Once you master the following standard rules of capitalization, you will be able to capitalize most words without consulting other sources.

II.A. Capitalize the first word of a sentence.

The sentence above is an example; so is this one.

Note: In most writing, capitalization of a sentence following a colon is optional, but be consistent. Some documentation styles specify whether such sentences should be capitalized, so if you are writing a research paper following a particular documentation style, see the appropriate guidelines.

II.B. Capitalize proper nouns and trade names.

Capitalize the names of people; places; political, racial, and religious groups; institutions and organizations; sacred writings; brand and trade names; ships, planes, and trains; monuments; awards; and specific academic degrees and courses.

Karen O'Neill	University of Michigan
the Dead Sea Scrolls	Catholic; Protestant; Judaism
the Bible (or the Holy Bible)	the Koran
Twenty-first Street	United States Post Office
Colorado River	the Spirit of St. Louis

the South	Purina Cat Chow
Congress	League of Women Voters
Calculus 101	Master's of English Education

Exceptions: Do not capitalize directions, ideologies, or philosophies (unless derived from the name of an individual, as Marxism).

After Ken left Philadelphia, he drove *south*.

Shelly is an *idealist*.

Many Russians feel they were better off under *communism*.

II.C. Capitalize proper adjectives and abbreviations.

Capitalize adjectives and abbreviations derived from proper nouns.

the French language	Palestinian soldiers
Cooper's hawk	Appalachian quilt
Japanese maple	Boston terrier
IRS	UCLA

Note: There are exceptions: for example, *Venice* but *venetian blind*, *French door* but *french fry*. If in doubt, check a dictionary. See also section III, Abbreviations.

II.D. Capitalize official and personal titles.

Capitalize a title (or rank) immediately before the name of a person.

Dr. Stephanie Winters	Professor Celia Kincaid
Justice Sandra O'Connor	President Dwight Eisenhower
General Colin Powell	Reverend Jamison
Mr. Jacob Turner	Ms. Shannon Maguire

Exception: When no name is given, do *not* capitalize a title.

The professor encouraged the class to share their opinions.

The president of the United States visited flood victims.

II.E. Capitalize titles of literary and other artistic works.

Ordinarily, capitalize the first and last words as well as all major words in the title of a literary or artistic work.

Last week Jack read the autobiography of William O. Douglas, *Go East, Young Man: The Early Years*.

Erma J. Fisk's *The Peacocks of Baboquivari* is an unusual story of an elderly woman who lived alone for five months in the foothills of Arizona, recording and banding birds.

At the Louvre, we saw Leonardo Da Vinci's *The Mona Lisa*.

Note: Rules for capitalizing titles of works differ from one documentation style to another. If you are writing a research paper and following a particular style, check the appropriate guidelines.

II.F. Capitalize calendar items and historical periods.

Capitalize months, special weeks, days, holidays, and historical periods.

April	New Year's Day
Tuesday	Right-to-Read Week
Easter	Middle Ages
the Renaissance	the Great Depression

Exceptions: Do not capitalize seasons or centuries.

our spring break	the twentieth century	in the winter

II.G. Capitalize events and documents.

Capitalize wars, treaties, constitutions, and other important events and documents.

World War II	Treaty of Versailles
World Series	United States Constitution
Rose Bowl game	Magna Carta
the Louisiana Purchase	Battle of Gettysburg

Exceptions: Do not capitalize laws, theories, or hypotheses:

nature's laws	theory of relativity
code of Hammurabi	Mendelian principles

III. ABBREVIATIONS

III.A. USE ABBREVIATIONS APPROPRIATELY

When writing, avoid unnecessary abbreviations. Use only conventional abbreviations that can be easily understood. Use abbreviations in your list of works cited but generally not in the text of your research paper. If you do use an abbreviation in the text, be sure to define it. Except for addresses and documentation, spell out the names of countries, states, and possessions in the United States.

In many reference sources, you will find abbreviations. A key to the abbreviations is often placed in the front or back of the publication. In older works, you may find the punctuation slightly different than given here. Dictionaries may give two ways to punctuate some abbreviations. If in doubt about periods or spacing, check an up-to-date dictionary.

Abbreviation rules differ significantly from one documentation style to another, so if you are writing a research paper and following a particular style, check the appropriate guidelines. The examples that follow are based upon the *MLA Handbook for Writers of Research Papers*, 4th ed., by Joseph Gibaldi, and *The American Heritage Dictionary*, 3rd ed.

III.A.1. **Be aware that no periods or spaces appear between or after most letters that are capitalized.**

FBI	IBM	MD
PSAT	PhD	RN
IRS	EST	DNA

Some exceptions:

B.A.	J. R. Smith	Ms. Jones
U.S.S.	Scott Felder, Jr.	Mr. Daley
N.P.	S.S.	

III.A.2. **Use a period after each lowercase letter of most abbreviations that represent a word.**

p.m.	ed.	s.t.
a.m.	r.s.v.p.	e.g.
n.p.	p.p.a.	

There are many exceptions:

2nd	mph	rpm

III.A.3. **Use a period after most abbreviations that end with lowercase letters.**

Eng.	Univ.	wk.
dept.	mkt.	assn.
Sp.	Mar.	Ger.
Tues.	Fr.	yr.

IV. NUMBERS

IV.A. USE NUMERALS OR SPELLED-OUT NUMBERS APPROPRIATELY

Two basic systems for numbers above ten exist. Choose the system that is appropriate for your audience, and follow it consistently. Many writing handbooks tell you to spell out numbers that can be expressed in two words or less: *one hun-*

dred but *101.* Other guides, especially in business and technical writing, tell you to spell out numbers up through ten and use numerals for numbers above ten: *ten* but *11.* Both systems call for consistency and specify numerals in certain situations and spelled-out numbers in others.

IV.A.1. Begin sentences with spelled-out numbers.

Never begin a sentence with a numeral. Either spell out the number, or invert the sentence if the number is too large to spell out.

> Seventy-five students were enrolled in Computer Science 111 last quarter.

> Last quarter 250 students were enrolled in Computer Science 111.

IV.A.2. Spell out round numbers.

Round numbers (tens, hundreds, thousands, and so forth) and approximations should be spelled out.

> Experts estimate that we have enough coal to last two hundred years.

IV.A.3. Combine numerals and words to avoid large figures with many zeros.

> 25 million   300 billion   100 trillion

IV.A.4. Be consistent in writing numbers in parallel constructions.

> Sue bought three books, four pens, and two notebooks.

> The English department ordered 36 manila folders, 210 red pencils, and 15 large packages of typing paper.

> The chef ordered 18 heads of lettuce, 7 pounds of carrots, 6 bunches of celery, and 7 cabbages.

Note: If a small number is used in the same sentence with a large number but in a different context, the smaller number can be spelled out.

> Those *two* technicians are operating $12,000 computers.

IV.A.5. If two numbers occur together, either spell out the smaller number or else recast the sentence to separate them.

> In 1997, 3,532 students registered for fall quarter. [may be unclear]

> In fall quarter 1997, there were 3,532 students registered. [preferable]

> *four* 15-cent stamps

> 20 *five*-inch nail files

IV.A.6. Use numbers correctly in addresses.

Except for the house number *one*, express house numbers as numerals. If a street name is a number less than eleven, spell out the number. If the street name is eleven or higher, use a hyphen preceded and followed by a space to separate the house number from the street number.

> One Blaine Avenue
>
> 9 Blaine Avenue
>
> The furniture is to be delivered to 454 East Fifth Street.
>
> Grace lives at 1310-121st Street.

IV.A.7. Use numerals in dates, measurements, and decimals.

> March 15, 1997 [not March 15th, 1997] or 15 March 1997
>
> 6 feet 2 inches tall, 7 square feet, 3 inches, 4 minutes
>
> The temperature was 110 degrees [or 110°] Fahrenheit.
>
> The average age of our students is 27.5 years.

IV.A.8. For percentages, use the percent symbol or spell out *percent* as appropriate.

In ordinary usage, use a figure, followed by the word *percent* spelled out. In business usage, figures are sometimes used with the symbol for percent. The symbol for percent is always used in charts and tables.

> Ordinary usage: 50 percent
>
> Business usage: 50 percent or 50%
>
> Technical usage: 50%
>
> Charts and tables: 50%

IV.A.9. Ordinarily, use numerals for sums of money.

> $1.38 $454.06 $1,564
>
> $5, $10 [zeros are usually omitted for even amounts]
>
> eighty-nine cents [amount less than a dollar in ordinary prose]
>
> $0.89, 89¢, or 89 cents [business usage]

Note: In legal documents, spell out sums of money and then write the numerals in parentheses: "I agree to pay a monthly rental fee of one hundred ten dollars ($110)."

IV.A.10. Use numerals appropriately in expressions of time.

Use numerals except when the word *o'clock* is used: 6 p.m.; six o'clock.

IV.A.11. Use numbers in fractions appropriately.

Except in technical usage and in charts and tables, simple fractions are usually written out: one-third, one-eighth. Fractions mixed with whole numbers are written as numerals: 28½ cubic inches. (If the keyboard does not have a fraction key, a hyphen is added to make such mixed numbers clear: 28-1/2 cubic inches.)

Note: Instead of ordinary fractions, use decimals to express precise amounts. If a decimal fraction has a value less than one, place a zero before the decimal point: 0.628.

V. GRAMMAR AND USAGE

V.A. SENTENCE FRAGMENTS

A fragment is a portion of a sentence that is punctuated as if it were an entire sentence. Lacking a subject, a verb, or both, a fragment is an incomplete thought. A fragment may be a word, a phrase, a dependent clause, or any combination of words that deviate from the basic subject-verb (or verb-subject) sentence pattern.

Fragments are sometimes used deliberately, but if you use a fragment be sure (1) that you know how to avoid unintentional fragments, (2) that your reader will approve, and (3) that the fragment is appropriate in the context. To be effective, a fragment should have a purpose. For example, in conversation or written dialogue, fragments are common, but in formal writing they should be avoided in all but a few special circumstances. The most important special uses of the fragment are answers to questions, exclamations, and requests or commands.

When is the next meeting? Next Thursday at 2:30 P.M. [fragment answer to question]

What a shame!   No! Not really!   [exclamations]

No smoking.   Ready, get set, go!   [requests or commands]

V.A.1. Avoid using *-ing* words or infinitives as main verbs, thus creating a fragment.

Incorrect

Driving 100 miles a day to and from classes, *doing* complex assignments, and *raising* a family. I found that my undergraduate days were exhausting. [The first group of words is a fragment.]

Jim and Shane stayed home last night. The reason *being* that they were broke. [The second group of words is a fragment.]

First, the proper equipment *to get* out on the lake or pond. A canoe with a paddle or chest waders will do the job. [The first group of words is a fragment.]

Correct

Driving 100 miles a day to and from classes, *doing* complex assignments, and *raising* a family, I found that my undergraduate days were exhausting. [Join the fragment to the sentence with a comma.]

Jim and Shane stayed home last night *because* they had no money. [The fragment and the sentence could be joined with a comma, but the result would be wordy.]

First, *gather* the proper equipment to get out on the lake or pond. Either a canoe with a paddle or chest waders will do the job. [Add a verb to the first word group; the subject is understood to be *you*, meaning "you gather."]

V.A.2. Avoid treating phrases that merely add additional details as complete sentences.

Incorrect

Then there is the high-speed driver. *A real maniac.*

Kevin called his father collect last night. *To ask for a loan.*

The company refused to honor the warranty. *Even though I purchased the lawn mower only six months ago.*

Correct

Then there is the high-speed driver, a real maniac.

Kevin called his father collect last night to ask for a loan.

The company refused to honor the warranty even though I purchased the lawn mower only six months ago.

V.A.3. Avoid treating dependent clauses as complete sentences.

Incorrect

After I learned the market price for comparable antique tables. I decided to rescue mine from the attic and refinish it.

Correct

After I learned the market price for comparable antique tables, I decided to rescue mine from the attic and refinish it. [The introductory adverb clause is made a part of the sentence with a comma.]

V.B. COMMA SPLICES AND FUSED (RUN-ON) SENTENCES

Beginning writers sometimes omit punctuation between clauses in a compound sentence. (See chapter 8 for more on compound sentences.) This error results in a *fused sentence*, sometimes called a *run-on sentence*. A related error is the *comma splice*, which occurs when two clauses are joined (spliced) with a comma. Never use the comma alone to punctuate a long compound sentence. If you use a comma, you must also have a coordinating conjunction. Note also that a semicolon is required before a conjunctive adverb such as *however* or *therefore*. The examples below will help to clarify punctuation of compound sentences:

V.B.1. **Punctuate sentences correctly to avoid comma splices.**

Incorrect

Terrariums are costly at a flower shop, they are inexpensive to make at home.

Terrariums are costly at a flower shop, however, they are inexpensive to make at home.

Correct

Terrariums are costly at a flower shop, *but* they are inexpensive to make at home. (Coordinating conjunction and a comma)

Terrariums are costly at a flower shop; however, they are inexpensive to make at home. [A semicolon replaces the coordinating conjunction and comma.]

V.B.2. **Punctuate sentences correctly to avoid fused (run-on) sentences.**

Incorrect

The ordinance won wide support it was passed by a two-thirds vote.

Correct

The ordinance won wide support; it was passed by a two-thirds vote. [semicolon added]

V.C. PRONOUNS

Pronouns have different uses and therefore have different forms. A pronoun that is a subject is in the *subjective* case; a pronoun that shows ownership is in the *possessive* case; and a pronoun that acts as an object is in the *objective* case.

Pronouns also show person. *First person* refers to the individual who is speaking: *I (We)* will leave soon. *Second person* refers to the individual spoken to: *You* are very thoughtful. *Third person* refers to the people or things spoken about: *She (He, It, They)* will arrive soon. The following table will help you review the uses of pronouns.

V.C.1. **Use the correct case of pronouns.**

Subjective case. Use the subjective case for the following:

Subjects of main or subordinate clauses
I will act as chairman during Brad's absence.
Jane's party was the best *I* have ever attended.

Appositives identifying words in the subjective case
Only two people—*Ray and I*—decided to go.

Subject complements following linking verbs
The winners were *he* and Joan.

Case of Pronouns

	Subjective	*Possessive*	*Objective*
Singular			
First person	I	my, mine	me
Second person	you	your, yours	you
Third person	he, she, it	his, her, hers, its	him, her, it
Plural			
First person	we	our, ours	us
Second person	you	your, yours	you
Third person	they	their, theirs	them

Possessive case. Use the possessive case for the following:

To designate ownership
That hat is *hers.*
The committee was late in finishing *its* report.

Before a gerund (a verb form used as a noun)
Your not writing upset Mother.
Her drum playing angers the neighbors.

Objective case. Use the objective case for the following:

Direct objects, indirect objects, and objects of prepositions
Bradley hit *it* over third base. [direct object]
Jack sent *her* flowers. [indirect object]
The letter was addressed to *me.* [object of preposition]

Appositives identifying objects
The club elected two new members, Erin and *her.*

Note: After *than* or *as,* use the pronoun case that correctly completes your meaning.

My mother understands my sister better than *I.* ("than I do")
My mother understands my sister better than *me.* ("than she understands me")

Notice that *we* or *us* before a noun takes the same case it would if you dropped the noun.

We students have complained to the administration about this problem before.

It is difficult for *us* registered Independents to affect the primary process.

V.C.2. **Make sure that what each pronoun refers to is clear.**

Since a pronoun is a substitute for a noun or a noun phrase, a pronoun's meaning is apparent only when the reader or listener knows to what the pronoun refers. In other words, a pronoun should have a clear antecedent.

Unclear

The law firm of Creager and Colvin failed after *he* withdrew the operating capital and fled to Switzerland.

Teresa proofread my paper, but she didn't find a single *one*.

He believes in reincarnation, but he does not believe that *they* appear to the living.

It said in the newspaper that the election would be close.

Clear

The law firm of Creager and Colvin failed after *Colvin* withdrew the operating capital and fled to Switzerland.

Teresa proofread my paper, but she didn't find a single *error*.

He believes in reincarnation, but he does not believe that *the dead* appear to the living.

The newspaper reported that the election would be close.

V.C.3. **Make pronouns and their antecedents agree in gender, person, and number.**

Pronouns must have the same gender, person, and number as the word or phrase they refer to. Because gender and person seldom pose problems with pronouns (but see section V.C.4. on sexist usage), the discussion here is limited to agreement in number. The rule is simple: Use plural pronouns to refer to plural antecedents. Use singular pronouns to refer to singular antecedents.

Indefinite pronouns

Most indefinite pronouns indicate number. The plural forms seldom pose problems, but the singular forms are confusing, sometimes violating logic. For example, the word *everyone* means all, but *everyone* is singular and *all* is plural. An easy way to recall these eccentricities of usage is to remember that any pronoun containing *-one* or *-body* is singular. Listed below are the most common singular pronouns:

anyone	everybody	somebody
anybody	everyone	one
either	someone	each
neither	no one	

If you have trouble with *either, neither,* or *each,* then mentally add *one* and think: *either one, neither one, each one.* Likewise, in a word that has the suffix *-body,* substitute *-one:* for *anybody,* think *anyone;* for *somebody,* think *someone.*

Compound antecedents

In general, use a plural pronoun to refer to compound antecedents linked by *and:*

George and Martha are taking *their* time.

However, when a compound antecedent is preceded by *each* or *every,* use a singular pronoun:

Every cafe and restaurant in town has seen *its* business suffer.

Use a singular pronoun to refer to singular antecedents linked by *or* and *nor.* Use a plural pronoun to refer to plural antecedents linked by *neither* and *nor:*

A dog or a cat has *its* special needs during warm summer months.

Neither friends nor family members gave *their* approval to the marriage.

V.C.4. Avoid sexist use of pronouns.

Since the early 1970s we have become more aware that the English language discriminates against women in many ways. Some people object to word forms that contain the generic form *man* (meaning all people—the human race) and the use of the pronoun *he* when the referent could be female, as in "Everyone brought *his* toothbrush." Some people attempt to solve this dilemma by using *he/she* or other combinations, but none of these coinages is generally accepted. How then can writers best handle the problem of sexist language?

Use *he or she* and *his or her* sparingly. One *he or she* or one *his or her* will not disrupt the flow of a sentence, but the repeated use of these terms can distract the reader. Instead, rewrite sentences so that male and female pronouns are avoided. You can omit the third-person pronoun, repeat the noun, or pluralize the entire sentence. Consider the following correct examples:

If a person is insincere, chances are that *his or her* insincerity will be detected.

If a person is insincere, chances are that *the* insincerity will be detected. [preferable]

If *people* are insincere, chances are that *their* insincerity will be detected. [preferable]

As a way of avoiding sexist usage, people sometimes use the plural *their* when a singular personal pronoun such as *his* or *her* is called for. This colloquial usage is heard in sentences such as "*Everyone* should remember to take *their* ground cloth and hunting knife." But for most writing, this sentence would be considered incorrect. Standard usage would be as follows:

Everyone should remember to take a ground cloth and hunting knife.

All should remember to pack *their* rain gear.

Not *one* of the runners felt *she* had run *her* best. [All the runners are women.]

None of the new members remembered to wear *his* fraternity pin. [Only men have fraternity pins]

V.C.5. Use relative pronouns correctly.

There are only six relative pronouns, easily memorized because five begin with *w: who, whom, whose, which,* and *what.* The other one is *that. Which, what,* and *that* have the same form for all three cases. *Who* is in the subjective case, *whose* is in the possessive case, and *whom* is in the objective case.

Who is calling? [subject]

Whose gerbil is that? [possessive]

To *whom* it may concern: [object of preposition]

Relative pronouns are used to introduce adjective clauses. Sometimes these pronouns cause problems in punctuation and usage. In the first example that follows, the adjective clause (italicized) is nonessential—unimportant to the main idea of the sentence; *which* is used and the phrase is set off by commas. In the second sentence, the adjective clause is necessary for the sentence to be clear and complete; *that* is used and no commas are needed.

A dog, *which had no collar,* followed me home. [nonessential clause]

The dog *that is wearing the collar* is mine. [essential clause]

Note: Who and *whom* generally refer only to people. *Which* and *that* refer to animals, places, or things. Sometimes *who* is used to refer to animals with names, but such usage is unusual.

V.C.6. Avoid inappropriate shifts of person.

A careless shift in person can confuse your reader. Maintain a consistent point of view by writing in the same person: first person (*I, we*), second person (*you*), or third person (*he, she, it, they*).

Inappropriate

I always spend the morning hours on work that requires mental effort, for *your* mind is freshest in the morning.

Revised

I always spend the morning hours on work that requires mental effort, for *my* mind is freshest in the morning.

V.D. VERBS

Since verbs are the most complex part of speech in the English language, a full treatment of the topic is impossible here. Only the verb forms that commonly cause problems are discussed.

Six Troublesome Verbs

Present tense	Past tense	Past participle
lie (to recline)	lay	(has, had) lain
lay (to place an object)	laid	laid
sit (to take a seat)	sat	sat
set (to place an object)	set	set
rise (to get up)	rose	risen
raise (to lift)	raised	raised

V.D.1. Use correct verb forms.

The "troublesome six" verbs

Six verbs, sometimes called "the troublesome six," are explained in the following table. Use the correct form of these verbs. Remember that *lay, sat,* and *raise*—when used in the active voice—all require direct objects and that *lie, sit,* and *rise* do not take objects. This guideline should help prevent confusion. In the examples below, the direct objects are italicized.

Direct Objects	No Direct Objects
Please lay the *book* there.	Lie down, Rover.
Sharon laid her *coat* on the bed.	Sue has lain in the sun two hours.
Barry set his *briefcase* on my desk.	Harry sat there.
Jim raised the *blind.*	The sun rises at 6:30 a.m.

Try to be consistent in your choice of tense. Four verbs—*can, may, will,* and *shall*—are frequently misused because people mix tenses improperly. But if you understand the principal parts of verbs and remember the groupings listed below, you should be able to use these verbs correctly.

Present tense	Past tense
can	could
may	might
will	would
shall	should

If you have a question about the tense of a verb, consult your dictionary. Be aware that two or more forms are sometimes considered acceptable.

Principal parts of irregular verbs

The following list of irregular verbs and their principal parts is based on the *American Heritage Dictionary,* 3rd edition.

Present	Past	Past Participle
bear	bore	borne
beat	beat	beaten
become	became	become
begin	began	begun
bite	bit	bitten
blow	blew	blown
break	broke	broken
bring	brought	brought
burst	burst	burst
buy	bought	bought
catch	caught	caught
choose	chose	chosen
come	came	come
cut	cut	cut
creep	crept	crept
dive	dived	dived, dove
do	did	done
draw	drew	drawn
drink	drank	drunk
drive	drove	driven
eat	ate	eaten
fall	fell	fallen
find	found	found
fling	flung	flung
fly	flew	flown
forget	forgot	forgot, forgotten
freeze	froze	frozen
get	got	gotten, got
give	gave	given
go	went	gone
grow	grew	grown
hang (suspend)	hung	hung
hang (execute)	hanged	hanged
hit	hit	hit
hurt	hurt	hurt

Present	Past	Past Participle
keep	kept	kept
know	knew	known
lead	led	led
leave	left	left
lend	lent	lent
let	let	let
lose	lost	lost
ride	rode	ridden
ring	rang	rung
rise	rose	risen
run	ran	run
say	said	said
see	saw	seen
shake	shook	shaken
shine (the sun)	shone	shone
shine (to polish)	shined	shined
sing	sang or sung	sung
sink	sank or sunk	sunk
speak	spoke	spoken
spring	sprang, sprung	sprung
stand	stood	stood
steal	stole	stolen
sting	stung	stung
strike	struck	struck
swear	swore	sworn
swim	swam	swum
swing	swung	swung
take	took	taken
teach	taught	taught
tear	tore	torn
tell	told	told
throw	threw	thrown
wear	wore	worn
write	wrote	written

V.D.2. Use *be* correctly.

The verb *be* should not be used as if it were a complete verb. Except in a few special instances (see the discussion of the subjunctive mood in section V.D.6. of this handbook), some other form of *be* or a helping verb such as *will* is required.

Incorrect

I *be* a college student.

I *be* going there.

Mrs. Beck, you *be* leaving soon?

Correct

I *am* a college student.

I *am* going there.

Mrs. Beck, *will* you *be* leaving soon?

V.D.3. Make subjects and verbs agree in number.

Use singular verbs with singular subjects; use plural verbs with plural subjects. Verb agreement is sometimes a problem, particularly for foreign students. But if you remember—when using the third person—that adding an *s* to a verb makes it singular, this principle should help. (Adding an *s* to a noun makes it plural.) Here are some third-person examples:

Singular	*Plural*
is	are
was	were
has	have
skates	skate
drives	drive

Words between the subject and verb

Words and phrases that appear between the subject and the verb sometimes mislead. In the following sentences, the verbs are plural to agree with the plural subjects:

The letters, along with the package, *were* mailed today.

The word *package* is not the subject. But because *package* comes immediately before the verb, it may seem natural to use *was*. This is not correct. In the following sentence *were* is correct:

The letters and the package *were* mailed this morning.

The package and the letters *were* mailed this morning. [preferable]

Compound subject linked with or or nor

Another troublemaker is the sentence that has a singular and a plural subject without *and*. Then the subject nearest the verb determines the agreement of the verb:

Neither the cookies nor the fruitcake *was* fresh.

Neither the fruitcake nor the cookies *were* fresh.

Inverted word order

In questions and in statements beginning with *there*, the subject usually follows the verb. Be careful that the verb agrees with the subject.

Are the photocopies ready to be picked up? (photocopies *are*)

There *is* only one clerk at work today. (clerk *is*)

Relative pronoun subjects

In a clause beginning with a relative pronoun—*who*, *which*, or *that*—look for the pronoun's antecedent to decide whether the verb is singular or plural.

People who *litter* should be fined heavily. (people *litter*)

This house, which *needs* some work, could be a bargain. (house *needs*)

V.D.4. Use the active voice of verbs unless there is a good reason for using the passive voice. (See chapter 8.)

Use the active voice in most sentences. The active voice occurs when the subject is the doer of the action expressed by the verb. The passive voice occurs when the subject is not the doer of the action expressed by the verb.

Sergei Grinkov *won* an Olympic gold medal twice. [active voice]

Twice an Olympic gold medal *was won* by Sergei Grinkov. [passive voice]

V.D.5. Avoid inappropriate shifts of tense, voice, or mood.

Inappropriate shifts in the tense, voice, or mood of verbs can be distracting and even confusing for the reader.

Inappropriate

Before he *went* to school, he *drinks* three cups of coffee. [needless shift from past to present tense]

Before he *went* to school, three cups of coffee *were drunk* by him. [needless shift from active to passive voice]

Go to school, and *you should* drink only one cup of coffee first. [needless shift from imperative to indicative mood]

Appropriate

Before he *went* to school, he *drank* three cups of coffee. [Or: Before he *goes* to school, he *drinks* three cups of coffee.]

Before he *went* to school, he *drank* three cups of coffee. [Both verbs are in the past tense and active voice.]

Go to school, and *drink* only one cup of coffee. [Both verbs are in the imperative mood.]

V.D.6. Use the subjunctive mood correctly.

The subjunctive mood is the form of a verb used to express doubt, desire, probability, a condition contrary to fact, or a hypothetical situation. The subjunctive appears in three ways: (1) in *if* clauses indicating unreal conditions; (2) in *that* clauses after verbs expressing requests, suggestions, wishes, or commands; and (3) in a few idioms.

Use the subjunctive to indicate unreal conditions.

My husband acted as though he *were* an expert at ironing until he scorched a shirt. [He is not an expert at ironing.]

In Chicago's traffic jams, I felt as if I *were* having a bad dream. [I was awake, not having a dream.]

Terry could fix that leak if he *were* here. [Terry is not here.]

Use the subjunctive in *that* clauses after verbs expressing requests, suggestions, wishes, or commands.

Her boss asked that she *remain* in the building during her coffee break.

The company requires that I *be* on duty at 8:00 A.M.

The committee agreed that Jane *be* given released time to complete the project.

Henry moved that the meeting *be* adjourned.

Use the subjunctive in a few idioms.

If this *be* true	Far *be* it from me
Come what may	Long *wave* the stars and stripes!

V.E. USE *LIKE* CORRECTLY

Use *like* as a preposition.

Jenny looks *like* her aunt.

Like me, Bill enjoys jazz.

It is not *like* him to be late.

I feel *like* resting.

It looks *like* rain.

He walks *like* a duck.

Use *like* as an adjective to mean "similar, equal, or alike."

I used one-half cup of butter and a *like* amount of flour.

My grandmother used to say, "*Like* father, *like* son."

Use *as if*, not *like*, as a conjunction to connect two clauses.

Incorrect

None of the teenagers lit their cigarettes *like* they were used to smoking.

Hazel acted *like* she was angry with me.

Correct

None of the teenagers lit their cigarettes *as if* they were used to smoking.

Hazel acted *as if* she were angry with me.

V.F. MODIFIERS

One frequent error, found not only in student writing but also in advertisements, newspaper articles, and other media, is tangled syntax or scrambled word order. Words or phrases are misplaced in sentences; sometimes important words are omitted. These offenses interfere with clarity and violate logic. Two common offenders are discussed here: misplaced modifiers and dangling modifiers.

V.F.1. Avoid misplaced modifiers.

Misplaced modifiers are simply modifying words or phrases (adjective or adverb) that are out of place. They sneak into places where they do not belong. For example, *only* is an impudent pest that cuts into line ahead of other words. Although *only* may seem small and harmless in the wrong place, don't overlook its misbehavior. Yank it back where it belongs, close to the word it limits. Consider some examples:

Misplaced

"Who says kids *only* like junk food?" [an ad for spaghetti]

"If *only* your feet could talk." [an ad for a podiatrist]

"If you *only* inspect your draft sentence by sentence, you can easily overlook how its parts work together." [a textbook]

Revised

Who says kids like *only* junk food?

If your feet could *only* talk.

If you inspect your draft *only* sentence by sentence, you can easily overlook how its parts work together.

The adverbs *almost* and *even* are other frequent offenders. Like *only*, they should be placed exactly before the word they modify.

Misplaced

She *almost* used the entire bottle of bath oil for one bath.

I *even* felt worse after I took the medicine.

Revised

She used *almost* the entire bottle of bath oil for one bath.

I felt *even* worse after I took the medicine.

Clauses and phrases may also be misplaced in sentences, often leading to unintentionally humorous misreadings:

Misplaced

Jane wore a flower in her hair *that was pink*. [What was pink?]

Dick kept an odd-shaped piece of jade in his jacket pocket, *which he considered lucky*. [What was lucky?]

A spider dropped off the piano stool as I opened the door *into a large web*. [Did the spider web have a door?]

I easily spotted the rare bird *using high-powered binoculars*. [Was the bird using binoculars?]

Revised

In her hair Jane wore a flower that was pink. [Or: In her hair Jane wore a pink flower.]

Dick kept an odd-shaped piece of jade, which he considered lucky, in his jacket pocket.

As I opened the door, a spider dropped off the piano stool into a large web.

Using high-powered binoculars, I easily spotted the rare bird.

V.F.2. Avoid dangling modifiers.

Dangling modifiers are phrases that lack a referent: the noun or pronoun needed to make the phrase clear and logical has been omitted. Usually, dangling modifiers cling precariously at the beginning of a sentence. Here are two examples from student papers:

Dangling

When only a youngster in grade school, *my father* instructed me in the art of boxing. [Who was in grade school?]

After standing up well under the two-year exposure test, the *manufacturers* were convinced that the paint was sufficiently durable. [The manufacturers stood up well?]

Revised (Referent has been added.)

When *I was* only a youngster in grade school, my father instructed me in the art of boxing.

After *the paint* stood up well under the two-year exposure test, the manufacturers were convinced that it was sufficiently durable.

Note: Whenever you include an *-ing* phrase (participial phrase) at the beginning of a sentence, check to see that the word it modifies immediately follows it, or rewrite the sentence to make that word the subject of the first clause. Probably the best way to find tangled syntax is to read your writing aloud and listen carefully. Does each sentence make sense? Beware of answering in the affirmative too quickly. Writers know what they mean. The question is whether each sentence will be clear and logical to readers.

VI. SPELLING

Some tips

Many people suffer feelings of inferiority because of problems with spelling. They seem to believe that they are less intelligent than people who spell accurately. But not all very bright people are good spellers. I remember one ninth grade student, a physician's daughter, who was a brilliant student except for her spelling. Her themes were filled with misspelled words. Once, after she had corrected a theme, a word was misspelled in a different way. When asked why she hadn't used a dictionary, she replied, "Oh, I asked Dad." This example illustrates the need for spelling tip number one: *Use a dictionary; don't ask someone about the spelling of a word.*

The mystery of poor spelling has not been completely solved. But we do know that incorrect pronunciation sometimes leads to incorrect spelling. Students who mispronounce words frequently misspell those same words. In the left list below are some common misspellings due to mispronunciation:

Incorrect	*Correct*
congradulations	congratulations
discribe	describe
discription	description
goverment	government
enviroment	environment
interment	internment
secratary	secretary
Artic	Arctic

miniscule	min*u*scule
sposed	s*up*posed
then (used in comparison)	th*an*

If you are unsure of the spelling or pronunciation of a word, look it up in a dictionary. Then practice writing and saying the word correctly.

In working with students, I've found that the best spellers are those who can visualize words. During spelling bees, students would write words on scraps of paper, in the air, or on a corner of the blackboard to see how the words looked. They told me that remembering the appearance of the word aided in recalling the correct letters.

If you can strengthen your mental images of any problem words, you can improve your spelling. One way is to keep a list of frequently misspelled words and to practice writing them. (Chances are there will be fewer than a dozen.) After you have looked up the correct spelling of each word on your list, write each one at least a dozen times.

Association aids for improving spelling

One way to improve spelling is to devise an association that will help recall a correct spelling. For example, one student who had difficulty with the word *occasion* could not remember whether it had two *c*'s and one *s* or vice versa. She looked the word up several times until she devised this sentence: "Twenty-one is a special occasion." Twenty-one (21) reminded her that occasion had 2 *c*'s and 1 *s*. Listed below are some other associations to help you recall certain spellings.

- A *secretary* is a keeper of *secrets*. [An *e* follows the *r* in both words.]
- *separate* has *a rat* in it. [An *a* follows the *p*.]
- *there, their, they're*

  there: Without the *t*, *there* becomes *here*. [Both words refer to location.]

  their: Without the *t*, *their* becomes *heir*. [Both words refer to ownership.]

  they're: This is a contraction of *they are*. [The apostrophe indicates that *a* has been omitted.]

- *principal and principle:* The following sentence should help you remember that *principal* refers to someone or something of importance: The *principal* points of his speech were. . . . On the other hand, *principle* refers to a code, law, or doctrine.

  The *principal* of our school was a *pal* to the students.

  The Tenth Commandment is a difficult *principle* to follow.

- *prejudice:* Just remember that *prejudice* means to *pre-judge* something.
- *stationery* and *stationary:* Remember that you write on an envelope. [Both *envelope* and *stationery* have *e*'s.] Something *stationary* stays in one place. [two *a*'s]

- *maneuver:* When you are riding a horse, the mane is in front of you. Just remember that the *mane* is before the *u.*

You may want to devise your own association aids for words that give you trouble.

Other spelling aids

- Only one English word ends in *-sede: supersede.* Only three words end in *-ceed: exceed, proceed, succeed.* All other words of similar sound end in *-cede: precede, recede,* and so forth.

- Drop the final *e* in most words when the suffix you are adding begins with a vowel: *chang(e)ing, hop(e)ing, purchas(e)able.* (In a few instances, however, the final *e* is kept: *changeable, knowledgeable, peaceable.* And some words can be spelled either way: *salable, saleable; livable, liveable.*) Usually the final *e* is kept when the suffix begins with a consonant: *hopeful, vengeful, homeless.*

- *Pre* means "before." *Per* means "through, to, for, by each," or "by means of." *Pro* means "in favor of" or "acting as."

  preschool: before school

  perceive: to become aware of directly through the senses

  procapitalism: in favor of capitalism

- Plurals of words ending in *y* are formed as follows: When a consonant precedes the final *y,* change the *y* to *i* and add *es: company, companies; lady, ladies; cherry, cherries.* Exception: plurals of proper names, for instance *the Kelleys.* When a vowel precedes the *y,* keep the *y* and add *s: monkeys, attorneys, byways.*

- To form the plural of nouns ending in *ch, s, sh, x,* and *z,* add *es: matches, gases, bushes, taxes, buzzes.* This rule also applies to the singular forms of verbs ending in these letters.

- When adding a suffix that begins with a vowel, double a final consonant if the word meets all of these criteria: (1) It is one syllable or is stressed on the final syllable; (2) there is only one vowel in the word or in the final syllable; (3) the word or syllable ends in a single consonant. The following words meet all these criteria: *rap, rapped, rapping; occur, occurred, occurrence; fit, fitter, fittest; repel, repelling, repellent.* Note that for words ending in *e,* the *e* is dropped but the remaining consonant is never doubled: *write, writing* (not *writting*).

- A modification of this rule applies when the pronunciation of the word changes after the suffix is added. For example, *infer* becomes *inferring* (doubled final consonant) because the stress remains on the final syllable; but it becomes *inference* (no double consonant) because here the stress shifts to the first syllable. A related modification is seen in words such as *offer, offered, offering* and *order, ordered, ordering.* The stress is always on the first syllable, and thus the consonant is not doubled.

Six ways to improve spelling

Probably the biggest factor in any improvement is motivation. If you resolve to refine your spelling skill and follow a plan, your spelling will become better. Here are six techniques to aid you:

1. **Use a dictionary to check words if you are unsure of their spelling.** A spelling-checker or pocket dictionary to carry and a desk dictionary in a convenient place at home are helpful.

2. **Pronounce words correctly.** If you leave out letters or syllables in pronunciation, you may leave them out when writing the word.

3. **Compile your own spelling list.** Review this daily for a few weeks. Look at each word. Then shut your eyes and see if you can spell it correctly.

4. **Write misspelled words correctly several times so that you can visualize their correct spelling in your mind.**

5. **Familiarize yourself with the memory association aids.** Then devise some of your own.

6. As a last resort, if you cannot recognize misspelled words, ask someone to mark them. Then get out the dictionary and correct the spellings yourself. With practice your spelling ability will improve, and you will be able to catch more of your errors.

VII. GLOSSARY OF USAGE

Some words in the English language are commonly confused because they look or sound alike. Other words used in conversation are sometimes mistaken for standard usage. This glossary will guide you in determining appropriate word choice for your college and business writing. The recommendations here are based on usage listed in current dictionaries. For clarity, misspellings and other unaccepted variations are listed after the standard word.

a, an   Use *a* before words starting with a consonant sound. Use *an* before words starting with a vowel sound.

- a bristlecone pine, a history, a quail, a sinkhole
- an aardvark, an egg, an infant, an honorable man

accept, except   *Accept* means "to believe," "to approve," or "to take" (as take an offered gift). *Except* means "without" or "excluding."
- Can he *accept* constructive criticism?
- All the children *except* Jane are here.

access, excess   The noun *access* is the "ability or right to enter, to use, or to approach." The verb *access* is used in a technological sense, as "to locate data." *Excess* means "too much" or "exceeding that which is normal and sufficient."

- It is impossible to gain direct *access* to the freeway from here.
- Lucinda can *access* those files easily.
- She stored the *excess* bread dough in the refrigerator.

adapt, adept, adopt   *Adapt* means "to make suitable for a specific situation." *Adept* means "very skilled; proficient." *Adopt* means "to take up and use as one's own," as an idea, word, or the like. *Adopt* also refers to the process of child adoption.

- Do you think you can *adapt* the part to make it fit?
- Jeff is *adept* at programming.
- When customers complain, Sarah *adopts* the tactic of "A soft answer turneth away wrath."

adverse, averse   *Adverse* means "harmful or unfavorable." *Averse* means "unwilling" or "disinclined."

- William has surmounted *adverse* circumstances before.
- Mike is *averse* to risk taking.

advice, advise   *Advice* is a noun that means "a view, opinion, or judgment." *Advise* is a verb that means "to counsel," "to inform" or "to recommend."

- His *advice* was to look for another job.
- I really don't know what to *advise*.

affect, effect   *Affect* is a verb meaning "to change or to influence." *Effect* is usually used as a noun to mean "result." As a verb *effect* means "to make" or "to implement."

- How will that *affect* your decision?
- What will be the *effect* of that decision?
- Can you *effect* an improvement in that procedure?

aggravate, irritate   *Aggravate* means "to make worse or more troublesome." *Irritate* means "to annoy," "to arouse someone to impatience or anger."

- Disparaging comments can *aggravate* a tense situation.
- Frequent wrong numbers *irritate* my father.

all ready, already   *Already* refers to time, meaning "previously." *All ready* means "prepared" or "available for action."

- Did you *already* clock out?
- Are you *all ready* to leave?

all right   *All right* means "satisfactory" or "proper." *Alright* is a common misspelling.

- It is *all right* to go in the kitchen; the floor is dry.

all together, altogether *All together* means "in a group." *Altogether* means "completely."
- The birds huddled *all together* to keep warm.
- Joe's answer was not *altogether* right.

allusion, delusion, illusion An *allusion* is "a reference" (often to a literary work). A *delusion* is a "mistaken idea." An *illusion* is "an erroneous perception of reality."
- He made an *allusion* to Hamlet.
- He suffers from the *delusion* that he is immortal.
- The ghost was an *illusion*, created with special lighting.

allot, a lot *Allot* means "to parcel out" or "to give a certain portion." *A lot*, used to mean "a large extent, amount, or number," is informal. **Alot** is a common misspelling.
- The government *allots* only one per family.
- He has *a lot* of confidence.
- Jill's grandmother is *a lot* better.

among, between Use *among* when referring to three or more units or people. Use *between* when referring to only two.
- Let's keep this secret *among* our family members.
- *Between* you and me, I like his beard.

amount, number *Amount* refers to a quantity or weight. *Number* refers to a numeral, unit, or indefinite quantity of items or individuals.
- The recipe called for a small *amount* of black pepper.
- The crowd *numbers* in the thousands.

an, a See *a, an.*

any, any other *Any* means "one, some, every, or all." *Any other* is used in a comparison. Do not substitute *any* (by itself), which in the following example would mean that Brian was faster than himself.

- Brian was faster than *any other* runner in his age group.
- You may select *any* of the top prizes.

appraise, apprise *Appraise* means "to evaluate or estimate the value." *Apprise* means "to give notice to or inform."
- Will you *appraise* this emerald ring for me?
- Did you *apprise* the prisoner of his rights?

around, about *Around* refers to "motion or direction." *About* means "approximately" or "almost." Although *around* is often used to mean *about*, this usage is not generally accepted.
- We drove *around* the block twice.
- I will stop by *about* 9 a.m.

assure, ensure, insure *Assure* means "to inform positively." *Ensure* means "to make sure or certain." *Insure* means "to cover with insurance." *Insure* also means "to make certain, especially by taking precautions."
- I *assure* you that every precaution will be taken.
- Checking the map beforehand will *ensure* that you find the right road.
- Did you *insure* the contents of your house?

averse See *adverse, averse.*

beside, besides *Beside* means "next to." *Besides* means "also."
- The scissors are lying *beside* my sewing basket.
- *Besides* my fishing equipment, I'm taking a picnic lunch.

between See *among, between.*

breath, breathe *Breath* is a noun; *breathe* is a verb. Both refer to inhalation and exhalation.
- The speech instructor advised taking a deep *breath* before starting to speak.
- *Breathe* deeply as you work out.

capital, capitol *Capital* refers to the "official place or city of government" or an "amount of money." *Capitol* refers to the "building that houses the official government offices."

- Denver is the *capital* of Colorado.
- We need more *capital* to fund the project.
- Sue visited the *capitol* building during her trip to the state *capital*.

censor, censure *Censor* is "to examine books, films, or other materials to remove or suppress what is considered objectionable." *Censure* is "to criticize severely or blame."

- The school board plans to *censor* books purchased for the school.
- The editorial *censured* a city council member for his failure to attend meetings regularly.

cite, sight, site *Cite* means "to quote." *Sight* refers to the ability to see or view. *Site* refers to location, as a building site.

- Can you *cite* his exact words?
- Can you *sight* Venus above the evening horizon?
- They selected a lovely wooded *site* for their new home.

complement, compliment *Complement* means "to complete or bring to perfection." *Compliment* means "to express praise."

- That floral arrangement *complements* your table setting.
- Brad *complimented* Cindy on her new shoes.

conscience, conscious *Conscience* is "the awareness of a moral or ethical aspect of one's conduct" and the desire "to prefer right over wrong." *Conscious* refers to "awareness of one's environment and existence."

- Jeannette returned the wallet to its owner to relieve her *conscience*.
- Is the patient *conscious* yet?

continual, continuous *Continual* means "recurring regularly or often." *Continuous* means "uninterrupted."

- Uncle Jake's *continual* complaining made our visit unpleasant.

- The flow of fresh air throughout the building is *continuous*.

council, counsel *Council* refers to a group of people who are delegated "to serve in an administrative, legislative, or advisory capacity." *Counsel* means "to give advice."

- Anthony is a member of the town *council*.
- The admissions office *counsels* students.
- Lawyers charge for their *counsel*.

criteria, criterion A *criterion* is a "standard, rule, or test upon which a judgment or decision can be based." *Criteria* is the plural of *criterion*.

- She gave only one *criterion* for the job: a strong back.
- He stated six *criteria* for the upcoming performance evaluation.

delusion See *allusion, delusion, illusion*.

effect, affect See *affect, effect*.

emigrate, immigrate When people *emigrate*, they leave their homeland to reside elsewhere. When they *immigrate*, they enter a different country to reside.

- My paternal ancestors, five brothers, *emigrated* from Wales in the late 1700's.
- They *immigrated* to the United States and traveled to the territory that later became Ohio.

eminent, imminent *Eminent* means "of high rank, station, or quality." *Imminent* means "about to occur, impending."

- Today is the birthday of that *eminent* inventor Thomas A. Edison.
- Skating on thin ice poses an *imminent* danger.

enthusiastic *Enthusiastic*, meaning to have great excitement or interest, is standard usage. **Enthused** is not accepted usage.

- Cody was *enthusiastic* about traveling to the Rocky Mountains.

except See *accept, except*.

excess See *access, excess.*

explicit, implicit *Explicit* means fully and clearly expressed; leaving nothing implied." *Implicit* means "implied or understood though not directly expressed."
- The doctor's directions were *explicit:* "Take one tablet with a full glass of water after meals."
- The company president has *implicit* trust in Sheila's judgment.

farther, further *Farther* refers to "physical distance" and *further* to a nonphysical dimension such as distance in time.
- We drove *farther* than usual the second day of our trip.
- If we go *further* back a few generations, we find other family members who also suffered breast cancer.

fewer, less *Fewer* is used in comparisons to refer to "individual units, things that can be counted." *Less* is used in comparisons to mean a smaller amount or "a mass of measurable extent."
- *Fewer* people attended the state fair this year than last year.
- Opals cost much *less* than diamonds of the same size.

flaunt, flout *Flaunt* means "to parade or display ostentatiously." *Flout* means "to show contempt for" or "to scorn."
- Lorrie *flaunted* her new engagement ring.
- Timothy *flouted* the dress code.

further See *farther, further.*

get *Get* means "to receive" or "to bring." The many colloquial uses of *get* should be avoided in college and business writing. (See a dictionary for other examples of colloquial usage.)
- Standard: Will you *get* a gallon of milk when you go out?
- Colloquial: I hope the frost doesn't *get* our garden.
- Colloquial: That really *gets* to me!

good, well *Good* is an adjective meaning "positive or desirable." *Well* is often used as an adverb to mean "satisfactorily or sufficiently" or "skillfully or proficiently." *Well* is also used as an adjective to mean "a satisfactory condition; right or proper."
- Jerry received *good* news this morning.
- Jeremy did *well* on his calculus exam.
- Henry is *well;* he has completely recovered from pneumonia.
- The project is going *well.*

hanged, hung People are *hanged.* Objects are *hung.*
- The convicted murderer was *hanged.*
- Derek *hung* the painting over the fireplace.

idea, ideal An *idea* is "a thought." An *ideal* is "a principle" or "a conception or model of something in its absolute perfection."
- Suddenly he had a delightful *idea.*
- Her *ideal* husband would be a wonderful father.
- Always be true to your *ideals.*

illusion See *allusion, delusion, illusion.*

implicit See *explicit, implicit.*

its, it's *Its* is the possessive form of *it. It's* is a contraction of *it is.*
- The dog has lost *its* collar.
- *It's* over seventy miles to the next town.

leave, let *Leave* means "to go out or away from." *Let* means "to permit or allow."
- Will you *leave* Jiffy at the kennel when you go to the lake?
- Please *let* me help you with those packages.

less See *fewer, less.*

let See *leave, let.*

loose, lose *Lose* is a verb meaning "to mislay." *Loose* is an adjective meaning "not tight" or "unconfined."
- Did you *lose* an earring?

- My watchband is too *loose.*
- An orangutan was *loose* in the park.

medium, media *Medium* is (1) an "intermediate course," the midpoint between two extremes; (2) a way that something is "transmitted or carried"; (3) "an agency by which something is accomplished or conveyed or transferred." *Media* is the plural of *medium.*

- The Internet is a *medium* that relays daily stock market reports.
- The *media* frequently refer to the escapades of the royal family.

moral, morale *Moral* is an adjective that refers to "judgment of the goodness or badness of human action and character." *Morale* is a noun that means "the state of the spirits of a person or group."

- The *moral* code of society seems to be changing.
- Employee *morale* is high at XYZ Company.

number See *amount, number.*

passed, past *Passed* is a verb that means "having moved on; proceeded." *Past* as an adverb means "beyond" and as a noun or adjective refers to time that is over. Do not write "*past* history" because all history is past.

- Jerry *passed* the bakery without stopping.
- Jerry drove *past* the bakery without stopping.
- Let's forget the *past* and look to the future.

patience, patients *Patience* is the ability to "bear pain, provocation, or annoyance with calmness." *Patients* refers to people who "receive medical attention, care, or treatment."

- *Patience* is a quality that is learned.
- The physician saw thirty-seven *patients* yesterday.

personal, personnel *Personal* refers to the private matters of an individual. *Personnel* refers to a group of people who work for an organization. (Note that *personnel* has two *n*'s.)

- Please don't ask *personal* questions.
- Their *personnel* are very courteous.

precede, proceed *Precede* means "to go before." *Proceed* means "to go" or "to continue."

- The Rose Bowl game *precedes* the Orange Bowl game.
- Let's *proceed* with the meeting.

quiet, quite *Quiet* means "free of noise." *Quite* means "very; entirely."

- Our dorm is rarely *quiet.*
- Your homemade apple pie is *quite* tasty.
- It is *quite* all right to park there.

quotation, quote *Quote* is a verb that means "to repeat or copy the words of (another)," usually citing the source. *Quotation* is a noun meaning "the act of quoting" or "a passage quoted."

- Do you plan to *quote* John F. Kennedy in your speech?
- A *quotation* from Winston Churchill might make an effective introduction.

real, really *Real* is an adjective meaning "genuine or authentic," "free of pretense or falsehood." (Avoid using *real* to mean "very.") *Really* is an adverb meaning "truly; genuinely."

- Her diamond is *real.*
- *Really*, I can't go with you.

regardless *Regardless* means "in spite of everything; anyway." **Irregardless** is redundant and nonstandard.

- Many people neglect to buckle their seat belts, *regardless* of the danger.

sight See *cite, sight, site.*

sometime, some time, sometimes *Sometime* means "an indefinite or unstated time." *Some time* refers to an amount of time. *Sometimes* means "occasionally."

- Stop in *sometime.*
- I haven't seen him for *some time.*

- *Sometimes* I feed the elephants at the city zoo.

stationary, stationery *Stationary* means "not moving" or "not capable of being moved." *Stationery* refers to writing materials.
- The tables in that restaurant are *stationary*.
- Would you like some monogrammed *stationery* for Christmas?

than, then *Than* is a conjunction indicating a comparison. *Then* is an adverb indicating time.
- Harrison likes pistachio ice cream better *than* chocolate.
- I will meet you *then*.

their, there, they're *Their* is "the possessive form of *they*." *There* is an adverb that refers to place. (*There* can also be used in several other ways.) *They're* is a contraction of *they are*.
- *Their* cars are parked on the street.
- Do you see that ten dollar bill lying *there* in the grass?
- *They're* the third couple from the left.

to, too, two *To* is a preposition meaning "toward," "in contact with," "in front of," or "constituting"; or the sign of an infinitive. *Too* means "also" or "more than enough." *Two* is the whole number following *one*; a couple.
- I walked *to* the town square.
- *To* ensure you arrive safely, check the cable that is towing your glider.

- May I go, *too?*
- *Two* robins built a nest.

try to *Try to* means "to attempt." **Try and** is not accepted usage.
- *Try to* pull up the cap of the bottle after the arrows meet.

two See *to, too, two*.

which, who Use *which* when referring to an object or an animal. Use *who* when referring to a person. (For more information about usage, see section V.C. on pronouns.)
- The black horse *which* is near the barn belongs to Stanley.
- *Who* did you say is calling?

who, whom *Who* is in the subjective case, *whom* in the objective case.
- These are the men *who* you thought were responsible. [*who* were responsible]
- These are the men *whom* you chose for the job. [you chose *whom*]

who's, whose *Who's* is a contraction of *who is* or *who has*. *Whose* is the possessive form of *who*.
- *Who's* the best candidate for the position?
- *Whose* Dalmatian is that?

your, you're *Your* is the possessive form of *you*. *You're* is the contraction of *you are*.
- Will you take *your* car?
- *You're* the winner of a trip to Tahiti.

Credits

Chapter 9   Page 120 Definition of "coelacanth" copyright ©1996 by Houghton Mifflin Company. Reproduced by permission from *The American Heritage Dictionary of the English Language*, Third Edition. Page 125 Definition of "gobbledygook" copyright ©1981 by Houghton Mifflin Company. Reproduced by permission of *The American Heritage Dictionary of the English Language*; entry for "gobbledygook" excerpted with permission of Macmillan General Reference USA, a Simon & Schuster Macmillan Company, from *Webster's New World Dictionary*, Second College Edition. Copyright ©1986 by Simon & Schuster, Inc. Chapter 16   Page 231 Definition of "work" from *The Oxford American Dictionary* reprinted by permission of Oxford University Press. Chapter 26   Page 449 Ellen Goodman, "A Very Human Search for Security." Copyright ©1979 The Boston Globe Newspaper Co., Washington Post Writers Group. Reprinted with permission. Page 451 Stephen Jay Gould, "Were Dinosaurs Dumb?" Copyright ©1978 by Stephen Jay Gould. From Stephen Jay Gould, *The Panda's Thumb: More Reflections in Natural History*. Reprinted by permission of W.W. Norton & Company, Inc. Chapter 27   Page 465 John Updike, "Still of Some Use." From John Updike, *Trust Me*. Copyright ©1987 by John Updike. Reprinted by permission of Alfred A. Knopf Inc. Chapter 28   Page 481 Arthur Guiterman, "On the Vanity of Earthly Greatness." Reprinted by permission of Louise H. Sclove; from Countee Cullen, "Yet Do I Marvel." Copyrights administered by Thompson and Thompson, New York, NY. Page 482 Countee Cullen, "Incident." Copyrights administered by Thompson and Thompson, New York, NY. Page 484 Joso, "The Barley Field," and Sora, "The Barley Field," from Harold G. Henderson, *An Introduction to Haiku*. Copyright ©1958 by Harold G. Henderson. Used by permission of Doubleday, a division of Bantam Doubleday Dell Publishing Group, Inc. Page 485 Emily Dickinson, ["I taste a liquor never brewed."] Reprinted by permission of the publishers and the Trustees of Amherst College from *The Poems of Emily Dickinson*, Thomas H. Johnson, ed., Cambridge, Mass.: The Belknap Press of Harvard University Press. Copyright ©1951, 1955, 1979, 1983 by the President and Fellows of Harvard College. Page 486 Archibald MacLeish, "Ars Poetica," from Archibald MacLeish, *Collected Poems 1917–1982*. Copyright ©1985 by The Estate of Archibald MacLeish. Reprinted by permission of Houghton Mifflin Company. All rights reserved.

Index of Authors and Titles

Note: Student writers are indicated by an asterisk.*

Subject Index

Note: Pages beginning with H are located in the handbook.